Achieving educational excellence

Achieving educational excellence

USING BEHAVIORAL STRATEGIES

Beth Sulzer-Azaroff
University of Massachusetts

G. Roy Mayer
California State University, Los Angeles

Holt, Rinehart and Winston
New York   Chicago   San Francisco   Philadelphia
Montreal   Toronto   London   Sydney
Tokyo   Mexico City   Rio de Janeiro   Madrid

Library of Congress Cataloging in Publication Data

Sulzer-Azaroff, Beth.
　　Achieving educational excellence using behavioral
strategies.

　　Includes bibliographies and index.
　　1. Learning, Psychology of.　2. Behavior modification.
3. Teaching.　4. Achievement motivation.　I. Mayer,
G. Roy, 1940–　　　II.　Title.
LB1065.S87　1985　　371.1'024　　85-5626

ISBN 0-03-071651-9

CBS COLLEGE PUBLISHING
Holt, Rinehart and Winston
The Dryden Press
Saunders College Publishing

Copyright Acknowledgments

For permission to use copyrighted materials, the authors
wish to thank the following:
Chapter 5 p. 92, from A. Cossairt, R. V. Hall, and B. L.
Hopkins (1973). The effects of experimenter's instruc-
(*continued on page 406*)

To Educators
who, regardless of the difficulty
of the challenge and
the paucity of support,
keep trying to guide their students
toward excellence

Preface

"Education for excellence" is the current rallying cry of the concerned public. We have been told in a number of commission reports that educational achievement has been slipping, and slipping badly during the past couple of decades. While the national economy requires workers with increasingly sophisticated skills, illiteracy grips more than 23 million adults and 17 percent of all twelve-year-olds in the United States. Achievement test scores have been falling, and military recruits are said to lack "higher order" intellectual skills.[1]

The problem does not end with declining academic performance. Valuable instructional time is replaced by the teachers' need to address motivational and management issues. Often, pupil misconduct creates an unpleasant classroom climate, and absenteeism, tardiness, and inattention compound the problem. Anger toward the schools is expressed as verbal hostility or even more directly in the form of vandalism and violence. (Not long ago, New Englanders were shocked to view on television the hundreds of thousands of dollars' worth of damage to a school library, laboratories, and classrooms committed by a group of local high school students on a drunken rampage.) As a result, educators become demoralized and withdraw from the field.

What can be done to reverse this dismal trend? Recommendations range from lengthening the school day or year, altering teacher training practices, and "getting tough" with students, to improving curricula and teacher salaries and providing merit awards for instructional excellence. Our gut reaction may be to applaud some of the recommendations while dismissing others. But gut reactions will not solve the problem. Instead, we need to look at the evidence to discover what conditions are apt to help students achieve educational excellence; what educational policies and procedures, rules and regulations, curricula, physical and social environmental arrangements, assignments, and teaching, consulting, and supervisory strategies have been found to promote and support improved academic and social performance. We must learn about effective educational strategies by examining the results of investigations that have been objectively conducted and analyzed. Or we need to research

---

[1] The National Commission on Excellence in Education (1983). *A Nation at Risk: The Imperative for Educational Reform*, U.S. Government Printing Office, Washington, D.C.

the problem ourselves. Such knowledge and skills are what this book is designed to help you acquire.

During the last quarter century, a new approach has evolved and matured to help us identify the factors or variables that influence behavior. Known as the experimental analysis of behavior, this approach focuses on behaviors of concern, carefully defines and determines ways to measure those behaviors objectively, and repeatedly tests selected variables to determine in what manner — to what extent, how generally and enduringly — those variables influence the behaviors.

This investigative tactic has been applied in the laboratory and in numerous fields — among many others, mental health, rehabilitation, medicine, business, industry, human services, and, of course, education. Over this time, scientific journals, texts, articles, and public presentations of findings of experimental analyses of behavior have increased to many thousands. National, international, regional, and local societies of behavior analysis have been formed and flourish. Why? One can only assume that this approach is meeting an important social need. People who are attracted to behavior analysis cite the appeal of its clarity, objectivity, directness, and ability to discover variables that systematically influence behavior. By applying those variables, practitioners concerned with the welfare of others (or even themselves) have been able to help remedy or prevent problem behaviors. Because the treatment methods tend to be positive and constructive, they are seen as benign and humane by those involved. Perhaps even more importantly, the analytic methods demonstrate how effectively the selected procedures affect the course of change over time, enabling the users to decide whether or not to continue or try another strategy.

This is not to say that behavior analysis is viewed with favor universally. Some say it is too technical, perhaps because it has adopted a language of precision. Others seem to find its animal laboratory origins unappealing. Many adhere to alternative methods or metaphors with which they are loath to part. The label "behavior analysis" frequently has been applied inappropriately to practices that superficially resemble the approach but actually lack its essential components, and critics understandably react negatively to such misapplications. Impatience with behavior analysis can stem from its failure to successfully have met a particular behavioral challenge, such as a universal cure for substance abuse or delinquency (even though it has made some impressive inroads into those extremely problematic areas). Often, the approach simply is misunderstood. One of our goals for this text is to try to deal with those concerns by explaining the terminology of behavior analysis, clarifying its attributes and methods, offering numerous real and hypothetical examples of its effective and humane application, and teaching you, the reader, how to make fruitful discoveries on your own.

Our main goal, however, is to contribute toward improving education by teaching about behavior analysis. To accomplish this we plan to present evidence of educational strategies that have been demonstrated to improve student learning, motivation, and deportment and to describe how these strategies might be applied conveniently, practically, and effectively in schools.

Why have we selected this goal? As parents, both of us are acutely concerned with educational effectiveness. As teachers who have taught and consulted at various levels, from elementary through postdoctoral, we empathize with the problems facing committed educators. We know the joy and satisfaction of seeing students learn in a supportive, pleasant atmosphere and want to help others to share that experience, as well. As private citizens, we are concerned that young people achieve the greatest possible competence to perform their jobs and live productively and contentedly, for this will improve the quality of their lives as well as the fabric of our society. We believe that educational excellence is achieved best by assuring that students progressing through school consistently succeed in accomplishing important and challenging tasks. This book is designed to teach you how to apply behavior analysis to help to accomplish that purpose.

For Whom Is the Book Intended?

Your attention to this preface suggests that you have an interest in educational improvement. You are our intended audience. Specifically, we have addressed ourselves to pre- and in-service teachers, consultants such as school psychologists and counselors, curriculum specialists, administrators, supervisors, concerned parents, and students. This book contains information and examples relevant for all these readers. As you skim the text you may note that the concepts rapidly become advanced and technical. Don't worry about that, because, in what we believe to be plain language, each concept and term is defined and illustrated in a variety of ways. A glossary is also offered in the back of the book to help you with any confusing terminology. Our students have told us that the material is readable and that on completing the text they felt they could identify and use the terms to read the technical research literature, to describe and explain the terms to others, and, for those who have practiced under supervision, to implement the strategies.

Although not essential, our students appreciate having completed a course in introductory psychology. This has permitted them to place behavior analysis within the broader context of psychology as a science and a profession.

Using the Text

You can use this text in different ways:

You can take it home and read it on your own, using it later as a reference source as you try out the suggested strategies.

If you are a serious student of behavior analysis, you will want to learn the definitions of terms, principles, and procedures. This will support your successful application of the strategies as well as enable you to read the current research literature. As we implied, this field is burgeoning, and new information is being discovered daily. With the knowledge and skill that the book is intended to provide, you should be able to examine critically new information as it is published.

Learning the Concepts

Our students have found that the best way to learn the many concepts of the book and how to apply them is to review the objectives before reading the chapter, and the study questions afterward. Most of them write out the answers to the study questions for the early chapters and continue to do so later on for any concepts with which they are experiencing difficulty. Some insist on writing out all study-question answers as an assurance to themselves that they really know the information in the chapter and are using it to their maximal advantage. ("Don't let your readers be fooled by the deceptively simple style," our students caution. "Each chapter is jam-packed with information.")

One concept that will crop up throughout the book is the importance of receiving reinforcement for progressing in small steps. A particularly effective way to accomplish this is regularly to take quizzes covering small quantities of the material after you have prepared yourself thoroughly. The data on more than a hundred studies (Johnson & Ruskin, 1977) have convinced us that the Personalized System of Instruction is an extremely effective instructional technique. With this system, known popularly as the "Keller Plan" (Keller, 1968), students prepare each chapter as above and then take a quiz over the material. Immediately afterward, someone—usually another student who already has demonstrated mastery of the material—scores the quiz and provides feedback. If the student being quizzed has scored 90% or above, he or she is credited with having mastered the unit and is permitted to progress to the next. Otherwise, a retake is scheduled. This continues until the mastery criterion is reached.[2] Using this method we are occasionally embarrassed, though simultaneously delighted, that our students know better than we do the contents of the text we have written.

Combining Text with Laboratory Experiences

The best way to learn to apply behavioral strategies successfully is to try them out under the guidance of a skilled supervisor, first with hypothetical cases, next with actual problems but under simulated conditions, and eventually with real people. We accomplish this by combining a series of laboratory and field experiences with the text. Using a manual (Sulzer-Azaroff & Reese, 1982), our students refer to fictional cases to set objectives, develop and use measures, and plan procedures and evaluation methods. These are tested out in role-play situations. Simultaneously, they follow the same format to design a self-management program to change a behavior of their own. Later, they apply the behavioral strategies systematically with an actual student or client. The manual and the students' supervisors (usually graduate students who have mastered the skills during a previous semester) provide sufficient guidance so that success is maximized. In this way our students not only learn to *say* what they should do, but actually *show* that they are capable of using the strategies effectively.

ACKNOWLEDGMENTS

No text of this scope is prepared without the input and assistance of a great number of people. The many youngsters, the personnel who serve them, and the students with whom we have worked have taught us much of what we know about effective, benign, and practical behavior-change strategies. We would like particularly to express our appreciation to the students who field-tested the manuscript, wrote study

[2]One set of multiple-choice questions with answers and three sets of short essay quizzes and answer keys for each chapter are available to bona fide instructors from the authors for the cost of reproduction and handling. Please send order on official stationery to Dr. B. Sulzer-Azaroff, Dept. of Psychology, Tobin Hall, University of Massachusetts, Amherst, MA 01003.

questions and quiz items, and gave us useful suggestions for improving its clarity. Our professional colleagues, through their writings and direct contact, also provided us with considerable material: principles, concepts and examples. Their names are scattered throughout the text.

Several people deserve a special note of thanks: Jennifer Scott, who prepared most of the study and quiz questions and their accompanying answer keys, and Susan Izeman and Richard Kirshen-Fleming, who proctored a number of students after they took the quizzes and made valuable suggestions for the improvement of various elements of the whole instructional package.

Considerable assistance with our writing style was provided by Nora Jacob and by Barbara Rosen. Barbara Mayer invested a tremendous amount of time and hard work in word-processing the manuscript and Kate Cleary also helped with many clerical chores.

To the dedicated educators like you, who prepare yourselves to guide your students toward excellence, we wish to express our heartiest appreciation. The fact that you are striving to improve your competence demonstrates how committed you are to doing your best. We hope that your efforts toward mastering this text are rewarded by your students' improved performance. That would be our best reinforcer.

References

Johnson, K. R., & Ruskin, R. S. (1977). *Behavioral instruction: An evaluative review*. Washington, D.C.: American Psychological Association.

Keller, F. S. (1968). "Goodbye teacher . . .". *Journal of Applied Behavior Analysis, 1*, 79–89.

Sulzer-Azaroff, B., & Reese, E. P. (1982). *Applying behavior analysis: A manual for developing professional competence*. New York: Holt, Rinehart & Winston.

Contents

part II
Principles and procedures: motivating, instructing, and managing behavior 61

part III

part IV

1 Introduction: strategies for achieving educational excellence

Goals

After completing this chapter, you should be able to:

1. Define and give illustrations of each of the following terms:
   a. Baseline
   b. Treatment, intervention, or program
   c. Collateral behaviors
   d. Contingencies
   e. Contingent relation
   f. Functional relation
2. Describe the three fictitious schools the authors use in their illustrations.
3. Explain the purpose of the book.
4. List five good teaching practices and provide an example of each.
5. Identify the similarities and differences between good teaching practices and applied behavioral strategies.
6. Describe and provide an example of the sequence of steps that applied behavior analysis follows.
7. List three major decision-making criteria used by behavior analysts in goal selection.
8. Describe the advantages of careful measurement.
9. Describe the withdrawal, multiple baseline, and multielement designs. Illustrate with your own example how an outcome can be verified experimentally.
10. Discuss why applied behavior analysis is less likely to be used exploitatively than other approaches.

The basketball rebounding off the spot on the schoolyard wall where a peace sign overlaps "The Fearless Devils" mingles its ping with a cascade of obscenities good-naturedly urging teammates to score another basket. A faint whiff of marijuana blends with the fumes of diesel trucks, the smell of boiling cabbage, overperked coffee, and the kitchen exhaust from a nearby Oriental restaurant. Teenagers gather in groups to watch the ballplayers or hunch conspiratorially, smoking and whispering. One youth, Juan, stands alone, shoulders rounded, hands thrust deeply into his pockets; he glowers at the others. It is 3:15 P.M. on a warm October after-noon and Washington Street Junior High School has just dismissed its students for the day.

Inside, Ms. Jackson peers down the hall before locking her classroom door securely and gets ready to attack the pile of papers on her desk before her. Down the hall, Mrs. Burnes is talking to the school counselor, K. C. Lee, and the principal, Manuel Rodriguez.

"Just when I thought I was making headway with Lucinda, this has to happen! You should have heard the language! 'I ain't gonna do this blankity-blank work!' and she tosses it off her desk, shoves her chair over, and storms out of the room. She banged the door so loudly that Mr. Lee heard it from his office way down the hall, didn't you, K. C.? And I'm sure I smelled alcohol on her breath, and there were bruises on her face and arms. I just don't know how we're ever supposed to accomplish anything in this place. No matter how hard I try, it seems to be a losing battle — you end up right where you started," Kate Burnes exclaims.

"You think you have problems," Mr. Rodriguez says. "This morning Juan Ortiz's mother comes barging into my office while I'm on the phone talking to the district superintendent. She starts pounding on the desk and demanding that I stop the other kids from picking on Juan. She tells me that if I can't keep order in this place, she's going to take matters into her own hands. She'll send over her brother — you know, the one who just got out on parole. I wouldn't be a bit surprised if he shows up here one of these days with a gun. I called the local precinct, but they say there's nothing they can do until something actually happens. They're too understaffed to follow up on all the threats that people report to them. Can you imagine! In other words, we have to wait for someone to be beaten up — or worse — before we can get any help from the police."

"I know what you mean, Manny," Mr. Lee adds. "Juan is in Pat Thomas's general science class, and he does have quite a problem. Pat asked for help, so I was in her room observing yesterday. The other kids tease him; they call him 'shrimp,' 'Momma's boy,' and a lot of other names I wouldn't repeat. She has tried almost everything — ignoring, scolding, advising Juan not to pay any attention. But of course he blows up and yells back and threatens to get them one of these days. Naturally, that just eggs them on. Can you imagine the difficulty that woman has, trying to conduct a chemistry demonstration with all that going on?"

No more than 15 miles away, another school is letting out. But the grounds of Franklin High School are manicured, and the youngsters who stream through its exits are dressed with careful and expensive casualness. Marissa, close to tears, avoids looking at Jeana as they amble slowly off the school grounds. "I can't believe I let it happen again. I don't

know what to do. My dad will kill me if he finds out."

"What are you going to do?" Jeana asks.

"I'm afraid to have an abortion. Besides, all they have to do is take one look at me. I look like such a kid. I bet they'd call my parents. Fourteen is too young to get married. Besides, I don't even know if it was Tommy or Fred. I never should have gone with them. I didn't know what I was doing. . . ."

Several of Franklin High's teachers have gathered in the lounge to decompress before they go home. "Can you beat that Richard Parker? His dad is one of the leading lawyers in town, his mom has at least three degrees and teaches philosophy at the community college, and he won't even try. I never saw a kid give up so easily. If it's not a problem he's seen a dozen times before, he won't even try," Ms. Martin says.

"He's the same way in my class," Mr. Genovese offers. "You give him an assignment and if it's not short and simple, he won't even begin to work on it. I'm sure he's bright enough. You should just get him talking about sports. I'll bet he knows the batting averages of every member of the Yankees for the past five years. The other day I overheard him talking about sports medicine — something about one of the players' knee operations. It was amazing how much he seemed to know about anatomy, but you'd never guess it from how he does in school. What a disappointment. After having his brother, Howard, I thought Richard would be an equal pleasure to have in class," the teacher says, shaking his head.

"I can imagine. Howard's in my senior social studies class, and his work is sensational. You should see the paper he just wrote on chemical waste disposal. He really has the knack of being able to see an issue from all sides, and he can write about it eloquently, too. I wish more of my students were like that," Dave Markham sighs.

"Well, I had one pleasant surprise today," Mr. Forsyth declares. "All of you know Freddie Farrel, whose dad is the night watchman at the foundry? Well, Freddie's coming along really well — designed this intricate model of the quarry area during prehistoric times and wrote a first-rate description to go along with it. Now if I can only find a way to prevent the other kids from teasing him about how 'squarely' he dresses. . . ."

By contrast, Willow Grove Regional School is isolated, its building many miles from any large center of population. Here there are only three classes: one primary—grades one through four; another middle—grades five through eight; and the other secondary—grades nine through twelve. Mrs. Olsen, teacher of the high-school-age group, also serves as principal because she has the fewest students. Most of the older youngsters have left school to farm with their families. Although the problems at Willow Grove may seem less dramatic, they are still acute.

"Not this, again!" complains one group of students who are clearly bored; while a few others counter with, "That's too hard." One 12-year-old, Billy, has not yet learned to read beyond the second-grade level. His teacher wants to have him tested to see if he might be mentally retarded, but the district school psychologist rarely finds the time to travel out to Willow Grove.

"Do you think we'll ever get a minute to breathe?" asks Mrs. Olsen, as Mr. Truax and Ms. Miller start sorting their materials. In one pile sit the papers to be graded; in the other, assignments for the next day. Ms. Miller sighs, "I have so many different assignments to plan for my students. It doesn't make sense to give them all the same work when their grade levels are so far apart. Oh well, it looks like one more night I don't leave before 7 P.M."

Although on the surface these schools seem very different, they share many of the same problems. The concerns of their faculties, students, and parents are the concerns of educators and parents everywhere:

- How can we encourage and sustain good academic performance by students?
- How can we establish and maintain a classroom atmosphere that is enjoyable and conducive to learning?
- How can we motivate youngsters to try their hard-

est and then to feel confident and satisfied with themselves when they do?
- How can we cope with the interpersonal and emotional problems of students and staff?
- How can we meet the requirements of an effective academic program, given limited human and material resources?
- How can we educate and guide teachers most effectively to manage, motivate, and instruct their students?
- How can we make the best use of counseling, psychological, and other support services?
- How can we work effectively with parents and other members of the community to gain their support for the school and its instructional program?
- In general, how can we plan the school environment so that teaching and learning are rewarding experiences?

Over the past couple of decades, our knowledge of the factors that influence the behavior of students, teachers, administrators, the public, and, indeed, of all living creatures has grown dramatically. In this text, we propose to share some of that knowledge with you, showing how it is applied effectively toward solving problems such as those just illustrated. From time to time, we'll return to those particular situations, because they typify so many of the problems faced by educators today. Naturally, those particular schools are figments of our imaginations, but the problems they encounter are very real. So bear in mind that when we refer to the Washington Street, Franklin, and Willow Grove schools and their students, staff members, and communities, no known living persons are being depicted. Yet the problems embodied by their situations are widespread and genuine.

For purposes of illustration, we also will draw on our own experiences. Besides teaching at the college and postgraduate levels, both of the authors of this book are parents. One of us has been an elementary school teacher and school psychologist; the other has been a high school teacher, counselor, and psychologist at the intermediate and elementary levels.

We've both spent considerable time out in the schools, consulting and doing research on problems like the ones we just described. We'll also call on the experiences that others have told us about and that we've read about in the published literature, thereby enabling you to see that the principles derived from empirical studies of behavior have general application; when applied correctly, they can produce dramatic improvements in the performance of students, teachers, other educators, and people everywhere.

Not that we pretend to have all the answers. We don't. But we believe that we have a methodology that has produced a substantial body of steadily increasing knowledge about human behavior. We hope to provide you with those guidelines that at the moment seem most productive. But perhaps even more importantly, we hope to equip you with a general strategy for solving or preventing the behavioral problems that you might encounter in your own role at school.

The methods involved are not new. They have always been "intuitively" practiced by successful teachers — as well as parents, managers, and, indeed, all sorts of people who work effectively with other people. Consider, for example, the following analysis of an actual experience.

GOOD TEACHING PRACTICES

A number of years ago, one of us was teaching at an inner-city school. Many of the students came from economically deprived homes. Few were strongly motivated to learn. Fighting and disruptions in the classroom were commonplace, and disciplinary functions took up an unusually large portion of the teachers' time. And yet there were some teachers who had model classes. Their students were learning, behaving maturely, displaying self-confidence; and they apparently respected and loved their teachers. These students were the same youngsters who in earlier years had proven difficult for other teachers to handle. What caused the metamorphosis? In retrospect, it became clear that those "superstar"

teachers were using good teaching practices. Here are some of the things they were doing.

Providing structure

They organized daily and weekly schedules and often incorporated suggestions that the students contributed. Individual and group programs were flexible enough to accommodate change, so that if one of the students had an exciting experience or if some event occurred unexpectedly, it was possible to adjust the schedule to capitalize on those situations. In general, however, students and teachers knew what they should do and when and where they should do it. They scheduled difficult learning activities, such as reading and arithmetic, for short periods of time initially, gradually increasing the duration and complexity. Enjoyable activities followed. After all the hard work had been done — at the culmination of units, for example — there were trips, parties, films, and musical performances.

Specifying rules clearly

Rules of conduct were specified at the beginning of the year and revised periodically thereafter. Students gave their input. They knew what constituted good classroom deportment. The teachers helped by translating prohibitions into prescriptions: instead of "Don't make too much noise," they'd offer, "Speak softly so others can concentrate." Having played a part in designating the rules, students felt more of a vested interest in upholding them and were more willing to cooperate. Sometimes the teacher and class found rules to be unreasonable or unworkable, so they revised them. For instance, an initial rule, such as "Stay in your seat," might later be modified to permit a student to leave his or her seat to sharpen a pencil, obtain and return materials, tutor peers, or carry out other valid activities.

Teachers worked hard to *catch the students being good* (a point emphasized by Bushell, 1973). Students received lots of attention when they followed the rules as specified. Privileges — such as helping the teacher, tutoring, or performing other prestige jobs — were distributed to those who followed rules. When the rules were broken, consequences that had been specified objectively were applied consistently. The students were proud of themselves for following rules that they themselves had designed, and the teachers were proud of their well-behaved pupils. This pride was apparent to the rest of the school.

Providing for active participation

Our super-teachers realized that effective teaching meant playing the roles of expediter, resource person, and consultant instead of just a dispenser of knowledge. The classes were structured so that all the children took an *active* part in their educational experiences. They read, wrote, sorted, constructed, organized, talked, listened to feedback, experimented; they played games, danced, sang, made up stories and poems, answered questions, solved puzzles, and did many other things. When they worked well, they knew it, either directly by seeing the products of their labor or indirectly by receiving the congratulations of their peers and teachers. Teachers rewarded achievement with attention, written or oral praise, comments on aspects of the performance that were particularly fine, and access to enjoyable activities and privileges. They spotted students with difficulties before a pattern of failure could develop and offered appropriate help and advice. For their part, the students gained the confidence that comes from a job well done.

Assigning tasks appropriate for individuals

The kind of successes described above can only occur when individuals are capable of performing their assigned (or self-selected) tasks acceptably. The successful teachers in our school constantly revised and refined their own instructional materials and hunted for new ones. They searched magazines and books on curriculum development, and they attended conferences and asked colleagues to share their successful experiences. Because such diversity

among student achievement levels existed in areas such as reading, spelling, and arithmetic, the teachers prepared many of the materials themselves. They would scout for easy but fascinating reading matter for those students who achieved slowly. They became well acquainted with each of their pupils and capitalized on the interests of each. The more capable students were allowed to follow their own interests, attaining the intrinsic rewards of succeeding at tasks that were sufficiently challenging but not overwhelming.

Today it is easier to teach students who possess a diversity of skills. Commercial materials offering a range of difficulty levels of high interest to children at various levels of development can be located with relative ease. A number of these have been broadly field-tested (Buchanan, 1965; Becker & Carnine, 1981). Literally hundreds of instructional products for handicapped learners have been developed since the Education for All Handicapped Children Act (PL 94.142) was passed in the United States in 1975. For advanced older students, individualized instructional programs and texts are commercially available in foreign languages, science, mathematics, statistics, electronics, and even contract bridge. Microcomputers are becoming more commonplace in school resource rooms, making individualized computer-assisted instruction a feasible option for almost any student.

The personalized system of instruction (PSI), originally developed for college students (Keller, 1968), also allows large groups of younger students to progress through instruction in various subject matters — from basic tool subjects to band music (Zurcher, 1977) — at their own individual rates and levels. It is particularly well suited to students who plan their schedules contractually with the teacher and who can read at a level sufficient to permit them to obtain information from the passage read. For example, McLaughlin and Malaby (1975) described sixth-grade students who served as reliable and accurate proctors (tutors) in a mastery learning program with their peers. Their arrangement resulted in the students completing more assignments and attaining improved grades. With programs and materials like these, successful teachers are addressing a wider range of student skills and needs ever more effectively.

Providing appropriate consequences

The model teachers in our school also accentuated the positive. They reinforced small improvements in academic, social, and personal behavior. And the consequences they provided were meaningful to the individual students. For some, telling others what they learned, or teacher attention, praise, or good grades sufficed. For others, applause or access to coveted privileges were delivered right after some small accomplishment. Positive consequences were presented consistently for gradual improvements. Jealousy was prevented by also allowing the rest of the group to profit from the efforts of their classmates; for example, the class got to have a party when one group of students completed its unit assignments.

BEHAVIORAL STRATEGIES AND GOOD TEACHING PRACTICES

Those of you who are familiar with the field of applied behavior analysis surely recognize that the model teachers in that school were using behavioral procedures very effectively, although they were probably unaware of having done so. In the same manner, over the whole span of human life on earth, teachers, parents, managers, and ordinary citizens have applied behavioral procedures to teach, train, or manage their own performance or those of others. So what we have to offer is hardly new to this century. What is new is the *manner* in which the procedures are applied. By describing various strategies for applying scientifically derived principles of behavior in a systematic and accountable way, we hope to help you to become a better educator.

APPLIED BEHAVIOR ANALYSIS

What exactly does it mean to apply scientifically derived principles of behavior in a systematic and accountable way — that is, to use applied behavior analysis? Are behavior analytic strategies effective? And if so, won't they be used exploitatively? It is our contention that, on the contrary, applied behavior analysis by its very nature is apt to be practiced in a particularly humane, sensitive, and responsible manner. Let's inspect how the method was used at Willow Grove Regional School for evidence to support this contention.

Thumbing through the pages of the *Journal of Applied Behavior Analysis* one day, Mr. Truax excitedly noted an article by Greer and Polirstok (1982). Those authors found that adolescent children, even those with problematic histories, were able to tutor eighth graders successfully in reading, to the mutual benefit of both tutors and tutees. The reading performance of both groups improved during their regular classes, as did their scores on standardized tests. This seemed like a promising possibility for Mr. Truax's class. But would that technique, tested by Greer and Polirstok in an inner-city school, prove effective in a classroom in which several grade levels were combined in the rural environment of the Willow Grove School?

To answer this question, Mr. Truax described the technique to his students, and they agreed to give it a try. For the initial **baseline,** * a representative measure of the behavior *prior* to any change in conditions, he recorded each student's scores on daily reading assignments for several weeks. (Conveniently, the assignments were of similar length and of very gradually increasing difficulty.) In the first **intervention** (also known as *treatment, change,* or *modification procedure*) phase, three boys who misbehaved often were then selected to tutor some of the other youngsters. The performance of the students they tutored — the tutees — was measured as previously and was found to have improved only

---

*All of the terms in this book that appear in **boldface** type are defined in the Glossary that begins on page 387.

slightly. As Greer and Polirstok (1982) noted, Mr. Truax found that his tutors failed to make approval statements when they should have.

So Mr. Truax added a second intervention. He and the tutors met for several sessions during their free period, and he showed them how to express approval. They practiced with one another until they had it right. Then during the tutoring sessions, Mr. Truax, aided by a highly responsible and respected student named Tim, observed to see how approval was being used. When tutors approved appropriately, Mr. Truax or Tim distributed points that could be exchanged later for special rewards and privileges. Results showed that rates of approval by tutors increased, and so did the tutees' performance in reading.

At that point, Mr. Truax wondered if the points were still necessary. So he stopped awarding points to the tutors when they approved appropriately. The tutors' rates of approving dropped, and so did the tutees' reading scores. After a couple of weeks, the teacher decided to reinstitute the point system and things once again improved. A **functional relation** between the intervention and student performance was demonstrated, because Mr. Truax found that by sequentially presenting and withdrawing the treatment conditions, or points, the change in praise and reading scores occurred *when* and *only when* the treatment was in effect. This observation showed that change was a *function* of the point awards. Fortunately, as time progressed, it was possible to diminish the number of points delivered slowly, as tutors began to use praise more comfortably as the program shifted over to a **maintenance** phase. Eventually, Mr. Truax only needed to compliment the tutors occasionally; yet their use of approval continued during tutoring, and the tutees continued to show improvement. One of the nicest aspects was that the tutors also behaved better in class and improved their own reading skills.

Selecting the behavior

This episode illustrated the essential steps followed in applied behavior analysis. What is it about this approach that makes it apt to be humane, sensitive, and responsible? As we have said, the very first thing that is done in applying behavior analysis is to select certain behaviors to be analyzed. This selection requires careful consideration rather than intuitive and haphazard treatment.[1] In our example, Mr. Truax needed to think carefully about the behaviors to be analyzed. He could have chosen to work on reducing the disruptiveness of his students or improving his own disciplinary skills. Instead, he applied a set of decision-making criteria:

1. What behaviors would be most advantageous to the class as a whole as well as to each of the members, himself included?
2. What behaviors would have not only short-range but also long-range payoff? How much extra effort would it take to see to it that they transferred or generalized across people, places or time?[2]
3. Could he arrange sufficient time, personnel, support, and other resources to follow through with this program and others like it?[3]

So he made a reasoned decision. Work on peer tutoring showed promise for all members of the class. The tutors stood to benefit through improving their own reading skills, and they might improve their conduct as well. Mr. Truax would be able to utilize his own time more effectively once the program was well underway, spending more time on teaching and less on managing.

After carefully weighing the alternatives and precisely identifying the behaviors to be tackled, Mr. Truax could involve others in the ultimate decisions as to whether or not to proceed. The students and

[1] If you are concerned with selecting objectives and an educational plan for a special-need student, we suggest you refer to Lovitt's "Writing and implementing an IEP" (1980). The general strategy recommended by Lovitt is consistent with the approach of this text.

[2] To reassure yourself that you have considered all possibilities here, refer to Drabman, Hammer, and Rosenbaum's generalization map (1979).

[3] Sulzer-Azaroff and Mayer (1977) and Sulzer-Azaroff and Reese (1982) include chapters on goal selection while a "mini-series" on target behavior selection appears in Issue 1 of the 1985 edition of *Behavioral Assessment*.

other appropriate parties could voice their opinions. If they preferred an alternate goal, that option could be discussed and negotiated in a "contractual" arrangement. The program then would be most likely to receive uniform support as all worked toward a common end.

Note how the program is designed with great care. You refer to records and obtain as much information as is useful in selecting appropriate long- and short-range goals, objectives, and procedures. You also analyze the system in which you will be operating to see if it will support the intended change. It would accomplish little for Mr. Truax to take great pains to train and supervise his students in tutoring if Mrs. Olsen, the principal, objected and couldn't be convinced that peer tutoring were a good idea. As all of us tend to do, you probably see more problems that you would like to tackle than your time and resources permit. So you need to set priorities, trying to target those goals that will most validly (Kazdin, 1985) accomplish as much as possible in the short and long run, for the greatest number of people at the least cost and effort. (Don't forget yourself. Your own satisfaction is a most important ingredient of being a successful educator.)

Contrast the above with this frequent occurrence: It's a bad day. The end of the grading period is approaching, and the students haven't been progressing to anyone's satisfaction. Neither their teachers, their parents, nor the students themselves are happy about the situation. A few pupils are misbehaving. The teacher scolds them or tries some other on-the-spot solution, possibly even asking some students to tutor one another. The next bad day she may try something else. But without a consistent purpose, consistent treatment is unlikely. Benefit is minimized. Additionally, the others involved haven't had an opportunity to express their concurrence with the goals, so they too may work at cross purposes, consequently accomplishing little.

Measuring the behavior

The next critical step, *devising measurement techniques*, further focuses attention on the value of the venture. You need to pose such questions as, "What does improvement in reading mean? Reading more words aloud correctly? Filling in blanks with a higher proportion of right answers or with an increasingly close match to a set of objective evaluative criteria? Writing descriptions or interpretations or critical commentary on the assigned passages?" You are forced to define the **operations** incorporated in the behaviors that have been selected. To do that you must say *who is to do what* and then add *under what circumstances and with what resources.* And you need to state the *standards* by which improvement will be demonstrated. In other words, you must specify **behavioral** or **instructional objectives.** Once that aspect is clarified, the ways to measure become more apparent. For oral reading, you would ask the student to read a passage, count the words read correctly and incorrectly, and compute the percentage or rate per minute of those correct or incorrect. For a critical interpretation, you might use a checklist to isolate and count those portions of the response that matched and those that didn't, and so on. (In Chapter 2, we discuss behavioral measurement in more detail.)

It is our contention that when you clearly specify behavioral objectives, not only will the procedures function more effectively, but the outcome will be more benevolent and advantageous to those involved in the long run. How? First, it brings you face to face with what it is you are striving for and says whether or not your goals are reasonable, too narrow, or too ambitious. This helps make your teaching more efficient and effective. Second, it enables you to communicate exactly what you are looking for to your students. Also, students can be involved in specifying objectives and measures. Either way, as a result, they are more likely to pursue the purpose. Third, in case you have found yourself defining objectives that might have some short-range but little long-range payoff, such as improving compliance but not proficiency, you can modify the plan before it is too late.

Next comes the construction of a **baseline.** The *selected behaviors are measured repeatedly over time, and a typical pattern of responding is re-*

vealed. Sometimes this pattern matches your expectations; sometimes it may surprise you.

The data may prompt you to modify the instructional environment in a simple way, such as changing a seating arrangement, the difficulty level of assignments, or the work group with which a student is to be affiliated. Alternatively, the baseline may help you to refine your objectives.

Because Ernie's oral reading is quite choppy and disconnected (disfluent), his teacher has concluded that he is a poor reader. Yet his daily written work is excellent. The objective for Ernie might be to increase his fluency in oral reading. Elmer, on the other hand, rarely scores above 50 percent on his assignments. His baseline indicates a need to assess his skills more closely and perhaps change the material he is assigned. Other students reveal reasonably high yet variable baselines; they do well on some days, not so well on others. It seems very appropriate to plan strategies to help them perform at a consistently high level.

You can see that using baselines can be very advantageous. They provide information that permits the system to be adjusted to each individual's own particular needs, to challenge students successfully yet reasonably. These are key ingredients for educational and personal success.

The important value of a *baseline* from an analytic viewpoint — that *it serves as a standard against which to assess any change during intervention* — also benefits the individual personally. For if an intervention has been in use for a while and if performance shows no improvement over baseline, then a different approach is indicated. Thus, the individual is not interminably subjected to an ineffective treatment. Other techniques are tried until, it is hoped, something effective is discovered. (Notice we do not assert that success is guaranteed, just that its likelihood is enhanced. Much remains to be learned about the conditions that influence human behavior and how to manage them optimally.)

The data revealed during treatment, of course, provide the most valuable information, both from a methodological and from a humanitarian perspective. If improvement is discernible, the treatment

continues; otherwise, as already indicated, it is modified. Recently, behavior analysts have begun to make it a practice to measure **collateral behaviors,** other behaviors not directly targetted for change but that might be positively or adversely influenced indirectly by the treatment. They ask themselves "what spin-off might be expected?" and refer to the research literature for guidance. In the Greer and Polirstok (1982) study, the tutors' on-task behavior in their own classes, outside of the tutoring sessions, was measured to examine the influence in the classroom of their involvement in tutoring. The study found that their rates of being on-task also improved in their classrooms. The measurement of such collateral behaviors can inform us about any potentially related value or harm to individuals or to the social group of which they are a part.

Selecting and implementing treatment strategies

Before you select treatment strategies or procedures, it is helpful to know what **contingencies** are currently in effect; that is, what events are reliable consequences for the behavior you have selected, what events precede the behavior as antecedents, and how they relate to its functioning. Note that contingencies can occur by happenstance, without anyone intentionally managing them; or they can be deliberately arranged, as were the points that Mr. Truax provided when the tutors approved appropriately. Whenever Ernie makes a mistake in oral reading, his teacher corrects him. The teacher never says anything when Ernie reads words correctly. Although his teacher is probably unaware of it, her attention is "contingent on" or, you might say, "dependent on" Ernie's errors. The contingent relation between the teacher's attention and Ernie's errors may be influencing his rate of producing errors. Each time Richard Parker is asked to tackle a new challenge, he sits in his seat and doodles or daydreams rather than complying. New challenges are the antecedent events that reliably precede doodling or daydreaming. Because those particular antecedent or consequential events *reliably precede or follow* *the behavior*, we say that there is a **contingent relation** between the two.

By examining the contingencies that are currently in effect, we can begin to guess how those events might function — that is, how they might be affecting a given behavior. Sometimes problems are solved simply by rearranging the contingencies. In Ernie's case, the teacher could try ignoring errors but saying something complimentary after the boy had read several lines in a row correctly. If Ernie's rate of producing errors dropped under those conditions, but rose again when the teacher returned to the former practices and again dropped when compliments were delivered contingent on correct reading, a **functional relation** between the behavior and the consequences will have been demonstrated, as it was with Mr. Truax's use of points and appropriate tutoring. (Similarly, functional relationships can be demonstrated between a behavior and those of its antecedents that reliably influence its rate of expression.)

Many productive behaviors yield reinforcement naturally, so contingency management is unnecessary. An exciting story, a pleasing passage of music, or an artistic product, for instance, may obviate the need to reinforce reading, listening, or crafting. In other cases, it may not be possible to manage the contingencies that appear to support a behavior. Profound pleasure may reliably accompany Marissa's sexual behavior, or it may be followed by lots of attention from her partners or even by something she says to herself: "I guess I must be pretty," or, "Now they can't ignore me." It would be very difficult to manage the first two consequences, though Marissa and her counselor possibly might work together on the self-statements. When contingencies can't be managed, other things can be tried. The program may be abandoned, or if feasible, more powerful or immediate consequences may be arranged to support some more adaptive behaviors to compete with the unwanted ones. (In Chapter 18 we will describe how Marissa's counselor helped her to cope with this problem by learning to be more socially assertive.)

After doing your best to identify the current contingencies, you also consider whether or not a simple rearrangement of the physical, social, or other aspects of the learning environment will rapidly accomplish the purpose. Otherwise, you will need to find out whether or not you have adequate resources — time, supplies, and personnel — or if those could be obtained. Mr. Truax turned to his students to meet his need for additional personnel. Next you ask, "What is the nature of the change to be accomplished? Is it intended to increase or reduce a behavior; to teach responses that don't currently exist; to broaden or narrow the sphere within which the behavior occurs; to keep it going over time, or what?"

Different procedures or procedural combinations are suited to each type of change. Chapters 4 and 5 contain methods for motivating or increasing the occurrence of behavior. Chapters 6 through 8 present procedures that can be used for instruction, and Chapters 9 through 12 focus on procedures for reducing or managing behavior. The procedures indicate how to arrange contingencies. But first you should be convinced that the goals are acceptable to those involved and that all generally concur regarding the planned procedures, particularly any that deviate substantially from standard practice. Thus, those involved might negotiate a "contract." Then an optimal time and place for implementing the program is selected, along with the methods you plan to use to analyze the outcomes experimentally. (Chapter 3 discusses these issues and evaluation in more detail.)

If you are faced with a particular problem in some academic area — handwriting, spelling, oral or written communication, reading, arithmetic — or in the social arena — social skills, attendance, vandalism, lunchroom behavior, or other behavior outside the classroom — then you will find Chapters 13 through 21 particularly helpful. However, the successful resolution of many of these problems involves a total staff commitment. Thus, Chapter 22 presents a variety of staff development strategies for effecting change among individuals and total staffs.

Evaluating the effects of treatment on the behavior

Lastly, the experimental verification aspect lets you know whether the treatment is responsible for the change, so you can make subsequent decisions — whether or not to keep it in effect; to try it with other behaviors or people, or in other places; to fade it out slowly; or whatever. Mr. Truax experimentally verified his outcome by sequentially presenting and withdrawing the conditions — a **withdrawal design** — and demonstrating a functional relationship. Other ways to verify the suspected contingent relation between the response and its antecedents and/or consequences include applying the treatment conditions on other behaviors, in other settings, or with other people — methods known as **multiple-baseline designs.** Verification also may be achieved by demonstrating that under discriminatively distinctive circumstances different conditions or different values of the same condition produce discernibly different patterns of a behavior — an analytic method known as a **multielement design**[4] (Sulzer-Azaroff & Mayer, 1977). These designs will be discussed in more detail in Chapter 3. If the results of your intervention were particularly promising, then you could tell others about it as so many have, thereby extending the benefit to more people.

ETHICAL ISSUES IN USING BEHAVIORAL METHODS

Does the foregoing necessarily imply that applied behavior analysis cannot be exploitive? No. As with any powerful set of procedures, people could apply this technology to their own advantage and the detriment of others. It is just rather unlikely. What despot would select goals on the basis of broad input, carefully define those goals, select measures of change, record and chart progress, analyze the out-

[4] *Alternating treatment* (Barlow & Hayes, 1979) and *simultaneous treatment* designs (Kazdin & Hartmann, 1978) also permit similar comparisons between different contingency arrangements.

come functionally, and tell others about it? (If nothing else, the person probably would worry about the project's records being discovered.) Nor is the field contributing anything to tyranny by analyzing procedures of behavior change per se. The world has long been acquainted with such powerful procedures as threats, punishment, and bribery to achieve selfish ends — ends that the despots may fail to communicate to themselves as well as to those they victimize. In Chapter 22 (Table 22.2) we present and respond to a set of frequently posed questions about behavior analysis, a number of which bear on ethical concerns.

At this point; we hope you will ask yourself what sort of an approach best safeguards the individual from exploitation. Is it one that considers what is best for the individual and others in the long as well as the short run, or one that treats difficulties as they arise with whatever means are at hand at the moment, regardless of future consequences? One that follows a prescribed plan, or one that is practiced intuitively? One that involves those concerned in the planning of strategies, or one that denies an attempt to influence, or that is based on a conviction that only those in charge know what is best? One that verifies the necessity for a procedure, or one that uses procedures arbitrarily? One that objectively notes change, or one that operates by guesswork? One that is designed to help people improve the quality of their lives, or one that pretends that interpersonal influence isn't happening, or that refuses to act on the grounds of unnecessary interference?

We believe that the careful, judicious planning involved in applying behavior analysis is to the optimal advantage of each individual student. By analyzing the **repertoire** of a student's behaviors and the environment within which learning takes place, the system helps the student to succeed. Because accomplishment is rewarding, learning becomes pleasurable. Increased competence and self-confidence result. What could be more humanitarian than that?

Summary

A major purpose of this book is to equip you with a general strategy for solving and preventing behavioral problems, **and for making your professional ca-**

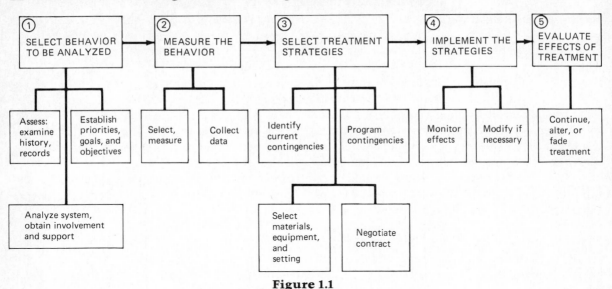

Figure 1.1
A five-step behavior analysis model.

reer and the activities of your students more meaningful and enjoyable through social and academic success. Several fictitious school situations were presented to illustrate the common concerns of many students, parents, and educators. The strategies that we will be describing in subsequent chapters for dealing with such concerns are based on solid principles that have been researched and substantiated. Although these strategies are hardly new and have been practiced "intuitively" by many successful educators, we emphasize how to use them systematically and, consequently, more effectively and humanely. We also show that behavioral strategies are not limited to application with students. We will provide many illustrations demonstrating their effectiveness on the behavior of staff members and others as well.[5]

The strategies are based on a behavioral analysis model consisting of five basic steps, summarized in Figure 1.1. Although every single step is not always necessary for every situation, we believe you will find the model helpful in approaching and effectively resolving major concerns. We also suggest that you consider certain practices throughout all steps of the program: (1) be ethical and accountable; (2) learn as much as you can about how to proceed by reading the literature, consulting with experts, and involving specialists; and (3) carefully record behavior and make any changes that the data dictate. Such an approach can best safeguard students and staff from exploitation while they progress toward achieving educational excellence.

[5]Literally thousands of books and papers have been written describing the application of behavior analytic procedures to just about every imaginable aspect of human performance: activities in the realms of health, business, family and community life, social relations, and many, many others.

Study Questions

1. In your own words, describe some of the problems common to the three fictitious schools.
2. Discuss the significance of the recent discoveries of factors that influence human behavior.
3. T/F   The authors plan to show you how to solve all your problems as an educator. Explain your answer.
4. T/F   Effective behavioral procedures are practiced "intuitively" by successful teachers. Explain your answer.
5. List and illustrate with your own original examples five good teaching practices.
6. In what way are "good teaching practices" similar to "applied behavior analytic procedures" and in what way are they different?
7. Next to each phase title, define the term and describe briefly what happened in Mr. Truax's adaptation of the study by Greer and Polirstok (1982).
   Phase title:
   Baseline
   Intervention
   Results
   Maintenance
8. (a) List three criteria for deciding what behaviors to select for change.
   (b) Why do you think these criteria are important?
9. Describe some other steps you might follow in selecting the behaviors you plan to try to change.
10. Imagine that you are organizing a program of behavior change with a teacher. Select an original illustrative problem and describe what you would tell her has to be done to measure the behavior and why.
11. Describe a novel situation in which it would be advisable to assess collateral behaviors.
12. Betsy writes out the answers to her study questions. Afterward she scores above 90 percent on the unit quiz.
    (a) Use this example to describe the term *contingent relation*.
    (b) Explain how she could find out if the contingent relation were a functional relation.
13. A colleague fears that behavior analytic strategies might be exploitive. Outline your response.
14. Summarize the steps you would follow in conducting a behavioral analysis program. Use your own original problem situation to illustrate each of those steps.

References

Barlow, D. H., & Hayes, S. C. (1979). Alternating treatment design: One strategy for comparing the effects of two treatments in a single subject. *Journal of Applied Behavioral Analysis, 12,* 199–210.

Becker, W. C., & Carnine, D. W. (1981). Direct instruction: A behavior theory model for comprehensive educational intervention with the disadvantaged. In S. W. Bijou & R. Ruiz (Eds.), *Behavior modification: Contributions to education.* Hillsdale, N J: Lawrence Erlbaum Associates.

Buchanan, C. D. (Ed.) (1965). *Sullivan associates program, programmed reading book.* New York: McGraw-Hill.

Bushell, D., Jr. (1973). *Classroom behavior: A little book for teachers.* Englewood Cliffs, N J: Prentice-Hall.

Drabman, R. S., Hammer, D., & Rosenbaum, M. S. (1979). Assessing generalization in behavioral modification with children: The generalization map. *Behavioral Assessment, 1,* 203–219.

Greer, R. D., & Polirstok, S. R. (1982). Collateral gains and short-term maintenance in reading and on-task responses by some inner-city adolescents as a function of their use of social reinforcement while tutoring. *Journal of Applied Behavior Analysis, 15,* 123–139.

Kazdin, A. E., (1985). Selection of target behaviors: The relationship of the treatment focus to clinical dysfunction. *Behavioral Assessment, 7,* 33–47.

Kazdin, A. E., & Hartmann, D. P. (1978). The simultaneous treatment design. *Behavior Therapy, 9,* 912–922.

Keller, F. (1968). Goodbye teacher. *Journal of Applied Behavior Analysis, 1,* 79–89.

Lovitt, T. (1980). *Writing and implementing an IEP.* Belmont, CA: Fearon Education, Pitman Learning.

McLaughlin, T. R., & Malaby, J. E. (1975). Elementary school children as behavioral engineers. In E. Ramp & G. Semb (Eds.), *Behavior analysis: Areas of research and applications,* Englewood Cliffs, N J: Prentice-Hall.

Sulzer-Azaroff, B., & Mayer, G. R. (1977). *Applying behavior analysis procedures with children and youth.* New York: Holt, Rinehart and Winston.

Sulzer-Azaroff, B., & Reese, E. P. (1982). *Applying behavioral analysis: A program for developing professional competence.* New York: Holt, Rinehart and Winston.

Zurcher, W. (1977, October). *A total PSI program for a junior high school band.* Paper presented at the Second National Symposium on Research in Music Behavior, Milwaukee, WI.

I Behavior analysis: an accountable system

"Behavioral procedures used to sound so impersonal to me," commented Mr. Rodriguez, the principal at Washington, to his staff. "Then I had a couple of long, heart-to-heart talks with Mr. Lee, and he has convinced me otherwise."

"How did he do that?" Ms. Thomas questioned.

"By pointing out a few things. For instance, the way we usually conduct our teaching is based on guesswork about what helps our students most. He indicated how behavioral methods use objective ways of finding out what is happening, so our own positive or negative biases don't get in the way. For instance, you have told us how you have tried all sorts of things to get Juan to pay attention. If you used a be-havioral approach you would identify some objective measures of paying attention. Those measures would show if any change occurred when you tried out your strategy; if any of those methods had even a subtle effect for the better or worse—but that wasn't the only thing."

"What else?"

"Well, you know how we select many of the things we are to teach by referring to our curriculum guides. But we do a lot of academic and nonacademic teaching that isn't written there—particularly when we teach work habits, fair play, and other kinds of social behavior."

"I know what you mean," chimed in Ms. Jackson. "Just yesterday we di-

15

gressed into a discussion about ethics in politics because of that episode in Washington last week. I'm sure the class learned a lot."

"That's great, Ms. Jackson. I'm sure they did. But what I'm talking about is teaching when we may or may not recognize what's happening. We may not stop to ask ourselves what we're trying to accomplish and how it will affect our students. Within the behavioral model, important objectives are specified, including ways of finding out if they are being achieved."

"That sounds pretty mechanical to me."

"Just stop and think about it for a moment," said Mr. Rodriguez. "Is it better to work toward unspecified goals that have not been carefully studied from the viewpoint of what's best for students and those in their environments, or is it better to identify objectives so that they become obvious?"

"I think I see what you're getting at. When an objective is clearly stated, we and the students (and maybe even their families and neighbors) can look at it and decide whether it really makes sense to pursue it. We don't waste time and confuse our students and ourselves about what we're trying to accomplish."

"That's the point. But there's even more."

"Really?"

"I'm referring to the theme of accountability that laces the behavioral model; in particular, how it analyzes procedures to determine whether or not they are effective with individuals. So much evaluation in the field of education has been concerned with group averages that the individual often has been lost by the wayside. Behavior analysis looks at the performance of individuals in relation to changes in the environment. That allows us to keep searching for effective strategies to apply to each person."

"In other words," Ms. Jackson said, "what you're telling us is that a behavioral approach is a humane approach, because it is responsive to the individual—by helping all of us recognize what we will be teaching and by letting us know how effectively our teaching is progressing with individual students."

"Yes. But there's still another benevolent aspect. That is the emphasis behavioral educators have placed on the positive. When feasible—and it seems to be so when goals are realistic and instruction is matched to the individual's current *repertoire*, or set of capabilities and levels of performance patterns—students are able to progress satisfactorily, in that way they are rewarded by their successes or perhaps by some other pleasant events.

"So," continued Mr. Rodriguez, "learning should be enjoyable. But it seems to me that the best part is that by learning more, students should be able better to face the world and maybe improve the quality of their lives. If that's the case, I'm convinced. At any rate, I'm ready to give it a try and hope you are, too."

We hope you, too, are ready to give behavior analysis a try. Now that you have been introduced, in the first chapter, to the behavioral approach, you probably are beginning to understand what Mr. Rodriguez was talking about. In this section of the text we will explain assessment and other aspects of behavioral accountability in broader detail. As you study this and the subsequent material, please continue to ask yourself how effectively, in contrast with others, this approach meets your humanistic concerns. We trust you will join with us in concluding that it can do so very well.

2 Assessing behavior

Goals

After completing this chapter, you should be able to:

1. Define and give an illustration of each of the following terms:
   a. Narrative recording
   b. Sequence analysis
   c. Reliable measurement or recording
   d. Permanent product recording
   e. Reactivity
   f. Transitory behaviors
   g. Discrete behavior
   h. Event recording
   i. Time sampling
   j. Continuous behavior
   k. Whole-interval time sampling
   l. Partial-interval time sampling
   m. Zone system
   n. Momentary time sampling
   o. Duration recording
2. Discuss the purposes of doing a sequence, or contingency analysis, and describe how it is done.
3. List the advantages and disadvantages of narrative recordings, and explain how they are conducted.
4. List and discuss the two critical factors on which precise behavioral assessment depends.
5. List, illustrate, and discuss the advantages of permanent product recording.
6. Describe and illustrate how, when, and when not to use event sampling.
7. Collect event data with someone else, and calculate your coefficient of agreement.
8. Discuss the conditions under which using each of the following recording systems would and would not be appropriate.
   a. Time sampling
   b. Whole-interval time sampling
   c. Partial-interval time sampling
   d. Momentary time sampling
9. Collect time sampling data with someone else, and calculate your coefficient of agreement.
10. Describe the PLA-Check observational system, including its advantages.
11. Discuss how and under what conditions to use duration recording.
12. Collect duration recording data with someone else, and calculate your coefficient of agreement.

Mrs. Parker checked her watch again—6:14, hardly any later than the last time she had looked. With the aroma of beef burgundy wafting through the house, she dropped into a chair and picked up the newspaper. But instead of relaxing and using the momentary respite to catch up on the day's news, she could barely concentrate. It had been a distressing afternoon—the boys' report cards had come in the mail. For Howard, it was straight A's again; but Richard got D's in English and math, even worse than the last time.

She had tried to calm herself before Richard arrived home from school, but his manner hadn't helped. When she had heard the back door shut, she called out to him, but he didn't respond. So she had gone to his room, knocked, and walked in. Richard was lying on his bed, staring up at the ceiling, arms folded under his head. He'd neglected to remove his track shoes, and flakes of semihardened mud were sprinkled all over his new tweed bedspread.

"Good grief, Richard. What's the matter with you? You don't answer when I call. And here you are; absolutely ruining your new spread."

"If all you want to do is yell at me, why don't you leave me alone? I didn't ask you to come into my room!"

"Well, it's our money that pays for your things. You never seem to appreciate what we do for you. Take your schoolwork, for instance. We keep asking you if you have homework, and we try to remind you to do it. You insist there isn't any, but now your report card comes and it's apparent that you haven't been keeping up. D's! Two of them. Sometimes I wonder if you're not doing badly just to spite us." Her voice had begun to quiver, and she felt tears starting to well up.

"Look, if you feel that way, why don't you just leave me alone?" Richard demanded.

The next morning, when everyone was calmer, Mr. and Mrs. Parker decided it was time to do something about the situation with Richard. With their son's grudging consent, they made an appointment to speak with Dr. Levy, the school psychologist. A week later, Mr. and Mrs. Parker sat down to discuss their concerns with Dr. Levy. Both expressed their fear that Richard might not be admitted into college if he continued to earn such poor grades, and they asked if perhaps he might have been assigned to the wrong track.

Mrs. Parker also commented, "Richard doesn't seem to try hard enough. He gives up too easily. I wonder if he does this because he has realized he just can't catch up to Howard?"

"That could explain part of the problem, but perhaps not all. Maybe some other factors are involved," the psychologist answered.

"Like what?"

Dr. Levy reviewed Richard's file with them, indicating a set of scores the boy had attained on a widely used achievement test. Reading vocabulary: grade equivalent—8.6; reading comprehension—7.5; arithmetic computation: 9.8; word problems: 7.7.

"That's not too good for a ninth grader, is it?" Mr. Parker asked. "It seems to me that Howard's scores were always much higher than that."

"Well, actually, on the whole, these aren't all that awful," observed Dr. Levy. "One thing that may be a problem for Richard is that many of the students here at Franklin score well above grade level. We're just a privileged group, and our students do well. It might be not only Howard's performance that is discouraging Richard, but that of Richard's peers as well.

"Let's look a little more closely at these scores," she continued. "It appears that Richard doesn't do as well when reading comprehension is involved—as, for example, with word problems in arithmetic."

"If that's all there is to it, let's send him to a private school where he can get closer personal attention," Mrs. Parker suggested.

"I'm not sure we're quite ready to make that decision yet. Part of the problem could have to do with the effort Richard puts out. You've noticed that at home. Why don't we talk to his teachers, and examine his performance more closely—not only the *products* he produces but also the *processes* by which those products are fashioned, such as his work and study habits and deportment. That's what we usually do in cases like these. We should also look at the social environment of the class and how it affects Richard. Then we can get together and plan our strategies. How does that sound?"

Both parents expressed their agreement, and a follow-up meeting was scheduled two weeks later.

And so the assessment process began.

TESTING AND INTERVIEWING

First, Dr. Levy wanted to meet Richard, so she invited him to her office to get acquainted. With the World Series going on, they had a lot to discuss. A star pitcher was suffering from an injured elbow, and Richard talked about the player's chances for recovery. Because Richard himself had some difficulty with his knee, he was especially interested in the topic and, as it turned out, was quite knowledgeable about human anatomy and physiology.

"Would you like to go into that field?" queried Dr. Levy.

"You mean sports medicine or exercise science or teaching gym? You must be kidding. Right now, I'm wondering if I'll make it through high school. I'm doing so terribly, my parents must be really discouraged."

"I wouldn't be all that worried. It's apparent that you've got a lot going for you. Why don't we do some detective work and see how we might be able to help?"

Dr. Levy began by assessing Richard's general level of intellectual functioning via an individual intelligence test. Richard was not required to do any reading, but he was asked to define lists of words, solve some problems, work a few puzzles, repeat sequences of numerals and perform other activities. When she later calculated the score, it fell within the superior range. Clearly, Richard had achieved a number of important skills well beyond those of many of his contemporaries.

Next, the reading specialist, Ms. Pear, conducted a diagnostic reading session. She presented prose passages to Richard and requested that he read them aloud. She also asked him many questions about the material he had just gone through. Richard read rapidly, she discovered, and often skipped over words or substituted others that fit the context or visually resembled the actual words in the passage. He apparently had developed some troublesome habits that probably were interfering with his comprehension. Following a summary discussion of her findings, she and Richard agreed that he probably could profit from some help in reading skills.

After that, Richard and the guidance counselor,

Mr. Kay, met to discuss a number of topics, including how the boy typically went about doing his homework. Apparently, when he did it, Richard followed no regular format—sometimes he wrote down assignments, other times he trusted them to memory; sometimes he did homework in his room, other times in the living room in front of the TV. Because he worked out regularly with the track team each afternoon, Richard was often too tired to concentrate on homework in the evening. Instead, he would resolve to set the alarm early in the morning and catch up. Unfortunately, he reported that for some reason the alarm failed to awaken him most of the time. It was a good thing his father had to catch an early train and made sure his son was awake in time for the bus.

Before they parted, Mr. Kay offered to help Richard with his study habits and to work with Dr. Levy to see if anything else could be done to help him to improve his school achievement. Richard thanked him and shrugged his shoulders with a parting, "I guess it can't hurt."

BEHAVIORAL ASSESSMENT

Although much useful information was gained from the tests and interviews, Dr. Levy and Mr. Kay recognized that most of it constituted either a limited sample of Richard's performance or was based on hearsay evidence. The most valid way of finding out about the social environment of the class and Richard's performance would be to see for themselves. So the psychologist and the guidance counselor arranged with Richard and his teachers to observe him and others repeatedly in his math, English, and physical education classes. To determine where they later might focus their attention, they started by using a **narrative recording** system.

Narrative recording

During their initial visits to the classes, both observers seated themselves as unobtrusively as possible.

As if producing a script for a play, they jotted down, as it was occurring, *a narration of what was transpiring* in Richard's classes. Here are some excerpts. Note how they read like a script to a play:

- *Math class*. Assignment written on board: "Do pages 72–3 on simple equations." Several students ask questions. Teacher reviews procedure for class. Richard sits quietly as teacher speaks. Then turns to assigned pages and does work. Talks to boy next to him and they compare answers. Teacher remains at desk correcting papers.
- *English class*. Discussion of homework questions over a story all were assigned to read. Teacher calls on students who raise hands to answer questions. Richard sketches space vehicles, gazes out of window (looks bored). . . .
- *Physical education*. Discussion of aerobic exercises for a few minutes, then all practice. Teacher circulates around gym, correcting and complimenting students' efforts. Several students are asked to demonstrate, Richard among them. He looks toward me and smiles a little sheepishly. . . .

Sequence analysis

Afterwards, Dr. Levy took those narratives and, using a format developed by Goodwin (1969), did a **sequence analysis,** examining them in terms of what preceded and what followed Richard's productive and nonproductive performances. For example, see the analysis below.

Setting: Math Class
Teacher: _____ Date: _____ Time: _____
Ongoing Activity: Class working on assignment in book. Teacher reviewing aloud.

Antecedents	Behavior (Richard)	Consequences
Teacher writes assignment on board.	Takes out book; turns to page.	None for R. Another student raises hand; asks question.
Teacher explains assignment.	Looks toward teacher.	None visible.
Teacher turns to work at his desk.	Begins working.	Teacher ignores R. and other students working.

Setting: P.E.
Teacher: _____ Date: _____ Time: _____
Ongoing Activity: Aerobic exercises — lectures, practice, and demonstrations.

Antecedents	Behavior (Richard)	Consequences
Teacher discusses aerobic exercises.	Watches.	Teacher asks students for review of how aerobics work and who benefits from them.
Several students raise hands.	Watches.	Teacher comments on other students' responses.
Teacher asks students to practice.	Does exercises.	Teacher circulating; compliments R.
Teacher calls on R. and others to demonstrate.	Demonstrates (and smiles in my direction).	Teacher indicates positive aspects of performance; other students watch and try to do same.

Sequence analyses often suggest factors that may relate to students' problematic performance in school, such as the nature of the assignment, patterns of teacher-student interactions, and others.

They also may clue us about ways the environment can be improved to remedy the situation. In Richard's case, we begin to suspect that aspects of the content of his classwork and his interactions with his teachers may be supporting his current behavior. The extended sequence analyses in math and English have shown that when Richard does what he should, he is ignored; when he strays from the assignment, he is corrected. During a discussion in physical education, however, his teacher compliments him, and other students are very responsive to his contributions. Perhaps providing Richard with materials of interest, along with approval by teachers and peers for being productive, would aid his improvement.

Sequence analyses do not necessarily require the presence of outside observers. Sometimes teachers can conduct such analyses by themselves. For instance, Ms. Thomas could record Juan's interactions with his classmates on the playground or during lunch, and perhaps she might generate some guesses about what events provoke Juan or sustain his surliness.

PRECISION IN RECORDING

Narrative recordings approach the measurement of actual behavior much more closely than do test scores and retrospective reports. They are not as precise as some other strategies of behavioral assessment, though, because they tend to be subjective. Each observer may note different aspects of ongoing events. If we want to find out what actually is happening, we need to use techniques of assessment that are *standard* — that enable different observers to record the same event the same way. If one observer noted that Juan stood alone and glowered, and another that he seemed to be plotting "something dire," that wouldn't help anyone to know what was actually going on or what might be done to change it.

Precise behavioral assessment depends on two critical factors: clearly *defining* the behavior of concern; and devising a recording system that will yield uni-

form or *reliable* data. Vague terms like "surliness," "boredom," or "lack of comprehension" need to be redefined so that anyone handed the definitions would be able to score their presence or absence. Such redefinition is accomplished by providing a description of what physically occurs. Perceived boredom during instructional activities may be described as "looks out of window, doodles, yawns," and so on. Lack of comprehension may be noted as "answers questions or carries out instructions incorrectly," and so on. When the performance can be seen or heard distinctly — and recorded in specific descriptive details — observers are more apt to agree about what is transpiring.

Reliable recording is another matter. Sometimes that is readily accomplished; other times not. We are fortunate, though, that applied behavior analysis has evolved a number of methods that permit performance to be recorded precisely. These methods should permit you to assess directly most of the classes of behavior that concern you as a teacher, administrator, or specialized provider of psychological or educational services. Some of these methods can be used by teachers with relative ease. Others are more amenable to application by consultants or other outside observers. Even with the latter category, though, the system can be adjusted for use by teachers or even students recording their own behavior. (Later in the book, we supply many examples of students conducting self-recording.) Here we shall describe some of these methods.[1]

Recording products of performance

After conferring with Richard's teachers, Dr. Levy decided to look more closely at his academic performance. The most simple and obvious thing was to examine the academic work the boy had produced over the past several weeks — worksheets, reports, homework, and so on. This material would provide

[1] In subsequent chapters, we discuss dealing with specific problem areas, such as classroom management, social skills, vandalism, instruction, and so on. In those chapters you will learn about additional measures that have been used to assess change in those areas. For further information, consult the articles referenced within the text.

a sample of his typical patterns of academic response. The psychologist also looked at his teachers' grade books, computing sets of items completed correctly and reviewing Richard's grades on assignments and whether or not the work had been embellished with doodles.

Products of this type are relatively easy to measure reliably, because they are durable and can be assessed repeatedly by the same or different people, permitting us to estimate our reliability readily by comparing one measurement against another. If both agree, then we are more confident that our system is sound. If not, we can keep referring to the product to redefine or revise our way of scoring it until agreement is reached.

Another advantage of an enduring or **permanent product recording** is that it can be assessed at a time or place different from that in which it was produced, thereby avoiding a situation in which the person being observed reacts to the presence of people from the outside by behaving in a nontypical fashion. Richard might complete his written assignment with far greater care than usual in the presence of Dr. Levy. Such **reactivity** would produce misleading evidence, so it was fortunate that she could retrieve his previous work.

Sometimes the product of a behavior of concern remains in the environment and can be measured more readily after people depart. The amount of litter in a lavatory, cafeteria, or playground provides one example; the costs of repairing vandalized school property is another.

When litter is used as the product that is to be measured, then individual pieces of litter usually are counted (Bacon-Prue, Blount, Pickering, & Drabman, 1980; Chapman & Risley, 1974; Mayer, Nafpaktitis, & Butterworth, 1981). Chapman and Risley (1974) counted pieces of litter that were larger than two inches in diameter. Excluded were those that were indigenous to the surroundings, such as twigs, rocks, leaves, trash containers, lawn furniture, or intact toys. Later, in Chapter 20, you'll see how products of vandalism are used as evidence in support of the effectiveness of particular behavior change strategies.

Recording transitory behavior

Many behaviors, however, do not leave an enduring product, such as litter, broken glass, or assignments handed in to the teacher. Smiling, reading, or computing aloud, making a threat, paying attention to the teacher, teasing . . . these are examples of **transitory behavior.** They must be recorded when they happen. If you want to record fleeting behaviors, you will need to observe and record the behaviors as they occur. In that case, to minimize *reactivity* to your presence, you should try to be as unobtrusive as possible and visit several times until people ignore or *adapt to* your presence.

Frequency or event recording. The simplest method of observing ongoing behavior is to count how frequently each event takes place. Dr. Levy could count the number of times one of Richard's teachers called on him or the number of times he answered a question. Mr. Truax could count the *rates per minute* of the words Billy read correctly and the words he read incorrectly.[2] Assuming that the behaviors were sufficiently *discrete*, that their beginning and end were clearly distinguishable, all she would have to do is to make a hatch mark each time it occurred. If she wanted to convince herself that she were counting reliably, she could ask someone else—the teacher, Richard, or another outside observer—to count, too. They could then estimate their **reliability** by comparing how closely they agreed by taking the totals derived by each and dividing the smaller total (i.e., the number of agreements) by the larger total (i.e., the number of agreements plus disagreements). The larger the quotient, the better the agreement. Other examples of events that lend themselves readily to frequency recording are: the number of times that a student sharpens a pencil, contributes to the class discussion, or attends a job interview; the number of times a teacher calls on a particular student, makes a praise statement, or delivers a reprimand; the number of times the prin-

---

[2]Ogden Lindsley, developer of *Precision Teaching*, advocates using frequency in time, (i.e., rates per minute) as goals and standard measures.

cipal visits; or the number of assertive statements a client makes in a social skills training session.

If the behavior of concern occurred either very frequently or infrequently, particular events could be missed. To convince ourselves better of the reliability of our recording when a behavior occurred often, two or more observers could use a recording form designating blocks of time, say every 15 seconds. Marks designating each occurrence of the event then are placed within their corresponding time blocks and later compared for the total within each time block. Such a system would be useful for measuring the number of times Lucinda leaves her seat or the room, or how often she throws her work on the floor, or the number of times Richard volunteers to answer a question or attempts to solve a problem. On Figure 2.1 you see two forms on which two observers recorded the number of times Lucinda left her seat during a 6-minute observational period.

Below the sample forms, we have calculated a coefficient of agreement to estimate how reliable our observational system might be. Because the definitions of out-of-seat behavior were precisely specified (no simple task—try it, you'll find out), the quotient was reasonably high, sufficiently high to convince us that our definitions and recording methods were designed adequately.

Students can also be taught to collect event data. The observers in the Cleveland school (MacPherson, Candee, & Hohman, 1974) were elementary school students, 9 to 11 years of age. They were taught to record instances of talking while the aide speaks, out-of-seat, and various forms of quarreling in their school cafeteria. For accurate scoring they earned praise and tokens exchangeable for various rewards and privileges, such as an early lunch period, snacks, and the use of audiovisual equipment. They received the rewards or privileges regularly during training and intermittently afterward. The observers worked in pairs, each sitting at an opposite side of the lunchroom, marking a recording sheet divided into three rows of twelve squares each. Each row corresponded to one of the three target behaviors; each square, to a 5-minute interval. Observers made a tally mark in the box designated for that particular

5-minute interval each time they noted any of the target behaviors. Reliability was assessed by comparing the number of intervals in which both observers agreed on the exact frequency of the target behavior and dividing by the number of 5-minute intervals scored for that day. Observers were assigned to different partners during one phase to prevent any one pair from developing an erroneous pattern of agreeing.

Time sampling. Unfortunately, it is not always possible to limit measurement to discrete events that readily can be counted. Many behaviors of concern to school personnel are of such a nature that it is difficult to keep track of the count or tell when they begin and end—they are **continuous behaviors.** Try counting the number of times a student twirls her hair, or see if you can keep track of episodes of "attending" in class or showing depression. Even when behaviors are defined with exquisite precision, you will find out how difficult counting them can be. It probably will be impossible for you to count hair twirls accurately, or identify the moment a student begins looking at his work, or note when his back hunches over and his mouth turns down at the corners. Event recording also can yield distorted estimates when the behavior of concern is capable of varying widely in duration. (Say, for instance, Lucinda has left her seat only once—but she stayed out of it throughout the whole period.) In such circumstances, time sampling can save the day, providing the behavior occurs on the average of at least once every 15 minutes (Arrington, 1943).

Let us see how Richard's attending and his teachers' responses were recorded by Dr. Levy. First Dr. Levy prepared to assess Richard's attending and his nontask and disruptive behaviors and to record how his teachers responded to him. She defined each of Richard's behaviors:

1. Attending (A): Directing eyes and/or head toward work, doing assignment, answering questions aloud, and so on.
2. Disruptive (D): Tapping pencil, tearing paper,

OBSERVATION FORM 1

Person Observed _Lucinda_   Date _10-2_   Time _850_

Behavior _Out of seat_

Observer _K. C. Lee_   Definition: No part of lower portion of body touching chair.

15	30	45	60	15	30	45	60
—	—	|	—	||	—	—	||
—	—	—	—	—	|||	—	—
||	—	|	—	||	—	|	|

OBSERVATION FORM 2

Person Observed _Lucinda_   Date _10-2_   Time _8:50_

Behavior _Out of seat_

Observer _N. Rodriguez_   Definition: No part of lower portion of body touching chair.

15	30	45	60	15	30	45	60
—	—	|	—	(|)	—	—	||
—	—	—	—	—	(||)	—	—
||	—	|	—	(|)	—	|	|

Number of time blocks in which both agreed exactly: 21

Number of time blocks in which number did not match exactly (indicated by circles): 3

Total number of blocks (agreements plus disagreements): 24

agreements: 21

$$\frac{\text{agreements}}{\text{agreements} + \text{disagreements}} \Big\} \frac{21}{24} = .875$$

Figure 2.1
Calculating agreement scores.

talking without permission, throwing papers, and so on.

3. Nontask (N): Looking out of window, doodling instead of attending or working, working on material other than that assigned, and so on.

For the teachers, she defined their responses to Richard like this:

1. Approval, verbal or nonverbal (+): Praise, nod, smile, "O.K.," pat on the back or other positive feedback, either spoken or gestured.
2. Disapproval, verbal or nonverbal (−): Negative statements, such as "Wrong" or "No;" frown; corrections (e.g., "Add that again"; "The word doesn't say, 'dessert,' it says 'desert.'") or other negative gestures or comments.
3. Neutral (0): No discernible reaction to Richard.

Dr. Levy used a behavioral assessment instrument that looked like the one in Figure 2.2.

Although she could have used a stop watch to cue her, Dr. Levy instead selected an audiotape player. A prerecorded tape prompted her, via an ear plug, to observe Richard or the teacher for 10 seconds and to record the symbol designating what she observed during the next 5 seconds: "Observe, record 15; observe, record, 30. . . ." For the first 5 minutes she recorded Richard's behavior; for the next 2½ minutes, the teacher's. This pattern continued until the recording sheet was completely filled in. Then she added any comments she thought to be relevant.

Actually, Dr. Levy used two different varieties of **time sampling**[3] when she observed. Wishing to be conservative in her estimate of Richard's attending behavior, she only would record an *A* if the boy were attending *throughout the full 10-second interval.* Naturally, using this approach caused some of Richard's attending to go unrecorded if he had been momentarily inattentive during any particular interval. So the estimate was conservative. (Any be-

haviors that occurred during the 5-second "record" interval were ignored.) That method is called **whole-interval time sampling.** It is used any time you want to assess performance conservatively, particularly any performance that you are trying to increase, such as remaining on-task, presenting a pleasant facial expression, sustaining relaxed muscles or holding a musical note—among many others.

For inattentive or disruptive behaviors and the teacher's responses to them, Dr. Levy followed a different format—scoring the interval with the appropriate symbol *as long as any single instance of the behavior occurred.* That way, she would not miss any instance of those categories. So, for example, if Richard spoke briefly with a neighbor while the teacher was explaining something to the class (or Lucinda shouted out a four-letter word, or Juan nudged one of the other children), the behavior would be noticed. This method is called a **partial-interval time sampling** system, because as long as any part of the interval can be scored for a particular act, the total interval receives the designation. Once a *single* episode of the behavior is observed, the entire interval is scored for that behavior. Frequencies are *not* counted within the interval. As you can see, Richard need not have been whispering throughout the full 10 seconds (nor Lucinda swearing, nor Juan nudging). Similarly, Richard's teacher may compliment him for a correct answer or for obeying directions during a part of a teacher-observed, ten-second interval; the praise would be recorded, too.

This method does *overestimate* how much of the time a student disrupts or a teacher shows approval. For the disruption, though, we can live with such overestimations, for when the data suggest improvement, we know that even a brief expression of the behavior has not occurred. In terms of the teacher's use of approval, if a partial-interval system were not used, it would probably be impossible to score any instance of approval, as the response would not be likely to last the full ten seconds. To assure yourself that you understand what these two different time-sampling systems mean, refer back to Figure 2.2. Calculate the number of intervals scored for each category and describe what the recordings mean.

[3]To avoid distorted indices of agreement, be sure your system allows you to score every interval. Provide a way of recording the absence of the behaviors you have pinpointed for measurement.

BEHAVIORAL ASSESSMENT INVENTORY

Observer's Name _Levy_____ School _Franklin_____ Date _10-15____

Teacher's Name _Ms. Martin_____ Time _1⁴⁰__ Activity _Math_____

STUDENT/ OR TEACHER	15"	30"	45"	60"	75"	90"	105"	120"	135"	150"	TOTAL A/+	D/-	N/0
S Richard	a	a	a	a	N	a	a	a	a	N	8	0	2
T Ms. Martin	O	O	O	O	O	O	O	O	O	-	0	1	9
S Richard	a	N	N	a	a	a	a	a	a	a	8	0	2
T Ms. Martin	O	O	-	O	O	O	O	O	+	O	1	1	8
S Richard	a	a	N¹	N	N	N	N	N	N	N	2	0	8
T Ms. Martin	O	O	O	O	O	O	O	O	-²	O	0	1	9
S Richard	N	N	N	N	N	a	D³	N	a	a	3	1	6
T Ms. Martin	O	O	O	O	-²	O	-	O	O	O	0	2	8
S Richard	a	a	a	a	a	a	a	N	a	a	9	0	1
T Ms. Martin	O	O	O	O	O	O	O	O	O	O	0	0	10
Total: Student / Teacher											30/1	1/5	19/44

Comments:
1. Looking at Magazine instead of assignment.
2. Told to put away magazine.
3. Bangs desk.

Figure 2.2
Sample of a Behavioral Assessment Instrument.

Show your statement to a colleague or your instructor and see if that person agrees.

It should be apparent to you that time sampling of the type just described can be a fairly complex method of observation. Precise and reliable scoring is achieved best when great care goes into defining behaviors, training observers, and calibrating their results. Consequently, before Dr. Levy would feel confident that the data she collected were reliable, she would enlist the aid of a colleague and check to see how closely their independent observations matched.

In Richard's case, Dr. Levy turned again to Mr. Kay for help. Together they reviewed the definitions of the behaviors they planned to record. Then, viewing a video recording of another student's classroom behavior, they practiced together. Because the audiorecorder they used to signal each interval was equipped with dual earplugs, they could rely on the same tape to keep them on track, so both scored the same intervals at the same time.

After 10 minutes they compared their scores cell by cell. Then they computed their coefficient of agreement by adding all the agreements[4] and dividing by the total agreements plus disagreements. At first their score was quite low — .54. But after they refined their definitions and practiced a little more, they eventually reached agreement scores in the high eighties and nineties. When the two observed Richard in his classes, they did agree quite well; their average agreement scores reached into the low nineties. Thereafter, at least once during each intervention phase they would repeat the process to assure themselves that their recording techniques had not drifted away from the original plan.

Recording continuous behavior for large numbers of students outside the classroom can present additional problems. The **zone system** has been found useful for recording such behaviors. It is analogous to the time-sampling system, except that in addition to dividing time up into small intervals, space is divided similarly. The observer watches all the students within a particular area (e.g., a section of the cafeteria or playground) regardless of how many students there may be. Any one single instance of a behavior that can be scored is marked when it occurs within the time interval in that particular area. The observer scores behavior within one zone several times in a row before moving on to the next. Naturally, to obtain as representative a picture as possible of what actually is happening, each zone should be relatively small and should provide approximately the same opportunity as the others for the target behaviors to occur. It helps to sketch a map onto the recording sheet to remind observers of the location of each area.

Willow Grove Regional School was experiencing behavior problems in areas outside the classroom. Ms. Miller, who enjoyed graphic arts, volunteered to prepare a schematic drawing of the corridor, the lunchroom, and the playground. Then she and the other teachers designated three zones in the corridor, nine in the lunchroom, and nine in the playground. Boundaries were identified by sketching in familiar objects: the water fountain, fire door, steam table, home plate, willow and spruce trees, and other landmarks. The target behaviors were defined as operations, and the teachers then went out in pairs to test the system. They identified the first playground zone and found that it was occupied by several children playing kickball, so the number of occupants changed from moment to moment. Watching that zone only, they observed one student teaching another how to position his foot and yet another student teasing a player who had just made a poor play. The first met one of their definitions of "kindness" (i.e., instructing another in a skill); the second was scored as "disruptive" (teasing, hitting, swearing, handling clothing or belongings, and the like). A child in the adjacent area made a nasty remark, but that was not included in the scoring because the incident did not occur within that particular zone. After scoring for six 10-second intervals, each of which was separated by a 5-second recording interval, the team moved to a spot from which they could observe the next zone. The sequence of recording for six intervals then was repeated. Comparing their scores interval by interval and zone by zone, the teachers found that some of the definitions had to be refined. Also, the boundaries of two zones were confused, so those were clarified; then the staff was ready to begin.

Several older children were asked if they would be willing to assist in the program. Three agreed to help do the observing, and they were trained to score until their ratings agreed with those of their partners

[4]Both Powell (1984) and Ary (1984) discuss the distortions that time sampling can introduce, underscoring the importance of using the system as conservatively as possible when using it to estimate the influence of an intervention. Hopkins and Hermann (1977) suggest a method for calculating random — chance interobserver agreement against which to interpret indices of reliability — especially important when occurrence of the behavior is very frequent or infrequent.

and the trainers on an average of more than 80 percent of the intervals. Three other students became playground monitors who learned to deliver tokens appropriately for the targeted reinforceable behaviors. The teachers checked to see that scoring and the implementation of the system were conducted reliably. First they checked regularly; once satisfied that the system was operating smoothly and fairly, they only needed to supervise occasionally.

The number of intervals scored for the desired and undesired behaviors then were tallied for all zones for each day and recorded on a chart posted at the lunchroom entrance. Once the token phase was implemented, a noticeable decrease in noxious behavior could be seen on the chart, along with a powerful increase in positive interactions. The social environment of Willow Grove School was improving, and the data were there to verify it.

Sometimes it's easier to record continuous behaviors mechanically. For example, electronic meters have been used to record noise levels. A noise level monitor that would stop accumulating points when the noise exceeded a preset level in a cafeteria was used in a program by Mayer et al. (1981) and a microphone, amplifier, and sound-level meter were used in a study by La Rowe, Tucker, and McGuire (1980). In both cases, the meter was set at a threshold level, beyond which noise levels were judged unacceptable. When the noise level exceeded the threshold, a visible light was activated. The light only remained on for a second in Mayer's program, permitting each light flash to be counted.

Momentary time sampling. Without a doubt, you occasionally will face situations in which you would like an estimate of the rate at which a behavior is occurring, but you can't observe what's happening full time because you must be involved in other activities. Besides the solutions of using mechanical devices or involving others—consultants, volunteers, peers, or the students themselves—you can collect the data yourself, by using a **momentary time-sampling** system.

Having found out about Richard's difficulties with reading comprehension, Dr. Levy wondered if

his difficulties during math class might surface when he was presented with word problems (according to the standard definition), in contrast to straight numerical calculations. Although Ms. Martin, his math teacher, was occupied with helping all the other students as well, she agreed to glance over at Richard periodically, to note whether or not he was attending during computation or while doing word problems. Each time Richard was in class, Ms. Martin took a small filing card imprinted like the one in Figure 2.3.

Because she became so involved in her activities, Ms. Martin was pleased to be cued to record Richard's attending. She activated a tape recorder at the beginning of class. Every 5 minutes, it was programmed to say a number ("one," "two," . . .) softly enough not to disturb the class. (You could use a wrist watch alarm, musical tone, a parking timer, or a light flash operated by a timer to cue yourself instead.) At that moment, Ms. Martin glanced over at Richard and noted whether or not he was attending to his work, placing a check in the appropriate column. By the end of the 50-minute class, Ms. Martin was able to record Richard's attending ten times, and in this way she obtained a rough estimate of the behavior. Although much of Richard's attending had to be overlooked, after a sufficient number of classes a pattern emerged, showing how Richard attends as a function of his assignment. Suppose the percentage

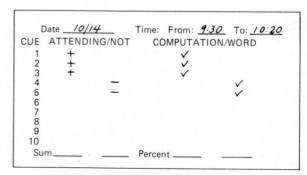

Figure 2.3
Recording card for momentary time sampling.

of his attending during computation were indicated on a graph by solid dots connected by a solid line, and his attending during word problems was shown as an open circle connected by dashed lines on the same graph. Would you be able to tell if the nature of the assignment affected Richard's attending? Examine Figure 2.4 and describe what you see.

Certainly the estimates obtained by Ms. Martin were rough, yet eventually the data were adequate to provide some useful information—that Richard's inattentiveness primarily was confined to those times when word problems were involved. This finding further supported his need for assistance with reading comprehension.

Had circumstances dictated a need for more valid estimates of a student's performance, say in the case of deciding whether or not to "mainstream" Tom, a student in Ms. Hollingsworth's special class at the Washington Street School, the system would need to be revised. Perhaps Tom's potential teachers were concerned that he might not be able to stay on-task as long as their other students. Mr. Lee could spend some time observing the students in those classes as well as recording Tom's performance in Ms. Hollingsworth's room. In this case, the time intervals would be shorter and would occur more frequently—for example, each 10 seconds over a 1-hour period, broken up by a few rest periods. This method of time sampling would yield a reasonably representative estimate of the proportion of time that Tom and the other students remained on-task. A close match between the two would provide evidence in support of the transfer. (Reliability here would be estimated in the same manner as described above: by involving a second trained observer and deriving a coefficient of agreement, matching each pair of scores for each observation.)

Perhaps it has occurred to you that to estimate the level of on-task behavior of the class to which Tom might be transferred, Mr. Lee probably would want to measure the behavior of the class in general, rather than that of one or two students. What he could do, then, would be to observe a different student each 10 seconds until all had been observed, repeating the cycle after the performance of all had

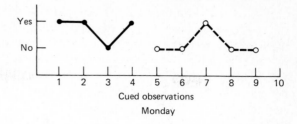
Cued observations
Monday

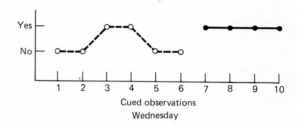
Cued observations
Wednesday

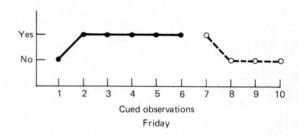
Cued observations
Friday

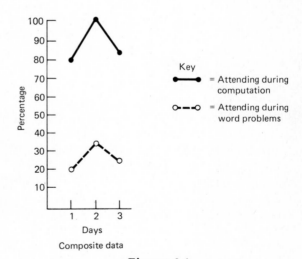
Days
Composite data

Figure 2.4
Graphic representation of Richard's attending, as recorded by teacher.

been recorded. Alternatively, using slightly longer intervals, at the end of each he could count the number of students who remained on-task divided by the total number of students present. This result would yield an estimate of the proportion of students who continued to stay on-task throughout the session.

A system like the one just described, in which every given number of minutes the teacher or another simply counts the number of students who actually are engaged in the assigned activity at that moment, is called **PLA-Check**—*PL*anned *A*ctivity Check (Risley & Cataldo, 1973). PLA-Check has been used widely in educational, day-care, and other human service settings to measure the extent to which participants are engaged in planned activities. The validity of PLA-Check has been demonstrated by noting that ratings by laymen and professionals of the quality of various classroom activities have matched closely the PLA-Check estimates. The device probably would be an excellent choice for measuring change among students of Willow Grove School. Given the staff's concern that the diverse students attending the school use their time as productively as possible, teachers could use PLA-Check to assess which sorts of alterations in the educational environment produced the highest levels of productive engagement by students.

Duration recording

In some instances, the length of time a particular event persists will be of concern—for instance, how long Amanda Rodriguez, the principal's daughter, practices piano, Marissa expresses herself assertively during a role-playing session, Juan participates in group activity, or Richard spends obtaining Ms. Pear's help in reading. Assuming it is possible to discern clearly when a behavior begins and ends, and it doesn't switch on and off too rapidly, you simply can measure accumulated time by activating a stopwatch.

To demonstrate the accuracy of your recording, periodically work in pairs, scoring independently and being sure that the clicking of your watch is not seen or overheard by your partner. At the end of the observation session, see how closely the two durational recording totals match by dividing the smaller total by the larger. If the quotient approaches .90 or beyond, you've probably agreed closely.

Occasionally you will be interested in estimating the duration of a behavior, the beginning and end of which is difficult to identify. Ms. Miller senses that her students waste considerable time switching from one activity to the next. She asks Ms. Heinz to help by timing the students from the moment when she signals the class to the moment when all get down to work. So Ms. Heinz positions herself in the back of the room prepared to operate her stopwatch. But what happens?

One child appears to be starting to work, takes out her book, but then drops her pencil, and begins to talk with her neighbor. Another wanders about the room for awhile; another asks to be excused; another asks Ms. Miller to please repeat her instructions. In a frenzy of clicking the stopwatch off and on, Ms. Heinz finally gives up in confusion, because it is difficult to tell exactly when "getting down to work" actually begins and ends.

The next day, she tries another tactic. Using a partial interval time sampling technique, she scores each interval as off-task as long as *any* student is doing anything except performing the assignment as given or engaging in an explicitly permitted alternate behavior. Now she and Ms. Miller can estimate how long it takes the class to complete the transition. All they have to do is to add the intervals between Ms. Miller's signal and the interval when all were on task. They find this method for estimating duration to be simple and convenient. When they test it for agreement by both simultaneously recording several times and find it acceptably reliable, they decide to continue to use it. First the system will be used to establish a representative standard against which to measure any subsequent change—a baseline. (You will learn more about this in the next chapter.) Then if they decide to try to shorten transition times, they can continue, using the system to measure the influence of the *interventions* they will try.

Summary

In this chapter we have guided you across a lot of ground. You have seen how the behavioral approach addresses a global problem area, like students' failure to achieve or to conduct themselves appropriately in the social milieu of the school, and how it analyzes and refines the problem until it can be measured. You start by gathering as much information as possible about the issue of concern and then investigate more closely by seeing and hearing and counting, rather than depending only on the indirect reports of the concerned parties. In addition, you do not rely on a single observational period, when what you observe may or may not depict accurately what is typically happening. Rather, you collect direct measures of behavior repeatedly under various circumstances to estimate as well as possible what is acutally transpiring. (In the next chapter we describe how that is accomplished.)

A variety of assessment procedures were presented. Testing and interviewing were reviewed briefly. The majority of the chapter, though, dealt with behavioral assessment. The first direct observational recording system introduced to assess behavior was narrative recording. It consists of an observer recording exactly what was occurring at the moment it happened. The outcome of a narrative recording reads like a script to a play. A sequence analysis was the next assessment method discussed. Its purpose is to assist the observers in identifying specific antecedents *and* consequences that may be influencing the current behavior and to help them decide what might be done to remedy the situation.

More precise behavioral assessment methods are used to record the level or rate at which a targeted behavior occurs. These involved permanent product recording; frequency or event recording; whole, partial, and momentary time sampling; and dura-

Table 2.1

Selecting an observational method

Observational method	Select observational method when behavior				
	Produces durable product	Is transitory	Is discrete	Is roughly equivalent in duration each time expressed	Is continuous
Permanent product	x				
Event		x	x	x	
Duration		x	x		
Time sampling[a] (whole, partial, and momentary[b])		x			x

[a]The behavior should occur at least once every 15 minutes if time sampling is to be useful.

[b]In most cases, for teachers to be able to use momentary time sampling, the behavior needs to occur fairly often; for example, somewhere about 10 percent of the observed time or more. Otherwise, occurrences of the behavior are not likely to be recorded.

tion recording. Each method was discussed along with how to calculate its interobserver reliability.

As illustrated in Table 2.1, permanent product recording is used when the behavior leaves an enduring product such as a completed assignment or a broken window. All the other behavioral assessment methods are used for recording transitory behaviors. Event recording is used to keep track of behaviors that are clearly discrete (though you should be sure the behavior doesn't occur so rapidly as to cause you to lose count) and are roughly equivalent in duration. Duration recording is used to keep track of discrete behaviors when the length of time a particular event persists is of concern. The time-sampling methods are used to record nondiscrete or continuous behaviors that occur at least once every 15 minutes.

As an important aside, we hope you have noted how the behavioral approach can be practiced with a sensitive concern for human values. Did you notice that our students are often involved in planning and carrying out systems of measurement and programs of intervention? Can you see how the objective and precise determination of behaviors on which to target guards the performance of the people concerned from biased or arbitrary treatment? There is little room for subterfuge or deception in such an approach. Everything is clear and above board. As in the case of Richard Parker, his family, and the relevant staff of the Franklin High School, all involved can join forces in a cooperative effort toward improving the situation of concern in as efficient and effective a manner as feasible.

Study Questions

1. List the kinds of information that interviews can and cannot provide.
2. Identify and describe the information that can be obtained from two types of standardized tests.
3. Provide an original example of a narrative recording.
4. Tim's teacher wants to develop a sequence analysis in order to better understand his behavior during English class. Describe the task that should be completed before beginning the sequence analysis.
5. Mary threw her crayons on the floor after her teacher had requested that she put them away. The teacher's request is the _____.
6. Tom was required to pick up the pieces after he broke his mother's vase. Picking up the pieces is called a _____.
7. You have been observing Susan at recess.
   (a) Use your imagination and narrate an episode of an event you could have observed.
   (b) Construct a sequence analysis of the episode (including at least three behaviors).
8. Identify the information that a sequence analysis can provide.
9. Examine the sequence analysis in Question 7(b) and describe three things about Susan's behavior.
10. T/F It is not always required that an outside observer do a sequence analysis. Justify your selection.
11. Narrative recordings tend to be:
    (a) subjective
    (b) objective.
    Explain your choice.
12. On what two critical features does precise behavioral assessment depend?
13. Two observers are visiting a math class to record how often the students are bored.

(a) Identify one problem with their plans.
(b) Suggest a solution.
14. (a) Describe an original behavior that would not be appropriate for event recording.
(b) Support your answer.
15. Karen's art teacher wants to know if she is completing her assignments in art class. Describe one way he could find this out most easily. What recording procedure do you think is most appropriate?
16. Mark is learning to make salads in his group home. Each night two of his teachers examine the salad to determine if it has been completed. His teachers compare their scores at the end of each week to estimate their _____.
17. (Refer to Question 16.) The teachers' data agree only 50 percent of the time. Suggest a solution to this problem.
18. (a) Explain (1) reactivity and (2) permanent product recording.
(b) Explain and illustrate with an example the advantages of using permanent product recording.
(c) Describe a method you might use to estimate how much chewing gum is stuck to the gymnasium floor, without having to count each wad of gum.
19. (a) Provide two original examples of behaviors that can be measured more readily when people are not present.
(b) Justify your selection of these examples.
20. The school psychologist wants to observe Bob to see how often he leaves his seat during science class. However, she is afraid that he will remain seated more often in her presence and this will affect the data. Describe how such reactivity might be prevented.
21. (a) Provide an original example of a behavior best assessed by counting its frequency.
(b) Support your answer.
22. Describe one method for calculating an estimate of reliability.
23. (a) Identify a behavior that occurs very frequently or infrequently.
(b) Describe the most appropriate observational system for that behavior.
(c) Demonstrate that you can accurately cal-

culate reliability for the recording system you selected.
24. (a) Provide an original example of a behavior inappropriate for event recording.
(b) Support your answer.
25. (a) List and (b) operationally define three behaviors so that they can be recorded reliably.
26. Provide an original example of time-sampling recording and sufficient instructions to enable a naive observer to implement the system.
27. (a) Define whole-interval time sampling.
(b) Does it over- or underestimate the occurrence of a behavior?
(c) Explain why.
28. Operationally define three behaviors for which whole-interval time sampling would be appropriate.
29. (a) Define partial-interval time sampling.
(b) Does it over- or underestimate the occurrence of a behavior?
(c) Explain why.
30. Time-sampling recording is being used to assess how often Steven sucks his thumb. The behavior was defined as his thumb touching his lips, tongue, or teeth. Ten-second intervals are used and a mark is placed in the box if the behavior is exhibited at any time during the interval.
(a) Is this whole- or partial-interval recording?
(b) Explain your choice.
31. Describe how observers can be trained and assessed to ensure reliability.
32. List one advantage to using momentary time sampling.
33. (a) Define and (b) provide an example of momentary time sampling.
34. (a) Describe and (b) offer an original method for assessing on-task behavior of a class.
35. (a) Describe PLA-Check.
(b) Under what circumstances would its use be appropriate?
36. (a) Provide an example of duration recording.
(b) Provide fictitious data and calculate a reliability score.
37. Describe a system for measuring duration

when it is difficult to discern the beginning or end of a behavior.

38. A representative standard against which to measure any subsequent change is called a _____.

39. Referring to Table 2.1, solve the following problem: Sarah wants to determine how many times she goes to the water cooler in a day. Pilot observations revealed that she went to the water cooler fewer than ten times a day. Using the table, select the appropriate recording system.

References

Arrington, R. E. (1943). Time-sampling in studies of social behavior: A critical review of techniques and results with research suggestions. *Psychological Bulletin, 40,* 81–124.

Ary, D. (1984). Mathematical explanation of error in duration recording using partial interval, whole interval, and momentary time sampling. *Behavioral Assessment, 6,* 221–228.

Bacon-Prue, A., Blount, R., Pickering, D., & Drabman, R. (1980). An evaluation of three litter control procedures: Trash receptacles, paid workers, and the marked item techniques. *Journal of Applied Behavior Analysis, 1,* 165–171.

Chapman, C., & Risley, T. R. (1974). Anti-litter procedures in an urban high-density area. *Journal of Applied Behavior Analysis, 7,* 377–383.

Goodwin, D. L. (1969). Consulting with the classroom teacher. In J. D. Krumboltz & C. E. Thoresen (Eds.), *Behavioral counseling cases and techniques.* New York: Holt, Rinehart and Winston.

Hopkins, B.L., & Hermann, J.A. (1977). Evaluating inter-observer reliability of interval data. *Journal of Applied Behavior Analysis, 10,* 121–126.

La Rowe, L. N., Tucker, R. D., & McGuire, J. M. (1980). Lunchroom noise control using feedback and group contingent reinforcement. *Journal of School Psychology, 18,* 51–57.

MacPherson, E. M., Candee, B. L., & Hohman, R. J. (1974). A comparison of three methods for eliminating disruptive lunchroom behavior. *Journal of Applied Behavior Analysis, 7,* 287–297.

Mayer, G. R., Nafpaktitis, M., & Butterworth, T. W. (1981). *Dealing with disruption and mayhem in the school lunch area.* Office of the Los Angeles County Superintendent of Schools, Downey, CA.

Powell, J. (1984). On the misrepresentation of behavioral realities by a widely practiced direct observation procedure: Partial interval (one-zero) sampling. *Behavioral Assessment, 6,* 209–219.

Risley, T. R., & Cataldo, M. F. (1973). *Planned activity check: Materials for training observers.* Lawrence, KS: Center for Applied Behavior Analysis.

3 Being accountable

Goals

After completing this chapter, you should be able to:

1. Define and give an illustration of each of the following terms:
   a. Baseline
   b. Graph, illustrating the ordinate, abscissa, and vertical broken lines (be sure each aspect of the graph is labeled clearly)
   c. Functional relation
   d. Task analysis
   e. Delphi method
   f. Behavioral goal
   g. Operational statement
   h. Instructional objective
   i. Functional skill
2. Identify two basic purposes of collecting an adequate baseline.
3. Describe how a cumulative graph differs from a "typical" graph.
4. Observe an individual. Allow for adaptation; collect and graph the baseline data.
5. List two major reasons for assessing the environment.
6. Describe and provide an original illustration of several ways for assessing the results of a behavioral intervention (i.e., show that the treatment strategies are responsible for bringing about a desired change in performance).
7. Describe the importance of consumer satisfaction in evaluating the results of a behavioral intervention program.
8. Describe how behavioral goals are individualized for students.
9. Describe the purpose of behavioral objectives and how they differ from behavioral goals.
10. Discuss why it is important to develop objectives that include various skills that you want to teach.
11. List and discuss five guidelines for selecting the most important and feasible instructional objectives for a student.
12. List and discuss several factors that should be considered in assessing for individualized student planning.

"Boys and girls, beginning today we are going to try something different in social studies," explained Mrs. Olsen. "Instead of everyone doing the same assignment, we'll be working in groups. Each group will elect a leader, who will take charge of giving out materials and seeing to it that the job for the day gets done. Today you'll get assignment sheets and need to select a project."

"What group will I be in?" asked Chris.

"You'll find out in a minute; I'm just about to hand out the list."

After all the students discovered which groups

37

they were to join, Mrs. Olsen instructed them to assemble in different sections of the room, where each quickly elected a leader.

"Oh look," exclaimed Pam. "On this sheet it says we should learn more about the post-World-War-II presidents. It looks as if we won't all have to read the same thing and take a test over it. Instead we can pick one president and tell about that person's life some other way. We can write a poem, a play, a short story, or a song that tells about important events in their lives."

"Hey, that's for you Chris," exclaimed Henry.

"Yeah. Truman, Truman. What rhymes with Truman?" and Chris began to hum and pretend to strum a banjo, while the others laughed. "I'd better do a little reading about him to get some ideas."

"Well I'd be awful at that," sighed Pam. "I can't even carry a tune."

"Don't worry," advised Chris. "You're really good at art projects. Here it says you can do a montage."

"That's not a bad idea. My dad saves old magazines. I bet I could find some good pictures. Any ideas about which president I should pick?"

The group continued its discussion, planning who would do what and how information would be obtained. By the end of the period, although some of the students still would need guidance from their teacher in selecting their projects, many were ready to go.

While all this was happening, Mrs. Olsen had set her wristwatch alarm to signal every 10 minutes, as she had been doing during the social studies period for the past three weeks. Each time it sounded, she paused for a moment to count and record how many students were engaged in the assigned activity (according to a preset definition). At the end of the class, more students were scored as being on-task than on any previous day.

"This idea of building on student's interests does seem to be working," she told herself. "But maybe that's just because it's novel. I wonder what will be happening a few weeks from now; or whether I'll find it a nuisance."

When a strategy of change is to be put in effect, it is reasonable and appropriate to be concerned about whether or not it is needed and likely to ac-

complish its purpose. Any change in routine requires extra effort and a period of adjustment, so we will really want to know if carrying out our plans will be worth it. Mrs. Olsen had consulted her grade book and saw that few students were doing exceptionally well in social studies. To see how productively they were using their time, she used a PLA-Check recording method. The data indicated that considerable time was being wasted during that period. She also had asked students to rank their most to least favorite activities. Not surprisingly, lunch and recess headed the list; but social studies, math, and English tied for last place. The combination of data informed her that something different needed to happen.

Mrs. Olsen's plan has a good chance of working, because she evaluated the situation from many perspectives before diving in. By continuing to monitor performance during the time her modified procedures were in effect, she would be able to assess the nature of the change. If the data told her that the system were working, she would want to find out how dependable the method was and how general, so she could try it out in one of the other subject areas, like math or English.

It is natural that when we think we have identified a serious problem, we want to correct it as rapidly as possible. This was the case with Richard Parker's parents and teachers, also with the teachers of the Washington Street School who were concerned with mainstreaming Tom and helping Juan and Lucinda to get along better with their peers. All had a clearer picture of the difficulties they faced and some notion of how to address them. But all of us need to be patient. First, we should find out the extent of the problem; then, determine how the system in which we are operating will support our goals and procedures. When we are adequately informed, we can pinpoint exactly where we hope to go by specifying our objectives and planning how to get there by selecting promising behavioral strategies.

In this chapter, we cover that territory. We will discuss collecting baseline data to determine the extent of the problem and examining factors pertinent to assessing the system. You will find that many behavioral strategies are ideally suited to remedying academic and social problems of students. However, these strategies also can be used preventively to train and manage staff and to make more efficient and effective our pursuit of the educational aims of our nation, communities, and schools.

COLLECTING AND GRAPHING BASELINE DATA

As any educator knows, all of us have our good and bad days. Certainly that would be the case with the students and staff with whom we are becoming acquainted in this book. Richard might surprise his teacher periodically by working especially hard and turning in accurately completed assignments, but we know that he has not been doing so consistently. If observational recordings were limited to one session alone and taken on an atypical day, the resulting information could be misleading. To avoid the biasing effects of insufficient data, those involved in behavior analysis have made a practice of collecting enough data to permit a pattern of typical responding to emerge. Those data, as mentioned in Chapter 1, are used to construct a **baseline** or standard against which subsequent change will be measured. The baseline data, then, are collected over a number of sessions.

Much as we would like to provide you with a rule about the number of sessions or data points necessary to generate an adequate baseline—one that *really* represents a typical pattern of performance—that is not possible. All we can say is that if the behavior varies little from session to session, fewer points will be required; if it bounces around unpredictably, then more will be necessary. If the behavior never or hardly ever occurs, you will need very few data points—just enough to convince yourself that the behavior indeed was missing. Where data are retrievable by searching through permanent products—such as work folders, attendance records, or grade books, like Mrs. Olsen's—longer baselines cost little time and effort to generate. Observational

recording, on the other hand, requires more time, skill, and effort; thus, understandably, you will be tempted to minimize the time you spend in that activity. In most cases, you probably will want to record baseline over a period of a week or two, for a minimum of five sessions.

With Richard, Dr. Levy and Mr. Kay were able to obtain his teachers' planning books and the papers the student had completed over a 2-week period. From that information they constructed several graphs, permitting a pattern of his typical performance to emerge.

In constructing the graphs, they used a standard format for displaying Richard's data. Let's look at three of the graphs that Dr. Levy and Mr. Kay put together (see Figures 3.1, 3.2, and 3.3.) They illustrate the following points for you to note when constructing a graph:

1. The **ordinate,** or vertical axis, indicates the measures: the level, rate, or percentage of the behavior.
2. The **abscissa,** or horizontal axis, indicates the time dimension, usually expressed in days, sessions, or weeks.
3. Both the ordinate and abscissa are labeled clearly so the information presented can be understood at a glance.
4. Changes in conditions or treatment phases are indicated by vertical broken lines.
5. Each treatment phase is labeled clearly.
6. Usually only one set of data is plotted on a graph. However, when more than one are plotted, be sure to use different symbols and/or connecting lines for each.
7. Lines connecting data do not cross the vertical broken lines. They are discontinued between each treatment condition.
8. When several data values are at the zero level, raise the zero point above the abscissa level on the ordinate, as in Figure 3.3, so the points may be seen clearly.
9. Label the graph to describe briefly the data displayed. The labels should make it possible for another person to understand the graphed data without needing additional information.

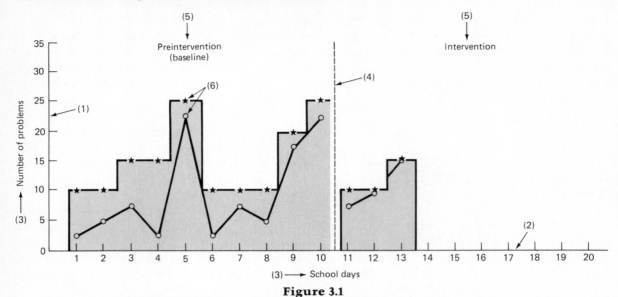

Figure 3.1
Number of problems accurately completed by Richard (○) in contrast with the number assigned to him (⋆).

In Figure 3.1 you can see the pattern produced by the data points when the frequency of each is plotted. In math class, for example, the number of problems assigned varied from day to day, and so did Richard's rate of accurately completing them. The baseline before the horizontal dashed line (between days 10 and 11) shows that indeed Richard rarely completed his assignments accurately.

If you are more interested in patterns produced by single responses over time, a cumulative record can

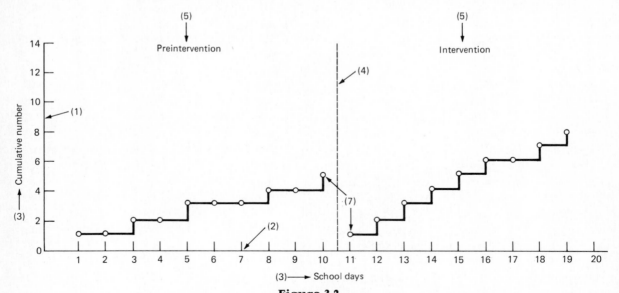

Figure 3.2
Cumulative number of English assignments completed by Richard.

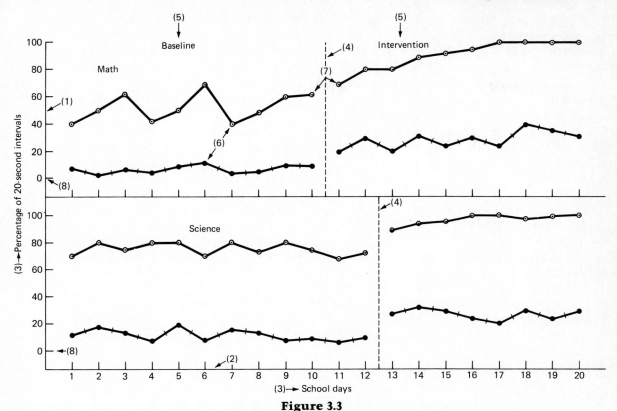

Figure 3.3
Percentage of intervals in which Richard attended throughout (⊙) and in which his teacher communicated approval at least once (●).

depict them clearly. In English class, for instance, Richard is given one assignment each day. Sometimes he completes it, and sometimes he doesn't. On the cumulative graph in Figure 3.2, notice that each data point is added to the previous total, so you always can see how many of the performances have accumulated from the beginning. When the response accumulates slowly, the slope of the curve generated by connecting the points is flatter; when responses accumulate rapidly, the slope is higher. We have found this cumulative frequency graph reinforcing to students. When behaviors such as homework, assignment completion, or punctuality are graphed as "yes" or "no," the downward movement on a regular graph can be discouraging. A cumulative frequency graph avoids such downward movements.

In Figure 3.3 you see displayed the data collected every few days by Dr. Levy during Richard's math and science classes. Plotted are the number of 20-second intervals scored for Richard as *attending* for the full interval, and the number of intervals in which the teacher signaled approval toward Richard some time within the interval.

Notice that during the baseline conditions, prior to any intervention, Richard behaved differently in math and science, and the teachers of those classes responded differently toward him. In math, Richard paid attention irregularly and not very often. His teacher displayed little approval toward him. In science, he paid attention more often and his teacher did express approval toward him occasionally. Data of this sort tell us a couple of important things: first, that Richard is capable of paying attention fairly well; and second, that the teacher's approval and Richard's paying attention seem to be paired with one another. (Although at this point, we cannot tell which behavior, if either, produces the other.)

Should you decide to count rates of responses per a given time block, you may find the standardized universal behavior chart (Johnson, 1970) very useful. The chart can be adjusted to include cumulative or logarithmic functions as well as other frequency counts.

ASSESSING THE SYSTEM

The intensive assessment of Richard Parker's behavior provided a number of critically important bits of information. We learned about his strengths and deficiencies and the circumstances that might promote or interfere with his performance in school. Once that information is gathered, the people who will be involved in designing a program of change to remedy Richard's difficulties are at an advantage. As we shall see later on, knowing what strengths upon which to build and what antecedents and consequences to arrange can be enormously helpful.

Richard's repertoire of behaviors, however, does not express itself in a vacuum. We recognize that behaving individuals are constantly interacting with and being affected by their physical and social environments. It is these environments that must be managed if change is to occur. So for Richard, it will be necessary to provide training in reading comprehension and study skills. Altering his teacher's mode of responding to the student also probably will help. For instance, if Ms. Martin were to redistribute her attention toward Richard so that she made a point of noticing him while he was on-task, he might put out more effort in class.

Another reason for assessing the environment is to locate the features that will support or impede improvement once an intensive effort to change behavior has been terminated. What sense would it make to teach Marissa that she should encourage her male admirers to join her in socially acceptable group activities, if the facilities for such activities are unavailable? What good would it do to teach the students of Willow Grove School to tutor their peers if the school board objected to this on philosophical grounds? We need to know as much as possible about available resources, bases of support, and probable interference before we launch into designing a program of change. For if the system pulls one way and we pull the other, we are bound to be the losers.

Many segments operate within the educational system: governmental and district-wide laws and policies; personnel at district, school, and community levels; material resources and services; and other social, political, and economic aspects. You need to consider each to decide whether or not to proceed with a particular plan designed to improve the performance of your students. To simplify the process for you, we present in Table 3.1 a partial list of activities for assessing the support and resources. You might wish to consider these prior to investing major effort in a particular program of change.

Table 3.2 illustrates a needs assessment that can be used to evaluate your current school climate and discipline practices. While the information obtained from Table 3.1 helps you to know what kind of support you might expect, the needs assessment describes the current situation. As you progress through this text, you will begin to understand how the elements contained in this survey can affect pupil and teacher behavior. (For instance, in Chapter 7 we discuss the importance of clearly stating and communicating rules and regulations governing student behavior.) For a program to manage conduct at Washington Street Junior High, these elements include:

- Involvement of all affected parties—administrative, staff, student, parental, and community representation—in the development, implementation, and evaluation of the discipline program.
- Clear communication among all those involved.
- Provision for both individual differences of students *and* staff, including appropriate consequences, programs, and academic materials.
- Reliance on positive rather than punitive methods of control.

Table 3.1
Suggested activities for assessing environmental support and resources

I. District Level
  A. Inform and request support from each of the following:
    1. Superintendent.
    2. Person(s) with the major responsibility for overseeing data and programs in the area on which you plan to work (e.g., vandalism, attendance, discipline, etc.).
    3. Director of special services and/or others recommended by the superintendent.
  B. Locate supplemental resources such as the instructional materials center or other repository of extra books and materials.
  C. Familiarize yourself with any district-wide programs and policies that have been or are operating in your targeted area.

II. School Level
  A. Inform, request support, and discover information about each of the following:
    1. *Principal.* The principal's leadership role; his or her view of instructional and professional staff and school's strengths and weaknesses; programs supported; years in school; related background information; how principal is viewed by staff; degree to which he or she uses praise; behaviors; particular staff member he or she reinforces or recognizes more than others; availability to staff; and degree of rapport and interaction with students.
    2. *Vice-Principal* (when applicable). Obtain same information as for the principal, plus how that role differs from the principal's.
    3. *Secretary.* Attitude toward principal, instructional, and professional staff; years at school; attitude of staff toward secretary; strengths and weaknesses; interests; control over communications; and nature and degree of administrative responsibilities held.
    4. *Psychologist/Counselor.* Attitude toward staff and project; knowledge of behavioral approach; days per week at school; role; and background.
    5. *Custodian.* Role and attitude of staff and students toward custodian and vice versa.
    6. *School Staff.* Are there cliques? Views of psychologist, principal, and faculty leaders; gathering places for breaks, lunch, etc.; and current philosophical orientation.
    7. *Special Staff and Services.*
      a. *Remedial Reading Teachers.* Time spent at school; approach used in remediation; materials available; relation to staff; and willingness to cooperate.
      b. *Librarian.* Level of training; time available; relation to staff; and availability of high interest/low vocabulary materials.
      c. *Resource Specialist.* Level of training; number of days or time spent at school; relation to staff; any behavioral approaches used; and available materials.
      d. *Available Aids/Volunteers.* Degree of responsibility and training.
      e. *Student Council and Student Officers.* Degree of leadership and responsibility.
      f. *School Security Personnel.* Responsibilities; relation to students; number; and visibility.
      g. *School Nurse and Attendance Clerk.* Responsibilities and available information.
  B. Any school-wide programs and policies that have been or are operating in your targeted area.

III. Community Resources
  A. Inform, request support, and discover information about each of the following:
    1. *PTA.* Size; involvement; support funds; chairperson's telephone number; degree to which members are interested in supporting a project in your targeted area; and other leaders in the group.
    2. *Library.* Location and availability of films, records, tapes, etc.
    3. *Community Recreation.* Local programs; involvement; size; time; and location.
    4. *Description of Immediate Neighborhood.* Perception of school; socioeconomic status; and neighborhood service organizations that may be willing to help.
    5. *Local Educational Supply Stores.* Those available.
    6. *School Advisory Council.* Role.

This table is an adaptation of one developed by Mayer et al. (1983).

Table 3.2
Constructive discipline needs assessment for evaluating school climate and discipline practices

	Classroom			Schoolwide		
	Much improvement needed	Some improvement needed	Acceptable	Much improvement needed	Some improvement needed	Acceptable
1. Specific Discipline Problems						
a. Appropriate social skills in relating to teachers and peers.						
b. Vandalism (theft, property damage, fire).						
c. Attendance (truancy and tardiness).						
d. Classroom disruption and nonattending.						
e. Campus cleanliness.						
f. Task completion.						
g. Student compliance.						
2. Statements of Rules and Regulations						
a. Involve student, parent, and teacher input in development, implementation, and evaluation.						
b. Stated clearly.						
c. Stated positively.						
d. Kept updated.						
e. Communicated at least annually to students and parents.						
3. Consequences to Deter Behavior						
a. Involve student, parent, and teacher input in development, implementation, and evaluation.						
b. Stated clearly.						
c. Applied consistently.						
d. Communicated at least annually to students and parents.						
e. Provide for student differences by revising the consequences as necessary.						

f. Emphasize constructive alternatives over punitive methods for reducing undesirable behavior.

4. Consequences (Positive Incentives) to Foster Behavior

a. Involve student, parent, and teacher input in development, implementation, and evaluation.

b. Stated clearly.

c. Applied consistently.

d. Communicated at least annually to students and parents.

e. Communicated through negotiated behavior management contracts.

f. Revised to provide for student differences.

g. Include approval statements more frequently than disapproval statements.

h. Used to acknowledge *improvement*, not just exemplary behavior.

5. Administrative and Staff Involvement

a. Ways provided for staff, students, and parents to make suggestions regarding school and classroom policies and programs.

b. Regular feedback regarding staff satisfaction with administrative action and policy implementation sought.

c. The administration acts promptly on faculty requests and suggestions regarding discipline policy.

d. Good teaching is positively recognized and appreciated by the administration.

Table 3.2
(continued)

	Classroom			Schoolwide		
	Much improvement needed	Some improvement needed	Acceptable	Much improvement needed	Some improvement needed	Acceptable
e. School authorities take prompt action when disciplinary referrals are made.						
f. Assistance is provided on request in designing a behavior management program that takes into account individual differences.						
g. Assistance is provided in matching student reading skills, with appropriate materials and assignments.						
h. In-service training is provided for staff members to acquaint them with disciplinary policies and procedures *and* to enhance their behavior management skills.						
i. Teachers confer with and assist one another regarding methods of maintaining discipline.						
j. Positive notes are written and positive comments are made to and from teachers, support staff, administrators, and parents.						
k. Teachers are provided with various rewards and notes that can be used with students.						

This table is an adaptation of one developed by Mayer et al. (1983).

ASSESSING RESULTS OF BEHAVIORAL INTERVENTIONS

Of greatest concern to all of us is our students' academic, social, and personal growth. We hope that the methods we employ will improve students' achievement, deportment, and satisfaction with their peers and themselves. Indeed, the major portion of this text is devoted to helping you to accomplish that end.

But how are we to know when a program of intervention has been successful? By demonstrating measurable change as a function of the intervention; that *when and only when* the intervention has been in effect over time, does reliable change take place. To do that sort of functional analysis, we begin by assessing the baselines of the behaviors most in need of change. After investigating probable sources of dependable support (material and social), from administrators and community members, we then select a promising strategy of change and analyze its effects. For Richard Parker, the strategy probably would include such tactics as more frequent teacher approval of his paying attention in class, plus some intensive work in reading comprehension and study skills. For Marissa, she might be trained in the social skills that would permit her to maintain rewarding social relationships without getting into trouble. For Juan, social skills training, too, probably would help, as would teaching him how to smile and enjoy himself in constructive social situations. For encouraging the staff of Willow Grove School to tailor assignments to match student repertoires, the most appropriate strategy might involve in-service training and regular feedback.

As the selected tactics are applied, data collection continues, exactly as in baseline. If we observe a desired change in performance, one that lasts over time, we may begin to suspect that our tactics have been effective. But can we be sure? Only if we can show that applying the intervention and change in performance coincide reliably. To demonstrate this influence, the tactic may be presented repeatedly across settings, subject areas, people, or behaviors in *multiple baseline* fashion. Or it is presented, withdrawn, and then presented again according to a

withdrawal arrangement. Only if the performance improves coincidentally with the presentation of the intervention can we conclude that the change is a function of that intervention. If no such reliable change occurs or if change occurs regardless, we have failed to demonstrate a *functional relation* between change in performance and the intervention. Notice that behavioral strategies are *not* applied on faith or sustained because they have worked effectively with others. You might start there, but you always put them to the test with the people directly involved.

In Figure 3.3, we showed you the graph of Richard's performance in class after his math and science teachers had increased their rates of communicating approval to Richard when he was working well. Richard received tutoring in reading comprehension and study skills on days 4 and 7, respectively. This multiple baseline across subject areas showed that it was *only* when each teacher's rates of approval changed that Richard paid better attention.

We have seen how to determine the effectiveness of a behavior change strategy on Richard's behavior. Now let us look at how we might do the same for staff behavior.

At Willow Grove School, as you may have guessed, the staff had been taught how important it is to capitalize on students' levels of preparedness and interests, which, for example, had produced a temporary increase in Mr. Truax's rates of adjusting his assignments accordingly. However, rates now had returned almost to previous levels. It appeared as if something had to be done to reinforce the change. Having explored the topic in the literature, Mrs. Olsen became convinced that providing feedback to all the teachers (herself included) would increase or maintain the rates. She examined each teacher's lesson plan daily, counting the academic subjects for which assignments had been adjusted to individual levels of interest and preparedness by means of grouping or offering independent work. Then she calculated a percentage based on the proportion of the total assignments that had been matched to individuals. For 1 week, she did this to establish a baseline. Then for 1 week she sent a daily note to the other teachers, indicating the percentage for that day and congratulating them for improvement when merited. During this phase, the rates of matching increased substantially. Providing that sort of feedback did take time, however—about 15 minutes a day. So Mrs. Olsen wondered if it was really necessary. To determine if the increase were a direct function of the feedback, she withdrew it for a week. Noticing a drop as the week progressed, she decided to reinstate feedback. Take a look at Figure 3.4 and see what happened. (Note that Mrs. Olsen used a withdrawal design.) Are you convinced that individualizing assignments is a function of feedback conditions? She was, and so are we!

Sometimes educators are curious about whether one method is preferable to another for a particular student or group of students. Ms. Hollingsworth thought she noticed that her pupils seemed to respond better when she asked them to do something in a nice tone of voice rather than when she gave orders in an authoritarian fashion. Deciding to test out her theory, she defined each style of giving instructions. She then decided to measure student compliance by using a PLA-Check type system, aided by the student teacher, who collected the same data for reliability purposes. After taking baseline in both places, Ms. Hollingsworth then used one style when teaching in one section of the room and the other when teaching in another place, measuring compliance a number of times in each place. The data plotted on Figure 3.5 show that indeed the

pleasant instructional style produced a higher rate of compliance.[1] You can use this *multielement design* to compare any of your own methods, provided you pair each different method with distinctly different situations (or *stimuli*) to measure the same behavior.

Consumer satisfaction

Without a doubt, demonstrating that a particular arrangement of the environment effectively changes the performance of concern is the key factor that we need to assess. But it is not the only one. Recall how aspects of the physical and social environment also may play an important role in determining whether or not a particular intervention will receive ongoing support. If key people feel especially awkward about using a particular tactic, misunderstand it, or find that it requires too much time, money, or effort, they may discard that tactic despite its proven effectiveness. One way to avoid this potential pitfall is to ask those key people how satisfied they are with the program.

After a 2-month period of providing feedback to her staff—by then on a semiweekly basis instead of daily—Mrs. Olsen was convinced that the feedback played an important role in encouraging her staff to modify their methods of instruction. But she still

[1]This example was inspired by Madalyn Tyson's doctoral dissertation at the University of Massachusetts, Amherst, 1983.

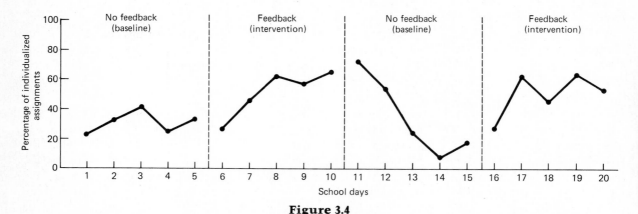

Figure 3.4
Percentage of assignments adjusted to students' levels of preparedness and interest, as a function of feedback.

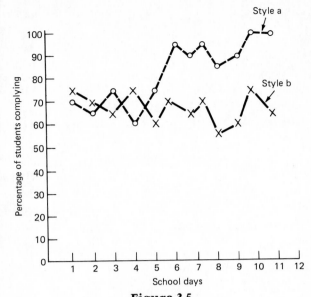

Figure 3.5
Average percentage of students complying in subjects in which style "a" (o--o)—gentle; or style "b" (x—x)—authoritarian—were used.

Table 3.3
Questionnaire[a]

Dear Students:

For a while now, your teacher has given you work that may not be the same as what other children in your grade are doing. We want to know how you like this. Please circle the letters that tell how you feel about what you are asked.

1. How do you like having your own work to do?
   a. I don't.
   b. A little.
   c. A lot.

2. How hard is your work in school?
   a. Easy.
   b. Just right.
   c. A little hard.
   d. Too hard.

3. Do you like school more or less than before?
   a. Less.
   b. The same.
   c. More.

4. How much are you learning in school now?
   a. Less.
   b. The same.
   c. More.

5. How often do you help other pupils?
   a. Very often.
   b. Sometimes.
   c. Never.

6. How often do other pupils help you?
   a. Very often.
   b. Sometimes.
   c. Never.

7. Tell us what you think about this new way of doing things.

[a]To be read aloud to students who read below third-grade level.

wondered if the time and effort involved for all were worthwhile. So she decided to ask the members of the school board, teachers, parents, and students about it by distributing a questionnaire for them to fill out anonymously. Table 3.3 illustrates the questionnaire she administered to the students.

The questions asked of staff, parents, and school board members were different, of course. When Mrs. Olsen analyzed the information she had gathered, she found it very useful. For instance, while a few of the students said they didn't like doing different work from that of their peers, most said they liked school better and felt they were learning more. The parents were even more enthusiastic, reporting that their children brought more work home and completed it with greater accuracy than previously. Several volunteered that their children seemed more eager to go to school, and one mother even reported that her daughter's previously frequent morning stomachaches seemed to have disappeared. School board members expressed the concern that the method might be more costly, although it hadn't

been so far; however, they noted, if students attended school more regularly and scored higher on achievement tests, any minor increases in costs would have been worth it. From the teachers she learned that the new approach seemed to make their teaching job more satisfying. Students were progressing better and disrupting less. Because extra effort was involved, the method would be far too difficult without student teachers and peers tutoring one another. Once the teachers got into the swing of planning for individuals, though, it began to get easier, as the material they developed could be used over and over again with different students. One of the teachers asked if the school might purchase a computer terminal and the staff receive training in the use of computers as instructional tools so that teachers might share units with other schools in the region.

Now Mrs. Olsen felt confident that matching instruction to individuals' levels of preparedness paid, and she decided to continue supporting it in every way possible. She would investigate other resources in the region and elsewhere, look into costs for computer hookups and continue to supply feedback to the teachers for offering the adjusted curricula.

Program evaluation

When we examine the functional effects of a particular intervention and the satisfaction expressed by its consumers, we are assessing how well our strategies of educational change are achieving our purposes. It is essential, however, that we do not lose sight of the big picture: the more global purposes of schooling. We also need to evaluate how closely the outcomes of our educational programs match our broad goals and objectives.

Each of the constituencies within a school system will have its own priorities. Parents want their children to profit by acquiring knowledge and skills that will enhance the quality of their lives. As representatives of the public, school board members probably will share that goal while also feeling responsive to taxpayers, who hope that costs will be kept to a minimum. Depending on their levels of maturity and other factors, students will have some goals, while professional educators will have others.

One way to approach evaluating a program is to examine its anticipated outcomes in relation to the outcomes it actually has achieved. Has the district been able to operate within its budget? How closely? Have as many graduates been able to obtain jobs as predicted? How much discrepancy exists between the original prediction and the actual number of jobs obtained?[2]

As educators, we may have indicated that we plan to raise the average standardized test scores of our students by a certain percentage. Rapidly we will realize, though, that to accomplish this noble purpose, we must break that goal down into a set of smaller goals that will enable our grand goal to be achieved, and those goals must be stated in such a way that we will be able to measure change both as it takes place and afterward. This process is accomplished by pinpointing carefully what students are to learn.

Pinpointing goals

At Washington Street School the staff decided it had best determine a method for evaluating how effectively it was serving its students.

"What do we want our students to learn?" asked Mr. Lee.

"To read."

"To love learning."

"The skills to allow them to earn a living."

"To appreciate good literature."

"To get a sense of fulfillment out of life."

"To be scientifically literate."

As splendid as these educational goals are, you can see that they are very broad and have been stated rather vaguely. Guiding students toward achieving such amorphous ends would be like directing someone to a location in a city without specifying an address or providing a phone number or a street map. The person ultimately might find the place, but how many blind alleys and wrong turns would have been traversed along the way?

Analyzing tasks. What, then, needs to be done? Mr. Lee explained that the goals must be broken down into their component parts, as a series of steps the student is to follow.

---

[2]This type of question could be posed if you were using a "discrepancy evaluation" system of program evaluation, in which obtained outcomes are compared to expected outcomes.

"Then, each step must be identified precisely. This strategy is called **task analysis.**[3] What do you say we try doing a simple task analysis to see what it's like? Look, I've a bowl, a whisk, a hot plate, frying pan, a fork, salt, butter, and an egg."

"Are you hinting that we might be about to do a task analysis for scrambling an egg?"

"You guessed it, Manny."

"But that's so easy," protested Pat Thomas.

"We'll see," responded Mr. Lee with a wry smile. "Why don't we write down the steps here on the board."

The group listed:

• Crack the egg.
• Break it open.
• Whisk it with a pinch of salt.
• Melt the butter.
• Scramble the egg in the hot pan.

"Is that it?" inquired Mr. Lee.

"Sure. We said it would be simple," responded Mr. Rodriguez.

"Shall I give it a try?"

"Why not? Go ahead, K. C."

Mr. Lee took the egg and cracked it against the table top as the white began to drip onto the surface.

"Into the bowl! We should have said that," called out Kate Burnes.

As the egg plopped into the bowl, it was joined by a few fragments of eggshell. Referring to the task analysis he poured a sizable amount of salt into his palm and prepared to dump it into the bowl.

"Hold it. That's too much salt."

"You said a pinch. With all the practice I've had pinching my little Jade's cheeks lately, I'm used to hefty pinches. Maybe we'd better change that part to a measure. Is a quarter of a teaspoon O.K.?"

Assured of their acquiescence, he changed the item. Then he picked up the whisk, obviously ready to begin beating the egg.

"Hey, wait," called out Burt Cole. "You're about to mix in all those pieces of egg shell."

"Well, I don't see anything about shells on the list? Do you Burt?"

"Then add 'remove any egg shells.'"

Mr. Lee started to use his fingers.

"Use the fork. Ugh!" said Ms. Jackson in a tone of mock disgust.

Adding "with a fork" to the previous notation, Mr. Lee chased a few bits of eggshell unsuccessfully about the bowl.

"Any real chef knows the best way to remove egg shells is to use one of the intact halves. Try that, K. C.," advised Pat Thomas.

The challenge met, Mr. Lee again altered the task analysis, and the process continued until at last the egg was cooked and served (minus egg shells) to the staff in minute portions on crackers.

"You have definitely made your point, K. C. Task analyses have to be complete and tested out so they can be revised if necessary," summarized Mr. Rodriguez.

"That's true. It is especially important that they be tested with the group for which they are intended. I was obviously intentionally giving you a hard time, but just think if I were one of Ms. Hollingsworth's students, who was learning to cook for the first time. Without the precise list we were forced to generate here, the student might well fail."

"O.K. You've made those points graphically clear," said Ms. Jackson. "But I'm concerned with teaching much more complicated material, like scientific concepts. Would a task analysis be relevant for me?"

"Let's see. Can you suggest a general goal?"

How about considering the goal "scientific literacy?" What constitutes scientific literacy—that is, how can its components be stated precisely? And how can they be defined in behavioral terms?

Suppose you, our readers, were to try to dissect the goal of "scientific literacy" into all the steps the student must perform to achieve it and then to specify those learning tasks as instructional objectives. You could begin alone or by consulting experts. In the present case, you would be apt to study curriculum

[3]We return to the topics of task analyses and objectives in Chapter 17.

guides, read articles on the topic, and confer with experts. You might even start out by adapting the **Delphi method,** in which a panel of experts is asked to supply a certain number of items to include in a behavioral definition of "scientific literacy." These terms then would be compiled and the panel asked again to select a certain number of the most critical. The process would continue until a particular number of items clearly has risen to the top. Those would be the items to be analyzed into a sequence of tasks.

For the sake of discussion, suppose that among the components of "scientific literacy" you have identified the following:

- Distinguishing among at least five different branches of science by providing appropriate examples of experiments particular to each.
- Listing and explaining a set of basic concepts of physics, chemistry, biology, geology, and psychology.
- Defining *scientific method.*
- Assessing the adequacy of reports about scientific findings communicated in the popular media.
- Identifying the scientific foundations of a set of recent technological advances.
- Correctly using particular scientific instruments.

As you can see, even these tasks need to be subdivided further and then resubdivided until they consist of a sequence of steps that are manageable and attainable. For instance, the item on using instruments could include this specific point: "Preparing a set of slides to be viewed through a microscope and depicted in drawings." At last we have presented a task that can be achieved within a reasonable series of learning activities. This **behavioral goal** contains an **operational statement** of what is sought; it is phrased in observable and measurable terms. We can observe and count the number of slides and drawings completed.

At this level of analysis, the sequence of tasks may be adjusted to the students who are to perform them. (This applies to social as well as other tasks, too.) The student's current repertoire of skills are tested to see which, if any, he or she already has acquired. Those skills need only to be reviewed or possibly set aside if appropriate. Other aspects of each student's performance also are considered: the size of the step the individual learner can accomplish successfully (some steps may be recombined, others further broken down to match his or her particular requirements); the most suitable sensory mode or modes in which to present instruction (visual, auditory, tactile, etc.); variations in the arrangements of steps; and so on.

Developing objectives

With tasks matched to individual learners, both students and instructors will want to know if students are progressing and when they have accomplished a given skill. You can provide this information by preparing **behavioral** (in the present case *instructional*) **objectives.**

Behavioral objectives state exactly what students are to learn to do, under what set of circumstances, and to what degree of proficiency. In other words, they are objective statements of the performances that constitute behavioral goals. Instructional objectives, as with any form of behavioral objectives, state (1) student *actions*, (2) *givens* or *conditions* — times, places, materials, and instructions — and (3) the *criteria* or *standards* by which acceptable achievement is assessed. When teachers and students know exactly what performance is expected of them, under what conditions and according to what standards, the learning process tends to be focused and efficient.

Let us examine the task identified above: "Preparing a set of slides to be viewed through a microscope and depicted in drawings." We can guess what is involved, but are not completely sure. So let us develop the objective.

- *Action.* Prepare slides to be viewed through a microscope and depicted in drawings.
- *Under what circumstances.* Access to the specimens, a microscope, slides, covers, an array of tools and 6 hours in the laboratory.
- *Standard of performance.* When the student has

produced one drawing of each of four different specimen slides, and the instructor can identify each specimen correctly on the basis of the sketch without any additional information, the task will be fulfilled.

Now the student knows exactly how the assignment is to be completed, and the instructor knows what skills need to be taught and what materials must be supplied. Both know when the skill has been acquired adequately and when it will be appropriate to progress to the next objective.

Identifying all performances you plan to teach. Task analyses and their constituent instructional objectives may include various skills. In the skill we just broke down into objectives, several different kinds of behaviors were incorporated: cognitive behaviors, such as being able to distinguish one specimen structure from another; motor behaviors, like handling slides and scalpels; performances, which included eye-hand coordination; and others. Some of the skills you are concerned with teaching also might include affective aspects, like satisfaction or enjoyment, for example, a student saying, "I liked doing that," or choosing to do the task again, and so on. It is important for you to recognize the full array of performances you plan to have students achieve, so none that may be crucial is overlooked and so you can adjust your teaching to the specific purposes you've identified.

To illustrate, we will relate an episode experienced by our team while teaching a course in applied behavior analysis. Substantial effort had gone into preparing study questions, quizzes, and answer keys designed to cover critical material. We found that when students had completed the course, most were able to define terms and explain concepts very well, but only a few could apply the principles toward solving novel behavioral problems. When we examined our study materials, we found that most of the questions were of the "recall" and "explanation" varieties. The students had been asked to tell what they had read in the text. They were not asked to solve behavioral problems. So we revised the materials to include many situations for which students were instructed to propose solutions. Their ability to handle novel problem situations improved accordingly.

This experience formed the basis for a series of studies examining the relation between study materials and the conceptual skills that students learned. In one of the investigations (Chase, Johnson, & Sulzer-Azaroff, 1985), we found that if students were given practice in defining terms on tests covering the material they had studied, they defined terms well. If they were asked to develop their own original examples of a concept, they performed best in that mode. If they were asked to examine and see whether examples appropriately illustrated the concept or not, that was the skill they learned best. Yes, there were instances of carry-over from one mode to another, but such transfers were minor compared to the relation between the skill taught and the skill demonstrated.

You also need to identify *where* and *with whom* the skills are to be expressed. Just because children practice careful penmanship in your class, that doesn't mean they automatically will in someone else's, any more than you practice the same social skills with your family that you do with your senior supervisors. If you want generalization across behaviors, settings, or people, you must plan for it rather than leaving it up to chance.

The moral of the story is to *pinpoint exactly what the student should be able to do at the end of the instructional or behavioral intervention, and teach to that end as directly as possible.* It makes little sense to instruct a young child in writing manuscript letters or a surgeon in performing a delicate operation only by lecturing them on the subject, without providing an opportunity for guided practice. Similarly, do not limit study or test items to questions about names and dates if your aim is to enable your students to analyze historical events in a particular way. Do provide them with practice, and ask questions calling for that sort of an analysis. If you want them to transfer or generalize that learning to novel situations or subject matter, provide them with experience in many different situations.

If you want the modified behavior to persist, indicate for how long and at what level. (See Chapter 17 for a more detailed discussion of generalization and maintenance.)

This fundamental maxim of good teaching is not restricted to cognitive learning, either. It applies to social, motor, and affective learning as well. Just as an effective coach teaches skills in isolation where they can be studied, as well as in a game situation where they can be applied, behavioral instruction sees to it that students engage in a performance — or as close to that performance as possible — in the location and in the manner they will be expected to do it in the future. As you read our coverage of teaching particular subject matters later on, you'll see how this point has been put to use to teach handwriting, sports, compositional writing, reading, and so on. You also will note in subsequent chapters how social skills and instructional and classroom management techniques are taught according to this precept. Children like Juan even can be directly taught to smile as Cooke and Apolloni (1976) and Hopkins (1968) have done, and their depressive behaviors successfully treated (Frame, Matson, Sonis, Fialkov, & Kazdin, in press; Reisinger, 1972). In such instances, the components of the behavior and the circumstances under which those components are to be expressed are pinpointed precisely so instruction can be adjusted as closely to the end goal as possible. (See Chapter 17 for a more detailed discussion of developing objectives.)

Matching people and objectives

In theory, given infinite time, resources, and instructional talent, it should be possible to teach any physically intact human being anything by breaking down the skill into smaller and smaller parts until those parts are finally of a size that the student can acquire. In fact, it is amazing how such an approach has worked successfully, even among people whose development has been delayed severely — enabling them to acquire highly complicated functional skills: vocational skills like assembling electronic parts or bicycle brakes (Walls, Ellis, Zane, & VanderPoel, 1979); self-care skills, like brushing

their teeth (Tyson, Tyson, & Sulzer-Azaroff, 1983); or skills for the community, such as using coins appropriately (Lowe & Cuvo, 1976).

That sort of fine-grained analysis of learning goals takes time and often large expenditures of funds, patience, and other resources. Life is not long enough, nor support sufficient, to enable students to master every conceptual, motor, social, and affective skill we think is important. For practical purposes, then, some selection techniques must be applied. To this end, goals must be analyzed in relation to individual students so that the most important functional and feasible instructional objectives are chosen for each. This argument was made by Brown, Nietupski, and Hamre-Nietupski (1976), who emphasized the importance of age-appropriate, *functional*, and socially significant teaching objectives for severely handicapped individuals. As Donnellan (1980) has indicated, many instructional objectives do not meet those requirements. Instead, one often can see retarded teenagers playing with toys suitable for preschoolers, such as blocks or wooden beads, rather than learning how to prepare food, perform the housekeeping chores that adults need to do, and master skills to function in the community and get along with peers.

If you are in a situation in which you must select some objectives in preference to others, consider the following factors.

Will the objective benefit the people whose behavior is to be modified; will it be functional for them not only in the short run but also in the long run? Having Tom spend an hour a day coloring the pictures on his worksheets may keep him occupied but will it help ease his transfer into a regular classroom? It might be possible to teach Richard to accept his deficiencies and not become upset when he receives a poor grade and thereby avoid some of his emotional outbursts, but how would that help him later on? Improving his reading and study skills probably will help him improve his grades and avoid becoming distressed; those skills also will serve him in later life.

Will the objective benefit others in the individual's social environment? Does it lend itself to instruction in a natural way, so it can be practiced and reinforced along the way?[4] Juan himself might benefit from learning how to express his frustrations by learning how to fight more effectively. While this might alleviate his depression, it would not be supported by others around him. Conversely, teaching him formally as an incidental aspect of his natural social activities to be assertive in a pleasant way would more likely be well received and supported and thereby maintained by his peers and teachers.

Is the objective one that can be achieved in a reasonable time period? All of us operate best when receiving reinforcement regularly. Easier objectives, ones that build on previously acquired knowledge and skills, will be achieved more readily than difficult ones. Rather than insisting that teachers at Willow Grove School adjust assignments for all students in every subject all at once, for instance, they might be asked to match assignments to students' levels for one group in one subject.

Will the objective take more time, money, and effort than those involved are willing to spend? It might be useless to target an objective that requires a personal computer for each student or that the staff work evenings and weekends. Then, we should find out how much support we should anticipate for our objectives.

Can the objective meet multiple needs? Some skills meet more than one purpose. Teaching Richard general study skills will help him with all his subjects. Enabling Marissa to assert herself will pay off not only in helping her to avoid her sexual misadventures, but it also may help her to establish more wholesome relationships with other people.

Additionally, Kratochwill (1985) reports that criteria for selecting target behaviors are becoming conceptually and empirically explicit. His list of conceptual criteria includes: physical danger, likelihood of the target behavior being maintained, positive rather than negative properties, importance for the development of other behaviors, flexibility or adap-

tation to the environment, and effectiveness in changing existing contingency systems to promote long-term positive development. Empirical criteria include (Kratochwill, 1985, pp. 3, 4) "consistency with developmental or local norms, relevance to successful performance, positiveness as rated through social validation, capacity for discriminating between skilled and nonskilled performance, and if left untreated would result in negative prognosis."

OTHER FACTORS IN THE ENVIRONMENT

Other factors besides subject matter area, skill deficits, general "ability" (i.e., achievement), and social interactions between the student and peers and the teacher must be considered in assessing for individualized student planning. Sometimes the physical environment can influence performance. Some students have been found to eat faster while "easy listening" music is played and slower with rock music (Van Horn, Mein, Rich, Tison, Trout, Watterson, & Wilfong, 1981). Crowding seating arrangements and the presence of distracting objects might sometimes impair a student's academic performance.

How activities are scheduled or sequenced, how much time is allocated to different assignments and how presentations of materials are paced (Becker & Carnine, 1981; Strong & Traynelis-Yurek, 1982; Van Houten & Little, 1982) also may have an effect.

How specific learning tasks relate to one another also can be important. With Richard, we saw how his skill deficit in reading comprehension probably influenced his performance in several of his classes. Most academic work requires that the student has achieved a set of basic prerequisite skills: paying attention for an adequate length of time, following complex instructions, completing assignments, using basic tools such as writing implements, and possessing social skills adequate to permit the student to work productively in a group setting.

In subsequent chapters (e.g., Chapters 17 and 18), you will see how many of these variables have been analyzed to assess their influence on student behav-

---

[4]*Incidental teaching* is a technique involving arranging the natural environment to attract children to desired materials and activities. The teacher instructs and reinforces target behaviors, such as initiations of elaborated requests, by permitting the student access to the item or activity. (McGee, Krantz, Mason, & McClannahan, 1983).

ior. If you suspect that some of these may be adversely affecting one of your students, a fellow staff member or you can test it out. Take baseline data under conditions as they are. Modify the suspected conditions and continue collecting data and see if any improvement occurs. If so, replace the original conditions and see if the earlier pattern of behavior returns. If it does, reimplement the change. Or if you are not willing to return to the original conditions with that person, repeat the analysis with other people or with the same person under different conditions or with other behaviors. Then you will have verified to your own satisfaction the rationale for sustaining the modified conditions.

You may have recognized by now how important it is to become well acquainted with both the people whose behavior is targeted for change and the environment in which the objective is to be expressed. You need to know the person's skills and deficiencies, rates of learning different types of material, and ways of being motivated. You also must be aware of what human and material resources are available and what kind of commitment other people have made to supporting the objective. Only when a strategy — be it instructional, training, or therapeutic — is matched to the individual and the environment will success and consequent reinforcement be forthcoming.

SELECTING A COURSE OF ACTION

All were now ready to do some educational planning for Richard. A planning meeting was held, attended by Dr. Levy; Mr. Kay; the reading specialist, Ms. Pear; Richard; his parents; and the science teacher, Mr. Forsyth. Dr. Levy summarized how Richard had scored considerably above average on the individual I.Q. test. Ms. Pear described Richard's excellent vocabulary, but she also commented that Richard's reading comprehension score was below grade level. She offered to work with him individually to help him correct that problem. Dr. Levy summarized Richard's academic performance. His work was uneven; he showed many indications of performing well, but those indications were inconsistent; and his work could be done more neatly and with greater care. The guidance counselor, Mr. Kay, concurred, pointing out that Richard worked hard in math and science but wasted lots of time in English. Mr. Kay also mentioned that the teachers attended to Richard infrequently in English and math, but relatively more often in P.E. and science. "That's easy for me," commented the science teacher, Mr. Forsyth. "Richard, you really do well in my class. You have lots to contribute. If only your exam grades were better, you'd probably be making A's consistently. Maybe the work you do with Ms. Pear will help you there."

The conference ended with a plan for Richard to receive help with his reading and for him to work toward increasing the number and percentage of completed assignments. He'd also try to increase his on-task behavior in English to at least 70 percent each day. Mr. Kay offered to continue recording a few times a week to see how well Richard was coming along. Each Friday he would send a note to the Parkers summarizing their son's records for the week. If Richard's goal for the week were met, he would earn a special privilege, such as tickets to a sports event, a ride to a place of his choice, extra spending money, a book, or other things that could be added at a later time.

When the meeting adjourned, Richard's parents thanked the staff for their efforts on behalf of their son and expressed their relief that he wasn't stupid after all. "I never thought he was," replied Dr. Levy. "But this is just the beginning. If Richard is to catch up sufficiently, he'll have to work hard. With the cooperation of all of us, he has a good chance of doing that over the rest of his high school years."

Summary

Before implementing a treatment program, it is important to select a method to measure the target behavior, as described in the previous chap-

ter, and use that measure to determine the extent of the problem—the baseline. Next, the degree of material, administrative, community, and social support for the program must be determined. The program should be implemented only if sufficient support can be generated for it.

We recommend also that you select a method for evaluating the effectiveness of your program. Only then will you know if your program of intervention was responsible for any obtained behavior change.

You are now ready to specify in detail the objectives that you want to teach. Each objective includes an action, the circumstances under which it will be performed, and a criterion level to help you determine when it has been accomplished. Your objectives, along with a measure of consumer satisfaction and a means of evaluating its effectiveness, help you to determine the success of your behavior change program; it is an accountable approach.

Selecting appropriate goals and objectives is not always an easy task. Several guidelines were provided for choosing the most important and feasible goals and objectives. Other factors that you will need to consider to promote individual success, such as the physical environment, scheduling activities and others, also were highlighted for your use.

The next step is to implement the treatment program. Let us now turn our attention to procedural strategies and tactics of intervention.

Study Questions

1. Define *baseline*.
2. Discuss the basic purposes for collecting an adequate baseline.
3. List the ten points to note when constructing a graph.
4. Paul wants to graph his self-management data. He is interested in patterns produced by single responses over time.
   (a) Suggest a type of graph capable of depicting this information clearly.
   (b) Draw a sample graph of the type you identified in question 4(a).
   (c) Describe how it differs from a typical graph.
5. State the information you could obtain about Richard from Figure 3.3.
6. Discuss the importance of assessing a person's physical and social environments.
7. List several segments operating within the educational system that need to be considered when designing a program.
8. Explain the purpose of administering a needs assessment.
9. List the four elements contained in a needs assessment survey.
10. The teachers at the Hillside School have been using a behavioral program to reduce noise in the lunchroom. Provide them with a method to determine if their tactics are effective.
11. Briefly describe the program conducted at Willow Grove School to increase teachers' rates of adjusting assignments to individual student needs.
12. List several reasons why a particular intervention might not receive support.
13. One way to avoid the problem of staff discarding a strategy is _____.
14. Provide one way to evaluate a program.
15. Define *task analysis*.
16. Describe the Delphi method.
17. List the components of putting on a sock.
18. Define behavioral goal.

19. Discuss in detail adjusting the sequence of tasks to the student. (Be sure to include all the aspects of the student's behavior to be considered).
20. Define *instructional objective*. (Compare it with *behavioral goal*.) Be specific.
21. Write an instructional objective for *hanging a picture*. (Be sure to include three parts.)
22. Provide an original example illustrating the need for identifying all performances that you plan to teach.
23. You want your students to be able to play basketball. Discuss ways that you (a) would and (b) would not test their skills in basketball. (Support your answer.)
24. Give an original example of a complex skill you might teach to a severely developmentally delayed person by using a task analysis.
25. State the five factors that should be considered when you must select some objectives in preference to others.
26. (a) Use these factors and select one of your behaviors to target for change.
    (b) Justify your selection.
27. Discuss environmental factors that affect your performance on a test.
28. Provide factors about the test itself that could affect your performance.
29. Describe a method for determining if there are any factors adversely affecting one of your students.
30. State the information you should know about the individual and the environment to help ensure that your program will be a success.
31. Describe a plan for selecting a course of action for a student who needs help.
32. Select the operational statement from the examples below:
    (a) Hand raising is defined as lifting the hand at or above shoulder level.
    (b) Record each time Susie is angry.
    (c) Susie is tired and hungry.
33. Karen is recording Jon's on-task behavior during math class. His teacher said that he is on-task more often now that Karen is observing him. (a) Label his increase in on-task behavior with the appropriate term and (b) discuss how it can affect the baseline.
34. List the various skills that should be included in a behavioral objective.

References

Becker, W. C., & Carnine, D. W. (1981). Direct instruction: A behavior theory model for comprehensive educational intervention with the disadvantaged. In S. W. Bijou & R. Ruiz (Eds.), *Behavior modification: Contributions to education* (pp. 145–210). Hillsdale, NJ: Lawrence Erlbaum Associates.

Brown, L., Nietupski, J., & Hamre-Nietupski, S. (1976). The criterion of ultimate functioning and public school services for severely handicapped students. In L. Brown, N. Certo, K. Belmore, & T. Crowner (Eds.), *Papers and programs related to public school services for secondary age severely handicapped students*, Vol. VI, Part 1. Madison, WI: Madison Metropolitan School District, 1976. Republished: *Hey don't forget about me: New directions for serving the severely handicapped*. Reston, VA: Council for Exceptional Children, pp. 2–15.

Chase, P. M., Johnson, K. R., & Sulzer-Azaroff, B. (1985). Verbal relations within instruction. Are there subclasses of the intraverbal? *Journal of the Experimental Analysis of Behavior*.

Cooke, T. P., & Apolloni, T. (1976). Developing positive social-emotional behaviors: A study of training and generalization effects. *Journal of Applied Behavior Analysis, 9*, 65–78.

Donnellan, A. M. (1980). An educational perspective of autism: Implications for curriculum development and personnel development. In *Critical issues in educating autistic children and youth* (pp. 53–88). U.S. Department of Education, Office of Special Education.

Frame, C., Matson, J. L., Sonis, W. A., Fialkov, M. J., & Kazdin, A. E. (In press). Behavioral treatment of depression in a prepubertal child, *Journal of Behavior Therapy and Experimental Psychiatry*.

Hopkins, B. L. (1968). Effects of candy and social reinforcement, instructions, and reinforcement schedule learning on the modification and maintenance of smiling. *Journal of Applied Behavior Analysis, 1,* 121–229.

Johnson, J. M. (1970). A universal behavior graph paper. *Journal of Applied Behavior Analysis, 3,* 271–272.

Kratochwill, T. R. (1985). Selection of target behaviors: Issues and directions. *Behavioral Assessment, 7,* 3–5.

Lowe, M. L., & Cuvo, A. J. (1976). Teaching coin summation to the mentally retarded. *Journal of Applied Behavior Analysis, 9,* 483–489.

Mayer, G. R., Butterworth, T. W., Spaulding, H. L., Hollingsworth, P., Amorim, M., Caldwell-McElroy, C., Nafpaktitis, M., & Perez-Osorio, X. (1983). *Constructive discipline: Building a climate for learning.* (Available from the Office of the Los Angeles County Superintendent of Schools, 9300 E. Imperial, Downey, CA 90242).

McGee, G. G., Krantz, P. J., Mason, D., & McClannahan, L. E. (1983). A modified incidental-teaching procedure for autistic youth: Acquisition and generalization of receptive object labels. *Journal of Applied Behavior Analysis, 16,* 329–338.

Reisinger, J. J. (1972). The treatment of "anxiety-depression" via positive reinforcement and response cost. *Journal of Applied Behavior Analysis, 5,* 125–130.

Strong, M. W., & Traynelis-Yurek, E. A. (1982, May). *Behavioral reinforcement within a perceptual-conditioning program of oral reading.* Paper presented at the Eighth Annual Convention of the Association for Behavior Analysis, Milwaukee, WI.

Tyson, M., Tyson, W. M., & Sulzer-Azaroff, B. (1983). *Programming across complex skills.* Unpublished manuscript.

Van Horn, R. W., Mein, K., Rich, B., Tison, C., Trout, C., Watterson, M., & Wilfong, S. (1981). Environmental psychology in the classroom: Four studies. *Education and Treatment of Children, 4,* 171–178.

Van Houton, R., & Little, G. (1982). Increased response rate in special education children following an abrupt reduction in time limit in the absence of a token economy. *Education and Treatment of Children, 5,* 23–32.

Walls, R. T., Ellis, W. D., Zane, T., & VanderPoel, S. J. (1979). Tactile, auditory and visual prompting in teaching complex assembly tasks. *Education and Training of the Mentally Retarded, 14,* 120–130.

II Principles and procedures: motivating, instructing, and managing behavior

"Another lost day," complained Rudy Smith. "That's what happens when you've got a class full of jocks. All they can think about is tomorrow's game. History is the last thing on their minds."

"It's been the same way in my class today," replied Dave Markham. "I must have reminded the group to get back to work 40 times. The weather seems to be the most important thing at this point, so they kept looking out the window trying to predict the condition of the field."

"Maybe," Rudy offered, "we should start giving out M & M's to get them to work, like they do in elementary school."

"Don't think I haven't been tempted," said Dave. "But my wife tried that with her fifth graders and it didn't work. I don't think that B. Mod stuff is any good. It's just a fad."

"I agree," concurred Rudy. "Once I tried using a token system. Gave the kids poker chips that they could turn in for prizes and that didn't help at all."

"Hold on. Just a second!" interrupted Arlene Levy. "Just using M & M's and tokens doesn't necessarily mean you're using behavior modification procedures as they should be used. Much more is involved."

"Like what?" challenged Mr. Smith.

"Well, for one, not all children like M & M's; or even if they did, maybe Dave's wife didn't give enough or gave

61

them at the wrong time or their parents objected—I know I would. I wouldn't want my Jenny getting candy. Who knows?"

"Do you think that's what happened with my token system?" asked Mr. Smith. "Maybe the kids didn't like the prizes."

"That could have been what happened. You know, Rudy, most of our students have enough pocket money to buy what they really want. It often takes a bit of deprivation for things to be reinforcing."

"It sounds like what you're saying, Arlene, is that behavioral procedures need to be adjusted to different students."

"That's exactly what I mean. No one method is going to work for everyone. You need to alter your procedures to match the individuals involved—and that goes for us as well as our students."

"How do we do that?"

"The best way I know is for you to learn about general principles of be-havior; then turn them into procedures by matching them to your students. Of course, it helps to learn about how others have done this, so lots of examples can come in handy."

"I'm game," agreed Mr. Smith. "I'd be willing to give it another try if you think it will help my students to learn their social studies. Where do I start?"

Dr. Levy offered to share some books and articles on the topic and to continue the dialogue. She also volunteered to visit their classes when they were ready to test out their procedures.

Part II of this text is designed to provide you with that kind of information. It will describe a number of basic behavioral principles and illustrate how they have been applied effectively in educational and other settings. By the time you complete Chapters 4 to 12, you will have learned a set of these fundamental principles and gotten many ideas about how you can translate them into methods for addressing the problems that face you as an educator.

4 Identifying and delivering behavioral consequences

Goals

After completing this chapter, you should be able to:

1. Define and give illustrations of each of the following terms:
   a. Reinforcer
   b. Stimulus
   c. Punisher
   d. Aversive stimulus
   e. Positive reinforcer
   f. Primary or unconditioned reinforcers
   g. Positive reinforcement
   h. Negative reinforcement
   i. Punishment
   j. Premack principle
2. Differentiate between negative reinforcement and punishment.
3. Describe how the strength of a given reinforcer may be influenced.
4. Describe what can be done to identify effective reinforcers.
5. Describe and illustrate how a specific neutral stimulus can be turned into a reinforcer.
6. List several reinforcers appropriate for a group.
7. Discuss what factors should be taken into consideration when reinforcement depends on the group's level of performance.
8. Discuss the advantages of teaching peers to identify and reinforce desired social and academic behavior.
9. Describe a peer reinforcement program.
10. Discuss the advantages of teaching students to reinforce their own behavior.
11. Describe how to teach a youngster to reinforce his or her own behavior.

The first thing you noticed when you walked into the classroom was a boy standing on a desk, while the other students laughed and pointed at him. Only one or two of the dozen or so were seated and working.

"You see what I mean?" the teacher complained to the consultant. "These youngsters were hand-picked as being mathematically talented. I know they all come from good families. I just don't understand why they are so impossible."

"It really is going to be difficult to test out the new curriculum you are developing if they keep behaving like this. I can understand why you're asking for help."

"I know I need it. This is a new experience for me. My earlier work with gifted high school juniors and seniors obviously didn't prepare me for a group of spirited 10-year-olds."

"Hey, teacher. Look at me!" called one of the boys as he executed a cartwheel across the floor.

"Me too!" — as another walked on his hands.

Another forced an exaggerated belch, provoking groans from some of the others; while a couple approached their teacher.

"I can't work. Can't you shut them up?"

"O.K. you guys," responded the teacher in a firm tone. "Enough is enough. Back to the salt mines," and the uproar temporarily subsided.

To the consultant, it seemed apparent that attention from their teacher, in any form, reinforced the students' actions. Seeing them working and terminating the disruption reinforced the teacher's method of handling the situation. But neither the teacher nor the students seemed to be aware of how their behavior was being influenced. So the consultant met with the teacher later on and tried to explain what was happening. Since the teacher was dubious, they decided to try an experiment.

They clearly defined unacceptable off-task student behavior by specifying each of the actions in that category. For example, they included being out of seat or handling materials belonging to others without permission, asking questions or making comments irrelevant to the assignment, and so on. Then, the consultant measured each student's on- and off-task behavior, being certain to establish — through revising and refining the definitions — that regardless of who did the observing, the same specific information would be recorded. After demonstrating to their mutual satisfaction that the students were indeed off-task a good deal of the time, they selected a promising strategy. Instead of looking at, talking to, or helping students who were not attending to the task at hand, the teacher and his teaching aide would redistribute their attention — now providing it to those students who were hard at work.

An amazing thing happened. As the teachers walked about the room offering assistance, commenting positively on work of high quality, and ignoring students while they were off task, the measures began to indicate a major drop in off-task behavior. The youngsters began to get down to work in earnest, and it was at last possible to start assessing the curriculum materials.

In fact, change came so fast and endured so well — for weeks — that everyone began to wonder if some other factors might have been responsible. Perhaps, they pondered, the group finally had gotten into the swing of things — enjoying the challenge of the novel materials and its success with the curriculum.

Maybe the students were maturing as time passed, or some other unknown factors were responsible. How could they find out?

They decided to return to the original conditions of the classroom. The teachers again would listen to or correct students who interrupted, wandered, or made irrelevent comments. They'd leave alone those students who were working hard. Again, change was swift. The calm of the past several weeks was rapidly displaced by chaos. Convinced after a week or so that the manner in which they distributed their attention really *did* matter, the teachers switched back to the experimental procedure. Peace and progress were restored once more, never again to be put to the test.

REINFORCERS DEFINED

That actual episode probably helped you figure out what *a **reinforcer** is: a **stimulus*** (an object or event) *that follows a particular behavior and increases the strength* (rate, duration, etc.) *of that behavior*. Notice that for a stimulus to be called a reinforcer, it must be a *consequence* of a behavior and function to *increase* or *sustain* the behavior. In the situation just described, attention and praise were obviously reinforcers, because they increased or maintained the on-task behaviors of the students. But attention or praise is not automatically reinforcing. Some people *decrease* their rates or intensities of doing something when that action is praised by certain people under particular circumstances. In such cases, praise would not be a reinforcer. Instead, it would be a **punisher.** Consequently, before labeling an event a reinforcer, it must have followed the behavior *and* increased or sustained it.

Types of reinforcers: positive and negative

The episode described above also illustrates many important features of the reinforcement procedure. For example, it shows how two different types of events influenced the behavior of students and teachers. In that situation, several influences were operating on the behavior of each member of our cast of characters — the students, the teachers, the consultant, and the curriculum development team. First, the teachers had found themselves in an aversive, or punitive, situation. They were eager to exchange the **aversive stimuli** — the students' unruly and inattentive behavior — for **positive reinforcers** — data giving evidence that students were beginning to learn, progress, and enjoy their math class. Those latter positive stimuli also would reinforce the performance of the consultant, and so would the satisfaction and appreciation of the teachers and the curriculum development team. For the students, as quickly became apparent, it was the teachers' attention and approbation that functioned as powerful reinforcers.

As you can see, *positive* and/or *aversive* stimuli may be involved in the reinforcement process. We work to maximize positive reinforcers, as we work to rid ourselves of aversive stimuli. Yet both positive and aversive conditions can serve to increase or maintain behavior. How can this be? It has to do with whether the reinforcer is added or subtracted as a consequence of the behavior. A behavior increases or maintains when it is followed by the addition of a positively reinforcing object or event. A behavior also *increases* or *maintains* when it is followed by the *subtraction* or *removal* of an aversive object or event (see Figure 4.1). We'll discuss that **negative reinforcement** process in greater detail shortly.

Once the rationale was explained, our teachers began to redistribute their attention to students who were hard at work. They were told that this behavior would remove the aversive student off-task behavior and gain them the positive reinforcer, improved student learning. Their initial attempts were strengthened by the positive comments of the consultant. Then, sure enough, after a few days of trying the method, student deportment began to improve and that evidence contributed even more reinforcement.

Everyone's behavior is controlled by contingent events of various kinds. Assuming the appropriate preconditions have been in effect, we tend to repeat performances that are followed by certain stimuli that are by their nature reinforcers, such as food, beverages, or sexual activity, or that are followed by the removal of painful or irritating events. The stimuli involved are called **primary** (or **unconditioned**) **reinforcers** or **aversive stimuli.**

Stimuli that have become reinforcing as a result of our histories of learning **(secondary** or **conditioned reinforcers)** also may promote repetition of behaviors. Because each of us has a unique history, conditioned reinforcers vary between people. For some (again, the preconditions having been met) they can be activities like water skiing or playing field hockey or the harmonica; for others, it may be collecting the latest commemorative stamp, obtaining a new sports car, spending time with someone special, or leaving class early. Many of us find a commendation from a respected supervisor or peer very reinforcing; and for most of us, our jobs have their rewarding aspects. If you are a teacher, signs of student progress can be very reinforcing. In addition, again, as a function of our individual past experiences, particular events may become *conditioned* as *aversive stimuli*: frowns or disagreement from a loved one; the entrance of a supervisor who has recently reprimanded us or a student who complains frequently; a certain numeral on the bathroom scale; and too many more.

You may not always be aware of which reinforcers influence your behavior. You may or may not notice that what you do to terminate irritants — like

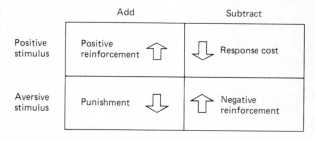

Note that both positive and negative reinforcement increase behavior. As you've probably already guessed, response cost, like punishment, reduces behavior. Yet, like negative reinforcement, response cost involves the removal of a stimulus. Response cost will be discussed in more detail in Chapter 11.

Figure 4.1
Definition of terms.

noise or a perceived threat to your authority — has been negatively reinforced and is therefore apt to continue. For example, if reprimanding has been effective in quieting your class, you will probably continue to reprimand. It worked — it eliminated or diminished the noise for a while. Thus, your reprimanding was negatively reinforced. Similarly, without realizing why, you could be acting to produce a positive reinforcer, such as giving a warm smile or frequently calling on a student who usually responds with a correct answer.

Perhaps you are a specialist — a consultant, resource person, supervisor, administrator. Besides your intentional attempts to influence others — through planned training, supervision, or consultation — the responses you get will in turn influence you, often without anyone being aware of what is happening. Some may accept your advice enthusiastically; some grudgingly. Some compliment you on your counsel. How does this influence the frequency and quality of your interactions?

Negative reinforcement and punishment

You may be having difficulty understanding negative reinforcement and identifying when you or others are being influenced by it. Negative reinforcement often is confused with punishment. If you will remember that *punishment decreases behavior*, while *reinforcement* — positive or negative — *increases behavior*, the confusion can be reduced. Both negative reinforcement and punishment involve an aversive consequence such as scolding, misbehavior, crying, or hitting. For example, when a youngster misbehaves, her teacher might scold her. If the scolding reduces the misbehavior, the scolding is a punisher. *When a consequence reduces a behavior, we say that the behavior was punished.* But what about the behavior of scolding? What consequence followed from it? Scolding was followed by the termination of the misbehavior; in other words, scolding worked (at least for the moment). Her teacher probably will scold again the next time a similar misbehavior occurs. Despite the teacher's awareness of the "rule" that punishment has many disadvan-

tages, the negatively reinforced scolding will tend to be repeated. (Although rules can and often do govern our behavior, as we shall see in a later chapter, contingencies that are directly experienced can be even more powerful.)

Along the same lines, when 2-year-old Mervis has a temper tantrum and his mom picks him up to soothe him, and the tantrum subsides, his mother will probably repeat her response the next time he has a tantrum. His mother's picking Mervis up has been negatively reinforced, while his tantrum behavior has been positively reinforced. Unless other factors are introduced into the situation, both behaviors will increase over time.

Let us go over a few more illustrations to make sure you can discriminate negative reinforcement from punishment and positive reinforcement. Kevin's sister Debbie stands in his way so he can't see the TV program. He pushes her out of the way. She leaves. Why is he likely to push again? Because the act got her out of his way — terminated the aversive situation. What affected Kevin's pushing? Negative reinforcement. What influenced Debbie's standing in the way? Punishment. She stopped standing in the way.

Debbie's mom is upset because the trash is overflowing in the kitchen. She nags Debbie to empty it. Finally, Debbie empties the trash. What was the outcome of the mother's behavior of nagging? Negative reinforcement — her nagging led to the trash being emptied. What was the consequence to Debbie for emptying the trash? Negative reinforcement — taking out the trash stopped the nagging.

To summarize, then, both punishment and positive reinforcement involve presenting or adding a stimulus following a behavior. Positive reinforcement results in an increase of the behavior. Punishment results in a decrease in the behavior. Negative reinforcement also increases behavior, but in this case a stimulus is reduced, subtracted, or removed — rather than added — as the consequence of the behavior. We suggest that you review each example and ask yourself: is a stimulus added, as in positive reinforcement or punishment; or is it subtracted, as with negative reinforcement, following the behavior? Does the behavior increase? Then it has been positively or negatively reinforced. Or does it decrease as a result of the consequence? Then it has been punished. These questions should help you distinguish the three procedures. (See Figure 4.1 for a summary of these terms.)

REINFORCER SELECTION

Now you realize that regardless of whether or not we recognize them as such, each of us has a distinct set of reinforcers that influence our behavior. Yet we don't wish to imply that the strength of a given reinforcing event is invariable. The reinforcing potential of a stimulus can and often does change as a function of time, prior history, concurrent events, and many other factors. If a long time has passed since your last meal, then a juicy steak, a pizza, or a bowl of chicken soup could exert strong control over your behavior. But if you just had finished dining, then the reinforcing properties of those foods probably would be minor. Similarly, even a highly preferred activity, like playing tennis, should lose its ability to reinforce at the end of the fifteenth set.

Nevertheless, for most of us, some events provide reinforcement virtually always, regardless of time or place. Such events include money, attention and approbation from respected individuals, the availability of options from among which we can freely select, and so on. So in choosing reinforcers to accomplish a given purpose, you might begin with one of those generally effective reinforcers, as we did with teacher attention in the math class. But if that is not successful, you could try something else.

We've experienced situations in which attending to selected behaviors produced little effect, particularly with underachieving and unruly students. In one case, the teacher timed and placed her attention optimally, but the attention paid by the students' peers when they misbehaved neutralized her efforts. This pattern of misbehavior was difficult to control without resorting to punishment, which the teacher and we rejected. So instead, we introduced a token system that consisted of check marks, a given number of which could be exchanged for items or activities highly desired by the students. The check marks were distributed while students were hard at work and when they had accomplished their assigned tasks. (In one situation, a check mark was given for each correctly completed item from the workbook.) That did it. Change was achieved. Then, after several months, we found it possible to delay gradually the delivery of those contrived reinforcers through altering the economy — by raising prices and by substituting activities more natural to the school environment, such as allowing extra time in the library, gym, or shop. Yet progress continued.

Suppose you were employed by the Washington Street School and were determined to do something to assist Juan, the loner who was teased so often. How would you apply reinforcement? You could teach him how to approach other students so they would be likely to invite him to join their activities, and show him ways to reinforce their treating him with consideration. As he began to practice those skills you could signal your approval with a wink, a smile, or a touch. (The techniques for teaching productive social skills like these have been the subject of much recent study and are the topic of Chapter 18.)

Every organization rewards its staff members for doing their jobs, and schools are no exception. Salaries, progress reports, informal feedback, preferred schedules or assignments, raises, and promotions are familiar to those of us who are gainfully employed. Some people are fortunate enough to find the work itself reinforcing and might be tempted to do their jobs regardless of those other rewards. While students ordinarily are not given wages to learn, the natural school environment contains many other potential reinforcers for them. Obvious ones include good grades, promotion, class placement, and positive feedback — both written and oral — from teachers. As we've seen earlier, accomplishment, attention, and praise may prove quite influential; so can access to preferred school activities and such privileges as permitting a student to tutor a peer.

Should you find yourself at a total loss to identify an effective reinforcer for one of your students or staff, or even for yourself, try applying the **Premack principle.** This principle states that high-frequency behaviors may function as reinforcers of low-frequency behaviors. Research (Konarski, Johnson, Crowell, & Whitman, 1980) has indicated that other factors, such as response deprivation, may influence the extent to which a given activity is reinforcing at that particular time. (It seems that if a particular response that has not been accessible to an individual for a while becomes available, such as going to the movies if you are a busy student, engaging in the response will be relatively more reinforcing.) Despite variations in *how* reinforcing an activity is at a given time, in general the Premack principle holds. We and our students (many of whom are teachers, counselors, and psychologists) have applied it to our own behavior and find that the principle functions very well indeed. For instance, one of the authors showers each morning, but for 4 days out of 7, she doesn't permit herself to take a shower until she has done her aerobic exercises. Students don't have control of many of the reinforcers — such as money or course credits — that influence their behavior, so they need to be creative about finding something they can control, such as their leisure-time activities. We have asked them to record in a diary what they do during their unstructured time. Some find that they play games — tennis, racquetball, or pool — or musical instruments. Others do lots of gourmet cooking, knit, or go on outings with their families. Many regularly watch favorite television programs or visit singles bars. Some write poetry, jog, or spend time drinking coffee and gossiping with their friends in person or on the phone. Whatever the activities, the students then may decide to restrict access to one or more of those that they do with high frequency, permitting themselves to engage in those activities only when they've met a prespecified increase in their selected low-frequency activity: studying, writing, exercising, practicing an instrument, relaxing, or whatever they've chosen. The same approach has proven useful with children and youth as well.

Notice that one individual's high-frequency behavior may be another's low. It is also possible that a formerly low-frequency behavior may increase to such an extent that it ultimately may begin to acquire reinforcing properties of its own. For instance,

one graduate student wanted to learn to play the guitar. Because she never could seem to get down to practicing, she wouldn't permit herself to begin preparing dinner until she had practiced according to schedule. Eventually her playing improved so much that she really enjoyed herself and no longer needed to arrange the dinner-preparation contingency. In fact, playing and singing began to be so much fun that she could then play and sing to reinforce another low-frequency behavior.

In one of our school projects, students were allowed access to various activity centers or to select some other privilege from a "menu" when they'd done their reading assignments correctly. To our delight, some of the students made such excellent progress in reading that they began to select recreational reading in the classroom or library as their reinforcer. Then reading work no longer required artificial reinforcement. Recreational reading could be used to reinforce improvement in other subject areas!

If your school has a high pupil:teacher ratio and your students seem to enjoy assisting one another, something that might help all of you is to teach the students to tutor one another responsibly, and then permit them to do so as a reward for having done their own assignments well. Richard Parker, the undermotivated Franklin High School student, would probably jump at an opportunity to assist the coach, while some students of rural Willow Grove School who complete their work quickly might be pleased to help those just behind them.[1] As an added bonus, they would have their own skills reinforced in the process.

---

[1] The skills involved in effective tutoring are relatively simple to learn: how to present material, ask questions, check the accuracy of the response, provide reinforcing or corrective feedback, and act in a generally friendly manner. We have taught tutoring or proctoring skills to undergraduate and graduate college students (Johnson & Sulzer-Azaroff, 1978), to those in preschool (Weidenman & Sulzer-Azaroff, 1980), at primary (Ramey & Sulzer-Azaroff, 1979) and secondary levels, and even to students with special needs, such as those whose development has been delayed or who have interpersonal or emotional difficulties. The key to success seems to have been adequate training plus regular supervision and feedback, with appropriately practiced skills receiving much approbation.

TURNING NEUTRAL STIMULI INTO REINFORCERS

We've encountered instances in which reinforcers natural to the school environment failed to affect the performance of some individual students. In those cases, we turned to other reinforcers that *were* effective. Although we ourselves have no concern about rewarding progress with whatever it takes — within reason — some school personnel are reluctant to "pay students for learning" throughout the students' school careers. Because reinforcement is so important in education, it is indeed fortunate that the science of human behavior has taught us ways to turn neutral stimuli into reinforcers.

Neutral stimuli can become reinforcers by being paired with other stimuli that already have shown themselves to be powerfully reinforcing. If grades or praise fail to reinforce at first, they may be paired repeatedly with access to privileges, such as being monitor, or even with something tangible like a snack or a trinket. If you start out by presenting the neutral stimulus, "What a fine row of nice round O's you made, Carla," and follow it immediately with something known to be rewarding for that student, "Here's a sticker," and do this often enough, then the neutral stimulus — the teacher's compliment — will begin to signal that something good is about to happen. (It also would help to tell Carla that if she pleases you, you will let her know it and some of those times you will give her a special reward.) The pairings should be very frequent at first, perhaps continuing over several days or weeks. As you begin to see signs that the formerly neutral stimulus seems to be taking hold (Carla may begin to smile when her efforts are praised, or she may begin to solicit praise — "Teacher, how is this O?"), then the pairings can occur less and less often. You also may introduce a delay between the formerly neutral stimulus and the previously more effective one — very slowly at first, then gradually increasing the delay over time. (Again, it would help to explain. "You are writing so nicely, Carla, that I'm saving a sticker to give you when you finish.")

How do you know if your stimulus is becoming a reinforcer? Measure changes in performance. This is one reason why behavioral practitioners are so careful about recording data. For it is the individual's behavior that informs us whether or not a particular strategy is effective. Drop the smiling-face stickers too abruptly and Carla's percentage of well-formed letters may begin to diminish. Accordingly, it is essential that you define your responses carefully, keep clear records and watch for improvement or deterioration from day to day. Don't be afraid to drop back a little if necessary, temporarily increase the number of pairings, and reduce the delay between the two stimuli. Once performance has been recovered, you can try again, this time progressing more gingerly than before.

REINFORCEMENT AND GROUPS

At this point we can hear your plaintive cries: "What do they expect of me? I teach a dozen subjects a day, and my students' abilities vary from one to another. How can I treat each student individually for each of the many academic skills and social behaviors we are trying to promote?"

If you teach at the upper levels, you are probably responsible for a large number of students. Or you may be a pupil personnel specialist with a huge caseload. If you are a principal or supervisor, you may be responsible for a whole school or division. All of you share similar concerns. Fortunately, you needn't despair. There are reinforcers that are influential with large as well as small groups of individuals. We've already seen how praise and attention can do the trick in some situations. Among others that are generally reinforcing are social events like parties and dances, games, opportunities to play records, free time, a change in the schedule or in academic requirements, field trips, special assemblies featuring musical performances, plays or films, and many others. In subsequent chapters we will find out how to make use of these effectively and will present specific techniques of reinforcement that have worked with whole groups of students: being able to display the school banner for a week; being complimented via announcements over the public address system;

receiving points, certificates, or access to recreation or special activity rooms; being dismissed early; and many more.

Even if the members of your group are so diverse that no set of reinforcing events is appropriate for all of them, you can still use a general reinforcer like a point, certificate, voucher, or token. Each of the members of a whole class could earn the same number of points as a reward for a good hour's work, but each could exchange his or her own set of points for different backup reinforcers. Some might select tokens, contributed by a local merchant, good for playing electronic games; others might choose to spend extra time in the library or to be monitor for a day.

It is important to remember that when you select a general standard of performance for all the members of a group, each member must be able to achieve the standard. Otherwise one unsuccessful individual can spoil it for the rest, who, in turn, might become antagonistic toward that person. Standards must be set so that they can be gained with a reasonable, not an inordinate, amount of effort. "Yesterday everyone made at least an 85 percent on the assignment. Today, let's see if that can be raised to 86 percent (not 100 percent)."

Check your records of student performance closely so that the modified standards you set are realistic. "Last week all of you worked hard without getting out of your seats for 20 whole minutes. Today, if that can be stretched to 22 minutes (not 30), we'll let each of you try for the lucky number. The one who gets it will be able to select the game for recess."

When reinforcement depends on the performance of the group, rather than each individual, the more able students often begin to tutor the poorer ones. Further, contingencies based on the group's performance often result in superior achievement by most of its members (Hamblin, Hathaway, & Wodarski, 1974; Van Houten & Van Houten, 1977). In contrast, students working for individual reinforcement tend to be concerned primarily with their own performance, rather than assisting one another.

It usually is not necessary to resort to giving prizes or contrived privileges to staff members; a simple statement about what's been accomplished can be very effective. "It's nice that so many more of you are remembering to compliment the students for clearing off their tables in the lunchroom. Those tables have never looked so good before!"

In many classrooms today, students have different levels of skill. If the members of your group vary so much in their performance that a single standard would be inappropriate, then it is necessary to subdivide the group. You might, for example, have a couple of students with special learning disabilities; requiring them to meet the standards of the larger group clearly would be inappropriate. That subgroup should be given its own standards to meet, standards that are readily within those students' grasp. Then you could reinforce the performance of each subgroup that achieved its own standard, or the performance of the whole group if all the subgroups met theirs.

The point to remember is that you need to be practical and realistic in selecting reinforcing contingencies. But you first should be sure that the standards you set are reasonable and can be achieved. If they are, you'll probably find, as we did in some of our research on group contingencies (Frankosky & Sulzer-Azaroff, 1978), that the members of the group begin to help and to cheer one another on. When that happens, the morale of the group as well as its members' achievement will improve (Hamblin et al., 1974).

REINFORCEMENT BY PEERS

Do not feel as though you need to be the sole provider of reinforcement or that you need to teach each student individually. You also can encourage peers to identify and reinforce desired social and academic behavior. Reinforcement from peers can be especially powerful and can be dispensed by them more frequently and immediately than you might be able to. In case you need to be reminded of the power of reactions by a student's peers, wait for a pleasant day and spend some time watching a group of youngsters play an informal team game like soft-ball or soccer. Look at the expression of the young-ster who executes a key play successfully as her peers cheer her on; note the chagrin of the player who fumbles and is criticized by his teammates. Those messages are deeply felt. Just as the rest of us do, though, peers apply contingencies irregularly and often aversively. So if you'd like to harness peer approval, you might need to arrange conditions to support it.

An elementary school teacher, Mrs. Smith, wanted to encourage peers to comment positively on the good things that classmates and the teacher were doing.[2] She assembled the students and told them that because so many good things were happening in the class, it was not possible for her to notice them all. Would the children help? Of course! So she told them about the "Secret Pal Game":

"Each week the names of all the students, the teacher, and the aide will be placed in a hat. Each member of the class will draw the name of the person who is to become your secret pal this week."

Players were charged with four responsibilities: (1) not to divulge the name of the secret pal; (2) to observe the secret pal and notice when that person did something especially nice; (3) to write the nice act down on a form; and (4) to place the form in the secret pal's envelope, stapled to the bulletin board.

Then the teacher and children proceeded to carry out each of the responsibilities. First the teacher acted as a secret pal, being careful to provide many examples of positive comments: "I've written these: 'Sidney picked up the trash around the lunch table.' 'When Gail looked sad because her cat's new kittens had to be given away, Rob comforted her.' 'Fred's hair was so neatly combed today.' 'Rhoda helped Frank by checking the spelling on his composition.'"

The children quickly caught on and wrote similar messages, for which the teacher complimented them.

Because it was near Valentine's Day, the forms were shaped like hearts (see Figure 4.2). Several were

[2]Based on Smith and Mayer (1978).

Figure 4.2
A message to a secret pal.

distributed to each member of the class, and the game began in earnest. Occasionally the teacher commented when she noticed that some students' envelopes already contained notes from their secret pals; she reminded the others of their responsibilities. By the end of the week each envelope contained at least one message. The class was assembled. How excited and pleased the children were as the names of their secret pals were revealed and their messages read aloud!

"Can we play it again?" they pleaded.

"Sure. But this time I have some different forms for you. What shape is this?"

"I know," squealed Sidney. "It's George Washington's hatchet."

"Good for you. Now pick the names of your secret pals and be sure that you send them at least one positive message, like the ones you heard today. But in case you see someone else who's done something especially nice, you can write an extra message to that person too. I'll probably do that also."

They continued to play the game throughout a good part of the school year, varying its format once in a while. During one period when the number of compliments seemed to be flagging, the teacher displayed a colorful bar graph, called a "Compliment Meter." The total number of compliments for the week was tallied and recorded on the bar graph, and the children worked hard to increase the level the next week—and were successful. After a few weeks, the compliment meter was taken down, but the compliments continued to be given at a reasonable rate. The best part was that the students actually began to increase their natural rates of complimenting one another even as the "Secret Pal Game" gradually was phased out. The children had learned what fun it was to give and receive compliments.

We have seen similar methods used successfully by teachers at the upper elementary, junior high, and secondary school levels and by counselors with small groups. Staff and supervisors have used games like this to promote positive feedback among themselves. In one case, the game was entitled "I Spy." Participants filled out a form like the one you see in Figure 4.3.

At Charter Oak High School, in order to raise funds, a service organization sold "telegrams" that consisted of carnations plus positive notes. In some schools teachers and supervisors send one another "Success-O-Grams" (see Figure 4.4), and students

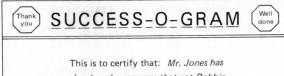

This is to certify that: *Mr. Jones has developed a program that got Robbie completing his lessons. A fantastic program and teacher!*

Sent by *Mrs. White* on *September 27, 1981*

Figure 4.4
"Telegram" for staff and students.

communicate their support during exam week and other times of stress by sending a message designed to help the receiver feel "warm and fuzzy"—a "Fuzzygram" (see Figure 4.5).

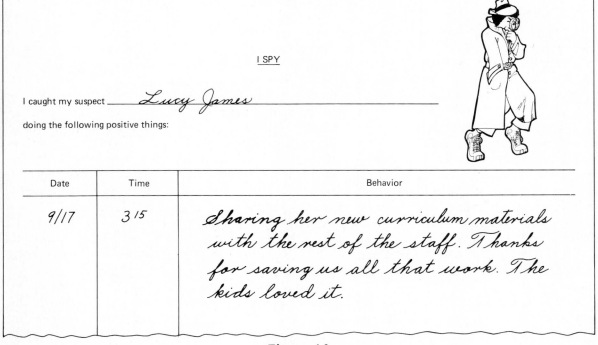

I SPY

I caught my suspect ___Lucy James___

doing the following positive things:

Date	Time	Behavior
9/17	3¹⁵	*Sharing her new curriculum materials with the rest of the staff. Thanks for saving us all that work. The kids loved it.*

Figure 4.3
Promoting positive feedback among staff.

FUZZY GRAM

(outside)

To:

Debbie

From:

Mrs. Geis

For: _Debbie has patience &
contributes to vocabulary
review.
Debbie knows how to
behave, and she
always has a kind
and pleasant word
for me. She knows
how to study. It is
a pleasure to see her
apply herself._

(inside)

Figure 4.5
A method for communicating support.

There are various ways to teach staff to increase its use of praise for good conduct.[3] One method we've seen used effectively is "reinforcement bombardment." Members form small groups of five or fewer people. Each then talks for about 2 minutes on a topic about which he or she is excited—a student's recent success, an accomplishment of his or her own. Meanwhile, the others list all the positive things they can think of regarding the content and style of the presentation. These, along with positive verbal explanations, then are given to each speaker at the end. We've found that writing things down often helps people to later voice their comments orally, and this situation is no exception. We also have observed that positive comments and notes to students increase when staff members are encouraged to write one another positive notes and place them on a "Warm Fuzzy" or "Thank-U-Board" located in the faculty lounge (see Figure 4.6). When teachers use and experience positive feedback from peers, they may be more inclined to provide similar positive feedback to their students.

Although game formats can be novel and fun for adults as well as children, there are other ways to prime members of an organization to deliver positive feedback to one another. One of us keeps a suggestion and comment box for students and staff at our learning center. Written responses are tacked to the bulletin board so those who take the time to write either positive messages or constructive suggestions know that their communications have been received and appreciated. We regularly model positive feedback in our classes, and the students catch on quickly. So when the group is asked to comment on a presentation by a class member, we frequently hear such statements of specific praise as, "You were so well organized and your handouts were so clear; it was really easy to follow your presentation." Or, "Compared to your last report, this was much more comprehensive. You must have spent lots of time gathering and sorting your material." Needless to say, we and the recipients of the praise communicate our appreciation for such helpful comments, so they continue.[4]

We also arrange our curricula so that individual students can display their special talents. One assignment requires students to discover a unique skill of their own, then to teach it to their peers. We have learned skills ranging from knitting, selecting photographic filters, foot massage, folding birds from paper, and decorating cakes to changing spark plugs and distinguishing different woods from one another (see Sulzer-Azaroff & Reese, 1982, Chapter 8). Such an activity provides its own natural source of peer reinforcement, as students always are impressed by the special expertise among their classmates.

You can teach peers systematically to become monitors, as Smith and Fowler (1984) did. Five- to seven-year-olds in a remedial kindergarten were taught by means of instructions, quizzing, and role playing to show they understood the monitoring procedure. They were to give points to children who performed correctly during transition times. Points permitted the children to play outside. The monitors did their best jobs when they were given corrective feedback, rather than when left entirely on their own.

An indirect method of promoting peer approval is to arrange a contingency in which the performance of one individual results in reinforcement for all members of the group. Max and Dick were students in a special education class (Kazdin & Geesey, 1977). At various times when they were being attentive, the two could earn points either for themselves alone or for the whole class. The children could exchange their points for special rewards, such as free time, stickers, or a soft drink. During those times when Max or Dick earned for the class, they were more attentive than when they earned only for themselves. Perhaps one reason why they paid attention at a higher rate during the "earn-for-the-group" condition was that their peers prompted attentiveness and gave them approval when they were being attentive. (Peers could well have punished inatten-

---

[3]That teachers often can profit from training in the use of approval has been posited by Forehand and Wells (1977), citing evidence from White (1975) and Heller and White (1975) that natural rates of approval by the teachers they observed were extremely low.

[4]Teachers also use more praise when they model and role play giving praise during training (Sloat, Tharp, & Gallimore, 1977).

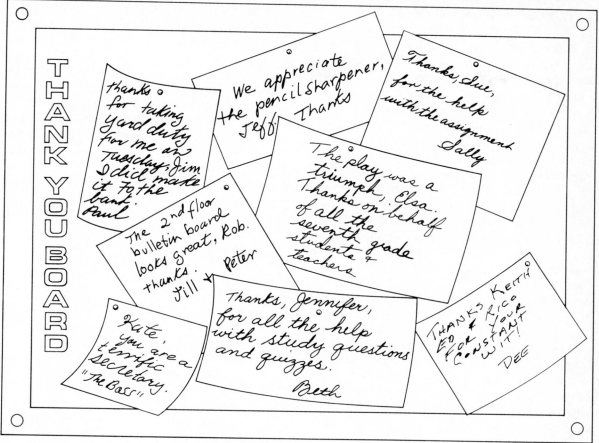

Figure 4.6
Thank-you board.

tion as well. To avoid such a situation, teach your students by modeling and instruction how to prompt and praise, and be certain that the target child can readily meet the criteria for reinforcement.)

Another form of group contingency actually did promote positive comments from peers and improved rates in reading (Van Houten & Van Houten, 1977). Students were divided into two teams during reading class. During one phase of the study, each individual student's accomplishments was posted publicly; during another, the scores of the team as a whole were posted as well. While rates of lesson completion increased during the individual phase, the increase was far greater during the "team" phase. Peer comments were monitored and were found to have increased substantially during the "team" condition. So it is likely that the peer comments contributed to the differential effect. The authors were then clever enough to capitalize on the findings by training peers to collaborate by commenting positively on production. Production rose even further. You might try a system like this. You could have teams elect a captain whose job it would be to coach the students to perform accurately and rapidly. Or you might consider training students to tutor one another, as discussed in the next chapter.

REINFORCEMENT BY ONE'S SELF

Relying on other people to furnish reinforcement does have its limitations, though. Others are not always there, and often, even if they are, they may be busy attending to other things. So one especially beneficial way to ensure that a contingency remains in operation is for individuals to reinforce their own behavior.

Harry and Larry were fifth-grade students in an "open classroom" containing thirty children (Szykula, Saudargas, & Wahler, 1981). Neither performed well in arithmetic. They made many errors and rarely completed assignments. With so many students, the teacher couldn't readily supply the attention required for the boys' progress. So they were taught to record their own arithmetic performance. On 3-inch-by-5-inch cards Harry and Larry noted the number of problems assigned to them, how many they completed, and how many were correct. After recording as instructed for several days, each was awarded a prize. The boys then were asked to select as a goal the percentage correct they would try to achieve each day. Larry selected 80 percent, and his performance improved accordingly. Harry, who selected 60 percent, did not progress. So a reward condition was added. When Harry met his goal for the day, he earned pieces to a model van that he eventually could assemble. It was Harry who indicated whether or not he'd met his goal and who went to the cabinet to select the parts of the model he had earned. That method was successful, and Harry's accuracy began to improve. After a while the boys stopped self-recording, yet they continued to perform well. Then their teacher took a leave of absence, and things rapidly deteriorated with the new teacher. So the previously effective conditions again were implemented, with the same happy results.

A fifth grader was taught to manage his own behavior in math (Stevenson & Fantuzzo, 1984). This consisted of (1) setting a goal for the number of problems he wanted to complete accurately; (2) counting and recording on a chart the number of problems he correctly completed; (3) comparing the number with the predetermined daily goal; and (4) exchanging his gold stars for various items from a self-determined menu of reinforcers. He was taught to do this by the teacher's aide, who first role played the skills and then, after reviewing the descriptions of the tasks, had the boy practice in a series of simulated math drills. Praise was given for accurately completing the tasks and he was asked to practice any inaccurately performed tasks. During the actual implementation of the self-management program, the aide and the boy continued to meet weekly to review the procedures so they wouldn't deteriorate. Not only did the boy do better in math performance, but so did the boy next to him, who was not trained in self-management. Also, the deportment of both improved in school and at home.

These examples show that students can learn to reinforce their own behavior. Actually, many examples of the successful use of self-reinforcement have been reported in the behavioral literature. Severely retarded children and other developmentally disabled people (e.g., Fowler, Baer, & Stolz, 1984; Shapiro & Klein, 1980), children with a fear of failure (Stamps, 1973), underachieving children (Edgar & Clement, 1980), college students working on study skills (McReynolds & Church, 1973), and teachers trying to enhance their self-esteem (Hannum, Thoresen, & Hubbard, 1974) have all used self-reinforcement procedures to improve their targeted behaviors. How can this be made to succeed? Sufficient research has not been conducted to enable us to respond completely to that question, but we can add our conjecture to those of Jones, Nelson, and Kazdin (1977). Jones et al. (1977) listed several external variables that may influence self-reinforcement:

- *History.* The student's prior involvement in a program of training to learn self-administration of reinforcers, as well as the length of time the target behavior has been treated by external contingencies, can be influential. (We would recommend for the present that you apply external contingencies for a lengthy time period, sufficient to establish firmly the behavioral change prior to shifting control over to the student; and that you provide an intensive program of training in self-administration of reinforcers.)

- *Criteria-setting.* Criteria for assessing success can be imposed externally or set by the students themselves. Goals can be lenient or stringent. Each influences the outcome of a program. The results of several studies on goal-setting suggest that the most promising approach is for individuals to set fairly stringent goals for themselves.

- *Self-monitoring.* A system that incorporates self-reward usually also includes self-monitoring, with clients observing and recording their own behavior. The very act of observing and recording has been found to influence behavior. Yet separating self-monitoring from self-rewarding isn't always possible, so the degree to which the two factors interact remains unclear. However, Richards (1981) concluded that "with students motivated to self-monitor and change their behavior ... self-reinforcement may occur naturally. Hence, self-reinforcement may not add to the processes inherent in self-monitoring a valued behavior" (p. 163). Self-reward, then, may be most useful when natural reinforcers are too weak or delayed. Because self-monitoring generally has led to improvement in target behaviors, you would be well advised to incorporate self-monitoring within any selected system of self-reward.

- *Surveillance.* The presence of an external agent who does or could monitor how people reward themselves can influence the course of events. Such an agent may cue different kinds of behavior, depending on who he or she is: a teacher, peer, consultant, or someone else. Even if an external agent is not intentionally monitoring the self-administration of reinforcement, subjects may feel the agent's presence. Whether or not to arrange for surveillance will depend on your own circumstances. The data you collect will indicate if any one particular kind of surveillance helps.

- *Instructional Sets.* In most studies of self-reinforcement, subjects are taught how to perform the target behavior as well as how to self-reinforce. Clear instructions may help individuals practice self-reinforcement successfully. It is not necessary for the external agent to define target behaviors or methods for self-reinforcing. In many of the self-management projects undertaken by our students, they assume the responsibility for performing both functions. Our role as instructors is to assess the clarity and feasibility of the students' plans and to supply appropriate feedback. If you are planning a group program that includes self-reinforcement, the members of the group could jointly define how to perform the target behavior and how to self-reinforce.

- *External Consequences on the Self-Reinforcing Behavior.* Accurate reporting often is externally rewarded, or inaccurate reporting is penalized, a necessary action in some cases, as in the study by Speidel and Tharp (1980), when subjects awarded themselves undeserved reinforcers. If it is to be used at all, a system to reward or penalize accurate or inaccurate self-reinforcement from the beginning probably is preferable. We have found in some classroom projects that if we praised honest recording during initial phases of a program, accuracy tended to persist.

- *External Consequences of the Target Behavior.* Both purposely arranged and unintentional contingencies may operate on the target behavior. A program might provide, for instance, for publicly announcing rewards earned. Such a practice or even an altered behavior may prompt approval or negative reactions by others. These consequences can influence the target behavior. If a target behavior has changed satisfactorily and durably for an extended time period, then it is probably best to avoid highly contrived external reinforcing methods. Those that come naturally shouldn't hurt. But if, as in the study by Szykula et al. (1981), self-reinforcing fails to produce the intended results, it may be judicious to turn to some supplemental reinforcing contingencies. Eventually, you might try to remove the external reward gradually to see if self-reinforcement takes over enough to permit the improvement to persist.

Control of contingencies

No matter how reinforcing a particular stimulus might be, you won't be able to apply it if it is not under your control. We already have seen instances of this in the situation in which peer attention was reinforcing misbehavior. If the schedule of your school is not something you can control, special activities during school time would not be an appropriate selection of reinforcers. At times, try as you might, powerfully functioning reinforcers are so beyond your control that almost nothing you do seems to work. You should not blame yourself for being unable to attain the impossible. Rather, you should shift your focus to other important elements within the system that may be more amenable to change (see Chapter 22).

Summary

We have defined two very important behavioral procedures: positive and negative reinforcement. These procedures affect your behavior and the behavior of those with whom you work every day. When you are aware of the impact of reinforcement on your behavior, you are better able to control what you do and to influence others more effectively.

To reinforce behavior successfully, you should try to identify the consequences that are maintaining or increasing that behavior. To aid you, we remind you of these few simple but very important rules:

- First, each individual is unique and has a unique history. For each, different sets of reinforcing objects or events are effective. The only way to find out is to test them.
- Second, the value of a reinforcer at a given time and place may vary according to other contingencies and factors.
- Third, should you find yourself at a loss with a particularly difficult case, find out what that person does most often during free time. Ask the person to keep a detailed diary of activities for a few days or weeks, indicating the time when each began and ended. If this is not possible, observe and record the individual's activities yourself as often as you can. Then, high frequency pursuits can be selected as reinforcers.
- Fourth, general reinforcers, such as points and tokens, are useful with groups because they can be exchanged for different backup reinforcers. They also can be paired with more natural consequences, such as praise and recognition, so that eventually those natural consequences will acquire more powerful reinforcing properties. Meanwhile, the points and tokens gradually can be phased out and replaced by more natural consequences. Frequently, reinforcers such as praise can be identified as being effective among most members of a group. For those for whom praise fails to work, it will be necessary to select other reinforcers and pair them with praise.
- Finally, the reinforcers you select must be under your control. You must be able to arrange the environment so that the reinforcers will follow only certain selected behaviors. Peers frequently control many reinforcers. Thus, we described a variety of methods of encouraging peer recognition of desired behavior. These methods include making some of your reinforcement contingent on group performance, rather than on the performance of each individual,

and a variety of peer reinforcing pro-grams. Control of reinforcing contin-gencies often can be achieved, but sometimes such control is impossi-ble. Do your best within current cir-cumstances, but don't expect miracles.

Throughout the remainder of this book, you'll see an extensive array of reinforcers that people have been able to utilize effectively. As you continue reading, we hope that you find suffi-cient possibilities for your own situation.

Study Questions

1. Define *reinforcement*.
2. Susie is given a piece of candy each time she hands in a neat spelling paper. Her spelling papers become sloppier and sloppier.
   (a) Is candy a reinforcer?
   (b) Support your answer.
3. (a) Identify an event that is a reinforcer for you.
   (b) Support your answer.
4. Define *positive reinforcer*.
5. Define *negative reinforcer*.
6. Compare and contrast positive and negative reinforcement giving an original example of each.
7. Illustrate how a behavior can be both posi-tively and negatively reinforced.
8. List four primary reinforcers.
9. Another name for a *primary reinforcer* is
   _____.
10. Compare and contrast punishment and neg-ative reinforcement.
11. (a) Define punishment and (b) provide an ex-ample of it.
12. When Jimmy takes out the trash his mother says, "Well, it's about time." He has been taking the trash out less frequently.
    (a) Label the mother's statement "Well, it's about time" with the appropriate term.
    (b) Support your answer.
13. Use the terms *positive reinforcement*, *nega-tive reinforcement*, and *punishment* to com-plete the following statements.
    (a) The procedure(s) that reduce(s) behavior is (are) _____.
    (b) The procedure(s) that involve(s) the ad-dition of a stimulus is (are)
    _____.

(c) The aversive procedure(s) is (are)
    _____.
14. Does the reinforcing potential of a stimulus remain constant? (Support your answer with an example.)
15. Mrs. Jones wants to use popcorn as a rein-forcer for her class. Use this example to dis-cuss, in detail, reinforcer selection.
16. Mr. Walker will not be able to question his new students or to observe them to deter-mine what is reinforcing for them.
    (a) Provide two stimuli that would have a high probability of being reinforcing for his students.
    (b) Support your choice.
17. Narrate an original example that demon-strates that you understand the term *token system*.
18. Tim's classmate takes his toys away from him during play time. Provide several skills Tim could learn to help solve this problem.
19. Describe the reinforcement you receive for taking a course.
20. Define *Premack principle*.
21. Describe how you might use the Premack principle to increase one of your behaviors.
22. Discuss the relation between response depri-vation and the Premack principle.
23. Provide an original narrative demonstrating that a neutral stimulus can become a rein-forcer. (Be sure to plan for when the neutral stimulus has become a reinforcer.)
24. Discuss, in detail, the importance of measur-ing changes in performance.
25. (a) List three reinforcers well suited for a group.
    (b) Assume that the members of your group

are so diverse that no set of reinforcing events is appropriate for all of them. Describe a method to reinforce their behavior successfully.

26. Now that you have devised a method for reinforcing the behavior of your group, describe in detail the standard of performance required for them to be eligible to receive the reinforcer. (Be sure to consider subgroups.)

27. Under what circumstances would you want to reinforce the academic achievement of the group rather than of individuals?

28. Discuss the advantage and disadvantage of involving peers in a program of reinforcement.

29. Develop your own variation of the reinforcement strategies such as the "Secret Pal" game or "Reinforcement Bombardment."

30. Provide at least three methods for increasing positive feedback in the classroom.

31. Mrs. Kane set up a program to increase Joe's on-task behavior. When he reached the criterion level for on-task behavior, all of the children in his class would receive a reinforcer of their choice. Unfortunately, Joe's peers began to punish him when he was off-task. Provide several solutions to this problem.

32. Devise a plan to reinforce a student's appropriate interactions with her peers. (a) List and (b) briefly discuss the seven external variables that may influence self-reinforcement.

33. Discuss your control of reinforcers and how this relates to your effectiveness as a behavioral manager.

References

Edgar, R., & Clement, P. (1980). Teacher-controlled and self-controlled reinforcement with underachieving black children. *Child Behavior Therapy*, 2, 33–56.

Forehand, R., & Wells, K. C. (1977). Teachers and parents: Where have all the "good" contingency managers gone? *Behavior Therapy*, 8, 1010.

Fowler, S. A., Baer, D. M., & Stolz, S. B. (Eds.). (1984). *Analysis and Intervention in Developmental Disabilities: Special Issue: Self Management Tactics for the Developmentally Disabled*, 4, New York, Pergamon.

Frankosky, R. J., & Sulzer-Azaroff, B. (1978). Individual and group contingencies and collateral social behaviors. *Behavior Therapy*, 9, 313–327.

Hamblin, R. L., Hathaway, C., & Wodarski, J. (1974). Group contingencies, peer tutoring, and accelerating academic achievement. In R. Ulrich, T. Stanchnik, & J. Mabry (Eds.), *Control of human behavior modification in education*. Vol. 3. Glenview, IL: Scott, Foresman, 333–340.

Hannum, J. W., Thoresen, C. E., & Hubbard, D. R. (1974). A behavioral study of self-esteem with elementary teachers. In M. J. Mahoney & C. E. Thoresen (Eds.), *Self-control: power to the person*. Monterey, CA: Brooks/Cole.

Heller, M. S., & White, M. A. (1975). Rates of teacher verbal approval and disapproval to higher and lower ability classes. *Journal of Educational Psychology*, 67, 796–800.

Johnson, K. R., & Sulzer-Azaroff, B. (1978). An experimental analysis of proctor prompting behavior in a personalized instruction course. *Journal of Personalized Instruction*, 3, 122–130.

Jones, R. T., Nelson, R. E., & Kazdin, A. E. (1977). The role of external variables in self reinforcement: A review. *Behavior Modification*, 1, 147–178.

Kazdin, A. E., & Geesey, S. (1977). Simultaneous-treatment design comparison of the effects of earning reinforcers for one's peers versus for oneself. *Behavior Therapy*, 8, 682–693.

Konarski, E. A., Jr., Johnson, M. R., Crowell, C. R., & Whitman, T. L. (1980). Response deprivation and reinforcement in applied settings: A preliminary analysis. *Journal of Applied Behavior Analysis*, 13, 595–609.

McReynolds, W. T., & Church, A. (1973). Self-control, study skills development and counseling approaches to the improvement of study behavior. *Behaviour Research and Therapy*, 11, 233–235.

Ramey, G., & Sulzer-Azaroff, B. (1979). *Generalization effects of involving behaviorally disordered children as teachers*. Paper presented at the annual meeting of the American Psychological Association, New York.

Richards, C. S. (1981). Improving college students' study behaviors through self-control techniques: A brief review. *Behavioral Counseling Quarterly*, 1, 159–175.

Shapiro, E. S., & Klein, R. D. (1980). Self-management of

classroom behavior with retarded/disturbed children. *Behavior Modification, 4*, 83–97.

Sloat, K. C., Tharp, R. G., & Gallimore, R. (1977). The incremental effectiveness of classroom-based teacher-training techniques. *Behavior Therapy, 8*, 810–818.

Smith, E. V., & Mayer, G. R. (1978, September). The secret pal game: Students praising students. *The Guidance Clinic*, pp. 3–6.

Smith, L. K., & Fowler, S. H. (1984). Positive peer pressure: The effects of peer monitoring on children's disruptive behavior. *Journal of Applied Behavior Analysis, 17*, 213–227.

Speidel, G. R., & Tharp, R. G. (1980). What does self-reinforcement reinforce: An empirical analysis of the contingencies in self-determined reinforcement. *Child Behavior Therapy, 2*, 1–22.

Stamps, L. W. (1973). The effects of intervention techniques on children's fear of failure behavior. *Journal of Genetic Psychology, 123*, 85–97.

Stevenson, H. C., & Fantuzzo, J. R. (1984). Application of the "Generalization Map" to a self-control intervention with school-aged children. *Journal of Applied Behavior Analysis, 17*, 203–212.

Sulzer-Azaroff, B., & Reese, E. P. (1982). *Applying behavior analysis: A program for developing professional competence*. New York: Holt, Rinehart and Winston.

Szykula, S. A., Saudargas, R. A., & Wahler, R. G. (1981). The generality of self-control procedures following a change in the classroom teacher. *Education and Treatment of Children, 4*, 253–263.

Van Houten, R., & Van Houten, J. (1977). The performance feedback system in a special education classroom: An analysis of public posting and peer comments. *Behavior Therapy, 8*, 366–376.

Weidenman, L., & Sulzer-Azaroff, B. (1980). *The effects of a reciprocal peer interaction on the social behavior of special needs preschoolers*. Invited paper presented at the Association for Behavioral Analysis, Dearborn, Michigan.

White, M. A. (1975). Natural rates of teacher approval and disapproval in the classroom. *Journal of Applied Behavior Analysis, 8*, 367–372.

5 Making reinforcement work

Goals

After completing this chapter, you should be able to:

1. Define and give an illustration of each of the following terms:
   a. Programmed instruction
   b. Prompts
   c. Physical guidance
2. List what should be done to maximize the effectiveness of reinforcement.
3. Describe several ways of making immediate reinforcement more feasible in instruction, classroom management, and consultation.
4. Discuss under what circumstances continuous versus intermittent reinforcement should be used and explain why.
5. Describe each step in setting up a peer tutoring program.
6. Present an argument for implementing a peer tutoring program.
7. Describe several ways of communicating the conditions for delivery of reinforcement.
8. Illustrate the application of reinforcement by describing some ways you might apply it to yourself, a student, or colleague.

"Listen everyone. I know how excited you all are about the trip to the state capital next week," Mr. Truax commented, "but I really want to make sure that you learn something, too, besides seeing the sights and eating a lot of junk food."

A chorus of "Oh no's" and moans was the reaction.

"Whoa! Hold on. Just because you're going to learn something doesn't mean it necessarily won't be fun."

"I don't get it," said Brad. "Can you tell us how we're supposed to do that?"

"Better than that, I'll show you. It's a beautiful day today, so we're going to go on a sort of a treasure hunt. Here is a map and a list of things to find and do. We'll divide into teams and go down to the courthouse square. The team that gets the most done will win a prize. These are all things you can find

without crossing any streets. I'll stay in the center and your team captain will see to it that you stay together...." and he continued explaining how they would proceed.

Among others, the list of instructions included such items as:

- Find a building with a cornerstone over 100 years old. Draw a picture of the front entrance of the building.
- Look for a milestone and describe its color, shape, and make up a four-line rhyme about it.
- Look for a picture of someone running for office. Describe what the person looks like in three sentences.

When the class returned to school, it was time to see what had been discovered. Students from each team were elected to show and tell about what they had accomplished.

Billy showed his drawing.

"That's really good!" said one of the boys.

"I think so, too," agreed Mr. Truax. "Look how you have all the details, including the number. Old doors don't look like modern ones, do they?"

When Brad read his rhyme, the class giggled and applauded. After Fern read her description of the candidate for sheriff, Mr. Truax praised her, saying that she really managed to capture the man's strength of character.

By the time all the discoveries had been shared, Mr. Truax announced, "All of you did so well, I think we have a tie. So everyone will share in the prize," and from his desk he took out a box of cookies and distributed one to each of his pupils.

"Now I know what you meant, Mr. Truax," exclaimed Brad. "The hunt was lots of fun, but we learned plenty about our town that we didn't notice before. Can we do this when we go to the capital?"

"Capital idea!" he responded, as the students' simulated groans mingled with the "hurrahs" in the background.

. . . And you should have seen what wonderful pictures, stories, and poems the students produced on their trip to the capital!

Why did the activity work so well? Because besides building on natural learning opportunities, it incorporated effective reinforcement techniques. Reinforcers were *appropriate*, yet *varied*; they were *applied frequently*, with *minimal delay*, and the *conditions* under which the student would receive reinforcement were *communicated clearly*. In this chapter we discuss effective reinforcement, explaining how each of these factors influence behavior change.

AMOUNT OF REINFORCEMENT

Assuming you've found a way to select an appropriate *array* of consequences for a particular individual or group from the guidelines presented in the previous chapter, you next need to consider how much

of each to dispense. There is no set formula to determine that — it depends. Just as a particular stimulus must be tested to find out if, in fact, it does have reinforcing properties, you need to experiment with the quantity of reinforcers. The trick is to figure out how much is just enough, yet not too much. In the illustration of the math class in the previous chapter, apparently a little attention and some praise were sufficient to accomplish the change. Mr. Truax's class seemed to find approval from their peers and teacher, and the prize of a single cookie, adequately reinforcing. But if the behavior to be reinforced is very difficult for the person to perform, if it requires lots of effort or fails to occur because it is in competition with a different behavior already being heavily reinforced, then the reinforcement has to be substantial.

Remember Marissa, who feared she might be pregnant? Her sexual behavior might well have been exquisitely reinforcing at the time, while any negative consequences would be delayed. Even suppose her pregnancy turned out to be a false alarm. Would the scare have been sufficient to discourage her from further sexual activity? Perhaps. Perhaps not. Given the dramatic rise in pregnancies among young teenagers, despite the fact that a substantial proportion know how pregnancy occurs, one has to conclude that the negative consequences of abstinence are less powerful than the positive ones of indulging in sex. The sexual behavior is immediately reinforcing, physically and socially, while an unwanted pregnancy is delayed and low in probability.

Marissa's close call might have scared her into seeking advice from the guidance counselor on how to avoid encountering such difficulties again. In a situation like that, the girl would need all the assistance she could get. She and Dr. Levy could discuss and select the skills she would like to learn, such as how to select her male companions with greater care, decline a proposition gently but firmly, and restrict her activities to situations in which she would be less likely to become aroused. Marissa also might want to be able to accept that being without a date for a while was not the world's greatest tragedy. To learn and apply skills like those, her efforts would need to be reinforced powerfully and substantially.

Marissa and Dr. Levy might negotiate a contract. In it, Marissa would agree to attend and participate fully in counseling sessions; in exchange, each time she did so, she would be excused from study hall and instead permitted access to the library or recreation room, where she could participate in crafts activities and listen to her favorite albums. So strong a reinforcing consequence would not be necessary if her goal were only to increase her grade by a certain number of percentage points, because Marissa is a reasonably hardworking student and is pleased when she earns a good grade. For school work, a small reinforcer, such as a little more specific feedback or praise, would be sufficient.

TIMING OF REINFORCEMENT

You've probably noted that the activity that is more immediately reinforced tends to be repeated. Although most of us have learned by long hard experience to delay our gratifications, we still find especially sweet those occasions when we don't have to wait. When your class or staff has accomplished something special, you wish your colleagues or supervisors could see it then and there. How many times have you heard the wistful plaint, "If only ———— had dropped by just then!"?

Many behavioral programs incorporate immediate reinforcement, undoubtedly because the procedure is so effective. The direct tie between the action and the reinforcer informs the individual exactly what behavior is to be repeated. The episode of Mr. Truax's lesson in social studies with which we opened this chapter shows how helpful immediate reinforcement can be. Attention, comments, and praise were presented when the students performed well. Those youngsters were able to make the connection almost immediately. In the case in which we resorted to a token system, it would have been impractical to try to deliver powerful reinforcers immediately. One just couldn't drop everything and permit students to go on a field trip every time they completed an assignment correctly. Instead, we added immediate supportive contingencies by pre-

senting points as the students finished and delivering the backup reinforcers as soon as feasible thereafter.[1]

It is important to note that our own behavior also is influenced when we implement behavioral programs. Inspired by reading and hearing about the dramatic successes of others, we may be tempted to undertake especially ambitious programs the first time we plan to apply behavioral procedures. Unfortunately, these do not always produce the desired results; or even if there is progress, it is often slow. In such cases, reinforcement in the form of improved student achievement or conduct either fails to occur or is delayed substantially. The tendency is to give up altogether: "I tried it, and it didn't work." You will want to avoid such a risk, so we suggest you heed the advice of Krumboltz and Thoresen (1969) and "select a specific workable behavior problem where results can be observable within a short period of time" (p. 154).

If you function in a consultant's role, you must be particularly careful to provide your consultees with immediate reinforcement whenever feasible. Should immediate reinforcement prove impractical, you can aid staff to tolerate the delay between their presenting you with a problem and its solution. Add supportive reinforcers, such as approving and recognizing not only the ultimate outcomes but also the behaviors constituting the process—the staff's implementation of the program you have suggested. We have found that many teachers experience difficulty when they first try ignoring students' disruptive behavior and attending to and approving acceptable behavior. In one case, a teacher couldn't seem to ignore the antics of one particular student. We helped the teacher by displaying numbered cards in sequence, from the back of the room, each time he praised the boy. After several days, the teacher no longer needed the cards. Apparently the data indicating improvement in the student's behavior were sufficient to reinforce his continued efforts.

Note how keeping careful records also helps us to

---

[1]Should you wish to read about token economies in greater detail, you might refer to Ayllon and Azrin (1968) or Kazdin (1982).

keep trying. Two or three additional problems out of a hundred completed accurately every few weeks may not be at all apparent to us. But when we've counted and graphed those results each day, the rising trend becomes evident and our extra efforts are rewarded. (By the way, as mentioned in the previous chapter, there is no reason why the students can't chart their own daily performance, as long as we closely supervise and reinforce accurate recording intensively in the beginning. Many modern instructional programs provide charts on which students keep their own progress records.)

Immediate reinforcement can be built into instructional programs at all levels, from the most basic to the most advanced. We incorporate immediate reinforcement in our university training by using the "Keller Plan," also known as the "Personalized System of Instruction (PSI)," as a main component. One feature of this system is frequent quizzing. Students are assigned a specific number of units to master. (In some cases, there are options from among which they select a set.) They prepare by studying the material and answering a set of study questions that covers the key concepts of the assignment, just like those at the end of each chapter in this book. Once they feel ready, they come to our Mastery Learning Center to take a quiz. As soon as they have finished, the paper is graded by another student who previously has demonstrated mastery over that material and who has been trained to practice effective tutoring skills. Our findings are consonant with those of an extensive number of studies that have examined PSI (Johnson & Ruskin, 1977). We've found that our students enjoy learning and retain their knowledge especially well with PSI.[2]

[2]Greer (1984) reports a number of successful applications of PSI in elementary, junior high, and high school. In reviewing individualized systems of instruction in secondary schools, Bangert, Kulik, and Kulik (1983) have suggested that secondary students "may need more stimulation, guidance, support, and constraint than individualized systems ordinarily provide" (p. 152). They also suggested that group pacing might prove beneficial. We believe that "contracting" also might produce stronger effects.

Quizzes covering the material in this text are available to bona fide instructors from the authors at cost. Please write letters of request on official letterhead stationery.

There is a quid pro quo, though. Writing good study and quiz questions and answer keys takes quite a bit of time. We need to remind ourselves of the value of this program and that it will take less time to prepare the next time we teach the course. This strategy can help us to tolerate the *delayed* gratification of outstanding student performance. Otherwise we might not be willing to expend the effort.

In **programmed instruction,** as described by Skinner (1958), students are engaged actively in the learning process. Short segments of instructional material are presented, followed by a question or request for the student to do something using the information. The student then performs accordingly. When a program is matched carefully to the ability of the student, most of the student's responses are correct, and then the student is provided with instant feedback as to the correctness of the response. Assuming that being correct is reinforcing for the student, then his or her efforts are reinforced immediately and almost every time.

The increasing presence of inexpensive personal computers makes it feasible and practical to provide this sort of programmed instruction to a vast number of students. Curriculum developers who design and evaluate instructional programs for individuals with differing abilities probably will provide the best educational service. For instance, Richard Parker is a student who makes little effort in math word problems. He probably would profit from a program of short, simple, interesting problems that are sufficiently challenging for him to feel he has accomplished something when immediately informed that his response was correct. His brother, Howard, on the other hand, might do better with much longer and more complex problems. Howard also probably could tolerate a reasonably lengthy delay in receiving feedback on the correctness of his response.

Don't despair if your budget does not permit such equipment. Teachers have recognized the need for immediate feedback for a long, long time and have been able to accommodate that need. Permitting students to correct their own papers with answer keys, or to correct each other's work, is one way of providing more immediate feedback instead of keeping them waiting for the teacher to grade each paper. Another is for a more advanced student, teacher's aide, volunteer, or another teacher to do it. Not all of your students need immediate feedback on all their work. Select those who are most in need at one particular time and concentrate on them. Naturally, other reinforcing events will follow later for those students who haven't had the advantage of your immediate attention.

Providing immediate reinforcement is not limited to book learning, either. It can be used in coaching sports and other motor activities and in training social, emotional, or personal skills. One clever application of this principle was used by Smith, Schumaker, Schaeffer, and Sherman (1982) to increase seventh graders' participation in and the quality of discussions during social studies. Each day a student was designated to record points given by the teacher whenever another student contributed a relevant question, answer, or comment. These points were converted into weekly grades, which contributed 25 percent to their overall grade. Awards of points also were paired with statements of praise. Quality was increased by attributing "star quality" to certain categories (e.g., giving a reason). Such contributions earned students 3 points and occasional praise. Both objective observational data and ratings by 46 independent judges supported the findings of major improvements in percent participation and quality of discussions.

Parents have been taught how and when to respond appropriately to their children by wearing an ear plug that receives radioed messages from their coach immediately following an interaction with the child or children. The coach then tells the parents when they're doing well and when they need to change their tactics (Bernal, 1969). This system also is used to train practice teachers in formal classroom instruction, in physical education in the field or gym, and elsewhere. We provide our proctors-in-training with instant feedback by engaging them in role playing and by videotaping their performance. The videotape then is played back, and the performance can be interrupted at any time or the taped segment repeated for discussion. Even without a vid-

eotape recorder, it is still possible to interrupt a role playing or practice session to provide the appropriate consequences right away.

When Marissa and her counselor meet to practice various social skills, immediate reinforcement will prove extraordinarily helpful. Suppose one day they decide to practice a sequence in which Marissa is being cajoled into going for a ride to get a few beers. She and her counselor plan a reasonable set of firm but inoffensive refusals, like, "I'd really like to spend some time with you, but I don't want to go out for beer. How about we walk down to the teen center and listen to. . . ." Marissa plays her own role; her tone of voice is weak, and she sounds indecisive. Interrupting her, the counselor models an expression of stronger resolve and confidence, and Marissa tries again. As Marissa shows improvement, her counselor nods her strong approval. Reinforcement is immediate.

Once a behavior has been changed as anticipated and regularly practiced under natural circumstances, you should begin to plan to introduce reinforcement after some time has elapsed. Delay of reinforcement has a practical advantage, in the sense that the dispenser of the reinforcement needn't stop everything to deliver the reinforcers. It also appears that delayed reinforcement enhances generalization and resistance to periods of nonreinforcement (i.e., extinction).

Several 4- and 5-year-old children received stickers or points that they could exchange for toys by engaging in one of the following behaviors: offering to share, commenting positively about activities, maintaining appropriate study posture, or conversing with peers (Fowler & Baer, 1981). The points or stickers were earned for performing the target behavior during one period of the day. Data were recorded during that period (the contingent setting) as well as later on (the generalization setting). The rewards were presented at one of three times: following a short delay, right after the contingent setting period, or much later in the day. Children tended to practice the target behavior to a greater degree during the generalization period of the delayed reward condition.

Mayhew and Anderson (1980) did a similar study with two adolescent retarded boys whose work habits in class were selected for improvement. The study consisted of several phases: baseline, during which no reinforcers were given; an immediate reinforcement phase, during which tokens were delivered right away during class for appropriate working behavior; or a later reinforcement phase, when the boys were shown a videotape of their performance. Each of those reinforcement situations was followed by a baseline phase. While immediate reinforcement produced superior results, it also was found that the appropriate behavior persisted longer during nonreinforcement phases following delayed reinforcement than following an immediate reinforcement phase.

Delays should be introduced gradually, just as more natural reinforcers are. As always, the performance of the student informs us when a delay may have been introduced too abruptly. If so, we need to retreat temporarily to an earlier phase. In our classroom token economy, we first set up point exchanges right after the reading class, although we placed tangible rewards in a paper bag and stored them until dismissal time. After a while, the exchange time was delayed until the end of the day. After several weeks, exchanges were held on alternate days and ultimately, once a week—an arrangement similar to many pay schedules.

In this section you have seen how it is possible to incorporate immediate reinforcement within the school routine—in instruction, classroom management, and consultation. Sometimes, arranging to reinforce immediately may take a little ingenuity, like using an electrical beeper to cue you to deliver reinforcers on time or finding or designing programmed curriculum materials. Yet the effort will be worth it, for in the early stages of behavior change, immediacy of reinforcement is an especially powerful feature. Later on, you'll be able to relax in the knowledge that not only is delay acceptable, but it actually will promote durability and generality of the altered behavior. Now let us go on to another important feature: the frequency with which reinforcement is delivered.

FREQUENCY OF REINFORCEMENT

How often do you reinforce a behavior that you want to increase or maintain? If it has been reasonably well established, then you reinforce only every once in a while. Your students have learned to start their work right away. So every once in a while you comment, "What a pleasure this class is. You all get down to work so fast!" But try very hard not to take things for granted and totally neglect reinforcing a behavior that has improved earlier. You don't need to provide reinforcement every time. In fact, by reinforcing intermittently, you are raising the likelihood that the behavior won't stop or *extinguish* if reinforcement is not forthcoming later on. (Later you'll see how intermittent reinforcement of an unwanted behavior can create all sorts of difficulties— for exactly the same reason, because *intermittently reinforced behaviors tend to persist.*)

But probably you are more concerned with behaviors of another category: those that are being established or strengthened, or those that need *to increase* in *rate.* Here *reinforcement should be continuous or as close to continuous as is reasonably feasible.* That's why our math teachers continually circulated about the room, because it permitted them to comment positively very often. For Marissa, *every time* she practices or improves in giving a good assertive response during role playing, her counselor nods approval and provides specific feedback with praise: "Now that time, you did that very well. Your eye contact was good. You looked straight at me. Your tone of voice was firm. You smiled and appeared friendly and not at all threatened. You made me feel as if I'd like to go with you to the teen center."

Increasing frequency of reinforcement with peer tutors

At Willow Grove School, Mr. Truax, teacher, and Mrs. Olsen, principal, are concerned about the fact that Billy, a 12-year-old who only reads at second-grade level, needs some more practice. Yet no one has sufficient time to listen to the boy read. So Mr.

Truax and Mrs. Olsen decide to ask Billy to tutor a couple of the children in Ms. Miller's class who are learning some of the words that Billy clearly has mastered. Billy, enthusiastic about becoming a "teacher" himself, agrees to stay after school for a few sessions, during which Mr. Truax will show him how to teach. The boy is shown how and practices holding word cards, praising correct answers, prompting incorrect ones, and learning other tutoring skills while Mr. Truax uses an observation form to check the skills which Billy practices correctly[3] (see Figure 5.1). At the end of the training session, Mr. Truax and Billy go over the observation form together, and the skills that were practiced correctly that day are marked "good." Billy also is taught how to observe and rate his own performance. When Billy has been trained adequately, he tutors his students once or twice after school. Mr. Truax watches, and after the session he lavishly praises all successful attempts and gently corrects those that need to be improved. In a few days, Billy and his students start working in a corner of Ms. Miller's room, and Mr. Truax then can begin to supervise less frequently. Now Ms. Miller has the observation form and when she gets a moment, she watches Billy and his students; then she checks the form to give him when the tutoring session is finished. Billy also fills out an observation form of his own. For a few days after school he and Ms. Miller compare their ratings, and day by day he increases the accuracy of his self-scoring. Eventually, Billy is able to rate his own performance independently, thus supplying his own reinforcement.

You can see how this sort of program might be very successful as well as beneficial to a number of people. First, there are the youngsters who are tutored. They have increased opportunities to practice their reading or other skills. An older child reinforces each correct response with praise, and those correct responses should become well established. Then there is Billy himself, who now receives consistent reinforcement of several types from a number of different sources. He practices reading words he's already mastered and knows they are correct.

[3]Based on Ramey and Sulzer-Azaroff (1979).

Also, two teachers provide him with specific feedback about his practice of the tutoring skills. Because he has been so carefully trained and supervised, that feedback is almost always positive, as is the feedback he provides himself. Because Billy uses those skills properly, his students respond well to him, and they learn. That, too, is consistently reinforcing. And, following their initial investment of time and effort, Mr. Truax and Ms. Miller find that their undertaking is consistently reinforcing for them, as they have saved time in the long run. Mrs. Olsen, who has been observing this process with much interest, decides to institute a similar program among her own students and finds that more learning and less boredom result.

Not only have model students become successful tutors, but even those who are academically or developmentally delayed, hyperactive, or behaviorally disordered have been taught to tutor successfully. Effective teaching was just the beginning, though. Their own learning increased and their conduct improved in the process as well.

If you want to run a successful peer tutoring program, it is important to follow a few important steps, as was done with Billy:

1. The routine should be worked out clearly in advance so all participants know who is to do what, where, with whom, using what materials, for how long, and to what end. You could list each step on a wall chart and provide tutors with individual check lists that they could mark as they complete each step, while you verify their activities from time to time.

2. Tutors usually need to be trained and supervised. They must be able to perform the following skills: assess and score performance accurately; cue without overprompting by not providing extraneous hints; model and reinforce good behavior; be friendly; and praise, deliver rewards, and correct errors appropriately. Written rules for conducting specific tutoring sessions and self-checks can help, but they may not be sufficient. You probably will need to practice with the prospective tutors, modeling the appropriate behaviors yourself, then asking them to practice in role-

Remember to ...

___ 1. Have the lesson ready.

___ 2. Talk clearly.

___ 3. Be friendly.

___ 4. Tell the student when he is right.

___ 5. Correct mistakes. STOP! Give the right answer. Have the student do it.

___ 6. Praise good work!

___ 7. Make the lesson fun.

___ 8. Do not give TOO MUCH help.

___ 9. Fill out the daily sheet.

___ 10.

Figure 5.1
Peer-tutoring checklist. (Source: Ramey and Sulzer-Azaroff, 1979.**)**

playing sessions. It also will pay to observe the first several sessions that any student conducts, providing reinforcement and corrective feedback as merited. If necessary, compliance with the routine can be reinforced with privileges, tokens, or points as Greer and Polirstok (1982) did to increase rates of approval by the tutors. Often, just the prestige of being a tutor is sufficient, though; and students, eager to do a good job, sustain their levels of performance with feedback to themselves or from the tutees, observers, or teacher.

3. Tutor selection should be based on a careful match. The tutor's own repertoires of skills should slightly exceed those of the tutees. If the tutors themselves have not mastered the material to be taught, they can teach erroneously. If their skill levels are substantially beyond those of their tutees, they will not benefit from the increased exposure to academic tasks afforded by the tutoring experience.

Let us examine a few additional illustrative tutoring programs and see how those steps have been included.[4] Jane, Norman, and Brady, three children between 9 and 10 years old, were students in an ungraded open-environment class (Dineen, Clark, & Risley, 1977). Although they were of average intelligence, their reading, math, and spelling achievements were considerably delayed. In an attempt to enhance their spelling performance, the children were taught to identify several sets of spelling words. Then they were trained to tutor one another. Teachers modeled appropriate tutoring, had the students imitate, and then played the role of tutees. When the students displayed acceptable tutoring skills, they were praised. Each student then was assigned to teach the other two students a list of 15 words. Depending on the number of words the tutees learned, the tutor was awarded items from a reinforcing menu. Both tutors and tutees gained from the experience, as tutors learned almost as much as their tutees. In addition, those youngsters who had the honor of being selected to tutor apparently

gained some prestige, improved their own academic skills, and were treated by others with more respect than in the past. Can you imagine what a pleasure this might be for a youngster like Billy?

The advantage to tutors as well as tutees in an inner-city school (much like the Washington Street School) was demonstrated in similar fashion by Greer and Polirstok (1982). Each of three ninth graders with histories of serious discipline problems served as a tutor of five eighth graders, whose reading scores were a couple of years below grade level. To highlight the necessity for training and reinforcing the appropriate use of feedback in tutoring, the tutors first were observed to note their natural use of social reinforcement. Rarely did they naturally praise tutees. A new phase of the study then was instituted, during which tutors were taught to approve very often and were given points for the number of approvals they delivered each session. These could be exchanged for additional shop classes, certificates from a fast-food chain, opportunities to use audiovisual materials, and letters to the tutors' parents praising their work. As rates of approval rose, so did the tutees' correct reading responses. But the tutors themselves also gained during that phase, remaining on-task more in their own classrooms and performing better on their own reading assignments. In addition, both groups showed substantial improvement over previous gains on their standardized reading scores. In this particular case, though, it was necessary to sustain the point system for tutors to continue praising, for when points were withdrawn temporarily, approval rates dropped and so did tutee and tutor learning and performance. (Perhaps if tutors had been trained initially and simply had been praised for use of good tutoring skills, they would not have become dependent on the points. If you are considering a peer tutoring program, you first might train your tutors intensively and then supervise and provide differential praise often during initial tutoring. If approval rates remain inadequate, then at that point you could introduce a reward system for approval.)

Peer tutoring need not be restricted to students who need extra help. It is an effective method at all levels of education, from the most fundamental pre-

---

[4]For a review of peer tutoring, see Devin-Sheehan, L., Feldman, R. S., & Allan, V. L. (1976).

school level to highly advanced professional and technical training. For example, when teachers were taught behavioral procedures and then taught other teachers what they had learned, similar results to those described above were obtained (Jones, Fremouw, & Carples, 1977). Not only did student disruptiveness decrease at least as much in the tutees' classroom as in the tutors', but two of the three tutors who profited least from the original training were able to achieve further reductions in disruptiveness as a benefit of instructing other teachers in the approach. Similarly, the effective use of peers as tutors has been demonstrated amply by the numerous published studies of the personalized system of instruction (Keller, 1968).[5] Peer tutoring or proctoring is an essential element of PSI. Proctors usually are students who already have mastered the content of an instructional unit and who grade the performance of other students being assessed for their mastery of the material. Researchers at the college level have found that it pays to train proctors to prompt appropriately, score accurately, and provide positive feedback—and it helps if their grade depends on how effectively they exercise those skills. And, as reported in previous studies, proctors also profit from the experience by having their own learning reinforced.

We have returned to the topic of peer tutoring to demonstrate that despite the apparent logistical difficulties that teachers might face in attempting to reinforce frequently and consistently, there are feasible alternatives. Perhaps you have noticed that several of our earlier examples also incorporated continuous or near-continuous reinforcement within their systems. In one case, the teacher tried to attend as often as possible to children who were hard at work. The token programs permit points or checks to be presented each time a unit of behavior is completed appropriately, and the programmed texts and teaching machines provide the same sort of consistency. You will want to arrange for frequent reinforcement in your own setting if you are trying to encourage your students, *or* clients, to increase the rate of a particular behavior. This is also the case for staff.

[5]See Johnson and Ruskin (1977).

Using frequent reinforcement with staff

Yes, staff needs frequent reinforcement during its initial efforts to change their behavior, just as students do. If you are functioning as a trainer, supervisor, or consultant to an instructional staff, your success will depend, in large measure, on the extent to which trainees receive regular and frequent reinforcement. Indeed, if your staff receives consistent reinforcement you may find that it is less likely to suffer burnout. The importance of this has been borne out in several studies (MacDonald, Gallimore, & MacDonald, 1970; Holden & Sulzer-Azaroff, 1972; Hunt & Sulzer-Azaroff, 1974; Fox & Sulzer-Azaroff, 1982). Each included some system for providing regular positive feedback to teachers or teaching-parents as they practiced their newly acquired instructional or management skills. Often feedback is done in person, but we have found that adequate support can be provided while the going is slow by providing charts, telephone calls, and notes, and also by encouraging peers to provide positive recognition of the newly acquired skills. Dustin (1974, pp. 423–424) stressed how important it is for change agents to possess such tenacity while change is taking place:

> One reason that institutions change superficially has to do with ineffective behaviors on the part of the change agent. These proponents of change "burn out," or move on, before the change is fully implemented. It is necessary that a change agent possess tenacity to follow through and to return to the same tasks and the same individuals time and again.

Once change is well established, the frequency of praise, phone calls, charts, and graphs can be reduced gradually until you almost can dispense with them entirely.[6] This occasional **intermittent**

[6]Use a gradually increasing **ratio schedule** (one that requires progressively more responses before they are reinforced) in the beginning to promote a high rate of response; shift to an **interval schedule** (one that requires progressively more time before the responses are reinforced) after the response pattern is high and stable.

reinforcement, and the support provided by the consultees' peers, enables you to reduce the amount of time you need to devote to any one consultee while supporting the durability of change. Cossairt, Hall, and Hopkins (1973, p. 100) have found in their study on principals as agents of change for teacher performance that praise by teachers maintained and even increased when they themselves were praised intermittently for using it. They concluded that:

> This would seem to indicate that the excuse that principals and supportive staff do not have time for the social reinforcement of teacher behavior is invalid. Operant principles of reinforcement systematically applied would therefore seem to be functional in helping principals and consultants accomplish their primary goal, which should be improving instruction. It would also seem that this could be done with a minimal amount of time and effort. (Reprinted with permission of the authors and publisher. Copyright © 1973 by the Society for the Experimental Analysis of Behavior, Inc.)

COMMUNICATING CONDITIONS FOR REINFORCEMENT DELIVERY

Recently, a local station televised a public hearing on the topic of school buses. Parents started by expressing their anger at the transportation department's failure to maintain the vehicles adequately. Before long, the focus began to shift, as both parents and bus drivers alike began to voice their concern about misbehavior on the school bus. Drivers said that they worried that the distraction caused by children running up and down the aisles, fighting, and shouting might result in an accident. Apparently this sort of problem is hardly limited to that one community, as we will discuss in Chapter 21. What's to be done? Where does one begin?

A good place to start is by specifying rules. Rules are identified and clearly defined, with input from all those concerned—the bus driver, parents, teachers, and particularly the youngsters themselves. The students know the difference between acceptable and unacceptable conduct: "Remain seated," "Speak

softly," "Keep your hands and feet to yourself." They just fail to abide by those rules.

That is only the initial step. The next step is more difficult, but it is essential. When rules are followed, those acceptable behaviors are reinforced according to the prescribed methods described earlier. In one case reported in the literature (Ritchl, Mongrella, & Presbie, 1972), the students who rode a particular bus really enjoyed popular music. So whenever all were seated quietly, rock music was played. If the students became noisy or disruptive, the music was shut off for a specified time. The method worked extremely well, and disruption on that bus essentially was eliminated.

This example shows us how important it is to indicate clearly the conditions under which reinforcement will occur and to apply reinforcement optimally when the behavior occurs under those conditions. What you're trying to accomplish is to teach the learner to *discriminate*[7] the conditions under which a particular behavior will be reinforced; in this case, what will happen when the behavior matches the rules. This is not to suggest that discrimination is a *necessary* step, just a desirable one. The very same procedure probably would have worked even if the rules hadn't been specified. But it probably would have taken longer to accomplish the happy results.

Because *behavior tends to increase more rapidly when the conditions under which it will be reinforced are communicated clearly*, many behavioral programs incorporate this feature. The establishment of classroom and school *disciplinary codes*, or rules, includes this procedure. Another example is *goal setting*. A group of eight young people between the ages of 16 and 21 were enrolled in a school program (Kelly & Stokes, 1981). Each had previously dropped out of school and needed remedial academic training. Funds were available to pay them for their progress. In one phase of the study, the students and the teacher negotiated a reasonable goal for the math, English, and reading items they would com-

---

[7]Stimuli that signal that a given response has a probability of being reinforced under the conditions in effect are technically labeled *discriminative stimuli* and often are abbreviated as S^D. These are discussed thoroughly in Chapters 6 and 7.

plete the following week. Then if the goal were reached, they'd receive their pay that week. This arrangement was compared to one in which the students' pay depended on their attendance. Needless to say, performance was far superior when goals were set and money was given contingent on their accomplishment. (See Fellner & Sulzer-Azaroff, 1984, for an extensive discussion of goal setting.)

How about the experiment with the math class that we discussed in the previous chapter? There, *rules* were simpler. Because they were clearly defined, they were easy to follow. It took almost no time for the students to recognize what constituted being on-task and that only on-task activities would gain attention and praise.

Contractual arrangements have been used for various purposes to signal which responses will be reinforced: for example, establishing weight goals or caloric intake for control of obesity or setting goals for application of specific management techniques by teachers or parents. In fact, numerous books and articles have been written on behavioral contractual arrangements, because they have been found to be so effective a method for changing behavior (Blechman, 1974; Dardig & Heward, 1976; DeRisi & Butz, 1975; Homme, Csanyi, Gonzales, & Rechs, 1970). Sometimes telling or writing the conditions under which a particular response is likely to be reinforced doesn't quite accomplish the purpose. Marissa's counselor might have told her how to respond to pressure, and she might even have written down the guidelines. Yet the skills are so complex that Marissa probably still would fail to catch the exact nuances of that complicated behavior. So her counselor not only told her what to do, but she also showed the girl by modeling the appropriate skill herself. Then Marissa caught on.

There are still other methods for communicating the conditions under which a particular response is apt to be reinforced: prompting and guiding. Verbal **prompts** are often used to cue a verbal response, like a word or concept. "If you want to be able to discriminate between the terms 'ordinate' and 'abscissa,' the vertical and horizontal axes of a graph, respectively, remember that the word 'abscissa' has a *b*, and *b* stands for 'bottom.' " This sort of a prompt will help you to respond "abscissa" next time someone asks you about labeling the horizontal axis of a graph; the condition, a horizontal line, begins to signal that the response, "abscissa," will be reinforced. A gesture or verbal reminder also can help us to perform a nonverbal response correctly — like showing the motions to be copied or telling how to do it. (Keep your eye on the ball!)

Physical guidance helps communicate exactly how a particular body movement should be executed so that it will receive reinforcement. Marissa's counselor might show and actually position her shoulders so her posture communicates a message of "firm resolve." Marissa would feel how her body was positioned and could also see it in a mirror. That would help Marissa to begin to gain reinforcement for practicing the response when requested to do so. (Later on, of course, she will practice the response, not on request, but when natural conditions call for it. But that kind of more complicated teaching, along with a more detailed discussion of communicating conditions for reinforcement delivery, are presented in Chapters 6 and 7.)

APPLYING REINFORCEMENT STRATEGIES

Now you should begin to think about your own situation and some of your own behaviors, or perhaps those of students and staff that you would like to see increase.[8] Then see how each of the rules of effective reinforcement can apply in those circumstances. But if you decide to try out reinforcement, don't forget to consider such ethical issues as whether you are justified in attempting to accomplish that change and whether you should obtain the informed consent of the individuals involved or their guardians. Also, be certain to select a clear, objective method for measuring the behavior, and do measure and graph it several times before beginning so that you can see where you're starting. Then when you try out your program of reinforcement, continue to

[8]Should you wish to involve yourself in a more structured training program to learn how to apply these behavioral procedures, refer to Sulzer-Azaroff and Reese (1982).

measure so you can see if things are working as planned.

Sometimes you might begin to wonder if the change really resulted from your management of reinforcement. Try discontinuing the program for a while to see what happens. If the data show that the behavior is beginning to drop back, then you'll know how important your program was to its success, and undoubtedly you'll want to reintroduce it. Or you might want to try out the program with a few other people, or at different times or places, or with other behaviors to see if it has the same results. If it does, you should be quite convinced that the program is effective. If not, you'll probably need to adjust the program to those special circumstances.

Then someday, should you wish to terminate your program, be sure to do so with great care—slowly lengthening the time between the behavior and reinforcement and reducing the frequency with which you reinforce. Gradually restrict the amount of reinforcement and supplant any artificial reinforcers with more natural ones, gradually diminishing rules (or fading), prompts, and other cues for communicating which behaviors are to be reinforced. If your data tell you that change is sustaining, then you are terminating your program in just the right way. But if things begin to disintegrate, go back to the point where they were working successfully; reestablish the behavior, and then progress even more gingerly than before. Perhaps then you will have accomplished your purpose.

Summary

In this chapter we have given you some very important facts about ways to increase behavior through reinforcement. You've learned that a behavior increases optimally when reinforced immediately and consistently with an object or event that is appropriate to the individual under those circumstances. The amount of reinforcement must be just enough to keep the behavior going, but not so much that the individual becomes sated with it. That, of course, depends on the reinforcers you select and on factors such as how long the individual has been deprived of the reinforcer, among other things. We also mentioned how important it is to communicate clearly the conditions under which a particular behavior will be reinforced—either verbally or via modeling or guidance. Finally, we asked you to begin to apply these strategies to your own situation so you can practice using the concepts.

Study Questions

1. Discuss how to determine the appropriate amount of reinforcement to dispense.
2. State several reasons for reinforcing a behavior immediately.
3. Mr. Brown would like to reinforce his students' good behavior immediately. However, this is not always possible. Offer a suggestion for solving his problem.
4. The teachers in the Oak Street School have heard about behavioral programs and would like to implement one in their school. What advice would you give them on selecting a behavioral problem for their first program?
5. The students in the basic math group do not want to record their performance. What advantage of recording performance would you offer them?
6. Reinforcement is built into a Personalized System of Instruction (PSI) course. Provide evidence to support this statement.
7. (a) Describe and (b) list the benefits of programmed instruction.
8. The staff of the Bayberry School realizes that its students would benefit from the immediate feedback that a computer can provide. However, no funds are available to support

purchase of a computer at this time. Suggest several alternative means for providing immediate feedback to their students.

9. The Lawsons have immediately reinforced their son's homework completion and his behavior has been changed as anticipated. Discuss in detail whether or not they should delay reinforcement.

10. Describe how a delay in reinforcement should be introduced.

11. Provide reasons for intermittently reinforcing a behavior.

12. Under what conditions should reinforcement be delivered continuously?

13. Describe in detail an appropriate method of training a student to be a peer tutor.

14. List several advantages of using peer tutors. Be sure to discuss advantages for the student, peer tutor, and teacher.

15. (a) Identify and (b) discuss the important steps to follow for achieving a successful peer tutoring program.

16. Use an original narrative to demonstrate the successful training of a peer tutor.

17. Dr. Johnson plans to use proctors in her college-level psychology course. Offer several suggestions to help ensure success of the program.

References

Ayllon, T., & Azrin, N. H. (1968). *System for therapy and rehabilitation*. New York: Appleton-Century-Crofts, 1968.

Bangert, R. L., Kulik, J. A., & Kulik, C. (1983). Individualized systems of instruction in secondary schools. *Review of Educational Research*, 53, 143–158.

Bernal, M. E. (1969). Behavioral feedback in the modification of brat behaviors. *The Journal of Nervous and Mental Disease*, 148, 375–385.

Blechman, E. A. (1974, July). The family contract game: A tool to teach interpersonal problem solving. *Family Coordinator*, 269–280.

Cossairt, A., Hall, R. V., & Hopkins, B. L. (1973). The effects of experimenter's instructions, feedback and praise on teacher praise and student attending behavior. *Journal of Applied Behavior Analysis*, 6, 89–100

Dardig, J. C., & Heward, W. L. (1976). *Sign here: A contracting book for children and their parents*. Kalamazoo, MI: Behaviordelia.

DeRisi, W. J., & Butz, G. (1975). *Writing behavioral contracts: A case simulation practice manual*. Champaign, IL: Research Press.

Devin-Sheehan, L., Feldman, R. S., & Allan, V. L. (1976). Research on children tutoring children: A critical review. *Review of Educational Research*, 46, 355–385.

Dineen, J. P., Clark, H. B., & Risley, T. R. (1977). Peer tutoring among elementary students: Educational benefits to the tutor. *Journal of Applied Behavior Analysis*, 10, 231–238.

Dustin, R. (1974). Training for institutional change. *The Personnel and Guidance Journal*, 52, 422–427.

Fellner, D. J., & Sulzer-Azaroff, B. (1984). A behavioral analysis of goal setting. *Journal of Organizational Behavior Management*, 6, 33–51.

Fowler, S., & Baer, D. M. (1981). "Do I have to be good all day?" The timing of delayed reinforcement as a factor in generalization. *Journal of Applied Behavior Analysis*, 14, 13–24.

Fox, C. J., & Sulzer-Azaroff, B. (1982). *A program to supervise geographically dispersed foster parents' teaching of retarded youth*. Unpublished manuscript.

Greer, R. D. (1984). *The teacher as strategic scientist*. Paper presented at the Sixteenth Banff International Conference on Behavioral Science.

Greer, R. D., & Polirstok, S. R. (1982). Collateral gains and short-term maintenance in reading and on-task responses by some inner-city adolescents as a function of their use of social reinforcement while tutoring. *Journal of Applied Behavior Analysis*, 15, 123–139.

Holden, B., & Sulzer-Azaroff, B. (1972). Schedules of follow-up and their effect upon the maintenance of a prescriptive teaching program. In G. Semb, D. R. Green, R. P. Hawkins, J. Michael, E. L. Phillips, J. A. Sherman, H. Sloane, & D. R. Thomas (Eds.), *Behavior analysis and education—1972*. Lawrence, KS: University of Kansas.

Homme, L., Csanyi, A. P., Gonzales, M. A., & Rechs, J. R. (1970). *How to use contingency contracting in the classroom*. Champaign, IL: Research Press.

Hunt, S., & Sulzer-Azaroff, B. (1974, September). *Motivating parent participation in home training sessions with pretrainable retardates*. Paper presented at the

American Psychological Association, New Orleans, Louisiana.

Johnson, K. R., & Ruskin, R. S. (1977). *Behavioral instruction: An evaluative review*. Washington, D.C.: American Psychological Association.

Jones, F. H., Fremouw, W., & Carples, S. (1977). Pyramid training of elementary school teachers to use a classroom management "skill package." *Journal of Applied Behavior Analysis, 10,* 239–253.

Kazdin, A. E. (1982). The token economy: A decade later. *Journal of Applied Behavior Analysis, 15,* 431–445.

Keller, F. S. (1968). Goodbye, teacher. . . . *Journal of Applied Behavior Analysis, 1,* 79–90.

Kelly, M. L., & Stokes, T. R. (1981, November). *Contracting and goal setting to increase the academic productivity of disadvantaged youth*. Paper presented at the annual meeting of the Association for Advancement of Behavior Therapy, Toronto.

Krumboltz, J. D., & Thoresen, C. E. (Eds.). (1969). *Behavioral counseling cases and techniques*. New York: Holt, Rinehart and Winston.

MacDonald, W. S., Gallimore, R., & MacDonald, G. (1970). Contingency counseling by school personnel: An economical model of intervention. *Journal of Applied Behavior Analysis, 31,* 175–182.

Mayhew, G. L., & Anderson, J. (1980). Delayed and immediate reinforcement: Retarded adolescents in an educational setting. *Behavior Modification, 4,* 527–545.

Ramey, G., & Sulzer-Azaroff, B. (1979, September). *Generalization effects of involving behaviorally disordered children as teachers*. Paper presented at the annual meeting of the American Psychological Association, New York.

Ritchl, C., Mongrella, J., & Presbie, R. L. (1972). Group time-out from rock and roll music and out of seat behavior of handicapped children while riding a school bus. *Psychological Reports, 31,* 967–973.

Skinner, B. F. (1958). Teaching machines. *Science, 128,* 969–977.

Smith, B. M., Schumaker, J. B., Schaeffer, J., & Sherman, J. A. (1982). Increasing participation and improving the quality of discussions in seventh-grade social studies classes. *Journal of Applied Behavior Analysis, 15,* 97–110.

Sulzer-Azaroff, B., & Reese, E. P. (1982). *Applying behavior analysis: A program for developing professional competence*. New York: Holt, Rinehart and Winston.

6 Control by antecedents: differential reinforcement

Goals

After completing this chapter, you should be able to:

1. Define and illustrate the use of each of the following terms and procedures:
   a. Discriminative stimulus (S^D)
   b. Natural discriminative stimuli
   c. Artificial discriminative stimuli
   d. Fading
   e. Delayed prompting
   f. Transfer of stimulus control
   g. Setting event
   h. Rule-governed behavior
   i. Contingency-shaped behavior
   j. Extinction
   k. Differential reinforcement
   l. Discriminative control
2. Discuss the importance of being able to identify S^Ds and setting events.
3. Explain the function of fading and delayed prompting.
4. Describe the difference between rule-governed and contingency-shaped behavior.
5. Describe why a particular S^D may fail to evoke a behavior.
6. Identify and list two basic rules for applying extinction.
7. Describe and illustrate how an S^D, such as a classroom behavior rule, is developed.

The faculty of Washington Street Junior High was excited! Earlier, Mr. Lee, the counselor, had talked about effective reinforcement, and everyone's interest was piqued. Now several members had asked him if, during in-service training, he would teach them more about behavioral instruction in order that it might cure all their teaching woes. Mr. Lee replied that while such miracles were beyond his capabilities, he'd be pleased to share some of the findings from the analysis of behavior and a few strategies that the teachers might use to evaluate problems of concern to them.

Now it was Wednesday afternoon. The students had been dismissed early to free faculty for the bi-weekly in-service meeting. Everyone listened attentively as Mr. Lee narrated how behavorial methods have helped students to improve their performance in reading, handwriting, spelling, creative art and writing, social studies discussion, and other areas. He described how reinforcing contingencies increased rates of academic response; how the timing with which materials were presented influenced accuracy of performance; what instructional prompts were and how they were faded; and other concepts.

Taking notes furiously, the audience became increasingly confused. Ms. Jackson held up her hand. "Could we slow down a little? You're losing me. You've used so many new terms and concepts that it's getting difficult to follow." Others nodded their agreement.

Mrs. Burnes added, "We're pretty familiar with terms like reinforcement and contingencies because we learned about them earlier. But now we hear you mentioning **extinction, differential reinforcement, discriminative stimuli, setting events, prompting, fading,** and so on. Could you explain those to us?

"Sure," replied Mr. Lee. "I just wanted to start out by letting you know that behavioral approaches are often more complex than just applying reinforcement—and they can have an impact on academic learning, as well as on students' conduct in school. When we move into this realm, we need to examine not only the events that follow learning activities, but also those that precede and accompany the behavior. Over the course of this in-service training program, we'll analyze examples so we can see how each type might influence rates and quality of academic performance, deportment, and other classes of behavior. But for the time being, let's concentrate on the events that occur before the response of concern—the antecedent stimuli. Allow me to begin with a general introduction.

"Think of a learning episode as if it were a theatrical production, like the performance of *West Side Story* the drama club presented last year. Of course, the central aspect of a play is the *acting*—the lines and movements of the actors. Maria's, Tony's, and the others' songs, lines, dances, and expressions constituted the major aspect of the play. The acting is like the academic behavior with which we are concerned. But acting just doesn't happen in a vacuum. It is influenced by all sorts of events. What are some of them?" Here are the replies that he jotted on the board:

1. The script
2. The director's instructions
3. The stage set
4. The applause and rapt attention of the audience
5. The actors' reactions to hearing themselves perform well
6. The props and costumes
7. The musical score and accompaniment
8. The lines of the other performers *or* the prompter's whispered lines
9. The stage directions
10. The actors' stage fright (and they all laughed!)

"Yes. All of these factors affected the performance—some early in the preparation of the production, some later, some during the actual performance, and some afterward."

Mrs. Burnes exclaimed, "I'll never forget the glow on Carmen's face when she was presented with the bouquet after playing Maria so beautifully!"

"It's not hard to identify a few of the events as reinforcers, then, is it?—The applause, rapt attention, flowers, congratulations, and so on. Right," said Mr. Lee. "But what other sorts of events do we see? What are the events that directly precede a particular acting sequence?"

"That's pretty obvious—the script tells them exactly what to say, and the stage directions what to do," offered Ms. Jackson.

"That's true. They certainly were important in the beginning. But later the actors didn't need the script. It was the lines of the other players that prompted them."

"Or the prompter," Mrs. Burnes noted.

"Yes. Now you're indicating another important set of elements. The script tells the actors what to say or do, and when. When they follow through correctly, that produces reinforcement or avoidance of aversive consequences, like flubbing their lines. So they learn that following the script will be reinforced. They *discriminate* that behaving and speaking in accordance with the lines of the script will set the stage or occasion for reinforcement. The script is a stimulus, not a reinforcing stimulus, but a stimulus that helps them to discriminate the conditions of reinforcement. This is why we call those antecedent stimuli **discriminative stimuli.** They tell the performer that the behavior will be reinforced under those special circumstances," said Mr. Lee.

"But you yourself agreed that the script only does its job in the beginning. Later on, it's the others' performance that cues the correct response," another teacher commented.

"Yes, I did. The very same performance can be cued by different discriminative stimuli. If you stop and think about it, as teachers, we often attempt to substitute one set of discriminative stimuli for another, hoping to exchange natural cues for artificial prompts."

"Oh, I get it," piped up Ms. Jackson. "The script is an artificial set of prompts that the players need to rid themselves of as soon as possible. Otherwise it wouldn't be much of a play. I can just see Tony and Maria doing their love scene, scripts in hand."

"You've got it. The whole idea is first to evoke the specific response with whatever prompt it takes. In this case it is the script. What might it take initially in a Spanish course?"

"Lines from the text," the Spanish teacher offered.

"Or words written on the board or spoken by the teacher or on a tape cassette. How about in arithmetic?"

"Maybe a pocket calculator, or tangible objects to count, or pies to cut."

"How about P.E.? Let's say, teaching how to swing a bat."

"I do it by hanging on and guiding the student through the swing," the P.E. teacher, Mr. Cole, said.

"All of that is true. But we don't provide those prompts forever, do we?"

"No. Little by little we try to get rid of them so the responses eventually occur under the circumstances that call for them naturally."

"Like?"

"Like asking them to solve a problem without the pocket calculator or the pie," the math teacher said.

"Like having them swing correctly when the ball comes toward them," the P.E. teacher added.

"Yes. Those are the **natural discriminative stimuli,** that is, those that will be encountered in the real world. *We wouldn't be doing our jobs if we never weaned our students from those artificial prompts,*" Mr. Lee stressed.

He went on, "Now, you saw how the discriminative stimuli are swapped gradually. (By the way, you people wouldn't mind if I used the abbreviation 'S-D'—it's written like this: S^D. It's a pain to keep saying 'discriminative stimuli' all the time.) Anyway, when you *gradually* substitute the natural for the **artificial S^Ds,** hoping that the natural S^Ds will take control—that they eventually will *set the occasion for* the key behavior—you are using a procedure called **fading.** One S^D 'fades in' as the other more artificial one 'fades out.'"

"I do something like that," broke in Ms. Hollingsworth. "Like the other day Tyrone was working on a new set of word cards. Tommy helped by holding the cards, counting to himself for a few seconds, then if Tyrone didn't answer, Tommy said the word. Each time he presented the set of cards, he waited a few seconds longer. Before you knew it Tyrone was anticipating the—I guess you'd call it—the prompt. So the word—the natural S^D—finally began evoking the correct response."

"Yes," answered Mr. Lee. "That's a very good way of transferring control over to natural stimuli—similar to what we've been discussing. In this case the procedure is called **delayed prompting,** or sometimes **stimulus delay,** because of the delay between the natural and the artificial antecedent stimuli. A psychologist by the name of Touchette has worked with this technique" (Touchette & Howard, 1984).

"Aren't fading and delayed prompting something like what we do when we're trying to exchange natural for artificial reinforcers?" Mrs. Burnes asked.

"Yes, fading S^Ds and delayed prompting have much in common with altering the quality of reinforcers. Both start by using stimuli that effectively control that particular behavior for the individual and gradually substitute other stimuli that eventually *should* control the behavior. They do differ, though, in terms of where they exert their influence."

"Sure," Ms. Thomas chimed in. "Reinforcers follow the response; S^Ds come before it.

"But how about those other things remaining on the list? They don't exactly function the same way, do they—I mean the stage set, costumes, props, and so on?"

"You're right," Mr. Lee said. "Those stimuli tend to be present throughout. They do not cue, nor do they reinforce particular responses. Yet they certainly do influence the acting in a general way. Did any of you watch a rehearsal without scenery, costumes, or props? Contrast that with the cast's performance on opening night," said Mr. Lee.

"I did. The difference was striking. The players were so much more convincing when the set was in place and they had their props and costumes," Ms. Jackson commented.

"Well, antecedent stimuli like those fall into another category. They influence behavior in a more global way; they do not evoke only specific responses. Rather, they alter broad patterns of responding. These are, in a sense, S^Ds that simultaneously control a wide range of behaviors—like when you're tired or hungry, the stimuli presented by your internal environment evoke general irritability. (Yes, the source of stimulation can be internal!) Such stimuli are called **setting events.**[1] Now can you see why I like to use the theatrical metaphor?"

"Do setting events always need to be present right there?" asked Mr. Rodriguez. "I remember I used to get terrible stage fright. My voice would quiver and my knees would knock all morning, even before I left for school, on days whenever I knew I'd have to get up in front of a group. That was before I learned to ham it up." The staff laughed, and he responded with a courtly bow.

"Yes, events that took place previously, or that happened early in the day, can influence your performance later on. In 1977, Krantz and Risley found that children in a kindergarten class were far more inattentive following an antecedent period of vigorous activity than following a rest period.

"But before going any further," said Mr. Lee, "I think we've done just about enough today. I hope that now these terms mean more to you than they did an hour ago. We've been overly simple, just so we can start with a common vocabulary. Later, we'll see how S^Ds and setting events may influence complex learning and performance. A lot of exciting work has been done with discriminative stimuli. Wait 'til you hear how fading and delayed prompting systems have been designed to help children you'd never expect to be able to, to read and do arithmetic without making any mistakes at all in the process. But we should reserve that discussion for another time. Meanwhile, why don't you try to identify some examples of S^Ds and setting events in your classes?"

[1]Wahler and Fox (1981) go into this topic in quite a bit of detail, arguing that this is an area of much needed research.

DISCRIMINATIVE STIMULI AND SETTING EVENTS ILLUSTRATED

Two weeks later the group reconvened. Mr. Lee asked for examples of S^Ds and setting events. A fair number were offered. Here are some he wrote on the board:

Discriminative stimuli	Setting events[2]
Text passages	Weather: humidity sunshine, etc.
Instructions for solving problems	One's nutritional state
The problems themselves	A bad experience earlier in the day, like being
Written assignments on the board	beaten by a parent or getting into a fight
Rules of conduct in class	Awareness of being pregnant, nauseous, etc.
Anxiety symptoms	
Model letters for handwriting	Other salient physical sensations
Modeled demonstrations of:	A pep talk
dance steps	A motivating film
hand positions for the typewriter	Summer/Christmas vacation on the way
using shop equipment	Being told to hurry or
the good conduct or misbehavior of others, such as responding to commands rapidly, or smoking, using drugs, and so on	to work slowly and carefully
	Noise, movements of others in the room
	Objects in the room, colors, decorations
Signals by the coach	A pleasant atmosphere or a "coercive" one
	The density of people or furniture in a room

"Hey," said Mr. Rodriguez. "Isn't one of those in the wrong place?"

"You're right," Mr. Lee answered. "Who can find it?"

[2]Specific instances of some of the setting events listed here might function as S^Ds. For example, falling rain, a weather condition, could cue opening an umbrella.

"It's anxiety symptoms, I think," Mrs. Burnes offered. "That would affect performances of all kinds, wouldn't it?"

Mr. Lee agreed and transferred "anxiety symptoms" to the column on the right.

He commended the faculty for the extensiveness of the lists. "Naturally, we'd have to be much more precise to enable us to utilize those stimuli in some way — you know, to define them operationally. For instance, could we refine the term 'coercive' operationally? Let's try the term 'coercive atmosphere.'" Participants began to list the events that they felt constituted a coercive atmosphere, such as a high proportion of scolding, threats, and other aversive management techniques — ridicule, overly rigid rules of conduct, and so on. All agreed that many of the other items listed would need to be treated similarly before a teacher could proceed.

"Why do you think it is important for us to be able to identify the antecedent conditions — the S^{D}s and setting events that influence behavior?" asked Mr. Lee.

"Well, for one, if we know what event or events set the stage for a particular response, we can modify the frequency of the response by presenting, taking away, or withholding that stimulus," responded Ms. Thomas. "I do that with my science classes. I give them rules for conducting experiments, and they follow through pretty well. When I ask the students to copy down what's on the board, they do it. So my rules and instructions must be S^{D}s."

"That's a good example of **rule-governed behavior,**" Mr. Lee replied, "because the behavior reliably follows the S^{D}s — your rules and instructions."

Mrs. Burnes commented, "I wish I had the same good fortune with students in my English class. The other day I suggested that they copy down the homework assignment. When I walked around the room and looked at what they were writing, there was Lucinda writing all right, but it wasn't the assignment. I wouldn't dare tell you what she *was* writing, but you see words like it all over the playground wall!"

Mr. Lee explained that Mrs. Burnes had pointed out something very important about antecedent stimuli. "They do not universally occasion the same response by everyone. If they did, things would be much simpler. All you'd have to do is present them once to achieve the desired effect. For example, if you observed that a particular event like the instruction 'watch your verb tenses' consistently produced correct use of verb tenses, then you could just present that antecedent event — the instruction — and all your students would use the correct tense."

"I'm getting the impression," she answered, "that the consequences of behavior are the most important, because unless they are contingent on the antecedent-response combination, the antecedent won't gain control."

"Hey, good for you. You've really caught a subtle but terribly critical point," Mr. Lee nodded enthusiastically, "about the difference between **contingency-shaped** (like receiving reinforcement for using correct verb tenses) and rule-governed (like saying "watch the verb tenses") behavior. In 1974, Skinner said that an individual following rules and other instructions may learn the behavior more quickly but, and I quote, 'does not behave precisely as one who has been directly exposed to the contingencies, because a description of the contingencies is never complete or exact (it is usually simplified in order to be easily taught or understood) and because the supporting contingencies are seldom fully maintained'" (p. 125).

"I'm not sure I get his point entirely," interjected Ms. Jackson.

"Let me try with another example or two. Here's one we should all resonate to. You know many rules for keeping yourselves in good shape physically — like?"

"Exercising regularly."

"Avoiding sweets."

"And too much booze."

"Eating nutritious food."

"Keeping regular hours."

"Exactly — and we all follow those rules, just like we always follow the Ten Commandments, right?"

When the hilarity subsided, they discussed why rules often were broken, realizing that many behaviors produced rather immediate and powerful reinforcement, sufficient to override the influence of a rule they might recite to themselves.

"That's why it is so important, sometimes, to come in with a way of supporting a response that is different from the one that usually gains us heavy reinforcement. Although we'll come back to this point on another day, maybe one more example will help. Any ideas?"

"What about what we're learning in these sessions, Mr. Lee?" asked Mr. Rodriguez. "Aren't you giving us rules for managing and teaching our classes? Are you saying that if we've used other — presumably less effective — methods in the past which have been shaped by reinforcing contingencies that we might have a tough time shifting over to these new ones?"

"Absolutely. Now you are beginning to understand how important it is for you and me and other willing staff members to visit classrooms and give teachers positive feedback or for the teachers to self-reinforce as they try out their new strategies; and why we'll want to keep at it at least until other more natural forms of reinforcing feedback, like seeing the students learning better and faster, reliably override the previous forms of reinforcement. On that note, let's take a break and have some of those tempting refreshments that Mrs. Burnes and Mr. Cole brought today. After the break we will continue our discussion and look at several applications."

USING ANTECEDENT EVENTS TO CHANGE BEHAVIOR

Notice that *two critical factors related to antecedent events* in the above Washington Street Junior High illustration have been identified: (1) when they can be identified and controlled they can be used to alter performance; and (2) antecedent events do not necessarily affect everyone in the same way. This being the case, and assuming you could identify an antecedent stimulus that *did* function to change behavior, you'd need to ask yourself whether or not the person attempting to produce the

change could manage that antecedent stimulus. If you look at the list of S^Ds generated by the Washington Street School faculty, you'll see that some of them — signals, instructions, demonstrations, references to sample models, and so on — easily could be managed by the teacher or students. Others would be difficult to control, such as the modeled misconduct of other youngsters. The same is true for the setting events. You could give pep talks, or show inspirational films, or slow down or speed up the pace of your instruction. Your students could ask to move to a quieter location or might eat a good breakfast, but the weather and holiday schedules are neither under their control nor yours.

Sometimes you can influence setting events that wouldn't ordinarily be yours to manage. Many schools provide nutritious meals to poorly nourished children. Assisted by skilled professionals, parents have been helped to control their aggression toward their children. Often parents will cooperate with a request that their child get more sleep or come to school with adequate school supplies. Insofar as the weather is concerned, although we certainly can't do anything to change it, we can and do modify its effects by selecting proper clothing; building shelters; using heating and cooling systems, humidifiers, dehumidifiers; and so on.

Often, all you need to do is a little creative brainstorming to find ways to harness the S^Ds that influence the performance of concern. But how about the times you are unsuccessful when you arrange stimuli, intending to evoke a particular response? What do you do then? You first must find out if under the conditions in effect (also *antecedent stimuli*) the key stimulus is discriminative for that individual or not. If it isn't, you can try to remedy the situation through instruction; or you might select a different and more effective S^D. Sometimes a stimulus temporarily fails to evoke a particular behavior. That may happen when some other more powerful stimuli (reinforcing, aversive, discriminative, and so on) are exerting their influence at that moment. Amy hasn't recorded her assignment because the bell has signaled lunch period and she's thinking about how she can avoid being victimized in the lunchroom. Roberto hasn't eaten since last evening; the lunch bell cues him to get ready to be first in line, instead of recording his assignment. Food, right away, is a much more powerful reinforcing contingency for someone who hasn't eaten for a long time than is the consequence of not jotting down an assignment for the following day's class. If you were Mrs. Burnes, what would you do to determine whether or not your instructions to copy down the assignment were discriminative, at least under some circumstances? Probably you would see if Amy or Roberto followed the instructions at other times, instead of only just before lunch. If they did, then you could present assignments at a different time. If not, then you might choose to bring the desired response under discriminative control. Let us see how this might be accomplished.

TEACHING FOR DISCRIMINATIVE CONTROL

How do you think antecedent stimuli acquire control over particular responses? They acquire this control when a specific response is differentially reinforced, that is, reinforced only when it occurs under particular stimulus conditions and not reinforced, or placed on **extinction,** otherwise. To understand **differential reinforcement** better, let us turn now to extinction and its role in teaching discriminative control.

Extinction and differential reinforcement

"Time for the third graders to read," announces Ms. Heinz.

Lena and Sonya rush over to sit on either side of her, their faces wreathed in pleasure at having attained the prized places next to the student teacher.

Ms. Heinz asks the students to open their readers to the story about how Rover tipped over the paint and got paw prints all over the front porch. As they chuckled in recollection, the children found the correct page.

"Will you please start, Sonya?"

Sonya began, the others following along in their own books and Ms. Heinz nodding and smiling periodically:

"Father was brushing the steps with fresh white paint. Just then Mother called. 'Father, can you help us open this, it is—sick. . . .'"

A pause, then, "Boys and girls?" All waved their hands vigorously. "Lena?"

"It is stuck."

"Good for you, Lena. You remembered that the middle sound was 'uh' as in 'up' and you saw the 't' there. Sonya, would you like to try it again?"

The next time Sonya tried, she read the word correctly and Ms. Heinz nodded her approval, signaling her to continue.

What sort of procedure did Ms. Heinz use immediately following Sonya's error? We know it was not punishment, as she did not present an aversive stimulus, such as "no" or "wrong." Surely, as nothing was added or subtracted, it was not positive or negative reinforcement—and for good reason. Either form of reinforcement would serve to *increase* the error. Nor was it response cost, as she did not subtract any reinforcers. What actually happened right after Sonya made her mistake was that Ms. Heinz *withheld* a reinforcing stimulus, the approval she had been delivering in the form of nodding and smiling. *When a stimulus that previously had followed a response no longer does, and the subsequent rate of the response then diminishes, we label the operation "extinction."*

At this point we could add another column to the matrix presented in Figure 4.1 (see Figure 6.1).

Extinction is a natural phenomenon in much of life. We greet the mail carrier and he returns the greeting. We continue to say hello, but one day there is no response. Eventually we stop hailing him. We flick a wall switch and the room fails to light up. After a few more trials, we give up. We work extra hard on our reports and are commended for our efforts. Then no more approving comments are delivered. Eventually we do not work as hard on our reports.

When we apply extinction to other individuals, we may not be aware of doing so, just as we may not realize when we are reinforcing others. For instance,

	Add	Subtract	Withhold
Positive stimulus	Positive Reinforcement[a] ⬆	Response cost ⬇	Extinction ⬇
Aversive stimulus	Punishment ⬇	Negative reinforcement ⬆	Recovery[b] ⬆

The arrows indicate the direction that behavior changes: ⬆ denotes an increase, ⬇ a decrease.

[a]The distinction between the addition of a positive stimulus and the removal of a negative one is, in a sense, arbitrary. If a person is in a cold room and puts on a sweater, we can say either that the added warmth was positively reinforcing or that the subtracted cold was negatively reinforcing. The critical feature of reinforcement is that the rate of the behavior increases; not that the stimulus is positive or aversive.

[b]When a response that ordinarily produces an aversive consequence occurs without the usual detrimental effects, the response is reinforced negatively, which in turn brings about recovery of the behavior. Such a procedure is of limited utility in education.

Figure 6.1
Definition of Terms.

Mr. Rodriguez starts out a meeting with, "Did you hear the one about the dog who sat at the bar stool . . ." and his staff begins to look out the window or at their watches. "Oh, I guess you've heard it before. We'd better get on with our work." Or a relative enters with a new hair style. No one notices. The next time the family gets together, she is wearing her previous coiffure.

Yet it is certainly possible to apply extinction intentionally. You do this when you want to reduce the future frequency of a response—errors, tasteless jokes, irritating behaviors, or whatever. For example, Stanford drives his mom to distraction by whining for all sorts of costly, nonnutritious food items whenever they go grocery shopping. She has had it. Henceforth no matter how much he cajoles, she will not give in. Never, ever again. Eventually—even while it may get temporarily worse—assuming she has stuck to her guns, his whining subsides.

If you want to apply extinction to reduce responses for purposes of instruction or management, you need to know what reinforcing events are maintaining the behavior so that those events can be ter-minated. Analyzing the sequence of events can be useful in this process. Astute observers often can identify likely reinforcing contingencies, which, assuming they can be controlled, may be withheld henceforth. If the rate of the response drops as a result, the key reinforcer has been identified.

Under many circumstances, attention is a powerful reinforcer. Should your observations suggest that a problematic response is being sustained by your attention, you can plan to ignore the behavior thereafter. But if it is supported by the attention of others or by some other reinforcer, even if you totally ignore the behavior, little will be accomplished. (You will have to make sure that the others also withdraw their attention, or else you will need to try something else.) If Mr. Rodriguez amused himself with his jokes, he probably would continue to tell them despite the disinterest of his staff.

In Chapter 11, we will discuss how planned ignoring and other methods of extinction are used to reduce conduct problems. In this chapter, we emphasize the role played by extinction in *differential reinforcement* and *stimulus control*. You should recognize at this point, though, that extinction may take a while to accomplish its purpose and that it may have some troublesome side effects: that the behavior could get worse before it starts getting better; that it may be accompanied by some undesirable side effects, such as aggression and escape; and that the response may crop up unexpectedly from time to time even after you thought you had disposed of it entirely. We suspect, though, that these negative aspects are less serious in cases involving differential reinforcement, as the procedure provides opportunity for reinforcement as well as extinction.

Applying extinction

Regardless of your purposes in applying extinction, heeding a couple of basic rules will help. Most importantly, it is essential that you consistently withhold the reinforcer that is sustaining the response when it is unwanted. Also, be sure that no alternative reinforcers are supplied to the behavior at that time. If so, under those circumstances the response will be reinforced some of the time and not at other times. This intermittent reinforcement, as you already know, produces patterns of responding that are especially enduring. Had the staff occasionally smiled as Mr. Rodriguez began his stories during their meetings, he probably would have continued and would be more likely to keep on telling jokes in the future.

Using extinction in differential reinforcement

Ask yourself under precisely which circumstances the response is and is not acceptable. You need to know exactly what the different circumstances are so you can permit or encourage the response when it is supposed to happen and "place it on extinction" (in behavioral jargon) when it is not. Sonya's reading "sick" would be perfectly acceptable, and consequently reinforceable, had the printed word read "s-i-c-k" instead of "stuck." As that was not the case, her use of the incorrect label had to be eliminated.

When a response is reinforced under some circumstances and not under others we call the procedure **differential reinforcement.** Conceptually, differential reinforcement is as simple as that. Two procedures are operating: reinforcement and extinction. In practice, you may find it more complex, as your differential application of the two types of consequences requires that you be extremely vigilant and that your timing be excellent. Let us illustrate with a few examples.

Mrs. Burnes has asked George to sketch out a backdrop for the play that the class is rehearsing. Sam has offered to design advertisements for the show. George hurriedly dashes off a reasonable representation of some trees and a road. Sam labors over his sketch, finally producing a form that is just about recognizable as a house. Mrs. Burnes approaches and is ready to compliment George when she recalls that he has worked more carefully in the past and produced much higher quality work. So instead she withholds her praise and says something noncommittal: "I'm looking forward to seeing how this turns out as you continue working on it."

With Sam, her inclination is just the opposite, as his product is far more primitive than George's. But she notes that Sam has applied a few suggestions she has given him about perspective. So she compliments him on that aspect of his work. Had Mrs. Burnes failed to remind herself about the skill levels of each student, she very well might have inadvertently reinforced George's rush job and placed Sam's efforts on extinction.

Marissa seeks out Dr. Levy for some help. She knows that the psychologist is broad-minded, sympathetic, and understanding, yet she is having a difficult time describing her problems. Dr. Levy helps her by listening and watching very carefully as they chat about seemingly inconsequential things.

"I saw this old movie on TV the other night. It was so corny. First they held hands, then they kissed. Then at the end she gets pinned and you're supposed to think they get married and live happily ever after."

Dr. Levy could have responded by talking about some of the movies she had seen lately, or she could have given Marissa a lecture on how times change.

Instead, she differentially reinforced the crack in the door. "I agree. By today's standards, that does seem pretty corny. Kids today act differently, don't they?"

Marissa continued by describing how "kids in general" were acting now. Again, Dr. Levy was able to ignore irrelevant cues and pick up on key statements, reinforcing them with particular attention and thereby helping to "shape" Marissa's revelation of what concerned her.

Too much time is wasted during transitions in a number of classes at Washington Street School, so Mr. Rodriguez suggests that the teachers have all their materials and assignments arranged and that they select some reinforcing events to use when their students get to work rapidly. As he tours the building following class changes, he makes a point of stopping in at a few rooms in which he notices that students have started working right away. In each, he compliments the class and teacher. He does not visit those classes when the students take too long settling down.

Mr. Cole is determined to help all the boys and girls in his physical education classes learn to play soccer well and to enjoy it. Although it takes lots out of him, he runs along with them and shouts positive feedback at the moment he sees a player follow through according to his instructions. Meanwhile he ignores less perfect movements. Mr. Cole knows how important timing is, how immediate reinforcement works best. He also knows that it is essential that he not reinforce the improper style inadvertently. Unfortunately, using a very inefficient kick, Sam scores for his team. Regardless of what Mr. Cole says, Sam may well repeat that style of kicking, as long as it works once in a while. Remember, we cannot control all reinforcers.

Here you have seen differential reinforcement at work. When the distinctive properties of the different antecedent stimuli are clear to learners, differential reinforcement teaches them to *discriminate* one stimulus from another, for example, "sick" from "stuck." Differential reinforcement also is a key element of other more complex behavioral procedures: shaping, other forms of stimulus control, chaining, and so on. You will learn more about

some of those procedures later. At this point, let us see how differential reinforcement operates to bring behavior under the control of antecedent stimuli.

DIFFERENTIAL REINFORCEMENT AND STIMULUS CONTROL

"Mervis, see, I have a surprise for you—a cookie." The words "Mervis . . . I have a surprise for you," precede Mervis's receiving a treat. Before long, even from another room, when the boy hears, "I have a surprise for you," he approaches his mother. Because receiving a cookie has been paired with the antecedent event, his mother's invitation, the phrase acquires **discriminative control**—reliably occasioning Mervis's approaching his mother. Without her offer, he receives no cookie and he learns "no offer equals no cookie."

Much academic instruction is designed to bring students' responses under discriminative control:

"This is the letter 'i.' Say 'i.'"

"I."

"Very good. What is this letter?"

"I."

"Terrific. You can tell that this is an 'i.'"

Or, "Look at the following words: Gato, perro, pajaro. Which is the word for bird?"

"Pajaro."

"Great! You've really got it."

Note that discriminative control is acquired in the same way as the earlier example of approaching when promised a surprise: particular antecedent-response combinations are differentially reinforced. Of course, the combination of the antecedent stimulus with the response needn't be reinforced every time. But to take hold, there must be some confirmation that the combination is appropriate. Often this confirmation is delivered in the form of a nod or smile by the teacher or other students. Sometimes the teacher reinforces (negatively) by not correcting. Naturally, we would urge you *during the early phases of instruction to present immediately and regularly an effective, positive reinforcer following the selected stimulus-response combination; to differentially reinforce that combination in contrast with combinations that you would not want to strengthen. Later, you gradually could phase out the* frequency with which you had been delivering the reinforcer and introduce more natural and delayed reinforcing stimuli, such as a nod or a smile, or else just permit progression to the next task.

Summary

Several concepts were introduced in this chapter: discriminative stimuli, fading, setting events, extinction, and differential reinforcement. Each is integral to effective classroom instruction. The discriminative stimulus (S^D) occasions behavior because if the behavior occurs in the presence of the S^D it is likely to be reinforced. Artificial or intrusive S^Ds, though, like extra directions or physical guidance, need to be faded and replaced by more natural S^Ds.

Both discriminative stimuli and setting events are antecedent stimuli that influence behavior. Setting events, though, are more complex than discriminative stimuli. When they precede and/or overlap subsequent simple discriminative stimulus-response interactions, they influence in a more general way how ensuing behavior is expressed. For example, fatigue from insufficient sleep the night before could be a setting event for a student's tears after receiving a low test grade.

Differential reinforcement, a combination of extinction and reinforcement, is another very important concept. You must be able to understand and use differential reinforcement effectively to develop discriminative stimuli to teach or change behavior reliably. Now that you have been introduced to many of the basic stimulus control concepts, let us turn to the next chapter and learn how to apply stimulus control effectively.

Study Questions

1. Mrs. Berryman is concerned because Timmy frequently fails to pay attention in class. State the types of events that she needs to examine before attempting to solve Timmy's problem.
2. (a) Define and (b) provide an original example of antecedent stimulus.
3. Define discriminative stimuli.
4. The letters CAT written on the blackboard cue Sarah to say "cat." Provide three other stimuli that could also cue this response.
5. All of the following examples function as S^Ds for the class's quieting down.
   (a) Select the preferred S^D.
   (b) Justify your selection.
      (i) The teacher scolds them.
      (ii) The teacher asks them to begin working.
      (iii) The teacher asks them to be quiet.
6. (a) Define and (b) provide one example for each of the two types of S^Ds that could cue you to write your name on your quiz.
7. (a) Provide an original example of fading and (b) demonstrate your ability to define it by labeling the critical features of your example.
8. You are using delayed prompting to teach a set of words in a foreign language. Describe how you do this.

9. Compare and contrast fading and altering the quality of reinforcers.
10. (a) Define and (b) provide three examples of setting events for a behavior of your choice.
11. At a training meeting, Mr. Wang asked if setting events always needed to be present to affect the behavior. (a) Answer his question and (b) use an example to support your answer.
12. Operationally define (a) two S^Ds and (b) two setting events of your choice.
13. Mr. Santos is very busy this semester and does not want to spend time identifying the antecedent stimuli affecting his students' behavior. Discuss in detail why it is important for him to do so.
14. Define rule-governed behavior and compare it to contingency-shaped behavior.
15. The lunch bell rang and all of the students in Mrs. Berger's class closed their books and headed for lunch except for Terri. Give a behavorial description of Terri's failure to go to lunch.
16. (a) Which of the following are most important. (b) Justify your selection.
    (i) consequences
    (ii) antecedents
17. Describe how antecedent events may be utilized effectively and tell a limitation of these events.
18. Mr. Jones has established that Korine does poorly on tests she takes a few days prior to a holiday. Now that he has identified the functional antecedent stimulus for her behavior, what should he do next before instituting a program?
19. The teachers at the Green Street School noticed that many of the children did not pay attention during gym class when it was chilly. Offer two suggestions so that they will be able to manage this setting event.
20. Mr. Bowers was unsuccessful when he assigned his students to design an original experiment. Explain this failure from the perspective of stimulus control.
21. You believe that Mary fails to write her name on math quizzes because the cue "Name _____" on a math quiz does

not function as an S^D. Describe a method to determine if your assumption is correct.
22. (a) Define and (b) provide an original example of differential reinforcement.
23. When Steven made funny faces behind his teacher's back the class used to roar with laughter. However, the class has stopped laughing, since the teacher has threatened them with loss of recess. Steven has been observed to make funny faces less and less frequently.
    (a) Identify and (b) define the procedure that is operating on Steven's behavior.
24. Discuss the relation between a sequence analysis and extinction.
25. Steven's teacher is excited to discover that he no longer makes funny faces behind her back now that the class is ignoring this behavior. She has been reinforced by the success of her plan and now intends to ignore all of his inappropriate behavior.
    (a) Identify a problem with her idea.
    (b) Offer an alternative suggestion.
26. Discuss in detail the problems that could arise when using extinction with differential reinforcement.
27. Carolyn plans to begin to use extinction to help one of her colleagues refrain from making derogatory racial remarks. Provide her with a list of guidelines to ensure that she appropriately applies the procedure.
28. The two procedures operating during differential reinforcement are _____ and _____.
29. Differential reinforcement teaches people to discriminate one stimulus from another and is a key element of other more complex behavioral procedures. List three of these procedures.
30. (a) Define and (b) provide an original example of discriminative control.
31. You want the children in your class to read the word sun when they see the letters s - u - n in their books. Describe how you can ensure that the letters s - u - n gain discriminative control over their behavior.
32. Compare and contrast setting events and S^Ds.

References

Krantz, P. J., & Risley, T. R. (1977). Behavioral ecology in the classroom. In S. G. O'Leary & K. D. O'Leary (Eds.), *Classroom management: The successful use of behavior modification.* New York: Pergamon Press.

Skinner, B. F. (1974). *About behaviorism.* New York: Alfred A. Knopf.

Touchette, P. E., & Howard, J. S. (1984). Errorless learning: Reinforcement contingencies and stimulus control transfer in delayed prompting. *Journal of Applied Behavior Analysis, 17,* 175–188.

Wahler, R. G., & Fox, J. J. (1981). Setting events in applied behavior analysis: Toward a conceptual and methodological expansion. *Journal of Applied Behavior Analysis, 14,* 327–338.

7 Applying principles of stimulus control

Goals

After completing this chapter, you should be able to:

1. Define and illustrate the use of each of the following terms and procedures:
   a. Critical features
   b. Irrelevant features
   c. S^Δ
   d. Weak or incomplete stimulus control
   e. Modeling
   f. Model
   g. Imitative prompt
   h. Self-modeling
   i. Graduated guidance
   j. Progressive delay
   k. Response delay
2. Identify the S^D, response, and reinforcer from an observation of another person's behavior, your own behavior, or an illustration.
3. Explain why trial and success are emphasized rather than trial and error.
4. Explain the concept of *antecedent stimulus control*, illustrating why school rules possibly might not be followed and how this problem can be remedied.
5. List and discuss why each of the ten main steps for developing classroom and school-wide rules or conduct codes can contribute to the effectiveness of a program.
6. Identify the critical features of a concept.
7. Describe and illustrate how to use critical and irrelevant features in teaching a complex behavior or concept.
8. Differentiate between *incomplete stimulus control* and an S^Δ, with an explanation and example.
9. Identify the S^Δ, response, and reinforcer from an observation of another person's behavior, your own behavior, or an illustration.
10. Differentiate between Pavlov's conditioned stimulus and an S^D.
11. List and discuss the importance of the factors that should be considered when selecting a model.
12. List and discuss how a teacher or group leader can use prompting and reinforcement methods to enhance imitation.
13. Describe how a knowledge of stimulus control can facilitate self-management.
14. List several additional prompting strategies and describe how to use two of them.
15. Describe how to use fading effectively.
16. Discuss the pros and cons of using errorless learning strategies.

When Mr. Lee covered the topic of applying principles of stimulus control, he asked faculty members to identify from their own experience antecedent-response combinations that they wished people would learn and some that they would like to teach.

"So we can see how general this topic is, let's select examples relating to classroom management; instruction at a fundamental level, such as a simple identification task; instruction at a more complex level, for instance, an evaluative or subtle conceptual task; and everyday life."

"Let's start with everyday life," suggested Mr. Cole. "Here's one of my favorites: in the presence of a 'No Smoking' sign, people do not smoke."

Then the others joined in.

"When I'm telling about the troubles I had in school, my wife listens and responds."

"When I pass an ice cream parlor, I don't go in."

"When it's 5 o'clock, I prepare chicken, meat, or fish, two vegetables, and a salad, instead of pizza or other convenience foods."

"When I hand my child something he has requested, he says, 'Thanks.'"

"When it's 11 o'clock at night, I go to bed."

"If the posted speed limit is 55 m.p.h., I drive at less than 60 m.p.h."

"When a garbage can is available, people throw their litter into it instead of on the ground."

"When the principal, Mr. Rodriguez, visits my room, he comments on something nice that he sees going on."

The suggestions that teachers gave for discriminative stimuli they might use to manage their classes more effectively were fairly easy for them to generate.

"When rules of conduct are presented or posted, the students follow them."

"When students need to leave the room, they signal by raising their hands. Then the students don't leave until they receive permission."

"When a student begins to make me feel angry, I count to ten and practice my diaphragmatic breathing."

"Good," commented Mr. Lee. "You're identifying some S^Ds for yourselves. Can you think of any others?"

"When the students are working on assignments at their desks, I circulate and commend those working hard."

"If I want to give out a homework assignment, I write it on a transparency the night before and project it during the first five minutes of class, and then

I compliment the students who I see copying it down."

"Aha," Mr. Lee exclaimed. "You now are aware of the three essential parts of the contingency—how the antecedent-response combination is paired with reinforcement! Those last two examples show you just how it happens. How about the simple identification tasks?"

"I think I have one," said Ms. Hollingsworth, the special education teacher. "Several of my students have such severe deficits that they haven't yet mastered some of the most rudimentary skills. I'd like them to learn to label letters and numbers correctly, and to copy model letters and the stories we write together."

"Yes," Mr. Lee replied. "In each case, there is an antecedent stimulus that you'd like to have evoke a response. Now you realize that when the S^D-response combination occurs, it is very important to reinforce immediately afterward."

The other participants added a few examples of their own.

1. When a textbook asks students to solve a particular problem, they respond correctly, such as giving the right answer to the question, "What is the formula for the circumference of a circle?"
2. When they're asked to perform a particular experiment, they use the correct equipment.
3. When a ball is pitched, the students watch it instead of looking at the bat, their feet, or the other kids.

"That makes me wonder," interrupted Mr. Rodriguez. "Whatever happened to trial and error? Can't people learn to discriminate by having their wrong responses punished? That's how I learned!"

"Sure! You're raising a perfectly appropriate point," answered the counselor. "Nature often teaches us to discriminate that way. We learn not to touch a hot stove by getting burned. We learn to watch where we're going by injuring ourselves when we don't. We learn to share, take turns, and make requests politely because the members of our social groups respond negatively when we don't. Don't forget that when we talk about reinforcement, it can consist of the presentation of a positive event *or* the removal or avoidance of an aversive one. Here we've been trying to emphasize 'trial and success' instead of 'trial and error.' Can you guess why?"

"Probably for the same reason it was stressed earlier when we studied positive methods of classroom management," offered Mrs. Burnes. "So the kids will respond well. So they enjoy learning and don't experience the unpleasant side effects that often accompany punishment: escape, avoidance, fear, anxiety, and aggression. I can understand that. The other day my husband and I were playing bridge. I kept playing second hand high instead of low, and of course we'd go down. I got so frustrated, I wanted to scream. His sarcastic comments didn't help, either. For a while there I wondered what I was doing at the table and began to despise the game. It wasn't until we bid and made a slam that I started to feel better."

For a few minutes, the participants shared similar stories. They recognized that life dishes out lots of punishment for incorrect responses to particular conditions, but that when possible, it would be preferable for them to try to incorporate positive reinforcement for correct responses in their teaching. Mr. Lee added that there probably were cases in which they might want both to reinforce the proper response positively and punish the improper one. He asked for a case in point.

"In my science class," replied Ms. Thomas, "students had better learn that certain chemicals, like hydrochloric acid, need to be stored properly because they are so corrosive. That sort of mistake I *never* fail to punish. What I guess I'd better begin to concentrate on is adding positive reinforcement when they do it right. That never occurred to me before."

Ms. Hollingsworth gave a similar example. A few of her students enjoyed doing woodwork. She would plan to use the combined set of contingencies to maximize the pupils' correct use of potentially dangerous tools.

Suddenly Mr. Rodriguez spoke up. "You know, every once in a while we discuss our school rules—how they aren't followed. I'm beginning to understand why. Part of it has to do with follow-through; another part with our focus on punishment."

"Another probably has to do with the way we state and communicate the rules and the penalties for breaking them," added Ms. Jackson.

"Would we be taking you too far afield, Mr. Lee, if we spent some time on the subject?" asked the principal. "Maybe this is the right moment for us to pursue that."

"Not at all, Mr. Rodriguez. I can see that the others are just as eager as you. This will be an excellent way to apply some of the concepts we've been discussing. You know, I recently sent for a paper on developing classroom and school-wide rules and conduct codes that I heard were working very well in inner-city schools like ours. While we take our break, I'll try to dig it out of my file. Then maybe we can all take a look and try to figure out why they seem to be working. This also will help us understand how rules and other verbal antecedents affect behavior."

In the subsequent sections we will describe several frequently used categories of antecedent stimuli: verbal stimuli, such as rules, instructions, and concepts; modeling; forms of physical, visual, and sensory prompts; and how to shift stimulus control over to the antecedent stimuli that should naturally control the responses.

VERBAL ANTECEDENTS

Verbal antecedents, such as rules and instructions, are among the simpler cases of stimulus control. As you see how these stimuli acquire their controlling properties, you will find that the same processes apply to more complex forms of other verbal and nonverbal performances that are controlled by antecedents, such as conceptual learning, imitating, and responding to different prompts and cues.

Rules

The steps to follow for developing rules that effectively manage student behavior were summarized by Mr. Lee from a paper by Mayer et al. (1983). They included:

1. *Know your situation*, being sure to familiarize yourself with district policies. Assess your school to determine prevalent problems. Plan to involve all concerned parties: Administrators, staff, students, and parents.
2. *Communicate rules*. At the beginning of each school year, or in the case of transfer students, when they arrive, see to it that school and classroom rules are communicated to all pupils. Rules are better understood (as well as accepted, supported, and enforced) when *all concerned parties are represented among the developers of the codes*. Thus, yearly review by all concerned parties is recommended.
3. Whenever possible, *state each rule positively*, so students know what they *should* be doing — an instructive approach — rather than what they should *not* do, which is only suppressive. Table 7.1 displays some examples.
4. *Limit the number of classroom rules to no more than five or six, and determine that they are consonant with the school-wide policies.* Too many rules are difficult to learn, follow, and enforce. School and classroom codes must not conflict with one another. Otherwise those involved will become confused, as the two sets work at cross-purposes.
5. *Circulate a draft* of the school code to all concerned parties and seek a legal review. Revise on the basis of input and obtain administrative approval.
6. *Teach the rules to staff, students, and parents.* Staff can become familiar with the school codes in meetings and workshops. Display class rules prominently, discuss, and, if it seems appropriate for your class, role play positive and negative examples of the rules. Distribute copies to all the students and their parents. Ask parents to discuss the rules with their youngsters and return a signed form to the school to the effect that they have done so.
7. *Reinforce rule following but do not reinforce rule breaking.* If the rule is to raise one's hand for recognition before speaking, the teacher should recognize only those students who raise their hands and ignore those who speak without permission. Based on input from the students, identify and apply consistently supplementary incentives as well, both at the classroom and the school-wide level. For instance, if a whole class has abided by school rules for a certain number of weeks, you could invite them to a special assembly, party, or sporting event; or you might distribute lottery tickets to each student for a school-wide drawing. When rule following is differentially reinforced, the environment soon will cue (i.e., serve as an S^D for) students' adherence to the rules.
8. *Phase out incentives and reminders gradually.* Do this only when rule following has reached a high and consistent level of acceptability. Slowly decrease the frequency with which incentives are delivered and begin to remind the students less and less often. If you progress too quickly, you will find out about it, because the problematic behaviors will start to reemerge. Retrench and begin again.
9. *Classify infractions into two categories:* those that can be tolerated temporarily (most); and those that are definitely intolerable; that is, that present a clear danger. The former category might include daydreaming, littering, calling out, leaving one's seat without permission, or working on a nonassigned activity (playing). In the latter category you could include acts such as fighting, hitting, lighting fires, damaging property, and wielding weapons.
10. *Select consequences for infractions.* Again, with input from those concerned, identify what should be done after infractions have been committed. For minor ones, identify and reinforce the correct behavior when others express it, or wait until the student is following the rule and then reinforce. (Chapters 9 and 10 provide and illustrate a number of such constructive alternative procedures to punishment.) *Only punish major infractions.* (See Figure 7.1 and Chapters

Table 7.1
Illustrative classroom rules

Positive examples	Negative examples
(Try to state your rules like these samples.)	(Try to avoid stating rules negatively.)
1. Raise your hand before asking questions.	1. Don't talk without raising your hand.
2. Listen carefully to teachers' instructions.	2. Don't begin work until you have listened to instructions.
3. Follow directions.	3. Don't ignore directions.
4. Cooperate with your classmates.	4. Don't interfere with the work of your classmates.
5. Work on assigned tasks.	5. Don't work on anything other than assigned tasks.
6. Complete your assignments on time.	6. Don't waste time.
7. Treat others as you would like to be treated.	7. Don't be rude to your classmates or use foul language.
8. Bring books, pencil, and paper.	8. Don't forget your work materials.
9. Be in your seat before the tardy bell rings.	9. Don't be late to class.
10. Keep your hands, feet, and objects to yourself.	10. Don't touch, hit, or kick others or throw objects.

Illustrative schoolwide rules

The student will:

Follow directions.

Stay in supervised, assigned areas.

Walk when the appropriate bell rings.

Use equipment appropriately.

Use restrooms and drinking fountains for intended purposes only.

The student will refrain from:

Chewing gum on campus.

Teasing, insulting, or provoking other students.*

Bicycle or skateboard riding on campus.

Throwing food during meals.

Smoking.

Stealing.

Acting disrespectfully.*

Damaging school property.

Using or carrying drugs.

Using or carrying weapons.

These illustrative rules first appeared in Mayer et al. (1983). Items marked with an asterisk (*) would be further defined as observable behaviors.

11 and 12 for potential punitive consequences for major classroom and school-wide infractions.) Consistently and immediately use the consequence that is the most educative and least intense of those that have been demonstrated effective for that particular student's behavior.

Examine Figure 7.1 to see how "Constructive Discipline" differs from those traditional disciplinary strategies that have relied totally on punishment to reduce behaviors.

When the Washington Street School staff examined the main points from the document, they agreed that the ideas made good sense. They also were able to identify a number of the points that had been brought to their attention in workshops, such as: tailoring consequences individually, differentially reinforcing with care, emphasizing the positive, involving participants, maintaining consistency, and others.

Can you add a few more by yourself?

As he wrapped up their very productive session,

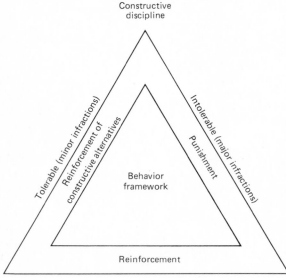

Figure 7.1
A triadic model of discipline. (*Source:* Mayer et al., 1983.)

Ms. Jackson complimented Mr. Lee for helping them so much. "Although many of us have been using many of those concepts sort of intuitively, it's really helpful to see them combined in such a meaningful and useful way. But aren't we spending an awful lot of time on management issues? You hinted that we would be learning about how stimulus control fits in with instruction. That's *my* main concern."

"And mine as well. Before we meet again, why don't all of you try to develop some illustrations of complex learning. We'll be able to use them as examples as we go along."

Complex learning

The next time they met, Mr. Lee asked for their examples of complex learning.[1] No one responded. "I guess this is a tough one. Let me try first. Maybe then you'll be able to supply some of your own," he offered.

"In 1976, Miller and Weaver were teaching an introductory psychology course at the freshman college level. Included in their syllabus were several concepts the students were to learn to identify and correctly discriminate from others. A lesson consisted of an introductory section in which the concepts were presented to the students. The instructors provided a definition along with examples of the concept from everyday behavior, plus instructions on how to identify whether or not a situation exemplified the concept. Next, 20 fictional examples of everyday situations were presented. Most illustrated the concept under study. Several did not. The task was for the students to select the examples that correctly illustrated the concept and reject those that did not.

"Some correct examples seemed to defy common sense," he went on. "For instance, to illustrate reinforcement, they included a situation in which a behavior increased in rate when it was followed by a spanking. Correct responding depended on the student's ability to identify the presence or absence of

---

[1]We return to complex learning in Part III of this text.

critical features that distinguished that concept from a different concept. **Irrelevant features** such as names, settings, behaviors, and other stimuli were varied. The items then were sampled to constitute a quiz. Correct answers were reinforced with points toward a grade, as usual. If more than 10 percent of the answers were incorrect, the student was required to do extra work and take an alternate form of the quiz," Mr. Lee concluded.

"Let's examine that illustration to see how it fits into what we've been discussing," he suggested. "First, what are the S^Ds for the concept 'reinforcement'?"

"The critical features of the concept. Probably they included the features '*a stimulus*,' '*that follows as a consequence of the response*,' and '*that increases the rate of the response*,'" ventured Ms. Hollingsworth.

"And the response?"

"That's easy. 'Labeling the concept.' You don't need to ask us for the reinforcers, because they're pretty obvious—the grades and avoiding extra work," she said.

"Now can you come up with some of your own?" asked Mr. Lee.

"I guess I do something like that when I try to teach scientific principles," Ms. Thomas said. "I want the students to be able to explain why a can collapses when we pump out the air, and things like that. The S^D is the request for the principle and the response is the correct statement. I also encourage them to give other examples, just like you're doing here."

"Yup. I guess my instructional methods here would be another example."

"I've got one," offered Mr. Cole. "I've been trying to teach my students the meaning of good sportsmanship. We defined it and gave several examples and counterexamples. Then when we see instances of good sportsmanship during group games, we try to point them out. But we also point out examples of poor sportsmanship. We haven't talked about wrong S^Ds yet, have we? We don't only reinforce the right response to a particular S^D or punish a wrong response, do we? Don't we also withhold reinforce-ment or punish the response when it follows an antecedent stimulus that should not evoke that response, even though it may be perfectly appropriate for evoking some different response?"

Identifying the S^Δ, response, and consequence

"Now you're getting the full picture," said Mr. Lee. "You surely wouldn't want your students to label name-calling as an example of good sportsmanship, but you might want them to apply the good sportsmanship label when teammates call out words of encouragement. The antecedent stimulus 'words of encouragement' should evoke the response 'good sportsmanship.' The antecedent stimulus 'name-calling' should not. The latter kind of antecedent stimulus is not called an S^D. It is, instead, an **S-delta**[2] (abbreviated like this: S^Δ). The S^Δ signals that if the target response is expressed in the presence of that stimulus, the response will *not* be reinforced. After a while the response no longer occurs when the S^Δ is presented. This happened when an inappropriate example was presented in the study on conceptual instruction we just talked about. If the example did not contain the appropriate critical features for the selected response—the label for a particular concept—the student earned no points toward the grade.

"S-deltas, then, can acquire just as much control as S^Ds," the counselor continued. "Both, given the appropriate histories, can reliably influence the behavior they precede—but in contrasting directions. The S^D will begin to *evoke* a response; the S^Δ to *suppress* it. *This is not the same as* **weak** *or* **incomplete stimulus control**—the situation that happens when the learning history hasn't reinforced sufficient pairings of the antecedent-response combination—like when a difficult concept hasn't been

---

[2]Sulzer-Azaroff and Mayer (1977) have identified three types of discriminative stimuli: S^D, S^Δ, and S^{D-}. The S^Δ acquired its discriminative properties by being paired with extinction conditions, whereas the S^{D-} acquired its by being paired with punitive consequences. Both S^Δs and S^{D-}s inhibit behavior. We have used the S^Δ here more generically to include the S^{D-}.

paired sufficiently with reinforced examples. Now, can we come up with one or two other examples of complex instruction, this time including both the concepts S^D and S^Δ together?"

"I'd love my daughter, Amanda, to learn the difference between high-quality and trite music," said Mr. Rodriguez. "I haven't been too successful, though, because all I seem to do is indicate what I consider to be dreadful by asking her to shut it off or turn it down. I guess if I want her to learn, we — or at least I — had better take a course in music appreciation so I can find out the critical features of good music. Then I can reinforce her listening when the music matches only *those* features, so those features can become S^Ds and trite music will become S^Δs."

The home economics teacher said, "I've been trying to teach my pupils how to eat more nutritiously. We've identified many of the critical features of a nutritious diet. I hope the items from the basic food groups that they see in the cafeteria displays will act as S^Ds, while junk foods will become S^Δs for eating. Although coming up with a powerful enough reinforcer to offset the intrinsic reinforcement of junk food will be quite a challenge."

"Those are both good examples," said Mr. Lee, as he passed the potato chips. "Now, before we continue, are there any questions?"

"I have one," Ms. Jackson said. "I've learned about Pavlov and his dog. The sound of a bell is paired repeatedly with meat powder, and the dog eventually learns to salivate to the sound of the bell alone. The bell is a conditioned stimulus that elicits the response. Isn't that just like an S^D?"

"In one way, yes," responded Mr. Lee. "Pavlov's conditioned stimulus and our discriminative stimulus both come before and evoke a response. But in the Pavlovian conditioning situation, the salivating response was physiological, and the original unconditioned stimulus (or UCS) was meat powder. It *elicited* the response every time. When the bell was paired with the meat powder many times, just its sound alone began to elicit salivation. The bell became a conditioned stimulus (or CS). S^Ds depend on *reinforcement* to acquire their control over behav-

ior, and the behaviors are of a different category — one that many would call 'voluntary,' but that Skinner has labeled 'operant' because the behavior 'operates' on the environment and causes it to react."

"What I want to know," asked Mrs. Burnes, "is does each student need to experience differential reinforcement in order to learn? I'm sure my students learn vicariously by watching and listening to others."

Mr. Lee replied that she was certainly correct, and what Mrs. Burnes was referring to was called **modeling.** Now let us discuss modeling in some detail.

MODELING

When we hear the word *model*, we think of an ideal figure or a form to be duplicated or imitated. The word "model" is ascribed to people who have characteristics that are exemplary in some respect: "Her ballet performances are models of grace"; "His involvement in community activities shows him to be a model citizen"; "That principal is a model of excellence." The skills and attributes of behavioral models are reinforced through approbation, esteem, respect, or even material rewards. On the job, the model worker is often rewarded with a promotion, bonus, or raise. When people are exposed to the behavior of a model, it is little wonder that the model prompts (that is, it functions as a *discriminative stimulus* for) imitation. The imitated performance also has a chance of producing reinforcement for the imitator — as when an employee notes that a coworker has been promoted, so the employee imitates the coworker's performance.

When we discuss the term model from a behavioral perspective, we recognize that the model is not necessarily always engaging in an ideal performance — only that the individual's behavior does prompt imitation from observers. And we recognize, to our distress, that under natural circumstances reinforcement is not restricted to exemplary behavior. If Fred attracts the full attention of the teacher and the class, his mischievous acts may well be repeated and imitated by others. Because modeling can prompt observers to imitate a full array of behaviors that are desired, unwanted, or neutral, you will want to learn as much as you can about how it functions.

Using modeling effectively

If an observer has only to watch another person behave in order to perform similarly, then the behavior need not be learned painstakingly, component by component. In fact, this shortcut to learning helps young children to develop skills very rapidly. They watch, listen to, and not always but often successfully mimic what their friends and elders do and say — whether good, bad, or indifferent. When they fail, it may be due to not yet having mastered the components of the complex behavior. Little Mervis, watching his playmate Frieda pulling a toy train, immediately follows her lead. But after seeing Frieda mount her tricycle and pedal away, Mervis is unable to imitate her successfully because he has not yet learned how to place his feet on the pedals or to push them in a rotating motion. If you plan to teach via modeling, you should recognize that the method only can work if the learner already can perform the components that constitute the action to be imitated.

There are other factors to consider as well. Who should be selected to serve as a model? What methods should cue imitation? How should one follow up once the model's behavior has been imitated adequately? A discussion of these factors follows.

Selecting models

Similarity. People are more likely to imitate others who share attributes with them: a physical resemblance, affiliation with the same group, similar talents or deficiencies, and so on (Kazdin, 1974; Kornhaber & Schroeder, 1975; Statland, Zander, & Natsoulas, 1961). However, the particular attributes that appear to facilitate imitation or serve as S^Ds vary among individuals. For example, physical resemblance may foster imitative behavior by Pete, but not by Jim. Friendships often are based on shared skills and interests, which could be one reason why friends tend to mimic one another in dress, social behavior, and activities. You can capitalize on this by selecting a member of a group of friends who is especially competent in the behavior to be performed as a model.

Peers who are not necessarily close to one another also may serve as perfectly effective models, especially if performers possess some overlapping qualities. Students enrolled in the same class or studying the same subject do have much in common. Perhaps that is why peer tutoring is found to be a promising instructional method. Peers successfully have taught one another all sorts of academic skills, like spelling (Dineen, Clark, & Risley, 1977) and social skills such as engaging in social play (Ragland, Kerr, & Strain, 1981). Colleagues, too, can teach each other effectively by demonstrating skills and explaining facts. In one study (Jones, Fremouw, & Carples, 1977), teachers so successfully taught their colleagues strategies of classroom management that disruption decreased in *both* their own and their colleagues' classrooms.

Self-modeling. What can you do when there doesn't seem to be a likely model around? The student may be different in so many ways from other members of a group that imitation is highly unlikely. If you have pupils with severe disabilities, you surely understand what a problem this can pose, for the skill levels of peers may be way beyond those of the student who could profit from modeling. Here is an especially clever ploy: use **self-modeling**. (Who could be more similar?)

Self-modeling works like this: the student is videotaped while performing a particular skill. The tape then is edited to remove weak performance and external prompts. Only the exemplary performance is retained. (This differentiates *self-modeling* from *self-observation*.) The taped performance then is shown to the student to prompt imitation. This method has been used to teach social skills (Hosford, 1980) and to instruct children handicapped by spina bifida how to swim (Dowrick & Dove, 1980).

Competence of model. Naturally, if you are trying to cope with problem behavior, you don't want to select models whose performance is identical to that of the learners. Rather, you would select people who share much in common with them but who are also competent to perform an acceptable alternative to the problem behavior. Suppose you were organizing a counseling group to increase socially acceptable responses to difficult situations, such as offers of drugs. You would be certain to include some peers with shared characteristics—ethnic, cultural—but who also were highly effective in avoiding pressure to abuse drugs. This concept of the importance of exposing learners to peers with more advanced competence has been used as an argument in support of mainstreaming handicapped youngsters among their more capable peers (Mann, 1975).

Prestige. When you select a model, you are much more likely to accomplish your purpose if that person holds some prestigious position within the group (Bandura, Ross, & Ross, 1963). Sometimes this is the student who tends to answer questions correctly or the youngster who has some special talent or skill, like George who can draw so well, or Sam the star basketball player, or Maria who won an award for her science project. Prestigious individuals are observed to receive reinforcers often, in the form of good grades, social approval, or material success, thereby prompting imitation by others who would like to share in those rewards.

At one time, one of us was consulting with the psychology staff of a large institution for the retarded. In several buildings on the grounds, the staff had instituted successful token programs. Residents were progressing well as a result. In other buildings, it seemed impossible to accomplish any changes in the strategies that staff used to motivate residents' learning. So it was suggested that a highly competent and popular staff member be sought to assist. Such a person was located and asked if he would be willing to accept temporary assignment in each of several buildings, to set up token economies there. He agreed. Before long, staff members of those buildings also were actively engaged in conducting the programs.

Multiple models. There may be some advantage to employing multiple models rather than just

one. Several models exert more influence than a single one (Barton & Bevirt, 1981; DeRicco & Niemann, 1980). Also, if you always select the same person as a model, the individual may become disaffiliated from the group—that is, rejected as a "teacher's pet" or some other more colorful description.

Prompting imitation

Highlighting resemblance between observers and models. You already have seen that similarity between models and observers is important. The similarities may not always be apparent, though. What you might do, in that case, is point out the resemblance between the model and the observer. You could indicate that the model enjoys the same sorts of activities, shares a common heritage, or has had similar experiences. The findings of several investigators (Bandura, 1968; Byrne, 1969; Byrne & Griffitt, 1969) support the value of emphasizing the resemblance between models and imitators. Have you noticed how commercial advertisements often use models who resemble the intended consumers, and how the ads frequently communicate this resemblance? "Mrs. Blue, a person who loves cats just the way you do, uses Farfel Cat Food."

Rehearsing behavior. Imitation will not necessarily occur spontaneously. Despite modeling to facilitate sharing, Rogers-Warren, Warren, and Baer (1977) found that preschool children did not share. Barton (1981) found the same thing when modeling was used as the sole procedure, so he then successively introduced some additional elements into the program. He conducted training sessions during which the children were told and shown how to share and then were asked to rehearse or practice sharing. That "behavioral rehearsal" or "role-playing" program did effectively promote sharing in the regular group. Once the children began to share more, their rates increased even further when they were prompted and praised for sharing in the group setting. [Behavioral rehearsal also is used frequently to teach other prosocial skills like donating (Rosenhan & White, 1967), classroom management techniques (Jones et al., 1977), and a wide array of complex performances.]

Providing rationales. Another way to prompt imitation is to offer a rationale for the behavior. This technique seems to become increasingly effective as youngsters mature (Poche, Brouwer, & Swearingen, 1981). When you provide rationales, explanations, and/or rules for governing the model's behavior, you may enhance not only imitation but also generalization and retention (Braukmann, Maloney, Fixsen, Phillips, & Wolf, 1974; Zimmerman & Rosenthal, 1974). We are applying this rule throughout the book. For example, we just provided a series of rationales for following specific procedures to promote imitation.

Maintaining simplicity of modeled performance. You also should be careful to avoid modeling a behavior that is too complex for the audience. Try to imitate operating a complicated instrument or performing a complex dance step or tennis stroke you recently have seen executed by an expert, and you will see what we mean. What you should do instead is to break down the complex performance into simpler components to be demonstrated one at a time. As each part is imitated competently, it can be joined with the next until the full pattern is smoothly executed.[3] Think what you would do if you were a counselor and were trying to teach a student, firmly but politely, how to refuse an offer to share some drugs. Undoubtedly, you'd break the response down into its parts: eye contact, gestures, tone of voice, verbal statements, and so on. Videotape machines can be especially helpful here, as they permit replay as often as necessary, and some permit the demonstration to be conducted in slow motion.

Reinforcing the behavior of the model. You have seen that under natural circumstances those people whose behavior is reinforced

[3]In Chapter 8 you'll learn more about how to break down complex behavior for more effective instruction.

tend to be imitated. Following that lead, you should try to reinforce the behaviors you would like to see imitated.

Providing consequences for imitation

Reinforcing imitative acts. By now you know that the only way to produce a durable change in behavior is to assure its consistent reinforcement intensively for a while and then, after it reaches an acceptable level, irregularly but persistently. No matter how effective your modeling techniques are in prompting a particular behavior, don't expect that behavior to maintain independently since reinforcing the model's performance is not always sufficient to promote imitation in and of itself. Barton (1981) found that when children who shared were praised, the others in the group did not necessarily copy them. Later on, though, when the latter group members did share and were praised for doing so, their rates of sharing increased. A similar discovery was made by Ollendick, Dailey, and Shapiro (1983). While working on puzzles, some children were praised; others were not. For a while the "observing" children increased their performance in the same way the models did. But after a time, the number of puzzles correctly placed by the observers began to drop back. When observers received intermittent praise for puzzle placement, though, they performed as well as the models. Perhaps over time, the coupling of the two events—reinforcing the models' *and* the observers' performance—would begin to exert some discriminative control over the children's behavior. In other words, this tactic is similar to highlighting the resemblance between the model and the observer. Both can make the conditions for reinforcement more salient.

As always, you need to examine the environment to assess whether or not the natural conditions will provide sufficient reinforcement for the behavior. If not, you need to provide supportive contingencies. Ms. Thomas knows that she will need to keep praising the other children for imitating the exemplary work habits of their peers. But some of the things they imitate will turn out to be reinforcing for the children, so she will be able to remove her extra support. For instance, if any of the students eventually matches Sam's skill in playing ball, George's in drawing, or Maria's in science, they probably will find the activities sufficiently rewarding to keep them going.

Be careful, though, about what imitative acts you reinforce. Rogers-Warren and her colleagues conducted a series of studies with preschool children, examining the relation between what children *say* and what they *do* in terms of how sharing was modeled. In one case (Rogers-Warren et al., 1977), the children were shown how to share by adult models whose *verbal* reports of sharing were reinforced. Then the children were asked if they had shared. Their reports were reinforced whether or not they were true. The children increased their reported rates of sharing, regardless of whether or not they actually had. Only when verbal reports that corresponded with what the children really had done were reinforced, did the rates of sharing increase. You may be able to promote imitation by reinforcing verbal reports of imitation, but first you must be sure that what the reporter says corresponds to what the reporter does. In the absence of accurate information on correspondence between saying and doing, we suggest that you stick to reinforcing deeds rather than words.

OTHER PROMPTING STRATEGIES

You have seen how behavior can be encouraged by means of instructions, rules, and modeling. In the first two, the prompts were verbal, and in the last, they were visual. All sorts of other prompting strategies are available for you to use as well. You select the ones that are closest to the critical S^Ds and that *do* evoke the response successfully. For instance, teachers long have utilized mnemonic devices to cue their students' recall: Rhymes ("Thirty days hath September . . ."); acronyms (UNESCO); neologisms ("mvem jsunp" is a pair of "words" we learned to help us remember the names and positions of the

planets); graphic cues such as pictures; partial answers; sounds; tastes; textures; lights; colors; physical guidance; and all sorts of combinations of these and more. You will notice that the study questions at the end of each chapter often make use of various prompting strategies to help you acquire difficult discriminations.

PROMPTING SELF-MANAGEMENT

Prompting strategies, or the principles of stimulus control, also can be used to assist students to manage their own behavior. For example, if studying at a particular time and in a special place is reinforced regularly, then after a while that ambience should begin to set the stage for studying.

That was Fox's (1962) assumption when the students in his experiment selected a room in which they would study only French. To avoid the students' pairing nonproductive study time with time in the room, they were asked to leave after completing only short translation assignments. Reinforcement was provided in the form of immediate knowledge of results and a chart on which their hourly rates of translation were plotted. Systems similar to these are used by productive fiction writers. Irving Wallace, author of *The Prize* and many other successful novels, has described his own work schedule and those of other well-known writers (Wallace, 1977). They have a separate place in which to work and set a time schedule. They also record their accomplishments, such as pages written, which presumably serves a reinforcement function.

Your students also can do something similar. They might set up a place in a certain area of the room where they perform only certain tasks. Then, they could record their own progress, and if that feedback were not sufficiently reinforcing, they could reward themselves or show their products to someone else who could verify the report and dispense immediate reinforcement. A contract could be drawn up that specifies the amount of time and the number of products to be accomplished (e.g., problems completed, questions correctly asked and answered, and so on) and the type of recording and reinforcement to be applied for the span of the contract. (Under some circumstances, you might want to find an objective source of verification, such as parallel recording by a fellow student or another person who is often in that area.) When a contract similar to this was drawn up by college students, Bristol and Sloane (1974) found that those students who had been progressing poorly in the past improved on their test performance.

If you would like to promote such a self-management program in your setting, then plan ahead to increase the likelihood that the system will work. Examine your physical arrangements. Provide contractual and self-recording forms as a means for verifying accuracy of recording and reporting. Establish a strategy for permitting students to reinforce their performance accurately, plus a mechanism for encouraging students to set challenging but achievable standards of performance for themselves. You may be pleasantly surprised by the results.

TRANSFERRING STIMULUS CONTROL

"Cues, props, prompts, models," protested Mr. Cole. "Whatever happened to spontaneity? How will my kids ever play a sport well enough to enjoy it if they are continually spoon-fed with all that help?"

"Any of you could ask the same question about your subject areas," responded Mr. Lee. "Eventually most forms of artificial support should be eliminated, leaving only the natural, critical antecedent stimuli to set the occasion for the appropriate response: the words on the page, the science and math problems, the instruction to play ball, and all the others we mentioned last time. Do you remember that we did raise this issue earlier when we first talked about control by antecedents, using the metaphor of a stage play?"

"Yes, I remember. We talked about transferring stimulus control. But how do we do it?" Mr. Rodriguez asked. "I agree with Burt Cole. We surely don't want students to become too dependent on all those

extra cues. But how do we keep performance from falling apart?"

"It is not complicated at all, but as with so many things, it does require vigilance and patience," Mr. Lee answered.

Remove prompts gradually

He proceeded to remind the group that if fading is used, it must be conducted gradually. Here is the essence of his explanation: prompts should be taken away slowly, not all at once. If you review class rules daily and the students have been following them regularly, begin to fade by reviewing the rules on alternate days, then twice and later once a week. If you use a pictorial prompt to help a pupil remember the name of a letter, then once the student consistently labels it correctly, starting with the most artificial or intrusive prompt, you should stop using the picture a bit at a time, but not completely or right away. (In Chapter 15 on reading we illustrate this method of fading.) If you have to imagine yourself at the beach in a bathing suit on a lovely warm sunny day, listening to the palm trees sighing in the wind, to prompt yourself to avoid entering an ice cream parlor, and you have followed through well as a result, begin to reduce the scope of the image a bit at a time.

Introduce progressive delay

Another way to shift or transfer stimulus control is by focusing on the time dimension. We discussed this other procedure in Chapter 6: **progressive delay** (Bradley-Johnson, Sunderman, & Johnson, 1983; Touchette, 1971; Touchette & Howard, 1984). (Sometimes the procedure is called *stimulus delay*.) Recall that what you do is to present the antecedent stimulus that is supposed to control the response, wait a few moments, then supply an artificial prompt such as telling an answer or a portion of it. Follow correct responses by repeating trials in which the presentation of the artificial S^D is delayed a little longer. Follow incorrect responses with a delay that is shortened. Eventually, what happens is that the student begins to respond before the artificial prompt is given. This is called the "moment of transfer." This procedure has been used successfully to teach normal preschoolers to discriminate easily confused letters and numbers (Bradley-Johnson et al., 1983); severely retarded children to discriminate different orientations of the letter E (Touchette, 1971) or difficult numerals, letters, and words (Touchette & Howard, 1984); mentally handicapped youngsters to follow simple motor instructions (Striefel, Bryan, & Aikins, 1974); and handicapped adults to perform practical assembly tasks (Walls, Haught, & Dowler, 1982).

Let us see how this progressive stimulus delay procedure might work in a school setting. The students in Mr. Markham's class are learning about natural resources. They have been taught that farm land is apt to be found in flat regions, well fed by water; that forests tend to be located in more mountainous areas; and other general principles. So when they are discussing the economics of a particular area, they need to know about its natural resources. During the initial work on this unit, Mr. Markham displays a map that indicates elevations and water resources. Later, he delays unrolling the map for a while; then he delays longer and longer until the students don't seem to need to refer to it at all. In a sense, we guess you could say that they have "memorized" where particular natural resources are located.

George is struggling to learn how to kick a soccer ball in a selected direction. Mr. Cole demonstrates a sequence of movements for George, and the boy imitates him. As George begins to get the hang of the movements, Mr. Cole begins counting silently — 1001, 1002, and so on — to help himself gradually increase the delay before he shows George the move once again. Before long, the student has "anticipated" his teacher and makes the correct move before the demonstration is presented.

Try graduated guidance

If you want to fade *physical guidance* gradually, you can use the **graduated guidance** technique (Foxx & Azrin, 1972). The way you go about it is gradually to remove the pressure you exert in guiding the movement. Also, you shift the locus of your

assistance further and further away from the body parts that eventually are to take over control.

The Parker family is planning to attend a neighborhood picnic and softball game. Howard, who has never been particularly proficient in sports, hopes to join in but is worried because in the past it seemed that every time he came up to bat, all he could produce was a pop fly. So he asks his brother, Richard, to help him with his swing. Richard stands behind him, places his hands and arms over Howard's and guides his brother's movements. When Richard begins to feel that Howard is swinging in the proper manner, he starts to loosen the pressure on his hands and arms. As Howard continues to practice the swing, Richard continues to reduce his hold and at the same time moves his hands to his brother's wrists; next to his lower arms; and eventually, with only the lightest touch, to his shoulders. Then he breaks contact altogether. Howard has learned to swing "errorlessly" as a result. (Naturally this would have to be followed by considerable reinforced practice and probably with a number of refresher guidance training trials, as previously established patterns tend to crop up from time to time.)

You might find this method of teaching and fading especially useful when training any of a variety of physical skills: practicing sports movements, operating shop equipment, fashioning forms in the arts or crafts studio, performing music or dance, and many others. Not that physical guidance is all that new; coaches, trainers, and teachers have used the technique throughout the ages. What *is* new is the systematic method of fading, in which the steps are so slightly graduated in size from one another that errors are not permitted to occur, and incorrect movements are not expressed; therefore, steps do not need to be corrected or unlearned.

Try response delay

There is another method of antecedent control you can use to reduce the likelihood that errors will occur: the **response delay** procedure. Very simply, what this entails is preventing the student from responding immediately by requiring a preset time delay between the S^D and the response (Dyer, Christian, & Luce, 1982). The technique was used with three residents of a facility for autistic children to teach receptive and expressive language. In two of the cases, the child was to point to an object according to its proper pronoun reference or to its function. In the third case, the child was to follow a motor instruction, such as "Raise your right hand." The response delay aspect was managed by holding the child's hand for a 3- to 5-second interval before permitting the response. For these three children at least, the delay procedure appeared to evoke better performance than the no-delay condition. The authors suggested that because having their hands held seemed to have been aversive to the children, the delay might be introduced instead, by removing the stimuli to be touched from the child's reach during the interval.

In essence, the response delay procedure is one that appears to inhibit impulsiveness by supplying an interval during which the student can overtly or covertly apply self-prompting strategies, such as verbal instructions or images. It would be as if we stopped and waited for a few moments to remind ourselves of the bidding in a hand of bridge to guess where particular cards lay before playing out the hand, or as if we covertly rehearsed the sequence of steps we should follow in preparing to taxi our plane down the runway or to execute a complex dance

routine. (Some of our best friends call those behaviors "thinking"; many of our close colleagues would label them "cognitive processing.") At any rate, the procedure is worth applying when your students tend to respond too rapidly and therefore incorrectly.

Now it is your turn to try to apply methods for transferring stimulus control. Refer back to the other examples that were posed at the beginning of the chapter. You may well find it profitable to describe to yourself, a peer, or an instructor how you would attempt to produce control by those antecedent stimuli, and how you would fade any artificial prompts.

The role of data in transferring stimulus control

The other key point about transferring stimulus control is that data on performance should serve as a guide. As you probe periodically to see how well the behavior of concern is coming under stimulus control, plot the data on a graph. A simple way to do this is to plot the number or percentage of behaviors correctly practiced without any artificial assistance. When the data consistently demonstrate the response to be near perfect, it is time to switch over to

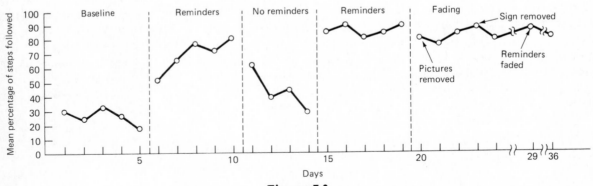

Figure 7.2

Mean percentage of steps followed by students gathering correct equipment for science projects. Note that Ms. Thomas stopped collecting data daily when the pattern had been well established.

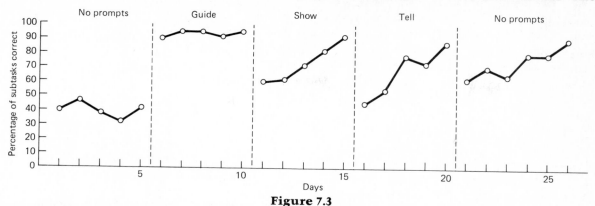

Figure 7.3

Percentage of subtasks performed correctly by Howard when swinging a bat. The steps illustrate a fading sequence from most to least intrusive prompt. Notice that Howard's performance during the "Guide" phase approaches 100 percent. This result is understandable because his coach has major control of his movements.

a fading mode. If performance deteriorates, turn back temporarily to reestablish the acceptable rate and then try again, the next time more gingerly. Observe in Figure 7.2 what happened when Ms. Thomas worked on teaching her students to gather the correct equipment, helping them first by reminding them daily and posting a sign with instructions and pictures. Then note how performance deteriorated when she stopped all three aids at once, what happened when she replaced them, and finally what resulted when she removed the reminders one at a time.

If you anticipate that your students will learn the selected antecedent-behavior combination very slowly, we suggest that you plot performance as a function of prompt level. That will help all of you to see the bits of progress as they occur and to decide when to fade each category of prompt. In Figure 7.3, we show how Howard learns to swing a bat. First he is guided physically. Next his brother models the swing for him, a less intrusive prompt. Next he only uses verbal reminders. Ultimately, Howard swings pretty well with no extra help at all. The subtle progress he was making probably would be lost on you without your own very useful aid — a graph. (We do not recommend that you fade using graphs to assist your educational decision making. They

bring to light information that may be obscured in casual observation, given the practical limitations on our time and efforts.)

To prompt or not to prompt?

It would be appropriate for you, at this point, to ask whether it is really preferable to block the occurrence of errors by using prompts prior to the response instead of permitting errors to occur and then correcting them. You would have a point in posing this question, as prompting and fading do take imagination, time, and effort. Also, our students do need to learn perseverance in the face of failure. All we can say is that if it is very important that a response be performed without error, the errorless method is preferred. So you might invest your resources in using an errorless approach to teach surgical procedures, operation of dangerous equipment (i.e., a drill press), performance under hazardous conditions (driving on ice or flying through clouds), and work with expensive materials that could be destroyed when handled improperly (as may occur when cutting a diamond). We also recommend that you use errorless procedures to teach correct responses that repeatedly have been expressed incorrectly in the past, as in the case of Howard's batting form and with students who have lengthy histories of failure. Using prompts to prevent errors also is useful particularly for long and difficult tasks, in contrast to short and simple ones (Haught, Walls, & Crist, 1984). Remember that what is easy or difficult depends on the skills of the individual and should not be judged on the basis of what we presume would be easy or difficult for us.

Summary

We have looked at a variety of applications of stimulus control principles as they relate to following rules and instructions; teaching concepts; using modeling and other prompts; and managing one's own behavior. We then showed how artificial prompts are withdrawn by fading them gradually to shift control from artificial to critical antecedent stimuli. These are not always easy tasks for educators. Thus, a number of practical techniques and illustrations were presented in each section.

To illustrate using stimulus control to promote good conduct in school, we listed ten steps for you to follow to increase the likelihood of students following directions and rules. We also recommend yearly review once an effective behavior code has been established. That would help ensure continuing student and staff involvement, as well as permitting accommodation to differences in the school population and environment that might occur over time.

To teach complex concepts, the first step involves identifying and teaching students the critical features that you want to become the controlling S^Ds. Then, when you have presented the key aspects to the students, you give a number of examples, discussing how each correctly or incorrectly illustrates the complex concept and why. Finally, the students need to practice identifying examples that correctly illustrate the concept and rejecting those that do not. You should be sure to follow each correct response with immediate reinforcement during the early phases of learning, and then gradually reduce the frequency of reinforcement as the students become proficient in identifying or behaving in accordance with the concept.

A second type of discriminative stimulus was introduced in order to permit you to fully understand complex learning: the S^Δ. In contrast to the S^D, which occasions behavior, the S^Δ suppresses behavior. When the S^Δ is present, it signals that if the behavior occurs it is not likely to be reinforced, as when the incorrect response is not reinforced in complex learning and differential reinforcement.

Modeling was introduced as another specific stimulus control procedure. It is used to teach many classes of behavior. We discussed a variety of factors that can influence the likelihood that a model's behavior will function as an S^D to evoke imitation. We showed how an appropriate model is selected, how imitation may be cued, and how you should follow up once the model's behavior has been imitated.

A knowledge of stimulus control also can be used to teach people how to achieve more control over their own behaviors, such as completing assigned work and showing initiative. Several strategies for promoting self-management were presented.

We closed the chapter with a discussion of when and how to fade intrusive or artificial S^Ds, such as those that frequently are introduced to teach complex concepts and skills. Several techniques were provided for accomplishing this end, such as stimulus and response delays and graduated guidance. We also illustrated and discussed the pros and cons of using errorless learning strategies. However, our illustrations of fading and other stimulus control concepts do not end here. Because they are integral to classroom instruction and behavior management, you will encounter additional illustrations throughout most of the remaining chapters. Thus, be sure you have mastered these concepts before progressing further.

Study Questions

1. List the three basic parts of a contingency.
2. Describe why learning by trial and success is preferred to learning by trial and error.
3. (a) Provide original examples of two situations in which punishment would be acceptable. (b) Justify your selection.
4. (a) Identify and (b) briefly summarize the steps to follow for developing rules that effectively manage student behavior.
5. Provide three rules for the lunch area that are examples of constructive discipline.
6. The Washington Street School staff identified a number of important points to remember. List five of these points.
7. (a) Write a sample quiz question. Identify (b) the critical features and (c) the irrelevant features of your example.
8. (a) Define and (b) identify the S^Ds for the concept *extinction*.
9. When her friend rolled the ball to Kerry, Kerry kicked it. Identify (a) the S^D and (b) the response.
10. Define *S-delta*.
11. Compare and contrast the control exerted by S^Ds and S^Δs.
12. Sue believes that Pavlov's *conditioned stimulus* (C.S.) and Skinner's *discriminative stimulus* are exactly the same. How would you explain to her the differences between them?
13. Define modeling.
14. (a) Provide an example of a model whose behavior you have imitated. (b) Discuss possible reasons why you imitated that person's behavior.
15. Tim pokes Sally in the back as his friends cheer him on.
    (a) Could Tim's performance serve as a model?
    (b) Support your answer.
16. Sally watched her older brother write her name in cursive writing. She tried to imitate his behavior, but was unsuccessful. Provide a possible explanation for her failure.
17. You want to learn a new sport.
    (a) Select a person to model the behavior and (b) identify the similarities between yourself and that person.
    (c) Explain why those similarities are important.
18. (a) Provide three situations that would be ideal for self-modeling. (b) Describe why you would prefer self-modeling to standard modeling in those situations.
19. Illustrate how you could use self-modeling to teach a child effectively how to ask to join a group of peers playing a game.
20. Mr. Kelsey will be selecting models for his gym class. Offer him some guidelines for selecting models that possess the appropriate levels of competence.
21. Discuss the relation between prestige and modeling.
22. List the advantages of using multiple models.
23. Tom will model baseball throwing for Harry. Harry has never met Tom before and seems somewhat intimidated by Tom's superb throwing. Offer a suggestion to the coach that could increase the likelihood of imitation.

24. Sarah modeled sharing, yet the class did not spontaneously imitate the behavior. Provide a possible explanation and a suggestion for improving the situation.
25. List the advantages of providing rationales for the desired behavior.
26. Break down the behavior of putting on a coat into small components so it can be imitated more easily.
27. Discuss in detail the effects of reinforcing the desired behavior when using modeling. (Be sure to refer to both the model and the imitator.)
28. Describe the correct method of reinforcing imitative acts.
29. Identify the problems found by Rogers-Warren et al., when they reinforced verbal reports of sharing.
30. List original examples of three prompting strategies.
31. Describe in detail how a desk can become an S^D for studying.
32. Sue wants to promote a self-management program in her class so her students will increase the amount of time they study. Discuss how she can plan ahead to increase the likelihood that her system will work.
33. Define fading.
34. Describe the appropriate method of fading prompts.
35. (a) Define and (b) provide an original example of *progressive delay*.
36. Define *moment of transfer*.
37. (a) Identify and (b) describe the procedure used to fade physical guidance gradually.
38. (a) Provide an original example and (b) label the critical features of the response delay procedure.
39. Under what circumstance should you not fade the use of graphs?
40. Under what circumstances is errorless learning most appropriate?
41. State one potential disadvantage of errorless learning.

References

Bandura, A. (1968). Social-learning theory of identificatory processes. In D. A. Goslin & D. C. Glass (Eds.), *Handbook of socialization theory and research*. Chicago, IL: Rand McNally.

Bandura, A., Ross, D., & Ross, S. A. (1963). Imitation of film-mediated aggressive models. *Journal of Abnormal and Social Psychology, 66*, 3–11.

Barton, E. J. (1981). Developing sharing: An analysis of modeling and other behavioral techniques. *Behavior Modification, 5*, 386–398.

Barton, E. J., & Bevirt, J. (1981). Generalization of sharing across groups: Assessment of group composition with preschool children. *Behavior Modification, 5*, 503–522.

Bradley-Johnson, S., Sunderman, P., & Johnson, C. M. (1983). Comparison of delayed prompting and fading for teaching preschoolers easily confused letters and numbers. *Journal of School Psychology, 21*, 327–335.

Braukmann, C. J., Maloney, D. M., Fixsen, D. L., Phillips, E. L., & Wolf, M. M. (1974). An analysis of a selection interview training package for predelinquents at achievement place. *Criminal Justice and Behavior, 1*, 30–42.

Bristol, M. M., & Sloane, H. N., Jr. (1974). Effects of contingency contracting on study rate and test performance. *Journal of Applied Behavior Analysis, 7*, 271–285.

Byrne, B. (1969). Attitudes and attraction. In L. Berkowitz (Ed.), *Advances in experimental social psychology*. Vol. 4. New York: Academic Press.

Byrne, B., & Griffitt, W. (1969). Similarity and awareness of similarity of personality characteristics as determinants of attraction. *Journal of Experimental Research in Personality, 3*, 179–186.

DeRicco, D. A., & Niemann, J. E. (1980). In vivo effects of peer modeling on drinking rate. *Journal of Applied Behavior Analysis, 13*, 149–152.

Dineen, J. P., Clark, H. B., & Risley, T. R. (1977). Peer tutoring among elementary students: Educational benefits to the tutor. *Journal of Applied Behavior Analysis, 10*, 231–238.

Dowrick, P. W., & Dove, C. (1980). The use of self-modeling to improve the swimming performance of spina bifida children. *Journal of Applied Behavior Analysis, 13*, 51–56.

Dyer, K., Christian, W. P., & Luce, S. C. (1982). The role of response delay in improving the discrimination performance of autistic children. *Journal of Applied Behavior Analysis, 15,* 231–240.

Fox, L. (1962). Effecting the use of efficient study habits. *Journal of Mathematics, 1,* 75–86.

Foxx, R. M., & Azrin, N. H. (1972). Restitution: A method of eliminating aggressive-disruptive behavior of retarded and brain damaged patients. *Behaviour Research and Therapy, 10,* 15–27.

Haught, P., Walls, R. T., & Crist, K. (1984). Placement of prompts, length of task, and level of retardation in learning complex assembly tasks. *American Journal of Mental Deficiency, 89,* 60–66.

Hosford, R. E. (1980). Self-as-a-model: A cognitive social learning technique. *The Counseling Psychologist, 9,* 45–61.

Jones, F. H., Fremouw, W., & Carples, S. (1977). Pyramid training of elementary school teachers to use a classroom management "skill package." *Journal of Applied Behavior Analysis, 10,* 239–253.

Kazdin, A. (1974). Covert modeling, model similarity, and reduction of avoidance behavior. *Behavior Therapy, 5,* 325–340.

Kornhaber, R., & Schroeder, H. (1975). Importance of model similarity and extinction of avoidance behavior in children. *Journal of Clinical and Consulting Psychology, 43,* 601–607.

Mann, P. H. (Ed.) (1975). *Mainstream special education: Issues and perspectives in urban centers.* (USOE Project No. CEG-O-72-3999 [609]). Reston, VA: Council for Exceptional Children.

Mayer, G. R., Butterworth, T. W., Spaulding, H. L., Hollingsworth, P., Amorim, M., Caldwell-McElroy, C., Nafpaktitis, M., & Perez-Osorio, X. (1983). *Constructive discipline: Building a climate for learning.* (Available from the Office of the Los Angeles County Superintendent of Schools, 9300 East Imperial Highway, Downey, CA 90242.)

Miller, L. K., & Weaver, F. H. (1976). A behavioral technology for producing concept formation in university students. *Journal of Applied Behavior Analysis, 9,* 289–300.

Ollendick, T. H., Dailey, D., & Shapiro, E. S. (1983). Vicarious reinforcement: Expected and unexpected effects. *Journal of Applied Behavior Analysis, 16,* 485–491.

Poche, C., Brouwer, R., & Swearingen, M. (1981). Teaching self-protection to young children. *Journal of Applied Behavior Analysis, 14,* 169–176.

Ragland, E. U., Kerr, M. M., & Strain, P. S. (1981). Social play with children: A study of the effects of teacher-mediated peer feedback. *Behavior Modification, 5,* 347–359.

Rogers-Warren, A., Warren, S. F., & Baer, D. M. (1977). A component analysis: Modeling, self-reporting, and reinforcement of self-reporting in the development of sharing. *Behavior Modification, 1,* 307–322.

Rosenhan, D., & White, G. M. (1967). Observation and rehearsal as determinants of prosocial behavior. *Journal of Personality and Social Psychology, 5,* 424–431.

Statland, E., Zander, A., & Natsoulas, T. (1961). The generalization of interpersonal similarity. *Journal of Abnormal and Social Psychology, 62,* 250–256.

Striefel, S., Bryan, K. S., & Aikins, D. A. (1974). Transfer of stimulus control from motor to verbal stimuli. *Journal of Applied Behavior Analysis, 7,* 123–135.

Sulzer-Azaroff, B., & Mayer, G. R. (1977). *Applying behavior analysis procedures with children and youth.* New York: Holt, Rinehart and Winston.

Touchette, P. E. (1971). Transfer of stimulus control: Measuring the moment of transfer. *Journal of the Experimental Analysis of Behavior, 15,* 347–354.

Touchette, P. E., & Howard, J. S. (1984). Errorless learning: Reinforcement contingencies and stimulus control transfer in delayed prompting. *Journal of Applied Behavior Analysis, 17,* 175–188.

Wallace, I. (1977). Self-control techniques of famous novelists. *Journal of Applied Behavior Analysis, 10,* 515–525.

Walls, R. T., Haught, P., & Dowler, D. L. (1982). Moments of transfer of stimulus control in practical assembly tasks. *American Journal of Mental Deficiency, 87,* 309–315.

Zimmerman, B. J., & Rosenthal, T. L. (1974). Observational learning of rule-governed behavior by children. *Psychological Bulletin, 81,* 29–42.

8 Instructional strategies: chaining and shaping

Goals

After completing this chapter, you should be able to:

1. Define and give an illustration of each of the following terms:
   a. Response repertoire
   b. Chaining
   c. Backward chaining
   d. Shaping
   e. Successive approximation
   f. Differential reinforcement of high rates (DRH)
2. Describe and illustrate the dual function and the important ramifications of a chain's components.
3. Describe and illustrate how to use chaining effectively.
4. Describe and illustrate how to use shaping effectively.
5. List and illustrate four different ways of shaping behavior.
6. List the six criteria to guide you in setting up a shaping program.

The mantle of smog that ordinarily hung over the city had lifted and was replaced by a crisp Indian summer day. Ms. Hollingsworth's class had been behaving especially well for the previous day or two, and she decided to take them over to the park to play. One of the primary objectives for her special class was to teach the students to interact positively with one another; a second was to enable them to acquire skills that would permit them to participate with their contemporaries in "regular" classes. Learning to play team sports like softball, touch football, and soccer seemed to meet both requirements. So Ms. Hollingsworth planned to use this time to teach her pupils how to play softball. She would show them how to pitch a ball, hit it, and run from one base to another, using the knowledge she had gained recently via in-service training. All she would have to do was prompt the correct responses by means of instructions or demonstrations, or if necessary, by guiding their movements and then slowly fading those prompts until the response was executed adequately. This process worked pretty well when she taught the group how to run around the bases. Pitching, hitting, and catching the ball were another story altogether. No matter how well the teacher told or showed them how to perform, none of the students except Tyrone and Lisa seemed to be able to connect, and those two already played regularly. Not knowing what to do next, Ms. Hollingsworth brought up her problem at the next in-service meeting. Mr. Lee received her inquiry with interest.

"That's an excellent example to use for this next section on instruction," he said. "Today we'll be discussing what to do when a response simply hasn't been learned; when no amount of careful differential reinforcement helps, because the behavior is absent from the person's **repertoire** of responses—

you know, those things the person has already learned to do. For instance, you could tell me, show me, or even guide my hands to the proper buttons on the control panel of an airplane, but that wouldn't enable me to pilot it, because I don't possess the requisite skills. Sure, some of the operations are a matter of bringing my responses under stimulus control — I do, after all, know how to push a button, so all I'd need to learn there would be when to do it. But when it comes to a complicated performance, like maneuvering the flaps, I'd have to learn the response itself."

He continued, "Complex performances of the kinds we've been discussing, that are missing from the repertoire and need to be learned, can be taught in one of two basic ways: either by shaping or chaining, depending on a number of other factors. But before going into that, let's generate a few other examples of the kinds of behaviors we're talking about. Who can identify a behavior that is absent from someone's repertoire; so stimulus control procedures, by themselves, wouldn't be sufficient?"

"One I can think of," said Ms. Thomas, "is Juan's approaching the other children in a friendly way and asking them to play. I don't think I've ever seen him smile or make eye contact with the others. I doubt he can do it."

"That's a good one. You'll see how social skills like those have been taught when we study that topic later on. How about some academic performances?"

The teachers volunteered a number of examples:

"Handwriting — both manuscript and cursive. Some of my students can't even hold a pencil properly, much less form the letters correctly."

"Using the card catalogue."

"Reading words of more than one syllable."

"Following multiple instructions — either those I give, or those in their workbooks or on activity sheets."

"Conversing in a foreign language. They can say individual words, read, and write them, but conversing aloud is a lost cause."

"Basic arithmetic, like long division, multiplication with two or more digits, and so on."

"Participating in group discussions during my social studies class."

"Writing a critical paper. All they seem to do is regurgitate the book."

Mr. Lee responded, "Those are all illustrations you might keep in mind as we're summarizing the general approach to teaching via shaping and chaining. Soon afterward, we'll review how others have used those procedures separately or combined with stimulus control techniques to enhance academic performance."

CHAINING

Chaining is a procedure that is designed to link together behaviors that the individual already can do separately into a smooth, unitary, complex performance. Using the author card catalogue in the library is an example of a complex behavior that we usually must teach formally. The first steps in teaching such a complex behavior are to list each behavior that is involved and to make sure that the students can perform the component behaviors that will link together to form the complex behavior, namely:

1. Going to the library.
2. Locating the card catalogue.
3. Using the alphabet to find the section containing the first letter of the last name of the author whose work they're seeking.
4. Using the alphabet to locate the cards corresponding to the particular author.
5. Finding the card for the author containing the book title they're seeking.
6. Reading the card and copying down its code number.
7. Matching the number with numbers posted on the sides of the shelves.
8. Finding the shelf that should include the code number.
9. Following the numerical sequence on the backs of the books until the specific book is located.

What is the reinforcer in this sequence of responses? Locating the book. All the other components of the chain of responses help the person get there by serving two functions: reinforcing progress—"You've completed one more step"—and cuing or producing stimuli that prompt the next response (Thvedt, Zane, & Walls, 1984)—"Let's see. Here's the section for authors whose last names begin with the letter H; next I use the alphabet to find H-E." If you want to use technical language to describe these dual functions of the components of a chain, you could say, *"Each link functions as a conditioned reinforcer for the previous link and as a discriminative stimulus for the subsequent one."*

This dual function of the members or links in the chain that constitute a complex behavior have some important ramifications for instructional effectiveness. We already have discussed how the immediacy of consequences influences the effectiveness with which the response is reinforced. The more immediate the consequence, the better, at least in the initial stages of reinforcement. If you examine the sequence of simpler responses in the chain "using the author card catalogue," you will see that some occur very close in time to the reinforcer—"finding the correct shelf"—and some are quite remote—"going to the library" or "locating the card catalogue." Which of the component responses will be reinforced most optimally? "Locating the shelf," because, assuming the book is on the shelf, that act will be reinforced more immediately than the preceding ones.

We also have learned earlier that when an event frequently accompanies reinforcement, that event begins to acquire reinforcing characteristics of its own. Because locating the shelf is often paired with finding the book, locating the correct shelf begins to be reinforcing; and it reinforces the previous link, matching the numbers on the sides of the shelf. As the chain of responses is practiced repeatedly, links earlier and earlier in the chain become reinforcing. Eventually, each response is reinforced by the next, and the sequence begins to be expressed as a single cohesive unit. Thus, if the student engages in any behaviors between any link that are not part of the desired chain, the desired complex behavior has not

occurred. For example, if the student went to the wrong floor after going to the library, then the correct chain was not established fully. Similarly, if Mrs. Burnes wants her students to come in from recess, walk to their seats, sit down and attend, but Lucinda, after sitting down, talks to a neighbor rather than attending, then the desired chain has not been established. *The sequence must be expressed as a single cohesive unit.*

Using chaining effectively

You might ask a couple of questions about the best way to use chaining to teach a complex behavior, like doing long division or participating in a group discussion. Should you teach all parts of the chain at once or a few at a time? If you do teach a few at a time, with which do you begin?

At this point, the evidence seems to weigh in favor of teaching a few of the components at a time (the *part* method) rather than the full sequence at once (the *whole* method), at least when the chain consists of many links and the students have problematic learning histories. A group of mildly and moderately retarded adults were being evaluated regarding their potential for vocational rehabilitation (Walls, Zane, & Ellis, 1981). They were to assemble three different apparatuses—a carburetor, a bicycle brake, and a meat grinder. The clients were trained to assemble by the *whole* method with one apparatus: step one, followed by step two, followed by step three, and so on until all steps were followed. They were taught by the *part* method with another apparatus: steps one and two were performed in sequence until learned; then steps one, two, and three were performed until smooth; and so on until all the steps were learned. When taught by the *whole* method, clients made many more errors than when the links of the chain were added one by one.

We would guess, in the absence of extensive evidence, that relatively simple chains—those consisting of only a few links—are acquired just as well by the *whole* as by the *part* method, as Blake and Williams (1969) found with paired associate learning. If your student seems to be experiencing difficulty acquiring a fairly complicated skill composed of many responses, however, then you should try the *part* method.

Do you always start with the first two links in the chain when using the part method? Is there perhaps a better place? You *could* begin with links in the middle or at the end. How do you decide? As always, you probably will want to capitalize on opportunities for early reinforcement. That could mean that you would begin with the *last* two links in the chain, because latter links are closest to the reinforcer. In fact, it is just that sort of **backward chaining** that has been used to teach handicapped learners skills that are highly complex for them, such as tying their shoes, dressing themselves, and so on.[1]

If some of the component responses seem to be "intrinsically reinforcing" (i.e., in a sense, rewarding for their own sake) for the student, you also might consider starting there. Ms. Hollingsworth noticed that her students really seemed to enjoy running and tossing the ball back and forth. She decided to begin her instruction with those responses, right in the middle of the chain that constitutes "playing softball." Unfortunately, any recommendations we may offer here are speculative because little research has examined this issue.

Although backward chaining seems to be a promising approach, Walls et al. (1981) compared backward and forward chaining (within another phase of the study that we discussed above) and found that the clients made no more mistakes with forward than with backward chaining. If you are deciding where to begin, ask yourself how likely it is for your students to be able to sustain their performance under any of the various arrangements, and try out those that appear most promising. If one doesn't work, then try another. At any rate, be sure to provide adequate reinforcement as the segments link up — praise or whatever else is effective with those students. Reinforce at the end of the two-, then at the end of the three-, then at the end of the four-component sequence, and so on. Eventually when the full sequence is thoroughly acquired, the natural reinforcer — solving the problem correctly, getting the book, winning the game, carrying on a conversation, and so on — should begin to sustain the complex behavior, and you slowly can dispense with the intermediate reinforcement you've used along the way.

Just as you can supplement with reinforcers during the chaining process, you also can use prompts ["salient enough to be discriminated" (p. 667), suggest Thvedt et al., 1984] to help occasion the segments of the response, so that they are expressed in the appropriate order. These prompts can be in the form of verbal instructions, demonstrations, pictorial representations, or physical guidance, among others. "Remember! Hold the bat at this angle. Watch the ball. Swing and follow through when it reaches this point." If you show or say the instructions sufficiently often, learners may begin to cue their own responses by repeating the instructions to themselves covertly. (Didn't you do the same sort of thing when you first learned to drive a car, or swing at a golf ball, or serve in tennis?) You then fade those discriminative stimuli as each component smoothly links up with those adjoining. Here fading can be tricky. You don't want to prompt so long that the students become overly dependent on the prompt — like needing to consult a cookbook every time they boil an egg or referring to the manual while driving. Nor do you want to fade too quickly, so that the sequence disintegrates — as when all instructions are removed simultaneously and major components begin to be omitted[2] or expressed in the wrong order (first swinging the bat, then watching the ball). Of course, a different type of prompt (e.g., "Now let's combine the two, watching the ball *and* swinging.") also can lend temporary support. Once the full com-

---

[1] Marc Gold has produced a series of training films that illustrate the use of backward chaining to teach self-help skills to the retarded.

[2] An example familiar to us is training in an industrial task. Trainees often are shown the full operating sequence, including those links specifically designed for safety. Then they are turned loose. Often the links that serve a safety function, such as donning protective clothing or turning off equipment before cleaning or servicing it, are omitted by novices, unless they are prompted to include those components via peer examples or by means of specific prompts plus reinforcement for complying with the prompts.

plex sequence is performed correctly as a unit, make sure it is reinforced optimally and then try to speed up the rate with which it is expressed. Differentially reinforce the behavior whenever the time to express it shortens.[3]

Review

Before progressing any further, pause to synthesize what you've learned about chaining and see if you can apply it. Pretend you are a participant in the in-service program conducted by Mr. Lee. He asks you to take one of the complex skills that the members listed and, in a manner similar to analyzing a task, to break it down into the series of components that form the response chain. Now describe the steps you would follow in teaching that chain. Tell what links you would teach first and why. Plan how you might supplement with intermediary reinforcers and discriminative stimuli. Then add the system you will follow for gradually removing those supplementary aids. If you have an instructor or peer who is studying this material, ask that person to provide you with feedback about your plan. Of course, the best way to assess any plan is to try it out, comparing it with some standard procedure to see which does a better job of training skills of comparable complexity and difficulty.

SHAPING

Mr. Rodriguez had been thinking about what Mr. Lee said about instruction, and the principal wondered if he might be able to apply the principles of chaining in his supervisory activities. Impressed by

[3]Sometimes people express unwanted chains, such as a series of accelerating emotional responses that ultimately terminates in a crescendo of aggression, or a sequence of components that leads to a self-abusive act or a seizure. Often careful observation will reveal the early segments of the chain. What you do to prevent the behavior is to break the chain as *early* as possible by interrupting, restraining, or if necessary punishing those initial segments. See Zlutnick, Mayville, and Moffat (1975) for an example of the modification of seizure disorders, and Fellner, La Roche, and Sulzer-Azaroff (1984) for an illustration of the reduction of self-stimulatory behaviors using this technique.

reports of the effectiveness of a highly formalized system of teaching at the elementary level called *direct instruction* (Becker & Carnine, 1981), he hoped his junior high school staff would be able to apply the main features of *direct instruction* in their own teaching: to *beat the clock* (or to *teach more in less time*) and to *control the details of what happens*. Specifically, teachers would need to:

1. Follow a very carefully organized and detailed sequence of instruction.
2. When appropriate, teach skillfully in small groups.
3. Be able to evoke unison responses.
4. Use signals to encourage all students to participate.
5. Pace presentations quickly.
6. Apply specific techniques for correcting and preventing errors (graphing errors, giving the correct answer in discrimination tasks, prompting the student to apply a multistep strategy, and others).
7. Use praise.

"If all I had to do would be to drop by from time to time and compliment their use of *direct instruction*, it would be easy to improve their teaching skills," Mr. Rodriguez decided. But before long, he recognized that this would be premature.

First, the system was rather sophisticated; and second, he was not certain that the teachers could express all the necessary component responses. To confirm his suspicions, he visited several classes, observing how staff members paced their instruction, whether or not they praised, how they corrected errors and how much detail they used to organize their instruction. As he had anticipated, they varied considerably. Ms. Jackson kept up a lively pace and her students remained highly attentive. Another teacher's pacing was erratic; sometimes there were long pauses during which she hunted for materials or seemed to be thinking about how to explain a concept. Having had extensive training and supervision in the use of praise, most teachers did apply it at least occasionally. No one asked his or her students to graph errors, and only a few used signals to cue responses.

"Teaching the use of signals should be relatively easy," the principal decided. "I can demonstrate how it's done correctly in class, let the teacher try, and then reinforce successful attempts. Afterward, I could provide feedback intermittently, a fairly uncomplicated discrimination learning procedure. But some of those others—rapid pacing, techniques for correcting errors—they're so complicated that even a chaining procedure probably would be insufficient. Some teachers may not even know how to draw graphs themselves." He decided that he would have to find out what to do when a person was not able to perform a particular response.

In fact, that was the topic of the next in-service training session: how to shape new responses. Again, various examples were offered—this time responses that needed to be taught from scratch:

- Holding a pencil; forming letters correctly.
- Participating in a group discussion.
- Writing a critical paper.
- Recording errors.
- Making friends and sharing and demonstrating other social skills.
- Comprehending textual passages.

The list continued to grow to such an extent that Mr. Lee called a halt. "The important thing to remember is that the shaping procedure can be applied to each of those types of behaviors, sometimes by itself, sometimes in combination with other techniques."

He explained how shaping was quite simple to describe although not always so easy to apply. "To shape, you find a behavior that the person *can* do that resembles as closely as possible the response to be taught, and you reinforce it as it changes successively, to make it more and more closely resemble the response you're trying to teach. It's as if you're trying to form an irregular piece of clay into a well-proportioned and finely finished object; little by little, you work at the task until it successively begins to resemble what you're trying to achieve. Recall how Carmen changed in the skill with which she performed Maria's role in *West Side Story?* She started out reciting her lines woodenly, but little by

little, the director kept congratulating her each time she improved, and we all know how terrific the final product was. This shaping method is called the method of *reinforcing successive approximations* because each time the response successively approximates the response to be ultimately achieved, it is reinforced."

Maloney and Hopkins (1973) used a shaping procedure to teach creative writing to elementary school children in grades four through six. Approximations were broken down into four steps: establishing a baseline and then writing an increased number of different adjectives, action verbs, and beginnings. They used a game format to reinforce each step. The students were divided into teams, and members of the team that produced the greatest number of items in a particular category won extra recess time and a treat. If both teams exceeded a preset level, both teams won. Data showed that as production within each category was reinforced, its rate increased. At the end of the study, the children's writing samples were shown to two independent raters. In general, the raters judged the third composition, the one with high numbers of action verbs, as most creative. Similarly, Glover and Gary (1976) taught eight fourth- and fifth-grade children a set of key categories of creative responses that have been identified by experts specializing in general creativity: number of different responses, *fluency;* number of verb forms, *flexibility;* number of words per response, *elaboration;* and statistical infrequency of response forms, *originality.* The task assigned the children was to list all the possible uses of an object, and responses fitting within those categories were sequentially reinforced in a manner similar to that used by Maloney and Hopkins (1973). Again responses in each category increased as a result. The students had taken the Torrance test of creativity (Torrance, 1966) at the start of the program. When they took it again at the end, their scores increased considerably. In both cases, component responses were shaped and chained into a highly complex response class labeled "creative performance."

Teaching a child how to make friends would be virtually no different. You would need to find out what the critical components are, and reinforce those responses as they grow to resemble each component more and more closely. If approaching a peer, making eye contact, smiling, and offering to share a toy were identified as the components, you would help the child learn each of those responses by practicing them, perhaps in a role-playing or game situation. Each response that changed slightly in the desired direction then would be reinforced. (In Chapter 18 on teaching social skills, you will see more examples of this kind.)

Using shaping effectively

Combine with stimulus control. There is no reason why you cannot combine stimulus control procedures with both your shaping and chaining instruction. Holding a pencil properly could be taught that way. First you could model or physically guide the approximation and gradually fade the guidance by shifting the locus of your assistance away from the body part to be moved and reducing the intensity of your movements as the approximation began to be expressed more and more independently [Foxx and Azrin (1972) have labeled this method *graduated guidance*, as we described in Chapter 7]. This technique has been used to teach all sorts of self-help and other motor skills. Parents often guide their children's learning of new skills that way—walking, riding a bike, swinging a racket or bat, brushing teeth, and so on—and so do teachers and coaches. The best results occur when approximations are reinforced with optimal effectiveness.

Selecting appropriate approximations. You will want to watch out for several pitfalls with shaping, however. One relates to the size of the steps or approximations that are selected for reinforcement. What step sizes constitute progress in comprehending reading? Would such steps as answering one additional question correctly each day suffice? The answer, of course, depends on the level of difficulty and the number of questions. Under some circumstances, for some children, that would be a reasonable schedule; for others it wouldn't. Mr. Rodriguez recognizes that his faculty is bright and mo-

tivated. He might be misled into thinking that they could grasp and apply all the key elements of *direct instruction* following one exposure to the topic. A much more reasonable approach would be to shape bit by bit, commenting positively each time he observed more of the elements being practiced in the classroom.

Steps that are too large to manage are one issue. Another issue is steps that are too small. Howard could master a mathematical concept the first time he read or heard about it. Fortunately, his teachers were sensitive to his ability to progress rapidly through large chunks of material. Had they insisted that he practice the same drills that his classmates did, he might have found math very boring and turned away from it. If your students progress at different rates, some needing to have each approximation broken down into smaller approximations and others able to combine tasks, you really need to assign tasks to match their capabilities if you want to maximize success and enthusiasm and minimize failure or boredom.

If misconduct is a problem in your setting, it could well be related inadvertently to the level of difficulty of the instructional materials. Center, Deitz, and Kaufman (1982) studied this issue. Fifteen students were assigned math problems that either matched or were mismatched with the students' levels of ability. When the problems were too difficult, the students tended to misbehave to a much greater extent than when they were capable of completing the assignments successfully. Similarly, another study (Mayer, Nafpaktitis, & Butterworth, 1985) found that the assignment of instructional materials that were inappropriately matched to the students' reading levels was related to school vandalism. These are only two of several studies that support the fact that students tend to misbehave more when their work assignments are too difficult for them. We might be tempted to dismiss these findings as so self-evident as to be unworthy of mention. Yet, tailoring assignments to individual capabilities is the exception rather than the rule in many classrooms in the United States. Consider, for example, how often student misconduct is addressed as a target first, rather than subsequent to a rearrangement of curricula to match the individual capabilities of each student.

Reinforce improvement, not the status quo. Another potential problem is to reinforce an approximation too heavily, so that the progress terminates there rather than at the goal. (Of course, you do want to reinforce the goal behavior heavily when it is reached, just not the approximations.) Some of Wanda's gymnastics movements are superb, and a great fuss is made every time she performs one. Other aspects of her routine are only slightly better than mediocre, however. The amount of reinforcement she gets for the expert movements are sufficient to reinforce the entire routine as it is practiced. Poor Wanda. She may never win a competition, unless some strategies for avoiding that situation are instituted (e.g., eliminating the expert movements from her routine temporarily).

Louie is just learning to write. He proudly brings his paper home to his mom, and she exclaims, "How wonderful. You've written, 'Dear Mom, I love you.'" Mom can read his writing and so can Louie. Louie writes better than some of the other students so his teacher continually praises his work, even though it stops improving. Louie could run the risk of writing like that from then on, at least while he is in that particular class. Some instructional programs in handwriting incorporate principles of behavioral instruction (e.g., *Write and See*, Skinner & Krakower, 1968). One of the big advantages of such programs is that they are designed to require ever-increasing improvement in quality of performance.

Now you should be able to describe how shaping is optimally conducted: start where individuals are currently performing, and reinforce changes that more and more closely resemble the behavior to be learned. You recognize that the step size differs for different individuals. For some, a giant step is manageable; for others it must be much less demanding. Then you reinforce just enough so the step is expressed more often than any other more distantly related to the goal, after which you move on as before. In case you reach a snag and seem unable to help

the student to progress to the next level, untangle the snag by breaking that particular step into smaller components, and proceed as before. When the goal behavior is reached, repeatedly reinforce it according to the guidelines described in Chapter 5 so that it will become firmly established.

Additional methods of shaping behavior

Notice that in most of the examples we have provided, the change has been in the form or **topography** of the response. The form of the response was continually altered until it looked a certain way (for instance, the correct swing of the bat), or different elements were added (e.g., the set of skills that composed creative writing, and so on). It is possible to follow the very same protocol to establish other aspects of performance as well. Panyan (1980)[4] lists four additional **dimensions of behavior** that can be shaped, besides changing the *form* of the response successfully. Other dimensions of the response may be altered: *lengthening the response or series of responses* (duration), as in increasing the time a student spends on task; *reducing the time to respond* (latency), as in the length of time it takes for a student to solve a particular problem; *expressing the same response more frequently* (rate), as in increasing the number of lines written within a set time period [this variation is commonly referred to as a distinct procedure called *differential reinforcement of high rates* (DRH)—see Sulzer-Azaroff & Mayer (1977) for further elaboration of DRH]; *changing the force of the response* (intensity), as in the force with which a softball is propelled. In each case, reinforcement would be reserved for changes in the desired direction—steps toward longer and longer series of responses, toward shorter and shorter latencies, toward higher and higher rates, toward greater and greater force. The starting place and the size or magnitude of the change required would follow the same principles as described above: you

---

[4]Panyan (1980) describes how to use shaping in considerable detail, including recording and prompting methods.

would start where the individual is currently functioning and proceed in steps appropriate to the capabilities of that person.

Ms. Hollingsworth is trying to teach Tom how to hit the softball. He has learned the form of the response through reinforcement of successive approximations of his motions. He even knows how to connect with the ball. Now he has to spend more time practicing hitting. Starting from the 5 minutes of hitting practice, the duration he spends practicing before his teacher praises his efforts is increased by half-minute intervals every 3 practice days. Sometimes he swings too late. Swinging with the optimal latency is reinforced naturally by his connecting properly with the ball, although this too can be manipulated by the speed with which the ball is pitched. Reinforcement of rates of hitting can be modified slowly to require more and more hits within a given time period. To shape intensity, concentric arcs could be drawn across the infield and outfield, and reinforcement delivered contingent upon the ball reaching ever-increasing distances. Tom will have a good chance of improving if his teacher follows the principles for effective shaping we have outlined above. Can you describe how she should apply those principles?

As you can see, we are dealing with some rather complicated subject matter. It would be difficult for anyone to keep track of each of the many categories indicated for each individual student. Ms. Hollingsworth probably would need to use some record-keeping system to remind herself and the students where to start each session. The students could help, too, by recording their own and each other's successes and failures. For topography, she could use a checklist that cited each component: angle of bat, starting position over shoulder, plane of swing, and so on. The catcher could rate the item aloud and another student check the move on a chart. Latency might be measured by using a stopwatch activated when the ball left the pitcher's hand and stopped when the swing started. The seconds then would be recorded by the observer. Hits within a time period would be measured by running the stopwatch for a fixed time period and recording the number of hits within that period. For intensity, the distance traversed by the ball could be measured and recorded.

Sounds like a lot of effort, doesn't it? If you agree, you should be recognizing that we need to shape our own behavior as well. Ms. Hollingsworth probably shouldn't try to record everything at once, unless she and the students who will cooperate in recording are already proficient data collectors. Rather, she should select one skill to record and begin herself; then after the system has been refined and simplified, the other students could be trained. Other categories can always be added later on in successive approximations.

Use the same principles described above to shape any especially challenging performance of your own or of staff you may be supervising, whether for a classroom management or an instructional goal. This admonition may be the most difficult for you to follow in this text. You may be tempted to rush out and try everything at once, but that is not likely to work too well. Instead, set some criteria for selecting your first actual attempt and allow those criteria to guide where you start. Achieve your first success, and then move on to the next. Here are some illustrative criteria:

1. How likely am I to succeed? (We too learn best by trial and success.)
2. How close is my current performance to the goal?
3. How critical is the goal? (Will it remove danger or severe discomfort, avoid major failure?)
4. How extensive will the improvement be? (Will many benefit?)
5. Will others support the change?
6. How much effort is involved?

Summary

Chaining and shaping are two procedures used to teach new behaviors. They are both integral to the instructional process. Chaining is used to combine simple behaviors that the individual already can do separately into

a single cohesive unit. Shaping is conducted by reinforcing successive approximations of a behavior until the desired performance ultimately is achieved.

Chaining is designed to teach complex behavior, consisting of multiple components. It is used most effectively when you teach a few of the components at a time, rather than the full sequence at once, unless the chain only contains a few links. Also, when possible, you can teach the chain, or complex behavior, by starting at the end, rather than at the beginning. The latter links are closest to the reinforcer.

Shaping stresses reinforcement for improvement, not for the status quo. It also stresses the importance of selecting appropriate approximations. Inappropriately selected approximations can handicap appropriate skill acquisition and can result in student misconduct. Thus, because chaining and shaping are instructional procedures that all teachers must use, we strongly recommend that every educator become skilled in their *effective* use.

Study Questions

1. (a) Identify and (b) define two basic ways to teach a behavior not already in a person's repertoire.
2. Susan wants to use chaining to teach her younger brother to put on his coat. List the first two steps she needs to complete.
3. (Refer to question 2.)
   (a) Identify the reinforcer for the sequence of responses.
   (b) State the two functions of the other components of the chain.
4. Discuss in detail the important implications the dual function of the links has for instructional effectiveness.
5. Harry can successfully perform each link in the chain, yet his teacher notices that he has not completed the chain successfully. Provide one possible reason.
6. (a) Compare and contrast the whole and part method of chaining, and (b) discuss the circumstances best suited for each method.
7. Mr. Baker understands how to use chaining appropriately but has never heard of backward chaining before. Use an example to explain this procedure to him.
8. Discuss in detail the controversy over the appropriate component at which to begin a chain. Be sure to consider the findings of Walls et al., (1981).
9. Mike wants to be sure to use reinforcement properly during chaining. Explain in detail the appropriate way for him to do this.
10. Identify four types of prompts that could help to occasion the segments during chaining.
11. Describe the appropriate way to fade prompts during chaining. (Be sure to include problems that may arise if they are not faded properly.)
12. For the science fair, Bill tried to teach Sarah to build a model of a heart. He used chaining, as the behavior was not in her repertoire. However, after 3 weeks of failure, he was advised to use shaping as well. State two reasons why he might have been given that advice.
13. Identify four behaviors that could be taught by shaping.
14. (a) Another name for shaping is the method of _____.
    (b) Explain why shaping is often called the name that you provided in part (a).
15. Describe in detail the steps you would need to take to teach a child how to make friends.
16. State the problems that will arise if successive approximations are (a) too small or (b) too large.
17. Identify a behavioral procedure that can be combined with both shaping and chaining.
18. Provide an original example of graduated guidance.

19. Mr. McCracken's students are usually well behaved. However, many conduct problems arise during math class. Discuss in detail possible reasons for the problems.
20. Use an original example to illustrate the problems that can be caused by reinforcing the status quo rather than reinforcing improvement.
21. Kelly is going to use shaping to teach one of her peers to paddle a canoe. Provide her with a set of guidelines to ensure that her shaping procedure is conducted optimally.
22. Monica always focuses on topography when she uses shaping. Identify four other dimensions of behavior that she could change with shaping.
23. (Refer to question 22.) For each of the dimensions, provide a system for measuring the target behavior.
24. (a) Which procedure, shaping or chaining, is designed to teach more complex behavior? (b) Justify your selection.
25. Provide an original example of shaping.
26. Describe how you might shape your own use of effective classroom management practices.
27. Compare and contrast the types of behaviors best suited for shaping and chaining.

References

Becker, W. C., & Carnine, D. W. (1981). Direct instruction: A behavior theory model for comprehensive educational intervention with the disadvantaged. In S. W. Bijou & R. Ruiz (Eds.), *Behavior Modification: Contributions to education.* Hillsdale, N J: Lawrence Erlbaum Associates.

Blake, K. A., & Williams, C. L. (1969). Retarded normal and superior subjects' learning of paired associates by whole and parts methods. *Psychological Reports, 25,* 819–824.

Center, D. B., Deitz, S. M., & Kaufman, M. E. (1982). Student ability, task difficulty, and inappropriate classroom behavior. *Behavior Modification, 6,* 335–374.

Fellner, D. J., La Roche, M., & Sulzer-Azaroff, B. (1984). The effects of adding interruption to differential reinforcement on targetted and novel self-stimulatory behaviors. *Journal of Behavior Therapy and Experimental Psychiatry, 6,* 33–51.

Foxx, R. M., & Azrin, N. H. (1972). Restitution: A method of eliminating aggressive-disruptive behaviour of retarded and brain damaged patients. *Behaviour Research and Therapy, 10,* 15–27.

Glover, J., & Gary, A. L. (1976). Procedures to increase some aspects of creativity. *Journal of Applied Behavior Analysis, 9,* 79–84.

Maloney, K. B., & Hopkins, B. L. (1973). The modification of sentence structure and its relationship to subjective judgments of creativity in writing. *Journal of Applied Behavior Analysis, 6,* 425–433.

Mayer, G. R., Nafpaktitis, M., & Butterworth, T. (1985). *A search for the elusive contingencies of school vandalism. A correlation study.* Manuscript submitted for publication.

Panyan, M. P. (1980). *How to use shaping.* Lawrence, KS: H. & H. Enterprises, Inc.

Skinner, B. F., & Krakower, S. A. (1968). *Handwriting with write and see.* Chicago, IL: Lyons & Carnahan.

Sulzer-Azaroff, B., & Mayer, G. R. (1977). *Applying behavior analysis with children and youth.* New York: Holt, Rinehart and Winston.

Thvedt, J. E., Zane, T., & Walls, R. T. (1984). Stimulus functions in response chaining. *American Journal of Mental Deficiency, 88,* 661–667.

Torrance, E P. (1966). *Torrance tests of creative thinking.* Princeton, NJ: Personnel Press.

Walls, R. T., Zane, T., & Ellis, W. D. (1981). Forward and backward chaining and whole task methods. *Behavior Modification, 5,* 61–74.

Zlutnick, S., Mayville, W. J., & Moffat, S. (1975). Modification of seizure disorders: The interruption of behavioral chains. *Journal of Behavior Analysis, 8,* 1–12.

9 Reinforcing alternative behaviors: a constructive substitute for punishment

Goals

After completing this chapter, you should be able to:

1. Define and give an illustration of each of the following terms:
   a. Reinforcement of incompatible behaviors (Alt-R or DRI)
   b. Punishment
2. Explain how the *slot machine* or *activity table* may be used in an Alt-R procedure.
3. Identify four reasons why punishment tends to be overused.
4. List eight disadvantages of using punishment and give an example of each in the school setting.
5. Present a case for using constructive strategies such as an Alt-R.
6. Describe the disadvantages of using an Alt-R procedure.
7. Explain what must be done in order to use Alt-R effectively.
8. Describe a situation in which you have seen an Alt-R used.

The school was typical of many others in small towns in the midwestern United States.[1] The students came from varied socioeconomic backgrounds. Some were children of second- or third-generation welfare recipients, while others had middle-class and professional parents. This particular fifth-grade class was not unusual in that respect; but in another sense, it was distinctive. The students completed few academic assignments, and many were both disruptive and aggressive. The reputation of the class rapidly was becoming so notorious that even the better-behaved members of the class were avoided during recess. Yet if you watched casually, you realized none appeared to be markedly handicapped. Most had reasonable vocabularies and could solve practi-

cal problems. They could be quite ingenious in plotting escapades, and they demonstrated at least one spectacular accomplishment—they were never ignored!

The teacher of the class had volunteered for the job. Having had many years of successful experience, she felt confident that she could help these children to improve academically. But by the time several weeks had passed, she began to realize that this situation was different from any in her experience. Despite her skill in teaching academic material, she could not persuade this group to get down to work; nor could she control disruption to her satisfaction. When a behavioral consultant from a local university offered assistance, the teacher and school principal readily accepted.

Measures of social and academic performance verified that the students in this class did disrupt often and produced little. A decision had to be made: what

---

[1]Based on a study by Sulzer, Hunt, Ashby, Koniarski, and Krams (1971).

141

behaviors should be targeted for change? Many possibilities were considered:

- Reducing disruptive performance such as being out of seat, making loud noises, or hitting and teasing other children.
- Reducing off-task behavior — that is, any failure to engage in assigned classroom activities.
- Increasing the teacher's rate of attending to on-task performance (sufficient literature already had shown the efficacy of attention by teachers when systematically delivered following desirable behavior).
- Focusing directly on increasing academic productivity.

Which one do you think was selected?

Several of the alternatives were discarded fairly early. The teacher felt that if all she did was to concentrate on reducing disruption or off-task behavior by punishing her students, as many of her colleagues did, the pupils might indeed remain seated and appear to be in contact with the academic materials, but their learning would not necessarily be assured. Helping the teacher to redistribute her attention also was eliminated as a goal, because data had been collected that showed that she already paid attention to students while they were engaged in their assigned activities.

Suppose academic productivity were selected? It was reasoned that if the students began to work harder and more effectively and efficiently, they would have less time for getting into trouble; also, if they began to improve in their academic performance, the teacher would have many more opportunities to comment positively on those accomplishments. Success might even encourage those youngsters to begin to feel better about themselves and their abilities (a phenomenon later verified by Scheirer & Kraut, 1979).

That was the strategy adopted, because it was important that each individual achieve a reasonable degree of success. However, each also was tested individually to determine the levels at which he or she could read and spell well. Standardized achievement tests were administered first to obtain a gross pre-

measure; then assignments were designed, based on the levels at which students showed they could succeed. The instructional materials selected were programmed, in the sense that brief questions or tasks were presented and students were required to write an answer and check its correctness right away. After observing progress for a couple of weeks, the teacher began to deliver points for each correctly completed item, provided that overall performance was over 90 percent and that students had used the instructional program properly, without being observed to peek ahead for the correct answer. The points could be exchanged for prizes or special activities such as local trips, games, songs, musical activities, and so on.

The system worked; students took to it with enthusiasm. In fact, before long, they were working so busily that there was no more time to get into mischief. Probably because they were succeeding, they became less aggressive. The teacher had many more opportunities to praise their accomplishments, and it was apparent that they began to feel more satisfied with themselves. Finally, objective data indicated increases in academic productivity and decreases in disruptiveness, and the results of the standardized achievement tests administered at the end of the year were markedly better than in previous years.

Recently, a similar program was observed at an alternative junior high school for students whose maladaptive social or emotional behaviors had caused them to be separated from their own neighborhood schools. For these youngsters, free time in a recreation room equipped with a pool table and games seemed to be a fairly powerful reinforcer. During the initial phases of the program, students could spend time in the recreation room following a half-hour of on-task behavior. If they committed specific infractions, however, they were isolated briefly from the group. Although a reasonable classroom environment was maintained, students were showing little in the way of sorely needed academic gains. Academic performance then was added to the previous requirements. The students continued to earn periodic access to recreational activities, but it was granted on the conditions of keeping on-task and completing their assignments acceptably. Again, disruption and inappropriate emotional behavior remained minimal, but academic performance began to improve as well.

In another study (Weidenman, 1980), a 4-year-old girl had been placed in a special preschool class designed to enable children with special needs eventually to join their nonhandicapped contemporaries' classes—to be mainstreamed. She was a cheerful, attractive child but extraordinarily shy. In fact, over several weeks, no one had seen her talk spontaneously or play with the other children. The child's parents and school authorities were concerned because extreme social isolation often is paired with later social and emotional difficulties. In this case, an increase in social interaction rather than a decrease in social isolation was targeted for change. Arrangements were made to promote social interaction under the most comfortable circumstances. A game was designed for the child to play with a peer, under the guidance of an adult. The task was to take turns either describing pictures or holding pictures for the partner to describe. A successful response—any reasonably accurate verbal descriptions—permitted the child to advance a marker on a game board. When the marker reached particular boxes, the participant would earn a colored paper sticker. The comfortable arrangement of the situation and the delight the youngsters took in playing was apparently sufficient to encourage the little girl to begin to communicate with her partner. Fortunately, she began to sustain the communication beyond the game situation, into free play time, and after several months her social interactions were not discernably different from those of the other children.

REINFORCEMENT OF INCOMPATIBLE BEHAVIORS— DIFFERENTIAL REINFORCEMENT OF ALTERNATIVE (ALT-R) OR INCOMPATIBLE (DRI) BEHAVIORS

Take a moment to reflect on the various procedures used in these cases. You will notice some common aspects. In each case, a number of alternative behaviors were available for targeting. These, both unwanted and desired, were clearly specified. Possibly the most tempting and obvious next step would have been to try to change those behaviors that were most troublesome. Instead, a careful search helped identify those behaviors that would be positive and constructive; and even more importantly for our purposes here, behaviors were identified that could not coexist with the undesired ones. (A student who is working hard to complete his or her reading assignment is not engaging in off-task behavior, distracting peers, interfering with the classroom routine, and so on.) But to *ensure* the *incompatibility* of the targeted behavior with the noxious one, data were collected on both.

The targeted behaviors were treated just as any of the others that needed reinforcement. Reinforcers appropriate to each individual were delivered consistently, immediately, and in a quantity sufficient to promote an increase in the behaviors. (Severely noxious behaviors were not necessarily ignored altogether. Those considered dangerous or seriously disruptive were punished.) As always, the students were helped to sharpen their ability to discriminate the conditions under which reinforcement and any other planned consequences would be forthcoming, by being given clear rules for acceptable and nonacceptable performance. As a result, two aims were accomplished. The irritating behaviors diminished, and productive performance increased. **Alt-R (reinforcement of alternative behaviors),** then, *is a procedure designed to reduce a particular behavior by reinforcing a competing behavior as an alternative to the original one.* In these cases, the teachers were using Alt-R very effectively.

At this point, convinced by the logic of the Alt-R procedure, you may be wondering why this method is not applied as a matter of course. The procedure makes sense. It accomplishes two purposes at once and sounds as if it might be just as rewarding for staff as for students. (In our experience that certainly has been the case.) Yet so often teachers turn to punitive methods. Evidence from a survey by the American Association of School Administrators (Brodinsky, 1980), for instance, indicates that school systems have invested more time and energy in implementing punitive than preventive measures to deal with student misbehavior. Why does this happen? What kinds of reactions do those methods produce, and what can be done to change the situation?

Why punishment is used frequently

An inventory of our own reactions to irritating events in our lives probably will yield instances in which we have resorted to **punishment**—if not in the classroom, then surely within our family or community setting. We may be tired and not feeling up to par in the first place, and then a series of things go wrong: the washing machine breaks down and soapy water pours all over the floor; the baby breaks a piece of our best crystal; the dog has chewed up a favorite hand-embroidered pillow; and the kids come home from school demanding that they be chauffeured downtown for new band uniforms that cost too much. Somewhere along the way, we find ourselves beginning to lose control—snapping, growling, scolding, maybe even striking out, and what is worse, enjoying this behavior for the moment at least. The guilt and confusion come later. Why do we permit ourselves to let go? What a terrible example to set for the children! Will we ever be forgiven?

The fact is that aggression is a predictable reaction to punishment, as it is to nonreinforcement (i.e., *extinction*). Several researchers (e.g., Azrin & Holz, 1966) have found that laboratory animals actually will work for the opportunity to injure another creature when they themselves have been hurt or their regularly scheduled reinforcers have failed to be delivered. It is likely that when we experience aversive events, such as breaking a treasured object or losing a close companion, or when we are assaulted by a series of irritating circumstances, we react in the same way.[2]

Using punishment also can be rewarding in another way. In direct contrast to reinforcement, *punishment*, as you will recall from Chapter 4, *involves the delivery of an aversive stimulus* (rather than a reinforcing one) *that is presented as a consequence of a given behavior, resulting in the subsequent decrease* (instead of increase) *in the rate of the behavior.* Intense punishment, delivered immediately and consistently, under circumstances that can be discerned readily by the performer, eventually can reduce or possibly suppress a behavior completely. Punishment that is not used so optimally still may provide a brief reprieve from the noxious behavior. What sort of a condition has been arranged? A noxious behavior is followed by punishment. The noxious behavior stops, ergo, negative reinforcement for using punishment! We already have learned that regardless of whether the operation results in the presentation of a positive stimulus or in the removal of a negative one, reinforcement is reinforcement—the behavior on which it is contingent will tend to *increase in rate.* In the present instance, punishment therefore will tend to be used more often. So blowing up at the kids when they make unreasonable requests will be reinforced, provided that the requests are terminated for a while. What is apt to happen the next time? Blowing up has been reinforced. It probably will be repeated.

Teachers are no different from anyone else. Punitive strategies like expelling, isolating, and shouting at students and informing the authorities as a way of treating student offenses produce immediate reinforcement. After the teacher shouts, "Shut up," the students immediately become quiet. When the disrupting student is expelled or isolated in another room, he or she no longer causes irritation. Each such punitive act brings immediate results and relief (or reinforcement) to those administering the punishment. The misbehavior stops. Because punishment produces rapid results, the teacher is likely to use it again and again. It comes as no surprise, then, that research has shown that many teachers rely increasingly on such strategies for classroom control

---

[2]Here is a case in which it would be difficult, from an ethical perspective, to test this hypothesis. Rightly so, human rights committees would be up in arms at the notion of conducting experiments that involved systematically delivering painful stimuli to human subjects. Yet, undoubtedly you can see how important it is that we understand those factors that lead to aggression.

(Brodinsky, 1980; Heller & White, 1975; Thomas, Presland, Grant, & Glynn, 1978; White, 1975). For example, Thomas et al. (1978) concluded that teachers tend to disapprove three times more frequently than they approve.

Besides its potentially reinforcing properties, another reason for the widespread use of punishment, according to Brodinsky (1980), is the belief of many educators that "a student's misbehavior is usually willful and always entirely the student's fault" (p. 6). A harsh reality for many educators to accept is that many student behavior problems are evoked inadvertently by the actions of teachers, peers, and other educators rather than arising spontaneously from within the student. Numerous studies have shown us that teachers unintentionally can teach students to engage in disruptive activities by attending to those activities (Anderson, 1964; Ebner, 1967; Hall, Lund, & Jackson, 1968; Solomon & Wahler, 1973). Similarly, families may reinforce deviant behavior. Patterson, Ray, and Shaw (1968) found that families attended to such behavior an average of 30 percent of the time.

It is a well-established fact that specific behaviors change as a function of their environmental antecedents and consequences. Changes in curriculum, rules, consequences, and other aspects of the environment of the school can produce changes in student behavior. Thus, we must shift our emphasis from blaming and punishing the student to analyzing and changing the school environment.

A final reason why punishment is used as often as it is can be attributed to a lack of familiarity with more constructive alternative strategies, a point contended by Homer and Peterson (1980), MacMillan, Forness, and Trumbull (1973), and Woods (1974). Teachers may turn to punishment because it is the method with which they are best acquainted. This contention is supported by the fact that Rust and Kinnard (1983) found that teachers' use of corporal punishment correlated with their own experiencing of corporal punishment as young students. Yet, when it is the only tool used to manage classroom behavior, the long-range outcomes may well be counterproductive, for a punishment procedure has some potentially serious disadvantages.

Disadvantages of punishment

Certainly punishment often is applied in our society deliberately. We incarcerate criminals, levy fines and speeding tickets, and give demerits for infractions. But it takes an all-too-familiar example, losing our tempers, to dramatize some of punishment's disadvantages. In our rage we attempt to inflict pain (literally or figuratively), as our body physiology adjusts to permit us to fight or flee. We are aroused; our muscles become tense and our internal organs begin to alter their functioning. Sometimes this can produce a stomach ache, heart palpitations, or other uncomfortable sensations; but for the moment we may simply feel good, as our behavior is reinforced in the manner we described earlier. But that pleasure is often short lived as a learned barrage of self-blame succeeds the prior aggression. We are uncomfortable that we have relinquished control to our emotions — and for being at the mercy of our own unfortunate reinforcement histories.

The punisher is not the only one to react. Those who are punished also are affected. If punishment is sufficiently harsh (intense, noxious, immediate, and so on), the ongoing behavior of those punished will stop. They, too, may experience the same physical effects we do, but our social relationship also is disrupted temporarily. With the cessation of the punished behavior, other behavior stops too: conversation, pleasant activities, task performance, and so on. Fight-or-flight reactions may not be restricted to the internal organs; they actually may occur. The victims may become aggressive, or, when they lack sufficient control to be counteraggressive, they literally or figuratively may flee. Victims who experience defeat may shift over to blaming themselves. Further, if such punishment occurs often, it may begin to lose its effect. The person whose behavior we have been punishing gets used to or adapts to the punishment. The irritating behavior no longer terminates. So one of two things happens: we try some other technique that has worked in the past, or we increase the intensity of the punishment. In the latter case, actual violence may eventually occur, and we all are familiar with *its* negative aspects!

How does this translate to the school situation?

The principal criticizes the teacher's ability to manage her classes. As a result, the teacher becomes angry at the principal, perhaps sufficiently so that she feels justified in taking off a few days. If that happens often enough, she may decide to quit. What forms does the fight-or-flight response take among students? Violence, vandalism, disruption, noncompliance, rudeness, tardiness, absence, tuning out, and other forms of active or passive resistance. We don't mean to suggest that it is only the schools that are responsible for all of those distressing student reactions to excessive punitiveness. Punishment may occur at home or in the neighborhood, and its effects felt in school. Those same behaviors may be provoked by conditions other than punishment—response to the termination of reinforcement, imitation of peers' aggression or escape, or the experience of prior reinforcement for those acts. What we do wish to do is to alert you to the possibility that many of the most troublesome behaviors of students, as well as of educators, might just be traceable to an overemphasis on the use of punitive methods of management.[3]

The research literature is beginning to document cases in which punishment has been found to be related to some of the problems we have just identified. In one case (Boren & Coleman, 1970), the imposition of fines was found to be paired with an increase in absenteeism. In another with which we are intimately familiar (Mayer, Butterworth, Nafpaktitis, & Sulzer-Azaroff, 1983), average vandalism costs diminished in 23 schools as teachers, instead of punishing, increased their rates of praising and using other positive consequences for students' productive classroom behavior. Perhaps similar relations will be found between pupil truancy or tardiness, and staff absenteeism or burnout.

One more critical disadvantage to resorting to punishment too frequently is that the practice inadvertently may teach others to use it as well. Those in authority, such as principals and teachers, are often very prestigious. (No wonder. They are in charge of so many reinforcers that are powerful with teachers and students: salaries, promotions, job and assignment schedules, personnel reports, grades, the quality of the social environment, and so many others.) Many studies (e.g., Bandura, Ross, & Ross, 1963; Bandura, 1965) have shown that the behavior of prestigious individuals tends to be imitated. So if school principals or teachers are likely to lose their tempers, it would not be surprising to find that those they supervise also begin to show signs of doing likewise. In the area of child abuse, recent findings that abusing parents were often themselves abused as children (Conger, 1982) provide some indirect verification of these conclusions.

Notice we have not said that punishment does not work as a management tool. It does, when properly used. Nor have we contended that punishment should never be used. There are times when no alternatives are reasonably appropriate—in cases of imminent danger, severe disruption, or when other methods have been tried repeatedly and found ineffective. (But in the latter case, we would argue that it is the responsibility of the schools to teach their students systematically to respond to positive methods. See the section in Chapter 5 on turning neutral stimuli into reinforcers for ways this might be accomplished.) What we have tried to emphasize is that punishment may do more harm than good. In the long run, it could cause people to punish more often and to harm themselves and their victims by injuring them, if the punishment is physical, or by impairing social relationships and promoting aggression or escape, self-blame, imitative aggression, and other harmful side effects.

WHY USE CONSTRUCTIVE STRATEGIES?

Using punishment to escape from a distressing situation is quite understandable, as the previous discussion has shown. Selecting positive constructive alternatives requires much more advance planning and patience. We cannot await a noxious event and deal with it on the spot as with punishment. Instead, we

---

[3]Does it strike you as ironic, as it does us, that while physical discipline of children by parents is considered child abuse, a crime in many locales, the same action by educators under the label of "corporal punishment" is broadly condoned—if not encouraged—in the vast majority of states in the United States?

need to identify the behaviors to be increased and to arrange the events that are to precede and follow them, which means extra effort.

Is it worth it? We think so, for several reasons. The first, and most obvious, reason is that teaching is our business. By focusing on constructive performance, we help our students to acquire new knowledge and skills, as appropriate. Second, positive reinforcement makes learning pleasurable. Pleasant events follow progress, enhancing the school environment for students and teachers. It is much nicer to hear kind things about one's accomplishments than criticisms about one's failings. This positive attitude toward the school also may have some more tangible payoff. We would guess that there is less truancy, violence, and vandalism in schools in which the positive is emphasized than in those in which aversive control predominates. Recent evidence supports this assumption, as you will see in the sections on those problem areas later in the book.

Achievement and success also are tied to improved self-concepts. In an extensive review of studies designed to increase educational achievement by enhancing self-concept, Scheirer and Kraut (1979) concluded that improved self-concepts do not necessarily increase school achievement, but vice versa: "In this view, self-concept change is likely to be an outcome of increased achievement with accompanying social approval, rather than an intervening variable necessary for achievement to occur" (p. 144).

Finally, there is some evidence that reinforcement of alternative behavior may be judged by the public to be more acceptable than punitive methods (Kazdin, 1980, 1981). Those who use procedures that are approved of by the public should receive more reinforcement in the long run.

EFFECTIVELY REINFORCING ALTERNATIVE BEHAVIORS

The key to successful use of the Alt-R procedure is to find alternative behaviors that cannot coexist with the behavior targeted for reduction. A staff member cannot be absent if he or she is present, nor

can a student be tardy if he or she has arrived on time. While working constructively, a student is not apt to be disrupting. Then, once the alternative behavior is selected, you should reinforce it as effectively as you know how: immediately, consistently, with sufficient reinforcers of the right kind for that individual or group. You also should carefully avoid reinforcing the behavior that has been targeted for reduction. If it is a behavior that may have been sustained by attention, it will have to be ignored. But Alt-R takes time to produce its effects, so occasionally you might need to add a procedure that works faster. If the behavior is dangerous, severely disruptive, or otherwise intolerable, you may find it necessary to punish it directly; yet at the same time, you seek some positive alternative behaviors to nurture, too.

Perhaps you feel that this advice is easier said than done. You have racked your brain for methods of reinforcing positive alternatives, checked out our earlier chapter on reinforcement and failed to identify a promising strategy that would work in your situation. You might appreciate hearing about some creative solutions that others have devised when they were similarly stumped.

ILLUSTRATIVE APPLICATIONS OF REINFORCING ALTERNATIVE BEHAVIORS

Reinforcing alternatives to attendance problems

Is absenteeism a problem at your school? Reinforce attendance. Some firms give lottery tickets to employees who come to work for a set number of days. You could try this approach with students or staff when they do come to class or meetings.

We have tried this method a few times. A series of six workshops over a 5-month period was held for teachers, pupil personnel workers, administrators, and other educational specialists from eight junior and senior high schools. Teams of five staff members were to attend from each school. Each attendee received one ticket for attending the first time, two the second, and so on. Extra tickets were distributed to members of those teams whose members were all present. At the end of the workshop, the ticket stubs were placed in a bowl and several winning tickets were drawn. Prizes included aspirin, a mint, a bottle of wine, a certificate exchangeable for an hour of an administrator's time, release from duty in the lunchroom, and other items and privileges. Attendance at the workshops remained high, even increasing slightly over time.

Student attendance also can be rewarded by using a **slot machine game.** Those who meet the criteria, such as attending for a given number of days in a row, are allowed to select one of several overturned paper cups under which slips of paper have been placed. The slips contain certificates that can be exchanged for special privileges or activities: selecting the game for physical education, earning points toward a grade, prizes, access to popular toys for a given time period, free time, a preferred assignment as monitor, and so on.

Tardiness can be avoided by increasing the incentives for prompt arrival at class. One teacher wrote a few answers to homework or quiz problems on the blackboard early in the morning, erasing them prior to the late bell. Another distributed tickets for a drawing early in the day. If important and interesting things happen early in a session, promptness will be reinforced.

Reinforcing alternatives to disruptions and improving work habits

Mrs. Olsen, who teaches the secondary grades and serves as principal at Willow Grove Regional School, expressed the following concern shared by herself and the other members of her staff: "How do I get my students to do their assignments instead of engaging in competing activities?"

She had two basic choices: reducing off-task and increasing on-task behavior, or increasing productivity. As we already have discussed, if you can get two results for the price of one, that makes sense. Much research has shown that when students are academically productive, they are less apt to be off-task

(Sulzer, Hunt, Ashby, Koniarski, & Krams, 1971; Hay, Hay, & Nelson, 1977). Yet the converse is not necessarily true (Hay et al., 1977). Depending on how it is defined, being *on-task* doesn't have to mean that the student is producing very efficiently. Pam, a tenth-grade student in Mrs. Olsen's class, could be fulfilling all the requirements to receive reinforcement for on-task responses, looking at her assignment, marking with her pencil and having her page open to the proper place; however, she could be writing the initials of her boyfriend on her paper or be conjuring up an entrancing fantasy. If reinforcement contingencies instead encouraged Pam to produce answers to questions, write summaries, illustrate or critique an assigned passage, or some other productive performance, she would be less likely to waste her own and others' time.

Earlier you saw how disruptions in a class could be reduced by reinforcing academic performance. In the Sulzer et al. study (1971), students were given points exchangeable for rewards and privileges for workbook items that were completed correctly. The pupils really became involved in their work—so much so that classroom disruption and general off-task behavior essentially vanished. You'd better watch out for one pitfall here, though. A system like this could promote very high rates of production, both accurate *and* inaccurate. Providing that students completed enough correct items, they would get paid off handsomely, despite errors here and there. As Klein (1975) found, this arrangement could cause them to rush and work carelessly. Sulzer et al. avoided the problem, fortunately, by insisting that accuracy levels not fall below 90 percent if students were to be permitted to collect their own points. This level was reasonable, as all students had been preassessed and assigned material on which they had demonstrated their ability to perform very accurately.

Working diligently on an academic task has not always been found to be incompatible with disruptive behavior in all reported instances. Ferritor, Buckholdt, Hamblin, and Smith (1972) found that their students continued to misbehave as they worked for their reinforcers. They concluded that both academic productivity and classroom conduct had to be targeted to restore a reasonable learning environment. We suggest, though, that you start by reinforcing productivity first. If that results in improved academic performance but not in better conduct, you then could add the second element. But before resorting to a classroom management tactic, recheck the material to see if it is tailored appropriately to the students' current level of performance; also examine your reinforcing contingencies to assess their potency. At least temporarily, you could supplement these less obtrusive ones that you are currently using with more powerful reinforcers, such as rewards or privileges.

Mrs. Olsen might try praising academic productivity, later to discover that her students showed some nice academic gains. If disruption continued, though, she could add some other more powerful features to her system, such as self-recording of accurate performance, home report cards, or maybe special activities such as a disco dance on Friday — contingent on all the students' setting and reaching goals for the other four days of the week. Because all students would stand to benefit, they might try to avoid disrupting or distracting each other.

In case none of these alternative methods effectively reduces off-task behavior, you naturally would turn to some other Alt-R strategies or other methods for reducing disruption directly. (Refer to Chapters 10, 11, and 12 for additional methods of reducing undesired behaviors.) Next we illustrate some other techniques that incorporate the reinforcement of alternative behaviors. These were implemented successfully to increase quiet and on-task behavior while reducing noise and other forms of disruption.

The curriculum for five primary-level grades in Rochester, New York (Cowen, Jones, & Bellack, 1979), included both individual and group work. Several times a week, about one-third of the pupils in each class would meet for group instruction with the teacher in a reading circle. Meanwhile, the other students were supposed to be doing their own assignments individually. Instead, many left their seats, ran around the room, talked to one another, and disrupted in other ways. To cope with the situation, the teacher was given a stopwatch to activate as long

as all were working appropriately. In case a student disobeyed one of the classroom rules, the teacher was to stop the watch, call the student by name, review what the student was supposed to be doing, and if necessary remind the student that time was being wasted. As all resumed working, the watch then was reactivated. When 15 minutes of work time accumulated, the class was permitted to select an activity from a menu of reinforcers, and its members could engage in the activity for the number of minutes remaining from a one-half hour period. If everyone worked for the first 15 minutes, that would mean that the remaining 15 minutes could be used for the reinforcing activities. Of course, each disruption reduced the time for those activities. As you might have anticipated, disruption diminished dramatically, and both teachers and students expressed their pleasure with the system.

In a classroom in the Van Wig Elementary School, students had a habit of shouting out answers. The teacher and students agreed that a better approach would be for students to raise their hands when they had something to say. For a few weeks, a timer was set — first for intervals as short as a few minutes, then gradually for longer intervals. Whenever the timer sounded,[4] one of the students who had remembered to follow the rule about raising hands was permitted to take a turn at the slot machine. The slips of paper beneath four or five paper cups were changed regularly. Sometimes the player could win a special privilege, such as being line leader or scorekeeper. Others won free time, early dismissal, or time in a special resource room. Sometimes the class was divided into groups, and all members of a group that had conformed to the rule were permitted the reward that had been selected. As you might imagine, students then encouraged one another to remember what they needed to do to become eligible for a chance at the slot machine. One published study (McReynolds, Gange, & Speltz, 1981) reported

---

[4]If you prefer a more subtle signal, try recording a series of chimes or musical notes on a cassette tape. Just record the sound, push the fast forward button, stop, and record again. Many pocket calculators and digital watches also can be set to produce a pleasant alarm to remind you periodically to implement your reward system.

that students not only continued to be engaged with their work but also completed more problems when all members of a group were required to remain on-task for a set number of minutes in order for *any* to play a game afterward.

It may be appropriate in your situation to select several target behaviors to work on at once. The class can be asked to identify a complete set of on-task behaviors: doing assigned work such as reading or writing, or listening, remaining seated, communicating in a soft voice, and other activities incompatible with disruption. Then some method of systematically reinforcing adherence to those rules is added. This rule could be as simple as writing on the blackboard the names of those students who remain on-task, or it could be more complicated if necessary by providing a slot machine or a turn at the **activity table,** where they could engage in preferred tasks or games.

Activity tables have a similar function, except that craft supplies such as clay, collage materials or other media, interesting books or periodicals, audio-visual equipment with earphones (records, tapes, television, films), games, or other special materials are displayed. When a signal from a timer sounds or when students complete an assignment without violating the rules they are allowed to spend a preset period of time at the table. Should it be necessary to reinforce rule-following more often, point cards may be checked every few minutes by the teacher, a monitor, or the students themselves (assuming a method for verifying accuracy of self-scoring can be arranged). Then, once a set number of points is earned, these points can be exchanged for time at the table (or a turn at the slot machine).

If you are dissatisfied because you pay too much attention to misconduct or want to increase your own rate of reinforcing academic productivity or on-task behavior, you might use the Alt-R method to manage your own behavior. You could arrange a signal to remind yourself to stop and say or do something reinforcing, or you might set a daily goal for yourself: "During each class I will comment favorably at least three times when the group is working well." You could use a counter or a scorecard to note how you are doing. You very well may find that the number of times you scold or criticize drops as your rate of reinforcing positive classroom behavior increases.

Summary

Many of the pitfalls of using punitive strategies were presented in this chapter. Punishment promotes fight-and-flight reactions as well as negative attitudes toward oneself and school. The use of punitive strategies often is reinforced by the immediate relief they provide. Thus, we often find ourselves overusing punishment. Students may adapt to such an overuse, diminishing the effectiveness of punishment as a reductive strategy. When, on occasion, punishment is called for, then it is important that it function effectively. To avoid a situation in which reasonably benign forms of the procedure might cease to be effective, we must avoid ex-cessive reliance on punishment, applying constructive alternatives instead.

Alt-R is one such constructive alternative. When carefully selected alternatives to an undesirable behavior are positively reinforced, the student not only learns to behave more appropriately, but the undesirable behavior also diminishes because both desired and undesired behavior cannot occur simultaneously. The Alt-R procedure can produce long-lasting results when the desired alternative behaviors are properly strengthened and maintained. In this chapter, we saw how various programs were used to increase alternative behaviors. The Alt-R pro-

cedure is constructive, makes learning and school pleasurable, and promotes self-confidence and positive attitudes toward the school.

To reduce behavior optimally, alternatives need to be selected carefully to ensure incompatibility with misbehavior; appropriate reinforcement techniques should be used; and reinforcement must be withheld totally from the undesirable behavior. When used alone, Alt-R will reduce a behavior more slowly than when combined with punishment, but the delay usually is justified because the negative side effects of punishment are avoided when punishment isn't used. The many advantages of Alt-R should convince you of its value as a regular classroom management procedure.

Study Questions

1. The children on bus 3 are constantly misbehaving. The school personnel would like to select one behavior to target for change. Provide them with at least two suggestions to help them make a wise choice.
2. Mrs. Smith wants all of her students to achieve academic success. Devise a plan to increase the likelihood that this will happen.
3. List the advantages of having your students succeed academically.
4. (a) Offer a target behavior for each of the problem behaviors below.
   (b) Support your answer.
   (i) Yelling during class.
   (ii) Teasing peers.
   (iii) Stealing toys from peers.
5. (a) Define and (b) provide another name for Alt-R.
6. Provide a criterion for selecting a target behavior for a program using Alt-R.
7. Describe the appropriate method of reinforcing a target behavior.
8. Alt-R is going to be used to eliminate Tom's doodling on his papers.
   (a) Will additional procedures be required?
   (b) Support your answer. (Be specific.)
9. (a) Develop a program using Alt-R to change one of your behaviors and (b) support your answer.
10. T/F Teachers are more likely to use punishment than praise. Support your choice with evidence.
11. Define *punishment*.
12. Using punishment can be rewarding.
    (a) Use an example to demonstrate that this statement is true.
    (b) Label your example with the correct term.
13. Discuss in detail three reasons for the widespread use of punishment.
14. (a) Describe several physiological changes that occur when someone loses his or her temper.
    (b) Provide one reason for the occurrence of the physiological changes.
15. List six or more negative effects of punishment on the person being punished.
16. Provide at least five fight-or-flight responses likely to be seen among students.
17. Discuss the conditions that can provoke the same fight-or-flight behaviors as a response to punishment.
18. Mr. Morten, the school principal, is especially careful to avoid using punishment, except when absolutely necessary. Provide a reason for his behavior.
19. Under what circumstances is punishment acceptable?
20. Present a strong argument for the use of Alt-R in the school.
21. Discuss the relation between self-concepts and school achievement.
22. Mr. French wants to select alternative behaviors to reinforce in order to reduce problem performance in his classroom. Provide him with a guideline to aid him in his selection.

23. State in detail the proper method for reinforcing alternative behaviors.
24. Several psychologists agree that Cathy's fire setting needs to be terminated rapidly. What procedure will they probably use? Why?
25. List an alternative behavior to reinforce for each of the examples below.
    (a) Absenteeism.
    (b) Mistakes on tests.
    (c) Unanswered test questions.
    (d) Hitting peers.
26. Provide an original solution to the problem of tardiness among staff.
27. Discuss the relation between academic productivity and on-task behavior.
28. (a) List one pitfall to reinforcing academic productivity.
    (b) Offer a solution.
29. Design plans to increase working diligently on an academic task and to eliminate disruptive behavior. (Include two plans—one more obtrusive than the other.)
30. Create an original narrative demonstrating that several behaviors can be targeted for change at once. (Be thorough.)
31. Develop a program using Alt-R to change a teacher's behavior.
32. Discuss the advantages and disadvantages of using positive strategies.

References

Anderson, D. E. (1964). *An application of behavior modification techniques in the control of hyperactivity of a braindamaged child.* Unpublished M.A. thesis, University of Oregon.

Azrin, N. H., & Holz, W. C. (1966). Punishment. In W. A. Honig (Ed.), *Operant behavior: Areas of research and application.* New York: Appleton.

Bandura, A. (1965). Behavioral modification through modeling procedures. In L. Krasner & L. P. Ullman (Eds.), *Research in behavior modification.* New York: Holt, Rinehart and Winston.

Bandura, A., Ross, D., & Ross, S. A. (1963). Imitation of film-mediated aggressive models. *Journal of Abnormal and Social Psychology, 66,* 3–11.

Boren, J. J., & Coleman, A. D. (1970). Some experiments on reinforcement principles within a psychiatric ward for delinquent soldiers. *Journal of Applied Behavior Analysis, 3,* 29–37.

Brodinsky, B. (1980). *AASA critical issues report. Student discipline, problems and solutions.* AASA, 1801 N. Moore St., Arlington, VA 22209. (#021-00334).

Conger, R. D. (1982). Behavioral intervention for child abuse. *The Behavior Therapist, 5,* 49–53.

Cowen, R. J., Jones, F. H., & Bellack, A. S. (1979). Grandma's rule with group contingencies—A cost-efficient means of classroom management. *Behavior Modification, 3,* 397–418.

Ebner, M. (1967). *Observation of changes in reinforcement schedules as an outcome of successful behavior modification.* Unpublished doctoral dissertation, University of Oregon.

Ferritor, D. E., Buckholdt, D., Hamblin, R. L., & Smith, L. (1972). The noneffects of contingent reinforcement for attending behavior on work accomplished. *Journal of Applied Behavior Analysis, 5,* 7–17.

Hall, R. V., Lund, D., & Jackson, D. (1968). Effects of teacher attention on study behavior. *Journal of Applied Behavior Analysis, 1,* 1–12.

Hay, W. M., Hay, L. R., & Nelson, R. O. (1977). Direct and collateral changes in on-task and academic behavior resulting from on-task versus academic contingencies. *Behavior Therapy, 8,* 431–441.

Heller, M. S., & White, M. A. (1975). Teacher approval and disapproval on ability grouping. *Journal of Educational Psychology, 67,* 796–800.

Homer, A. L., & Peterson, L. (1980). Differential reinforcement of other behavior: A preferred response elimination procedure. *Behavior Therapy, 11,* 449–471.

Kazdin, A. E. (1980). Acceptability of alternative treatments for deviant child behavior. *Journal of Applied Behavior Analysis, 13,* 259–273.

Kazdin, A. E. (1981). Acceptability of child treatment techniques: The influence of treatment efficacy and adverse side effects. *Behavior Therapy, 12,* 493–506.

Klein, R. D. (1975). A brief research report on accuracy and academic performance. *Journal of Applied Behavior Analysis, 8,* 121–122.

MacMillan, D. L., Forness, S. R., & Trumbull, B. N.

(1973). The role of punishment in the classroom. *Exceptional Children, 40*, 85–96.

Mayer, G. R., Butterworth, T., Nafpaktitis, M., & Sulzer-Azaroff, B. (1983). Preventing school vandalism and improving discipline: A three-year study. *Journal of Applied Behavior Analysis, 16*, 355–369.

McReynolds, W. T., Gange, J. J., & Speltz, M. L. (1981). Effects of multiple individual and group operant contingencies on student performance. *Education and Treatment of Children, 4*, 227–241.

Patterson, G. R., Ray, R. S., & Shaw, D. A. (1968). Direct intervention in families of deviant children. *Oregon Research Institute Research Bulletin, 8*, No. 9.

Rust, J. O., & Kinnard, K. (1983). Personality characteristics of the users of corporal punishment in the schools. *Journal of School Psychology, 21*, 91–105.

Scheirer, M. A., & Kraut, R. E. (1979). Increasing educational achievement via self concept change. *Review of Educational Research, 49*, 131–150.

Solomon, R. W., & Wahler, R. G. (1973). Peer reinforcement control of classroom problem behavior. *Journal of Applied Behavior Analysis, 6*, 49–56.

Sulzer, B., Hunt, S., Ashby, E., Koniarski, C., & Krams, M. (1971). Increasing rate and percentage correct in reading and spelling in a fifth grade public school class of slow readers by means of a token system. In E. A. Ramp and B. L. Hopkins (eds.), *A New Direction for Education: Behavior Analysis, 1971.* Lawrence, KS: University of Kansas, Project Follow Through, Department of Human Development.

Thomas, J. D., Presland, I. E., Grant, M. D., & Glynn, T. (1978). Natural rates of teacher approval and disapproval in grade-7 classrooms. *Journal of Applied Behavior Analysis, 11*, 91–94.

Weidenman, L. E. (1980). *The use of a reciprocal peer interaction as a means of evaluating a pre-school mainstreamed classroom.* Unpublished doctoral dissertation, University of Massachusetts.

White, M. A. (1975). Natural rates of teacher approval and disapproval in the classroom. *Journal of Applied Behavior Analysis, 8*, 367–372.

Woods, P. J. (1974). A taxonomy of instrumental conditioning. *American Psychologist, 29*, 584–597.

10 Positive classroom management: modeling and differential reinforcement procedures

Goals

After completing this chapter, you should be able to:

1. Define each of the following procedures, and give an example of how each procedure can be used to reduce the frequency of a behavior of a student or colleague.
   a. Modeling
   b. Differential Reinforcement of Low rates of behavior (DRL)
   c. Differential Reinforcement of Diminishing rates of behavior (DRD)
   d. Differential Reinforcement of the nonoccurrence (or of zero rate) of a behavior (DRO)
   e. Momentary DRO
2. Describe the technique the authors suggest to help you increase your use of modeling.
3. List the advantages and disadvantages of methods of differentially reinforcing low or diminishing rates of behavior.
4. Describe the Good Behavior Game, including steps that can be taken to minimize its disadvantages.
5. List the advantages and disadvantages of DRO.
6. Describe how the Good Behavior Game can be modified to incorporate the DRO procedure in place of reinforcing diminishing rates of behavior.
7. Complete Table 10.1.
8. Describe when a punitive rather than a positive procedure should be used to reduce behavior.

The holidays were just a few days away, and excitement was building. The noise during lunch break had been deafening, and even though it was time for students to return to work on their science reports, many of the youngsters continued to mill around, talking animatedly, arguing, teasing. Roberto nudged a book off the corner of Eric's desk and hee-hawed heartily in response to Eric's outraged "Hey!" Karen and Susie squirmed uncomfortably, girding themselves in anticipation of a fight. Ms. Thomas, herself somewhat edgy, drew a deep breath and glanced about the room. Noting that Sam had sat down and taken out his work materials, she walked over, touched him on the shoulder and commented, "It's so nice to see how quickly you are getting down to work, Sam. I guess that star ball players like you know how important good timing is!" Taking the cue, Eric shrugged his shoulders and began to arrange his books, and most of the others followed suit. Attention withdrawn from Roberto, he too returned to his seat and prepared to work. "That's the way, Eric, Tony, Susie. Nice going, Karen, Roberto!" Continuing to circulate about the room, Ms. Thomas stopped from time to time at someone's desk. At one point she exclaimed, "What an excellent drawing. It really shows how that part of the experiment was done. Take a look at George's drawing, people. Isn't it great?" As she approached Eric, she softly commented, "I'm glad you didn't let him get your goat!" Then she waited a few moments until Roberto had been hard at work. "Nice work, Roberto. Is there anything I can help you with?" Then to the class in general, "This is more like it. The way you're all working so hard, I wouldn't be surprised if some of your projects are accepted for the science fair. Wouldn't it be fantastic if this class could produce a winner this year? Remember how proud the whole school was of Maria last year when she brought home an honorable mention?" Before long, their irritability vanished, and the students immersed themselves in their science activities.

As you might well imagine, this scenario could have resulted in a very different outcome. Many of us might have succumbed to shouting, scolding, or sarcasm, contributing even further to the general discomfort. Perhaps this would have restored order temporarily, but what would it have accomplished in terms of the quality of the students' work and their enthusiasm for it? Based on what you have read in Chapter 9, you probably recognize that losing one's temper contributes little. In the present episode, the results were just what we would have hoped for. What was responsible?

One thing you've probably identified is the teacher's use of reinforcement of alternative behaviors (Alt-R). Reinforcement was delivered as a function of behavior that was not compatible with disruption. But Ms. Thomas also employed some other highly effective positive procedures: modeling and differential reinforcement of the omission of behavior. In this chapter, we explore these and several other methods for reducing disruption and enhancing the social environment of the classroom.

MODELING

Modeling was discussed as a stimulus control procedure in Chapter 7. We pointed out that the behavior of selected models (or — to be more technically correct — the *stimuli* produced by the model's be-

havior) can prompt or set the occasion for imitation (i.e., it can function as a discriminative stimulus for imitation). In this chapter we show how modeling can serve as an effective tool for managing conduct in the classroom. However, regardless of whether modeling is being used as a classroom management procedure or as a stimulus control procedure for a different purpose, the same guidelines as those contained in Chapter 7 apply for using it effectively. Thus, we suggest you review as necessary and follow those guidelines whenever you use any modeling strategy.

Modeling can be a most useful classroom management procedure, as was illustrated above — Ms. Thomas achieved control in her class by first using Sam's behavior as a model for others in the class and then Eric's, Tony's, Susie's, Karen's, and Roberto's behavior as they too started performing appropriately. As a procedure for reducing behavior, it incorporates the strategies for Alt-R discussed in the previous chapter and it shares all of its advantages and disadvantages. However, though modeling does not necessarily work rapidly, it can reduce behavior faster than Alt-R alone, because modeling prompts alternative behavior that you frequently will be able to reinforce differentially. Also, as with Alt-R, a major advantage of the modeling procedure is that it focuses the teacher's responses on positive behavior. As we mentioned previously, there is a tendency for us to respond disproportionately to negative behavior: "Roberto, sit down!" "Eric, be quiet!" "Stop that!" "Don't you know any better?" "Get back over here!" Modeling procedures help to turn the tables so the students who are behaving well get their share of recognition.

In case you find it difficult to notice and point out models of good behavior, you might try this strategy: *use the minor misbehaviors you do notice to cue yourself to find several students who are engaging in constructive alternatives and reinforce those behaviors,* as illustrated earlier with Sam and the other students. Take care, however, when you put this suggestion into practice. Just as reinforcing the desired behavior by a model can prompt others to imitate, reinforcing unwanted behavior can do the same. Although the caution may seem obvious to you, it is worth emphasizing, because all of us inadvertently reinforce behavior we would prefer not to see repeated. For example, Witt and Adams (1980) showed that observers will imitate either appropriate behavior, such as working hard, or inappropriate behavior, like playing with a pencil, if the teacher attended to the behavior.

Similarly, two classroom teachers of our acquaintance were practicing modeling procedures with their high school classes. One reported that she had given up using the suggested strategies, attending only to those students who were on-task when minor infractions occurred. An inquiry revealed that one student had solicited the teacher's response by saying, "Teacher, I'm working quietly, too. See?" And she did. Another student did likewise and, again, the teacher responded, "Yes, you're working well, too." Before long, to the teacher's distress, the whole class was soliciting attention. So she concluded that the strategy hadn't worked. The other teacher had a similar initial experience. But in her class, as soon as a student openly requested recognition, she paused to analyze the situation and decided that this sort of thing could get out of hand. So she ignored the bid for attention in favor of the other students who were hard at work. For her, the strategy worked like a charm in each of her three classes—one standard, one remedial, and one advanced math group. So in the course of your normal working activities, if you are tempted to attend to behavior or to comply with a request that you wouldn't want repeated, resist; otherwise others may test to see if the same ploy will work for them.

Differentially reinforcing low and diminishing rates of behavior

Mrs. Olsen has set herself the goal of involving more students in group discussions. One problem is that a few of the children generally dominate, while the more docile students rarely enter into the discussion. Chris is a case in point: he asks all sorts of provocative questions and ventures his opinions forcefully, regardless of whether or not his teacher has called on him. Because Chris contributes interesting information and stimulates worthwhile interchanges,

Mrs. Olsen is reluctant to shut him off altogether. She would prefer simply to reduce his involvement to enable the others to have their opportunities to speak. Finding that asking him politely to restrain himself only worked for a short while, she decides to use a **differential reinforcement of low rate (DRL)** procedure. In the **DRL** procedure, *a behavior is reinforced only if it occurs following a specific period of time during which it did not occur* (Ferster & Skinner, 1957). Chris and Mrs. Olsen agree that if he waits 3 minutes after participating, she will call on him at the next opportunity. If not, she will ignore what he says and require him to wait 3 more minutes for his next opportunity to participate.

Notice that the DRL schedule is designed to reduce behavior by reinforcing a response that has been preceded by a specific time interval without the target behavior. Because a reinforcer is forthcoming when the response has followed a period without responding, the rate of responding eventually should drop to that set by the rules of the contingency.

Other differential reinforcement methods for diminishing response rates (DRD)

It may be difficult for teachers or staff who work with groups of students to attend as closely to the time as DRL requires, however, so in practice a similar, more practical method often is used—a differential reinforcement method for diminishing response rates (DRD).[1] Instead of presenting a reinforcer following the targeted response only if it occurred after it was *not* expressed for a fixed time, a *reinforcer is delivered "if the number of responses in a specified period of time is less than, or equal to, a prescribed limit"* (italics added) (Deitz & Repp, 1973, p. 457).

As in our example with Chris, Deitz and Repp (1973) were concerned with reducing talk-outs in two different classes. During one phase of their study, a maximum number of three talk-outs per 50-

---

[1]We elected to use this abbreviation (DRD), although it is not standard in the field.

minute period was permitted. The students were told that if the criterion was met, they would be rewarded with, in one case, extra play time; in another, with a couple of pieces of candy at or near the end of the day. In a third case, a high school class in office procedures, the problem was different. Here the students entered into the class discussion but digressed from the academic topic, relating social events instead. Deitz and Repp implemented four differential reinforcement phases, each of which permitted fewer digressions than previously, until during the fourth phase none was permitted at all. Meeting the DRL requirement for the first 4 days of the week permitted the class to spend the fifth period as they pleased. The troublesome behavior diminished in tandem with the differential reinforcement requirement, to the extent that during the last phase the students no longer were changing the subject to inappropriate topics. A year later, Deitz and Repp (1974) reported using a similar procedure with gold stars and no backups as reinforcers. The procedure effectively reduced talk-outs in one case and talk-outs and out-of-seat episodes in another.

Another way to arrange contingencies to diminish response rates is to require turn-taking. In our example with Chris, he might be called on only after another student has had a turn; then after that rate stabilized, two students would have their turns, and so on until his rate was proportional to that of the other students. If you try this method, record your actions as precisely as feasible, so that you can see if the system is working. As in many other instances of shifting over to less and less reinforcement, too large a step will interrupt progress. If your records indicate improvement was only temporary, and the prior problem has returned, test your schedule for extending the time by dropping back a few steps and then see if the progress can be recaptured.

The Good Behavior Game. The Good Behavior Game is a well-known classroom management technique for differentially reinforcing diminishing rates of misconduct. It was first described by Barrish, Saunders, and Wolf (1969) to help teachers manage seriously disruptive classroom behavior. Since then, numerous educators have reported suc-

cessfully using the game or some variation of it in grades ranging from the primary through secondary.

To play, you divide the class into teams, each consisting of students who typically exhibit equivalent rates of the problem behavior. Then, with the help of the class, you list several rules on the board, such as, "No throwing objects, whistling, and talking out." If a member of a team violates a rule, the team is penalized by receiving a mark next to its name. First an initial criterion level that is challenging but achievable for the students is set with the class for a period or the full day; for example, the level might be no more than six infractions. The team that has received fewer than the criterion number of marks wins. One or more teams can win the game. However, if all teams receive penalty points beyond the criterion level, the team with the fewest marks against it wins. Winners are allowed special privileges such as free time, tickets to a game, special time for projects, homework, or other previously negotiated reinforcers. The losing team members remain working on their assignments. Once the game has been played successfully at the initial criterion level two or three times, the level is lowered; for instance, from six to three. *The object,* of course, *is to reinforce lower and lower rates of student misbehavior until the desired level is reached.*

The Good Behavior Game is easy to implement, and most students enjoy it. However, an individual or two may decide not to play. So what do you do? There are several ways you can handle the situation. Harris and Sherman (1973) placed the dissenters on a team of their own, rather than penalizing other teammates. All consequences remained the same as before except that each check mark above the selected criterion meant that the members of that team were required to spend 5 minutes after school. This procedure proved effective within a few days. In fact, "After the fifth day of this condition, the students on the third team asked to be returned to their former teams; the teacher allowed them to do so" (Harris & Sherman, 1973, p. 416). Both teams went on to win the game on subsequent days. Similarly, Butterworth and Vogler (1975) isolated any student who committed two violations (only the first counted against his team). Further, the student was not permitted to participate in any special privileges that his team might have won and had to make up the lost time before or after school.

The Good Behavior Game just described mainly focuses attention on negative rather than positive behavior. To avoid this problem, several successful adaptations of the game have been developed. One involves dividing the class into six or eight teams. The class lists five to seven behaviors for which points can be earned and five to seven behaviors for which points can be lost. Before the end of a day, negative marks are subtracted from the positive points of each team. Bonus points are given to any team that receives no negative marks. The rest of the game remains the same. Below, we describe a different successful variation that used an Alt-R version of the game, instead, to reduce disruptive library behavior (Fishbein & Wasik, 1981).

Advantages and disadvantages of methods for differentially reinforcing low or diminishing rates of behavior

These procedures are tolerant, in that they accept the occurrence of a given behavior. Like Alt-R, they can be convenient, effective, and they make use of positive reinforcement to reduce behavior. While the person who uses Alt-R searches for positive alternative behavior to reinforce, those who use these differential reinforcement methods focus on negative or excessive behavior, thereby encouraging more attention to undesired behavior. To guard against this excessive focus on the negative, these procedures should be combined regularly with Alt-R. Now we turn to a method designed not to reduce but to eliminate troublesome performance: **omission training,** or DRO.

POSITIVELY REINFORCING THE OMISSION OF BEHAVIOR

The kids have been needling Freddy again. "What a haircut! Did your mom put a bowl over your head to trim it?"

"Tough luck. I bet your parents won't even give you the money for the class trip next month."

"How come you're always hiding over there looking like you're hard at work? Trying to butter up the teacher?"

Freddy hangs his head, shrugs his shoulders and momentarily raises his hands as if to fend off his tormentors. So intently are they enjoying his discomfort that they fail to notice that Mr. Forsyth, their teacher, has been watching the whole episode.

"Okay, you guys. That's just about enough. Freddy does work especially hard. You should be encouraging him instead of making his life miserable! And Freddy isn't the only one you tease. I think that between today and tomorrow we'd better find a way to deal with this sort of thing." The next day they reviewed the problem. Together they decided that the students would earn points for every period in which there had been no teasing.

"Alright," commented Mr. Forsyth, "there will be 20 periods between now and the trip, so let's see—the class will have to earn 15 points to be eligible to go. Just to make sure we all understand each other, we'd better carefully define what we mean by teasing."

Mr. Forsyth then asked the class to describe what teasing was and wasn't. The students reviewed several recent episodes to test the definition and drew up a chart to be checked for each class period in which no teasing took place. Because all stood to gain or lose, the students began to encourage each other to avoid teasing, and things began to improve. Once in a while someone forgot and the group lost its point for the day, but there was a margin for error, so no one became terribly upset at the loss. By the time the day of the field trip came along, the group had earned 17 points. All, including Freddy, went and had a grand time.

The procedure Mr. Forsyth was using is labeled **omission training** or **differential reinforcement of the non- or zero-occurrence of a behavior,** and it is usually abbreviated **DRO** (Catania, 1979). *In the DRO procedure a reinforcer is delivered following a period of time during which a targeted response has not* *occurred.*[2] Omission training may be familiar to you. Reinforcers are delivered at the end of 30 minutes if Lucinda hasn't sworn during that time or if Richard hasn't crumpled up his paper. The class will earn an extra 5 minutes of recess if no one talks out without permission.

Ms. Miller is helping Mary Heinz, the student teacher, to reduce her criticisms of the students. They select the period during which the student teacher frequently criticizes. It takes place while the students are doing seat work, between 1:30 and 2 P.M. Ms. Miller takes a sheet of paper and divides it into ten columns, one for each 3 minutes. Then each time she notes a criticism, she makes a hatch mark under the appropriate column heading. After several days, she has noted that Ms. Heinz has been able to omit criticizing for two or three blocks of 3 minutes in a row. Those data inform them that a DRO interval of 5 minutes would be reasonable. So subsequently, she signals approval following each 5-minute block during which Ms. Heinz has not criticized. For several weeks, they keep the procedure in effect, and Ms. Heinz finds herself complimenting the students' accomplishments and improvements rather than criticizing their failures. The students' work begins to improve, and the seat-work period has become more pleasant for all. Ms. Miller slowly reduces her frequency of delivering approval. The natural reinforcing contingencies—namely, improved student performances—have taken control.

Advantages and disadvantages of DRO

Omission training can be very powerful, but there are some tricky aspects to it. The time base must be adjusted to the individual; otherwise the reinforcers will not be forthcoming often enough to promote

[2]If the targeted behavior does occur within the preset interval, the interval can continue to termination with subsequent occurrences of the target behavior ignored (technically *omission training*), *or*, following the target behavior, the interval can be reset (technically *DRO*). The former is more manageable in a group, but differences in effectiveness remain to be demonstrated (Catania, personal communication, 1982).

enduring change. (You can do this as Ms. Miller did, by referring back to baseline rates.) Later, as performance improves, the time intervals can and should be lengthened gradually. Also, because the delivery of a reinforcer depends on time rather than on a particular response, whatever the individual *is* doing at that moment is in risk of being reinforced. Lucinda hasn't sworn for 30 minutes but at the end of that time, she is doodling on her paper instead of doing her work. Because the rule calls for a reinforcer to be delivered at that moment, her doodling could be reinforced. If her teacher, Mrs. Burnes, is lucky (and Lucinda is, too), the next time a 30-minute time interval is completed, Lucinda will be doing something more productive, permitting that behavior to be reinforced and any previous damage should not be too severe. (Or to help reduce such problems, the rules can be elaborated to include other behavior to be omitted. Or the DRO can be combined with an Alt-R procedure; during the interval, swearing must be omitted, but a certain amount of productive work must be included.)

Probably the most challenging aspect of the DRO procedure is that it demands considerable vigilance, enabling the targeted behavior to be detected when it occurs within the interval. Otherwise, we may find ourselves inadvertently reinforcing the very behavior we are trying to reduce. Such surveillance may prove more difficult than we can manage under some circumstances. With the best of intentions, Mrs. Burnes loses track of Lucinda's swearing because she is concentrating on some of the other students. She inadvertently has delivered a reinforcer when the rules prohibit it. What alternatives are there for people who must divide their attention? One solution is to target behavior that produces products—doodling would be discernible on a worksheet. Barton and Madsen (1980) helped some retarded youngsters to reduce their drooling by presenting them with reinforcers following gradually longer time periods during which they did not drool. A similar program was conducted by Bennett (1980) to reduce vomiting. The procedure didn't require that the children be observed continually because the responses produced their own evidence.

Another solution is to use a sampling system, one

that is very similar to the momentary time-sampling observational system that we described in Chapter 2. Time is broken down into short intervals — shorter than those used when omission training is to include the whole interval. The underlying assumption, as with momentary time sampling, is that if intervals are short enough, the behavior sampled will approximate actual ongoing behavior. Instead of continually observing for any instance of the target behavior, *you observe and reinforce nonoccurrence only at the moment when the interval has terminated.* Let us label this modified DRO procedure **momentary DRO.**[3]

Sanford sucks his thumb very frequently. On his desk his teacher has placed a timer and two plastic containers, one of which is filled with play money. Sanford is shown how to set the timer for approximately four minutes and how to turn it so he can't see its face in the interim. When the timer signals, Sanford checks to see where his thumb is (and so does his teacher). If it is not in his mouth, he moves a play dollar to the empty container and his teacher congratulates him for not sucking his thumb and for following the rules of the game. (Play money can be exchanged for any of several preferred activities.) Sanford resets the timer as previously. He and his teacher return to their usual activities, and the process is repeated. In case the timer sounds and Sanford's thumb is in his mouth, and he properly resists awarding himself his "token," the teacher lavishly praises his adherence to the rules. Over several days, the teacher should need to check concurrence less frequently. As Sanford's rate of thumb sucking begins to decrease, the intervals can be gradually increased until the thumb sucking has been totally eliminated.

Momentary DRO certainly seems simpler to use than whole-interval DRO, but does it work as well? The answer is maybe. Repp, Barton, and Brulle (1983) studied this question with four boys who exhibited some mildly disruptive responses. The two different forms of DRO were compared and, in gen-

eral, the whole-interval DRO schedule fared better than the momentary one. There was an exception, though; momentary DRO did the job just fine after a phase in which the disruptive responses had already been reduced by means of whole-interval DRO. If you stop to think about this, the findings should not surprise you. Since, during the previous phase, disruption was reduced to a minimum, the boy rarely disrupted during the subsequent momentary DRO phase. So reinforcement would not be likely to occur in close proximity to a disruptive act. In contrast, when the momentary DRO came first, because the rates of disruption were still fairly high, it is probable that the reinforcers were delivered closely upon the heels of some disruptive act.

The overall picture should look familiar: first, a pattern of performance is well established by means of a very powerful contingency requirement, in this case five minutes without one single disruptive act (analogous to using a very powerful reinforcing contingency to modify and firmly establish a modified pattern of performing, such as a very dense schedule); then we see that solidly established pattern being maintained by a weaker set of contingencies, in this case reinforcement every five minutes, provided no disruption was occurring at that moment (analogous to the intermittent reinforcement we know to sustain established performance over time). So when in doubt, we suggest you start with short, whole intervals to diminish the behavior to an acceptable level. Then after that level has stabilized, you can switch over to the momentary DRO. Once you again achieve stability of change, you might then begin to stretch the size and vary the length of the intervals.

Let us illustrate how you might follow these suggestions in your setting. Target the behavior to be changed. With the temporary help of another person, like a guidance counselor or aide, take baseline recordings of the performance. Select an initial DRO interval. If the target behavior occurs only very rarely, start with a lengthy interval; if very frequently, a short interval; and use the whole-interval DRO. When the rate drops and stays infrequent, you can change to momentary DRO. Set a criterion level for the switch-over, say two weeks in a row

---

[3]Technically, this schedule is a tandem fixed time (FT) DRO or variable time (VT) DRO (Catania, personal communication, 1982).

with the target behavior occurring no more than __ times within the interval. Then switch to the momentary DRO. After a few days, the teacher can assume the management of the procedure.

The same method also can be used with groups of students. When you are ready to transfer control of the momentary DRO to the teacher (or a monitor or to students to manage for themselves) you can divide the group into a few subgroups. Set a timer or play a tape on which you've recorded a series of chimes about every __ minutes.[4] When the signal sounds, check each group to see if the behaviors are occurring. If not, award the group a point. At the end of the session, tally up the points. The group with the most, or the groups whose members have earned more than some set criterion number, then are awarded some special privilege. This game is very similar to a variation of the *Good Behavior Game* (Barrish et al., 1969). There is a basic difference, though. In the Good Behavior Game, a mark is given following a violation of the rules, instead of as in the momentary DRO method when the violation is *not* occurring. We suspect that the outcomes of either procedure would be similar insofar as reduction of the targeted behavior is concerned, but some day research may show differences in collateral effects, such as enjoyment of the game as well as of school.

Omission training—either whole or momentary DRO—has been shown to operate effectively as a classroom management tool (Repp & Deitz, 1974). Even given the practical adjustments just described, there is one remaining disadvantage to using it in isolation: DRO requires that you focus on the behavior to be reduced. Meanwhile, acceptable alternative behaviors will go unnoticed unless you have targeted them as well. Consequently they may undergo extinction, rather than being strengthened as appropriate. This point has been dramatically supported in a study by Leitenberg, Burchard, Burchard, Fuller, and Lysaght (1977).

Six families with sixteen children aged 2 to 10

participated in a study that compared the effectiveness of Alt-R and DRO in reducing conflict. Sibling conflict was defined as physical and verbal attacks including hitting, pushing, throwing objects, taking another's belongings, making threats, name calling, and so on. During the DRO phase, children were praised and given a penny following each 1-minute interval in which there was no conflict. Instances of conflict were neither reinforced nor criticized; rather, they were ignored. During Alt-R, praise and pennies were distributed following episodes of appropriate interactions, such as playing, helping, or sharing. Both procedures were equally effective in reducing sibling conflict, but only during Alt-R did the children increase their appropriate interactions. The point is, if you elect to use a DRO procedure, don't assume that other behavior necessarily will improve. If you want to see improvement as well, target that behavior and reinforce it. Here is an excellent example of what we mean. A fourth-grade class was particularly disruptive in the school library. The children were noisy, failed to use the library as intended for reading or reference, pushed one another, and when they touched each other while walking on the carpeted floor they transmitted electric shocks to one another. Together, the librarian and the class developed a set of rules for appropriate conduct in the library (Fishbein and Wasik, 1981, p. 91):

(a) If you talk, talk quietly. (b) Choose a library book or look at library materials during the library period. (c) When walking, be very careful not to shock one another. (d) Treat one another with respect at all times, being careful not to push or fight.

The class was divided randomly into two teams. The librarian looked up several times during the period and awarded a team a point only if all its members were following the rules. To win the game, a team needed to obtain three out of four possible points. The winning team(s) could choose between working on an art project or hearing a story read by the regular classroom teacher during the last ten minutes of the afternoon. Any losing team would continue with its regular classroom work. Both

[4]Erken and Henderson (1976) have prepared a contingency management package, *The Practice Skills Mastery Program*, consisting of a series of tapes with beeps recorded at sequentially longer variable intervals.

Table 10.1
A comparison of constructive alternatives

| Procedures | Illustrative behavior | | |
	Asking for help	Calling out without raising hand	One of interest to you _____ _____
Alt-R	Positive reinforcement of asking for help	Positive reinforcement of hand raising	
Modeling	Positive reinforcement of *other* student's asking for help	Positive reinforcement of *other* student's hand raising	
DRL	Positive reinforcement of asking for help after an interval of not asking for help	Positive reinforcement of calling out after an interval of not calling out	
DRD	Positive reinforcement at the end of intervals containing reduced rates of asking for help	Positive reinforcement at the end of intervals containing reduced rates of calling out	
DRO	Positive reinforcement following interval of not asking for help	Positive reinforcement following interval of not calling out	

teams usually won the game, and there was no report of a student or two who didn't play the game. Perhaps the more positive nature of this variation of the Good Behavior Game, plus involving the students in establishing the rules, resulted in "increased student motivation to behave appropriately" (Fishbein & Wasik, 1981, p. 93).

COMPARING CONSTRUCTIVE ALTERNATIVES: AN ACTIVITY

Alt-R was presented in the previous chapter, and modeling, DRL, DRD, and DRO were described in this one. It will be easier for you to discern the differences among these procedures and to use each more effectively if you practice using the terms appropriately. In Table 10.1 we have illustrated how each procedure operates on the same behaviors. Think about how you might use this procedure to correct a minor yet irritating behavior of your own, or that of a student or colleague, and complete the third column of the table.

Summary

Several constructive alternatives to punishment were presented: modeling, and various ways of reinforcing low, diminishing, and no (zero) rates of a behavior. As with the Alt-R procedure, each relies on positive reinforcement to reduce inappropriate behavior. Unlike punitive procedures, each should help maintain or increase positive statements about oneself, school, and work. While convenient and effective, they do not necessarily provide immediate relief. These procedures, then, are recommended for reducing behavior that can be tolerated temporarily. Due to the problems associated with punitive procedures, these constructive alternatives are generally preferred. Punishment is best reserved for cases of danger to oneself or others, or for severe disruption.

All of these constructive alternatives to punishment can be combined. In fact, using positive reductive procedures in preference to punishment permits your instruction to be more positive and constructive.

Study Questions

1. List several positive classroom management procedures.
2. Define *modeling*.
3. Provide an original example of how modeling can be used to reduce a disruptive behavior in the classroom.
4. Discuss the relation between Alt-R and modeling as a reductive procedure.
5. State several advantages of combining modeling with Alt-R.
6. Mrs. Cedar finds it difficult to attend to appropriate model behavior in her classroom.
   (a) Offer a suggestion.
   (b) State one problem that could develop if she takes your suggestion.
7. Define DRL.
8. Greg is helping his peers with their science projects. His teacher is pleased to see that he has learned to assist others but is concerned with the fact that he ends up doing most of the work on their projects. She plans to use DRL to solve this problem.
   (a) Is DRL an appropriate procedure to use?
   (b) Support your answer.
9. Provide an original example of the use of DRL.
10. Mr. Spencer uses DRL to reduce the frequency of Tom's continuously asking irrelevant questions. Unfortunately he finds it difficult to attend as closely to the time as is necessary to run his program successfully. Describe an alternative method of DRL that would solve his problem.
11. Discuss one method, other than DRL, which can be used successfully to reduce talk-outs.

12. List (a) the advantages and (b) the disadvantages of DRL.
13. Describe the Good Behavior Game in detail.
14. Several students in Mr. Weber's class decided not to play the Good Behavior Game with the rest of the class. Provide him with several ways to handle the situation.
15. Suggest one original variation of the Good Behavior Game that would focus the teacher's attention on positive behavior.
16. (a) Define and (b) provide several other names for DRO.
17. Describe in detail a program using DRO to eliminate pushing in the lunch line.
18. List (a) the advantages and (b) the disadvantages of DRO.
19. Provide an original example of DRO combined with an Alt-R procedure.
20. Mrs. Burnes is unable to constantly observe Sally. List four behaviors that would be appropriate for DRO considering that Mrs. Burnes must attend to a large number of students.
21. (a) Define and (b) provide an original example of momentary DRO.
22. Describe the variation of the Good Behavior Game that uses momentary DRO.
23. Mr. Borden made all of the practical adjustments described in this chapter before beginning a program using DRO.
   (a) State one problem that still may arise.
   (b) Offer a solution.
24. The school lunch room is much too noisy. Describe in detail a plan to reduce the noise using the more positive variation of the Good Behavior Game.

25. Carol constantly pleads for later deadlines. Fill in Table 10.1 using Carol's problem behavior.
26. Under what circumstances should a punitive procedure be used to reduce behavior?
27. Offer a number of ways to minimize the disadvantages of the Good Behavior Game.
28. List (a) the advantages and (b) the disadvantages of using modeling.

References

Barrish, H. H., Saunders, M., & Wolf, M. M. (1969). Good behavior game: Effects of individual contingencies for group consequences on disruptive behavior in a classroom. *Journal of Applied Behavior Analysis*, 2, 119–124.

Barton, E. J., & Madsen, J. J. (1982). The use of awareness and omission training to control excessive drooling in a severely retarded youth. *Child Behavior Therapy*, 3, 16–18.

Bennett, D. (1980). Elimination of habitual vomiting using DRO procedures. *The Behavior Therapist*, 3, 16–18.

Butterworth, T. W., & Vogler, J. D. (1975). The use of a good behavior game with multiple contingencies to improve the behavior of a total class of fifth-grade students. *Los Angeles County Division of Program Evaluation, Research and Pupil Services Newsletter*.

Catania, A. C. (1979). *Learning*. Englewood Cliffs, NJ: Prentice-Hall.

Deitz, S. M., & Repp, A. C. (1973). Decreasing classroom misbehavior through the use of DRL schedules of reinforcement. *Journal of Applied Behavior Analysis*, 6, 457–463.

Deitz, S. M., & Repp, A. C. (1974). Differentially reinforcing low rates of misbehavior with normal elementary school children. *Journal of Applied Behavior Analysis*, 7, 622.

Erken, N., & Henderson, H. S. (1976). *Practice skills mastery program*. Logan, UT: Mastery Programs, Ltd.

Ferster, C. B., & Skinner, B. F. (1957). *Schedules of reinforcement*. New York: Appleton.

Fishbein, J. E., & Wasik, B. H. (1981). Effect of the good behavior game on disruptive library behavior. *Journal of Applied Behavior Analysis*, 14, 89–93.

Harris, V. W., & Sherman, J. A. (1973). Use and analysis of the "good behavior game" to reduce disruptive classroom behavior. *Journal of Applied Behavior Analysis*, 6, 405–417.

Leitenberg, H., Burchard, J. D., Burchard, S. N., Fuller, E. J., & Lysaght, T. V. (1977). Using positive reinforcement to suppress behaviors: Some experimental comparisons with sibling conflict. *Behavior Therapy*, 8, 168–182.

Repp, A. C., Barton, L. E., & Brulle, A. R. (1983). A comparison of two procedures for programming the differential reinforcement of other behaviors. *Journal of Applied Behavior Analysis*, 16, 435–445.

Repp, A. C., & Dietz, S. M. (1974). Reducing aggressive and self-injurious behavior of institutionalized retarded children through reinforcement of other behaviors. *Journal of Applied Behavior Analysis*, 7, 313–325.

Witt, J. C., & Adams, R. M. (1980). Direct and observed reinforcement in the classroom. *Behavior Modification*, 4, 321–336.

11 Extinction, response cost, and timeout

Goals

After completing this chapter, you should be able to:

1. Define and give an illustration of each of the following terms:
   a. Aversive stimuli and procedures
   b. Extinction
   c. Spontaneous recovery
   d. Response cost
   e. Timeout
2. List and provide an example of each of the four major unpleasant side effects that should be anticipated as a result of using aversive procedures.
3. List four things teachers can do to help prevent the occurrence of punishable offenses, and explain why each can help prevent such behavior.
4. Identify situations in which the use of aversive procedures might be appropriate.
5. Describe how peer cooperation might be achieved to obtain extinction conditions.
6. Describe what you should be prepared to do in order to use extinction effectively.
7. List and provide examples of the advantages and disadvantages of extinction.
8. Describe the difference between extinction and Alt-R.
9. List the advantages and disadvantages of response cost.
10. Describe ways of avoiding or reducing disruptive reactions to the use of response cost.
11. Describe what needs to be done to use timeout effectively.
12. List the advantages and disadvantages of timeout.
13. Describe how to avoid abusing timeout procedures.
14. Differentiate between extinction, response cost, and timeout by citing definitions, explanations, and examples.

"Get away from me, you idiot!"

Mrs. Burnes looked up just in time to see Amy's head thud into the closet door, with Lucinda standing over her.

"What's going on here, Lucinda?" the teacher rasped.

"That scrawny little witch pushed me. I told her to stay away!"

"It was just an accident," Amy countered, gulping back her tears. "I tripped on that book."

"That does it, Lucinda! Let's go. Harry, you watch the class while we go down to Mr. Rodriguez's office."

"Let go of me."

"Okay. But you march!"

An hour later, Mrs. Burnes burst into the teachers' lounge, where her colleagues were relaxing before returning to their classes. Her hair in disarray, knuckles white, she confronted Mr. Lee.

"I've had it," she snapped, breathing hard. "You

tell us how we should be positive and reinforcing, patient and understanding. How on earth are we supposed to do that when we have to put up with this sort of thing?" She related the episode of the morning. "When *I* went to school, nothing like this ever happened. We didn't even dare to whisper in class for fear of getting rapped across the knuckles with a ruler."

"At my school in the South," Ms. Jackson responded, "it was the paddle. Get into a fight or sass the teacher and off you went to the vice principal's office. I remember more than once hearing some kid yelling through the door. We used to cut a wide swath as we passed his office, I can tell you that."

"Sometimes I wish we could do something like that here," sighed Mrs. Burnes. "For a few minutes there, I cheerfully could have inflicted bodily harm on Lucinda."

"Well, I'm glad we don't," said Mr. Lee. "Anyway, even though it's still used a lot in other regions of the country, I've yet to see a convincing piece of research that supports using corporal punishment in school."[1]

He shook his head, then continued, "Most of the time, it's applied arbitrarily and inconsistently, so the rules don't have a chance of being learned; and often punishment happens after a lot of time has passed. In fact, in many states, principals are the ones to administer the punishment and a witness has to be present. If and when that happens, it's so late that the punishment hardly affects the behavior it was supposed to diminish."[2]

"I understand that," Mrs. Burnes said with a shrug. "I can guess where Lucinda gets it from — parents whose only response is to use brute force — so what else can we expect from her? It would be silly

for me to go around complimenting her every 15 minutes for *not* beating up her classmates."

"No. You're right. That isn't reasonable," Mr. Lee responded. "Some behaviors can't be tolerated — when they're dangerous to those around the misbehaving students or to the offenders themselves. We can't stand by patiently while a student improperly handles a sharp tool or a harmful chemical, or when others are being threatened or actually physically abused. At the same time, the other students have a right to be educated. So if someone is constantly disruptive, despite our best efforts, we should find a way to put a stop to it."

"I agree with that," Ms. Thomas chimed in. "But I also think that we teachers have rights too, and we should be able to perform our jobs under reasonable circumstances. It's kids like Lucinda who cause so many well-qualified teachers to abandon teaching. Kate Burnes is one of the best. We need to do everything to help make her enjoy her job."

"I'm convinced," Mr. Lee answered, as they all arose to return to work. "For our next in-service meetings, let's discuss ways to handle and reduce intolerable behavior. As long as we have to use such strategies sometimes, we might as well do so as effectively as possible."

A few days later, Mr. Lee opened the in-service session with a review of the positive approaches to reducing behavior and a caution that most of the procedures he would discuss that day were aversive — unpleasant or punitive. Aversive procedures can be valuable, he told the teachers, in reducing undesirable behaviors or at least in teaching students to discriminate acceptable from unacceptable performance (Bandura, 1965a, 1965b, 1965c; Marshall, 1965). However, because of their punitive nature, aversive procedures tend to have some unpleasant side effects. These can include avoidance, escape, or aggression; and those reactions might be transferred to the people administering the procedure as well as to other events, people, and physical properties of the environment. Punitive instructional, motivational, or management practices could well be the source of many instances of truancy, tardiness, vandalism, inattention, hostility, and other counterproductive student reactions.

---

[1]According to Friedman and Hyman (1979), only 2 of the 50 states in the United States clearly prohibited the use of corporal punishment during the year of their survey.

When corporal punishment *is* avoided it is generally "not on the basis of an objective evaluation of scientific data but rather on the basis of ethical, philosophical and sociopolitical considerations" (Gardner, 1969, p. 88).

[2]See Rose (1981) for a behavioral analysis of corporal punishment in the schools.

He also briefly reviewed some of the things the teachers could do to help prevent the occurrence of punishable offenses in the first place: involving students in specifying and enforcing rules of conduct; matching assignments to students' capabilities and interests; providing choices; consistently pairing rules and consequences, so the rules begin to govern the behavior; and making academic achievement and school in general as reinforcing as feasible. (See Chapters 4 to 8 and 13 to 22 for elaborations of these points.)[3]

This and the next chapters are concerned with the kinds of procedures to which Mr. Lee referred — strategies for reducing intolerable conduct. These include extinction, response cost, timeout, overcorrection and other forms of contingent effort, and punishment. These procedures and the stimuli paired with their application are labeled **aversive** for two reasons: because they reduce the subsequent rates of the behaviors to which they are contingently applied, and because the recipient tends to try to avoid or escape from them. As with reinforce-

ment, these procedures are defined not by their structure or intended outcome but solely by their reductive influences on behavioral patterns. Events not evoking those reactions are not aversive and indeed may be reinforcing, as in the case of a chronically naughty child who solicits scoldings or spankings because that is the best way to command attention. We caution you to reserve application of aversive procedures for cases in which it is ethically justifiable; that is, when the behavior is dangerous or severely disruptive, or for situations in which you have given positive approaches a fair trial and have failed to bring the offense under control within a reasonable span of time.

SPECIFIC AVERSIVE PROCEDURES

Aversive procedures can be categorized according to whether they involve presenting, withholding, or withdrawing of (or terminating) a particular stimulus. (The kind, amount or intensity, duration, quantity, and other characteristics of the stimuli also influence the effectiveness of these procedures.) Table 11.1 highlights some key elements of the procedures to be presented. We first will discuss each separately,

[3]Tyson (1983) found that when teachers offered choices and gently requested rather than brusquely commanded, some students tended to cooperate to a greater extent.

Table 11.1
Aversive procedures

Procedure	Present/withdraw/ withhold	What	How much/how long
Extinction	Withhold	Previous reinforcers	Completely
Response cost[a]	Withdraw	Reserve of reinforcers	N quantity
Timeout[a]	Withdraw	Reinforcing environment	T time
Overcorrection[b]	Present	Requirement to restore environment to improved state and to practice overly correct form of relevant behavior	N repetitions and/or T time
Other contingent[b] effort procedures	Present	Requirement to expend effort	N repetitions and/or T time
Punishment[b]	Present	Aversive event	I intensity

[a]These procedures are often labeled punishment as well — some call them "negative punishment" because the stimulus is withdrawn.

[b]These procedures might be grouped under the general label "positive punishment" (see Catania, 1979, p. 113).

defining it and discussing a few key aspects particular to that procedure. Afterward, in Chapter 12, we present a set of general rules for effectively using any of these procedures.

EXTINCTION

You became acquainted with extinction earlier, in Chapter 6, when we discussed *differential reinforcement*. There, as here, extinction was used to reduce the rate of a particular response. In Chapter 6, we were concerned about a behavior not occurring following a particular antecedent event; otherwise that antecedent stimulus might begin to evoke the undesired instead of the desired behavior. To avoid this problem, the desired behavior was reinforced (e.g., with a sign of approval): "Right," "Okay," "Go on," or a positive grade or evaluation. Sometimes the consequence was attention or even a more powerful reinforcer. When the inappropriate response occurred, reinforcement was withheld. The same is true here, when you hope to modify deportment. In this case, you block delivery of those reinforcers that previously had been attained.

You may remember Pam and Chris, students in Mrs. Olsen's class at Willow Grove School. Pam was off-task so often that her progress was impaired. Chris tended to dominate the conversation, often digressing to irrelevant topics. When a sequence analysis of each student's performance was carried out, it appeared that Mrs. Olsen paid Pam little attention when the girl was working busily, but quite a bit when she wasn't. Chris's digressions often were followed by praise or the close attention of his peers. Assuming that each of those events was the crucial reinforcer in its situation, extinction could be applied by making sure that the reinforcer was withheld. After casually discussing her plan with the two students, Mrs. Olsen gritted her teeth and said nothing when Pam looked out the window, doodled, or otherwise wasted time. For Chris, the problem was more difficult. The teacher could withhold her attention to his digressions, but the other students'

responses would be more difficult to manage. Perhaps, they discussed, if she consistently set an example, the other students would begin to follow her lead. Mrs. Olsen also could provide reinforcement when students did ignore Chris's irrelevant comments, so she talked with the class about setting up a reinforcing activity for the group when its members were able to ignore Chris's digressions. With Pam, Chris, and the other class members agreeing to the plan, it had a good chance of succeeding.

Using extinction effectively

When you use extinction to reduce a behavior, you need to recognize how the procedure usually operates and adjust your plans accordingly. We have learned earlier that a regularly reinforced behavior will become well established, especially if the reinforcement was initially quite dense but later occurred intermittently and gradually less and less often. Such a behavior tends to persist for a long time, even when reinforcement no longer continues. Therefore, it is often necessary to sustain extinction conditions for a long time, until the behavior eventually subsides.

Advantages and disadvantages of extinction

The predictable attributes of the procedure also influence its value. Because it takes time for extinction to have its effect, it usually is best to avoid using it on dangerous or intolerable behaviors, for you would need to reduce rapidly any performance that threatens the safety of others, such as hitting or throwing dangerous objects at people.

Extinction can be used to reduce behaviors that are tolerable to some extent, though, such as swearing, digressing from the topic of discussion, or being off-task; but Pam and Chris can be expected to continue to express those problem behaviors that have been fashioned by a long history of intermittent reinforcement before they begin to subside. In fact, during the earliest stages of extinction, the problematic behaviors may temporarily worsen, even to the extent that they are expressed in rapid bursts. Pam is likely to increase temporarily the amount of time that she is off-task. Similarly, Chris can be expected to increase the number of irrelevant comments he makes. Should Freddy intentionally ignore his classmates' teasing, it might worsen before slacking off.

Even after the problem behaviors have subsided, they may crop up periodically without any clearly apparent reason[4]: Pam starts looking out the window again. Such **spontaneous recovery** (or resurgence, Epstein & Skinner, 1980) can prove particularly risky, because at those times, people may be caught off guard and inadvertently provide the reinforcer; or they erroneously might conclude that the procedure failed and revert to their previous practices, which would make things worse than ever. The individuals with the problematic behaviors begin to learn — with or without an awareness of what is happening — that all they have to do is to keep behaving as they have been and eventually the reinforcer again will be forthcoming.

Another possible pitfall in using extinction is that, as with the other procedures discussed in this chapter, it may be accompanied by escape or aggression. You will know what we're talking about if you can recall your reaction the last time you used a pay phone and were cut off in the middle of a conversation without any coins left with which to contact the operator; or when a vending machine failed to deliver your purchase or return your change; or when you spent hours preparing a gourmet meal and no one complimented your efforts. Revenge would have been so sweet.

One nice thing about using extinction is that you may not need to do anything, nasty or otherwise. It takes little of your time, although much of your attention. So if you plan to apply the procedure, be sure you have identified the reinforcer(s) that has or have been supporting the behavior, and be certain the reinforcer(s) can be withheld. In addition, anticipate that change will occur slowly and that you

[4]Epstein (1983) argues convincingly that responses "resurge" lawfully — depending on many factors, such as schedules with which old and new behaviors are reinforced, the duration of the reinforcement, and others.

may have to contend with aggression or escape responses.

You also have a responsibility to see to it that reinforcement is provided at other times to compensate for the person's loss. It is a natural reaction to seek reinforcement. If it is not obtained via productive means, other strategies will be used. So if Mrs. Olsen manages to implement her extinction procedure, she would be best advised to provide reinforcement to Chris and Pam at other more appropriate times; otherwise her success may be limited.

Here is another example. Suppose one of the teachers in your school is continually complaining that the students are rude, the paperwork requirements excessive, the classroom supplies scarce. She suffers from a lack of appreciation, inadequate support, and on and on. Her complaints make her and everyone else increasingly more miserable. Provided you were very tactful about it, you could mention the issue to her and, with her concurrence, the staff collectively could ignore the complaints henceforth. All of you sustain the treatment, while complaints ebb and flow, until they do begin to diminish. Be fair, though. Your colleague deserves some form of attention. Try to give it when she makes a positive or constructive statement. In the beginning, you might even be especially attentive to neutral remarks, such as comments about the weather, or find something about her to compliment — a new outfit or, preferably, a recent accomplishment. Eventually that teacher may surprise you pleasantly by offering constructive comments.

Does some of this sound familiar? It should. We are only a step away from a procedure about which you read previously: *reinforcing incompatible behaviors*. The only thing you would need to add is to target the particular behaviors to be reinforced. Then *voilà*, you have Alt-R.

Extinction, as we have seen, is a fairly benign but often slow-acting strategy. It requires perseverance and patience, and you must anticipate some temporarily unpleasant side effects. Know, too, that stimuli paired with extinction conditions can acquire aversive properties. Do not be surprised if your previously complaining colleague temporarily avoids you and the others or the place where you all tend to gather. If you must reduce a behavior rapidly, you would be ill advised to rely solely on extinction. Rather, for behaviors that are dangerous or severely disruptive, you may need to consider trying one of the procedures we describe next.

RESPONSE COST

"Quick. Hide it. She's coming!"

Ms. Hollingsworth rounded the corner of the school building just in time to notice Tyrone attempting to conceal a shiny object in his pocket.

"Is that what I think it is? Let me see."

Tyrone abashedly hands her a pocketknife.

"You know that this breaks one of our important school rules, don't you? What is the penalty for that?"

"I guess our group loses 20 points," he said.

The other boys and girls protested, "We told you not to. Now look, we'll miss our extra recess for at least a week."

Items that could be used as weapons had been banned from the school ever since a student in a fight was slashed badly by a boy wielding a knife. The students were all familiar with the rule, but occasionally the temptation to gain their peers' attention by challenging such regulations was too great.

To prevent such occurrences, Ms. Hollingsworth had assembled her class to develop a set of rules. They had suggested several "do"s and "do not"s. Among the "do"s were actions such as working quietly, helping each other, asking for permission to leave the room, and so on. The "do not"s included throwing objects, teasing, swearing, hitting, carrying weapons, taking objects belonging to others, and performing additional acts the teacher or students felt should not be permitted.

To encourage the students to comply with the rules, Ms. Hollingsworth had suggested a game. She had divided the class into teams, according to the students' seating arrangements. Each morning every team was given 10 points. Then at the end of the morning and afternoon sessions, teams whose mem-

bers had followed all the "do"s and avoided all the "do not"s would be awarded 5 additional points. Points would be deducted for violations committed by team members: a few for the less-severe infractions, such as teasing or swearing; more for those considered dangerous, such as bringing potentially dangerous objects to school. A half hour before each school day ended, the teams tallied up their points. All teams with 17 or more points (or the team with the highest number) got to select an activity from a *reinforcement menu* — a game, free time, special assignments, or privileges. The system worked well, as the students encouraged one another to remember to follow the class rules. Having caused his team members to lose so many points — and thus, extra recess time — discouraged Tyrone from ever bringing a pocketknife to school again.

The technical label for the penalty procedure is **response cost,** as it involves *withdrawing a specific quantity of reinforcers contingent on a response.* In the case just described, the response of carrying a knife resulted in a cost to the team, causing its members to lose a quantity of reinforcers — in their case, extra recess time or other reinforcing events. Perhaps you already have recognized that our society also applies practices resembling response cost in its attempts to manage misbehavior. These practices take the form of fines and penalties: loss of yardage in football, traffic fines, cash penalties for lack of compliance with particular safety and health regulations, and others.

Using response cost effectively

Response cost has been used effectively as a tool of classroom management, in ways similar to those described above.[5] The procedure also has been implemented to decrease off-task behavior and consequently increase completion of academic tasks by hyperactive children (Rapport, Murphy, & Bailey, 1982) as well as to reduce stealing in elementary school classrooms (Switzer, Deal, & Bailey, 1977). In

[5]Also see applications of the "good behavior" game (Barrish, Saunders, & Wolf, 1969; Fishbein & Wasik, 1981; Harris & Sherman, 1973).

the latter case, the authors worked with three classes in which stealing was a severe problem. First they attempted a typical ploy: presenting weekly lectures on honesty. As you might have anticipated, this accomplished little; stealing remained high. Then a group contingency was invoked. The entire class would lose its free time if any stolen objects were not returned within a set time, while the class would earn extra free time if no thefts occurred at all on that particular day. This approach essentially eliminated the problem for the remainder of the study.

Advantages and disadvantages of response cost

In addition to demonstrating itself to be an effective method of reducing behavior, response cost can be relatively easy to implement, particularly if the reinforcers subtracted are symbolic rather than real. It is easier to subtract points or reinforcing activities than to snatch away a reinforcing object. But do not be surprised if your application of response cost generates the same sorts of fight-or-flight reactions we already encountered with other reductive strategies. (Recall your own reactions the last time you realized you were being signaled by a police officer to pull over.)

With special planning, however, you can avoid particularly disruptive reactions. Arrange, as we have done successfully in our work, to return a portion of a fine paid by a penalized student if he or she returns to work right away. Alternatively, at the beginning of a session, provide a bonus pool of reinforcers — points or tokens, for instance — but keep them under your management. Subtract a predetermined number contingent on infractions, delivering any that remain in the pool at the end of the session. (If you use this tactic, though, we caution you to avoid delivering the bonus reinforcers after a misbehavior occurs. It would be best to wait until a few minutes of good behavior have transpired first. Can you guess why?)

Mrs. Burnes might attempt to halt Lucinda's aggressive outbursts by using response cost, or perhaps by trying the game Ms. Hollingsworth used, as described earlier. In case other students appeared to place undue pressure on Lucinda, thereby possibly evoking the very behavior targeted for elimination, Lucinda could be placed in a team consisting of a small group of helpful and supportive peers or, if need be, on a one-person team. In the latter case, each time she attacked another child, only she would lose some reinforcers.

Response cost requires that individuals have in their possession some reinforcers that can be contingently removed. If that condition does not hold, you might turn to a closely related procedure: timeout.

TIMEOUT

As the bus pulled away from the state capitol, heading toward a nearby amusement park, Mr. Markham heard a pop and sizzle and his sensitive nose picked up a familiar aroma. Approaching Tommy and Fred, he noticed them hurriedly closing their brown paper bags.

"That wouldn't be beer, boys, would it?"

"So what if it is?"

"You know that's against the rules. Every student was sent a letter clearly stating that alcoholic beverages and drugs would not be permitted during the social studies outing. You'd better give that to me. And I'm afraid you'll have to stay on the bus with the driver while we're at the park."

As the other students debarked, Mr. Markham instructed the two boys to sit far apart, under the driver's supervision. They remained there until the group departed again an hour later.

The procedure Mr. Markham used is called **timeout,** as the boys' *access to reinforcement was withdrawn for a period of time.* With timeout, the *opportunity for reinforcement is removed,* in contrast to extinction, wherein a usual reinforcer is just withheld. Timeout also differs from response cost in that no actual reinforcers are removed — only the opportunity to gain them is, for a specific amount of time. Yet, as with all the procedures included in this chapter, timeout resembles the other two by demonstrating a reductive effect. In the present instance, Tommy and Fred have lost access to the reinforcing experience of spending an hour at the amusement park with their friends.

As with response cost, a semblance of the timeout procedure is used regularly to try to control misdeeds in our society, taking the form of jail sentences, time in a penalty box, disciplinary suspensions from work or school, and so on. In schools, teachers long have used isolation as a management tool. We say a "semblance is used," though, because often those practices do not actually conform to the definition of timeout. Either the opportunity for reinforcement has not been totally blocked or the period of time is not preestablished. Indeterminate prison sentences, periods of solitary confinement, and removal of an individual from an aversive situation are not instances that conform to the definition of timeout.

Using timeout effectively

To use timeout effectively, you must be sure that what you intend to be a period of nonreinforcement is not actually reinforcing. For instance, Tyrone has a bad habit of leaning back in his chair so that it rests on the two rear legs alone. Twice he has fallen over, once bumping the child behind him and once narrowly avoiding injury to himself. The next time Ms. Hollingsworth notices Tyrone sitting that way, she sends him to sit behind the file cabinet. Relieved of the distraction, Ms. Hollingsworth continues with her math lesson. After a little while she is distracted again, as she sees Tyrone peeking from behind the cabinet and making funny faces. The other children are giggling and no longer are attending to their work. Tyrone does not seem to be suffering in the least. Do you think his rate of leaning back in his chair will diminish?

This example illustrates some of the pitfalls that might face your attempts to use timeout. First, the environment was not arranged to block reinforcement. Second, the time period was not fixed, and Ms. Hollingsworth forgot where Tyrone was. Third, Tyrone succeeded in avoiding an unpleasant situation. He performed poorly in math and did not enjoy it one bit. By removing him from math class, Ms. Hollingsworth inadvertently was reinforcing the behavior she had hoped to eliminate. The frequent management practice of sending unruly children to the principal's office also may backfire for similar reasons. We have known cases in which the principal or school secretary has taken advantage of a culprit's presence to send him or her on errands or have that student answer the telephone — high-status jobs in those schools.

What Ms. Hollingsworth might have done instead was to find a location in which Tyrone could not attract the attention of the other students or engage in other pleasant activities. To avoid losing track of Tyrone — and not be tempted to overuse the procedure by ridding herself of his irritating presence — she could set a kitchen timer or wrist alarm. The signal then would prompt her to recall Tyrone to the group, assuming he was not misbehaving at the time. Otherwise she could reset the device for another couple of moments to cue her again to observe Tyrone and determine whether or not his conduct merited his return to the group. Finally, she would extend every effort to make math class more reinforcing for Tyrone, perhaps by adjusting his assignments to his capabilities or interests or by providing him with the assistance he needed to receive the reinforcement intrinsic to success. Otherwise she had better select a different reductive procedure for classes that Tyrone did not particularly enjoy, such as seating him away from the others for a period of time during which he still would be expected to participate in the lesson but not receive other reinforcement. [This procedure has been labeled **contingent observation** by Porterfield, Herbert-Jackson, and Risley (1976).] Or possibly she might use response cost by removing some of his points or attempt one of the procedures described in the next chapter.

If you have met with little success in using timeout, you too may need to make similar adjustments. What changes does the following episode suggest to you?

A 16-year-old retarded client failed to cease spitting and injuring himself despite being isolated following such acts. So Solnick, Rincover, and Peterson (1977) reasoned that perhaps the boy's normal environment needed to be made more reinforcing. After new toys, verbal prompts, and praise were added to that environment, the timeout procedure began to take effect.

Perhaps you would like to use timeout as a general management procedure for handling serious infractions by any member of a group, as Murphy, Hutchinson, and Bailey (1983) did to control aggression on the playground. Aggressive acts during organized games were treated with a two-minute timeout on the bench for the offender.

If it were not feasible to remove several offenders from the group at once, you could, instead, remove the reinforcing environment from them, which Foxx and Shapiro (1978) accomplished by providing each of their severely retarded students a ribbon to use as a necktie. If a child engaged in one of a specifically designated set of misbehaviors, the tie was removed for three minutes or longer, if necessary, until the misbehavior stopped. Treats and praise were delivered to the children every few minutes, provided they wore their ties. In a regular classroom, this procedure could be effected by designating a section of the room as the **timeout area.** Students committing particular violations could be moved to that place for a fixed interval, as well as separated from one another, of course. While seated in that location, they would not be called on or permitted to interact with others in the class. Naturally you would have to reinforce heavily the other students' withholding of attention from the offenders during the interim.

Advantages and disadvantages of timeout

One nice thing about using timeout is that you need not present any aversive events. All you have to do is separate the individual from the reinforcers for a while. In that sense, timeout should be fairly benign. Provided that the offenders comply with your instructions to initiate the timeout period, it is a relatively simple procedure to use. It also features the added advantage of removing from your immediate presence an individual whose behavior has been irritating to you or others in the environment. But that advantage, as we have seen, also can become a source of difficulty.

In our experience, timeout frequently is abused as a procedure. Probably because it is negatively reinforcing to the user, timeout tends to be overly selected as a management tool. We have seen timeout used as a convenience to staff, rather than as an educative tool: students have been sent to timeout for being off-task for a while or for causing minor distractions and other seemingly minimal problems; the procedure has been used capriciously, without preset times; sometimes students were forgotten for extended periods. We have experienced situations in which personnel have contended that by using their idiosyncratic versions of timeout, they had demonstrated that they were knowledgeable in the skills of behavior modification (or behavior therapy or applied behavior analysis).

Any temptation to abuse this procedure can be avoided in the following ways: reserve timeout for the modification of behaviors that are clearly intolerable, and check any legal restrictions on the way you intend to use it. Also, verify your procedure with your organization. Consult written statements of policy regarding timeout and obtain the informed consent of the student's parent or guardian before using any timeout arrangement that departs from standard practice in a major way or that involves isolating the student completely. For example, many state laws require psychologists who work in institutions to submit proposed timeout programs to a review committee. Use a safe area, readily supervised. Then, as always, collect careful data, baseline first, then rates of the problem during the timeout intervention. If the behavior does not appear to diminish after several days, modify the procedure; check for inadvertent reinforcement and control it, or else turn to another strategy. Also, adopt a system for reminding the teacher when the timeout period is over. Short timeouts are preferred, because once the student has been exposed to the longer durations, the briefer ones may lose their effect. If people using timeout are required to record when the individual entered into and was released from timeout, they will be apt to adhere to the specific procedure more rigorously.

As we have seen, you must be able to manage the critical reinforcers if timeout is to have any effect. With some students, that will not be possible. For them, being separated from the ongoing school activities may be a pleasure, giving them time to relax, fantasize, self-stimulate. The timeout procedure will not work. If that is the case and you have tried or rejected using response cost and extinction, you may find that requiring the student to expend effort as a consequence of severe misconduct may rectify the situation. We will turn to this procedure, among others, in the next chapter.

Summary

Three aversive procedures were presented in this chapter: extinction, response cost, and timeout. To help you recognize each and differentiate among the three, as well as identify the contingent effort and punishment procedures, we included Table 11.1. Note how extinction involves withholding reinforcers from a previously reinforced behavior, while response cost and timeout both involve withdrawing reinforcers or the opportunity for reinforcement. When response cost is used, a predetermined quantity of reinforcers are withdrawn following each occurrence of the targeted behavior. Timeout, on the other hand, involves withdrawing the opportunity to receive reinforcement for the behavior over a prespecified time period, either by removing the student from the reinforcing environment or by removing the reinforcing environment from the student. Both response cost and timeout reduce targeted behavior rapidly, while the effect of extinction tends to be slower.

In the next chapter we discuss contingent effort procedures, punishment, *and* general guidelines for effectively applying all the procedures listed in Table 11.1. Thus, before selecting and using any aversive procedure, be sure to read the guidelines presented in Chapter 12.

Study Questions

1. Discuss (a) the advantages and (b) the disadvantages of using aversive procedures. (Did you notice that the word *aversive* does not include a *d*?)
2. List several ways to prevent the occurrence of punishable offenses before they happen.
3. In this chapter, both the procedures and the stimuli paired with their application are labeled aversive for what two reasons?
4. State the similarity between the definition of reinforcement and the definitions of the aversive procedures.
5. Under what circumstances are aversive procedures ethically acceptable?
6. List a set of criteria used to categorize aversive procedures.
7. (a) Define and (b) provide an original example of *extinction*.
8. Design a procedure for using extinction to eliminate Tom's hitting his classmates. (Be sure that all of the students in his class are involved.)
9. Describe in detail the course followed by a behavior undergoing extinction.
10. List three behaviors that are (a) appropriate and (b) inappropriate candidates for an extinction procedure. Justify your selection.
11. Jean's father frequently buys her candy when she whines at the checkout counter. Thus, he intermittently reinforces her inappropriate behavior. He plans to put her whining on extinction. Describe in detail the

changes he is likely to see in her behavior as time progresses.

12. Define *spontaneous recovery*, and give an example from your own behavior.

13. Discuss the importance of understanding spontaneous recovery.

14. Provide one original example of (a) escape and (b) aggression as side effects of extinction.

15. Describe the advantages of using extinction.

16. List three steps that should be considered when instituting an extinction procedure.

17. Provide one of your major responsibilities when you use extinction.

18. Describe the relation between extinction and Alt-R.

19. Use an original example to demonstrate that a stimulus paired with extinction conditions can acquire aversive properties.

20. Define *response cost*.

21. Provide three original examples of response cost.

22. List (a) the advantages and (b) the disadvantages of response cost.

23. Discuss ways to avoid especially disruptive reactions to response cost.

24. (a) Define and (b) provide an original example of timeout.

25. Compare and contrast timeout with (a) extinction and (b) response cost.

26. Provide two original examples of timeout as it is applied in our society.

27. State three pitfalls that might face you in your attempts to use timeout.

28. Mr. Morgan requires that Betty sit alone isolated from the reinforcement of her peers for three minutes whenever she throws papers in class. Unfortunately, he is very busy attending to the other students and often forgets to invite Betty to rejoin the class at the end of the three minutes. Suggest a way to help Mr. Morgan solve his problem.

29. A teacher is unable to remove several offenders from a group simultaneously. Provide a solution (using an example to illustrate).

30. List (a) the advantages and (b) the disadvantages of using timeout.

31. Describe ways in which abuse of timeout can be avoided.

32. Discuss how you would go about selecting a duration for a particular timeout situation.

33. (a) Provide three fictitious examples of children whose problematic behaviors would not be reduced by timeout.
(b) Support your answers.

34. Demonstrate that you thoroughly understand each of the aversive procedures by adding a fifth column to Table 11.1. Label the column "Example" and fill in the column with examples that illustrate the complete operation.

References

Bandura, A. (1965a). Influence of models' reinforcement contingencies on the acquisition of imitative responses. *Journal of Personality and Social Psychology, 1,* 589–595.

Bandura, A. (1965b). Vicarious processes: A case of no-trial learning. In L. Berkowitz (Ed.), *Advances in experimental social psychology.* Vol. 2. New York: Academic Press.

Bandura, A. (1965c). Behavioral modification through modeling procedures. In L. Krasner & L. P. Ullman, (Eds.), *Research in behavior modification.* New York: Holt, Rinehart and Winston.

Barrish, H. H., Saunders, M., & Wolf, M. M. (1969). Good behavior game: Effects of individual contingencies for group consequences on disruptive behavior in a classroom. *Journal of Applied Behavior Analysis, 2,* 119–124.

Catania, A. C. (1979). *Learning.* Englewood Cliffs, NJ: Prentice-Hall.

Epstein, R. (1983). Resurgence of previously reinforced behavior during extinction. *Behavior Analysis Letters, 3,* 391–397.

Epstein, R., & Skinner, B. F. (1980). Resurgence of responding after the cessation of response-independence reinforcement. *Proceedings of the National Academy of Sciences*, U.S.A., 77, 6251–6253.

Fishbein, J. E., & Wasik, B. H. (1981). Effect of the good behavior game on disruptive library behavior. *Journal of Applied Behavior Analysis, 14*, 89–93.

Friedman, R. H., & Hyman, I. A. (1979). Corporal punishment in the schools: A descriptive survey of state regulations. In I. A. Hyman & J. H. Wise (Eds.), *Corporal Punishment in American Education*. Philadelphia: Temple University Press.

Foxx, R. M., & Shapiro, S. T. (1978). The timeout ribbon: A nonexclusionary timeout procedure. *Journal of Applied Behavior Analysis, 11*, 125–136.

Gardner, W. I. (1969). Use of punishment with the severely retarded: A review. *American Journal of Mental Deficiency, 74*, 86–103.

Harris, V. W., & Sherman, J. A. (1973). Use and analysis of the "good behavior game" to reduce disruptive classroom behavior. *Journal of Applied Behavior Analysis, 6*, 405–417.

Marshall, H. H. (1965). The effect of punishment on children: A review of the literature and a suggested hypothesis. *The Journal of Genetic Psychology, 106*, 23–33.

Murphy, H. A., Hutchinson, J. M., & Bailey, J. S. (1983). Behavioral school psychology goes outdoors: The effect of organized games on playground aggression. *Journal of Applied Behavior Analysis, 16*, 29–35.

Porterfield, J. K., Herbert-Jackson, E., & Risley, T. R. (1976). Contingent observation: An effective and acceptable procedure for reducing disruptive behavior of young children in a group setting. *Journal of Applied Behavior Analysis, 9*, 55–64.

Rapport, M. D., Murphy, A., & Bailey, J. S. (1982). The effects of a response cost treatment tactic on hyperactive children. *Journal of School Psychology, 18*, 98–111.

Rose, T. L. (1981). The corporal punishment cycle: A behavioral analysis of the maintenance of corporal punishment in the schools. *Education and Treatment of Children, 4*, 157–169.

Solnick, J. V., Rincover, A., & Peterson, C. R. (1977). Some determinates of the reinforcing and punishing effects of timeout. *Journal of Applied Behavior Analysis, 10*, 415–424.

Switzer, E. B., Deal, T. E., & Bailey, J. S. (1977). The reduction of stealing in second graders using a group contingency. *Journal of Applied Behavior Analysis, 10*, 267–272.

Tyson, M. E. (1983). *An analysis of two styles of teacher-client interaction*. Doctoral dissertation, University of Massachusetts.

12 Overcorrection, contingent effort, and other forms of punishment

Goals

After completing this chapter, you should be able to:

1. Define and give an illustration of each of the following terms:
   a. Overcorrection
   b. Contingent effort
   c. Presenting punishing stimuli
2. Identify, discuss, and illustrate each of the four components of overcorrection.
3. Identify the similarities and differences between overcorrection and other contingent effort procedures.
4. Describe what must be taken into consideration when using nonrelevant forms of contingent effort.
5. Describe how physical guidance should be administered when used in connection with a contingent effort procedure.
6. Discuss the rationale for the authors' position on the use of corporal punishment in the schools.
7. Describe the effective use of contingent effort and punishment procedures.
8. Differentiate between extinction, response cost, timeout, contingent effort, overcorrection, and presenting punishing stimuli by providing definitions, explanations, and examples.

Ms. Hollingsworth had asked Mr. Lee to drop by to observe Tyrone. She felt the boy might be a good candidate for mainstreaming into a regular class but wondered about some of his social deficits. It proved a timely moment for the guidance counselor's visit, for once again Tyrone leaned back and fell over with a crash, this time landing squarely on Tommy's foot. Fortunately, neither was seriously hurt, but how about the next time?

"Timeout seemed to be working," Ms. Hollingsworth sighed after class. "I have this little wrist counter that I depress every time I see Tyrone leaning back," she explained, showing Mr. Lee the resulting graph (Figure 12.1).

"Yes, it certainly does seem to be working, but apparently from what we just saw, not fast enough. It's a good thing no one was seriously injured," he replied. "Perhaps we should consider trying **overcorrection**."

OVERCORRECTION

"What do I have to do?" asked the teacher.

"The idea is to *require that the offender expend extra effort as a function of the infrac-*

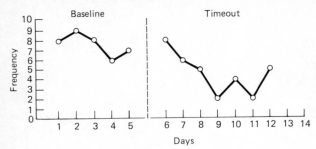

Figure 12.1

Number of times Tyrone leaned back in his chair.

tion.[1] You ask him to do two things: according to Foxx and Azrin's 1973 paper, he should first *overly correct the effects that the inappropriate act had on the environment*, and second *intensively practice idealized forms of the relevant behavior*. Correcting the environmental effects in this case would require

[1]Occasionally in the literature one finds some of the procedures presented in this section classified as "response cost." The operations differ, as Luce, Christian, Lipsker, and Hall (1981) have contended: in response cost, reinforcers are deducted; here, aversive events are *presented* in the form of work requirements. For this reason we have elected to differentiate these procedures and use the general term *contingent effort* to identify those that require additional work or effort as the consequence. However, as you will recall from Chapters 4 and 9, any consequence in which an aversive event is presented and results in a decrease in the behavior (including contingent effort) is a punishment procedure.

that Tyrone pick up his chair, dust it off, and place it where it belongs. He also would need to apologize to you and the class and, of course, to Tommy for the disruption, and straighten other chairs throughout the room. An overly correct form of relevant behavior might require that he repeatedly practice keeping his two feet firmly on the floor, back arched straight, his hands on the desk, with his eyes directed toward you or his work. Do you think you could try that?"

"That means I'll have to stop what I'm doing, but I'm used to that by now. So are the other students. They know to proceed with their work or take out a book. We're doing that already with the timeout program. But won't it take a little longer to carry out this overcorrection routine?"

"Yes. But experience has shown that it produces pretty rapid results."

"Then I guess the bother will be worth it," Ms. Hollingsworth decided.

Two weeks later, the graph looked much better (Figure 12.2).

Overcorrection is but one of several procedures involving **contingent effort** (Luce et al., 1981), or *a requirement that offenders exert themselves as a consequence of a misbehavior*. This exertion may take various forms. Rapidly performed work requirements repeatedly have shown their ability to reduce subsequent rates of a behavior. In fact, Foxx and Bechtel (1982) and Miltenberger and Fuqua (1981)

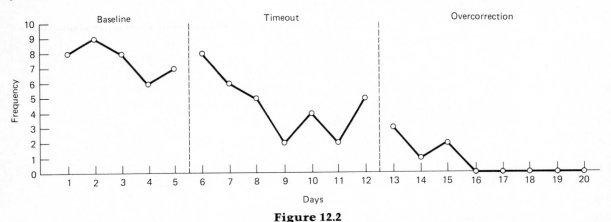

Figure 12.2

Number of times Tyrone leaned back in his chair, under treatment with timeout and then with overcorrection.

cited close to 100 studies in which overcorrection and other contingent effort procedures were employed on aggressive-disruptive, self-stimulatory, self-injurious, toileting, oral, and educational-social behaviors. We will consider other forms of contingent effort following our discussion of overcorrection.

Using overcorrection effectively

When Foxx and Azrin first described overcorrection in 1972, they indicated that it should contain four components: restitution, positive practice, education, and relevance to the offense through topographically similar responses.

The restitutional aspect of overcorrection requires that the offender restore the disrupted environment, not only to its previous condition but to an improved state. That is why Tyrone would be asked to apologize to everyone, to right and dust off his chair, and to reposition the other chairs in the class. If students observed to be embellishing school property with graffiti were required not only to remove their own productions but also to clean much larger areas, such as a complete wall, that would be another example of restitution.

The positive practice component of overcorrection mandates that the disrupter intensively practice overly correct forms of the relevant behavior, which helps the individual learn correct forms of the preferred alternative especially well. By having to practice sitting up straight with his feet firmly on the floor and his hands at rest on the desk or at work on his assignments for several minutes a number of times in a row, Tyrone should begin to acquire the more appropriate posture. Similarly we could ask our graffiti artists to repair or paint walls or to refinish furniture, enabling them to acquire new and more positive skills.

As you can see, both the restitutional and positive practice aspects of our overcorrection examples are relevant and educative. The work that offenders must do relates to their misconduct, and it teaches or increases acceptable alternatives. This approach compares favorably with more arbitrary and punitive kinds of required exertion that many teachers have imposed over the years, such as having students write some rule 500 times, press their noses to the blackboard, or hold their arms over their heads against the wall for extended periods. (Yes, these sorts of disciplinary practices still prevail.)

Some behaviors don't bother others but are harmful to the individuals themselves. In such cases, restitution can be personal. For instance, Sanford sucks his thumb, and his teeth are beginning to protrude. When he is seen with his thumb in his mouth at home or at school, he is sent to the sink to brush his teeth, rinse with mouthwash, and scrub his hands. Technically, this is designed to remedy the introduction of an unclean object into his mouth. Then he is asked to practice a task requiring proper use of his fingers, such as sorting many small objects or removing tacks or staples from the floor and all the bulletin boards in the room.[2]

In other instances, it is not appropriate to apply all four aspects of overcorrection. Positive practice has been used without the restitutional aspect to teach spelling in at least two cases by Foxx and Jones (1978) and Ollendick and colleagues (1980). In the first instance, each misspelled word was treated by having the student write (1) its correct spelling, (2) the correct phonetic spelling, (3) its part of speech, (4) its complete dictionary definition, and (5) five original sentences in which it was used correctly. (Those from the dictionary and the spelling text were not acceptable.) As a result, more than half the students increased their spelling grades by over ten percent, the equivalent of a full letter grade. Follow-up data indicated that their improvement sustained reasonably well the following year. In the second case (Ollendick et al., 1980, p. 647), learning-disabled students improved their spelling by means of a similar method:

> The child was required to (a) listen to the word pronounced by the teacher's aide, (b) pronounce the word correctly, (c) say aloud each letter of the word,

---

[2]To find out how the positive practice aspect of overcorrection has been used to correct self-stimulation and lack of visual attending by severely handicapped students, see Epstein, Doke, Sajwaj, Sorrell, and Rimmer, 1974; Foxx, 1977; and Foxx and Azrin, 1973.

and (d) write the word correctly. This sequence of remediation was designed to incorporate multiple channels of learning and was repeated five times for each misspelled word.

When the positive practice was combined with reinforcement for correctly spelled words, the students learned more effectively and enjoyed the process more than with either of the two procedures separately.

Research indicates that restitution may not always be necessary, even in situations in which it *can* be applied (Carey & Bucher, 1981). If restitution was eliminated, you could focus on the positive practice of the behavior you want to teach and the procedure wouldn't take so long. It would mean, though, that someone other than the student would gain the experience of expending effort to repair any damage.

NONRELEVANT FORMS OF CONTINGENT EFFORT

There will be times when you find yourself at a loss to figure out what relevant form of positive practice or restitution to administer. What is the positive antithesis of having a temper tantrum, swearing, or committing aggression against others? Although apologizing could serve as one form of restitution, how would one go about requiring "doing nothing" and then positively practice it? In that case, you may need to apply only the part of the procedure that involves an expenditure of effort. For example, you might have the student stand up and sit down ten times or run around the track. However, the procedure then no longer would merit the label *overcorrection:* "Procedures that employ topographically dissimilar consequences or responses are not overcorrection regardless of whether they share several common components and characteristics with overcorrection" (Foxx & Bechtel, 1982, p. 280).

Nonrelevant work prescribed contingent on the misbehavior nonetheless may prove effective, constructive, or useful. Running laps or doing push-ups

or sit-ups could constitute reasonable physical exercises. The performance of housekeeping chores might, minimally, benefit others. Consequences of those types have been found to reduce misbehaviors effectively. Arm and hand exercises have been used to reduce inappropriate foot movements and vocalizations (Epstein et al., 1974); 10 minutes of window washing has been used to decrease swearing (Fischer & Nehs, 1978); and **contingent exercise** — standing up and sitting down ten times — virtually eliminated aggressive acts and comments, such as "I'm going to step on your face" or "I'm going to kill you" (Luce, Delquadri, & Hall, 1980).

Using contingent effort procedures effectively

Should you decide to apply a contingency requiring the student to work in some form unrelated to the misbehavior, we urge you to consider carefully what that activity will be. First, there is always the possibility that the student may begin to avoid or dislike contingent effort activities, such as running or push-ups, because that activity has been used as an aversive consequence. Second, you should select a task that will benefit the student first, and then, only to some limited extent, others. Avoid activities that will reinforce yourself or others strongly, otherwise it will be tempting to overuse the contingency. So if Mrs. Burnes decides to use this sort of procedure to reduce Lucinda's aggression in school, she would be better advised to have Lucinda perform some physical exercise or remove and put away all items not belonging on the classroom floor, rather than having the girl wash her teacher's car.

We add another caution in case you plan to try one of these contingent effort methods: be reasonably certain that the student will cooperate, either when verbally instructed or physically guided to perform the strenuous activity. You do not want to find yourself engaged in a tug-of-war with a student, particularly one who may be larger or stronger than yourself. Before abandoning the idea, though, see if patience will work. You can wait until the student calms down, helping matters along by appearing relaxed yourself. You also can teach your students and yourself to relax by using the kinds of techniques that Cautela and Groden (1978) have found successful with adults and severely emotionally disturbed children: diaphragmatic breathing, imagery, and other methods. Another strategy for applying overcorrection with resistant students is to place them in a location where they can calm down. Then continue with the training. In a case reported by Matson and Stephens (1977), a female psychiatric client, June, had the unpleasant habit of picking up small objects and throwing them in the faces of other patients and staff. Overcorrection training consisted of having her apologize to each victim, and for five minutes pick up objects from the floor and throw them in the trash. Early in the program June became so disruptive that it was impossible to guide her through the overcorrection routine. So she was placed in a quiet room until she was no longer agitated, and then returned to the ward to complete the positive practice sequence.

If you do use physical guidance, apply only the least amount necessary, gradually reducing pressure and contact. Using excessive force while applying contingent effort procedures can (and has) caused injury. By gradually lessening the amount of guidance you provide, you should find, as Matson and Stephens did, that the individual will begin voluntarily to comply with the procedure before very long. If neither this nor any of the previously presented reductive strategies succeeds, however, you may need to turn to punishment.

PRESENTING PUNISHING STIMULI

As we have seen in Chapter 9, punishment is defined according to its effect on behavior. (Now is a good time to review that definition. See page 144.) Only if the subsequent rate of a behavior diminishes as a function of the contingent delivery of a stimulus can we say that punishment has occurred. Depending on the circumstances and the learning history of the individual, this punishing stimulus can be as mild as a quizzical look or as harsh as a beating. In actuality, some events that you might assume to be

punishing can be reinforcing, and vice versa. Tommy and Fred have firmly established roles for themselves as tough guys, providing them with status among many of their peers. Marissa is not the only one captivated by those charms. The boys would not welcome public praise from a school official for fear of being teased and branded with such labels as "teacher's pet." They carefully avoid soliciting praise from those senior to them.

In contrast, some people may find those events most of us would tend to label punishing, like being physically struck, to be reinforcing. Occasionally adults and possibly even some children actually seek physical pain, which will happen if the person's reinforcement history has been such that the physical abuse frequently served as a prelude to a powerful reinforcing event, such as sexual gratification, attention, or affection. This sequence of events should not be difficult to understand for those of us who have struck someone in a fit of frustration. Then, beset by remorse, we follow by offering consolation and begging the person's forgiveness. Fortunately, any such effects are reversible, if we dispense reinforcers under more appropriate circumstances; so the unwholesome cycle can be broken.

Using punishment effectively

As in selecting reinforcers, the best way to identify a punisher for an individual is by means of observational recording; see what events tend to reduce the individual's rates of expressing particular behaviors. Then ask yourself (and if appropriate, other concerned individuals, such as parents, advocates, or your supervisor) if the punisher is under your control and if you can apply it ethically and humanely to the benefit of the individual in question. (Recall that sometimes delivering punishment can be extremely reinforcing to the user.)

What is ethical or humane? That question is not readily answered. For a timid student like Amy, being corrected or scolded for giving an incorrect answer may constitute severe punishment, especially as she is so responsive to praise when she does answer correctly. For a child like Lucinda, whose life has been laced with physical violence, a scolding may have little effect. To find an effective punisher for Lucinda, one might have to select a stimulus that would inflict intense discomfort. That could do her injury and hardly would be considered humane. In her case the use of alternative strategies like response cost, timeout, or overcorrection would make more sense.

There are times when even dispensing severe discomfort might be justified, provided that it causes no physical injury. We have seen cases of self-abusive or violent clients who have blinded or severely injured themselves or their care givers. Often such people fail to respond to any of the more benign treatments, such as the reinforcement of alternative behaviors or of response omission; however, a few contingent exposures to a noxious odor, taste, sound, or other sensation rapidly eliminates the maladaptive behavior. What would be more ethically defensible—years of fruitlessly trying ineffective remedies justified on humanitarian grounds or a few days' worth of effective punishment for the abusive behavior?[3]

What about the ethics of using corporal punishment in schools? We are referring to paddling, spanking, rapping children with rulers across the knuckles, and so on. It seems to us that such tactics are often ethically indefensible. First, research on corporal punishment is very limited (Rust & Kinnard, 1983). Second, because policy or law in the many states permitting corporal punishment requires that it be dispensed in the principal's or other official's office with a witness present, delay becomes necessary, diminishing the effectiveness of the punishment. Third, we do know that delivering punishment often negatively reinforces the user, as it rapidly (though often temporarily) terminates the annoying behavior. As we learned earlier, events immediately following an act are especially powerful.

[3]Much has been written on the subject of aversive control as a behavioral strategy. For recent references on the topic, see Budd and Baer, 1976; Friedman, 1975; Goldiamond, 1975; Martin, 1974; Pollack and Sulzer-Azaroff, 1981; and Thomas, 1977. We strongly urge that you consult such resources and your organizational, state, and federal policies before using a procedure of this sort.

Last, we currently have available to us, as evidenced by the contents of this text, many alternative strategies for reducing behavior effectively. Why select a method that probably is only minimally effective and that tends to generate unwanted side effects—avoidance, escape, and transfer of negative reactions to other aspects of the school's social and physical environment—when other better possibilities exist? We can think of only two possible reasons: dispensing punishment *is* reinforcing, either vicariously to the observer or directly to the user; and/or school personnel and the public are uninformed about alternative, more effective, and benign management tools. If the latter is the case (and the data by Rust and Kinnard, 1983, suggest it may be), we should take on ourselves the responsibility for informing them!

ADDITIONAL GUIDELINES FOR APPLYING REDUCTIVE PROCEDURES

Now that we have described a number of aversive reductive procedures and discussed some features specific to each, let us turn to a set of additional guidelines for you to consider in applying any one of the procedures discussed in this chapter and the previous one. In particular, we will comment on how much, how often, and at what point(s) you will need to apply the method, and how you may combine it with other now familiar procedures to enhance its effectiveness.

Choosing the optimal intensity of the stimulus

For cases in which you present or withdraw a stimulus, you want to know how intense that stimulus should be and/or for how long a time it should continue. Laboratory research (Azrin & Holz, 1966) suggests that optimal reductions in rate occur with highly intense stimuli. So if all you were concerned about was getting the misbehavior under control as quickly as possible, you would select intensely aversive stimuli: very unpleasant and arduous work assignments, extreme response cost penalties, and lengthy timeouts.

In the long run, though, beginning with harsh consequences may not be to your best advantage. Aside from the compelling humanitarian and ethical objections raised by such severe punishment, the harshness may be unnecessary. Less severe contingencies often do produce the desired results. Relatively brief overcorrection durations have been found to accomplish the purpose in several cases (Carey & Bucher, 1983; Czyzewski, Barrera, & Sulzer-Azaroff, 1982), as have brief timeouts and light response cost penalties. Simply isolating one kindergarten boy in a small open booth for five minutes each time he acted aggressively caused not only his but also his classmate's rate of aggression to subside (Wilson, Robertson, Herlong, & Haynes, 1979). You also may find, as did Carey and Bucher when they compared short and long overcorrection durations, that the student will resist, act aggressively, and disrupt during the extended periods while tending to remain more cooperative during shorter ones.

Should it happen that your initial methods are ineffective, you still have the promising option of increasing the intensity of the consequences. One caution, though: *introduce the more intense condition sharply, not gradually; abruptly, not slowly.* (This is just the opposite of the way you begin to thin out reinforcers to attain durability and fade prompts to shift over to critical discriminative stimuli.) The reason for a sharp and abrupt introduction of more intense conditions is that individuals tend to adapt to stimuli that gradually increase in aversiveness. So a gradually increased intensity will have little effect. If requiring Lucinda to apologize to her victims and to pick up objects from the floor in her vicinity failed to diminish her aggression, then she might be instructed, instead, to apologize to each person in the room individually and to tidy up the room in a manner that required more exertion. That would achieve the ends better than demanding that Lucinda apologize to two students and later three and so on, as such altered intensities hardly would be discernible.

Planning when and how often to follow through

In considering when and how often to follow through, the rule you should follow is no different from that with reinforcement: act immediately and every time, at least initially. To have its optimal effect, the relation between the unwanted behavior and its negative consequences must be predictable, which will happen best if every time the behavior occurs, it immediately produces an aversive event. That is not to say that delayed or intermittent consequences have no effect — they might. People do, after all, learn to bridge time gaps with words and images. So a boy sent to the principal's office for his afterschool scolding might reduce subsequent rates of coming to school late, having imagined throughout the day how unpleasant the encounter would be.

But why employ delayed consequences when others — response cost, timeout, and punitive work assignments — are available to be dispensed immediately? Even if circumstances prevent you from administering timeout or overcorrection, you still can use the form of response cost that involves deducting points or tokens.

Because consistency and immediacy are so crucial, you should seek out procedures that will be *practical* for you to implement and that are *acceptable* to relevant others, particularly supervisors, administrators, and parents. If the procedure requires you to disrupt your routine too often or demands too much time, effort, and attention, you will be less likely to follow through. If supervisors or parents complain, you will hesitate.

Careful planning on your own or with the aid of a consultant will help you design a strategy to suit your needs. But remember, if your plan deviates sharply from standard operating procedures within your system, first check it out with your supervisor and, if appropriate, with parents and the school board or committee. A written document that simply and straightforwardly lists who will do what to whom under what circumstances should dispel confusion and simplify the process for assessing, arbitrating, refining, or modifying the plan. It also can serve as a basis for preparing an informed consent form to be signed by students and/or their parents or advocates. You too will find the document handy should anyone inquire or should you need to review the details of the plan.

Combining reductive methods with other procedures

We have mentioned little about reinforcement in this chapter, assuming that by now you have learned this lesson well: whenever possible, *reinforcement should be part of all programs of behavior change*. Continually scanning for good behaviors and reinforcing them, especially with people whose histories have been problematic, should become second nature to you. For instance, Mrs. Burnes tries to be alert to any instances in which Lucinda supports her peers and comments favorably on them, often simultaneously awarding some special privilege. (Even though praise alone has little effect on Lucinda now, pairing the two events eventually may increase the power of praise and certainly will help Lucinda discriminate the circumstances under which good things happen.) Because managing their own affairs seems so important to Tommy and Fred, they could keep their own records and select and dispense their own reinforcers (assuming, of course, that it was possible to verify and reinforce accurate self-recording).

On the other hand, you should try to block reinforcement for the undesired act by withholding it yourself and managing conditions in the environ-ment so others too sustain *extinction* conditions. You might plan to reinforce students' ignoring of a peer's behavior previously supported by their attention, and record your own successful follow-through.

Using *stimulus control* procedures in combination with reductive strategies also can enhance the latter's effectiveness. Discriminative stimuli help people to discern for which acts, and under what circumstances the aversive consequences will be forthcoming, which is why it is so important that *both* those who are to manage and those who might receive punishment pinpoint very precisely the unacceptable behaviors to be treated. For managers, clearly defining the unacceptable performance — what it consists of, where and when it must not occur — helps them to implement the procedures more consistently. For students, knowing the precise features of what is considered to be a misconduct should accelerate the process of change. Guiding individuals or groups to generate a list of rules of deportment is a good way to accomplish that end (see Chapter 7). The list can be posted publicly on a bulletin board or privately on an individual's desk to serve as a reminder. While you want to avoid the extra attention accorded by extensive sermonizing after a transgression, a brief explanation of why the disciplinary action was instituted also will help the student to discriminate unacceptable behavior: "Tyrone, weapons are not allowed. That will cost your group twenty points." "Tommy, Fred, alcohol is not permitted. You'll have to miss the amusement park." "Lucinda, pushing and hitting cannot be tolerated. You must go to Mr. Rodriguez's office."

Summary

This chapter completes our presentation of aversive procedures, including overcorrection, contingent effort, and other forms of punishment. Table 11.1 compared each aversive procedure discussed in the present and previous chapter. We suggest that you refer back to it for a review of how the procedures differ from one another.

Contingent effort requires offenders to exert themselves as a consequence of their misbehavior. Overcorrection is a special form of contingent effort in which the required responses are topographically similar, or relevant, to the infraction. Another form of punishment involves delivering an aversive consequence. Each form decreases

the rate of the behavior that it follows; but for a number of ethical and practical reasons, punishment should be reserved for serious infractions, as was initially discussed in Chapter 7.

Now that you are acquainted with a broad array of reductive procedures, you should be better prepared to handle conduct problems in school. We have presented some of the particular characteristics of each procedure and how, in general, each method may be applied most effectively. We have reminded you of the importance of quality, intensity, duration, timing, and schedule in planning reductive strategies and discussed how combining reinforcement of desired behaviors, extinction of undesired ones, and stimulus-control procedures can support progress. We hope this has given you grounds for optimism.

Do not be distressed, however, if you are not able to solve every disciplinary problem you face. As a staff member of an educational organization, you hold control of many important conditions that affect your students (or perhaps employees), but that control is not total. There will be times when your own strength and resources will not permit you to overcome the effects of lengthy histories and you may encounter many conditions that you are incapable of managing. It remains to be seen whether the strategies we have suggested for Lucinda, Tommy, Fred, Marissa, and the others would be sufficiently powerful to prevail over the previous and current events in their lives. All we can do is work with our own inner and outer resources, and try our best. Let us anticipate progress, not miracles.

Study Questions

1. Define overcorrection.
2. Sarah threw down and broke a vase in the classroom after she learned that she had gotten a score of 43 percent on her math midterm. Her teacher required her to don gloves, pick up the broken pieces, apologize to the class for disturbing them, put the flowers from the vase in a jar of water, and put the jar of flowers on the table.
   (a) Identify and (b) label the critical features of this example of overcorrection.
3. Provide an original example of *overcorrection*.
4. Define *contingent effort*.
5. List the four components of overcorrection.
6. Provide an original example illustrating that restitution is an aspect of overcorrection.
7. Dick put his bubble gum underneath his desk. As part of overcorrection, he was required to place his piece of gum in a paper towel and to throw it away. He had to throw the paper away ten times before he was allowed to continue to work on his science project.
   (a) Identify the component of overcorrection illustrated in the above example.
   (b) State one reason for including this component in an overcorrection procedure.
8. Jessica left her seat without permission during a film strip showing and began wandering around the room. Her teacher had heard about overcorrection and decided to try it. She had Jessica walk around the classroom 15 times. Discuss in detail why this is not an example of the appropriate use of overcorrection.
9. Identify three original examples of behaviors that are not disruptive within the social environment but are harmful to the individuals themselves.
10. Dean did poorly on his grammar quiz. He had not correctly identified the nouns, verbs,

and adjectives in the sample sentences. Describe how positive practice without the restitutional aspect could be used to solve this problem.

11. Discuss (a) the advantage(s) and (b) the disadvantage(s) of eliminating restitution.

12. Mr. Day believes that a procedure he is using could be classified as overcorrection, although he has some doubts about it. Provide him with a set of criteria to use when making this decision.

13. Provide three original examples of contingent exercise.

14. State two important considerations when selecting an activity unrelated to the misbehavior for contingent effort.

15. List two techniques that could help both you and your students relax.

16. Maryjane was very resistant when her teacher attempted to apply overcorrection. Discuss in detail strategies he can use to reduce or eliminate this problem.

17. Tiffany's teacher plans to use physical guidance the first time he applies overcorrection to eliminate her problem behavior. Provide him with some guidelines for using physical guidance appropriately.

18. Define *punishment*.

19. Provide an original example illustrating that an event thought to be reinforcing can actually serve as a punisher.

20. Brad frequently talks during class. His new teacher has been consistently scolding him when she observes this misbehavior. However, his rate of talking during class continues to increase. Explain in detail why the teacher's scolding is functioning as a reinforcer.

21. Describe the best way to identify a punisher for an individual.

22. The teachers at Smith Memorial School are trying to classify the procedures they use into two categories: ethical and unethical. Discuss the problem(s) with their plan.

23. Neil believes that there are a few circumstances under which dispensing severe discomfort might be justified. Provide support for his view.

24. State four reasons for not using corporal punishment.

25. List possible side effects of using corporal punishment.

26. Mrs. Simmons understands that punishment should be used only if absolutely necessary. She has difficulty understanding why it is used so frequently. Provide her with two possible reasons for its extensive use.

27. State the information you will need to know when choosing the optimal intensity of a stimulus that you will present or withdraw.

28. Discuss the reasons for not beginning to punish with extremely harsh consequences.

29. Brian plans to use long rather than short overcorrection durations. Identify a possible problem with his selection.

30. Mrs. Hicks needs to increase the intensity of the consequence for Adam's dangerous behavior. (a) Explain the appropriate way to do this (b) support your answer.

31. State the rule to follow when considering when and how often to follow through with aversive consequences.

32. Provide an original example illustrating that delayed or intermittent consequences can be effective.

33. Mr. Holder is searching for procedures to improve the behavior of the students in his class. Give him some advice to aid his search.

34. Mrs. Barrett is planning a strategy to reduce class disruptions. One of her colleagues has suggested that she produce a written document. (a) List the information that this document should contain. (b) Describe the purpose of a written document.

35. Discuss the relation between the procedures in this chapter to (a) reinforcement, (b) extinction, and (c) stimulus control.

References

Azrin, N. H., & Holz, W. C. (1966). Punishment. In W. A. Honig (Ed.), *Operant behavior: Areas of research and application.* New York: Appleton.

Budd, K. S., & Baer, D. M. (1976). Behavior modification and the law: Implications of recent judicial decisions. *The Journal of Psychiatry and the Law,* Summer, 171–244.

Carey, R. G., & Bucher, B. (1981). Identifying the educative and suppressive effects of positive practice and restitutional overcorrection. *Journal of Applied Behavior Analysis, 14,* 71–80.

Carey, R. G., & Bucher, B. (1983). Positive practice overcorrection: The effects of duration of positive practice on acquisition and response reduction. *Journal of Applied Behavior Analysis, 16,* 101–109.

Cautela, J. R., & Groden, J. (1978). *Relaxation: A comprehensive manual for adults, children, and children with special needs.* Champaign, IL: Research Press.

Czyzewski, M. J., Barrera, R. D., & Sulzer-Azaroff, B. (1982). An abbreviated overcorrection program to reduce self-stimulatory behaviors. *Journal of Behavior Therapy and Experimental Psychiatry, 13,* 55–62.

Epstein, L. H., Doke, L. A., Sajwaj, T. E., Sorrell, S., & Rimmer, P. (1974). Generality and side effects of overcorrection. *Journal of Applied Behavior Analysis, 7,* 385–390.

Fischer, J., & Nehs, R. (1978). Use of commonly available chores to reduce a boy's rate of swearing. *Journal of Behavior Therapy and Experimental Psychiatry, 9,* 81–83.

Foxx, R. M. (1977). Attention training: The use of overcorrection avoidance to increase the eye contact of autistic and retarded children. *Journal of Applied Behavior Analysis, 10,* 489–497.

Foxx, R. M., & Azrin, N. H. (1972). Restitution: A method of eliminating aggressive-disruptive behavior of retarded and brain damaged patients. *Behaviour Research and Therapy, 10,* 15–27.

Foxx, R. M., & Azrin, R. H. (1973). The elimination of autistic self-stimulatory behavior by overcorrection. *Journal of Applied Behavior Analysis, 6,* 1–14.

Foxx, R. M., & Bechtel, D. R. (1982). Overcorrection. *Progress in Behavior Modification, 13,* 227–288.

Foxx, R. M., & Jones, J. R. (1978). A remediation program for increasing the spelling achievement of elementary and junior high school students. *Behavior Modification, 2,* 211–230.

Friedman, P. R. (1975). Legal regulation of applied behavior analysis in mental institutions and prisons. *Arizona Law Review, 17,* 39–104.

Goldiamond, I. (1975). Singling out behavior modification for legal regulation: Some effects on patient care, psychotherapy and research in general. *Arizona Law Review, 17,* 105–126.

Luce, S. C., Christian, W. P., Lipsker, L., & Hall, R. V. (1981). Response cost: A case for specificity. *The Behavior Analyst, 4,* 75–80.

Luce, S. C., Delquadri, J., & Hall, R. V. (1980). Contingent exercise: A mild but powerful procedure for suppressing inappropriate verbal and aggressive behavior. *Journal of Applied Behavior Analysis, 13,* 583–594.

Martin, R. (1974). *Behavior modification, human rights and legal responsibilities.* Champaign, IL: Research Press.

Matson, J. L., & Stephens, R. M. (1977). Overcorrection of aggressive behavior in a chronic psychiatric patient. *Behavior Modification, 1,* 559–564.

Miltenberger, R. G., & Fuqua, R. W. (1981). Overcorrection: A review and critical analysis. *The Behavior Analyst, 4,* 123–141.

Ollendick, T. H., Matson, J. L., Esveldt-Dawson, K., & Shapiro, E. S. (1980). Increasing spelling achievement: An analysis of treatment procedures utilizing an alternating treatment design. *Journal of Applied Behavior Analysis, 13,* 645–654.

Pollack, M. J., & Sulzer-Azaroff, B. (1981). Protecting the educational rights of the handicapped child. In G. T. Hannah, W. P. Christian, & H. B. Clark (Eds.), *Preservation of client rights: A handbook for the practitioner providing therapeutic, educational and rehabilitative services* (pp. 61–82). New York: Free Press.

Rust, J. O., & Kinnard, K. O. (1983). Personality characteristics of the users of corporal punishment in the schools. *Journal of School Psychology, 21,* 91–105.

Thomas, D. R. (1977). Staff competencies required for the implementation of aversive and deprivation procedures. In B. Sulzer-Azaroff (Chair), *Competency certification for the behavioral practitioner.* Symposium conducted at the Annual Convention of the American Psychological Association, San Francisco.

Wilson, C., Robertson, S. J., Herlong, L. H., & Haynes, S. N. (1979). Vicarious effects of time-out in the modification of aggression in the classroom. *Behavior Modification, 3,* 97–111.

III Applications: improving instruction

"There is no doubt that my students are behaving better," commented Dave Markham to Arlene Levy. "But I still feel they can learn more than they do."

"True. Just getting students to be quiet and accommodating isn't all there is. Some of my colleagues ridicule what they call the 'dead-man's contingency.'"

"What's that?"

"Just imagine a class of students who do not misbehave in any way. If reinforcement is delivered only for that, the pupils could just as well be mannequins."

"Ah. Sounds like heaven—at least for a moment or two. But I know what you mean. We really want more than ideal deportment. Learning is what it's all about. I realize that behavioral strategies can be applied to improving learning as well as conduct, but I feel I need to know more about how that is done. Any suggestions for doing a better job of teaching social studies?"

Perhaps you share Mr. Markham's interest in learning how to improve the effectiveness of your own or your staff's instruction. If so, you will probably find this section especially helpful. We show how behavioral strategies have been applied to improving performance in a number of basic tool subjects, such as handwriting, spelling, communicating orally and in written form, reading, and arithmetic. Then we add a chapter that will tell you how to apply the strategies to any of a variety of subject matter areas, liberally adding illustrations from social studies, sports and recreation, and other areas. By referring to these examples and using your knowledge of behavioral principles to adjust the strategies to your particular situation, you should be able to increase your students' achievement.

13 Handwriting and spelling

Goals

After completing this chapter, you should be able to:
1. List and explain each guideline a teacher may follow in developing a prescriptive handwriting program.
2. Describe five methods of reinforcing correct spelling for which investigators have reported success.
3. Describe how to use spelling programs in which students effectively (a) determine their own performance standards and (b) are involved in gamelike activities.
4. Describe two successful procedures for tutoring spelling.
5. Explain how the tendency to revert back to spelling errors can be avoided or corrected.
6. Describe three methods of remediating chronic misspelling.

Many youngsters and even some adults experience difficulties with handwriting and spelling. In this chapter, we present guidelines for improving these skills. First, let us look at handwriting.

HANDWRITING

One of the worst problems that Ms. Hollingsworth's students had was their inability to form letters clearly enough to be read. "Good grief!" she exclaimed to her husband as she struggled over the written assignments she'd taken home to grade. "You'd think these were written in some extraterrestrial language! I can hardly make out what they're trying to say."

As in many classrooms, Ms. Hollingsworth had posted model letters above the blackboard and conducted daily instruction in handwriting. She would show the letter to be practiced, draw it on the board, point out its special features ("See, the tail goes below the line!"), ask the students to trace the letter in the air, and then hand out lined paper on which they were to copy the letter. A few of the students performed reasonably under those circumstances, but others made the strangest errors. Some inverted the letters; others couldn't seem to keep them on the lines. John embellished his with dots and curlicues; Penny erased more than she wrote, so that by the time she finished, her paper resembled a slice of Swiss cheese. Several students didn't even attempt to do the assignment. A few others seemed to try; yet in apparent defeat, they would bunch up the paper and throw it into the wastebasket.

Ms. Hollingsworth tried coping with the problem by consulting with curriculum specialists and using current source material on the topic, with the result that some of the students' writing began to improve. Yet, she reasoned, if everyone was to succeed in school and later in modern society, all would have to write legibly. She decided to turn to the principles and practices of behavior analysis for guidance in developing prescriptive writing programs for those students who had persistent writing difficulties. Here we present some of the guidelines she and other teachers might consider in attempting to meet the challenge.

Assess for skill versus motivational deficiency

Facility in handwriting consists of correct letter formation plus a reasonable rate of production. Tom, who always tries to please his teacher, laboriously copies letters from the board and manages to form them legibly; yet it seems to take him forever. Penny appears to make an equivalent effort but fails miserably, as her letters face in various inappropriate directions and run off at peculiar angles. Frank dashes off a line or two of chicken scratches and gazes out of the window for the rest of the period.

It might be reasonable to conclude that Penny and Tom shared skill deficits, while we are unsure about Frank. One way to find out is to increase reinforcement, at least temporarily. Ms. Hollingsworth could arrange a token system, as Miller and Schneider (1970) did; she might permit the students to go out and play when they did their writing assignments accurately and/or rapidly (Hopkins, Schutte, & Garton, 1971; Salzberg, Wheeler, Devar, & Hopkins, 1971) or offer some other enticing reinforcing items or events contingent on adequate performance. Then, assuming that the reinforcers are known to be effective for each participating youngster and that the pupils apparently are trying their best, the teacher should be able to sort out those who are capable of producing letters accurately at a reasonable rate from those who aren't. Under those circumstances, Tom, for example, probably would perform as usual, accurately but slowly, while Penny might make her typical errors. An improvement in Frank's rate or accuracy would suggest that the teacher should arrange supplementary reinforcement during writing drills, while a lack of improvement would suggest the need to assist him to develop his skills.

Assess for and correct enabling skills

Sometimes, the problem that manifests itself as poor writing skill is caused by a more fundamental lack of preparedness, which in turn affects all of the letter formations. The student may be unable to hold the pencil, position the angle of the paper correctly, draw freehand lines and curves, and so on. Deficits of this kind often can be remedied by prompting or shaping. For example, when some of their young handicapped students did not profit from instruction and modeling, Rayek and Nesselroad (1972) placed different colored dots on the pencil and on the corresponding part of the child's hand at every point where it was supposed to come in contact with the pencil. You also can reinforce successive approximations to the correct form by praising those aspects that are improving, and, if necessary, by providing additional reinforcement. It might help to use graduated guidance — to guide the student's motions physically, letting up on your assistance gradually as the student begins to take over the correct movement. (See Chapter 8 for a description of graduated guidance.) Miller and Schneider (1970) selected skills like holding a pencil, drawing straight and curved lines at different angles, as well as drawing freehand lines and varieties of shapes, as prerequisites to instructing 4- and 5-year-old Head Start children to print letters.

Certainly, some difficulties with writing are related to sensory or other physical disabilities. A student who sees double images surely will have a hard time distinguishing the correct placement of lines and curves, as will the child with other visual limitations. Naturally, where such problems are suspected, a thorough ophthalmologic (vision) examination should be provided and, if possible, the disability corrected. It also is possible that the central nervous system is implicated in some children's writing problems. Again, suspected cases should be referred to a specialist in psychoneurology for diagnosis and treatment, if feasible.

Where suspected physical causes are not readily remedied, the student still deserves to receive optimal instruction. Interestingly, many students with lengthy histories of severe disabilities have profited from behavioral training in handwriting. An example is provided from a study by Lahey, Busemeyer, O'Hara, and Beggs (1977). Working with four students who had exhibited severe perceptual-motor disorders, the authors pinpointed several features of handwriting and figure drawing on which the pupils needed to improve: legibility; proper left-to-right sequencing; and orientation with not more than a 20-degree deviation. For each correct response, the teacher awarded a token valued at $\frac{1}{3}$ of a cent or, in one case, a raisin. For an incorrect response, the child was informed as to the nature of the error and shown how to perform the task correctly. As a result, not only did the trained responses of these children improve, but their formation of untrained letters and figures also showed improvement. Just as many people with orthopedic handicaps can be helped to function better by means of prosthetic devices, it seems that many children suspected of having damage to their central nervous systems can learn important skills by means of effective instructional strategies.[1]

Emphasize critical features

The differences between one letter and the next can be quite subtle. If your pupils fail to discriminate such subtle differences, their formation of letters may suffer. For instance, **p** and **q** are often reversed. Notice that the primary difference is in the way the letter faces; the same difference exists between **b** and **d**. When students learn to discriminate the critical features of these aspects, they are less likely to err. Help them by emphasizing the key features, either by making the critical semicircle darker, like this: **d**, or perhaps by temporarily providing an artificial prompt, such as that shown in Figure 13.1, in which **d** and **q** look left toward the fork (assuming

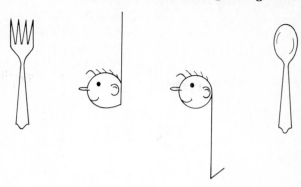

Figure 13.1
Emphasizing critical features: direction.

that standard place settings are part of your students' experience; otherwise use a different situation that is familiar, such as a mark, sticker, or ring on a particular hand, a window, or piece of furniture that is to the left of the room). Capital O and capital Q have only one key difference—the tail. Make a big deal about it. Figure 13.2 presents Q-ball the cat, with his tail emphasized to help students to remember the tail on the Q. Note how the artificial prompts are faded. (We return to methods for teaching subtle visual discriminations in Chapter 15.)

Shape to correct deficits in letter formation

It is very likely that some of your students (along with many adults, the authors of this book included!) exhibit skill deficits in manuscript or cursive writing. As in other related circumstances, you should shape the correct skill. But teaching a skill that requires especially fine motor coordination is

"Q-ball"
the cat

Figure 13.2
Emphasizing critical features: shape.

[1] See Rose, Koorland, and Epstein (1982) for a review of behavioral interventions with learning-disabled children and Epstein and Cullinan (1981) for a description of a model program for learning-disabled pupils.

easier said than done. Presenting reinforcement at exactly the moment a letter is being formed would require your constant vigilance. Instead you might arrange instructional material so reinforcement is built into the activity, as Skinner and Krakower (1968) and others have done. The Skinner and Krakower materials were designed to provide immediate feedback on the correctness of each writing response. The pages of the workbook were treated to reveal a dark line when a special chemical pen formed the letter correctly. Incorrect strokes produced only light yellow lines. Thus, the pupils could know immediately how well they had done. (We understand that it is possible to prepare similar materials from commercially available pens.[2])

A different, and more usable method for providing students with rapid reinforcement or corrective feedback for successively approximating accurate letter forms is to use plastic overlays, a system used by numerous educators (Fauke, Burnett, Powers, & Sulzer-Azaroff, 1973; Helwig, Johns, Norman, & Cooper, 1976; Jones, Trap, & Cooper, 1977; Trap, Milner-Davis, Joseph, & Cooper, 1978). Imprinted on the overlay are correct models or dashed outlines of letter forms that can be placed over the letter the student has produced. In the latter case, the letter is assessed by ensuring that the dashed overlay is properly positioned, then determining how well the letter meets certain criteria. How fully is it contained within the outline? Is it the correct length? When appropriate, are circles closed? Does it make contact with other strokes? Is it complete? Are the horizontal strike in the **t** and the diagonal stroke in the **x** in the correct places? [See the behavioral definitions and recording methods that Trap et al. (1978) used, reproduced on Figure 13.3.]

Jones et al. (1977) have shown that it is possible for first-grade students to use plastic overlays to self-record the correctness of their manuscript letter strokes after less than 120 minutes of practice and instruction. With such a system, shaping is accomplished by permitting more room for variability during the early phases of training. The most fundamental step uses broader outlines while more advanced steps use narrower outlines, so it is easier to be correct at first (Figure 13.4). Ultimately, the margin for error shrinks, until eventually the outline permits very little deviation at all (Figure 13.5).

We understand that some teachers use tracing paper instead of transparencies. The model letters can be seen clearly beneath a single thin sheet. After the student masters tracing the letters over such clear images, another sheet of tracing paper is inserted between the work and the model sheet. This diminishes the clarity somewhat. Again, as mastery is achieved with those diminished prompts, another sheet is inserted, and so on, until the student is writing without being able to see the model letters at all.

Consider backward chaining

It is not unusual for people to experience particular difficulty with portions of letters. Some of us omit loops or curves, while others slant portions of our letters in the wrong direction. Students with histories of poor handwriting need all the encouragement they can get. It is most rewarding when they are able to form letters that match a standard shape. They can do this by adding portions of the letter bits at a time, not starting at the beginning but at the end, as Skinner and Krakower (1968) did. For instance, instead of starting with the upswing on the letter **d,** they would begin with the last upswing (Figure 13.6).

Dashed lines may also be used to guide the proper motion temporarily. The student is almost guaranteed a good product. After this step is perfected for part of a letter, a new link is added, and so on until the student is forming the complete letter with the dashed prompts. Eventually the dashed lines at the end of the letter are faded out, until eventually no more dashes remain. The only prompts remaining are the letter charts with numbered strokes displayed across the front of the room. You can teach students to check those charts to assess the completeness of their letter strokes. Imagine how delighted

[2]One supplier is Marvy Color Tricks, Uchida of America, Woodside, N.Y. 11377.

The following criteria were used to determine the correctness of cursive letter strokes:

1. Containment: the strokes must be totally within the confines of the overlay boundary line.

Example:

correct 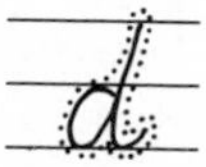   incorrect

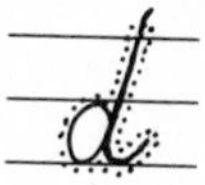

2. Length: each stroke not completing a circle or loop must begin and end between the small slash mark and the line forming the confines of the letter. With the exception of top of lower-case letters p and t, length will also be correct if it touches the line on the copy paper and is within the boundaries of the overlay.

Example:

correct 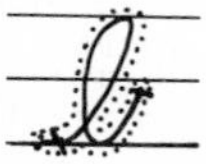   incorrect

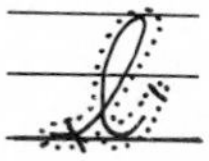

3. Closed circles: all letters, such as a, containing complete circles must be closed curves.

Example:

correct 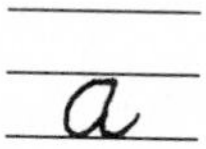   incorrect

4. Interstroke contact: all strokes must be in contact with other strokes except for the dot above i and j.

Example:

correct 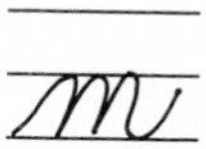   incorrect

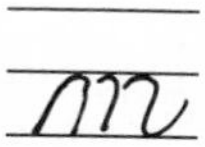

5. Completeness: the letter must be complete with all strokes present.

Example:

correct 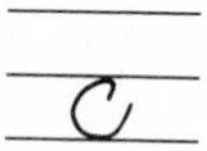   incorrect

6. The horizontal strike in the t and the diagonal strike in the x must intersect the other stroke near the center of the first stroke.

Example:

correct 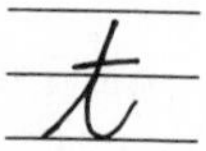   incorrect

7. The line on the overlay must align with the red baseline on the copy paper for the space completely across the paper.

Example:

correct    incorrect

Evaluation of the strokes by these criteria requires correct usage of the overlays. The overlays have sets of parallel lines that were drawn to match up with the red guidelines of the copy paper. The overlay was placed over the student's handwriting sample so that the line was directly over the red guideline until as many strokes as possible were within the letter boundary on the overlay.

Figure 13.3
Behavioral definitions and recording methods used for cursive handwriting (Trap et al., 1978).

they will be when they place a plastic overlay over their letters and see that they are perfectly formed![3]

[3]Plastic overlays are readily constructed by drawing the instructional material, photocopying it, and having a special plastic sheet run through a copying machine. Most commercial copy centers provide this service at a minimal cost.

Build on strengths

As always in the instructional process, we try to capitalize on the students' strengths and progress from their current capabilities. Consider the kinds of materials and implements that might produce initial success and the sorts of activities the student might

Figure 13.4
Guiding accurate letter formation, permitting a wide margin for error.

find intrinsically reinforcing. One student may be able to form very large letters on the board with chalk or a paint brush dipped in water. Another may find it fun to work with watercolors at an easel. If a thick crayon is easier to hold than a thin pencil (as it often is), start with the crayon. Tactile guidance in the form of yarn or raised or indented model letters might help. Naturally these temporary prompts would be faded gradually, following the suggestions already familiar to you, as soon as the student has mastered each step adequately. Neither Penny nor Ms. Hollingsworth would be pleased if Penny's legible writing only occurred when her letters were written on newsprint with a fat felt-tipped pen!

Teach students to instruct themselves

Penny found it especially difficult to form the **P** in her name. So Ms. Hollingsworth thought it might be worth the effort to spend some time with Penny alone while the other students went to the resource room. Following the instructional sequence used by Robin, Armel, and O'Leary (1975) she first modeled how to form the **P** correctly, instructing herself aloud, while Penny watched; next Penny joined Ms. Hollingsworth in the self-instructions; then Penny tried while both self-instructed; next Penny copied the **P** and self-instructed alone; and finally she whispered the instructions to herself. The general self-instructional format they followed was the same one that Robin and his colleagues described on page 182 of their report:

1. Question about the task: "What is it I have to do?"
2. Answer in the form of planning: "I have to make a 'P'."
3. Appropriate direct comment: "I have to go down, down, slow, stop at the bottom, stop."
4. Correction of error: "No, that's not straight; I have to make a straight line, like a stick."
5. Self-reinforcement: "It's done and I made a good letter."

Although Ms. Hollingsworth tried to encourage Penny to continue her self-instruction during regu-

Figure 13.5
Guiding accurate letter formation, permitting a narrow margin for error.

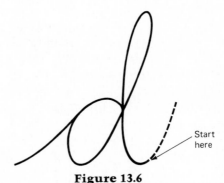

Start here

Figure 13.6
Guiding accurate letter formation, via backward chaining.

larly scheduled writing practice, the child rarely whispered the instructional guidelines she had been taught. Yet she did produce **P's** far superior to those of the past.

You too might try to teach some of your students to guide their production of letters via self-instructions, although you could find the individual training procedure time consuming, as Robin discovered. To avoid that difficulty, it would seem reasonable to test the procedure with a group instead. Guiding students to respond in unison is a well-established effective teaching technique, as Becker and his colleagues have shown (for example, Becker & Carnine, 1981).

Promote rate

Producing correctly formed letters is a major achievement, but it is not the whole picture. As discussed earlier, facility in handwriting includes performing at reasonable rates. These can gradually be accelerated via a schedule of **differential reinforcement of high rates (DRH).** The simplest way to do this is slowly to increase the required number of letters the student is to form correctly. Otherwise try what Hopkins and his colleagues did (1971). Decrease the time allotted for a standard assignment to be completed prior to permitting access to a reinforcing event. Be particularly watchful of the accuracy of letter formations at this time though, for increases in rates can be accompanied by diminishing accuracy. Major difficulties of that kind suggest a need to retreat temporarily to a lower rate requirement. When students show complete mastery of the letter over many trials for several days in a row at the slower pace, it is again time to initiate gradually the DRH requirement.

In the next section we proceed to spelling, another communication skill that is fairly uncomplicated to analyze, because it requires producing a sequence of letters that match a sample on a point-by-point basis. Yet, as with handwriting, the simplicity is deceptive. For many adults as well as children, spelling problems pose a serious barrier to effective communication.

SPELLING

"Where's Lena?" Sonya asked Ms. Miller. "She hasn't been to school all week."

"I just heard from her mother that she's been in the hospital to have her appendix taken out. She's home now but has to rest for a while before returning to school."

"I bet she must be lonesome and miss us."

"I imagine so, Sonya," the teacher answered. "Why don't we talk to the other children and see if they have any ideas about how to cheer her up."

The third graders got together and discussed the matter. Eventually, they decided that each would make Lena a get-well card and enclose a note telling her what had been going on in school during the past week. Ms. Miller agreed to collect their cards and notes and send them out.

That evening, Ms. Miller sat down to look through the third graders' greetings, chuckling as she read:

> Dear Lena,
>   I was sory to here you dond fil to wel. We hav ben workin hard in skool, but its O.K. cuz Ms. Miller is so nice and prety. Sarah got a hol in her new red swetr. Hope her mom dond give it to her. (You no what I mean!)
>
> Your frend,
> Sonya

Her laughter soon was replaced with concern. Sonya was not a problematic student. She read reasonably well and was quite good in arithmetic. She had some really creative ideas and got along with the other students. But her spelling was an obvious problem. This, Ms. Miller realized, was not an isolated case, either. Many of her students encountered difficulty in spelling. So Ms. Miller began to think about her regular approach to teaching the subject and what she might do differently.

At that time, Ms. Miller was selecting ten words for all the third graders and another ten for the fourth graders to learn each week. She would give them a pretest on Monday, mark the test, tell the students to study the words they got wrong, and give them another test on Friday. Occasionally, she would take a few minutes to point out difficult parts of words or discriminations, like the difference between homonyms, such as "to," "two," and "too." Some of the students caught on, while others didn't. Once in a while, when a spelling paper was especially poor, she would require the student to rewrite each misspelled word correctly ten times; but she wondered if that really did any good. For stories and compositions, she or her student teacher would circle misspellings in red and ask the child to look the words up in the dictionary and correct them.

Yet some students clearly did not profit from that exercise, either, as the same errors kept cropping up. So Ms. Miller consulted curriculum guides on spelling. She also assured herself that the students could read and comprehend the words assigned to them. She began assigning regular phonics drills and other exercises. Some visible improvement resulted, but still not enough to satisfy her that the students were learning as effectively as they might.

What would you do in Ms. Miller's place? Perhaps the most profitable thing you could do would be to revise your spelling curriculum entirely, substituting a Direct Instruction program (Dixon, 1977), a program demonstrated to have produced effects superior to those of any other Follow Through model programs (Stebbins et al., 1977). If that is not appropriate to your situation, you might turn, once again, to the general principles of behavior analysis. They may supply you with the help you would need; for as in other areas of academic skill development, behavioral procedures are being applied successfully to the remediation of many types of difficulties in spelling.

Reinforce correct spelling

Assuming that standard approaches were inefficient or ineffective, you could begin by encouraging the students to work harder. Learning to spell words correctly requires considerable effort. Students must focus on and consistently reproduce the letters in proper order. For some, this may be only a matter of increasing their rates of responding correctly. You could help them by carefully arranging reinforcing events. Probably the simplest way would be to permit those students who earned 100 percent on a pretest or on subsequent daily tests of the same words to use the spelling period for free-time recreational activities, a technique that Lovitt (1981) found to be quite effective. Or, if you assign tasks such as workbook exercises, you can make access to recreational activities contingent on completion of a particular percentage (e.g., 80 percent), a strategy that Rapport and Bostow (1976) found to result in major improvement in spelling by their 19 third-grade subjects.

A similar approach might help to increase the total number of correctly spelled words in creative writing exercises, as Trice, Parker, and Furrow (1981) found. In their case, a 17-year-old student was almost functionally illiterate. Instruction consisted of presenting him with cards on which open-ended questions were written, such as "What did your girlfriend do yesterday?" The student was to read the message, aided by the teacher if necessary, and write a response. During the phase that focused on spelling, the teacher counted the number of words spelled correctly and the number attempted but not spelled correctly. Points were awarded, two for each correctly spelled word and one for each word attempted but misspelled. If the total number of points exceeded the number of the previous session, the student was permitted to spend the remainder of the 30-minute period in free-time recreational activities. By the end of 45 sessions, he was attempting three times as many words as he had in the beginning, and his percentage correct improved substantially. Had this boy been fortunate enough to have access to a computer with word-processing capabilities, he could have used it to do his work. A program that checks spelling would then count for him the total number of words and the number incorrectly spelled, making the task far easier to accomplish. (Can you figure out how Ms. Miller might apply this sort of procedure with her poor spellers?)

Sometimes students need an especially powerful set of contingencies to encourage their early efforts at a difficult task, as was the case with a study conducted by Sulzer, Hunt, Ashby, Koniarski, and Krams (1971). Several fourth-grade students had participated in a remedial program to help them with various academic skills. When they scored at least 90 percent on their completed assignments, they were permitted to join the other students in a planned recreational activity. For some, this procedure was very effective, while for others, progress seemed inadequate. So the following year, the program was moved into the regular fifth-grade class. Various strategies were attempted in an effort to improve reading and spelling performance. The most successful tactic was to award a point for each assigned item that was completed correctly. Students could exchange the points for prizes and privileges, which encouraged the class to get down to work in earnest. After several months, it was possible to shift over from tangible rewards to activities more natural to the school routine, such as access to audiovisual programs and recreation. But in the meantime, the students had successfully progressed at double or triple their previous rates and also showed major improvements on standardized achievement tests.

A similar approach was used in a class for mentally handicapped fourth graders (Campbell & Sulzer, 1971). In that situation, the students worked very hard for access to special privileges, such as being monitor, sitting at the teacher's desk, carrying the athletic equipment, and so on. Much the same results were found by McLaughlin and Malaby (1972) in a similar program to increase completion of spelling and other academic assignments. The class was a regular fifth/sixth-grade combination of students from low socioeconomic backgrounds. For completing their assignments, the students earned points they could exchange every four days. As a result, they completed almost all their assignments. (You may be interested to know that during a different phase, when points were delivered for quiet behavior, students were quiet but their academic performance dropped off considerably. As we have often seen, the performance that was reinforced directly was the performance that increased.)

If you decide to use a token or point system to improve academic performance in spelling or any other academic skill area, consider involving the students by allowing them to determine how many points should be awarded for completion of particu-

lar assignments, as Lovitt and Curtiss (1969) did with a 12-year-old pupil who was enrolled in a class for students with behavioral disorders. The class operated on a system that enabled youngsters to earn points convertible to time in a high-interest room, where enjoyable activities were available. Initially, the teacher specified the value of each accomplishment. Then, in a second phase, the student was permitted to specify the number of points to be assigned for each. Although, not too surprisingly, the student was more liberal in his point allocations, he also produced considerably more during that phase.

You do have to be careful, though, if you permit your pupils to determine their own performance standards. As Felixbrod and O'Leary (1973) found, they might make their standards progressively more lenient, risking, perhaps, a reduction in performance rate. To counter this possibility while allowing students to continue determining their own standards, you could add one requirement, as McLaughlin (1982) did with great success in a special class for neurologically handicapped youngsters. The total number of words spelled correctly had to be higher than the number of the previous lesson. The author also noted that even further "increases in spelling performance were noted when students were trained through teacher praise and instructions to develop and maintain high performance standards" (p. 60).

Motivating children to improve their spelling by gamelike methods such as spelling bees is a long-established practice. The problem is that the poor spellers have little incentive to try because of their histories of failure, while the superior spellers receive the social reinforcement to which they probably have become well accustomed. Don't you wonder why such practices are continued? Perhaps the answer is that the victorious students enjoy the activity and this is reinforcing to the teacher.

It is possible, though, to capitalize on children's enjoyment of games while at the same time encouraging all of them to improve their spelling performance. Axelrod and Paluska (1975) accomplished that task in the following way: 22 third and fourth graders were divided into two teams, matched according to their baseline scores. The teacher assigned the class six words to learn to spell each day. On the following day, the students were tested on the words. The team with the highest total was the winner. The name of each member of the winning team was read aloud and winners were cheered. In case of a tie, both teams were designated winners. Although the students apparently enjoyed the game, it did not appear to help them improve their spelling. So a new phase was instituted in which members of the winning team were awarded prizes. During that phase, performance improved dramatically. Maybe the possibility of winning a prize was sufficient to encourage the students to work harder, or the contingency arrangement may have encouraged the students to tutor their team members, a possibility borne out by the teacher's observation, or both. (If you would like to use games to help your students to enjoy themselves while improving their spelling, we suggest you refer to Chapter 15.) Many reading games are readily transferable to spelling activities. While following through on this suggestion, think about how Ms. Miller could modify her current spelling program to make it more successful.

Involve tutors

You saw how the contingency arrangement reported by Axelrod appeared to encourage students to tutor one another. A similar result occurred when Evans and Oswalt (1968) arranged a contingency in which the spelling performance of one student could result in the whole class earning extra recess or story time. In one of the two cases examined, the others in the class offered the student assistance and encouragement, while in the second, such encouragement was not offered. However, you may not wish to leave the possibility of tutoring up to chance. Maybe you have some students whose spelling is so poor that they need much more intense individual instruction than you can provide practically. Besides referring to the sections on tutoring elsewhere in this book, you probably will find it informative to learn how this issue has been addressed in regard to spelling.

One possibility is to involve a parent as a tutor. This is what Broden, Beasley, and Hall (1978) did for

two boys. Dirk and Morris's mother was anxious to help her sons to improve their spelling — Dirk especially, because he was failing in many of his third-grade subjects. The mother was taught a set of tutoring procedures to follow three evenings a week. (The fact that she followed through was verified via audiotaped recordings.) On Tuesday evening, she presented a word list to the son she was working with and requested that he spell the words aloud. If the boy spelled the word correctly three times in a row, she praised him and proceeded on to the next. If not, she spelled the word correctly and asked her son to repeat it, until he spelled it correctly three times in a row. The next evening, the boy was to write the word down after having spelled it aloud correctly twice. Incorrectly written words were to be written correctly five times. Thursday evening, words were spelled orally once and written twice, with the same contingencies in effect. Both boys profited from their tutoring. Despite the fact that their teachers were unaware of the help they were receiving, the spelling test scores of both improved dramatically. Later comparisons showed that they retained the words for which they had received tutoring better than those for which they had not. Unfortunately, retention did decline over time, so the tutoring was not a complete success. (Careful programming for retention, as we shall see below, should prevent you from encountering such difficulties.)

We have repeatedly acknowledged that the very act of tutoring has been found to improve learning by both tutors and tutees. For this reason, it makes great sense to involve students as tutors of other students, with the objective of improving the spelling of both. Jane, Norman, and Brady were enrolled in an ungraded open-environment classroom containing 12 children of normal intelligence (Dineen, Clark, & Risley, 1977). Pretests covering 45 words indicated that each student spelled extremely poorly, achieving about one-third correct. So the three were trained in tutoring skills via modeling and role playing. Each then was assigned to teach a list of 15 words to one of the other two students according to this format: the tutor picked up a pile of 15 cards and read the top one aloud, then waited for the tutee to write it down and spell it aloud. If the response was correct, the card was placed in a *plus box*; if incorrect, the tutor spelled it aloud correctly while the student wrote it down. Then if the incorrect word was written and spelled correctly aloud by the tutee, the card was placed in a *minus box* to be reviewed again later, and the next word was presented. If the error persisted, the tutor repeated the oral presentation and asked once more for the oral and written response, until the student performed correctly. Then the procedure continued as earlier. After all 15 words were presented, the cards in the *minus box* were presented again, until all eventually were placed in the *plus box*. Then a test was administered to the tutee by means of a tape recorder. Both tutor and tutee were awarded special activities from a reinforcing menu based on the number of words the tutee spelled correctly. During the tutoring sessions, the teacher unobtrusively monitored the students. She praised them for working well or, if necessary, fined them by eliminating a portion of their afternoon snack or recess time if they didn't. (Only 8.5 percent of the interventions resulted in fines, while 91.5 percent resulted in praise.) Compared with a set of control words for which the students had received no tutoring, the words that they either tutored or for which they received tutoring were learned far better, with a 60-percent average increase for tutee words and a 45-percent increase for tutor words. Greenwood and colleagues (1984) found that their students' spelling similarly improved when they participated in peer tutoring.

Promote retention in spelling

Remember Dirk, whose mother tutored him and his brother at home? While he did well on his Friday tests, after several weeks Dirk apparently had lost much of his improvement, again misspelling many words. This development was not too surprising, as the boy probably had a history of intermittent reinforcement for spelling words incorrectly, a schedule that sustains performance very tenaciously. He could probably read the misspellings and perhaps others, also, could get the gist of what he was saying,

just as you probably did when you read Sonya's letter to Lena. In fact, misspelling can be reinforced inadvertently by the amused reactions of others. (Come on, now. Didn't you find yourself smiling when you read the get-well message?) Teachers also probably find it a nuisance to require that all misspelled words be corrected; so, again, the careless guess is reinforced.

This tendency to revert back toward errors can be avoided or corrected in several ways. The most benign is to provide opportunities for regularly reinforced practice. You are probably better off doing this a few words at a time, using a technique known as **distributed practice,** rather than doing many words all at once, which is known as **massed practice** (Reith et al., 1974). It is also a good idea to intersperse known words among the unknown ones, as Neef, Iwata, and Page (1980) found with six mentally retarded adolescents. Even though, in one phase, very dense reinforcement was provided for correctly spelling only new words, the students performed better when words they already knew were interspersed in the assignment. Probably the reinforcement provided by the review, as well as their frequent success, helped them improve their performance.

Excellent results in learning and retention of spelling have been reported for students who have participated in Follow Through programs using the Direct Instruction (DISTAR) curriculum (Becker & Gersten, 1982). Undoubtedly the instruction in DISTAR, which is presented according to a prepared script, provides for review as well as for regular reinforcing and corrective feedback.

Regardless of the approach you take, don't leave retention up to chance. Arrange to reinforce correctly recalled words during regular review exercises, and only drop such review when words consistently are spelled correctly over long time periods.

Perhaps you have encountered a student who chronically misspells particular words, despite your best efforts. Letter reversals among learning disabled youngsters are an example. Lovitt (1981) assessed and modified such a problem among seven 9- and 10-year-olds in a learning disabilities class. He developed a list of 40 words, each of which either began or ended with **b** or **d** and contained a short vowel. To prompt the students to discriminate between the two letters, the **b** initially was drawn in red, the **d** in blue. Then the students rehearsed reading and writing each word, receiving feedback and assistance as needed. Later, all letters were faded to black. Major decreases in the letter reversals resulted. (Turn to the section on reversals in reading in Chapter 15 for some other ideas along these lines.)

In case the correction procedures you use do not seem to be accomplishing what you hoped, you may need to try some more intensive methods. For instance, *positive practice* (Foxx & Jones, 1978) may be helpful. In the first part of Chapter 12 we provide two illustrations of how this procedure can be used to improve spelling. We suggest that you review this material if you have further concerns.

Another potentially useful technique has been described by Kauffman and colleagues (1978). Three children, two 8-year-olds and a 12-year-old, were encountering severe difficulties with their spelling. The standard method of showing them how to write the word correctly and requiring that they then imitate it was contrasted with a different procedure. Instead, the teacher imitated the child's misspelled word and, in the case of the older boy, indicated, by drawing a box around it, the portion of the word that was spelled incorrectly. The teacher then wrote the word correctly and asked the student to imitate the correct spelling. In all three cases, initial imitation of the student's incorrect spelling produced superior learning. The authors suggest that the imitated response of the teacher constituted an aversive event. Also, they speculated that highlighting the erroneous letters would enable the students to learn those letter sequences that constituted counter-examples of incorrect responses. That is, they learned more easily to discriminate correct from incorrect responses. Whether this finding is reliable for schoolchildren of all ages remains to be determined, but, in the meantime, it seems to be worth trying when other more positive methods fail.

Summary

Conceptually, handwriting is a very simple skill as it involves directly reproducing a model form. In practice, though, it can be extremely difficult, requiring highly refined eye-hand coordination. People write illegibly either because they do not work hard enough or because they lack the necessary skills. In the first case, the situation is remedied by enhancing reinforcing consequences, preferably by providing rapid feedback or else by supplementing reinforcers as a consequence of correct letter formations. When a skill deficit is involved, the student may need to discriminate the critical features of letters and receive considerable guided practice. Capitalizing on students' abilities can help them start out successfully and progress from there.

Spelling is difficult for many, regardless of other linguistic abilities, because the phonetic rules in the English language vary and there are many exceptions to those rules. For this reason, spelling instruction must be undertaken systematically. If your students are uniformly poor spellers, you probably should consider using a well-structured behavioral instructional program. More random spelling difficulties can be improved by encouraging students to make a greater effort by using game formats or, if necessary, other supplementary reinforcement methods. With children who have an especially difficult time learning to spell, you might try some sort of correction procedure, such as overcorrection, to remedy the difficulties. You must be careful not to assume that once a student has spelled a word correctly, he or she will continue to do so.

Rather, plan to keep errors from slipping back in by providing periodic review and by interspersing known words among lists of unknown words to be studied.

In the next chapter, we discuss another communication skill, written composition. Although composition in writing is far more complex because it requires synthesizing information and applying a variety of skills, you may find that some of the behavioral strategies for teaching compositional writing have relevance for spelling and vice versa. As you read about composition, ask yourself how some of the aspects of training might apply to spelling. Also, remember that correct spelling is a component of literate writing. The two must go hand in hand.

Study Questions

1. State two critical features of facility in handwriting.
2. Paul's handwriting is illegible. Design a method for determining whether or not his problem is a skill deficit.
3. (a) List at least three skills a child should master before being taught letter formation. (b) Describe two procedures that could be used to teach those skills.
4. State two physical problems capable of causing problems with writing.
5. Rachael has difficulty discriminating many subtle differences between letters of the alphabet. Suggest several ways of reducing this problem.
6. Describe the method developed by Skinner and Krakower (1968) to provide intrinsic reinforcement for correct letter formation.
7. Mr. Gerard is using plastic overlays to teach his students to write correctly. Each student is required to write the letter, place the overlay on top of the letter, and determine how well it meets the criteria. Provide at least four criteria of acceptability he could use.
8. Give an original example illustrating how shaping can be used to improve handwriting.
9. Carolyn does not believe that backward chaining can be used to teach children to form letters. Discuss how you would explain the procedure, as well as its benefits to her.
10. Dashed lines are S^Ds that almost guarantee a good written product. Describe how they can be used most effectively.
11. You are aware of the need to capitalize on your students' strengths in handwriting. State two considerations when trying to achieve this goal.
12. List the five steps of the self-instructional format for handwriting.
13. (a) Identify and (b) describe a method of accelerating handwriting rates.
14. Tom is concerned that increasing handwriting rates may result in decreased precision. Offer a suggestion to prevent this problem.
15. List several methods to encourage students to work harder.
16. Design an original program using creative writing exercises to improve spelling.
17. You have been chosen to select appropriate reinforcers for a spelling program. Discuss the reinforcers you would select. (Be sure to consider both the early and later stages of your program.)
18. State one very important consideration when implementing a token system.
19. (a) Identify a possible problem with permitting students to determine their own performance standards and (b) offer a suggestion.
20. (a) Create an original game to improve spelling accuracy and (b) state why you prefer your game to a spelling bee.
21. Ted's mother is concerned about his declining spelling test scores. Describe one way she could help him.
22. (a) Briefly describe and (b) design an original variation of the peer tutoring program imple-

mented by Dineen, Clark, and Risley (1977).

23. List several ways that incorrect spelling may be reinforced.

24. Define (a) distributed practice and (b) massed practice in spelling.

25. State the two advantages of using the Direct Instruction curriculum.

26. Mr. Norton's spelling program has been very successful. All of his students are spelling at least 85 percent of the words correctly. He now plans to terminate the program completely. Provide him with some constructive feedback about his plan.

27. Discuss how fading can be used to teach learning disabled children to spell.

28. Review and briefly describe the use of positive practice to improve spelling, as discussed in Chapter 12.

29. List several reasons for the success of the program by Kauffman and colleagues (1978), which utilized the imitation of the incorrectly spelled word.

30. Provide a list of guidelines for practicing words to prevent the student from reverting back to errors.

References

Axelrod, S., & Paluska, J. (1975). A component analysis of the effects of a classroom game on spelling performance. In E. Ramp & G. Semb (Eds.), *Behavior analysis: Areas of research and application* (pp. 277–282). Englewood Cliffs, NJ: Prentice-Hall.

Becker, W. C., & Carnine, D. W. (1981). Direct instruction: A behavior theory model of comprehensive educational intervention with the disadvantaged. In S. W. Bijou & R. Ruiz (Eds.), *Behavior modification: Contributions to education* (pp. 145–210). Hillsdale, NJ: Lawrence Erlbaum Associates.

Becker, W. C., & Gersten, R. (1982). A follow-up of Follow Through: The later effects of the Direct Instruction model on children in fifth and sixth grades. *American Educational Research Journal, 19*, 75–92.

Broden, M., Beasley, A., & Hall, R. V. (1978). In-class spelling performance: Effects of home tutoring by a parent. *Behavior Modification, 2*, 511–530.

Campbell, A., & Sulzer, B. (1971). *Motivating educable mentally handicapped students towards reading and spelling achievement using naturally available reinforcers in the classroom setting.* Paper presented at the annual meetings of the American Educational Research Association, New York.

Dineen, J. P., Clark, H. B., & Risley, T. R. (1977). Peer tutoring among elementary students: Educational benefits to the tutor. *Journal of Applied Behavior Analysis, 10*, 231–238.

Dixon, R. (1977). *Morphographic spelling.* Eugene, OR: E-B Press.

Epstein, M. H., & Cullinan, D. (1981). Project Excel: A behaviorally-oriented educational program for learning disabled pupils. *Education and Treatment of Children, 4*, 357–373.

Evans, G. W., & Oswalt, G. L. (1968). Acceleration of academic progress through the manipulation of peer influence. *Behaviour Research and Therapy, 6*, 189–195.

Fauke, J., Burnett, J., Powers, M. A., & Sulzer-Azaroff, B. (1973). Improvement of letter recognition skills: A behavior modification procedure. *Journal of Learning Disabilities, 6*, 25–29.

Felixbrod, J. J., & O'Leary, K. (1973). Effect of reinforcement on children's academic behavior as a function of self-determined and externally imposed contingencies. *Journal of Applied Behavior Analysis, 6*, 241–250.

Foxx, R. M., & Jones, J. R. (1978). A remediation program for increasing spelling achievement of elementary and junior high school students. *Behavior Modification, 2*, 211–230.

Greenwood, C. R., Dinwiddie, G., Terry, B., Wade, L., Stanley, S. O., Thibadeau, S., & Delquardi, J. C. (1984). Teacher-versus peer-mediated instruction: An ecobehavioral analysis of achievement outcomes. *Journal of Applied Behavior Analysis, 17*, 521–538.

Helwig, J. J., Johns, J. C., Norman, J. E., & Cooper, J. O. (1976). The measurement of manuscript letter strokes. *Journal of Applied Behavior Analysis, 9*, 231–236.

Hopkins, B. L., Schutte, R. C., & Garton, K. L. (1971). The effects of access to a playroom on the rate and quality of printing and writing of first- and second-grade students. *Journal of Applied Behavior Analysis, 4*, 77–87.

Jones, J. J., Trap, J., & Cooper, J. O. (1977). Technical report: Students' self recording of manuscript letter strokes. *Journal of Applied Behavior Analysis, 10*, 509–514.

Kauffman, J. M., Hallahan, D. P., Haas, K., Brame, T., & Boren, R. (1978). Imitating children's errors to improve their spelling performance. *Journal of Learning Disabilities, 11*, 33–38.

Lahey, B. B., Busemeyer, M. K., O'Hara, C., & Beggs, V. E. (1977). Treatment of severe perceptual-motor disorders in children diagnosed as learning disabled. *Behavior Modification, 1*, 123–140.

Lovitt, T. C. (1981). Graphing academic performances of mildly handicapped children. In S. W. Bijou & R. Ruiz (Eds.), *Behavior modification: Contributions to education*, (pp. 111–143). Hillsdale, NJ: Lawrence Erlbaum Associates.

Lovitt, T. C., & Curtiss, K. A. (1969). Academic response rate as a result of teacher- and self-imposed contingencies. *Journal of Applied Behavior Analysis, 2*, 49–53.

McLaughlin, T. F. (1982). Effects of self-determined and high performance standards on spelling performance: A multielement baseline design. *Child & Family Behavior Therapy, 4*, 55–61.

McLaughlin, T. F., & Malaby, J. (1972). Intrinsic reinforcers in a classroom token economy. *Journal of Applied Behavior Analysis, 5*, 263–270.

Miller, L. K., & Schneider, R. (1970). The use of a token system in project Head Start. *Journal of Applied Behavior Analysis, 13*, 213–220.

Neef, N. A., Iwata, B. A., & Page, T. J. (1980). The effects of interspersal training vs high-density reinforcement on spelling acquisition and retention. *Journal of Applied Behavior Analysis, 13*, 153–158.

Rapport, M. D., & Bostow, D. E. (1976). The effects of access to special activities on the performance in four categories of academic tasks with third-grade children. *Journal of Applied Behavior Analysis, 9*, 372.

Rayek, E., & Nesselroad, E. (1972). Application of behavior principles to the teaching of writing, spelling and composition. In G. Semb (Ed.), *Behavior analysis in education—1972* (pp. 171–184). Lawrence, KS: Project Follow Through. The University of Kansas Department of Human Development.

Reith, H. J., Axelrod, S., Anderson, R., Hathaway, F., Wood, K., & Fitzgerald, C. (1974). Influence of distributed practice and daily testing on weekly spelling tests. *Journal of Educational Research, 68*, 73–77.

Robin, A. L., Armel, S., & O'Leary, K. D. (1975). The effects of self-instruction on writing deficiencies. *Behavior Therapy, 6*, 178–187.

Rose, T. L., Koorland, M. A., & Epstein, M. H. (1982). A review of applied behavior analysis interventions with learning disabled children. *Education and Treatment of Children, 5*, 41–58.

Salzberg, B. H., Wheeler, A. A., Devar, L., & Hopkins, B. L. (1971). The effect of intermittent feedback and intermittent contingent access to play on printing of kindergarten children. *Journal of Applied Behavior Analysis, 4*, 163–171.

Skinner, B. F., & Krakower, S. (1968). *Handwriting with write and see.* Chicago, IL: Lyons and Carnahan.

Stebbins, L., St. Pierre, R. G., Proper, E. L., Anderson, R. B., & Cerva, T. R. (1977). *Education as experimentation: A planned variation model* (Vols., IV A–D). Cambridge, MA: ABT Associates.

Sulzer, B., Hunt, S., Ashby, E., Koniarski, C., & Krams, M. (1971). Increasing rate and percentage correct in reading and spelling in a fifth grade public school class by means of a token system. In E. A. Ramp & B. L. Hopkins (Eds.), *A new direction for education: Behavior analysis, 1971* (pp. 5–28). Lawrence, KS: Support and Development Center for Follow Through, Department of Human Development.

Trap, J. J., Milner-Davis, P., Joseph, S., & Cooper, J. O. (1978). The effects of feedback and consequences on transitional cursive letter formation. *Journal of Applied Behavior Analysis, 10*, 381–393.

Trice, A. T., Parker, F. C., & Furrow, F. (1981). Written conversations with feedback and contingent free time to increase reading and writing in a non-reading adolescent. *Education and Treatment of Children, 4*, 35–41.

14 Written composition and oral communication

Goals

After completing this chapter, you should be able to:
1. Describe the natural function of writing.
2. Discuss why compositional writing is often painful for students, and suggest an antidote. List specifically what can be done.
3. Describe how specific positive feedback can be used to improve creative writing skills.
4. Describe how the principles of effective reinforcement can be applied to writing.
5. Identify several features of writing critical for reinforcement, and describe methods of identifying other critical features.
6. Identify the behavioral procedures used to teach children to say the names of objects and events.
7. Describe how the classroom environment can be arranged to support students' appropriate practice of oral communication.
8. Describe how to improve conversational skills.
9. Describe a program for reducing spoken grammatical errors.

"Hello, Mr. Forsyth? This is Bill Farrel. You know, Freddie's dad."

"Yes, Mr. Farrel. I think I can guess why you called!"

"Gosh, I hate to be bothering you at home like this. I hope you don't mind."

"Not at all, Mr. Farrel. I know how difficult your upside-down schedule must be. Freddie mentioned that you work nights."

"Well, I just had to call to thank you for all you've done for Freddie. Ever since his story about the dinosaur prints came out in the *Gazette* yesterday, our phone hasn't stopped ringing. I even needed to take it off the hook for a while so I could get enough sleep. Everyone's calling to congratulate Freddie — and us, too. But I know that you deserve so much of the credit."

"That's kind of you to say, Mr. Farrel, but Freddie is the one who did the writing. He's quite a guy."

"But if you hadn't shown his work to Ned Callahan, it would never have been published, and if you hadn't taught him to be such a good writer, this couldn't have happened. Anyway, I just wanted to let you know how much we appreciate what you've done."

As he replaced the receiver, Mr. Forsyth smiled with satisfaction. It really was quite an accomplishment. His students were becoming much more skilled as writers. The previous month, Jeana's story had come out in the school literary magazine, and several other juniors were progressing just as well.

"It all started," he thought to himself, "when I sent that batch of compositions to Ned and asked him to have a couple of his staff writers judge them. But no. It began much earlier, the day I decided that I had to invest a major effort in helping my students to become better creative writers."

Mr. Forsyth had devoted a summer to reading as

much as he could about instruction and motivation of students in written communication skills. Besides reviewing his college texts and other articles (such as those included in the special issue on the psychology of writing in the Fall, 1982, edition of the *Educational Psychologist*), his conference notes, and the papers he'd gathered over the years, he also decided to explore what the behavioral psychology literature might have to offer. It already had proven useful for improving students' conduct, attendance, and other aspects of academic performance at Franklin. Perhaps it would be of use to him in this regard as well.

From last year, he recalled a conversation with Ned on the topic—especially his buddy's skepticism.

"Hey, listen. I've been in journalism for a long time—worked my way up to editor by doing every hack job you can imagine, so I know what it's like. Maybe you can teach kids skills like interviewing and reporting, but good writers—they're born, not made!"

That did it. Forsyth couldn't resist the challenge. How Ned laughingly had conceded defeat the day the results came through! Mr. Forsyth had given the journalists an unidentified mixture of pre- and postinstructional samples to rate. Several students' initial compositions were judged as dull, stilted, and technically limited, while their later work was rated interesting, witty, and stylistically sophisticated. In fact, Freddie's article on the local discovery of dinosaur prints was so fascinating that Ned had offered to print it in the *Gazette*.

Perhaps you too are tempted to share Ned Callahan's skepticism. We imagine some of your students avoid writing at all costs, even those who can tell fascinating stories aloud.

For instance, the group lunching with Chris is held in rapt attention as he narrates his great-grandfather's adventures in settling the wilderness: how he survived the hostile elements by learning from the natives; the time he found and raised a pair of young racoons apparently abandoned by their mother. . . .

"Oh, Chris," pleads Mrs. Olsen, who has been listening along with the rest. "If only you would write

that down just the way you said it. What a fine theme that would make."

"No way, Mrs. Olsen. Telling stories is fun. Writing them down is a drag."

Even if this sort of episode is more familiar to you than the earlier one, please permit us to try to provide you with grounds for hope. While we do not promise to teach you how to produce Pulitzer Prize winners regularly, we will try to show how to help your students become more skilled and willing writers. In this section, we narrate how several instructional researchers have applied the principles and technology of behavior analysis toward improving the creative writing of regular or special-needs students at the primary, high school, and, even, postgraduate levels. Perhaps their strategies for success will apply to your situation.

BEHAVIORAL APPROACHES TO COMPOSITIONAL WRITING

Behavioral approaches to instructing and motivating students to compose written work are similar to those used for other subject matter. While the most challenging difference is the difficulty we may encounter in trying to specify the requisite skills, we still attempt to arrange reinforcing and antecedent events as optimally as possible.

Audience reaction as a reinforcer

Let us begin by asking ourselves, "What is the natural function of writing?"

We write to evoke a response from the readers—who might even be ourselves—to amuse, guide, or inform them; to move them emotionally; and to enable them, in different ways, to share our experiences. We write stories to entertain; poems or love letters to produce images and feelings; directions to guide performance; reports to inform others; notes to guide our studying, and so on. The most natural way to motivate someone to write is to enable the author to experience the appropriate effect on the audience. If you ever have intended to write a humorous piece, and the reader to whom you showed it laughed while reading it, you will know what we mean. Unfortunately, seldom do our students ever receive that sort of reinforcing feedback from those who read their material.

Why is it so often the case that writing is painful for our students and, often, for ourselves? Perhaps, as Julie Vargas (1978, p. 24) contends, because instead of being reinforced, it so often tends to be punished by the reader:

> Teachers traditionally teach writing by giving assignments and hunting for errors in what students produce. Those who learn composition through having their papers corrected come under extremely strong control of the "critical audience" variable, so much so that writing becomes aversive.

As an antidote, she suggests that teachers focus more on thematic aspects, that they identify variables that produce good and bad writing, and establish appropriate instructional contingencies. By providing suitable exercises, for instance, the writer's efforts can be reinforced differentially by the reaction of the readers.

If, for example, the purported function of a composition is to communicate a set of directions, reinforcement should derive from the reader's appropriate follow-through. So Dr. Vargas asked both graduate students and sixth graders to write directions for something they knew how to do but their classmates did not. They could use equipment but could not communicate orally. When the directions failed to guide as anticipated, the author was required to revise or rewrite until they did, which, in turn, provided the reinforcement intrinsic to the exercise. It was pretty amusing when readers attempted to draw a piece of apparatus or a picture of a house guided solely by inadequately written instructions.

Other examples offered by Vargas include teaching description, style, and note taking. In each case she shows us how the audience exerts control and how the control can be managed constructively. For example, note-taking skills can be improved if the notes are used as a source for peer tutoring, because as the quality of the notes improves, so will the tutees' performance.

You should be able to capitalize on the fact that writing is supposed to evoke a particular response from the reader. Rather than just reading and correcting written assignments, try to plan activities that will supply their own rewards. Assign students to write jokes and read them aloud; see if the audience laughs. Ask them to provide clues for treasure hunts. Assign play and puppet-show scripts. Challenge your pupils to write book reports that will inspire their classmates to read those books, and help them to keep records of the number who do.

Specific positive feedback as a reinforcer

The sort of approach Vargas advocates makes considerable sense, but it might be premature for some of your pupils and can require a substantial effort from you. Many students lack the fundamental skills to enable them to participate at such a level. For them, the gap must be bridged between their initial faltering efforts and their production of quality prose. Also, teachers' limitations of time and/or imagination may restrict the extent to which they design and apply exercises involving audience reaction. Regardless, they should be able to provide specific positive feedback consistently. As you have seen, the tendency is to focus exclusively on errors, overlooking qualitatively good aspects. Instead, we can make a point of searching out positive examples of the skills we are trying to teach. Six sentences may be filled with jargon, while the seventh expresses its message simply and clearly. Why not congratulate the student for avoiding jargon in that sentence? If you find a description emotionally touching or a metaphor clever, let the student know. Indicate the point at which you laughed to yourself or where you were so intrigued that you felt compelled to continue reading. With enough effort, you usually can find several things to compliment. We review papers after editing or grading them to assure ourselves that they contain a reasonable number of specific complimentary comments.

Please notice that we are not recommending against your correcting or criticizing. For the sake of effectiveness and efficiency, you will need to handle mistakes. What we do suggest, though, is that you do this judiciously. Focus primarily on a few skills at a time and prompt the student to correct those particular errors. Then, of course, praise the improvement. You should strive for a reasonable balance between praise and constructively corrective statements.

If you want your pupils to be able to avoid receiving papers covered with spelling corrections, see if you can provide them access to a word processing program with a spelling check capability. (Although these are currently costly, prices continue to decline.) The spelling check will reduce their errors while they become better spellers in the process. (They will need to type in the word correctly themselves, once the program identifies the error.) By dispensing with your need to invest heavily in that aspect of grading papers, you can turn your attention to providing feedback on content and style. (As a matter of fact, word processors are now priced reasonably enough to be affordable to most school systems, and they should take considerable drudgery out of writing, revising, and evaluating prose material.[1]) By readily being able to correct and edit the material beforehand, it is possible for writers to produce impressive-looking printed copy, reinforcing to them and their readers.

Reinforcement strategies

Those of your pupils who are at the beginning stages, or who have experienced repeated extinction or punishment in their attempts to write, may require some more powerful reinforcing events to activate and sustain their efforts. As we have found in so many other circumstances, our knowledge of the principles of effective reinforcement such as immediacy, consistency, appropriate quality, and amount of reinforcement can come to the rescue.

[1]An example is The Writer's Workbench (Macdonald et al., 1982), which proofreads, comments on stylistic features of text, and provides reference information about the English language.

Immediacy and consistency. External feedback about one's writing usually follows an extended delay. It is impractical for teachers of large classes to assess lengthy written products and respond immediately. But they can return work as regularly and rapidly as possible. Our experience has indicated that some of the most effective teachers we know are those who provide qualitative feedback regularly and turn the papers back to their students very quickly. Other intermediate measures also are possible: assigning short exercises of the type suggested by Vargas—reading and acting upon written matter immediately; teaching students to recognize excellence in their own writing and to praise themselves for their accomplishments; circulating about the room during writing activities and commenting on sample sentences; allowing pupils to read their work aloud while you model and encourage reinforcing and constructively corrective comments from the audience. Also, although they provide no qualitative feedback, typewriters and word processors do yield immediate copy, which can reinforce intermediate steps in a laborious writing project.

Quality and amount. Particularly when a student's skill deficiencies limit access to natural reinforcers, you may find it helpful to supplement, temporarily, with more powerful extrinsic reinforcers. Let us illustrate from a number of cases.

Students in a fifth-grade adjustment class were awarded points for increasing word totals and diversity; the points could be exchanged for special activities (Brigham, Graubard, & Stans, 1972). As a result, they substantially augmented their total output.

A closely related procedure was used in an attempt to heighten the creativity of the stories written by fourth, fifth, and sixth graders (Maloney & Hopkins, 1973). Students were assigned to teams, and members earned points for the team by using different compositional variables. The team with the most points that day won, earning members treats and extra recess. If both teams exceeded a particular criterion, both could win. Points first were given for using different adjectives; later for different verbs; and then for both of those plus different sentence beginnings. As a result, diversity increased in each of those categories. Especially interesting were the findings obtained through subjective measurement: when two graduate students, in English and German respectively, were asked to rate subjectively a sample mixture of the compositions, papers produced during the latter two phases of the program were rated more creative.[2]

Third graders participated in a later project by the same authors (Maloney, Jacobson, & Hopkins, 1975). Lectures and requests had proved to be relatively fruitless strategies for encouraging the children to increase the variety of speech parts they used in their writing, so consequences, treats, praise, and free time were added. Performance improved and so did ratings by elementary school teachers who were unaware that a special project was being conducted. Improvement was particularly noticeable when the children's use of action verbs was most frequent.

In a similar vein, two high school teachers of English and biology, unaware of any special project, were asked to supply an overall quality rating of stories written by ten randomly selected eleventh graders (Van Houten & MacLellan, 1981). Again, their ratings mirrored improvement in certain compositional skills. In this particular case, students were taught how to increase the length of their T-units and to combine sentences. (T-units, or minimal term units, are used to measure subordinate clauses, Van Houten & MacLellan, 1981, p. 18): "The T-unit is a main clause plus any subordinate clauses or non-clausal structures attached to or embedded in it." The method used involved training the students to self-record the length of their T-units. Two teams were formed and individual scores and team averages were posted on a chart. The chart also indicated the best score for each of the individuals for the week, a score they were urged to exceed. Later, they were instructed on combining sentences, and this

was incorporated within the public posting system. Improvement occurred despite the absence of additional rewards.

Van Houten used public posting in another study designed to increase *writing rate* (Van Houten, Hill, & Parsons, 1975). Children in two fourth-grade classes had their writing timed and were taught to count the number of words they had written within a given period, which in itself increased the number of words they wrote per minute [as have self-recorded page counts by famous, highly productive authors like Anthony Trollope, Ernest Hemingway, and Irving Wallace (Wallace & Pear, 1977)]. Next the results were posted. Each time a student's score exceeded his or her previous high, the new record was posted on the chart. Rates increased even further. The most effective condition, though, was found to be one in which praise was added to the timing and feedback conditions. It is of further interest to note that in this series of studies peers frequently praised and applauded students who exceeded their highest score and those who made improvement. Also, not only did rates increase but so did the quality of the compositions (Van Houten, Morrison, Jarvis, & McDonald, 1974).

You need not be the one to have to manage extrinsic reinforcing events. The students may be able to manage them on their own. Thirty-seven third graders in a school in Auckland, New Zealand, were assigned to write stories four days a week (Ballard & Glynn, 1975). Rather than assessing 148 stories a week herself, the teacher taught the class members to self-assess and self-record. The pupils were taught to refer to a *good writing chart* for specific criteria and learned to count the number of sentences and action and descriptive words they used. Counting alone did little, but when points exchangeable for activities and privileges were added in sequential order for augmenting the number of each particular category, improvement resulted. Accuracy, although generally low, increased to reasonable levels in the phase in which reinforcement was contingent on accurate responses. Again, the effectiveness of the program was validated by the evaluations of independent judges.

---

[2]Skinner (1968) analyzed complex response classes such as creativity, problem solving, and others in the *Technology of Teaching.*

Antecedent strategies

Prompting by peers.

"Oh come, now, you don't mean to let on that you *like* it?"

The brush continued to move. "Like it? Well, I don't see why I oughtn't to like it. Does a boy get a chance to whitewash a fence every day?" (Clemens, 1875)

You may be amused to find that a variation of the ruse Tom Sawyer used to convince Ben Rogers to take over his chore of whitewashing Aunt Polly's fence has been experimentally verified in the classroom. The target performance was paragraph writing, though, instead of whitewashing fences (Van Houten & Nau, 1980). Prior to and following a 2-minute prewriting period, during which students reviewed their graded papers from a previous day, confederate peers made performance comments like these: "Did you write any paragraphs yesterday? I wrote __." or "I wrote __ paragraphs today. How many did you write?" (Van Houten & Nau, 1980, p. 59). Such prompts produced major increases in the percentages of paragraphs correctly written by other students.

Specifying the features critical for reinforcement. We have saved the hardest part for last. If you are planning to reinforce written exposition, you and your students need to know the discriminative stimuli; that is the rules, guidelines, and other circumstances under which reinforcement will and will not be applied. In other words you need to isolate the critical features of elements to be included in and excluded from their writing. We have seen some examples already: particular parts of speech, length of T-units, and others. Van Houten and Nau (1980) defined correct paragraphing as the placement of indentations each time there was a change of ideas within a story. Errors were counted when the student omitted the necessary indentation or included an unnecessary indentation. It

is relatively simple to communicate and monitor the inclusion of such features. But as you know, quality prose writing contains much more. It avoids cliches, excessive jargon, wordiness, digression, and other faults. [Refer to Table 14.1 to see how Vargas (1978) analyzes those faults operationally.] It includes finely polished material that enables the reader to share the writer's experiences.

You can identify the critical features of the subtler writing skills and techniques you want to teach by first identifying and then defining them as operations. Humes (1983) has done this for *planning, translating, reviewing,* and *revising.* For other skills, you might start with a basic text on the elements of style, such as the widely used book by Strunk and White (1979). You may need to rephrase some of their recommendations as operations,[3] but much of your work already will have been done for you. If further clarity is needed, one way to proceed is to select many writing samples. Then take these and sort them into two piles: one that contains the particular element and one that does not. Next ask yourself what features are common to each pile and how those features interrelate. These you will identify for your students and use as the basis for providing feedback.

Let us take the case of training your students to develop effective similes. You might gather a set of poems written by students over the years and identify as many similes as you can find. Then take each and categorize it as either effective or ineffective (and ask a respected colleague or two to do the same, if need be). Now ask yourself what particular stimuli prompted your behavior as you made your sorting decisions, and you will have the rules the students should follow.[4] As you read the next section, you will recognize how many of these concepts apply to oral communication as well.

---

[3]For assistance in operationally defining aspects of language, you may wish to consult Skinner's *Verbal Behavior* (1957), a text that includes a very thorough behavioral account of language.

[4]This tactic is based on a suggestion by Robert Mager in his helpful little book, *Goal Analysis* (1972).

Table 14.1
Teaching composition: example of faults in writing due to excessive control by verbal stimuli

Fault	Example	Analysis
Imitative behavior		
1. Plagiarism	(A passage is copied without credit)	In copying, control is formal point-to-point correspondence. At the time of writing, the writer is not under tact[c] control of the subject.
2. Redundancy (copying from oneself)	"The professor is making the student work too hard — harder than the student should have to work."	In redundancy, a writer repeats a point, echoing words already used. In the example, the redundant words "harder," "student," and "work" occur (instead of other words) because of the presence, in the writer's immediate environment, of the similar words he or she has just written.
Intraverbal control		
1. Cliches	"Dark as a tomb"	We call a phrase a cliche when the strength of part of it comes from the rest, rather than being under tact control. In this example, "as a tomb" derives its strength from association with the word "dark" rather than from the object or scene described.
2. Gobbledygook	"At the present time we are experiencing precipitation." (*Translation:* "It is raining . . .")[a]	Gobbledygook is a term coined by Congressman Maury Maverik to describe writing in polysyllables where simpler words will do. In gobbledygook, the direct tact is replaced by words deriving strength from other polysyllabic words.
3. Jargon and excessive use of abstractions	"For the variable responses to extinction, five of the six subjects extinguished faster following. . . ." (*Revision:* Five of the six preschool children pushed the button fewer times following. . . .) "The company implemented changes which should have increased productivity." (*Revision:* The managers sped up the assembly line.)	One cannot visualize what happened in these two examples because abstract terms cropped up from seeds in earlier pages, displacing the concrete words which would have come from stronger tact control. The revisions provide those words.
4. Wordiness	"It was used for fuel purposes."[b] "He is a man who"[b]	Extra words occur because of their association with a word already written. In the first example, "purposes" is unnecessary, but occurs because of the intraverbal chain, "used . . . purposes." Similarly "is a man who" is prompted by the word, "He." Both sentences would be stronger without the extra words.
5. Forced rhymes	"Pinocchio, In telling lies, Obtained a nose He could not disguise"	The necessity of rhyming, in the example, forced the use of "disguise" instead of the more direct word "hide." "Hide" would also have scanned better.

Table 14.1
Teaching composition: example of faults in writing due to excessive control by verbal stimuli (*continued*)

Fault	Example	Analysis
6. Straying off the topic	"Camps can be fun. This summer I went to camp Wildacre with my brother. My brother is older than me and he. . . ."	In the example, the writer strays off the topic when the word "brother" exerts intraverbal control over the sentences which follow.

[a]This example of gobbledygook was taken from Zinsser (1976, p. 14).
[b]These examples of extra words were taken from Strunk and White (1972, p. 18).
[c]"A *tact* is a verbal response occasioned by a nonverbal stimulus" (Catania, 1979, p. 236).
Reprinted by permission from Vargas, J. S. (1978).

ORAL COMMUNICATION

One thing that universally impressed Howard Parker's teachers at Franklin was his ability to answer questions and express himself eloquently when he presented ideas in class and even during informal conversation. Mr. Markham, his social studies teacher, mentioned more than once that Howard could explain certain subtle economic concepts better than he himself could. Carmen, at the Washington Street School, had a different talent in oral communication. When she recited in class, the whole group listened closely as she habitually applied the skills she had learned in the drama club, including timing and good intonation.

As in other aspects of communication, effective use of oral language is critical to producing a particular response in the listener, whether that response is to accept an explanation, help out, follow a direction, act amused or entertained, or offer a job. To participate in our society with reasonable success, people must be able to express their wants and needs, use words to assist and explain things to others, and converse socially.

Unfortunately, regardless of developmental, socioeconomic, and other factors that influence the acquisition of spoken language, many of our students are severely lacking in this area. They may not answer questions completely; they may have a hard time reporting events and explaining concepts; and their conversations may suffer from a paucity of expression. Deficits in oral communication handicap such youngsters academically, emotionally, socially, and economically. It is probably this recognition that has caused so much attention to be paid to the topic by behavior analysts. They have examined techniques for increasing functional spoken language, such as labeling objects; using different parts of speech; combining words into complex meaningful phrases, sentences, and conversational units; and other skills. While much of this work has been done with developmentally delayed youngsters (Garcia & De Haven, 1974; Lovaas, 1977; Schiefelbusch, 1971, 1978; Sloane & MacAulay, 1968), a lot is relevant to our present concerns.

If you were to invest the time in surveying reports of behavioral approaches to teaching oral communication skills, you would find that many of the behavioral procedures with which you are now familiar have been used. Children are taught to say the names for objects and events through modeling, prompting, fading, progressive delay, and reinforcement of successive approximations. Surely you do something similar when teaching new vocabulary words or foreign language equivalents. Many instructors use these techniques. For example, verbal recognition of objects or activities in English or a foreign language have been taught through progressive delay. To do this, you hold up an object, show a picture of the object or activity, or act out the activity, and then orally label it. After modeling the correct word, the students imitate it. Next, across successive trials, you gradually increase the delay between showing the object or the activity, and giving its label. Eventually, the students should begin to label the object or activity before the verbal prompt is given. Regardless of which procedure you use, however, if you are systematic in your approach, and use optimally arranged stimulus control and reinforcement strategies, your students probably are profiting from the experience.

You, also, probably recognize that many of the important aspects of oral communication are related very closely to those of compositional writing. As in teaching to compose in writing, you would pinpoint the skills to be taught and proceed from there to apply your familiar behavioral strategies. For instance, you could modify the techniques Vargas suggested for writing by substituting spoken activities. Because effective oral communication is so important to practitioners of behavior analysis, we include many such exercises in the training of our university students, such as asking them to teach a novel skill to their classmates. [See Sulzer-Azaroff & Reese (1982) for that and additional examples.] If supplementary reinforcement seems necessary, by audiotaping their oral presentations the students could self-record, tallying the number of descriptive terms, action verbs, new vocabulary words, special vocal emphases, pregnant pauses, or other skills being trained. If necessary, the tallies could be converted into points or tokens and backed up by reinforcing events or items.

Rather than elaborating extensively on this topic, permit us to supply a few illustrations of the application of behavioral strategies to improving oral communication. It is hoped that these examples and the resources we have cited will supply you adequately with ideas for tackling the challenges facing you in teaching effective oral communication.

Illustrative behavioral strategies

The Turner House Preschool is located in an economically impoverished area of Kansas City (Hart & Risley, 1980). As the children who attended had limited speaking skills, language training was a main focus of the program. To increase the quantity and complexity of the youngsters' spoken language, behavioral methods (i.e., reinforcement, shaping, chaining, modeling, prompting, fading, and so on) first were applied under fairly isolated conditions, so the children would not be distracted during instruction. Although the youngsters' repertoires of oral language increased substantially under those conditions, once they were back in the normal preschool environment, little carry-over was noted. So the environment was rearranged to promote incidental language learning. For instance, teachers began to prompt labels (Hart & Risley, 1974) and later more elaborate responses, eventually requiring that each child use the skill to obtain materials or assistance (Hart & Risley, 1975). If one wanted a particular toy, he or she was asked to explain why before it would be provided. Next, other children were involved so that the skills would carry over to the peer play situation. If a child wanted a particular item, the item was first handed to a peer and had to be requested by the child in compound form from that peer. The number of compound sentences expressed to the teachers and to the other children increased correspondingly.

To assess the importance of the outcome of the Turner House program, it was compared against data obtained from naturalistic observations of language production by preschoolers in two comparison groups. One was in a similar socioeconomic setting, and the other served middle-class children in a university community. Although their language had started out resembling that of the former group, by the end of the semester the performance of the children at Turner House was comparable to the rates by children in the latter location.

Incidental teaching procedures such as these have been found to teach not only new oral communication and other skills more effectively than traditional, highly structured teaching, but also have promoted greater generalization and spontaneity. An example is improved use of prepositions in natural settings by autistic children who had been taught those terms by means of incidental teaching (McGee, Krantz, & McClannahan, in press).

The key point of relevance here is that you should teach the linguistic skills that were pinpointed, but you should not stop there. Instead, arrange the environment to support appropriate practice of the skills as much as possible. As Hester and Hendrickson (1977, p. 316) have asserted, "The main purpose of any language-training procedure should be to provide language that is functional for the child in the natural environment." If the language you have taught is functional, it will tend to be practiced when necessary. Display a variety of materials that the students must request, or provide other opportunities to evoke natural verbal responses. Then, following the example of Rogers-Warren and Warren (1980), respond to the students' requests for materials or else attend to, acknowledge, or praise their application of newly acquired skills whenever and wherever possible. For instance, if you have been teaching the names of different geometric shapes and the students are working with wood or blocks, hand them materials only when they request those materials by using the proper descriptive term: "May I please have the triangular block?" "Sure, good you remembered that the three-sided form is a triangle." If they forget, ask another youngster to model the correct form or prompt it yourself before you deliver the appropriately requested item. Or suppose you use role playing to teach a skill for job interviewing: looking at the interviewer while conversing. You could model that skill under other circumstances and reinforce its practice by commenting positively when students use it during their less-formal interactions.

Teaching conversational skills

Being a good conversationalist is an important part of social effectiveness. Can it be taught? The answer is yes, as long as the components of the skill are pinpointed adequately. Minkin and colleagues (1976) used videotaped recordings of junior high school and university students to isolate some of the key features of effective conversational skills. They found three in particular: questioning, providing positive feedback, and spending a certain proportion of time talking. When instruction with rationale, demonstration, and practice plus feedback were used to teach those skills to four court-adjudicated predelinquent and delinquent 12- to 14-year-old girls, judges rated their conversational skills similarly to those of the university students. In another example, autistic adolescents were taught to practice assertiveness in

a game format designed to help them improve their conversational skills (McGee, Krantz, & McClannahan, 1984). If you were to attempt similar projects, remember how important it is to provide your students with repeated opportunities for reinforced practice under a variety of circumstances.

Spoken grammatical errors impede not only communication but social effectiveness. To paraphrase Professor Higgins describing why Liza Doolittle of *My Fair Lady* (Lerner & Loewe, 1956) was relegated to a lower social class, it was not her unkempt clothes and dirty face but the way she spoke that kept her in her place. If your students, for example, tend to use "is" and "are" incorrectly in a "wh . . ." question ("What is you doing?"), you can teach them the proper usage by applying the loose-training program developed by Campbell and Stremel-Campbell (1982) and tested with two language-delayed boys, aged 10 and 12. During two daily 15-minute training sessions, the teacher worked individually with each youngster, training other skills designated in the boy's individual educational plan. All correct uses of a "wh . . ." form plus the verb were reinforced whenever they occurred in a broader context. The teacher praised and repeated the child's correct response and awarded him a token. Incorrect uses were corrected and followed by a 2-second pause. The teacher then presented the correct form; when the child imitated it, he was praised and the teacher repeated the phrase, but the boy was not given a token. The skill was maintained formally within the free-play setting by continuous teacher praise and delivery of a token each three times it was applied correctly.

You should recognize that improperly spoken English tends to be modeled and reinforced regularly in a youngster's social milieu by parents and peers as well. In fact, using acceptable grammatical form is often punished. (Imagine Juan saying, "To whom are you speaking?" instead of, "Who are you talking to?" in response to a query from one of his peers in an informal social setting, and you will get the gist of what we mean.) The odds against overcoming such powerful support are formidable. For that reason, we suggest you select your targets of change very carefully. Pick only a few especially serious grammatical errors, and encourage their proper usage. For consistency of treatment, collaborate with your colleagues and enlist the help of pupils' peers by reinforcing their appropriate modeling and responding. Or, if necessary, as in a case by Garcia, Bullet, and Rust (1977), train the skill in the various settings in which it should be used.

Much as you might be tempted to correct every spoken error you hear, if most of the students in your school say it that way, try to restrain yourself. Sure, be certain that students are aware of the correct form; model it yourself so they can use it if they wish. But without an overall systematic program, change will be unlikely, and all you will succeed in doing is to impede communication and alienate yourself from your pupils.

Summary

Strategies based on behavioral principles can be used effectively to motivate and instruct students in compositional writing. By recognizing that producing a response by the reader is the natural function of writing, we can design exercises to help make writing more intrinsically reinforcing. Where further encouragement is needed, we can turn to methods for supplementing reinforcement: providing positive specific feedback and other promising reinforcing techniques. To guide our students to acquire compositional skills we proceed systematically by clarifying each performance of concern and then, in turn, providing differential reinforcement when they include it in their writing.

As with written expression, oral communication should function by producing a response from the audience. Effective speech accomplishes various social and academic purposes. To teach our students to speak effectively, it is best to provide them with the requisite skills via modeling, progressive delay, or more rigorous forms of behavioral instruction. Then follow through by seeing to it that the environment supports the change, either naturally or by arrangement.

Study Questions

1. State the key reinforcer for compositional writing.
2. Discuss why many people find writing aversive.
3. Provide one way that teachers can make writing more enjoyable for their students.
4. Describe how attempting to communicate a set of directions can improve composition writing.
5. Mrs. Schwarz wants her students to learn to take better notes. Provide an original example of a plan to accomplish this end.
6. List a number of advantages and two possible problems with the approach advocated by Dr. Vargas.
7. Mr. Green consistently has been underlining unnecessary words on Pat's papers hoping to reduce their frequency. Offer a more positive suggestion.
8. (Refer to question 7.) Provide Mr. Green with a simple means of ensuring that he carries out your suggestion consistently.
9. T/F It is recommended that you never correct or criticize student's work. Support your answer.
10. The Bakersfield School is considering teaching its students to use a word processor with a spelling check program. List the advantages of doing so.
11. Several of your students need to receive sup-

plementary reinforcers to activate and sustain their efforts. State four principles of effective reinforcement you should apply.

12. Mr. Carroll is unable to give his students immediate feedback on their lengthy written products. Discuss in detail the many alternatives that he has.

13. Discuss the importance of the *T-unit*.

14. Present an argument for reinforcing increases in writing rate.

15. Design an original program in which students manage extrinsic reinforcing events for themselves.

16. You plan to apply reinforcement in compositional writing, but have been told you will need to know the discriminative stimuli. Define and illustrate discriminative stimuli in this context.

17. List several critical features of elements to be (a) included in and (b) excluded from compositional writing.

18. Explain in detail how to identify the critical features of subtle types of writing skills.

19. T/F It is primarily lower-class children who lack good oral communication skills. Support your answer.

20. List four ways deficits in oral communication may handicap youngsters.

21. Discuss how teaching expository (compositional) writing and oral communication are similar.

22. The oral communication skills learned at the Turner House Preschool did not generalize to the normal preschool environment. Describe the method used by the experimenters to combat this problem.

23. State the main purpose of any language training procedure as assessed by Hester and Hendrickson.

24. Design an original incidental teaching program for promoting functional language.

25. State one essential criterion for teaching good conversational skills.

26. List the three key features of effective conversational skills.

27. Briefly describe the loose-training program developed by Campbell & Stremel-Campbell.

28. Discuss one possible reason for a student's improper use of spoken grammar.

29. Mrs. Cooper wants to correct every spoken error she hears. State (a) the disadvantages and (b) provide an alternative approach to the problem.

References

Ballard, K. D., & Glynn, T. (1975). Behavioral self-management in story writing with elementary school children. *Journal of Applied Behavior Analysis, 8*, 387–398.

Brigham, T. A., Graubard, P. S., & Stans, A. (1972). An analysis of sequential reinforcement contingencies on aspects of composition. *Journal of Applied Behavior Analysis, 5*, 421–429.

Campbell, R. C., & Stremel-Campbell, K. (1982). Programming "Loose Training" as a strategy to facilitate language generalization. *Journal of Applied Behavior Analysis, 15*, 295–301.

Catania, A. C. (1979). *Learning.* Englewood Cliffs, N.J.: Prentice-Hall.

Clemens, S. L. (1875). *The adventures of Tom Sawyer.* New York: Harper & Brothers.

Garcia, E., & DeHaven, E. (1974). Use of operant techniques in the establishment and generalization of language: A review and analysis. *American Journal of Mental Deficiency, 79*, 169–178.

Garcia, E. E., Bullet, J., & Rust, F. R. (1977). An experimental analysis of language training generalization across classroom and home. *Behavior Modification, 1*, 531–550.

Hart, B., & Risley, T. R. (1974). Using preschool materials to modify the language of disadvantaged children. *Journal of Applied Behavior Analysis, 7*, 143–256.

Hart, B., & Risley, T. R. (1975). Incidental teaching of language in the preschool. *Journal of Applied Behavior Analysis, 8*, 411–420.

Hart, B., & Risley, T. R. (1980). In vivo language intervention: Unanticipated general effects. *Journal of Applied Behavior Analysis, 13*, 407–432.

Hester, P., & Hendrickson, J. (1977). Training functional expressive language: The acquisition and generalization of five-element syntactic responses. *Journal of Applied Behavior Analysis, 10*, 316.

Humes, A. (1983). Research on the composing process. *Review of Educational Research, 53*, 201–216.

Lerner, A. J., & Loewe, F. (1956) *My fair lady.* New York: Chappell & Co.

Lovaas, O. I. (1977). *The autistic child: Language development through behavior modification.* New York: Irvington Press.

Macdonald, N. H., Frase, L. T., Gingrich, P. S., & Keenan, S. A. (1982). The Writer's Workbench: Computer aids for text analysis. *Educational Psychologist, 17*, 172–179.

Mager, R. F. (1972). *Goal analysis.* Palo Alto, CA: Fearon.

Maloney, K. B., & Hopkins, B. L. (1973). The modification of sentence structure and its relationship to subjective judgments of creativity in writing. *Journal of Applied Behavior Analysis, 6*, 425–433.

Maloney, K. B., Jacobson, C. R., & Hopkins, B. L. (1975). An analysis of the effects of lectures, requests, teacher praise and free time on the creative writing behaviors of third grade children. In E. Ramp and G. Semb (Eds.), *Behavior analysis: Areas of research and application* (pp. 244–268). Englewood Cliffs, NJ: Prentice-Hall.

McGee, G. G., Krantz, P. J., & McClannahan, L. E. (1985). The facilitative effects of incidental teaching on preposition use by autistic children. *Journal of Applied Behavior Analysis 18*, 17–31.

McGee, G. G., Krantz, P. J., & McClannahan, L. E. (1984). Conversational skills for autistic adolescents: Teaching assertiveness in naturalistic game settings. *Journal of Autism and Developmental Disorders, 14*, 319–330.

Minkin, N., Braukmann, C. J., Minkin, B. L., Timbers, G. D., Timbers, B. J., Fixsen, D. L., Phillips, E. L., & Wolf, M. M. (1976). The social validation and training of conversational skills. *Journal of Applied Behavior Analysis, 9*, 127–139.

Rogers-Warren, A., & Warren, S. (1980). Mands for verbalization. *Behavior Modification, 4*, 361–382.

Schiefelbusch, R. L. (Ed.). (1971). *The language of the mentally retarded.* Baltimore, MD: University Park Press.

Schiefelbusch, R. L. (Ed.). (1978). *Language intervention strategies.* Baltimore, MD: University Park Press.

Skinner, B. F. (1957). *Verbal behavior,* New York: Appleton.

Skinner, B. F. (1968). *The technology of teaching,* New York: Appleton.

Sloane, H. N., & MacAulay, B. D. (Eds.). (1968). *Operant procedures in remedial speech and language training.* Boston, MA: Houghton Mifflin.

Strunk, W., & White, E. B. (1972). *The elements of style* (2nd ed.). New York: Macmillan.

Strunk, W., & White, E. B. (1979). *The elements of style* (3rd ed.). New York: Macmillan.

Sulzer-Azaroff, B., & Reese, E. P. (1982). *Applying behavior analysis: A program for developing professional competence.* New York: Holt, Rinehart and Winston.

Van Houten, R., Hill, S., & Parsons, M. (1975). An analysis of a performance feedback system: The effects of timing and feedback, public posting, and praise upon academic performance and peer interaction. *Journal of Applied Behavior Analysis, 8*, 449–457.

Van Houten, R., & MacLellan, P. (1981). A comparison of the effects of performance feedback and sentence-combining instruction on student T-unit length. *Education and Treatment of Children, 4*, 17–33.

Van Houten, R., Morrison, E., Jarvis, R., & McDonald, M. (1974). The effects of explicit timing and feedback on compositional response rate in elementary school children. *Journal of Applied Behavior Analysis, 7*, 547–555.

Van Houten, R., & Nau, P. A. (1980). The effects of two types of peer comments on the use of paragraphing in written composition by elementary schoolchildren. *Child Behavior Therapy, 2*, 55–63.

Vargas, J. S. (1978). A behavioral approach to the teaching of composition. *The Behavior Analyst, 1*, 16–24.

Wallace, I., & Pear, J. J. (1977). Self control techniques of famous novelists. *Journal of Applied Behavior Analysis, 10*, 515–525.

Zinsser, W. (1976). *On writing well.* New York: Harper and Row.

15 Improving reading skills

Goals

After completing this chapter, you should be able to:

1. Describe two methods of encouraging students to read more for enjoyment.
2. Describe several reinforcing methods to increase the number of reading tasks students complete.
3. Offer some practical methods for tutoring students individually.
4. Define and illustrate the error correction procedure.
5. Describe how the A-B-C model applies to reading.
6. Explain how skill deficits in reading may be overcome by:
   a. Simple discrimination training
   b. Stimulus delay
   c. Stimulus fading
7. Discuss how fading methods can promote errorless learning.
8. List several reasons why students may fail to comprehend what they read.
9. Describe three methods to promote comprehension.
10. Describe how to enhance reading fluency.
11. Describe the Direct Instructional model and the SCORE program.
12. List the characteristics of effective programmed instruction.

The rain had been beating down in a steady stream for days, and the students at Willow Grove School once again had to stay in during recess. After having been cooped up for so long, they were becoming extraordinarily restless, and their teachers dreaded the noon break. To stave off the anticipated bedlam, Ms. Miller first had considered giving the class some drill work during their scheduled recess time. Then she rejected the idea, reasoning that the children needed a period of unstructured play during the day. Instead, she went to the library and borrowed a pile of attractive picture books, several of which had been her own favorites as a child. Placing the books conspicuously on the display shelf, she also laid out a set of educational games: word bingo, flash cards and matching pictures, and a scavenger hunt game

in the form of comprehension drill cards she had prepared herself. She hoped fervently that many of the students would be attracted to these activities, which would serve a double purpose: keeping the children occupied and helping them to improve their reading skills.

When the bell signaled recess, her hopes were dashed as a horde of students dashed over to the microcomputer, haggling over which of them would be first to play the video games. While the student teacher, Mary Heinz, took charge of that group, Ms. Miller struggled to calm the others who were chasing one another and tossing hats and paper wads. "Look," she pleaded. "Haven't you noticed the new books and games I've put out for you? Why don't some of you check them out?"

A few of the children shifted their attention over to those items, but the others persisted in contributing to the chaos. Ms. Miller sat down at her desk, rested her head on her arms and decided that the best thing she could do was to practice deep breathing until the next bell signaled the end of recess period.

Ms. Miller's experience was hardly unique. Given options, quite a few students probably would avoid any reading-related activity. Some have simply never learned to enjoy reading. Others have such limited skills that attempting to decode printed matter becomes an arduous task. Why would they choose to do something that involved reading when other more entertaining activities were available?

If we are to become a more literate society, we have a responsibility to encourage our students to take pleasure from reading and to supply them with tools that will enable them to do so adequately. More specifically, they should be able to recognize familiar words, figure out novel ones, comprehend what they are reading—and do all of this often and with facility.

Educators, curriculum specialists, and researchers have poured tremendous effort and resources into designing and implementing effective reading curriculum materials. Excellent textbooks, laboratories, workbooks, educational games, and audiovisual instructional materials are available commercially. In this section we do *not* intend to try to provide you with a complete guide to reading instruction. We assume that your school already has researched and found the best curriculum materials that it can afford and that teachers are trained and supervised in their proper use. Rather, we will describe some practices that, by incorporating behavioral principles, have successfully addressed several of the concerns identified above. As a reading specialist or classroom teacher, you may find these to be valuable supplements to the curriculum you currently are using.[1] We hope these suggestions will assist you as you struggle to increase your students' enjoyment of and proficiency in reading.

[1]For a thorough review of 51 applied behavior analysis studies in reading, see Delquadri (1983).

ENCOURAGING STUDENTS TO READ FOR ENJOYMENT

Have you noticed that many of your students who apparently enjoy reading come from families that place a high premium on written and oral language skills? Such youngsters are advantaged because their home backgrounds provide them with broad vocabularies and positive models. They observe their parents and siblings read; they probably are read stories, go to libraries, and participate in familial discussions involving information gleaned from magazines, newspapers, and books. These youngsters have learned from experience and example that reading can be fun, exciting, and informative. When they tackle novel or challenging printed matter, assuming they have adequate basic word-attack skills, they can figure out the words and grasp their meaning readily, as much of the vocabulary is already familiar to them.

A home in which reading is stressed, however, is no guarantee that all its children will acquire a love of reading. Nor does an impoverished background necessarily mean that a child will fail to learn what a pleasure reading can be. Our history books abound with examples of children like Freddy Farrel, whose accomplishments were not restricted by their modest roots. Regardless, there is little we as educators can do to change circumstances at home. Our responsibility is to enrich the school environment to provide optimal circumstances for promoting educational excellence. We must prevent students from being turned away by reading, and we need to help make this activity more appealing and rewarding. Let us see how some of our behavioral colleagues have accomplished this task.

Eight preschoolers studied by Haskett and Lenfestey (1974) were particularly bright and came primarily from professional homes. They apparently enjoyed many of the activities in their open-style class—playing with toys, listening to records, and engaging in art projects—but despite a nice selection of books, they avoided using the reading area. After several weeks, the teacher began to introduce new books into the reading area, assuring herself that the children noticed. This move was sufficient to attract a child or two to the area occasionally, where they could look at the books together or individually. The change during that phase, though, was hardly dramatic. Next, over several sessions, a few tutors and college students picked up books, went to various locations in the room and began to read aloud. Naturally, children came to listen and began paying more attention to books. They also spent more time looking at books independently than they had previously. It seemed that *modeling* reading and enabling the children to *sample* the reinforcement intrinsic to reading promoted their rates of interacting with books. The message is clear. If teachers want their students to interact with books, they can arrange to have the performance modeled by reading aloud to the class themselves or by involving other adults or children who are proficient in and apparently enjoy the activity. Once students experience how interesting a story or book is, they are more likely to pick it up and read it themselves.

INCREASING THE AMOUNT OF COMPLETED READING TASKS

One strategy to increase completion of reading tasks has probably already occurred to you: reinforce engagement in reading-related activities. Use reinforcing contingencies you know to be effective with your students when they complete their assignments or when they voluntarily engage in reading activities. For some students, extrinsic rewards delivered frequently might be the only effective reinforcers; however, a contingency as simple as "Grandma's rule" (Cowen, Jones, & Bellack, 1979) or public posting (Van Houten & Van Houten, 1977) could accomplish the purpose for many. In the Cowen et al. study, students simply had to accumulate 15 minutes of good work for the group to be able to select a reinforcing activity from a list of possibilities. They were helped to keep track of the time as it accumulated by being able to see a stop clock or watch that the teacher kept activated as long as the group was working. Van Houten and Van Houten posted the number of lessons completed by individuals as

well as by their total reading team, made up of members of the class. The team was publicly recognized as winning when its members increased the number of lessons they had completed over previous days. As this posting proceeded, an interesting thing happened. Particularly when student confederates modeled such encouragement, the children began encouraging one another to perform well, capitalizing on natural peer approval, a condition that appeared to promote the completion of more and more lessons.

Ms. Miller's scavenger hunt game consisted of a set of file cards directing the students to find particular objects in the room. She included words that the students needed to practice. For instance, one card said, "Find a blue block and put it in the scavenger hunt bag." (Interestingly enough, the children encountered no difficulty in decoding the word "scavenger," as the word described a game familiar to them.[2]) On others were written, "Look for a piece of chalk and put it in the bag," and, "Write three to five words about this game and put them in the box." Some of the children found this activity fun in and of itself. Others didn't. What might Ms. Miller do to engage her students' enthusiasm more actively?

Rosenbaum and Breiling (1976) worked with an autistic child using materials similar to those just described. They prepared a set of cards on which directions were written like, "Point to your nose," "Point to the cake," and "Point to the girl running." If the child performed the indicated action correctly, she was praised and given a treat. If not, the card was removed for 10 seconds and the experimenter modeled the correct response. After a pause, a verbal prompt was presented. Correct responses were rewarded as above; incorrect ones were followed again by a pause, then by physical guidance. The girl achieved 100-percent mastery of the 54 reading items within nine sessions.

---

[2]When preschoolers selected their own sets of words to learn to read, often the words were more complex than those the teacher selected, in a study by Sterling, Goetz, and Sterling (1984). Yet they learned those words as readily as the students who studied the easier, teacher-selected words.

Ms. Miller could employ similar teaching strategies to encourage her students to use her game; she could provide reinforcers for the right responses, either for correctly following individual instructions or for collecting a particular number of the indicated items. After a while, the activity might prove so enjoyable that the extrinsic rewards could be *gradually* eliminated.

A group of third graders selected on the basis of their difficulties with reading were involved in a word bingo game (Kirby, Holborn, & Bushby, 1981). Game cards were made up by arranging a matrix of boxes on which vocabulary words were written in random array, one word to a box. Playing in groups, the leader selected a word card from a pile containing matching words and read it aloud. When the children identified the word on their game card, they covered it. (During earlier stages, the word card was shown briefly; later this prompt was faded.) As in standard bingo games, the first player who covered a particular array of boxes correctly was the winner. Winners earned stamps on a wall chart, which could be accumulated and turned in at the end of the week for special reinforcing activities. The game permitted the participants to learn four sets of 24 sight-reading words successfully over 24 sessions. The intrinsic and extrinsic reinforcing contingencies clearly promoted acquisition of the words. This sort of activity is especially well suited to helping students learn to sight-read words that cannot readily be sounded out phonetically.

You can see how simply incorporating modeling and reinforcing events in your program can increase the amount of time students interact with reading materials. Below, we'll present additional examples of these kinds of approaches.

COPING WITH STUDENT NEEDS FOR INDIVIDUAL TUTORING

"Many of my students need individual tutoring. How can I as a teacher of a large group cope with this?" Perhaps you are already anticipating our response: find others to help. Research has shown that college students (Haskett & Lenfestey, 1974; Schwartz, 1977), student teachers, adult volunteers, paraprofessionals (Barnard, Christophersen, & Wolf, 1974), older peers (Ramey & Sulzer-Azaroff, 1979) or those of the same age (Robinson, Newby, & Ganzell, 1981) may effectively tutor students in reading.

In case you are concerned that these tutors might fail to perform properly, arrange to train and supervise them, as was done by Barnard et al. (1974) and Ramey and Sulzer-Azaroff (1979). (See pages 87–91 in this text.) With some careful planning, you can identify the rules for acceptable tutoring and reinforce adherence to them.

Just suppose you were a teacher of 18 hyperactive third-grade boys, some of whom required medication to calm them down, others who were aggressive or displayed perceptual difficulties such as reversals, and so on. It was your job to teach these children to read a list of 220 words, words that comprised 70 percent of the average person's everyday vocabulary. You were not permitted help from the outside. Those were the circumstances faced by Cynthia Smith, third-grade teacher of the Grant Elementary School in Springville, Utah (Robinson et al., 1981). With the assistance of the experimenters, a token system was developed that included two tasks involving reading and two tasks in which the student was to serve as a proctor. Here is how it worked: each day the student obtained a folder containing an assignment to learn a unit of words, four new ones and three review. With the aid of another student who had already learned that unit, he studied the words. When he was ready, he went to the teacher to be quizzed. If he could repeat and write the words correctly, Mrs. Smith gave him a green wrist token. Next he checked the wall chart to see who had not yet learned the unit and, with no special training or supervision, went to help that boy. When his student demonstrated mastery of the words, the tutor was awarded a yellow wrist token. Next, the procedure was repeated for a second assignment: arranging cutout words into coherent sentences, and helping another student to do the same. This activity earned him two more tokens, at which time he was permitted to play an electronic game for 15 minutes. Whenever a student passed a major-level test, he was permitted to play seven games on a pinball machine. Under those conditions, the students completed more than seven times the number of units as they had previously and progressed to more advanced reading texts. Although the teacher was able to shift reinforcing events gradually to activities more intrinsic to the school environment, all the students continued to perform well. Additionally, despite no directly arranged contingencies for conduct, the general deportment of the whole class improved noticeably!

Peer tutors also have had considerable success using an **error correction procedure** (Delquadri, Whorton, Elliott, & Greenwood, 1982). In this approach, the tutor requests the student to read orally for about 10 minutes. If the student says the wrong word, the tutor responds, "No, that's wrong. That word is _____instead of _____." Then the student is requested to reread the sentence correctly. Delquadri et al. (1982) used this error correction procedure successfully as part of a peer tutoring game in which teams competed against one another. Each student would earn three points for each sentence he or she read correctly. The teacher also awarded bonus points to peer tutors for doing a good job. These points would be added to the respective teams' scores. Winning the contest and the approval of their peers and teacher appeared to be sufficiently effective reinforcers, as no other extrinsic reinforcers were used.

Two other studies of peer tutoring have been described earlier (Greer & Polirstok, 1982; Ramey & Sulzer-Azaroff, 1979). You may recall that both involved behaviorally disordered students as tutors of other students, and that tutees' reading performance and tutors' social behavior were both monitored. In the former case, tutors were trained to use approval systematically, a condition that produced superior learning by tutees. Training alone, however, was insufficient, as tutors tended to use praise sparingly. So a system was introduced to reinforce the tutors' use of approval. Eventually, it became possible to remove the tokens used as rewards gradually; tutors continued praising occasionally, probably because their use of approval began to be reinforced by their tutees. In addition, as we noted earlier, in the Ramey

and Sulzer-Azaroff (1979) study, tutors were trained and supervised, receiving feedback periodically from the experimenter, again with similarly positive results.

Now, we leave it to you to figure out how Ms. Miller and the other teachers at Willow Grove School could take advantage of the findings of these studies to best serve all the students there. While you're engaging in that exercise, you also might consider some plans for the circumstances that now or sometime in the future might face you as an educator of students with widely disparate reading levels.

TREATING SKILL DEFICITS

"Motivation is not the problem. Some of my students show genuine skill deficits. What shall I do?" Because abundant materials are available for teaching reading skills, we assume that these students have not been able to learn from them. Perhaps they are unable to comprehend, read fluently, or quickly match words with their referents—objects, pictures, events, and so on. Beyond that, some may experience serious difficulty in identifying words or letters or in discriminating them from one another. For example, they may read "b" for "d" or "was" for "saw." Naturally, you would first refer for a vision examination any students suspected of having visual impairments, and see to it that any necessary corrections were carried out; but if the problem persists, what then?

Labeling words and letters

Consider, from a behavioral perspective, what reading is. At its most fundamental level, reading is the behavior of saying, aloud or silently, words that correspond to a set of written symbols. Of course, reading is much, much more (e.g., comprehending and so on); but for our present purposes, we are concerned with trouble that may arise at the level of basic word recognition. Using the familiar A-B-C approach, the written symbols constitute the *antece-*

dents (A), or stimuli to be discriminated; saying the words is the *behavior* (B); and what happens afterward (e.g., comprehension, praise, confirmation or correction, and so on) are the *consequences* (C). When one learns to read, the behavior of saying particular words or sounds is brought under the control of the antecedent stimuli, the written symbols. To teach reading, then, you must begin at the level of discrimination training.

It is fortunate that we recognize that basic reading skills involve discrimination learning, because then we can turn to the many principles of discrimination learning derived from experimental analysis of behavior. For instance, differential reinforcement, shaping, fading, and other methods that were intensively studied in the laboratory have considerable relevance for our present concern.

For example, when Ms. Hollingsworth shows Penny a figure that looks like this, *R*, Penny may reply with any of the following: "b," "p," "d," "q," or "r." Ms. Hollingsworth hopes to teach Penny to say the name of that letter and later to tell the sound that R makes. Penny will have to discriminate the R from other letters.

When people study discrimination learning with pigeons in a laboratory, they make sure the pigeon responds to different stimuli in different ways. Sometimes they present the stimulus alone at first, reinforcing the selected response (for instance, pecking) to the stimulus and gradually introducing one or more other stimuli. If the pigeon performs the selected response in the presence of those other stimuli, reinforcement is withheld. Usually the pigeon learns to perform the specified response—in this case, pecking—only in the presence of the critical stimulus. For more difficult discriminations, antecedents and consequences are arranged with greater care. If you watch Ellen Reese's films on operant learning, you will see a pigeon turning when the word "turn" is presented, and pecking in the presence of the word "peck" (Reese, 1978). If we saw a child doing similar things, wouldn't we say that the child was reading the words? How, then, do some behavioral strategies of teaching translate into reading instruction for the student who has severe difficulties learning to read?

Let's start with the least complicated method: simple discrimination training. Tom has learned to tell the boys' from the girls' restroom on his corridor by their location. When he goes to another part of the building, he is too embarrassed to ask someone to help him to identify the boys' room, so he waits uncomfortably until he returns to familiar territory. Ms. Hollingsworth suspects that this is happening, so she decides to teach Tom to read BOYS and GIRLS and to be able to tell them apart.

First, Ms. Hollingsworth double-checks by writing the two words on cards and showing them to Tom. He tries to respond, saying "bird" in response to the **BOYS** card and "goes" instead of **GIRLS.** In a way, this is promising because it shows that Tom is actually noting the first letter of each word and can produce the correct corresponding sound. At this point, Ms. Hollingsworth could simply compliment his correct production of those sounds and correct the other parts: "Well, Tom, you did know that this word began with the sound **b,** but we need to look more closely at the rest of the word. See, this part says "OYS." Can you make the sound?" Tom answers correctly, and Ms. Hollingsworth compliments him and asks him to try it again, this time combining the initial **B** sound with the **OYS** sound. When Tom succeeds, Ms. Hollingsworth praises him enthusiastically. Then they repeat the procedure with the word **GIRLS,** and again Tom succeeds and is complimented. A method like this often works, permitting teacher and student to move on to new words or phrases. But in Tom's case, when the two cards are mixed within a set of other words that include **BIRD** and **GOES,** the boy confuses them. Ms. Hollingsworth realizes that simple differential reinforcement is not sufficient; so she needs to try something else.

Stimulus delay. A prompting method that Touchette and Howard (1984) tested with three handicapped children might help here. The teacher presented a set of cards that displayed the letters, numerals, or words to be learned. To instruct, the cards were shuffled and placed in a row before the student. Targeting one item for instruction at a time, the teacher said "Point to the ___" (i.e., the designated card). Either every time, in one condition, or every third time, in another, if the student pointed immediately to the correct card, he or she received a token. Tokens could be exchanged for food, toys, or special privileges. If no response was forthcoming, the teacher waited a prescribed number of seconds and then pointed to the correct card. That prompt was sufficient to cause the student to imitate and thus perform correctly. Tokens were delivered for correct responses following the prompt, again either every single or after every third correct response. Teaching progressed by gradually delaying the time when the prompt would be presented, until the student reliably selected the correct card in advance of the prompt. Then another item in the set was taught in the same manner. Making almost no errors, the students eventually learned, regardless of the schedule or reinforcement, to identify most of the items on three different sets of cards. At the end of the project, all three sets were mixed together and two of the three students were still able to select almost every designated card correctly. [This **stimulus delay** or **delayed prompting procedure** also has been used successfully to teach easily confused letters, such as **b** and **d, m, n,** and **u,** and others (Bradley-Johnson, Sunderman, & Johnson, 1983) and various other skills such as language (Halle, Baer, & Spradlin, 1981), and manual signing (Smeets & Striefel, 1976).]

Stimulus fading. In case Tom appears to confuse features of the letters or words, **stimulus fading** could help. The words BOYS and GIRLS share some similar features, but there are noticeable differences between them too. Both are short and end with the letter s. All other letters are different. Ms. Hollingsworth rejects working on the initial letter sounds because Tom already knows them. Instead she decides to focus on the middle letters, the **OY** in **BOYS** the **RL** in **GIRLS**. Dropping the **S** for the moment, she draws the word **BOY** like this:

and says the sound for Tom. He repeats it correctly and is praised. Together they practice other words with **OY,** including, if possible, a word or two that Tom already knows: toy, coy, joy, Roy. Other words already familiar to Tom, but lacking the **OY** letters, are mixed in, but he continues to respond correctly because the large **OY** serves as a prompt. When he gets **BOY** correct every time, Tom is delighted with his success. Next Ms. Hollingsworth repeats the process with the **RL** sounds, using the size prompt to assist Tom in answering correctly. **BOY** is no longer confused with **BIRD,** nor **GIRL** with **GOES.**

Has Tom learned to read "boys" and "girls?" Not yet, because obviously he won't be presented with enlarged letters under ordinary circumstances. The size prompt will have to be faded gradually by reducing the dimensions of the oversized letters until they resemble the others. Then if Tom continues to label the words correctly, especially when they are mixed among others that share many key features in common with them, it is reasonable to conclude that he has learned to read the words correctly. Of course, the crucial test will come when he is taken to another part of the building and asked to locate the doors to the boys' and girls' restrooms. If he succeeds, all that needs to be done is to add the words to his set of known vocabulary so he can practice them periodically and work on reducing the latency or time between being presented with one of the words and saying it correctly. [Neef, Iwata, and Page (1977) have shown that interspersing known items during training in sight-reading helped students to learn their new words.]

A size prompt is relatively easy to use — but suppose it doesn't work? Other prompting techniques are available. You could use color or texture or intensity, or even superimpose a drawing that controls the response. The **OY** in **TOY** could be highlighted in red, while the other letter remains black (as Bradley-Johnson et al., 1983, did). Then, during subsequent trials, the color literally could be faded out, becoming grayer and darker until all red tints disappear. Or a string of yarn may be glued to the letters, gradually reduced to threads and ultimately removed. The **OY** may be presented as thick or dark letters. You can guess how those prompts would be faded. Whatever approach you take, you will know that a fading procedure has been successful when the student responds correctly in the absence of the prompt.

What do you do if the student still doesn't learn to make the critical discriminations? You have another option: you may superimpose a photograph (Corey & Shamow, 1972) or a figure drawing. Suppose Penny tries and tries but never seems to get the hang of making the appropriate sound for the letter s? Ms. Hollingsworth draws a picture that Penny recognizes, a snake:

"What does the snake say?" "Ssss." "See, the **s** looks like a snake and makes the sound 'sss.'". Penny catches on quickly, and at least produces an **s** sound when she sees the snake picture in a word:

Soon the figure drawing can begin to be faded:

Corey and Shamow (1972) faded their photographic pictorial cues by gradually reducing the intensity of the superimposed picture while sustaining the intensity of the letters forming the word. Under those circumstances, their preschool subjects learned the words much more effectively than when picture prompts were removed abruptly. In Figure 15.1, we have illustrated some similar ways we've seen to teach other letter sounds. Figure 15.2 shows the four steps of a fading program used by Mosher and Reese (1976) to teach safety words to retarded people. As the fading steps progressed, the size of the correct choice increased, until ultimately all words were of uniform size. In this particular study, students learned better when fading and nonfading trials were combined than when one or the other method was applied exclusively. In case you want to try this out for yourself, first attempt to match the Mandarin word for "soft" with the correct character in step 7, in Figure 15.3. Then notice how fading the size prompts could help you learn by trial and success.

Be careful, though, in choosing features of the letters you emphasize through pictorial prompts. You want to focus on the critical, not the noncritical, features of the form. The critical difference between a **g** and a **q** is the direction in which the tail moves. Focus on that feature, not on the noncritical aspects, because as Tawney (1972) found, emphasizing the critical aspects of forms will aid learning and retention of form discriminations.

Fading methods of the type described here work best when instructional stimuli are arranged so that the student makes few, if any, errors. For example, in the above illustrations the pictorial stimuli were replaced gradually by forms that ultimately became letters as they appear in textual materials. This gentle shift reduced the likelihood that students would make errors. Such *errorless learning* methods have been applied successfully with children with various types of learning disabilities, from those with minor perceptual difficulties to those with severely and profoundly delayed development. [We recommend the Etzel, LeBlanc, Schilmoeller, and Stella (1981), Mosher and Reese (1976), Sidman and Cresson (1973), and Sidman and Stoddard (1966) articles as sources if you plan to develop materials like these.]

When one of us was teaching primary-school students and they mixed up d and b, a pictorial prompt was used:

Students were told: "The d faces the classroom window, to your left, while the b faces the classroom door, to your right." How would *you* go about fading such prompts?

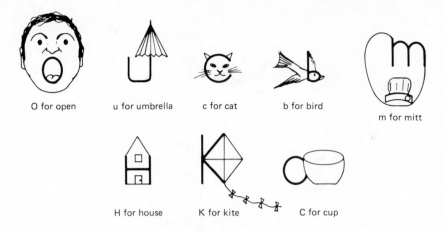

O for open   u for umbrella   c for cat   b for bird

m for mitt

H for house   K for kite   C for cup

Figure 15.1
Teaching letter sounds by superimposing pictures that prompt the correct phonetic sounds.

Figure 15.2
Emphasizing the correct choice by exaggerating its size: Four steps in a fading series for a study designed to teach safety words to mentally retarded students (from Mosher & Reese, 1976).

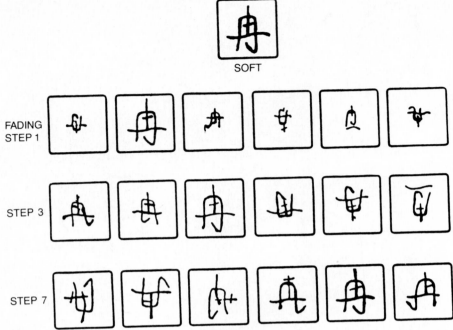

Figure 15.3

Examples of slides from a fading program. The first slide (top) showed the Mandarin word and its English translation. The first row illustrates the size difference between the correct and the five incorrect alternatives at the first step in the program. By the seventh step, all alternatives are the same size. Incorrect choices are variations of the same Mandarin word (from Mosher & Reese, 1976).

Promoting comprehension

There are probably all sorts of reasons why students fail to comprehend what they read.[3] The content of a passage may deal with unfamiliar material and thus make little sense. You know that feeling. Surely you've encountered the situation while reading texts for your courses. If children from rural areas are reading about problems specific to the city, they may have trouble comprehending the content,

and vice versa. During initial phases of instruction designed to increase comprehension, then, take care to use textual matter familiar to the students. That is why it often makes sense to prepare reading material dictated by the students themselves, in the form of *language experience charts* or stories. Or else, as a teacher, you can discuss what the story is about, elaborating on areas that may be unfamiliar to some students.

Inattentiveness to the material is another possible explanation for lack of comprehension. Lovitt (1981) promoted students' attention to details of written matter by using three strategies. First, the student was taught how to say facts about what he or she had read; the teacher would read a story aloud and then tell a series of facts about it, while the pupil tallied the number of facts listed by the teacher. Those facts were then reviewed by the pair. Next,

---

[3]For a conceptual and experimental analysis of rudimentary comprehension and reading skills, see Fields, Verhave, and Fath (1984). When "... a number of two-stimulus relations are established through training within a set of stimuli, other two-stimulus relations often emerge in the same set without direct training" (p. 143). The range of relations that can arise among stimuli and the ways in which three different forms of stimulus control function in that regard are described.

the student was asked to read a passage silently and then to recite facts about the passage. The pupil was given feedback on retelling for that particular instance and was told how that compared with previous days. For the last element, a trend line accelerating at a rate representing 25-percent growth per week was constructed. If the pupil's reading comprehension exceeded the trend line, he or she could select an event from a reinforcing menu of leisure-type activities.

Difficulty in comprehending textual material is not limited to young students, as we've already recognized. Students at higher educational levels may suffer from this problem as well. A group of college students was selected on the basis of their poor performance on the comprehension section of a standardized reading test (Glover, Zimmer, Filbeck, & Plake, 1980). Previously, the authors of the study had attempted to teach such students to use aids such as underlining to assist them in identifying the semantic base (meaning) of prose material. Yet the aids did not help. The authors reasoned that the students often underlined extraneous material and that any feedback they might have received was delayed too long to do any good. Therefore, they developed a system that allowed students to underline the minimum number of words within a five-line unit that gave the material meaning, and then to receive immediate feedback by comparing what they had done against an instructor's key. Tests on the content revealed that the immediate feedback helped the students to comprehend more effectively than they had previously.

Just think! Maybe this would be one solution to Richard Parker's difficulties. Perhaps he had developed poor reading comprehension habits that were difficult to break, which in turn could have impeded his learning in many areas, discouraging him from even trying any more. Teaching him how to identify the words that give the material meaning just might be the strategy that would help him to perform more satisfactorily in school.

If comprehension difficulties are a function of inattentiveness and you have access to computerized reading instructional programs, you may find that some of your students will attend closely to them.

Otherwise simple motivational techniques can encourage the student to attend more carefully to details, such as rewarding correct answers to questions about the material. In one of our studies (Sulzer, Hunt, Ashby, Koniarski, & Krams, 1971), fifth-grade students were required to answer fill-in-the-blank and other short-answer questions over the material they were reading. They earned points for each correct answer as soon as the reading class concluded. Points were exchangeable for items and activities identified on a chart, frequently referred to as a "reinforcing menu." The number of correct answers produced by the students increased as a result. We did worry that speeding up the rate also might encourage rapid but careless answering, so another feature was included in the system; we required students to score above 85 percent on review tests of the material. Otherwise, they'd be asked to repeat a unit, a process that would take them several days. Fortunately, that rarely happened.

It may be the case, in your situation, that simply supplying feedback rapidly and often will suffice to encourage your students to improve their reading comprehension. Try that before giving extrinsic rewards! If that doesn't help, add other reinforcers. Next, you could turn to some of the techniques described above.

Promoting fluency

It is not enough to enable students to read and comprehend accurately if they still take a year and a day to complete their assignments or reading materials. Reading fluently requires that a reasonable pace be sustained. Earlier, we discussed how various reinforcing contingencies could be used to enhance rates of decoding words and sounds. The same sorts of methods could apply to increasing rates of oral and silent reading. In essence, you use a DRH (differential reinforcement of high rates) procedure, reserving reinforcement for a pace that improves on previous speeds. For example, it takes Tom two minutes to read orally an experience chart one day. If he can read it in less than two minutes the next day, he receives a reward.

A number of researchers and developers of instructional curricula have devised methods to encourage higher pacing rates. One is an integral part of the *Direct Instruction* method (Becker & Carnine, 1981), which we will tell more about in a moment. In this approach, students often are asked to respond in unison to keep them attentive. This approach is paired with a reasonably rapid request for responses, a condition that has been found to improve accuracy of performance and to reduce off-task behavior. Strong and Traynelis-Yurek (1982) have reported working on a procedure designed to enhance word fluency: modeling and guiding by a tutor. The tutor and student read aloud and in unison a passage selected as matching the student's level. At times, the tutor begins to read louder and faster. If the student catches up and moves ahead, the tutor lowers his or her voice and continues to lag behind. Those authors may find that their students do improve their oral reading rates this way.

Strong and Traynelis-Yurek's method appears similar to one that has been attempted to promote more fluent speech among youngsters whose hearing is impaired, as the more natural the rhythm of speech, the greater is its intelligibility (Wilson & McReynolds, 1973). In the latter study, children read word lists or sentences in tandem with a vibrotactile stimulator. The idea was for them to match their oral reading with the pulses that they felt. Training consisted of differentially reinforcing paces of increasingly faster rates (a differential reinforcement of high rates, or DRH, procedure). Although the method did not improve the level of intelligibility of the students' speech, as anticipated, it did increase the rates of their oral reading. It would be interesting to use a similar technique to increase the pace of students' reading. For those without impaired hearing, a metronome, gradually accelerated, might be used to set the pace; or else light pulses or other signals could be used similarly to prompt increasing rates of reading.

THE DIRECT INSTRUCTION MODEL

"In our school it is not individual children or small groups who encounter difficulty with reading. The problem is more widespread than that. What can we do?" From our perspective, one of the most promising methods available is to implement Direct Instruction (Becker & Carnine, 1981; Becker, Engelmann, Carnine & Maggs, 1982). The Direct Instruction model (presented earlier in Chapter 8, page 134) uses its DISTAR materials to teach reading, mathematics, spelling, and other basic tool subjects throughout elementary school grades.[4] According to Becker and Gersten (1982, p. 76), these materials are

> designed to explicitly teach general principles and problem-solving strategies. Teachers and paraprofessional aides are trained to teach these programs in a fast-paced, dynamic fashion with high frequencies of unison group responses and systematic corrections of student errors.

The DISTAR, or Direct Instructional materials, are programmed carefully to incorporate many of the fundamental principles of behavior described earlier. For example, immediacy of feedback, both reinforcing and corrective, is provided to the younger children and is delayed gradually as they mature. To ensure that material is presented and followed with appropriate consequences in a proper manner, teachers follow scripts. Students respond aloud, which guarantees their active involvement; various other cueing and pacing strategies are used as well. Broad-scale research has shown that, based on standardized test scores and other measures, this program effectively enhances particular reading skills of retarded, autistic, non-English-speaking, bilingual, deaf, disadvantaged, and normal school and preschool children (Becker & Gersten, 1982; Becker, et al., 1982; Weisberg, 1983–1984). (Mathematical problem solving and spelling also have been found to improve significantly via DISTAR.) Also, the longer children are involved in the program, the better. Older children removed from the program main-

---

[4]Direct Instruction materials may be obtained from C. C. Publications, P. O. Box 23699, Tigard, OR, 97223 and from SRA, Science Research Associates, Inc., 55 North Wacker Drive, Chicago, IL, 60606.

tain previously obtained levels but fail to sustain their previously high rates of progress. In case your school is unable to afford DISTAR materials, it still would be advantageous to analyze and incorporate within your educational program as many of the features of Direct Instruction as possible.

Should insufficient personnel be your problem, paraprofessionals, student tutors, or parents could help by using a program like SCORE (Success Controlled Optimal Reading Experience, authored by Cradler, Bechthold, & Bechthold, 1973). SCORE is a sequential phonics program designed to teach pupils of any age who are deficient in basic word attack skills and/or reading below fourth grade level.

SCORE provides a self-contained tutor's kit, which includes a phonetically controlled, empirically derived lesson sequence ranging from individual sounds to four-syllable words incorporated into six booklets totaling 353 pages. Also included are a lesson timer, counter, manual, tests, and scripted record books. Student performance above or below a preset criterion in any of SCORE's 53 teaching units automatically signals the tutor to execute one of 3,000 predetermined alternate routes for the student. The program strategy ensures that each skill is mastered before a new skill is introduced. The mastery teaching strategies incorporated in SCORE are based on research by Block (1971) and Bloom (1973). Additionally, SCORE incorporates the specific behavioral learning principles summarized below:

- Continuous automatic adjustment of correct response rate at 90 to 92 percent correct so rapid learners aren't bored and slow learners aren't discouraged.
- Prompting strategies that include a special marker to reduce letter and word reversal errors, spaces between syllables that are gradually faded, and staggered letters to teach blending, etc.
- Active student involvement; they read aloud to a tutor producing from 150 to 400 correct, reinforced responses during each 10-minute tutoring session.
- Continuous reinforcement as a consequence of each correct response; the tutor clicks a tally counter after each to designate accumulating

points exchangeable for a reinforcer predetermined to be valued by the individual student.
- Tutors train and follow a script to provide corrective feedback for each incorrect response.
- Pacing and periodic reviewing. Each new element is gradually faded for review as new elements are introduced. The end of each unit provides a recycle/review page. If the student's performance falls below 100-percent correct in one of the review lists (recycle page), the unit is repeated. If preunit tests are passed at a 100-percent level mastery, the student may skip ahead to the next unit.

A federally funded, 3-year research project was conducted to evaluate and refine SCORE and validate tutor training procedures (Cradler, 1980). Because of the significant results in reading gains obtained by this and other studies, the U.S. Department of Education's Joint Dissemination Review Panel approved SCORE as an exemplary program for national dissemination.

READING INSTRUCTION AND THE NEAR FUTURE

There is hope for the Pennys, Toms, Richard Parkers, and other students with reading difficulties. As we've just seen, effective procedures exist for increasing motivation, concentration, comprehension, rate, and fundamental discriminative skills. Behaviorally based strategies have demonstrated their ability to teach students who are handicapped along with those who are very capable but lack some specific skills. Such strategies have been shown to help children from privileged as well as impoverished backgrounds.

We must acknowledge that many of these strategies are costly—in terms of time, forethought, or effort, if not in terms of money. For this reason, it is important that increasingly cost-efficient strategies and materials like the SCORE system be developed and disseminated.

One particularly hopeful sign is the current accessibility of small and relatively inexpensive computers. From today's perspective, practically every classroom should have regular access to computers within the near future. If so, it should be possible to teach reading via computer assistance.

Beware, though—it is not the computer hardware that will accomplish the task. It is the programmed material or software that will produce success or failure, and well-designed software of the kind we are describing will not be readily produced. If we have been sufficiently impressed by the potential of incorporating behavioral principles into instructional programming, then we will have to provide for:

- Adjustments of step sizes so that rapid learners aren't bored but slow learners aren't discouraged.
- Effective prompting strategies that are applied and appropriately faded.
- Mastery at each level before permitting the student to progress.
- Material that is intrinsically interesting.
- Students' active involvement.
- Consequences for correct responses that are appropriately reinforcing. (This may mean simply supplying intermittent feedback, or it may require the presentation of a game following a given number of right responses or an accelerating pace, depending on the individual student.)
- Corrective feedback that is helpful and nonpunitive.
- Pacing features.
- Periodic review.

Be careful not to be seduced into purchasing programs by merchants who use sales gimmicks to persuade you to buy their products. Be suspicious of appeals based solely on fun and enjoyment. Lovely pictures and pretty colors may seem attractive, but do they contribute or perhaps distract students from learning to read? It is your students who must benefit. Instead, as the report by the National Committee on Excellence in Education (1983) recommended for textbook publishers, *insist on seeing evidence of the programs' effectiveness* with students like your own. Otherwise, you may be better off learning to program the computer yourself and designing your own software. Refer back to the vast literature on programmed instruction from the 1960s, and you'll find out about many of the technical aspects of instructional programming [e.g., Skinner's *The Technology of Teaching* (1968); Markle's *Good Frames and Bad* (1969); and others].[5] If your program does an effective job, then you can arrange for its dissemination, and other students and educators can benefit as well!

[5]Teaching machines developed during the 1960s, following a few years of prominence, receded in importance as educational tools. It is our opinion that this happened primarily for two reasons. First, the machines were too costly at the time. Second, appropriate software was not available. Commercial materials were developed hurriedly to capture an enthusiastic potential market. Often principles of behavior were overlooked, and the programs failed to teach as anticipated. We hope that you will use the information we have provided to protect you and your students from a repetition of those events.

Summary

In this chapter we addressed various behavioral practices that have been shown to increase students' enjoyment of and proficiency in reading. Modeling and reinforcer sampling have been used effectively to increase the amount of time students spend reading. To increase the number of completed reading tasks, various reinforcement or feedback programs have been used effectively. Individual tutoring also can be beneficial to many students. Student teachers, adult volunteers, paraprofessionals, and peers can be taught to tutor students, assisting the teacher to meet better the needs of individual students.

To treat skill deficits in areas such as labeling words and letters correctly, comprehending, and reading fluently, we illustrated how a variety of behavioral principles and procedures have been used successfully. These behavioral principles and procedures, along with carefully programmed computers and the Direct Instruction model, all hold considerable promise for improving the reading skills of students in our schools today. Thus, we would encourage you to incorporate as many of these approaches as possible into your teaching practices. You may find, as we have, that your students' reading skills improve considerably.

Study Questions

1. Discuss several ways that families can encourage their children to read.
2. Describe the role of the educator in relation to reading.
3. Identify the two procedures used by Haskett and Lenfestey to encourage children to read.
4. Design an original program using modeling and reinforcement to increase the number of reading tasks completed.
5. Identify five groups of people who might be able to assist you with individual tutoring.
6. Refer to the study by Robinson et al. involving peer tutors and list the steps a child must complete before gaining access to the reinforcer.
7. Briefly describe an error correction procedure.
8. Sarah is a peer tutor. She was trained to use approval systematically, but provides it infrequently. Identify several solutions to this problem.
9. Use the A-B-C paradigm to describe reading.
10. Identify the level at which you should begin when teaching children to read.
11. List three behavioral procedures that often are used when teaching reading.
12. Tom can find the dates for Saturday and Sunday on his calendar but interchanges the two words when they are written elsewhere. Describe how you would use a size prompt to teach him to read these words correctly.
13. Size prompts do not help Susie. List several other prompting techniques that are available.
14. Provide an original example illustrating how pictures can be used as prompts to teach reading. (Be sure to describe how you will fade the prompt.)
15. Provide a guideline to follow when choosing features of the letters you emphasize through pictorial prompts.
16. Tim is gradually fading the prompts to ensure that his students make few, if any, mistakes. Identify the behavioral process.
17. Keith underlines words in the text when he is studying for a quiz in his behavior analysis class, but still fails to learn the critical features of the concepts he is studying. (a) Identify a possible reason for his poor understanding of the information and (b) provide a solution.
18. Define *reinforcing menu*.
19. Design an original program to improve reading comprehension.
20. (a) Identify and (b) define a behavioral procedure that may effectively increase rates of oral and silent reading.
21. State one reason why teachers might want to have their students read aloud in unison.
22. List two devices that can be used to increase the rates of oral reading by children with impaired hearing.
23. Describe the Direct Instruction model and SCORE programs.
24. Identify the populations aided by and describe how they have been helped by DISTAR.
25. Jim plans to purchase computer software for his reading class. List the important features he should seek in an educational program.

References

Barnard, J. D., Christophersen, E. R., & Wolf, M. M. (1974). Supervising paraprofessional tutors in a remedial reading program. *Journal of Applied Behavior Analysis*, 7, 481.

Becker, W. C., & Carnine, D. W. (1981). Direct instruction: A behavior theory model for comprehensive educational intervention with the disadvantaged. In S. W. Bijou & R. Ruiz (Eds.), *Behavior modification: Contributions to education*. Hillsdale, NJ: Lawrence Erlbaum Associates.

Becker, W. C., Engelmann, S., Carnine, D. W., & Maggs, A. (1982). Direct instruction technology — making learning happen. In P. Karoly & J. J. Steffen (Eds.), *Advances in child behavior analysis and therapy: Vol. 1* (pp. 151–206). New York: Gardner Press.

Becker, W. C., & Gersten, R. (1982). A follow-up of Follow Through: The later effects of the Direct Instruction model on children in fifth and sixth grades. *American Educational Research Journal*, 19, 75–92.

Block, J. H. (1971). *Mastery learning: Theory and practice*. New York: Holt, Rinehart and Winston.

Bloom, R. D. (1973). Learning to read: An operant perspective. *Reading Research Quarterly*, 8, 147–166.

Bradley-Johnson, S., Sunderman, P., & Johnson, C. M. (1983). Comparison of delayed prompting and fading for teaching preschoolers easily confused letters and numbers. *Journal of School Psychology*, 21, 327–335.

Corey, J. R., & Shamow, J. (1972). The effects of fading on the acquisition and retention of oral reading. *Journal of Applied Behavior Analysis*, 5, 311–315.

Cowen, R. J., Jones, F. H., & Bellack, A. S. (1979). Grandma's rule with group contingencies — A cost-efficient means of classroom management. *Behavior Modification*, 3, 397–418.

Cradler, J. D. (1980). Project SCORE, a tutorial reading system for the learning handicapped student. *Educational programs that work* (10th ed.). Washington, D.C.: U.S. Department of Education.

Cradler, J. D., Bechthold, D. L., & Bechthold, C. C. (1973). *Success Controlled Optimal Reading Experience*. Hillsborough, CA: Learning Guidance Systems.

Delquadri, J. (1983). *Reading: State of the arts as perceived from an applied behavior analysis paradigm*. Unpublished paper. Lawrence, KS: Juniper Gardens Children's Program, Bureau of Child Research, University of Kansas.

Delquadri, J., Whorton, D., Elliott, M., & Greenwood, C. R. (1982, May). *Peer & parent tutoring programs: A comparative analysis of the effects of packages on opportunity to respond, reading performance, and achievement scores of learning disabled disadvantaged children*. Paper presented at the Eighth Annual Convention of the Association for Behavior Analysis, Milwaukee, WI.

Etzel, B. C., LeBlanc, J. M., Schilmoeller, K. J., & Stella, M. E. (1981). Stimulus control procedures in the education of young children. In S. W. Bijou & R. Ruiz (Eds.), *Behavior modification: Contributions to education*. Hillsdale, NJ: Lawrence Erlbaum Associates.

Fields, L., Verhave, T., & Fath, S. (1984). Stimulus equivalence and transitive associations: A methodological analysis. *Journal of the Experimental Analysis of Behavior*, 42, 143–157.

Glover, J. A., Zimmer, J. W., Filbeck, R. W., & Plake, B. S. (1980). Effects of training students to identify the semantic base of prose materials. *Journal of Applied Behavior Analysis*, 13, 655–667.

Greer, R. D., & Polirstok, S. R. (1982). Collateral gains and short-term maintenance in reading and on-task responses by some inner-city adolescents as a function of their use of social reinforcement while tutoring. *Journal of Applied Behavior Analysis*, 15, 123–139.

Halle, J. W., Baer, D. M., & Spradlin, J. E. (1981). Teachers' generalized use of delay as a stimulus control procedure to increase language in handicapped children. *Journal of Applied Behavior Analysis*, 14, 389–409.

Haskett, G. J., & Lenfestey, W. (1974). Reading-related behavior in an open classroom: Effects of novelty and modelling on preschoolers. *Journal of Applied Behavior Analysis*, 7, 233–241.

Kirby, K. C., Holborn, S. W., & Bushby, H. T. (1981). Word game bingo: A behavioral treatment package for improving textual responding to sight words. *Journal of Applied Behavior Analysis*, 14, 317–326.

Lovitt, T. C. (1981). Graphing academic performances of mildly handicapped children. In S. W. Bijou & R. Ruiz (Eds.), *Behavior modification: Contributions to education*. Hillsdale, NJ: Lawrence Erlbaum Associates.

Markle, S. M. (1969). *Good frames and bad*. New York: Wiley.

Mosher, P. M., & Reese, E. P. (1976, April). *Task difficulty as a variable in teaching word recognition by fading and non-fading procedures*. Paper presented at the annual meeting of the Eastern Psychological Association.

The National Commission of Excellence in Education. (1983). *A nation at risk: The imperative for educational reform.* Washington, D.C.: U.S. Government Printing Office.

Neef, N. A., Iwata, B. A., & Page, T. J. (1977). The effects of known-item interspersal on acquisition and retention of spelling and sightreading words. *Journal of Applied Behavior Analysis, 10,* 738.

Ramey, G., & Sulzer-Azaroff, B. (1979, September). *Generalization effects of involving behaviorally disordered children as teachers.* Paper presented at the annual meeting of the American Psychological Association, New York.

Reese, E. P. (1978). *Skills training for the special child.* Distributed by Ellen P. Reese (writer/director), Hadleg, MA: Mount Holyoke College (film).

Robinson, P. W., Newby, T. J., & Ganzell, S. L. (1981). A token system for a class of underachieving hyperactive children. *Journal of Applied Behavior Analysis, 14,* 307–315.

Rosenbaum, M. S., & Breiling, J. (1976). The development and functional control of reading-comprehension behavior. *Journal of Applied Behavior Analysis, 9,* 323–333.

Schwartz, G. J. (1977). College students as contingency managers for adolescents in a program to develop reading skills. *Journal of Applied Behavior Analysis, 10,* 645–655.

Sidman, M., & Cresson, O., Jr. (1973). Reading and cross-modal transfer of stimulus equivalences in severe retardation. *American Journal of Mental Deficiency, 77,* 515–523.

Sidman, M., & Stoddard, L. T. (1966). Programming perception and learning for retarded children. In N. R. Ellis (Ed.), *International review of research in mental retardation* (Vol. 2). New York: Academic Press.

Skinner, B. F. (1968). *Technology of teaching.* New York: Appleton.

Smeets, P. M., & Striefel, S. (1976). Acquisition of sign reading by transfer of stimulus control in a retarded deaf girl. *Journal of Mental Deficiency Research, 20,* 197–205.

Sterling, L. K., Goetz, E. M., & Sterling, T. (1984). Acquisition and maintenance of basal and organic words. *Behavior Modification, 8,* 495–519.

Strong, M. W., & Traynelis-Yurek, E. A. (1982, May). *Behavioral reinforcement within a perceptual-conditioning program of oral reading.* Paper presented at the Eighth Annual Convention of the Association for Behavior Analysis, Milwaukee, WI.

Sulzer, B., Hunt, S., Ashby, E., Koniarski, C., & Krams, M. (1971). Increasing rate and percentage correct in reading and spelling in a fifth grade public school class of slow readers by means of a token system. In E. A. Ramp & B. L. Hopkins (Eds.), *A new direction for education: Behavior analysis.* Lawrence, KS: University of Kansas, Follow Through, Department of Human Development.

Tawney, J. W. (1972). Training letter discrimination in four-year-old children. *Journal of Applied Behavior Analysis, 5,* 455–465.

Touchette, P. E., & Howard, J. S. (1984). Errorless learning: Reinforcement contingencies and stimulus control transfer in delayed prompting. *Journal of Applied Behavior Analysis, 17,* 175–188.

Van Houten, R., & Van Houten, J. (1977). The performance feedback system in the special education classroom: An analysis of public posting and peer comments. *Behavior Therapy, 8,* 366–376.

Weisberg, P. (1983–1984). Reading instruction for poverty-level pre-schoolers: A seven year progress report. *Direct Instruction News, 3,* 16–18, 21.

Wilson, M. D., & McReynolds, L. V. (1973). A procedure for increasing oral reading rate in hard-of-hearing children. *Journal of Applied Behavior Analysis, 6,* 231–239.

16 Improving arithmetic skills

Goals

After completing this chapter, you should be able to:

1. Identify what to look for and describe how you might assess for difficulties in math.
2. Identify how to determine the elements you incorporate in your objectives.
3. Indicate what aspects constitute the antecedent, behavior, and consequence of an arithmetic operation.
4. Name the main source of reinforcement for doing math.
5. List and illustrate a variety of methods for enhancing reinforcement for doing math.
6. Describe how each of the following procedures and activities can be used to improve math skills:
   a. Chaining
   b. Managing specific antecedent conditions
   c. Modeling
   d. Self-instructions
   e. Prompting and fading
7. Describe how behavioral procedures may be applied to assist the talented math student.
8. Apply the behavioral strategies for improving math, reading, and communication skills to other academic skill areas.

"Again, Pam?" Mrs. Olsen questioned. "It seems to me you left your seat just a few minutes ago. How will you ever complete your assignment?"

Pam frequently left her seat during math class. Even when she did remain seated, however, her efforts were sporadic at best. She would attempt a problem or two, but typically she spent more time gazing out the window or over at Chris, who, as usual, seemed to know it all. It was no surprise that she barely made passing grades in math.

Mrs. Olsen attempted to get to the bottom of the situation one day after school, and called Pam in to discuss her history in regard to arithmetic. The girl said that she had had trouble with the subject for years, recalling an incident in second grade when she had been asked in front of the class to add a column of figures. She apparently had made a silly

error; and not only the other students but the teacher also had laughed at her.

"Math is just too much for me," Pam declared. "I get so worried, especially on tests, that I can't think at all. And when I try, I get it wrong. So what's the use?"

Mrs. Olsen had been doing a little reading about students like Pam, who experienced what is called "math anxiety"; and she found the topic fascinating. Tobias and Weissbrod (1980), for example, described various findings on mathematics anxiety, particularly as it related to women. In general, women take fewer math classes in school and have lower expectations of success for themselves in the subject. They also tend to attribute their failures to a lack of intelligence, while men fault their own lack of effort. Attempts to improve this situation among women have included various kinds of intervention, among them workshops directed toward relieving physical tension, providing positive math experiences, and other topics.

Mrs. Olsen decided that if she could provide students like Pam with more positive math experiences, they might begin to be less anxious about it. Then, if the problem persisted, she could refer the students for help in learning to relax when given difficult assignments.

ASSESSING DIFFICULTIES IN MATH

The obvious place to start, when a student like Pam experiences trouble with math, is to assess the situation. Does the difficulty reflect a motivational or a skill deficit? Or is it actually tied to the kinds of competing emotional responses usually labeled "anxiety" (i.e., tremors, palpitations, muscular tension, control by nonrelevant discriminative stimuli, and so on)? Once you assess the probable cause, the direction to follow will become apparent.

You could begin by looking over the student's file of papers to see if at least some of his or her class assignments have been done correctly. If so, you might conclude that the concepts are being mastered. It would be beneficial to examine the faulty papers closely to see if any operations are consistently in error. For instance, the student regularly may overlook numbers to be carried or add numerals instead of multiplying them.[1] If missing skills do not appear to be responsible, you might next observe the student informally during math class. Narrate what you see, particularly noting the apparent proportion of time spent on-task and any indicators of anxiety. Follow up by collecting relevant data.

If your informal investigations lead you to suspect deficiencies in the student's level of skill, you will need to find out more. Refer to the student's record to check his or her scores on standardized achievement tests such as the *Wide Range Achievement Test* (Jastak & Jastak, 1965), and then focus in more closely on the exact nature of the difficulties. A good place to start would be by referring to a task analysis of a mathematics curriculum, such as the excellent one offered by Resnick, Wang, and Kaplan (1973). Leonhart (1982) has shown how a task analysis can be used to assess arithmetic skills among a group of retarded students. If you have the time, you could assign the student a series of math operations from the task analysis, providing heavy incentives such as points or tokens exchangeable for preferred activities or items, to encourage hard work. After all, you want to find out if the student is capable of performing the various operations assigned—not, in this instance, what his or her typical performance is like. So you should provide optimal circumstances for success.[2]

SPECIFYING OBJECTIVES

Once you have diagnosed where the student's math difficulties lie, you are ready to identify the instructional objectives. You may have found that rate was the main issue. That being the case, you would formulate objectives incorporating rate building. If skill deficits are apparent, you would define the skill behaviorally and set criteria of acceptability. Glance at the objectives established by Resnick and his colleagues (1973) in Table 16.1, and you may find they have given you a head start.

In case you are convinced that you are dealing with a serious case of math anxiety, your objectives probably will include both rate and skill building, plus others calling for relaxation while the student performs math operations. Modifying physiological responses, such as muscle tension, palpitations, perspiration, and so on, probably should be managed by

---

[1]Should your school system be fortunate enough to have available the services of a math specialist, he or she will be able to conduct a far more sensitive and sophisticated diagnosis than we are suggesting.

[2]Maheady, Sainato, and Maitland (1983) showed that extrinsic rewards improved students' performance on standardized reading tests. Presumably the same effect could be accomplished with math.

Table 16.1
Objectives of the mathematics curriculum

Units 1 and 2: counting and one-to-one correspondence[a]
A. The child can recite the numerals in order.
B. Given a set of movable objects, the child can count the objects, moving them out of the set as he counts.
C. Given a fixed ordered set of objects, the child can count the objects.
D. Given a fixed unordered set of objects, the child can count the objects.
E. Given a numeral stated and a set of objects, the child can count out a subset of stated size.
F. Given a numeral stated and several sets of fixed objects, the child can select a set of size indicated by numeral.
G. Given two sets of objects, the child can pair objects and state whether the sets are equivalent.
H. Given two unequal sets of objects, the child can pair objects and state which set has more.
I. Given two unequal sets of objects, the child can pair objects and state which set has less.

Units 3 and 4: numerals[b]
A. Given two sets of numerals, the child can match the numerals.
B. Given a numeral stated and a set of printed numerals, the child can select the stated numeral.
C. Given a numeral (written), the child can read the numeral.
D. Given several sets of objects and several numerals, the child can match numerals with appropriate sets.
E. Given two numerals (written), the child can state which shows more (less).
F. Given a set of numerals, the child can place them in order.
G. Given numerals stated, the child can write the numeral.

Unit 5: comparison of sets
A. Given two sets of objects, the child can count sets and state which has more objects or that sets have same number.
B. Given two sets of objects, the child can count sets and state which has less objects.
C. Given a set of objects and a numeral, the child can state which shows more (less).
D. Given a numeral and several sets of objects, the child can select sets which are more (less) than the numeral; given a set of objects and several numerals, the child can select numerals which show more (less) than the set of objects.
E. Given two rows of objects (not paired), the child can state which row has more regardless of arrangement.
F. Given three sets of objects, the child can count sets and state which has most (least).

Unit 6: seriation and ordinal position
A. Given three objects of different sizes, the child can select the largest (smallest).
B. Given objects of graduated sizes, the child can arrange according to size.
C. Given several sets of objects, the child can arrange the sets according to size.
D. Given ordered set of objects, the child can name the ordinal position of the objects.

Unit 7: addition and subtraction (sums to 10)
A. Given two numbers stated, set of objects, and directions to add, the child can add the numbers by counting out two subsets then combining and stating combined number as sum.
B. Given two numbers stated, set of objects, and directions to subtract, the child can count out smaller subset from larger and state remainder.
C. Given two numbers stated, number line, and directions to add, the child can use the number line to determine sum.
D. Given two numbers stated, number line, and directions to subtract, the child can use number line to subtract.
E. Given addition and subtraction word problems, the child can solve the problems.
F. Given written addition and subtraction problems in form: $x + y$ or $x - y$; the child can complete the problems.
G. Given addition and subtraction problems in form: $x + y = \square$, or $x - y = \square$; the child can complete the equations.

Unit 8: addition and subtraction equations
A. Given equation of form $z = \square + \triangle$, the child can show several ways of completing the equation.
B. Given equation of form $x + y = \quad + \quad$, the child can complete the equation in several ways.

Table 16.1
Objectives of the mathematics curriculum (*continued*)

C. Given equations of forms $x + y = z +$ and $x + y =$ $+ z$, the child can complete the equations.

D. Given equations of forms $x + \square = y$ and $\square + x = y$, the child can complete the equations.

E. Given complete addition equation (e.g., $x + y = z$), the child can write equations using numerals and minus sign (e.g., $z - x = y$) and demonstrate relationship.

F. Given counting blocks and/or number line, the child can make up completed equations of various forms.

[a]Unit 1 involves sets of up to five objects; unit 2 involves sets of up to 10 objects.

[b]Unit 3 involves numerals and sets of up to five objects; unit 4 involves numerals and sets of up to 10 objects.

Table reprinted by permission from the authors, Resnick, Wang, & Kaplan, and the *Journal of Applied Behavior Analysis*, 1973, 6, pp. 679–710. Copyright 1973 by the Society for the Experimental Analysis of Behavior, Inc.

a trained specialist, such as a school or clinical psychologist, who has access to biofeedback equipment. If that describes yourself, you and your client may set objectives related to reducing such discomforts.[3] For the classroom teacher working with a student, however, it would be more practical to limit the objectives to completing tasks, paying attention, improving rate of performance, improving verbal behavior, and performing other actions that are readily accessible to monitoring in a group setting.

Sometimes standardized tests show that, on the average, students in a school or district perform substantially below grade level in math. In that situation, you may wish to consider a total program designed to promote higher achievement for everyone. By starting early—at the preschool or primary level—you may prevent difficulties from developing.

Remember, also, to identify objectives for your more capable and advanced students, to permit them to function with greater independence and to enrich their mathematical experiences. In the following sections, we offer strategies to assist you in coping with students' problems in math, but we also mention some approaches for more mathematically competent students as well.[4]

[3]In the workbook, *Applying Behavior Analysis: A Program to Develop Professional Competencies*, Sulzer-Azaroff and Reese (1982) have included a workshop and field activities designed to reduce anxiety. You and your student might find this format useful for designing a program directed toward lessening his or her math anxiety.

[4]We recognize that arithmetic is but one facet of mathematics but have chosen, for the sake of simplicity, to use the terms arithmetic and mathematics (or math) interchangeably.

A BEHAVIOR ANALYSIS OF ARITHMETIC OPERATIONS

- "Let's see now. Your total gasoline bill comes to $20.00, and you get a rebate of 3 cents a gallon. Just a sec while I figure that out."
- You are planning to recarpet your living room and need to calculate the requisite square footage.
- You anticipate moving and want to know how long it will take you to commute to work from your new home, traveling from your house to the train station and then from the station to your office.
- Uncle Sam wants a share of your income. You have to determine how much to give the government, without over- or underpaying.

From everyday life you undoubtedly could generate hundreds of additional illustrations that require mathematical computation. Conjure up a few more for yourself and then ask, from a behavior analytic perspective, just what sort of interrelation is involved between your behavior and the environment. Quickly, if you have not already, you will recognize that we are dealing with issues of stimulus control over chains of responses. A math problem constitutes the antecedent condition, the performance of the requisite chain of responses is the behavior, and, of course, the correct solution is the natural reinforcer (or the incorrect solution, the aversive consequence; Table 16.2).[5]

[5]Parsons (1972) has presented an excellent behavior analytic description of arithmetic behavior and program development.

Table 16.2
A contingency analysis of a math problem

Antecedent	Behavior	Consequence
Tax return form	Correct chain of behaviors: Calculate correct amount owed. Write out check. Enclose check and signed tax return in envelope. Stamp envelope and mail before April 15.	Avoid fine, emotional responses.
	Incorrect chain of behaviors: Any of the above components incorrect, missing, or out of sequence.	Fine or overpayment, emotional responses.

As educators, our task is to evoke the appropriate response to the problem. To accomplish that, we proceed just as we have all along, by discovering where among the A-B-Cs we should intervene. We must ask ourselves if the consequences are inadequate or inappropriate; if the behavioral chains include incorrect, disordered, or missing links; or if the critical features of the antecedent stimuli are not in control of the performance. Then we will know where best to focus our activity.

Let us begin with the simplest case: modifying consequences. Next, we focus on the performance of a skill, then on the mathematical problem and how its critical properties may gain adequate control over the skill.

IMPROVING ARITHMETIC: MODIFYING CONSEQUENCES

Unlike many realms of human activity, when it comes to arithmetic, a clear and distinct natural reinforcer exists: the correct answer. When the square footage of carpeting we have ordered matches the floor space exactly, our calculations are reinforced. When a critical period of time passes without the government auditing us, we breath a sigh of relief. Among adults, simply obtaining the same result on

rechecking an arithmetic calculation usually serves as sufficient reinforcement. In essence, reinforcement is intrinsic to most of the arithmetic operations with which we are concerned in our daily lives. Why is this not the case for many students?

Young children, in particular, may not yet have learned to self-check and verify the correctness of their answers, or to bridge the time gap between their responses and natural reinforcement. Older students may have found repetitious drill unpleasant or their efforts punished, so they are less likely to tackle their work. In either case, a reasonable strategy would be to increase reinforcement.

Enhance opportunities for success

You can enhance opportunities for success by interspersing relatively easy tasks within assignments, so the students frequently will produce the correct answers. Of course, to do that you need to know their levels of performance. Then, when they respond correctly, you should provide feedback as soon and as often as possible. Try circulating among the group with an answer key and checking problems as they are completed, or providing the key to students for them to check their work by themselves, or involving peers as proctors or tutors. Praise accomplishments regularly, when you know that praise is reinforcing for the students. Then as success becomes routine, gradually delay and reduce your frequency of praising.

As described earlier, in *Direct Instruction* (Becker & Carnine, 1981), primary school students are instructed in small groups at a rapid pace, using the DISTAR curriculum (Engelmann & Carnine, 1969). They respond in unison, are corrected when necessary, and are praised when appropriate. Just those features alone have been found to make a substantial difference in children's levels of performance. When combined with the careful sequential programming and administration that characterizes Direct Instruction, the curriculum has enhanced significantly mathematical problem solving among groups of disadvantaged youngsters participating in a Follow Through program over that of students in local comparison groups (Becker & Gersten, 1982). It seems, then, that if children's experiences with math are generally positive, productive, and intrinsically rewarding, they may not require supplementary reinforcers.

Boosting relevance and appeal of math activities

If success and praise are insufficient to encourage your students to achieve satisfactory results in math, you might ask yourself if the work can be made more relevant and interesting for them. Because arithmetic skills are integral to so many daily activities, you may be able to offer opportunities to practice those skills in ways more appealing to the students. We have seen teachers provide their pupils with important drill by involving them in planning and conducting shopping excursions — outings on which they can practice making change, determining unit costs, gauging appropriate quantities, and so on. Then purchases are used to prepare meals and party menus, activities that also necessitate applying arithmetic skills. Woodwork and other crafts, sports, music, dance, and computer games can involve mathematics; computations, relational and geometric concepts, and so on, may provide splendid opportunities for practice. Be careful, though, to tell the students if their answers are right or wrong, and, if appropriate, praise their efforts.

Supplementing with extrinsic reinforcers

Assuming you have done your best within practical limitations to plan interesting and relevant math assignments, and you recognize a need for your students to practice more intensively, you then might consider some extrinsic supplements: self-imposed, peer, group, parental, and other reinforcing contingencies.

A 7-year-old girl attending school in British Columbia was progressing reasonably well, but often failed to complete her arithmetic assignments (Johnston & McLaughlin, 1982). In fact, during baseline assessment she was found to have completed well below 60 percent of the problems assigned. On some days she finished almost none. For the intervention, the youngster was required to complete an assigned number of problems before being permitted free time for the rest of the period. Starting with a requirement of 30-percent completion, criteria were raised every few days until they reached 100 percent. In every instance, she met the requirement. Accuracy was recorded throughout and was maintained fairly well, particularly during three follow-up checks, when in the absence of the reinforcing contingency, the girl continued to achieve 100 percent (Figure 16.1).

Would you like your students to complete their arithmetic drill work accurately and rapidly? If so, you might use the method that McLaughlin (1981) did with a combined class of fifth and sixth graders in a low-income area of Spokane, Washington. The entire class operated on a token economy. Students could earn points for various productive academic and positive social behaviors, and they lost points for nonproductive academic behaviors and negative social behaviors. Rewards consisted of special activities and privileges, such as extra recess, projects, service as monitor, and so on. The students worked on multiplication of fractions. When they completed their assignments, each exchanged papers with a peer who graded it using an answer key. When points were awarded for accuracy and improved rates of performance, the youngsters gradually demonstrated substantial improvement in both areas. Sim-

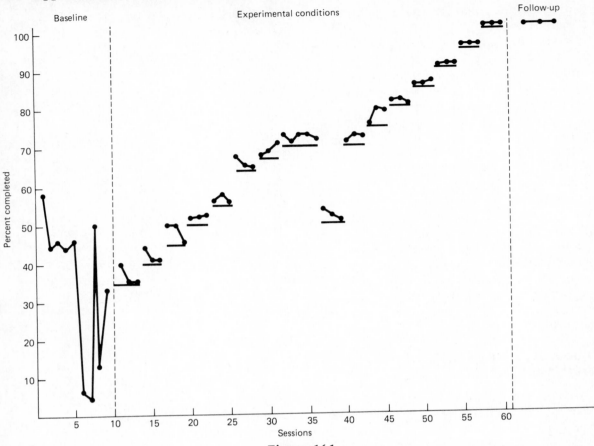

Figure 16.1

Improving percent of assignments completed. The percent of problems completed for each assignment during each of the experimental conditions. The solid horizontal lines indicate the reinforcement criterion set for each session (Johnston & McLaughlin, 1982).

ilar results were accomplished among three seventh graders (Schumaker, Hovell, & Sherman, 1977) when parents received a daily report card on their child's performance so they could award basic and special privileges accordingly.

Permitting pupils to check their answers themselves undoubtedly would save you considerable time; but their self-checking must be accurate if they are to learn correctly, particularly if students earn rewards for correct answers. You can well imagine that under the latter circumstances, as Hundert and Bucher (1978) found, the youngsters would be tempted to inflate their scores. The way around this difficulty is to place contingencies on accuracy of reporting. You can check publicly, as Hundert and Bucher did, penalizing inaccuracies and reinforcing accuracy; or you can randomly sample individual students' work and apply the contingencies. In our own work (Sulzer, Hunt, Ashby, Koniarski, & Krams, 1971) with children who used a programmed instructional text that supplied answers, we simply made a point of publicly praising individual students for using the material as intended, frequently in the beginning and intermittently afterward. Our careful observations convinced us that they continued to self-check accurately.

Sam, Kathy, and Randy attended a special class for children with learning and behavioral problems (McKenzie & Budd, 1981). While Randy performed reasonably well in math and had progressed to such an extent that he gradually was being phased back into a regular class, the other two children were not faring as well. So the teacher decided to ask Randy to tutor Kathy and Sam. The teacher trained and supervised Randy in helping without giving the answer, checking answers accurately, and, based on Kathy's and Sam's correct answers, praising and awarding points good for free time. Randy did his job well, and Sam and Kathy improved their percentage correct on division problems, even while Randy was not in the room. As a fringe benefit, Kathy and Sam remained on-task and were less disruptive during the peer tutoring. Should you be concerned that your tutors might be missing out on their own work, this need not be the case, as Conlon, Hall, and Hanley (1972) have shown. Their peer tutor solved as many arithmetic problems correctly while he was tutoring as he did when he was not. So again, this time with arithmetic, we find that well-trained and supervised peer tutors can accomplish a good deal.

Once students have acquired particular computational skills and you want to increase their rates of performance, you could examine and improve the schedules with which you distribute reinforcers. Follow the example of Lovitt and Esvelt (1970) and find out the students' baseline rates and use that to guide your adjustment of their reinforcement schedules. With their pupil, Lovitt and Esvelt noted a median rate of .8 correct answers per minute. When rules were changed so the student earned increasingly more points the more problems he solved correctly and the more rapidly he worked, his rate and productivity doubled.

If activity reinforcers don't quite do it, you might start out, temporarily, with tangible rewards like prizes, treats, trinkets, or toys that the children could rent for a time.[6] A class of Down's syndrome children received tokens exchangeable for treats for correct answers on the DISTAR (Engelmann & Carnine, 1969) arithmetic and language instructional programs. They learned better than counterparts from a class where children only earned praise (Dalton, Rubino, & Hislop, 1973).

In another case, 24 boys and girls in a second-grade class were asked individually to answer sets of arithmetic problems (Felixbrod & O'Leary, 1973). Some were informed that they could earn points exchangeable for prizes if they answered a given number of problems correctly. Of those students, half selected their own performance standards; the other half had performance standards imposed on them. Children in the reward conditions worked longer at the task than those receiving no rewards. Despite a gradually increasing leniency in setting performance standards, those who self-determined their rewards showed no drop in rate or accuracy over time.[7]

You also could try asking your students to specify point values for each accomplishment, as Lovitt and Curtiss (1969) did with a 12-year-old student in a class for children with behavior disorders. After first imposing point values for a while, the teacher turned over assignment of point values to the student. Under those circumstances, performance rose substantially, dropping back to its previous level when the teacher again resumed control. Particularly for adolescent youngsters, it seems especially promising to permit them to self-determine contingencies and standards as regularly as is feasible.

Sometimes repetitious rote drill can be made more

---

[6]You probably don't need to worry about pupils suffering from reduced interest in the subject after the rewards are withdrawn (Vasta & Stirpe, 1979), especially if the shift over to more natural contingencies is gradual.

[7]Exactly how much of the success could be attributed to setting of performance standards—S^Ds—and how much to the reward conditions cannot be determined, as both were introduced simultaneously. Research in occupational settings (e.g., Latham & Baldes, 1975) has shown that setting goals alone sometimes may produce increments in performance.

reinforcing by making a game out of it. Some of our graduate students who are teachers have reported successfully using a *quick-draw* math game to assist their students in learning the multiplication tables. To play the game, each student writes a different number (0 to 12) on one of 13 separate index cards. Two students are chosen to begin the game. Each takes one of the cards, concealing it; and, then, they stand back to back, approximately two feet apart at the front of the room. When the teacher says, ''Draw,'' the two students turn around and face each other, showing the number each has chosen. The first student to respond with the correct product remains at the front of the class. The loser sits down. The winner then chooses another student (alternating boys with girls) to challenge.

Peers can produce powerful support for one another when contingencies are arranged to harness this effect. McCarty and colleagues (1977) studied the arithmetic problem-solving performance of four adolescents residing in a psychiatric hospital. Two conditions were compared: one in which they worked for their own monetary rewards, the other in which each student had to complete at least three problems before any of the four could receive their money. The latter contingency produced increased performance rates, and peers aided one another on their work and redirected each other when they were off-task.

Be careful about the way you arrange group contingencies, though. When Ulman and Sulzer-Azaroff (1975) compared the number of arithmetic problems completed by a group of developmentally disabled adult students under one of three contingencies—no monetary rewards, an individualized reward, or a collective group monetary contingency—the individualized contingency won out. Why? Because in the group contingency, each earned the same amount, which was based on the average performance of the group. Those who stood to earn the most under the individual condition lost out in the group arrangements. (Interestingly, students in that study were institutionalized in a facility for the mentally retarded, yet they were able to tell which arrangement was to their greatest advan-

tage.) If you do use a group arrangement, then select it carefully to enhance production and peer support.[8]

TEACHING MATHEMATICAL SKILLS

Let us return for a moment to Mrs. Olsen's student, Pam. Although the girl's difficulties with math were in part motivational, the problem went still deeper. For that reason, simply rewarding her efforts would be insufficient. Pam had not acquired the skills to permit her to succeed. Enhancement of reinforcing contingencies will not accomplish the purpose if necessary skills are missing from a student's repertoire. Despite intense motivation, how effectively could you ski downhill without having the skill to do so? When a pupil lacks specific math skills, we need to arrange to teach those skills. Because our aim in teaching math is to bring chains of behavior under stimulus control, applying behavioral procedures known to promote chaining and stimulus control effectively should help. In this section, we illustrate how this end might be accomplished.

Chaining

Multiplying double digits, doing long division or geometric proofs, solving algebraic equations, calculating standard deviations, and performing most other mathematical operations call for a sequence of responses. Your students may be omitting some critical steps, like failing to carry, substituting incorrect links (as in adding rather than subtracting in long division), or performing steps out of order. In that case, you may find it useful to refer to the chapter on chaining (see Chapter 8). You probably will find yourself redesigning your instruction so that the students work on short segments initially, rather than on the full sequence. You also may solve parts of the problem for your students, still allowing them to complete the portions that are creating difficulty so

---

[8]See Litow and Pumroy (1975) for a discussion of this point.

Double-digit multiplication

1.
```
      42
    ×23
    126
   +84
    _66
   _____
```

2.
```
      31
    ×22
     62
    ×62
    --2
   _____
```

3.
```
      23
    ×21
     23
   +46
    ---
   _____
```

4.
```
      37
    ×54
    148
   +185
   ----
   _____
```

5.
```
      16
    ×72
     32
    112
   _____
```

6.
```
      94
    ×37
    658
    282
   _____
```

7.
```
      33
    ×23
     99
    _6
   _____
```

8.
```
      37
    ×64
    148
    --2
   _____
```

9.
```
      65
    ×37
    455
    ---
   _____
```

10.
```
      26
    ×18
    --8
    --
   _____
```

11.
```
      47
    ×52
    --
    ---
   _____
```

12.
```
      73
    ×61
   _____
```

Figure 16.2

One illustration of backward chaining.
To obtain the correct answer for problem type 1, the student needs only to complete the addition in the hundreds column. For type 2, only two columns need to be added, and so on for types 3 and 4. The box prompts are removed for 5, so the student needs to supply the correct number of digits. Adding with carrying is illustrated for 6 (assuming the student already can perform this operation; otherwise other problem types might need to be interposed). For problem type 7, the student begins to multiply, although part of that operation has already been completed. For 8, 9, and 10, more multiplication is required. By 11 the box prompts are removed, and by 12 the only prompt remaining is the line for the answer. Given sufficient reinforced practice with each problem type along the way and regular review of previously mastered steps, the student should make few errors. Can you figure out how to use backward chaining to teach long division or to solve a geometric proof?

they can experience some reinforced practice with those segments. Undoubtedly, you will enable the pupils to solve subsections of the chains accurately, smoothly, and rapidly before you add the next subset and, if necessary, use effective prompting and fading strategies to evoke accurate responses. Ultimately, you will ask your students to solve the problems completely, offering copious reinforcement as they succeed. We suggest you then intersperse those varieties of problems within the pupil's subsequent assignments to provide additional reinforced practice

as well as to encourage persistence. See Figures 16.2 and 16.3 for illustrative examples.

Managing antecedent conditions

The teachers at Willow Grove School had reorganized their approach to mathematics instruction. Work was assigned to students according to their actual performance levels; and occasionally, as with Pam, some worked on individualized assignments. Effective reinforcing contingencies were arranged.

We need to plan how much carpeting to order for our new offices. One office looks like this:

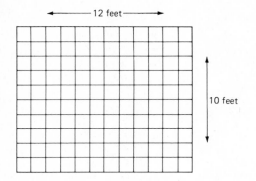

1. See that we have drawn the square feet for you. There are 10 rows of 12 squares each. We can either add up the 10 rows 12 times or we can multiply 10 times 12. That will tell us that we need____square feet of carpet.

2. Finish drawing the lines that show how many square feet you would need for this 7 × 10 office.

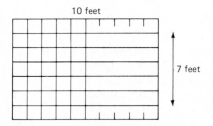

3. You will have 7 rows of____boxes each. Your example is 7 × ☐ . The answer is____square feet.

Figure 16.3
Backward chaining for determining square footage.
Notice how much of the work has been done for the student, almost guaranteeing initially correct answers. Again, the student is gradually required to do more and more of the problem.

For instance, students who completed their assignments would gain access during the last hour on Friday to special activities they themselves had identified: dances, games, cooking, crafts activities, and so on. Improvement was impressive, but the staff wondered if there might be room for any further gains. How about modifying antecedent conditions? Should they allocate specific instructional time to

math, or leave the pupils to their own devices? How should drills in rapid calculation best be arranged? If they scheduled group instruction, how active should the students be? What sorts of prompting strategies would be helpful?

At the moment, it appears that allocating specific instructional time to a subject, even when students attend passively, is better than allocating no time to it (Greenwood et al., 1984). Even 10 minutes a day devoted to whole group instruction in math produced major gains in Friday tests among inner-city school children. But arranging a class-wide tutoring game, which necessitated that pupils be engaged actively and increased their opportunities to respond, accelerated performance even further.

How time is managed also can make a difference, particularly when you are attempting to promote high rates of accurate performance. In a study by Van Houten and Thompson (1976), 30 minutes were allocated to arithmetic drill in a second-grade class. Records were kept of the number of correct problems per minute and the percentage correct. Two conditions were compared: the status of work when time up was called at the end of 30 minutes, versus progress noted each minute during the 30-minute period. In the latter, the children worked until a timer cued their teacher to instruct them to stop briefly and draw a line indicating where they were working at that moment. Then they proceeded on to the next 1-minute segment and so on. Surprisingly, the students accomplished considerably more within the 30-minute period with the 1-minute timing phase than in the standard situation.

How many drills per day are optimal? You can test this out in your own setting by varying systematically their number and/or distribution throughout the school day. When Raggio and Bitgood (1982) wondered how many 1-minute drills would be optimal for eight behaviorally troubled youths remanded to a supervised group home setting, they found that four drills per day—in contrast with one, two, or eight per day—produced the highest number of responses per minute. (This is not to suggest that you assign only four 1-minute drills to your students, only that you test various alternatives and select the most promising for your group.)

Other setting events, such as time of day, interspersal of drill throughout the day (rather than massed during a segment of it), prior and subsequent activities, features of the physical environment, and other conditions, to our knowledge, remain to be studied. It may be that antecedent conditions of those types can influence quality and rates of math performance.

Modeling

The show-and-tell method is the one typically used by teachers to explain arithmetic operations. The teacher explains how the problem is done and demonstrates, usually on the chalkboard. That is a reasonable approach and most students can learn that way. But if some of your students haven't profited from that form of group instruction, don't abandon the idea of using modeling. Rather, consider helping the child individually to promote closer attending, as Smith and Lovitt (1975) did. Working with learning-disabled children, they identified the categories of arithmetic computational difficulties their individual pupils were experiencing, for example, multiplication of numbers composed of several digits including a zero. Then they prepared worksheets containing those sorts of problems. To instruct, the teacher approached each student individually and demonstrated how to solve the problem. In several cases, she would leave the solution as a permanent model to which the child could refer. Sometimes

this was not necessary. Rapidly the students overcame their deficits.

If some of your students are functioning at the prearithmetic level, for instance, acquiring counting or relational skills, you probably permit them to manipulate tangible objects like blocks, sticks, wooden rods, or even small toys. In the event that instructions and modeling are not sufficient to evoke the appropriate response, physically guide each student in counting, matching, and so on, gradually fading the guidance as the student takes on increasing control. Leonhart (1982) found this approach very successful in aiding six severely handicapped students to progress through the Resnick et al. (1973) objectives.

Self-instruction

"Spring ahead; fall back."

"I have to make a right, then two lefts, and go 100 yards."

"To shift gears, first I press the clutch pedal...."

How many of us use cues like those to assist our recall? Instructing ourselves verbally can help us perform many intricate chains of behavior. The same is true for complex arithmetic skills, such as adding and subtracting with regrouping. Tom regularly forgot to carry when adding. Ms. Hollingsworth taught him a set of instructions she saw reported by Whitman and Johnston (1983; Table 16.3). By demonstrating the instructions herself, asking

Table 16.3
Example of self-instruction training sequence for addition with regrouping

Q. What kind of a problem is this? $57 + 35 =$
A. It's an add problem. I can tell by the sign.

Q. Now what do I do?
A. I start with the top number in the one's column and I add. Seven add 5 (the child points to the 7 on the number line and counts 5 spaces to the right) is 12. Twelve has two numbers. That means I have to carry. I put the 2 in the one's column (the child writes the 2 in the one's column in the answer) and the 1 in the ten's column (the child writes the 1 above the top number in the ten's column in the problem).

Q. Now what do I do?
A. I start with the top number in the ten's column and I add. One add 5 (the child points to the 1 on the number line and counts 5 spaces to the right) is 6. Six add 3 (the child counts 3 more spaces to the right) is 9 (the child writes the 9 in the ten's column in the answer). I got it finished so I'm doing good.

Tom to imitate, and reinforcing his gradual mastery of the instructions while she faded her prompts, Ms. Hollingsworth eventually taught Tom to repeat them to himself. Tom's accuracy increased substantially when he performed computations requiring regrouping, just as did that of the nine students described by Whitman and Johnston.

An 11-year-old boy in a class for children with behavioral disorders made a large number of errors in arithmetic (Lovitt & Curtiss, 1968). He was taught to verbalize the problem before attempting a solution. When he did that he made far fewer errors. So, you see, simple self-instructions sometimes can help.

You also can teach your students more complex self-instructions to use for various kinds of academic tasks, as Bryant and Budd (1982, p. 265) have done:

> (a) stop and look; (b) questions about the task (e.g., "What does the teacher want me to do?"); (c) answers to questions about the task (e.g., "That's right, I'm supposed to find the same"); (d) self-instruction to guide through the task (e.g., "This one looks like that one so I'll put an X on it"); and (e) self-acknowledgement (e.g., "I did a good job on this one").

Three children in a remedial preschool program were taught to use those self-instructions to help them complete worksheets, including finding-the-same items, following mazes, and sequencing sizes. To teach the self-instructions, the experimenter first modeled the task, then instructed aloud while the child performed it, then whispered the instructions as the child self-instructed aloud while performing the task. Next, the child performed the task while making lip movements; and finally the child said the sequence to himself or herself while performing the task. First training took place outside the classroom; testing occurred in the classroom. Later, minimal training was introduced directly in the classroom and students' performance in their assignments improved there correspondingly.

A group of fourth graders was taught an explicit strategy for translating word story problems into mathematical equations, in a study by Darch, Carnine, and Gersten (1984). Following a script, teachers taught a set of rules. The first was: "If you use the same numbers again and again, you multiply." Guided by the teacher in the beginning, students applied the rule to concrete models, such as boxes. Then they switched over to actual word problems. The words *each* or *every* cued that the same number was used again and again. Then division story problems were introduced by first referring to "number families" and the relationships between the "big number" and "two little numbers" in each family. Next students were shown how to analyze a set of numbers to see if the "big number" was given in the story. After some guided practice in solving several multiplication and division problems, they learned to apply two rules (Darch et al., 1984, p. 8): "If the big number is not given, the problem is a multiplication problem. If the big number is given, it is a division problem."

For the next step, students learned to ask two questions to help them identify whether a problem called for addition, subtraction, multiplication, or division. During practice, errors were corrected by modeling the correct response and asking questions from the previously taught explicit strategy.

When the outcome of teaching by that explicit method was compared with that of a group taught according to the instructions given in the teachers' guides of four basic arithmetic texts, it was found that the explicit method was far superior. After a couple of weeks the difference held, however, only for students who also received extra review lessons. Again, we see how important it is to provide for reinforced practice repeatedly after a skill is acquired.

General problem-solving strategies probably can help guide students to make their own mathematical discoveries. A talented youngster such as Richard's older brother Howard, who is so advanced in math, learned how to manipulate objects to figure out how to handle fractions. He also discovered for himself how to check sums by adding first from top to bottom and next in the reverse order. Howard enjoys math because finding out on his own is so reinforcing. Your students don't have to be mathematical whiz kids to discover things for themselves, as long as you arrange the environment appropriately. Provide them with tools such as these: objects to manipulate and/or relevant key questions or phrases, such as "What will happen if . . . ?" "What must I do every time to . . . ?" "How do the parts relate to one another . . . ?" "How is this like, and how is it different from . . . ?" "How many ways can I come up with the same answer . . . ?" "What is the formula for figuring out this sort of a problem . . . ?"

Mr. Truax noticed that many of his students learned mathematical formulas by rote, often recalling them incorrectly and not seeming to understand how they applied to reality. So he decided to provide many concrete examples and encourage the students to discover the general rules on their own. To teach the formula for determining square footage, he handed out piles of 12-square-inch floor tiles and asked the students to arrange them in various rectangular patterns. By handling the tiles, several of them recognized that square footage could be determined by multiplying the length by the width. Memorizing the formula was easier, too, as they could imagine the experience to aid their recall. Because of that success, Mr. Truax then used cooking activities to teach addition and multiplication of fractions. One student recognized that if he multiplied the numerator, he would have the correct answer; and he demonstrated this to the others. Most of the pupils later recalled how to multiply fractions because they remembered having to multiply one-half cups of butter and one-third cups of nuts by six to produce enough chocolate chip cookies for the whole class. On the basis of other work of ours (e.g., where we found that some language-deficient children learned to speak more easily when words were orally presented *and* signed simultaneously, Barrera & Sulzer-Azaroff, 1983), it seems that multiple sensory inputs might increase some students' learning and retention. In this hypothetical case, sight, touch, smell, and taste could serve as powerful prompts.

Learning by discovery can be a mixed blessing, though. Sometimes your students' great discoveries may be wrong or their strategies cumbersome. So examine their products and the methods used to produce them, providing corrective feedback if the outcome or process was in error, or encouraging more streamlined methods. Then, of course, reinforce correct solutions and clever efforts. If you show enthusiasm when your students make discoveries, they

probably will do the same for themselves and one another.

Prompting and fading to avoid errors and improve accuracy

Suppose your students make errors because they confuse written instructions, such as addition, subtraction, multiplication, and division signs. Technically, those antecedent stimuli—the symbols—do not evoke the correct operation. If so, one way to repair the difficulty is to apply procedures designed to help each antecedent stimulus to control the appropriate response. *Prompting and fading* the prompts is one way to accomplish that task.

A 9-year-old second-grade girl was reported by her teacher to have constant trouble retaining numerical facts. When presented with single-numeral addition problems the sums of which were greater than 10, she generally failed to give the correct answer. So Haupt, Van Kirk, and Terraciano (1975) tested out two different strategies to see if either might be more effective. For one condition, flash cards with covered answers were presented. If the youngster failed to give the correct response within two seconds, the cover was removed and the answer revealed. In the other condition, a *fading* condition, the answer could be seen easily through a cut-out window. Each time the child answered seven facts correctly within two seconds, a sheet of cellophane was added to those covering the answer, presumably making the answer increasingly less clearly discernible. The net result was that the girl made far fewer errors during the fading procedure and a week later showed that she retained more of the facts learned under that condition.

In a second experiment, the same authors worked with a 10-year-old boy who had trouble learning his multiplication tables. This time they compared a study condition, during which he repeated the tables to himself, versus a fading condition. In the latter, they placed a sheet of tracing paper over each answer, and the boy was instructed to trace each of the answers. Next, two sheets of tracing paper were applied and the process repeated. Ultimately, although the answers were obscured completely by several layers of tracing paper, the boy continued to supply correct answers. Although learning and retention were not perfect, posttests a few minutes and a few hours later demonstrated the superiority of the fading over the study condition.

Now that microcomputers are becoming more frequently available to schools, the opportunity is expanding for developing and applying training packages that contain not only fading, delayed prompting and other features capable of facilitating stimulus control, but also chaining and reinforcement as well. Because mathematics is logical and arithmetic problems have clearly correct answers, the subject is a natural for computer-assisted instruction. Assuming that we take advantage of those opportunities and design software in accordance with effective behavioral principles, in the foreseeable future, we should anticipate substantially improved math literacy among our youth.

Summary

We have illustrated in this chapter how behavior analysis can be used to improve arithmetic. The first step involves assessment to determine the specific concern, difficulty, or deficit. Once the problem has been isolated, the objective is developed. You are then ready to select and implement a strategy to resolve the difficulty or to teach new computational skills.

Part of the strategy is to assure sufficient reinforcement. Working out the correct answer to a math problem serves as a reinforcer for many students. However, for others, obtaining the correct answer is insufficient. Thus, we discussed a number of supplementary rewarding activities to help encourage higher rates of performance.

Supplementing reinforcement alone, though, may be insufficient. Computational skills and concepts must be taught. A variety of procedures and activities, such as modeling, self-instruction, prompting, and fading, were described to assist you in this task. Carefully applying those procedures while you combine them with appropriate reinforcement strategies can result in improved math performance.

At this point, you should recognize that many of the strategies that have been found effective in promoting high quality performance in arithmetic also may have relevance to other academic skill areas, as is also the case for the procedures you encountered in the previous chapters in this section. We hope that if your concern is in science, music, social studies, art, physical education, foreign language instruction, or another subject matter area, you will be able to transfer what you have discovered here to that case. In the next chapter, we present a number of examples of such applications.

Study Questions

1. Provide evidence that women are more likely than men to have math anxiety.
2. Describe the first step you should take when working with a student who experiences math anxiety.
3. Mrs. Baker examined John's papers and found that missing skills were not responsible for his low math grades. Identify the next step she should take in identifying the problem.

4. Your informal investigations lead you to suspect that Rebecca has deficiencies in her level of skill. Discuss the steps you might take to find out more.

5. Tina has a serious case of math anxiety. List at least three objectives that should be included in her behavioral program.

6. Identify several physiological responses that may be modified with biofeedback equipment.

7. List several objectives found to be practical when a classroom teacher is working with a student with math anxiety.

8. Use behavioral terminology to describe a difficulty a pupil is experiencing with math.

9. You want to discover where in the three-stage contingency your efforts are best placed. Identify the questions you would ask to determine this.

10. Provide a hierarchy to follow when attempting to bring sequences of responses under the control of the critical antecedents.

11. State the natural reinforcer for arithmetic.

12. The correct answer is not an intrinsic reinforcer for Jill. Offer several reasons for this.

13. Mr. Norton wants to enhance his students' opportunities for success with arithmetic. Provide a list of guidelines for him to follow.

14. Define *Direct Instruction*.

15. T/F Use supplementary reinforcers regularly when teaching arithmetic. Support your answer.

16. Create several original ways to make learning math more enjoyable.

17. Discuss (a) the advantages and (b) the disadvantages of permitting students to check their answers themselves.

18. Mr. Barton's students are reporting their scores inaccurately. Suggest several solutions to this problem.

19. Eric is going to be a peer tutor in his class. List at least four skills he will need to acquire.

20. Sam has acquired particular computational skills. Identify one behavioral dimension that could be targeted for change at that point.

21. Mrs. Quinn has tried using activity reinforcers with her students but found them to be ineffective. Offer a temporary alternative.

22. T/F Students should be allowed to specify point values for their accomplishments. Support your answer.

23. Describe the quick-draw math game.

24. Compare and contrast the effect of (a) individual and (b) group contingencies, using a mathematical illustration.

25. Under what circumstances would chaining be particularly beneficial in teaching arithmetic?

26. Mr. Holmes is debating whether or not he should allocate specific instructional time to arithmetic. Provide him with some advice.

27. How would you determine the optimal number of math drills per day.

28. Define the *show-and-tell* method.

29. Ken's teacher used blocks to model counting but found the method to be insufficient. Describe one alternative method of instruction.

30. Describe *self-instructing*.

31. T/F Children need to be mathematical whiz kids to discover things for themselves. Support your answer.

32. State (a) the advantages and (b) the disadvantages of learning by discovery.

33. (a) Use behavioral terms to explain carelessness.
(b) Identify two procedures to reduce the problem.

34. (a) Select an especially effective method for teaching multiplication and addition:
    (i) fading.
    (ii) repeatedly writing multiplication tables.
    (iii) studying.
(b) Support your answer.

References

Barrera, R. D., & Sulzer-Azaroff, B. (1983). An alternating treatment comparison of oral and total communication training programs with echolalic autistic children. *Journal of Applied Behavior Analysis, 16,* 379–394.

Becker, W. C., & Carnine, D. W. (1981). Direct Instruction: A behavior theory model for comprehensive educational intervention with the disadvantaged. In S. W. Bijou & R. Ruiz (Eds.), *Behavior modification: Contributions to education* (pp. 145–210). Hillsdale, NJ: Lawrence Erlbaum Associates.

Becker, W. C., & Gersten, R. (1982). A follow-up of Follow Through: The later effects of the Direct Instruction model on children in fifth and sixth grades. *American Educational Research Journal, 19*, 75–92.

Bryant, L. E., & Budd, K. S. (1982). Self instructional training to increase independent work performance in preschoolers. *Journal of Applied Behavior Analysis, 15*, 259–271.

Conlon, M. F., Hall, C., & Hanley, E. M. (1972). The effects of a peer correction procedure on the arithmetic accuracy for two elementary school children. In G. Semb (Ed.), *Behavior analysis & education—1972* (pp. 205–210). Lawrence, KS: The University of Kansas Support and Development Center for Follow Through, Department of Human Development.

Dalton, A. J., Rubino, C. A., & Hislop, M. W. (1973). Some effects of token rewards on school achievement of children with Down's syndrome. *Journal of Applied Behavior Analysis, 6*, 241–250.

Darch, C., Carnine, D., & Gersten, R. (1984, May). *Explicit instruction in mathematics problem solving*. Paper presented at the Annual Convention of the Association for Behavior Analysis, Nashville, TN.

Engelmann, S., & Carnine, D. (1969). *DISTAR™ Arithmetic 1: An instructional system*. Chicago: Science Research Associates, Inc.

Felixbrod, J. J., & O'Leary, K. D. (1973). Effects of reinforcement on children's academic behavior as a function of self-determined and externally imposed contingencies. *Journal of Applied Behavior Analysis, 6*, 241–250.

Greenwood, C. R., Dinwiddie, G., Terry, B., Wade, L., Stanley, S. O., Thibadeau, S., & Delquadri, J. C. (1984). Teacher vs. peer-mediated instruction: an ecobehavioral analysis of achievement outcomes. *Journal of Applied Behavior Analysis, 17*, 512–538.

Haupt, E. J., Van Kirk, M. J., & Terraciano, T. (1975). An inexpensive fading procedure to decrease errors and increase retention of number facts. In E. Ramp & G. Semb (Eds.), *Behavior analysis: Areas of research and application* (pp. 225–232). Englewood Cliffs, NJ: Prentice-Hall.

Hundert, J., & Bucher, B. (1978). Pupil's self-scored arithmetic performance: A practical procedure for maintaining accuracy. *Journal of Applied Behavior Analysis, 11*, 304.

Jastak, J., & Jastak, S. (1965). *Wide range achievement test*. Wilmington, DE: Jastak Associates.

Johnston, R. J., & McLaughlin, T. F. (1982). The effects of free time on assignment completion and accuracy in arithmetic: A case study. *Education and Treatment of Children, 5*, 33–40.

Latham, G. P., & Baldes, J. J. (1975). The "practical significance" of Locke's theory of goal setting. *Journal of Applied Psychology, 60*, 122–124.

Leonhart, W. B. (1982). *Acquisition and generalization of prearithmetic skills*. Unpublished manuscript, Manitoba Developmental Center, Behavioral Psychology Department, Box 1190 Portage la Prairie, Manitoba, Canada.

Litow, L., & Pumroy, D. K. (1975). A brief review of classroom group-oriented contingencies. *Journal of Applied Behavior Analysis, 8*, 341–347.

Lovitt, T. C., & Curtiss, K. A. (1968). Effects of manipulating an antecedent event on mathematics response rate. *Journal of Applied Behavior Analysis, 1*, 329–333.

Lovitt, T. C., & Curtiss, K. A. (1969). Academic response rate as a function of teacher- and self-imposed contingencies. *Journal of Applied Behavior Analysis, 2*, 49–53.

Lovitt, T. C., & Esvelt, K. A. (1970). The relative effects on math performance of single- versus multiple-ratio schedules: A case study. *Journal of Applied Behavior Analysis, 3*, 261–270.

Maheady, L., Sainato, D. M., & Maitland, G. (1983). Motivated assessment: The effects of extrinsic rewards on the individually-administered reading test performance of low, average, and high IQ students. *Education and Treatment of Children, 6*, 37–46.

McCarty, T., Griffin, S., Apolloni, T., & Shores, R. E. (1977). Increased peer teaching with group oriented contingencies for arithmetic performance in behavior-disordered adolescents. *Journal of Applied Behavior Analysis, 10*, 313.

McKenzie, M. L., & Budd, K. S. (1981). A peer tutoring package to increase mathematics performance: Examination of generalized changes in classroom behavior. *Education and Treatment of Children, 4*, 1–15.

McLaughlin, T. F. (1981). The effects of a classroom token economy on math performance in an intermediate grade school class. *Education and Treatment of Children, 4*, 139–147.

Parsons, J. A. (1972). The reciprocal modification of arithmetic behavior and program development. In G. Semb

(Ed.), *Behavior analysis in education* (pp. 185–199). Lawrence, S.: The University of Kansas Support and Development Center for Follow Through, Department of Human Development.

Raggio, S., & Bitgood, S. C. (1982, May). *Training in basic math: Effects of math operations and drills per day.* Paper presented at the annual Convention of the Association for Behavior Analysis, Milwaukee.

Resnick, L. G., Wang, M. C., & Kaplan, J. (1973). Task analysis in curriculum design: A hierarchically sequenced introductory mathematics curriculum. *Journal of Applied Behavior Analysis, 6,* 679–710.

Schumaker, J. B., Hovell, M. F., & Sherman, J. A. (1977). An analysis of daily report cards and parent-managed privileges in the improvement of adolescent classroom performance. *Journal of Applied Behavior Analysis, 10,* 449–464.

Smith, D. D., & Lovitt, T. C. (1975). The use of modelling techniques to influence the acquisition of computational arithmetic skills in learning-disabled children. In E. Ramp & G. Semb (Eds.), *Behavior analysis: Areas of research and application* (pp. 283–308). Englewood Cliffs, NJ: Prentice-Hall.

Sulzer, B., Hunt, S., Ashby, E., Koniarski, C., & Krams, M. (1971). Increasing rate and percentage correct in reading and spelling in a fifth grade public school class by means of a token system. In E. A. Ramp & B. L. Hopkins (Eds.), *A new direction for education: Behavior analysis, 1971* (pp. 5–28). Lawrence, KS: Support and Development Center for Follow Through, Department of Human Development.

Sulzer-Azaroff, B., & Reese, E. P. (1982). *Applying behavior analysis: A program for developing professional competencies.* New York: Holt, Rinehart and Winston.

Tobias, S., & Weissbrod, C. (1980). Anxiety and mathematics: An update. *Harvard Educational Review, 50,* 63–70.

Ulman, J. D., & Sulzer-Azaroff, B. (1975). Multielement baseline design in educational research. In E. Ramp and G. Semb (Eds.), *Behavior analysis: Areas of Research and Application* (pp. 377–391). Englewood Cliffs, NJ: Prentice-Hall.

Vasta, R., & Stirpe, L. A. (1979). Reinforcement effects on three measures of children's interest in math. *Behavior Modification, 3,* 223–244.

Van Houten, R., & Thompson, C. (1976). The effects of explicit timing on math performance. *Journal of Applied Behavior Analysis, 9,* 227–230.

Whitman, T., & Johnston, M. R. (1983). Teaching addition and subtraction with regrouping to educable mentally retarded children: A group self-instructional training program. *Behavior Therapy, 14,* 127–143.

17 A general strategy for improving academic performance

Goals

After completing this chapter, you should be able to:

1. Provide a synonym for Personalized System of Instruction (PSI).
2. Describe ten characteristics of effective behavioral instruction.
3. Discuss and provide an illustration of each of the four steps involved in designing academic instruction.
4. Identify three mistakes that many designers of instructional objectives make, and discuss what can be done to avoid each.
5. Describe and present an illustration of an instructional frame.
6. Describe PSI and what should be done to prepare study aids for a PSI program.
7. Discuss the educational importance of various instructional inputs.
8. Describe briefly some of the effects that behavior management procedures have had in the areas of physical education, science, social studies, and health and safety.
9. List the reasons why a student might finish objectives much more rapidly or slowly than planned. Discuss what can be done to rectify these situations.

"Well, we did it again!" exclaimed Dr. Levy. "Achievement test scores way above the norm. A good crop of candidates for the National Merit Scholarships and several awards from State U."

Each year, when the results of Franklin High School's standardized achievement tests came through, its staff, students, and community members were jubilant. A high proportion of the pupils scored in the upper ranges of the college admission test, many thereby gaining acceptance into their preferred schools. Regardless of grade level, the math, reading, and language scores were far above the national average. By contrast, results from the standardized achievement assessments at Washington Street School fell well below average, and those from Willow Grove hovered about midway — in the forty-eighth percentile.

From one perspective, we might conclude that academic performance was at its optimum at Franklin and needed little attention. The average score at Willow Grove was what one might expect, so why do things differently? As for the Washington Street School scores, it is commonly believed that children from economically deprived inner-city homes do poorly in school, so why bother tackling a hopeless task?

Is such fatalism justified? We're sure you will join us in responding with a resounding "no!" We already have seen numerous cases of individual students who obviously had potential, because they *did* improve in academic performance. By this time you surely have recognized our bias is that everyone can continue to learn, regardless of disabilities, deficits, or past performance. For the Tyrones, the Richard

Parkers, and the Billy's of this world, the challenge is greater; but consider how much room they have for improvement. Yet even for a model student like Richard's brother, Howard, there is always the possibility for growth. He can increase his performance rates and broaden his range of knowledge and skills—and doesn't he deserve the opportunity as much as his classmates do?

By now you have discovered many potential strategies for managing your students' conduct and encouraging them to get down to work. You have discovered how educational practitioners have applied behavioral principles and procedures to improve communication skills, as well as reading and arithmetic. We chose to emphasize those content areas because they are so essential to success in other academic and social realms. Yet students have profited from behavioral instruction in many other subject areas as well.

In this chapter, rather than exhaustively synthesizing the tremendous number of behavioral studies of academic tasks, we have chosen instead to offer a general strategy for improving academic performance. We will attempt to supply sufficient examples to enable you to devise methods that will meet your specific instructional needs. But please do not consider the illustrative cases as sacrosanct, to be followed as precisely as you might a recipe for a complicated cake; instead, refer to them as a source for reviewing the elements that constitute successful behavioral instruction.

CHARACTERISTICS OF EFFECTIVE BEHAVIORAL INSTRUCTION

Regardless of content, student attributes, or setting, if you were to examine effective behavioral instructional programs, you would note a number of common characteristics:

1. Knowledge and skills to be attained are pinpointed as observable operations. In *cognitive* or conceptual learning, this is especially important, so everyone knows what the student should be able to do with the information—for instance, reproduce something exactly, differentiate it from something similar, use it to solve a problem or to produce a product, or whatever.

2. Performance is defined, recorded, and reliably measured many times prior to, during, and following behavioral instruction.

3. The potential functions of the performance are identified to capitalize on them eventually as natural, intrinsic reinforcement. The ability to read, for instance, permits children to be captivated by a fascinating story, play enjoyable word games, follow instructions for constructing toys, learn dramatic roles, and so many other reinforcing activities. When teachers recognize such functions, they can incorporate them within the curriculum as early as possible.

4. When feasible, other aspects of the learning task are made to be heavily reinforcing. Assignments are sufficiently challenging so that their accomplishment is rewarding. (But they are not made so difficult that failure is likely.) Frequently, peer support is harnessed by arranging group contingencies, so that peers profit from the student's improvement and will tend to assist it. Instructional material is made interesting by including humor, suspense, clever examples, and so on, so that the learning activity has its own intrinsic worth.

5. Punishment is minimized by selecting learning activities for which pupils have the preparation necessary to permit them to succeed, and by emphasizing positive rather than only corrective or negative feedback.

6. If necessary, supplementary reinforcers—positive and perhaps even negative—temporarily are used according to the principles of effective instruction. These reinforcers may encourage the pupil to make an effort and respond more often. Performing correctly on a single occasion is considered insufficient. Rather, a student must be capable of repeating the response without error in rapid enough succession to meet the demands of the situation in which the response is to be applied. **Precision Teaching** (e.g., McGreevy, 1983) emphasizes rate building by

incorporating continuous monitoring and data-based decision making to encourage accelerating rates of correct responding.

7. Stimulus control methods are included, that is, prompting to evoke correct responses or help the student to identify or distinguish the critical features of an object, event, or concept to be discriminated, and fading to bring the responses under the control of the critical properties.

8. To facilitate appropriate generalization, many examples are provided: positive examples that include all critical and no erroneous features, and negative or counterexamples that contain inappropriate features or missing essential ones. (In this text we provide numerous positive examples of strategies that incorporate the critical features of behavior analysis. We also mention an occasional nonexample. Here's one more so you know what we mean:

> A teacher wanted to encourage her students to practice their multiplication tables. She promised that those who did would receive an A on their report cards.

Why is that a *nonexample* of a behavioral strategy? What features are incorrect or missing?)[1]

9. For purposes of efficiency as well as effectiveness, the pupils actively participate in managing instructional activities as much as possible. For example, they may collaborate or contract with the teacher in setting goals and standards of performance, record their own progress, tutor their peers, select and perhaps deliver their own reinforcers, and be involved in other ways. (To assure quality, naturally, systems for checking adherence to policies and procedures must prevail.)

10. Maintenance and retention are planned, not left to chance, by thinning out schedules of reinforcers, shifting over from artificial to natural ones, arranging opportunities for the recently acquired knowledge or skills to be expressed and reinforced naturally, and in other ways.

We probably should also mention some features that you would *not* always notice.

Students will not always be provided with fully individualized curricula or left completely alone to work independently and at their own paces. Assuming adequate preparation, they may be learning effectively in groups. Certain skills (e.g., oral communication, role playing, peer teaching, musical ensembles, games, and so on) require social groupings to be learned most effectively. Also, peers might serve as models, promoting observational learning (a factor we suspect to contribute to the success of Direct Instruction).

Many students have failed to learn to study at high rates when left to their own devices. [Perhaps that explains why the current data on individualization of high school curricula are not consistently promising (Bangert, Kulik, & Kulik, 1983).] Thus, to promote efficient learning, teachers may set the pace, until students demonstrate their capabilities for effectively governing their own rapid, high-quality progress. An example is the unison responding elicited from all members of the group being taught by means of Direct Instruction.

Nor is it the case that students left totally to their own discretion will assign themselves appropriate amounts of reinforcers. Teachers often find that they need to present self-reinforcement guidelines to which the students should adhere. Otherwise the instructors sometimes discover, as others have (Felixbrod & O'Leary, 1974; Jones & Ollendick, 1979; Wall & Bryant, 1979; Wall, 1983), that the pupils select increasingly lenient standards as time passes. [In our own work on self-selection of goals, we have advised that work groups select their goals from a given range. The suggested range was devised on the basis of prior performance and future challenge (Fellner & Sulzer-Azaroff, In press). The same sort of thing could be done for reinforcing consequences.]

For children whose preparedness differs widely from that of their peers, however, you likely would observe *both* well-programmed, small-group instruc-

---

[1]The study and quiz materials that we have designed to accompany this text, plus our *Applying Behavior Analysis Procedures with Children and Youth* (1977), include many examples and counter- or nonexamples.

tion (Becker, Engelmann, Carnine, & Maggs, 1982) and individualized instruction in use. Also, all students would be receiving encouragement and reinforcement for managing their time efficiently and learning on their own.

Should you see the need to modify your curriculum in a major way so that it conforms to the characteristics just described, take heart. You won't have to do it all yourself. DISTAR (Becker et al., 1982) may meet your needs if you are concerned with instruction at the primary level. The program includes three basic levels of reading, arithmetic, and language; also available are corrective reading and spelling.

Behaviorally sound instructional materials are being developed all the time (along with, unfortunately, many more that lack the necessary features). Examine new programmed and computerized instructional matter to evaluate evidence of effectiveness and to assess how closely it adheres to the characteristics described here.

Suppose you are faced with a situation in which you want to teach something for which effective instructional materials are unavailable. You might decide to develop the instruction yourself. If so, you may find the sequence of activities we suggest in the next section helpful.

DEVELOPING ACADEMIC INSTRUCTION

Assuming you have elected to design instruction to help your students achieve particular learning goals, you will want to have a method for proceeding. We suggest you first clearly specify your goals and objectives. Next prepare and assemble your instructional materials. Then plan and implement a system for managing the learning activities. Conclude by evaluating and, if necessary, revising the instructional activities. (Notice that the teacher plays the role of resource person and manager, rather than of singular source and communicator of knowledge.)

Now let us discuss and illustrate each of these steps.

Specifying goals and objectives

"I know what my students should accomplish. They should work hard to understand how history often repeats itself," said Mr. Markham. "Then they will know when international tension is apt to arise and how it might be prevented."

Let us use that goal statement to illustrate a number of important points.

Process versus product. Where is effort focused with a goal of the type offered by Mr. Markham? On the process by which the students reach the goal — their hard work — or on the product — the information or skill they gain and display? Our recommendation is that the product of learning, rather than the effort that goes into it, be emphasized. This perspective is supported by findings of Marholin and Steinman (1977) and others; working hard is no guarantee of a high-quality yield. If you are fearful that achieving the end product will be too delayed in time, break the task down into smaller components, each with a product of its own. When learning her part in *West Side Story*, Carmen received her reinforcement, not for the hours she spent memorizing, but for the number of lines she learned.

Another related hazard to be avoided is to focus exclusively on the *quantity* of outputs, rather than their *quality*. When children were required to work on an assignment for a particular time period prior to recess, they made fewer errors than when they were assigned a set number of pages to complete before they could go to recess — even though in the latter situation they produced more (Semb & Semb, 1975). If both quality and quantity are included in the criteria for receipt of reinforcement, however, as in Sulzer, Hunt, Ashby, Koniarski, and Krams's study (1971), the problem may not appear. Sometimes the effects of increasing the rate of production are paradoxical, and students begin to make *fewer* errors as they produce faster, as Van Houten and Little (1982) found when they increased math production rates by shortening the time limit. Why particular individuals respond by producing more or fewer errors as a function of rate of performance is unclear at this time. Probably factors such as the nature of the reinforcers, the type of skill and the proficiency with which it is performed, the learning history, social support system, and others may contribute. For present purposes, however, it is important that you recognize that quality and accuracy should be monitored to determine how they might be influenced by changes in rates of production.

Selecting and defining goals. Assuming you elect to emphasize products of learning, you will want to indicate exactly what goals are to be accomplished. Often this is done for you by your school system. Goals are set in curriculum guides, policies, and textbooks—not infrequently in the form offered by Mr. Markham. You may be dissatisfied by the nonbehavioral format of a goal statement or by the omission of certain subtle but important goals. How is one to find out when students "understand" a historical perspective? Is "understanding" enough?

We can suggest a couple of ways you can go about defining vaguely stated instructional goals. One is to design your own definition and try it out on a number of experts. Mr. Markham, for instance, might think about how understanding that history repeats itself could be demonstrated, and pose his description to a set of experts. He may decide that if students can describe three different kinds of events that have occurred almost identically at different times and places, he would be pleased. He asks the other social studies teacher, his former professor of history, and the social studies coordinator to see if they agree. If they do, fine. If not, he may need to continue the logical process until a satisfactory definition is achieved.

Alternatively, he could work backward. He might search through student reports or examination papers for the past several years to locate student products that exemplify the kind of understanding he is seeking. If he still finds it difficult to pinpoint the exact goals, he could sort the papers into a couple of piles, as suggested by Mager (1972) in his book *Goal Analysis*. In one pile would go superior examples; in the other, poor ones. Then he would look through the superior pile and try to extract the characteris-

tics of the most outstanding analyses. Maybe he would find that the best expression of understanding of the historical repetition of events not only included a description of several examples but also extrapolated to the present day; additionally it indicated various situations in which international law succeeded or failed to prevent the repetition of unfortunate historical events.

Should you be concerned with a motor, social, vocational, administrative or other not strictly cognitive (or, as behaviorists prefer to label it, *verbal*[2]) category of behavior, you might also select exemplary performance to help you define those goals. In his text *Human Competence*, Gilbert (1978) explains how exemplars may be selected and used in the process of engineering worthy performance. Not only can such models serve to elucidate the goal of an instructional, training, or management program, but they also should be useful in setting standards of acceptable performance and evaluating what reasonably might be and actually has been accomplished.

Mr. Markham still might be dissatisfied, despite having identified the best papers he could find.

"That's not all there is to it. I had a student a few years ago, name of Walter. Now he was really what I would call an outstanding student of history. It wasn't just the sophisticated content of his written work."

"What else was it?" asked his colleagues.

"The way he talked about issues. He was so convincing. Not just to me, but to other informed adults as well."

"Anything else?"

"Now that I think about it, there was—the way he spent his spare time, reading historical texts, participating in debates. He even joined a political science organization and attended its regional meeting."

"Isn't he the one who went on to law school? He was elected to the Town Board last year, I think."

"That's right. But getting back to setting goals, I don't think that election to public office is some-

---

[2]Skinner's *Verbal Behavior* (1957) analyzes the use of language as complex operant behavior.

thing I can ask of my current students, although you never know. It might help to get our funding increased," Mr. Markham added with a wry smile.

The point we are trying to make for you is to be careful to avoid analyzing goals in an overly simple way. Try to be as complete in specifying them as possible. If the goals primarily relate to verbal skills, are you content with simple memorization, or are you looking for evidence of comprehension, the ability to discriminate one concept from another, to combine or separate disparate ideas, to solve particular problems or create new information?[3] Ask yourself if *motor* actions or *social* performance — as in debating or attending meetings — play an important part. How about *affect* — the expression of emotions such as enthusiasm or of *style*, such as being convincing (naturally further defined)? You may consider the goal statement to be complete when you fully describe all the identified accomplishments and conclude that the ultimate performance would be truly exemplary.

Specifying objectives. Once Mr. Markham went through the process of identifying exemplary performance, he had to make some decisions.

"I think if all my students accomplished what Walter has, they'd all be A+ performers. But I should be reasonable. After all, Walter's parents spent years in the foreign service before settling down here. His mom is president of the local League of Women Voters. Things like that are out of my control."

"Which of his activities could you reasonably expect of your other students?" asked his supervisor.

"Well, writing clear answers to questions concerning the concepts we listed earlier, for one. Then a convincing presentation of oral arguments in class could be another. Reading and intelligent reporting on books about the topic should be O.K. too."

Mr. Markham continued his analysis further, until he had identified the goals for a major unit on international relations.

"How will you and the students know when they have accomplished the goals?" questioned his supervisor.

"That will be a problem. I know I have to define the *performance*, specifying the observable acts included in terms like 'clear answers,' 'convincing arguments,' and 'reporting intelligently' for them and for myself. The students also will want to know *how much, how long, when, where*, and *what other conditions and limitations* will be in effect, as well as the *standards of acceptability* (or *criteria*), so all of us can recognize when the goal has been reached."

As we have seen earlier in the text (see Chapter 3), what Mr. Markham realized was that he needed to specify his goals as *instructional objectives*. Here is an example of one such objective.

"On a five-item essay examination on the topic of cyclical trends in history *(condition)*, the student will list, describe, and illustrate with an actual historical episode *(performance)* each of the concepts listed on the answer key *(standard of performance)*, within the two-hour examination period *(limitation)*."

Now you should try. Specify another instructional objective for Mr. Markham and identify, as we have done, its special features.

Before ending this discussion on goals and objectives, permit us to caution you about a few of the traps into which many designers of instructional and behavioral management programs so often fall. Sometimes we mistakenly assume that once a performance is demonstrated or described, it can be expressed readily under all circumstances and will sustain forever afterward.

"All the students in my class demonstrated that they could secure the wood solidly with clamps and hold the saw properly. Yet, just yesterday, Mona put this great gash into her thumb."

Had the objective included a statement in which the proper performance would have to persist over each day of the full semester of shop class, Mona and

---

[3]Should you wish to check yourself for completeness of cognitive goals, you might examine Bloom's *Taxonomy of Educational Objectives* (1956) and Johnson and Chase's (1981) paper on a functional typology for verbal tasks.

her teacher might have arranged some contingencies, such as regular feedback or self-checking to sustain her safe practices. As we discussed earlier in our chapter on extinction, previously established behaviors tend to crop up again, especially when reinforcement of the newly acquired behavior is lacking. Watch yourself the next time you slice a carrot or potato. Do you hold the vegetable, the knife, and your hands in the safest position or do you do what seems easiest? The point is that *if long-term maintenance is what you want, you need to provide for it in the statement of the objective* (and, of course, during instruction).

Another frequent mistake is to assume that *saying* something is the same as *doing* it. (That shouldn't surprise us, because frequently the two are paired.)

"Just the day before the accident, Mona got 100 percent on the exam that covered safe use of the wood saw. How could she have done such a stupid thing?"

"Mrs. Green got an A in her course in behavior modification, so she must know that positive reinforcement is preferred to a reprimand. Yet just listen to her."

As authors of several texts on applied behavior analysis, both of us should be perfect parents, and our children, naturally, perfect too. Dare we confess that this is wishful thinking and that our behavior too is influenced by our prior histories, current conditions, and physical and other factors, in addition to the rules we recite to ourselves? While words may guide our performance sometimes, they are often insufficient. So specify your objectives for the direct expression of the behavior of concern, not just for a description of that behavior.

A last caution relates to *where* the performance is to be practiced. We teach social skills in the counselor's office and expect students to transfer them to a natural social setting; similarly, we teach arithmetic in the classroom, assuming it will be practiced in the gymnasium, shop, or in the community. Often such transfer does occur "spontaneously," but many times it does not. To avoid overlooking this factor in your statement of an objective, indicate *all*

the settings in which the performance should take place.

Other types of transfer or generalization of performance may be important when you specify your objectives. You might check them against the generalization map provided by Drabman, Hammer, and Rosenbaum (1979). In Table 17.1 we list the first eight elements in that map, adding our own illustrations.

By adding the element of *time*, Drabman et al. present eight more forms of generalization on their map. At this point you should be able to complete the map yourself by defining the form of generalization and illustrating it. We begin for you:

> Time generalization: Change in the performance by the target subject in the training setting that endures after the program contingencies have been withdrawn. Example: (You should supply it.)

Analyzing tasks. "I did all that, stated my objective as completely as possible," sighed Burt Cole, the physical education instructor. "But some of my students just don't seem to be able to do running broad jumps or 50-yard dashes very well."

Mr. Lee, the counselor, examined the objectives and agreed that indeed they were complete. "Maybe the problem has to do with the *size* or *complexity* of the objectives. Are you convinced that all your students are fully *prepared* to perform those skills, Burt?"

"Not really, K. C. Some of them have the funniest ways of moving their bodies. What should I do?"

"You might consider analyzing the tasks involved and breaking them down into their component *subtasks*. Then you could develop objectives for each. Those should be simpler and more fundamental. Perhaps that will make it easier for the students to learn."

"I guess I can do that. Let me give it a try and show you tomorrow."

The next day when the two met again, Burt Cole presented K. C. Lee with his task analyses. They resembled a pair designed by Cuvo and his colleagues (1982) for developmentally disabled students (see

Table 17.1
Illustrative objectives for selected categories of generalization

Maintenance: Continuation of the performance over time after the experimenter-controlled contingencies are sustained following the formal treatment program. After Mona has completed formal training in sawing—during which her instructor had praised her proper practice of the skill—she will continue to saw safely, while the instructor continues informally to praise safe sawing.

Subject generalization: Changes in the performance in nontarget as well as target subjects. While Mona is taught to saw safely, Wanda will watch and also learn how.

Behavior generalization: Changes in a behavior of the subject other than the targeted behavior. When Mona receives reinforcement for sawing wood safely, she also will saw metal safely in shop.

Subject-behavior generalization: Change in the nontarget behavior of a person whose performance has not been targeted for change. By watching Mona receive reinforcement for sawing wood safely, Wanda will saw metal more safely in shop class.

Setting generalization: Expression of the performance in a setting other than the one in which it is reinforced. Taught to saw safely in the shop in school, Mona will use the saw safely at home.

Subject-setting generalization: Change in the target behavior of a nontarget subject in a different setting. When Mona's safe sawing is reinforced in shop, Wanda will saw wood safely at home.

Behavior-setting generalization: Change in a nontarget behavior for a target subject elsewhere than in the treatment setting. After her safe sawing is reinforced in shop, Mona will slice carrots safely at home.

Subject-behavior-setting generalization: Change in the nontargeted behavior of a nontarget subject changes in a different setting. When Mona's safe sawing is reinforced in shop, Wanda will slice carrots safely at home.

Based on the generalization map described by Drabman et al. (1979)

Tables 17.2 and 17.3), but weren't refined to quite the same degree.

"The one problem I had was deciding how far to keep breaking down the tasks. After a while it seemed I was about to analyze them more than I needed to, so I just stopped."

"The crucial question is, 'Can the student perform the most basic subtasks? Is he or she prepared to succeed at that level?' If so, you've gone far enough. The best way to know is to try it out."

That is what Mr. Cole did. Before he knew it, most of his students had really improved in the skills he had analyzed. His objectives were reasonable.

All sorts of tasks can be analyzed, for all sorts of populations. Take a look at Table 17.4 to see the subcomponents that constitute learning to swim (McKenzie & Jaks, 1984). Mr. Markham may find that some of his students are unable to participate in a debate or don't know how to critique a book or an article. How might he analyze those tasks to identify

their subcomponents, so he can specify more basic objectives? Why don't you try doing that yourself.

Instructional input: preparing instructional materials and activities

By preparing their objectives carefully, Mr. Markham and Mr. Cole readily could identify what sorts of inputs would be important for their instruction. Mr. Cole decided to include *demonstrations* of the subcomponents of the motor skills he was teaching. He asked one of the more capable students to demonstrate the skills and recorded the demonstration on a videotape. He would be able to play and replay the tape, in slow motion if necessary, so the students could see exactly the form they were to imitate. (Later he would tape the students in action so they could assess their own performance and correct it if necessary.) He also took his task analysis and converted it into a checklist, so students would be able

Table 17.2
Task analysis for the standing long jump

Preliminary Activities
 1. Walk to starting line.
 2. Put feet perpendicular to line.
 3. Set feet as close together as possible.
 4. Put arms at sides, palms in.

Preparation
 5. Raise arms 135 degrees to torso.
 6. Turn palms away from body.
 7. Swing arms forward in circle.
 8. Bend legs at knees 45 degrees to ground.
 9. Bend torso at waist 45 degrees to ground.

Push Off
10. Swing arms forward.
11. Straighten legs.
12. Push off from toes.
13. Straighten torso.

In Flight
14. Swing arms backward over shoulder.
15. Bend legs upward at knees 45 degrees to ground.
16. Thrust arms forward and down.
17. Thrust hips forward.
18. Swing feet forward of body.

Landing
19. Land on heels.
20. Roll body weight forward.
21. Swing arms rearward.

Exiting
22. Step forward (either foot).
23. Raise torso.
24. Step forward (with other foot).
25. Walk out of back of landing pit.

This table was adapted from Cuvo et al. (1982). We appreciate their permission to include it.

to find out which performances they did and did not execute correctly.

Mr. Markham used his *task analysis* in a similar way. He prepared a *list of elements* of a good critique that he could give to the students so they could use it to check the completeness of their product. [Sulzer-Azaroff and Reese (1982) used a strategy like that to help their students prepare complete reports of their behavior analytic experiments. (See Table 17.5.)] To help the students to improve their debat-

ing skills, he videotaped a political debate. The students could use the sample to identify the critical features of good debating skills and to locate examples and nonexamples of those features.

When you are planning the instructional inputs that students will need to achieve the goals set for them, just refer to the objectives that have been identified. Those will suggest the types of materials, demonstrations, instructions, and other activities you might be able to use profitably. To determine

Table 17.3
Task analysis for the 50-yard dash

Preparation
1. Approach the starting line.
2. Place one foot near the starting line so that the foot is as close as possible but not touching the line and is in a position perpendicular to the line.
3. Extend the same side arm (as the foot used in step 2) forward.
4. Bend arm at elbow so that the forearm is parallel to the ground.
5. Clench fists.
6. Place other foot shoulder's distance apart and to the rear of the first foot so that the second foot forms a 45-degree angle to the starting line.
7. Extend the other arm rearward.
8. Bend arm at elbow so that the upper arm is parallel to the ground and the forearm is perpendicular to the ground.
9. Bend torso forward from waist to form a 60-degree angle to the ground.
10. Raise head.
11. Look toward the finish line.

Start
12. Swing rearward arm forward while swinging forward arm rearward.
13. Swing rear foot forward.

In Stride
14. Swing arms forward and backward using the shoulder as a pivot, keeping arms locked in a 90-degree position at the elbow.
15. Keep feet parallel during stride.
16. Bend torso slightly forward at waist to form about an 80-degree angle to the ground.

Finish
17. One stride away from finish line, bend torso forward to make contact with the finish ribbon.
18. Throw both arms rearward.

This table was developed by Cuvo et al. (1982). We appreciate their permission to include it.

exactly how to use those inputs, refer to the rules of effective instruction presented earlier in this text, especially the chapters on reinforcement, stimulus control, shaping, and chaining. Then you will be more likely to plan appropriate consequences and antecedent stimuli.

Consider how behavioral principles were applied toward planning instruction in beginning golf for adults (O'Brien & Simek, 1978). The skills were broken down sequentially into successive approximations, in backward form from a very short putt to, ultimately, a 200-yard shot from the tee (see Table 17.6). The trainees, adults at a local country club, would be required to master each of the approximations prior to moving back to the next. (An ex-

perimental comparison between a control group of conventionally taught golfers and those using this sequence demonstrated a statistically significant difference in favor of the behavioral method).[4]

Text material probably constitutes a major element of your curriculum. School textbooks often contain various study aids, such as objectives, problems, study questions, self-tests, and laboratory activities. Rarely, however, are those study aids assessed for effectiveness with particular student populations. You probably will need to do this yourself by

[4]In case you are interested in improving your own skills as a golfer, you might refer to Simek and O'Brien's (1981) book on the topic, *Total Golf*.

Table 17.4
Swimming: task analysis

1. Get in the water.
   Nose in the water.
   Face in the water.
   Open eyes under water.

2. Submerge for 3 seconds.
   Hold breath underwater 5 seconds.
   Hold breath underwater 7 seconds.

3. Blow bubbles.
   Bob at side 5 times.
   Bob and blow bubbles 5 times.
   Bob and blow bubbles 10 times.
   Bob and breathe, moving out to the rope with
   assistance.

4. Touch foot underwater.
   Touch toes to bottom.
   Touch bottom with hand.
   Sit on bottom.
   Pick puck up off bottom.

5. Push off side to teacher.
   Sit on side and push off to teacher.
   Stand and jump into water, holding teacher's hand.
   Stand and jump into water alone.

6. Sit on box and fall into water.
   Stand on box and jump into water, holding teach-
   er's hand.
   Stand on box and jump into water alone.

7. Hold onto side, face in water, for 5 seconds.
   Hold on to side, face in water, and let go.
   Prone float and recover.

8. Dead man's float 3 seconds.
   Jellyfish float 5 seconds.

9. Back float position (head back, body extended) hold-
   ing onto side.
   Back float position (head back, body extended) hold-
   ing onto side with one hand.
   Back float position (head back, body extended) with
   assistance.
   Back float position with light assistance behind
   neck.
   Back float alone 3 seconds.
   Back float alone 10 seconds.

10. Push off side, face in water, glide to teacher.
    Push off side, face in water, glide to rope.

11. Kick, holding on to side, face in water.
    Kick, holding on to kickboard, face in water, with
    assistance.
    Kick with kickboard across pool, face in water, with
    occasional assistance.
    Kick with kickboard across pool, face in water,
    alone.

12. Push off side and kick with prone glide to teacher.
    Push off side and kick with prone glide to rope.
    Push off side and kick with prone glide across pool,
    with assistance.
    Push off side and kick with prone glide across pool,
    alone.

13. Push off side and swim underwater.
    Swim underwater under obstacle.
    Swim underwater to rope.

14. Back glide with assistance.
    Back glide 3 feet to teacher.
    Back glide with kick with assistance to rope.
    Back glide with kick with assistance across pool.
    Back glide with kick to rope.
    Back glide with kick with occasional assistance
    across pool.
    Back glide with kick across pool.

15. Human stroke with arms—face in water—with
    assistance.
    Push off side, human stroke to teacher.
    Push off side, human stroke across pool with
    assistance.
    Push off side, human stroke across pool.

16. Finning with arms assisted across pool.
    Finning with arms 10 feet.
    Finning and kicking assisted across pool.
    Finning and kicking 10 feet.
    Finning and kicking across pool.

17. Sit—dive into water, holding teacher's hand.
    Sit—dive into water.
    Kneel—dive into water, holding teacher's hand.
    Kneel—dive into water.
    Stand—dive into water with assistance.
    Stand—dive into water.

18. Sit—dive into water and kick with prone glide to
    teacher.

Table 17.4
Swimming: task analysis (*continued*)

Kneel—dive into water and kick with prone glide to teacher.
Stand—dive into water and kick with prone glide to teacher.

19. Sit—dive off side, swim underwater.
Kneel—dive off side, swim underwater.
Stand—dive off side, swim underwater.

20. Bob at the side in deep water, holding the gutter.
Bob freely at the side in deep water.

21. Sit—fall into deep water with assistance.
Sit—fall into deep water.
Jump into deep water with assistance.
Jump into deep water.

22. Sit—dive from side into deep water.
Kneel—dive from side into deep water.
Stand—dive from side into deep water.

23. Jump off box into deep water, with assistance.
Jump off box into deep water.
Jump off diving board with assistance.
Jump off diving board.

24. *Stand—dive off diving board.*

25. Front crawl stroke arms—face in water—with assistance.
Push off side, front crawl stroke to teacher.
Push off side, front crawl stroke across pool with assistance (no breathing).
Push off side, front crawl stroke across pool (no breathing).

26. Rhythmic breathing at side 5 times.
Rhythmic breathing at side 10 times.
Rhythmic breathing at side 1 minute.

27. Rhythmic breathing with kickboard across pool, with assistance.
Rhythmic breathing with kickboard across pool.
Rhythmic breathing with kickboard across pool, with one arm stroking, with assistance.
Rhythmic breathing with kickboard across pool, with one arm stroking.

28. Combined front crawl stroke with breathing, across pool, with assistance.
Combined front crawl stroke with breathing, across pool.

29. Back crawl stroke arms and kick assisted across pool.
Back crawl stroke arms and kick with occasional assist across pool.
Back crawl stroke arms and kick alone for 10 feet.
Back crawl stroke arms and kick across pool.

30. Whip kick sitting on side.
Whip kick across pool in correct position with assistance.

31. Whip kick and elementary backstroke arms across pool, with assistance.
Whip kick and elementary backstroke arm across pool with occasional assistance.
Combined elementary backstroke across pool.

32. Hold breath underwater 10 seconds with eyes open.
Rhythmic breathing 10 times in waist deep water.

33. Prone float 10 seconds and recover to feet without assistance.
Prone glide 10 feet and recover to stand.

34. Prone glide with kick 20 feet and recover to stand.
Front crawl arm stroke in prone position 20 feet—legs trail.

35. Back float 10 seconds.
Back glide 6 feet and recover to stand.

36. Back glide with kick 20 feet and recover to stand.
Finning or sculling 20 feet—recover to stand.

37. Combined front crawl stroke 20 yards, breathing when necessary.

38. Combined stroke on back 10 yards, finning arms and flutter kick.

39. Begin swimming on front, turn over to back, and float or swim a few seconds and return to front again.
Swim 10 yards, change direction, and swim 10 yards back.

40. Stand in neck deep water facing shallow end, level off (swim to horizontal) and swim 20 feet.
Jump feet first into waist deep water and finish with a prone glide or crawl
Jump into deep water, level off and swim.
Stand—dive into water, swim 20 feet.

Table 17.4
Swimming: task analysis (*continued*)

41. Tread water 30 seconds.
    Elementary forms of rescue — reaching and extension assists.

42. Jump into deep water, level off, and swim 15 yards without touching bottom, change direction and swim back to starting point. Approximately halfway back, roll over to back and rest motionless (minimum paddling) for 30 seconds. Turn to stomach and swim to starting point.

Name _____

1. Open eyes underwater.

_____

2. Hold breath underwater 7 seconds.

_____

3. Bob and breathe, moving out to rope with assistance.

_____

4. Pick puck up off bottom.

_____

Developed by Tom McKenzie and Sharon Jaks, San Diego State University, San Diego, CA 72182.

Table 17.5
Checklist for written reports

Self-check	Instructor check	Task analysis
_____	_____	*Title:* Summarizes the emphasis or special characteristics of the study. These might include the population of subjects, the behavior, the setting, supporting personnel, apparatus, procedures, the experimental design, or innovative ways to measure validity, reliability, or generality.
_____	_____	*Author:* States the name and affiliation of the authors.
_____	_____	*Running Head:* Indicates the key words to be used as a heading on each page.
_____	_____	*Abstract:* Summarizes, in approximately 200 words, the problem or purpose, the variables investigated, the results and their implications.
		Introduction: Informs the reader about the nature of the problem and its significance. Presents and analyzes the *relevant* literature. Discusses any theoretical, legal, or ethical issues related to the topic, and justifies the research in terms of its implications for science and society. The introduction closes by describing the purpose of the study in terms of the goals, variables, procedures, and methods of evaluation.
_____	_____	Statement of the problem.
_____	_____	Its significance (for the individual, society, science).
_____	_____	Theoretical, ethical, legal issues.
_____	_____	Review of relevant literature.
_____	_____	References according to APA format.
_____	_____	Statement of purpose, including goals, variables, procedures, and methods of evaluation.
		Method: Describes exactly how the study was conducted in enough detail so that it might be replicated. Includes subjects, setting, personnel involved in the study, apparatus and materials, independent and dependent variables, procedures, and experimental design. The Method section should be organized according to the format outlined in the *Publication Manual* of the American Psychological Association (1983).[a]
_____	_____	Format and Headings, organized according to APA Manual.
_____	_____	*Subjects:* Age, sex, educational or other relevant background, special skills, deficits, problems. Species (if not human). How selected (if appropriate).
_____	_____	*Ethical provisions:* informed consent to goals, procedures. Methods for ensuring confidentiality, right to withdraw; participation of client, parents, agency personnel or others in selection of goals and procedures.
_____	_____	*Setting:* location (and rationale for selection); times, schedules (where relevant); relevant physical aspects of the setting.

Table 17.5
Checklist for written reports (*continued*)

Self-check	Instructor check	Task analysis
___	___	*Experimenters and other personnel involved in study* (where relevant): skills, training, responsibilities; previous experience with subject; extent of knowledge about design and procedures of the study; instructions, contingencies governing their participation.
___	___	*Apparatus and materials:* Name and source (manufacturer) of equipment; details of stimulus materials and how they were constructed and presented; description of validity and reliability of apparatus, materials, or test instruments. Include illustrations and measurements where appropriate, using metric system.
		Definition and measurement of behavior: (If subjects' task is simple — for example, pointing or pressing a lever — the behavior may be described under procedure.)
___	___	Operational definitions of all classes of behavior, including context and criteria and how they were recorded.
___	___	Recording procedures, rationale for selection, and methods for ensuring continuing reliability of observational recording. (Include index-of-agreement scores and approval forms for observational recording — where appropriate.)
___	___	Training of observers (where appropriate).
___	___	*Experimental design* and rationale for selection.
		Procedure: Precise description of treatment or level of independent variables or contingencies throughout all phases of the study. (If the procedure is complicated, include a table that summarizes the conditions.)
___	___	Length of sessions; duration of phases of study and criteria for proceeding to another phase.
___	___	Instructions (to subjects, other personnel).
___	___	Description of any unanticipated events that might have affected the results.
		Results: This section allows the reader to inspect and evaluate the data and to determine whether or not the author's subsequent interpretations and conclusions are justified. The data must be fully described. (It is not sufficient to say, "The data are presented in Table 1 and Figures 1–30" and proceed to the discussion.) In some studies, the results will be presented in sections, for example, Acquisition, Retention, Generalization; or Baseline, Treatment, Follow Up. Use subheadings that will assist the reader.
___	___	Data are quantified and replicable. (Any informal observations should be included in a separate section.)
___	___	Transformations of primary data are clearly described (and, if necessary, justified).

Table 17.5
Checklist for written reports (*continued*)

Self-check	Instructor check	Task analysis
_____	_____	Graphs and tables include legends (titles), are completely labeled, and are designed in accordance with APA format. Without reading the text, a reader should be able to look at a graph and describe the subjects, procedures, design, and results.
_____	_____	Descriptions of the results refer to the appropriate tables and figures.
_____	_____	If group data are presented, representative individual data should also be shown. (If not, state the percentage of individuals who reached criterion or responded in a particular way.)
_____	_____	If appropriate, supply statistical analyses and a justification for the particular analyses. Include name of test, test value, degrees of freedom, level of significance.
_____	_____	Reliability and validity of recording procedures if not already reported in Method section.
		Discussion: The interpretation of the results, their implications for science and society, and their relation to the literature.
_____	_____	The extent to which the results answer the experimental question posed. (Any ambiguities in the data should be described and discussed.)
_____	_____	Comparison with results of previous research (cited in introduction) and relation of results to one or more theories or issues.
_____	_____	Alternative interpretations of results (where relevant), with rationale for favored interpretation.
_____	_____	Generality and limitations of results.
_____	_____	Implications for science, society, and relevant populations. Include, where appropriate, a cost/benefit analysis.
_____	_____	Conclusions or recommendations that are not based upon empirical data should be identified as speculative.
_____	_____	Significance of study (data, design, procedure) for future research.
_____	_____	Questions for future research.
		References:
_____	_____	All references cited in text (none not cited).
_____	_____	Alphabetical order, in APA format (APA *Publication Manual*, 1983).
_____	_____	*Appendix* (If appropriate):
		Although not usually included in published reports, you (or your instructor) may want an appendix to your project report. An appendix could include your project proposal and form for informed consent, protocols or observational recordings, examples

Table 17.5
Checklist for written reports (*continued*)

of clients' work, raw data, or tables of the data that you have presented as graphs. If you are evaluating a workshop, append a copy of the participants' manual or handout.

General:

_____	_____	Grammar, spelling, punctuation (cf. *Webster's Third New International Dictionary*, pp. 16a–51a).
_____	_____	Proofed and corrected.
_____	_____	Generally active, not passive, voice.
_____	_____	Written in past tense.

From *Applying Behavior Analysis*, by B. Sulzer-Azaroff and E. P. Reese (pp. 391–394). Copyright 1982 by Holt, Rinehart and Winston. Reprinted by permission of CBS College Publishing, Inc.
[a]American Psychological Association (1983) *Publication Manual of the American Psychological Association*, (third edition).

trying out your materials and seeing how many of your students master them without additional help. When students do not master textual material adequately, you can add your own study aids or develop instructional material on your own.

As with the motor activities, text materials can be broken down into their component parts. These can be as small as the frames that are included in programmed instruction (Markle, 1969; Taber, Glaser, & Schafer, 1965), or as large as a few paragraphs or pages, as is done in the Personalized System of instruction, or PSI (Keller, 1968). A frame presents a small bit of information in a sentence or two, and asks the student to respond actively. Correct answers are maximized by using prompts that are faded gradually as the student progresses through the sequence. Figure 17.1 illustrates both a number of different frames plus various types of prompts. If you elect to prepare programmed instructional materials, we suggest you refer to the sources listed above. Developing programmed instruction requires some fairly sophisticated skills.

PSI is a system of instruction that permits a student to work independently at his or her own pace by examining prose passages with the aid of study questions, then demonstrating mastery of the material by passing unit quizzes that are scored immediately by proctors. Study materials are prepared for PSI by identifying key concepts to be learned and generating questions that the student should answer prior to being quizzed on a passage. If you plan to prepare study aids for PSI you should:

1. Identify each key concept in the passage.
2. Examine the list of concepts and ask yourself how the student should make use of each: by *knowing* — saying it back in the same words or in the form of a paraphrase; *discriminating* it from other concepts; applying it; *synthesizing* it with other concepts; *solving* a problem; using it to *evaluate* something; and so on. [Again, the papers by Bloom (1956) and by Johnson and Chase (1981) should come in handy here.]
3. Write a study question that will promote the kind of conceptual use you indicated above. For instance, if the concept is to be used to solve problems, provide sample problems. If it is to be discriminated from similar concepts, provide the concepts or examples and nonexamples and request the discrimination. If comprehension is the key issue, ask for explanations or for original examples of the concepts. Figure 17.2 offers a few examples. (Have you recognized our application of these principles in the study questions that accompany this text?)
4. Prepare a quiz to test the concepts you identified

Table 17.6
Experimental golf sequence and mastery criterion

Step	Shot	Mastery criterion
0	6" putt — large balls and hole	4 putts consecutively holed
1	10" putt between clubs	4 putts consecutively holed
2	16" putt between clubs	4 putts consecutively holed
3	2' putt clubs removed	4 putts consecutively holed
4	3' putt	3 out of 4 holed
5	4' putt some break	1 holed, 3 out of 4 within 6"
6	6' putt	4 consecutively within 6"
7	10' putt	4 consecutively within 12"
8	15' putt	4 consecutively within 15"
9	20' putt	4 consecutively within 18"
10	30' putt	4 consecutively within 24"
11	30' putt from fringe	Not tested
12	30' chip 3' off green 5 iron	4 out of 6 within 6'
13	33' chip 15' off green wedge	4 out of 6 within 6'
14	65' chip	4 out of 6 within 6'
15	15-yard pitch	4 out of 6 within 15' shaped down to 4 out of 6 within 6'
16	25-yard pitch	4 out of 6 within 10'
17	35-yard pitch	4 out of 6 within 15'
18	50-yard pitch	4 out of 6 within 15'
19	75-yard shot	4 out of 6 within 30'
20	100-yard shot	4 out of 6 within 40'
21	125-yard shot	3 out of 6 within 45'
22	150-yard shot	3 out of 6 within 54'
23	175-yard shot	3 out of 6 within 66'
24	200-yard shot from tee	2 out of 6 within 90'
25	Downhill lies, club selection, tee shots.	None

From an unpublished paper by Richard M. O'Brien and Tom Simek, Hofstra University. We thank the authors for their permission to publish this task analysis. The authors emphasize the importance of mastery to criterion at each step.

above. Quiz items do not contain prompts and often combine several concepts within one question. Here is one example: *Describe programmed instruction and give an original example of the material it includes.*

5. Prepare an answer key that includes each of the critical features that belong in the answer and any that do not belong. Assign a proportional point value to each aspect of the answer. Also in-dicate the numbers of the study questions that

Pictures:

 are used from time to time to prompt correct responses. Here a _____ prompt is illustrated.

Synonyms:

To provide conditions for trial and success, prompting helps the student to give the right or c _____ answer.

Antonyms:

The old way of teaching was through trial and error, but programming teaches through trial and _____ .

Questions:

This section discusses ways to use prompts in programmed instruction. Why is it frequently useful to provide such prompts?

Multiple choice:

Prompts are:
a. used in equal amounts in all frames in a sequence.
b. used only toward the end of an instructional sequence.
c. are used heavily in early parts of a sequence, are gradually changed from artificial to natural, and are finally faded completely by the end of the sequence.

Context setting:

Context setting also tends to make use of general knowledge. For instance, if the materials mentioned include cake, candles, and presents, it is fairly apparent that a _____ party is being discussed. When the discussion relates to methods of applying principles of the acquisition of behaviors to assist students to achieve a specific objective, it is fairly obvious that i _____ is being discussed.

Figure 17.1
Illustrative frames including prompts.

correspond to the quiz question, in case the student needs to be guided to review a particular passage.

Now you are ready to proceed. Distribute the study questions for the students to use with their reading. [The questions really should help your students to improve their performance, as Farnum and Brigham (1978) found with a social studies class of 24 fifth graders.] When each student is ready, permit him or her to take the quiz. Set a standard for mastery (usually 90 percent). Either you or a student

A. *Analysis:* Compare and contrast programmed instruction and the Personalized System of Instruction.

B. *Knowledge:* Which of the following illustrates a study question for PSI?
1. A small bit of information and provision for student responding is called a f———.
2. Provide examples and non- _____ when writing study questions.
3. List four rules for preparing study questions for PSI.

[The answer is (3). Why?]

C. *Comprehension:* Give an original example of a frame that includes a prompt.

Figure 17.2
Illustrative study questions designed to teach different forms of concepts.

(preferably someone responsible and socially skilled who recently has mastered the material) can then score the quiz. [As our research has shown (Johnson, Sulzer-Azaroff, & Maass, 1976), the student who assesses the quiz — the *proctor* — also will benefit from the experience.] If mastery has been demonstrated, permit the student to progress on to the next reading unit. If not, have the pupil study again and take a different form of the quiz. This process can be repeated as necessary until he or she achieves mastery.

We have found that it takes several hours to prepare a unit for PSI, including study questions, quizzes, and answer keys. We also have proctors keep records of problematic items, and we revise those items periodically. Access to word processors has made this task far simpler than it used to be.

Another time-saving device for both programmed and personalized instruction is the computer. Many varieties of instruction have been programmed for the computer and you should be able to use that instrument for these purposes without much difficulty. [Bennett (1984) has written a set of suggestions you can follow for evaluating microcomputer programs.] At least one study in introductory biology (Chamberlin, 1985) has shown that students learn just as well from a computer-proctor as from a human one. Some students even expressed more confidence in the quality control of the computer, although the majority in that investigation preferred the human contact of a peer proctor.

Precision Teaching. In the Precision Teaching method, developed by Ogden Lindsley, as students perform academically, their responses are recorded on a *celeration chart.* This allows students and teachers immediately to determine rates of correct and incorrect responses and to adjust goals and methods accordingly. Apparently the method has produced higher rates of fine quality academic performance than many others against which it has been compared (e.g., McGreevy, 1983). In a recent paper entitled *Pedagogy for Survival*, Douglas Greer (in press) summarized five concepts incorporated in *Precision Teaching.* These include the notions that (1) behavior change, including academic performance, is not additive but multiplicative. Students following Precision Teaching procedures often double their output weekly as they work toward their goals. (2) Behavior is unique within and between individuals as are their reactions to the environment. Therefore each student needs individual attention. (3) Learned behavior is specific to the circumstances in which it has been taught. If the intent is to have it be expressed under other circumstances — settings, times or places — it must be taught under those other conditions. (4) Behaviors are independent of each other. Changing one behavior will not necessarily produce change in another, even when dealing with such closely related responses as overt verbal statements and covert thought. While reciting something aloud, a student may be thinking something entirely different. (5) Behavior is shaped by consequences. This includes each of its particular facets, such as its uniqueness, independence, and specificity. (You might also refer to Lindsley's 1984 paper for additional information on this method.)

Asking questions and leading discussions are other forms of instructional inputs. The way a teacher asks questions can make a difference. Rather than requesting one-word replies, you probably have discovered that it pays to pose your questions to evoke multiple-word answers — for instance by requesting definitions, explanations, multiple-step answers, or students' views. Then, as Broden, Copeland, Beasley, and Hall (1977) found, your students will give more complete answers. Those authors also noted that if the teacher ignored answers in the form of incomplete sentences and called on another student to answer in a full sentence instead, the latter form of answering increased substantially.

The amount of participation in and quality of classroom discussion can be improved similarly through careful planning. You can increase participation, as Smith et al. (1982) did, by stating rules for discussion and by praising, restating, or paraphrasing the students' contributions aloud or on the blackboard. Participation also may be increased by planning an outline of discussion questions and by recording student contributions toward part of their grade. Quality can be improved by using the same consequences for students who provide reasons for statements, comparisons for different points, or examples supporting their statements.

Notice that we have said a good deal about demonstrations, written and computerized textual material, rules, asking questions, prompting, and other instructional inputs, but little about lecturing. *Lecturing* is placed at the bottom of the list for several reasons; we are convinced that critical information usually can be presented in written form so the student can study and review it independently. To learn effectively from a lecture, the audience not only needs to be adequately prepared but also must be very attentive and have excellent note-taking skills. There will be times, however, when lectures are the best form of input: when you want to motivate students by conveying your own excitement; when a topic or issue is current; or when your pupils require supplementary explanations of written matter or are incapable of reading the material due to skill or perceptual deficits. Fortunately, you can do a few things to overcome some of the limitations of lectures; you may tape them so students can review the presentations; provide written outlines, objectives, or worksheets; emphasize, repeat, and give many examples of the concepts you are trying to convey; or ask questions and encourage discussion and question-asking. Lecturing is one of the forms of instruction discussed by Skinner (1968) in his excellent text on the *Technology of Teaching*.

At this point you should have prepared and assembled all the instructional input you will need. Most of your work is behind you. Now you simply have to use it and manage the operation.

Managing learning activities

Mr. Markham's class responded well to the handouts and demonstrations he presented, and most of the students got down to work in earnest, accomplishing more than they previously had. But a few, like Richard Parker, dragged their heels.

"It's okay," Mr. Markham commented to Dr. Levy. "We can negotiate a contract. I'm pretty sure that will work."

It did! Richard found that the added assistance he received from the study aids provided by Mr. Markham helped him to comprehend the material better than he had before. The contract motivated him to keep going. (Should you wish to review material related to contracting, see Chapter 19 of this text and Reese & Filipczak, 1980; Schwartz, 1977; and others mentioned elsewhere in this book.)

Remember other strategies you can use to help your students get going and keep going: setting goals and performance standards (Brownell, Colletti, Ersner-Hershfield, Hershfield, & Wilson, 1977), helping students to develop self-control (O'Leary & Dubey, 1979; Rosenbaum & Drabman, 1979; Shapiro & Klein, 1980), establishing problem-solving strategies (Maher & Barbrack, 1982), and encouraging self-instruction (Bryant & Budd, 1982). A nice illustration is a study by Kelley and Stokes (1984). Eight economically disadvantaged high school dropouts negotiated contracts permitting them to earn money for academic production. Once the pattern was established, it maintained by means of goal-setting. We need not expand further on motivation here, as so much of this text's previous material has related to that topic. Instead we offer various examples illustrating the breadth of behavioral approaches to instruction and learning.

Behavioral instruction has addressed just about every aspect of educational activity: from the preschool to the most advanced levels of higher education; in business, industry, service professions, and the military. Thumb through specialty journals in advanced fields such as physics and engineering instruction. You will notice numerous illustrations, especially of adaptations of the Personalized System of Instruction, and of various forms of computer-assisted instruction (CAI). Investigate the innovative curricula of medical schools and executive training programs. You'll see what we mean. One small volume designed to teach fundamental behavioral principles to managers, *The One Minute Manager* (Blanchard & Johnson, 1981) remained on the best-seller lists for many months.

Within primary and secondary education, most content areas have been addressed by behavioral practitioners, including social studies, art, music, science, physical education, sports and recreation, foreign languages, vocational training, and many others. Features of effective academic instruction are emphasized, often along with innovative reinforcement strategies. For instance, the amount and quality of seventh graders' participation in *social studies* discussions increased when the students were informed of the criteria for quality contributions and when they received feedback and points toward a grade according to a group contingency arrangement (Smith, Schumaker, Schaeffer, & Sherman, 1982). Performance in *science* and social studies by junior high school students with academic and/or social problems improved and generalized as a result of their participation in a PREP program (Preparation through Responsive Educational Programs), an approach emphasizing individualized instructional and special reinforcement procedures (Friedman, Filipczak, & Fiordaliso, 1977). A point economy (backed up with rewards), social skills training, and training teachers and parents in behavioral principles were the key features of the reinforcement system.

Students' *athletic skills*, such as in football, gymnastics, and tennis (Allison & Ayllon, 1980), have shown dramatic gains following systematic use of verbal instructions, positive and negative reinforcement, positive practice, and timeout. Feedback and self-monitoring have led to improved performance

in football (Komaki & Barnett, 1977), soccer (Luyben, Hansen, Hardy, Leonard, & Romero, 1980), swimming (Koop & Martin, 1983; McKenzie & Rushall, 1974) and tennis (Buzas & Ayllon, 1981). As we have seen (Cuvo et al., 1982), handicapped youngsters too profit from this type of behavioral instruction. Perhaps it is no coincidence that Adam Buckminster ("Bucky") Cox, who won four world marathon and 50-mile running records between 1978 and 1981, when he was between five and eight years of age, or Kevin Dyer, the top medalist for 400-meter speed-skating at the International Special Olympics in 1982, both were coached by people with behavior analytic training: Ray Foster and Paul McCaffrey, respectively. In discussing the success of their swimming program, McKenzie and Rushall reported that "the swim club came from relative obscurity to provincial prominence. . . . At the provincial championships at the end of the study, the club placed second" (McKenzie & Rushall, 1974, pp. 205–206).[5]

Music and *art* have also been addressed by behavior analysts. For instance, Greer (1981) has cited more than 100 behavioral studies involving music, many of them relevant to educators. The studies cover music education; performance skills, such as learning to sing on pitch; and the use of music as a reinforcer.[6] Encouraging originality in painting exemplifies how behavioral strategies have been incorporated in teaching art. Three preschool girls were each observed as they painted at easels. When their teacher descriptively praised increases in the diversity of the forms the girls produced, form diversity increased (Goetz & Salmonson, 1972). Originality, in this case expressed as diversity of form, is, according to Torrance (1965), a key element of creativity.

Health and safety behaviors of school children are beginning to receive increasing attention. Pedestrian safety, prevention of abduction, and nutritional hab-

---

[5]See Martin and Hrycaiko (1983), Rushall and Siedentop (1972), and Rushall (1979) for further information on behavior analysis and sports.

[6]See Greer (1980) for a text on operant approaches to music education.

its are among the topics in those categories that have been behaviorally analyzed. Here are some examples. A six component training package plus immediate descriptive feedback was used to teach young elementary school children to cross streets safely (Yeaton & Bailey, 1978). Skills improved from 44 percent to 97 percent in one school and from 21 percent to 86 percent in another. Those high levels maintained one year later.

Children are being abducted at alarming rates. Modeling, behavior rehearsal, and social and occasionally tangible reinforcement were used to teach three preschool children to respond appropriately to suspects' solicitations, saying, "No, I have to go ask my teacher," and leaving. To examine the effectiveness of the preventive strategy, the children were approached by confederates who were young adult males. The men either simply asked the child to go away with them or added that an authority figure, such as a parent, approved. Sometimes they offered a surprise in the car (Poche, Brouwer, & Swearingen, 1981). Both right after training and at a 12-week follow-up, the youngsters expressed each of the appropriate responses very well.

Health status is affected by the food children consume. Young children from economically impoverished homes may refuse to consume the nutritious food offered them in school lunches. Madsen, Madsen, and Thompson (1974) reversed the situation by praising and giving small treats to children as they began to eat and when they finished their school meals.

Some of our own undergraduate and graduate students are interested in changing their eating habits. One method they have found quite successful is to record, graph, and sometimes publicly report the categories and amounts of junk and nutritious food they have been consuming.[7]

We should not forget *setting events* when we manage instruction. Time schedules, formats of grouping, sequences of activities, nonverbal signals, teachers' vocal tones, rates of presentation, and other activities can make a difference. Carnine and Fink (1978) examined the effect of training teachers to use signals and increase their rates of presentation of DISTAR material. The teachers learned the skills and the students made fine progress.

Not all of the factors identified have been analyzed systematically to determine what the best arrangements are. Here is *your* opportunity to engage yourself in scientific discovery.

Evaluating and revising instruction

When you prepare systematically, evaluation is a relatively simple thing to do. The objectives indicate what the *output* of instruction should be. You have already devised ways to measure that output via tests, checklists, and other devices. All you have to do is see how closely the two match—that is, to what extent the objectives were achieved. You may wish to plot progress by recording the data for the objectives actually accomplished on a graph that displays the objectives planned (see Figure 17.3)

If the discrepancy between planned and actual completion of objectives is large, then some revision is in order. Finishing much more rapidly than intended may suggest that the instructional activities are insufficiently challenging; finishing much more slowly, that they are too difficult, or that more guidance needs to be provided initially, motivational conditions should be augmented, or something else about the instructional process needs to be modified. Consider also whether or not you should select different objectives altogether.

You may have good reason for suspecting that particular students are failing because they lack necessary study skills. Perhaps they are incapable of sustaining engagement with a task for any extended time period. Maybe they interfere with their own and their classmates' learning by disrupting, rather than remaining seated and carrying out their assignments. It might appear that the teacher has omitted important preparatory activities or communicates or

---

[7]To assist you in planning programs to change eating habits, you might refer to the texts recommended by a colleague, Peggy Bentley, who is a nutritionist: Hamilton and Whitney (1979), Scheider (1983), Whitney and Hamilton (1981).

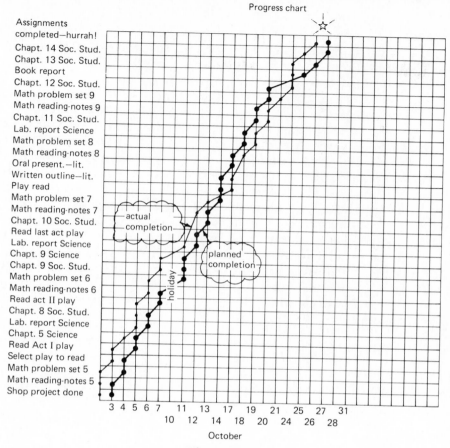

Figure 17.3
Contracted rate of progress for Richard for a variety of assignments. The dates on which the items are to be completed are marked down in the beginning (lower line). As Richard meets the standards for completing the assignments, he and his teacher place a dot on the corresponding date. If Richard keeps his progress above the minimal rate line, he earns extra time in the shop that week.

provides feedback in a counterproductive manner. Should such factors seem to be at work in your setting, you would be justified in examining those variables. In that case, you would have good reason for attempting to diagnose the problem by recording the relevant measures, such as the time the student is engaged in learning activities, the intervals during which disruption occurred, the nature or frequency of feedback, or completion of preparatory activities by the teacher. (Chapters 2 and 3 should help you here.)

Do not neglect the subjective reactions of the consumers of your instruction: the students and instructional staff. Ask them, by means of anonymous questionnaires, suggestion boxes, or interviews, to express their views of how and what they have been learning. Seek their constructive suggestions. Everyone might profit as a result.

Summary

The content of your subject matter aside, you now should be able to instruct more effectively by incorporating behavioral principles and procedures into your teaching practices. To guide you, we have offered a four-step model: first you select and clearly specify instructional goals and objectives, being sure to include provision for generalization over subjects, settings, and time. If necessary, you divide complicated tasks into their subcomponents and generate objectives from those. Second, you prepare all the instructional inputs you will need, such as textual materials, handouts, filmed models, questions, supplies, lecture outlines, and so on. Third, you carry out the instruction you have planned, supplementing it with motivational strategies as needed. Finally, you evaluate the effectiveness of the instruction by comparing your stated objectives against what has actually been accomplished. A wide discrepancy suggests the need for revision. You can get help in determining just what should be changed in the program by repeatedly collecting and analyzing data on the learning and instructional process and checking the reactions of the consumers of your services. You have seen numerous examples of ways that other teachers and providers of special services have instructed children and youth effectively by applying behavior analytic procedures. Now it is your turn. Go for it!

Study Questions

1. List the ten common characteristics of effective behavioral instructional programs.
2. Identify two ways that punishment can be minimized in a behavioral program.
3. Define (a) prompting and (b) fading.
4. The students at Lincoln High frequently complain that they are not being included in the management of their instructional activities. Discuss the possible solutions to this problem.
5. State at least six skills that may be taught effectively in groups. (Be sure to include examples that are not in the text.)
6. Mr. Spiegel read an article on self-reinforcement and is anxious to try this procedure with his students. (a) Identify a problem he might encounter when he uses this procedure, and (b) offer a solution to this problem.
7. _____ and _____ instruction are often used with children whose preparedness differs widely from that of their age mates.
8. Briefly describe DISTAR.
9. List the steps involved in developing academic instruction.
10. (a) T/F The process rather than the product of learning should be emphasized. (b) Justify your selection.
11. Discuss the issue of reinforcing the quantity of outputs versus their quality.
12. Describe one way that you could utilize the expertise of your colleagues when defining vaguely stated instructional goals.
13. Provide an original narrative illustrating how student papers could be used to define vaguely stated instructional goals.
14. Briefly summarize the advantages of using exemplars to define goals.
15. Select an instructional goal of your choice. List several ways that you can assess the performance of this skill.
16. Identify the critical features of an instructional objective.
17. Provide an original example of an instructional objective. (Be sure to label the critical features in your example.)
18. State the traps into which many designers of instructional and of behavioral management procedures so often fall.

19. Provide a guideline to follow when long-term maintenance is desired.
20. Several teachers at your school are concerned about transfer and generalization. Identify a source of assistance for them.
21. Jane stated her objectives as completely as possible, yet her students are still unable to perform the skills correctly. Discuss several reasons why this problem might be occurring.
22. Write a brief task analysis for a simple skill of your choice.
23. List the many types of instructional materials and activities from which a teacher can choose when designing an instructional program.
24. (a) Define and (b) provide an example of a *frame*.
25. Briefly summarize the main features of the Personalized System of Instruction (PSI).
26. Identify the types of materials you will need to prepare for a PSI course.
27. Describe the quiz-taking process in a PSI course.
28. Discuss the function of a *celeration chart* in Precision Teaching.
29. Juan will be leading his first discussion group shortly. Provide a list of guidelines for him to follow.
30. Discuss (a) the advantages and (b) the disadvantages of lecturing.
31. T/F Little can be done to overcome some of the limitations of lectures. Support your answer.
32. Present an argument for having students negotiate a contract.
33. Review the various fields and areas of concentration listed in the text that utilize behavioral principles. See how extensive a list you can generate.
34. Provide three original examples of setting events that might need to be considered when managing instruction.
35. Briefly describe the steps involved in evaluating and revising instruction.

References

Allison, A. G., & Ayllon, T. (1980). Behavioral coaching in the development of skills in football, gymnastics, and tennis. *Journal of Applied Behavior Analysis, 13*, 297–314.

Bangert, R. L., Kulik, J. A., & Kulik, C. (1983). Individualized systems of instruction in secondary schools. *Review of Educational Research, 53*, 143–158.

Becker, W. C., Engelmann, S., Carnine, D. W., & Maggs, A. (1982). Direct Instruction technology—making learning happen. In P. Karoly & J. J. Steffen, (Eds.), *Advances in child behavior analysis and therapy*, (pp. 151–206). New York: Gardner Press.

Bennett, R. E. (1984). Evaluating microcomputer programs. *Special Services in the Schools, 1*, 83–90.

Blanchard, K., & Johnson, S. (1981). *The one minute manager*. La Jolla, CA: Blanchard-Johnson.

Bloom, B. S. (1956). *Taxonomy of educational objectives*. New York: David McKay.

Broden, M., Copeland, G., Beasley, A., & Hall, R. V. (1977). Altering student responses through changes in teacher verbal behavior. *Journal of Applied Behavior Analysis, 10*, 479–487.

Brownell, K. D., Colletti, G., Ersner-Hershfield, R., Hershfield, S. M., & Wilson, G. T. (1977). Self-control in school children: Stringency and leniency in self-determined and externally imposed performance standards. *Behavior Therapy, 8*, 442–455.

Bryant, L. E., & Budd, K. S. (1982). Self-instructional training to increase independent work performance in preschoolers. *Journal of Applied Behavior Analysis, 15*, 259–271.

Buzas, H. P., & Ayllon, T. (1981). Differential reinforcement in coaching tennis skills. *Behavior Modification, 5*, 372–385.

Carnine, D. W., & Fink, W. T. (1978). Increasing the rate of presentation and use of signals in elementary classroom teachers. *Journal of Applied Behavior Analysis, 11*, 35–46.

Chamberlin, P. (1985). *A comparison of the effectiveness of computerized proctoring versus human proctoring* on *achievement of previously unlearned learning objectives when using Keller's personalized system of instruction*. Unpublished doctoral dissertation, University of Massachusetts, Amherst.

Cuvo, A. J., Ellis, P. J., Wisotzek, I., Davis, P. K., Shilling, D., & Bechtel, D. R. (1982, May). *Teaching athletic skills to mentally retarded students*. Paper presented at the annual meeting of the Association for Behavior Analysis, Milwaukee.

Drabman, R. S., Hammer, D., & Rosenbaum, M. S. (1979). Assessing generalization in behavior modification with children: The generalization map. *Behavioral Assessment, 1*, 203–219.

Farnum, M., & Brigham, T. A. (1978). The use and evaluation of study guides with middle school students. *Journal of Applied Behavior Analysis, 11*, 137–144.

Felixbrod, J. J., & O'Leary, K. D. (1974). Self determination of academic standards by children: Toward freedom from external control. *Journal of Educational Psychology, 66*, 845–850.

Fellner, D. J., & Sulzer-Azaroff, B. (In press.) Occupational safety: Assessing the impact of adding assigned or participative goal setting. *Journal of Organizational Behavior Management*.

Friedman, R. M., Filipczak, J., & Fiordaliso, R. (1977). Within-school generalization of the Preparation through Responsive Educational Programs (PREP) academic project. *Behavior Therapy, 8*, 986–995.

Gilbert, T. F. (1978). *Human competence: Engineering worthy performance*, New York: McGraw-Hill.

Goetz, E. M., & Salmonson, M. M. (1972). The effect of general & descriptive reinforcement on "creativity" in easel painting. In G. Semb (Ed.), *Behavior analysis & education* (pp. 53–61). Lawrence, KS: University of Kansas.

Greer, D. G. (In press). A pedagogy for survival. In A. Brownstein (Ed.), *Progress in the science of behavior*. Hillsdale, N.J.: Laurence Erlbaum.

Greer, R. D. (1980). *Design for music learning*. New York: Teachers College Press.

Greer, R. D. (1981). An operant approach to motivation and affect: Ten years of research in music learning. In *Documentary report of the Ann Arbor Symposium: Applications of psychology to the teaching and learning of music* (pp. 102–121). Music Educators National Conference, Reston, VA.

Hamilton, E. M. N., & Whitney, E. N. (1979). *Nutrition: Concepts & controversies*, St. Paul, MN: West Publishing.

Johnson, K. R., & Chase, P. N. (1981). Behavior analysis in instructional design: A functional typology of verbal tasks. *The Behavior Analyst, 4*, 103–122.

Johnson, K. R., Sulzer-Azaroff, B., & Maass, C. A. (1976). The effects of internal proctoring upon examination performance. *Journal of Personalized Instruction, 1*, 113–117.

Jones, R. T., & Ollendick, T. H. (1979). Self-reinforcement: An assessment of external influences. *Journal of Behavioral Assessment, 1*, 289–303.

Keller, F. (1968). "Goodbye teacher." *Journal of Applied Behavior Analysis, 1*, 79–89.

Kelley, M. L., & Stokes, T. F. (1984). Student-teacher contracting with goal setting for maintenance. *Behavior Modification, 8*, 223–244.

Komaki, J., & Barnett, F. T. (1977). A behavioral approach to coaching football: Improving play execution of the offensive backfield on a youth football team. *Journal of Applied Behavior Analysis, 10*, 657–664.

Koop, S., & Martin, G. L. (1983). Evaluation of a coaching strategy to reduce swimming stroke errors with beginning age-group swimmers. *Journal of Applied Behavior Analysis, 16*, 447–460.

Lindsley, O. (1984). *Precision Teaching*. Paper presented at the XVIth Banff Conference on Behavior Modification.

Luyben, P., Hansen, R., Hardy, J., Leonard, T., & Romero, J. (1980, May). *Behavioral athletics: Improving shooting accuracy on a college varsity women's soccer team*. Paper presented at the annual meeting of the Association for Behavior Analysis, Milwaukee, WI.

Madsen, C. H., Jr., Madsen, C. K., & Thompson, F. (1974). Increasing rural Head Start children's consumption of middle-class meals. *Journal of Applied Behavior Analysis, 7*, 257–262.

Mager, R. F. (1972). *Goal analysis*. Belmont, CA: Fearon.

Maher, C. A., & Barbrack, C. R. (1982). Preventing high school maladjustment: Effectiveness of professional and cross-age behavioral group counseling. *Behavior Therapy, 13*, 259–170.

Marholin, D., & Steinman, W. M. (1977). Stimulus control in the classroom as a function of behavior reinforced. *Journal of Applied Behavior Analysis, 10*, 465–478.

Markle, S. M. (1969). *Good frames and bad: A grammar of frame writing*. New York: Wiley.

Martin, G. L., & Hrycaiko, D. (Eds.). (1983). *Behavior modification and coaching: Principles, procedures and research*. Springfield, IL.: Thomas.

McGreevy, P. (1983). *Teaching and learning in plain English*. Kansas City, MO: Plain English Publications.

McKenzie, T. L., & Jaks, S. (1984). *A task analysis for swimming*. Unpublished manuscript.

McKenzie, T. L., & Rushall, B. S. (1974). Effects of self-recording in a competitive swimming training environment. *Journal of Applied Behavior Analysis, 7*, 199–206.

O'Brien, R. M., & Simek, T. C. (1978, August). *A comparison of behavioral and traditional methods of teaching golf*. Paper presented at the annual convention of the American Psychological Association, Toronto.

O'Leary, S. G., & Dubey, D. R. (1979). Applications of self-control procedures by children: A review. *Journal of Applied Behavior Analysis, 12*, 449–465.

Poche, C., Brouwer, R., & Swearingen, M. (1981). Teaching self-protection to young children. *Journal of Applied Behavior Analysis, 14*, 169–176.

Reese, S. C., & Filipczak, J. (1980). Assessment of skill generalization: Measurement across setting, behavior, and time in an educational setting. *Behavior Modification, 4*, 209–224.

Rosenbaum, M. S., & Drabman, R. S. (1979). Self-control training in the classroom: A review and critique. *Journal of Applied Behavior Analysis, 12*, 467–185.

Rushall, B. S. (1979). *Psyching in sports*. London: Pelham.

Rushall, B. S., & Siedentop, D. (1972). *The development and control of behavior in sports and physical education*. Philadelphia, PA: Lea & Febiger.

Scheider, W. L. (1983). *Nutrition: Basic concepts and applications*. New York: McGraw-Hill.

Schwartz, G. J. (1977). College students as contingency managers for adolescents in a program to develop reading skills. *Journal of Applied Behavior Analysis, 10*, 645–655.

Semb, G., & Semb S. A. (1975). A comparison of fixed-page and fixed-time reading assignments in elementary school children. In E. E. Ramp & G. Semb (Eds.), *Behavior analysis: Areas of research and application* (pp. 223–243). Englewood Cliffs, NJ: Prentice-Hall.

Shapiro, E. S., & Klein, R. (1980). Self-management of classroom behavior with retarded/disturbed children. *Behavior Modification, 4*, 83–97.

Simek, T. C., & O'Brien, R. M. (1981). *Total golf: A behavioral approach to lowering your score and getting more out of your game*. Garden City, NY: Doubleday.

Skinner, B. F. (1957). *Verbal behavior*. Englewood Cliffs, NJ: Prentice-Hall.

Skinner, B. F. (1968). *Technology of teaching*. New York: Appleton.

Smith, B. M., Schumaker, J. B., Schaeffer, J., & Sherman, J. A. (1982). Increasing participation and improving the quality of discussions in seventh-grade social studies classes. *Journal of Applied Behavior Analysis, 15*, 97–110.

Sulzer, B., Hunt, S., Ashby, E., Koniarski, C., & Krams, M. (1971). Increasing rate and percentage correct in reading and spelling in a class of slow readers by means of a token system. In E. Ramp & B. L. Hopkins (Eds.), *A new direction for education: Behavior analysis* (pp. 5–28). Lawrence, KS: University of Kansas, Department of Human Development.

Sulzer-Azaroff, B., & Mayer, G. R. (1977). *Applying behavior analysis procedures with children and youth*. New York: Holt, Rinehart and Winston.

Sulzer-Azaroff, B., & Reese, E. P. (1982). *Applying behavior analysis: A program for developing professional competence*. New York: Holt, Rinehart and Winston.

Taber, J. K., Glaser, R., & Schaefer, H. H. (1965). *Learning and programmed instruction*. Reading, MA: Addison-Wesley.

Torrance, E. P. (1965). *Rewarding creative behavior*. Englewood Cliffs, NJ: Prentice-Hall.

Van Houten, R., & Little, G. (1982). Increased response rate in special education children following an abrupt reduction in time limit in the absence of a token economy. *Education and Treatment of Children, 5*, 23–32.

Wall, S. M. (1983). Children's self-determination of standards in reinforcement contingencies: A re-examination. *Journal of School Psychology, 21*, 123–131.

Wall, S. M., & Bryant, N. D. (1979). Behavioral self-management of academic test performances in elementary classrooms. *Psychology in the Schools, 16*, 558–567.

Whitney, E. N., & Hamilton, E. M. N. (1981). *Understanding nutrition*. St. Paul, MN: West Publishing.

Yeaton, W. H., & Bailey, J. S. (1978). Teaching pedestrian safety skills to young children: An analysis and one-year follow-up. *Journal of Applied Behavior Analysis, 11*, 315–329.

IV Applications: improving conduct

"Did you hear what happened over at Lincoln Junior High last night?" asked Ms. Hollingsworth. "The police block is still up."

"Yup," Pat Thomas replied. "Two more kids in the hospital with stab wounds. And one of them apparently was an innocent bystander."

"How do you know that?"

"I have a friend teaching over there and she told me that the Jones boy was a pupil of hers—and that he was the type to stay out of trouble—avoided getting into those gang things."

"Thank goodness we haven't had the terrible problems Lincoln's experienced these past few years," added Kate Burnes. "We seem to be much better off, probably because Mr. Rodriguez

and K. C. Lee are so helpful and supportive. But still I worry."

"Me too. We continue to have our share of problems: fights, destruction of property."

"Our attendance records aren't as good as they should be," said Mr. Rodriguez, who had caught the tail end of the conversation. "The superintendent has been giving me a hard time over that."

"The thing I worry about most is what happens to our students when they leave our school," added Kate Burnes. "The neighborhood is crowded with unemployed dropouts. They don't know how to get along with each other or in society."

"True," responded Mr. Rodriguez. "I

was horrified to hear how many of the young people in our neighborhood have court records or actually have served time."

"I know that curing the deprivation and other social and economic factors that are at the root of these problems are beyond us," responded Ms. Thomas, "but there's got to be more that we can do to help. Maybe K. C. has some ideas."*

In their next conversation with Mr. Lee they all agreed that serious difficulties of the nature just described are not easily remedied. K. C. reinforced the conclusion that no simple solu-

tions exist. Yet he did explain that behavioral psychology is beginning to make some inroads into dealing with and preventing violence, vandalism, and other forms of antisocial acts. The strategies being developed are not restricted to correcting these acts, either. They also include methods for teaching youngsters how to be more effective socially, which should enable them subsequently to form productive relationships with peers, employers, and other segments of society.

In this part, you will encounter descriptions of a number of efforts that have been made to reduce violence and vandalism and to improve social skills, attendance, and deportment outside of the classroom. By studying about and improving on them, maybe you too will augment your contributions toward a better society.

---

*In this text we have elected to limit our focus to school-based programs. However, a vast literature on behavioral approaches to parenting skills is developing. For one example, see Sulzer-Azaroff and Pollack (1983.)

18 Improving social skills

Goals

After completing this chapter, you should be able to:

1. Discuss how social skills training differs from approaches that focus on pinpointing and eradicating problem behaviors.
2. Specify and discuss two major ways of identifying the specific social skills to teach. Include in your discussion how the two methods can complement one another.
3. Describe the purpose of carefully analyzing the social and physical environment prior to conducting social skills training.
4. Describe the changes in students' environments that can be anticipated when they are mainstreamed into regular classrooms.
5. Develop a social objective and explain how its inclusion would be appropriate in a social skills training program.
6. Identify and discuss the advantages and disadvantages of the two basic measurement systems presented by the authors.
7. Describe the purpose and type of information to seek when analyzing the antecedents and consequences of a social behavior you plan to teach.
8. List and describe each of the four basic steps in teaching social skills.
9. Explain why it is important to discuss the purposes and benefits with designated participants prior to the social skills training.
10. Describe the purpose served by skill cards.
11. Explain the purpose and the factors to consider when teaching students to prompt their teachers for attention and to use differential reinforcement.
12. Identify and discuss how each of seven steps can facilitate generalization and maintenance of newly acquired social skills.
13. Identify two designs that would be appropriate for evaluating the success of a social skills training program and two designs that would not.
14. Describe how to assess the generality, durability, and consumer satisfaction of the change.

"Hey, George—over here. Help me staple up this palm tree!"

"Mmm. Those burritos sure smell good."

"Wow. Look at the gorgeous colors in this embroidery."

"I like the wood carvings better. Look how pretty these figures show up on the purple velvet. Give me a hand and we can rearrange them all to look as good."

The multipurpose room was a hubbub of activity as the students planned for their international festival and bazaar. Over to one side, some boys were setting up for their Caribbean band performance, and every once in a while the sound of a guitar chord or drumbeat drifted across the room.

Juan Ortiz wandered casually toward the musicians, watching them out of the corner of his eye.

"Juan, why don't you give them a hand?" suggested Ms. Jackson, who had volunteered as faculty adviser for the festival.

"Who, him? He never wants to help," said one of the boys.

"Yes, I would. Here, let me move that drum for you," and Juan smiled a bashful smile. "Maybe I can sit in for a set or two on the bongos. I sometimes play them at home." As he beat out a quick rhythmic sequence, the other boys gathered around, their faces mirroring a combination of amazement and admiration. From across the room, Mr. Lee, who had been watching the event, caught Juan's eye momentarily and winked.

"Hey, Ms. Jackson. Can you get Tyrone out of the way?" complained Priscilla. "He's really being a pest. He keeps telling us how terrible our display looks and giggling his stupid laugh."

"They're always tattling on me," whined Tyrone, "and they keep calling me dummy."

"Another candidate for your social skills training program, Mr. Lee," said Ms. Jackson. "I can't believe the change that's come over Juan. The improvement in his academic work was one thing. After all, you helped us arrange for Juan's improvement, and we were in reasonable control of the situation. But getting along with the other kids—that's something I never thought I'd see!"

"It wasn't as difficult as you might think with Juan. He does have some talents and interests," the counselor offered. "Then, after experiencing success in his schoolwork, he began to feel better about himself. All he really needed to do here was to learn how to join a group, help out, share, and say some positive things when the time was right. I'm counting on the other kids to support the change naturally."

"With Tyrone, it's another matter, though," Mr. Lee went on with a sigh. "The remarkable progress he's made with Ms. Hollingsworth has convinced us that he has a pretty good chance of succeeding when he transfers. But because he's been in a special class for so long, he hasn't learned to get along with other youngsters his age from other classes. Also, when he moves into the regular eighth-grade class next year, it will be difficult for him because he's used to lots of attention from the teacher. It's a good thing we have several more months to work with him before he's mainstreamed!"

Mr. Lee was gratified to observe Juan's success. Although he would reserve judgment until the changes in Juan's social behavior maintained for a long time, he knew that the boy was on his way. But how had all this come about, and what was planned for Tyrone?

SOCIAL SKILLS TRAINING—WHAT IS IT?

Mr. Lee had been observing students like Juan and Tyrone for a long time. He noted not only that they lacked particular academic skills but other skills as well. Much of their trouble stemmed from the maladaptive ways they would interact socially with their teachers, peers, and others. The issue, then, was how to remedy the situation.

One approach would be to pinpoint the problematic behaviors and eradicate them. Or, he could use Alt-R, by *identifying and substituting constructive social behaviors*, social behaviors that would be apt to be supported by the social community, *and then teach them systematically*. It would be one thing to teach Juan to stop threatening his peers; it would be quite another to teach him how to support, cooperate, and communicate with them, and thus avoid being teased and angered in the first place. Using the first approach, Juan's nonthreatening behavior would evoke little reaction from others; in essence threats would be on extinction. Using the second approach—social skills training—Juan would be engaging in positive interactions so his constructive, positive social behaviors would be reinforced.

Social skills are important to people at all socioeconomic levels, not just to those from financially or culturally deprived backgrounds. Marissa, from her affluent surroundings, could also profit by acquiring the assertiveness skills to avoid involving herself in potentially dangerous, instead of safe, enjoyable, social activities. In keeping with the principle that behaviors to be selected for change should be constructive and likely to be supported naturally by the environment, social skills training is an excellent choice.

Certain social skills, such as attention, persistence on task, and compliance with teacher requests and directions, are important prerequisites for successful academic performance, a point emphasized by Cartledge and Milburn (1978). Ms. Hollingsworth, Tyrone's teacher, knows that Tyrone will need to learn how to get along with his new classmates without pestering them. Due to the limited size of her class, she has been able to pay considerable attention to him—complimenting his efforts and improvements frequently. She also knows her students very well and can usually tell, by watching their facial expressions or body language, when they understand and when they are or aren't listening. When Tyrone transfers into a larger class, things will be different. He will need to work longer or at least ask for feedback in an appropriate manner while doing classwork. If he is to succeed, he also must be able to solicit help when he needs it without disrupting the routine of the class. If he shows his appreciation to his teacher and peers, they will be much more willing to give him the help he needs.

Granted that social skills are critical to school success, then how do we begin? As in other instances of teaching skills to students, we start by assessing the performance of the individuals involved and the environments in which they are and will be functioning. This assessment results in identification of the necessary social skills and examination of the environment to predict how well it will support the change. Then specific objectives are designated, consent obtained, training conducted, and provisions made for assessing the behavior and increasing the probability that it will occur *and* be maintained in a *variety* of settings.

ASSESSING THE NEED FOR SOCIAL SKILLS TRAINING

Rating scales

Sometimes the social skills in which students need training are very obvious. Paying attention to the teacher is one of these. Teachers generally are aware of those students who are regularly inattentive, because they fail to direct their eyes in the proper direction during instruction and their questions or answers are irrelevant to the task. Other social deficits or excesses are extremely subtle. We look at a youngster and note that there is something odd about his or her behavior. We can't put our finger on it. A good way to initiate the process of identifying skills to be taught, in cases like those, is to refer to a rating scale, such as that illustrated in Figure 18.1, and to try to pinpoint the behaviors more specifically. Teachers, parents, and others who regularly interact with the students can fill them out. The students themselves may be asked to complete a modified form of such an inventory. Juan, for instance, might be able to respond to questions about how he initiates social contacts or converses with others. Marissa may well indicate her difficulties in avoiding certain kinds of peer pressure.

If you decide to prepare your own inventory, you might try to describe those nine behaviors that Mesibov and LaGreca (1981) identify as important areas for social skills training: smiling, greeting others, joining ongoing activities, extending invitations, conversing, sharing and cooperating, complimenting others, caring for physical appearance or grooming, and developing play skills. Others you could include are some that predict social acceptability as identified by Gresham and Nagle (1980) in their review of social skills training with children: participation, cooperation, and communication (Oden & Asher, 1977); greeting, asking for and giving information, extending an offer of inclusion, and effective leave-taking (Gottman, Gonso, & Rasmussen, 1975). For the components of socially effective assertiveness training, you could refer to Liberman and colleagues' (1975) text on personal effectiveness through assertiveness and social skills. You might find it helpful to see exactly how these and other authors described the operations involved in those categories.

Observation

Alternatively, if none of the skills listed above appear relevant to your particular case, you could pin-

When in situations in which the following would be desired, the individual—	Never	Seldom	About half the time	More often than not	Always
A. Pays attention as evidenced by:					
1. Directing eyes toward teacher (when teacher is talking or demonstrating).	1	2	3	4	5
2. Working on assignment (includes eyes directed toward assigned work).	1	2	3	4	5
3. Following instructions.	1	2	3	4	5
4. Asking questions related to tasks.	1	2	3	4	5
5. Answering questions when asked.	1	2	3	4	5
6. Volunteering answers.	1	2	3	4	5
7. Getting supplies with teacher's permission or upon request.	1	2	3	4	5
8. Nodding to communicate understanding.	1	2	3	4	5
B. Initiates social contact as evidenced by:					
1. Saying "Hi" or "Hello."	1	2	3	4	5
2. Introducing self by name.	1	2	3	4	5
3. Smiling during the interaction.	1	2	3	4	5
4. Asking questions about other person (name, likes, etc.).	1	2	3	4	5
5. Identifying common interests.	1	2	3	4	5
6. Sharing something about self.	1	2	3	4	5
C. Converses with others as evidenced by:					
1. Asking questions about other person(s).	1	2	3	4	5
2. Paraphrasing other person's meaning to communicate understanding.	1	2	3	4	5
3. Nodding following statement by others to communicate understanding.	1	2	3	4	5
4. Providing information about self or things others are interested in.	1	2	3	4	5
5. Discussing topics of common interest.	1	2	3	4	5
D. Expresses politeness and good sportsmanship as evidenced by:					
1. Saying "Thank you" or "I appreciated . . ."	1	2	3	4	5
2. Explaining why he or she is thanking the other person.	1	2	3	4	5
3. Complimenting and communicating what is being complimented.	1	2	3	4	5
4. Giving apology and communicating what apology is for.	1	2	3	4	5
5. Asking for permission.	1	2	3	4	5
6. Sharing objects with others.	1	2	3	4	5
7. Assisting others who desire assistance.	1	2	3	4	5

Figure 18.1
Social skills inventory.

When in situations in which the following would be desired, the individual—	Never	Seldom	About half the time	More often than not	Always
E. Demonstrates leadership qualities as evidenced by:					
1. Introducing others.	1	2	3	4	5
2. Providing understandable instructions.	1	2	3	4	5
3. Sharing ideas.	1	2	3	4	5
4. Distinguishing own ideas from those of others.	1	2	3	4	5
5. Pointing out which idea is best and why.	1	2	3	4	5
6. Initiating activities.	1	2	3	4	5
F. Negotiates differences as evidenced by:					
1. Stating own position.	1	2	3	4	5
2. Asking other for his or her position.	1	2	3	4	5
3. Paraphrasing other's position (stating other's position in own words).	1	2	3	4	5
4. Asking others for a solution.	1	2	3	4	5
5. Suggesting a compromise or telling other person what he or she has decided and why.	1	2	3	4	5
6. Seeking outside assistance when needed.	1	2	3	4	5
G. Handles criticism as evidenced by:					
1. Listening to complaint or accusation.	1	2	3	4	5
2. Paraphrasing (stating criticism in own words).	1	2	3	4	5
3. Clarifying (seeking to gain clearer understanding of criticism—"Do you mean . . .?").	1	2	3	4	5
4. Explaining own position.	1	2	3	4	5
5. Compromising, defending position, apologizing, or offering to make up for what happened.	1	2	3	4	5
H. Handles teasing as evidenced by:					
1. Ignoring it.	1	2	3	4	5
2. Making a joke of it.	1	2	3	4	5
I. Makes appropriate decisions as evidenced by:					
1. Stating problem.	1	2	3	4	5
2. Listing alternative choices.	1	2	3	4	5
3. Considering advantages and disadvantages of each choice (consequences, skills needed, accurate information gathered).	1	2	3	4	5
4. Choosing the best alternative choice.	1	2	3	4	5

Figure 18.1
Social skills inventory. *(continued)*

When in situations in which the following would be desired, the individual—	Never	Seldom	About half the time	More often than not	Always
J. Prompts teacher for attention as evidenced by:					
1. Waiting patiently and then requesting feedback.	1	2	3	4	5
2. Requesting help when needed.	1	2	3	4	5
3. Raising hand and waiting for permission before asking question.	1	2	3	4	5
K. Responds positively to teacher as evidenced by:					
1. Paying attention (See A, 1–7, above).	1	2	3	4	5
2. Providing verbal feedback that is appreciative or approving (e.g., ''Thank you,'' ''Oh, now I understand,'' etc.).	1	2	3	4	5
3. Providing nonverbal appreciative or approving feedback (e.g., smiling, nodding, etc.).	1	2	3	4	5
4. Sitting up straight.	1	2	3	4	5
5. Offering to help.	1	2	3	4	5
6. Following through when offers of help are accepted.	1	2	3	4	5
7. Greeting the teacher.	1	2	3	4	5
8. Inquiring how the teacher is feeling.	1	2	3	4	5
9. Complying with the teacher's requests.	1	2	3	4	5

Figure 18.1
Social skills inventory *(continued)*

point the behaviors yourself by observing what students with effective social skills do. Identify several students whose behavior within a category (e.g., greeting, conversing) is outstanding. Select those like Howard Parker, whose teachers frequently comment on how much they enjoy having him in class, and who is chosen for various positions of leadership by the other students. Ask those exemplary students to demonstrate the skills in question, for example, by having them orient visitors to the school. Observe how they carry out the task. Note what they say and do, including facial expressions, tone of voice, eye contact, types of questions asked, and so on. Place your narration in a sequential analysis, indicating antecedents, behavior, and consequences, and you then will be able to determine how particular behaviors are evoked, reinforced, ignored, or possibly punished. You also might con-sider videotaping the sequence—with appropriate permission granted, naturally—to facilitate your analysis and, as an added benefit, to preserve the modeled skills for later training, as discussed below.

Direct observation can be especially helpful in pinpointing social deficits as well. An example is a study by Blom and Zimmerman (1981) in which a girl was identified by means of a sociometric instrument as being unpopular. (Sociometric instruments determine an individual's relative popularity by asking members of the group to list their choices, from first to last, of peers to be included in an activity, such as a play group.) By observing the girl as she interacted with her peers, the counselor noted that she made limited contacts and that she failed to interact verbally in a positive fashion. These skill areas were then targeted for change.

ANALYZING THE SOCIAL AND PHYSICAL ENVIRONMENT

As with most other skill training, teach social skills so they will be sustained by the natural environment. For example, you may want to teach children to share toys. One way to do this would be to provide a small group of multipiece toys, which promotes sharing, as Deinzer, Feudo, and Shook (1982) found. But if the children who were taught to share spent most of their time with other children who refused to return the shared objects, sharing soon would cease. Similarly, it would be worth the time and effort to teach Tyrone to raise his hand and wait for permission to talk only if the teacher in the classroom to which he will be going usually ignores those who blurt out. Thus, one should assure that the natural environment will support the social skill to be taught. If the social environment does not uphold the behavior, it needs to be changed. If it cannot become more supportive, we recommend that a different behavior be selected, one that the environment does reinforce so that the behavior will have a reasonable chance of surviving.

When training students to develop social skills for the classroom, the teacher's cooperation is critical. If personnel other than the teacher are implementing the program, when it is relevant to the classroom they should discuss the training objectives with the teacher. Here is an illustrative objective:

> Students should show they are paying attention by making eye contact and through other ways: giving the teacher feedback when a concept is understood by smiling or nodding, and telling the teacher they understand.

Be sure the students' teachers concur that those behaviors are acceptable to them.

Teachers are more likely to cooperate with programs when they are consulted about training schedules, particularly if training is to take place outside the classroom or if an outside trainer is involved. Success probably will be accomplished more quickly if the cooperating teachers agree to the program and follow through by increasing the positive attention they give students as the youngsters practice their newly acquired skills in class. Fortunately, certain social skills—such as increased friendliness, expressions of appreciation for assistance, and other forms of social reinforcement—tend to produce a reciprocal reaction. A teacher to whom a smiling child says, "Thank you for helping. The way you explained that problem really made it clear," probably will react with a smile herself, and that can serve to reinforce the skill. Evidence to support this assumption has been found in numerous studies (Graubard, Rosenberg, & Miller, 1971; Polirstok & Greer, 1977; Seymour & Stokes, 1976; Stokes, Fowler, & Baer, 1978).

Easing children through the difficulties of mainstreaming and aiding especially quiet or withdrawn children requires that they be given a good deal of attention. Children can be taught to collaborate by learning how to prompt teachers to reinforce their efforts and to give them needed assistance. As Stokes et al. (1978) emphasize, "These skills may be especially important to young children who find themselves bereft of attention in classrooms, perhaps because they are labeled deviant, or perhaps because they do not represent a problem to their teachers" (p. 207), or, we might add, because their busy teachers are too preoccupied to provide attention contingent on progress.

We are beginning to learn what to anticipate when children are mainstreamed into regular classrooms. First of all, it stands to reason that the absolute amount of attention they receive probably will diminish, as they are competing with a larger number of students for the teacher's time. This abrupt shift in reinforcer density produces the same sorts of troublesome reactions as are found under extinction, or nonreinforcement, conditions. Second, unless some systematic preventive steps are arranged, such as the type of training we are discussing, we must anticipate that the attention the students do receive will be more negative than they previously have experienced. Support for this contention derives from several sources: Fink (1977) has shown that the interactions between teachers and handicapped students tend to be of the negative sort, while Bryan and Wheeler (1972) and Bryan (1974) found that although regular classroom teachers may give about the same low number of positive reinforcements to handicapped as to nonhandicapped students, the teachers criticized handicapped students twice as often as their peers. These findings are consistent with the results of long-standing research that has shown teachers to be more supportive of high-achieving students than of low achievers (Brophy & Good, 1970; de Groat & Thompson, 1949; Hoehn, 1954). It is because of this tendency that Thompson, White, and Morgan (1982) have recommended that teachers be encouraged to initiate more positive attention and give more positive feedback to handicapped and low-achieving students.

When students learn how to solicit teacher attention and feedback in socially productive ways (e.g., by waiting for an opportune moment, making good eye contact, smiling, asking politely) they can successfully reduce negative comments by teachers (Graubard et al., 1971). Additionally, they can feel more in control of the situation (Stokes et al., 1978), experience enhanced self-concepts (Graubard et al., 1971), and promote supportiveness, serenity, and responsiveness, as rated by themselves and peers (Nesbit, 1977).

SPECIFYING AND SELECTING OBJECTIVES

Once a particular social skill deficit has been identified and it has been determined that the environment can support the deficit's modification, specific objectives need to be formulated. As you recall, the objective specifies the particular skill to be taught, the conditions under which the behavior will or will not occur (don't forget to consider generalization of skills to other behaviors, settings, and times), and the standard for evaluating whether the desired change has been accomplished. For example, objectives for Tyrone and Juan may include:

- Tyrone is to raise his hand and wait for permission before asking a question during the math discus-

sion period at least nine out of each ten times he speaks aloud during a group lesson for five consecutive days.
- Tyrone is to be working on his assignments with his head and eyes oriented either toward the teacher when he or she is speaking or toward his assigned materials, unless he has permission to do otherwise, for 40 of the 45 minutes of English class for five consecutive days.
- Tyrone is to say "Thank you. I think I understand it now!" or a similar statement, at least three of four times his teacher answers his questions during English for five consecutive days.
- When teased, Juan is either to start discussing a topic he knows to be of interest to those involved, or ask a question, make a joke of the situation, or walk away for 90 percent of the teasing incidents for five consecutive days.
- Marissa will suggest a few safe alternatives every time she is invited to go for a beer, for a period of two weeks.

The standard for evaluating success of the treatment program should not be the ideal but that which is acceptable to all concerned parties. Thus, in the first two examples, a criterion level of approximately 90 percent was selected, while in the third, a level of 75 percent was chosen. Also, a frequency dimension needs to be added, specifying how often or over what period of time the criterion level must be achieved before all parties will be able to agree that the social skill has been learned. Thus, "for five consecutive days" was added to several examples' criterion levels to set a clear standard that includes the persistence of the desired behavior for evaluating the success of the treatment program.

MEASURING THE SOCIAL BEHAVIOR

The type of measurement system selected depends on the behavior to be measured, the precision sought, and the personnel available to do observations. A rating scale, such as the one illustrated in

Figure 18.1, can be administered easily by one person before and after treatment to determine if there has been a change in the treated social behavior(s). Such a system taps the reactions of the program's consumers—the student, the teacher, the parents, and any others who are important to the program. Assessing the satisfaction of consumers is an important element in judging the success of a program, and consumer satisfaction should never be taken for granted (Wolf, 1978).

Though obviously important, rating scales like these tend to be subjective and therefore subject to distortion when emotional issues are involved. For this reason, we recommend that the behavior be directly measured prior to, during, and following training. A number of tests of behavioral assertiveness exist. One, for example, is the behavioral assertiveness test (Eisler, Miller, & Hersen, 1973). For this test, students participate in role playing, which can be videotaped for scoring of components as Liberman and his colleagues (1984) have done. Tests of this kind could be very useful for Marissa to monitor her increasing social effectiveness. Or else you can design your own recording methods. For example, the percentage of teasing episodes that Juan ignores can be calculated. During how many intervals does Tyrone direct his eyes toward Ms. Hollingsworth when she is instructing? How often does he answer or ask questions related to the task? How often does he prompt his teacher for attention with phrases such as, "Have I been working carefully?" "How is this?" "Look how careful I've been!" "Look how much I've done!" and "Is this right?" How often does Tyrone attempt to reinforce his teacher's behavior differentially with comments such as, "Gee, it makes me feel good when you praise me"; "I like the way you teach this lesson"; "Fine"; "Right"; "I appreciate that"; "Thank you"; "Beautiful"; "Great"; "Super"; "Cool"; and "Right on?" How often does he signal by nonverbal approving gestures such as making eye contact, sitting up straight, smiling, raising his hand when appropriate, and nodding in agreement as his teacher speaks? Answers to such questions will provide you with a baseline or standard against which you can compare the effectiveness of your subsequent social skills train-

ing program's results. You probably can find an appropriate direct observational strategy from among those described in Chapter 2 to enable you to assess changes in the skills that result from training.

Once you have selected your observational system and the students have learned to ignore your recording of performance, you are ready to start collecting your observational baseline data. In addition, personnel permitting, you will want to obtain frequent interobserver reliability checks to reduce the possibility that observer bias might distort the validity of the data you have collected. Self recordings also should be checked for reliability by another observer, when feasible.

IDENTIFYING ANTECEDENTS AND CONSEQUENCES THAT CURRENTLY INFLUENCE THE SOCIAL SKILLS

Once the social behaviors to be taught are identified, their current antecedents and consequences should be analyzed to determine those that reliably influence the social behaviors. For example, let us analyze the antecedents to Tyrone's behavior of hand raising. *Does the classroom activity make a difference?* Is Tyrone more likely to raise his hand and await recognition from the teacher during class discussion, a math assignment, a lecture on English, or something else? *Does location affect his behavior?* Is he more or less likely to raise his hand when he sits near to or far from the teacher? Does it matter next to whom he sits? *Does the activity in which the teacher is engaged influence hand raising?* Is Tyrone more or less likely to raise his hand when the teacher is at her desk working or talking to another student? *Does the behavior of other students influence his hand raising?* Do they blurt out? Are they called on when they raise their hands? Is blurting out recognized? Do they avoid hand raising and other forms of participation?

The consequences to the behavior also should be analyzed to determine which are related to or influence the occurrence of the social behavior. *How does the teacher respond?* Is Tyrone called on or ignored when he raises his hand? Are his questions and answers treated positively by the teacher? *How do other students respond?* Do they ridicule hand raising? Do they ignore it? Do they give him attention if he blurts out? *Does Tyrone positively comment on his own behavior?* You would have to ask him what he tells himself about his question—did it help him, or did he conclude that it was stupid?

Answers to questions such as those posed above can help us identify possible discriminative stimuli and reinforcers that can be used in the treatment program. For example, let us say we discovered the following information:

1. Tyrone tends to raise his hand if his friend and neighbor Tom does, regardless of the activity and location of the teacher.
2. He is seldom called on when his hand is up.
3. When Tyrone blurts out, he usually receives teacher attention.
4. There is no evidence that he comments positively on his own behavior.

We might conclude that Tom probably would serve as a good model for Tyrone, and that if teacher attention could be made contingent on Tyrone's raising his hand rather than blurting out, it probably would serve effectively to reinforce his hand raising. Also, Tyrone probably would benefit from being taught to praise himself when he raises his own hand. A similar analysis of the A-B-Cs of Marissa's social effectiveness probably would help her and Dr. Levy, the school psychologist, select effective models and other antecedents and reinforcers.

DESIGNING AND CONDUCTING THE TREATMENT PROGRAM

The most common approach to teaching social skills involves four basic steps: (1) instructing and cueing students to perform and showing them examples of competent social skills *(modeling)*; (2) requesting them to practice the skills *(role playing)*; (3) *differentially reinforcing* the adequate aspects of their performance; and (4) encouraging and supporting their use of the newly learned social skills in a variety of settings *(generalizing and maintaining)*. For example, Bornstein, Bellack, and Hersen (1977) worked with four 8- to 11-year-olds whom their teachers referred to as excessively passive, unassertive, shy, and conforming. Each demonstrated at least three of the four following behaviors: (1) poor eye contact, (2) short duration of speech, (3) inaudible responses, and (4) an inability to make requests. More effective approaches to those behaviors were taught through the use of instructions, modeling, rehearsal, feedback, and practice in several different situations. Assertiveness for all subjects increased, and it was found to persist one month later.

Describing the purposes and benefits

Before starting a social skills training program with students, you should discuss the reasons why this type of training is being recommended, emphasizing how the particular skills to be trained will help them. Mr. Lee could tell Tyrone that the training might get him more friends in his new class, giving some examples of children like Tyrone who benefited from the same training. During this phase, you also can discuss potential goals and incentives and perhaps plan and negotiate a contract to help assure that the goals are mutually acceptable. Recall that students (and adults too) tend to cooperate with programs to a greater degree when they are consulted about them and do provide input. With a student like Marissa, who is rather mature and verbally skilled, entering into a mutually negotiated contract would probably help her to feel more adult and responsible, and thus more apt to work harder to achieve the purposes of the training.

Cueing the skill

Providing skill cards. Once the participants have been selected, you are ready to start treatment.

Goldstein, Sprafkin, Gershaw, and Klein (1980) recommended distributing skill cards to participants prior to the demonstrations. These cards contain the steps of the skill to be taught. These steps are similar to providing the student with a task analysis in the sense that the task is broken down into its components to make it easier to learn. For example, for paying attention when the teacher is talking, the following might be listed on Tyrone's skill card:

1. Look at the face of the person who is talking.
2. Nod once in a while to show you are listening.
3. Wait until the teacher stops talking before you talk.
4. Be ready to answer, to ask a question, or to react to what the teacher said.

Such a skill card has the added advantage of serving as a prompt, or S^D, reminding the student what to do and say, thereby increasing the likelihood of success.

Demonstrating the social skill to be imitated. Modeling was discussed in Chapter 7. To review briefly, a model should be selected who shares some similar characteristics with the student, who is competent in the behavior to be modeled, and who has prestige in the group. Also, several models should be used, not just one; and their modeled behavior should be reinforced. Tom is similar to Tyrone (i.e., he is of the same sex, approximate age, social status). Also, Tom is competent at raising his hand and is friendly, helpful, and a leader in the class. We already have observed Tyrone imitating Tom's behavior; thus, Tom would be a likely choice as a model. We would want to be sure the teacher called on Tom and praised him for raising his hand. We also would need to use additional students as models to prompt Tyrone's imitative behavior and be sure that the behavior is modeled under different circumstances or situations, so that he learns to practice the behavior when conditions vary.

A number of investigators have reported that not only can peers be used as models, but they also can be used effectively as tutors for teaching social skills (Lancioni, 1982; Strain, 1977; Strain, Shores, & Timm, 1977; Young & Kerr, 1979). For example, Lancioni (1982) successfully taught normal youngsters to tutor their withdrawn, retarded schoolmates in various prosocial skills.

Role playing the social skill

After the appropriate behavior has been demonstrated and the student has been shown *what* to do, discuss with the participants how that skill would benefit them. Then, encourage imitation or practice in *how to do the behavior* by asking the student to role play or rehearse the demonstrated behavior. As with goal and reinforcer selection, role playing works best when the student has been involved in selecting the behavior to be imitated and volunteers to take part. It is helpful to explain to the students why they should learn the modeled behavior. For example, if you are teaching students to cue the teacher for recognition and to provide positive feedback when he or she responds as indicated, you would point out how those skills could help them change their teacher's behavior. You also should keep the modeled performance simple or easy to imitate and emphasize the similarities between the observer(s) and models, since these similarities may not always be clearly apparent to your trainees.

An integral part of the program is to enable students to practice repeatedly the skills you are teaching them. If they are to observe, cue, and reinforce specific teacher behaviors, they need supervised experience in each task. For example, some students might tend to cue and reinforce any form of attention, even disapproval, unless you carefully teach them to discriminate among forms of attention through practice role-playing sessions. Also, cue or prompt with props such as tables and chairs to enhance the realism of the setting. Senatore, Matson, and Kazdin (1982) found that when the training sessions included such prompts, along with active rehearsal and fading of cues by the trainer, significantly greater change was obtained than when the clients only were asked to verbalize what they would say in a role-playing situation without the natural prompts.

to monitor its effects and be prepared to make modifications as necessary in the objective or treatment.

Differentially reinforcing the social skill

Once the student attempts to imitate the modeled behavior, provide or arrange for feedback or differential reinforcement. For example, when Tyrone raises his hand, his teacher should call on him and give him attention and praise. She should ignore blurting out and, instead, look for and call on Tom or another model who has his hand up. Tyrone also should be taught to comment positively to himself about his own hand raising.

Assuming your students are capable and willing, *assign homework* or arrange for them to *practice* the social skill in situations in which the behavior is likely to receive reinforcement. (Do not assign such practice, however, until the student has demonstrated mastery of the skill during role play.) Marissa could practice the sorts of assignments that Liberman et al. (1984) used, such as initiating and maintaining a five-minute conversation with a particular person or inviting someone to a recreational event. Goldstein et al. (1980) successfully used a strategy like this with junior high students. They suggest that to enhance the value of the homework for the students, have them write down where, when, and with whom they will try the skill, how they will observe and record the reactions of others and how they will reward themselves—that is, what they will say to themselves and what they will do for themselves—after performing the skill. After they have completed their homework, have them write down or describe what they did, what reaction they observed from others, and how they rewarded themselves. This information should be shared and discussed. And, based on the data collected by the student(s) and by an objective data collector, decide whether the skill should be continued as is or modified. Once the students have experienced success with the skill in the selected natural setting, assign the skill to be practiced in other settings. Continue

Teaching students survival skills

Occasionally, circumstances interfere with the necessary follow-through by classroom teachers, as discussed earlier. Students then can be taught the kinds of skills that permit them to cue attention and reinforcement from the teacher, and thereby survive despite those adverse circumstances. If you plan to instruct your students in these survival skills, you need to assess their deficits carefully to pinpoint those most critically needed.

When students are learning to prompt their teachers for attention, they must be taught to spread their bids across the work period rather than bunching them up at the beginning or end. Take care that the students don't irritate their teachers by prompting them too much at once. Also, if students learn to evaluate the quality of their work, they can restrict their bids for approval until it is merited. Then, when they judge their work acceptable (e.g., a page is finished without many mistakes; the student has worked carefully for a period of time), they can cue reinforcement from the teacher with phrases known to be acceptable to the teacher such as, "Have I been working carefully?" "How is this?" "Look how careful I've been!" and "Look how much I've done!" Try to discover and encourage the students to practice and use phrases that are most natural to them. To ascertain further an acceptable prompting level for a teacher, observe the class to determine acceptable rates used by other students. It helps to teach students to report accurately when and how many cues each gave and how the teacher responded to each by recording data simultaneously and providing them feedback (Risley & Hart, 1968; Rogers-Warren & Baer, 1976). Constant monitoring like this can provide valuable information regarding the appropriateness and effectiveness of the cueing program.

The second part of teaching survival skills consists of teaching the *students* to use differential reinforcement. For example, Graubard et al. (1971) assigned two teachers to each of seven 12- to 15-year-old students. Each student was given the responsibility "of accelerating praise rates and decelerating negative comments and punishment by the teachers" (p. 84). Students were trained in the following reinforcement techniques: (1) providing contingent verbal behaviors (e.g., "Gee, it makes me feel good and I work so much better when you praise me"; "I like the way you teach this lesson"); (2) asking for extra assignments; and (3) demonstrating contingent nonverbal behaviors (e.g., making eye contact, sitting up straight, nodding in agreement as their teacher spoke). The students also were taught not to respond and to turn their heads and look down when the teacher disapproved, scolded, or reprimanded them. These techniques were taught directly to the students and practiced repeatedly. Simulation techniques, role playing, and videotaping were used in the training. The behavioral procedures used by the students enhanced the teacher's use of positive reinforcement within a short period of time.

Similarly, Polirstok and Greer (1977) worked with an eighth-grade female junior high school student from a low socioeconomic area who was described as an extreme behavior problem. She was being referred to the Dean of Students for disciplinary action five to six times a week for verbally abusive language and other more serious offenses. Her counselor successfully taught her to deliver social reinforcement to her teachers when they were not disapproving of her behavior. The social reinforcement included statements such as, "Fine," "Right," "I appreciate that," "Thank you," "Beautiful," "Neat," "Super," "Cool," "Right on," and so on. Nonverbal approval consisted of smiles, pats, head nodding, looking at her teachers when they were talking, and raising her hand when appropriate. They also taught her how to receive praise and attention politely from others. The researchers observed four of her teachers (math, social studies, science, and Spanish). As the student practiced these skills, the approval rates of three of her four teachers increased, and the disapproval rates decreased for all four teachers. A follow-up 6 weeks later found that the teachers were pleased with the student's remarkable socialization and new-found maturity. Also, the student was referred to the Dean of Students only once after the training ended. She also frequently commented on "how much nicer she thought her teachers had become" (Polirstok & Greer, 1977 p. 75).

A final integral part of teaching survival skills to students is to train them in observational procedures. Observation must be used by students, not only to assist them in determining the appropriateness and effectiveness of the cues that they provide, but also to help them determine the appropriateness and effectiveness of their reinforcement. Is the teacher's behavior changing in the desired direction? Is the teacher providing increased reinforcement? Are there fewer reprimands? Through the use of observational procedures, students receive immediate feedback regarding their own effectiveness as change agents. They also can see quickly the benefits of their own behavior change. Different consequences should be used if those currently in effect do not influence the teacher's behavior to change in the desired direction.

In case this system sounds surreptitious, it needn't be. Teachers can be involved in the program from the beginning, participating in the skills to be trained and identifying the behaviors of their own to be targeted. After all, success will be mutually advantageous. The students will profit from being provided with a supportive environment for enhanced performance and a better quality of life; the teachers will benefit from the pleasure of receiving positive feedback from students and from any improvement in their own social interactions with their students. Most teachers we have encountered would like to attend to students and praise them more frequently and consistently, but they are too occupied with other matters to remember to follow through. The support provided by students who practice their own survival skills might be just what teachers need to enable them to acquire the habit of differentially reinforcing more frequently and consistently. Then, when the habit is well established, the responses of their students should be sufficient to sustain the change.

GENERALIZING AND MAINTAINING THE SOCIAL SKILLS

As you will recall, *generalization* is said to occur when a behavior learned under one set of conditions occurs under other circumstances. The academic skills Tyrone learned in his special education class should generalize to his regular class. Similarly, it was important that the skills Juan acquired in the counselor's office generalized to his classroom and elsewhere at school and home.

Generalization across situations is most likely to occur if each setting shares characteristics with the others. The greater the differences between the setting in which training takes place and that in which the skills are expected to be used, the more important it is to include generalization training within the program (Walker & Buckley, 1972; Walker, Hops, & Johnson, 1975). Social skills training, as we already have seen, often is conducted outside the classroom—in the office of a resource specialist, guidance counselor, school psychologist, or social worker. The trainer functions differently from the classroom teacher. Usually no more than a few students are involved, and their behavior in that setting may be quite different from that of the students in the setting where the skills are to be practiced. Under such circumstances, it would be surprising if generalization occurred spontaneously. As emphasized earlier, the same is true when students are shifted abruptly from special classes to regular ones for purposes of mainstreaming as mandated by Federal Regulation 94-142, the law that requires that students be placed in the least restrictive environment that is necessary to meet their individual educational needs.

Various steps can be taken to facilitate the generalization and maintenance of newly acquired social skills. [For more detail consult Stokes and Baer's "An Implicit Technology of Generalization" (1979) and Drabman, Hammer, and Rosenbaum's description of the generalization map (1979).] If mainstreaming is your concern, you should confer with the teacher designated to receive the student and observe the classroom to determine what materials are used and what rules students are required to follow. Then you would inventory necessary social skills. Typical ones include hand raising for the teacher's attention, cleaning up and caring for the students' own materials, working for extended periods of time without teacher attention, bringing supplies to school, and so on.

Next, if it is determined that the students have any skill deficits, they need to be taught the skills—particularly those supported by the natural environment. To teach these skills, you would begin to set up similar rules, substitute the instructional materials of the new class, schedule similar activities, and so on. In short, you gradually should make the training environment as similar to the natural one as possible, thereby increasing the likelihood that common discriminative stimuli will be shared by both settings, promoting or occasioning similar behaviors in both.

Simultaneously, you can teach the regular classroom teacher the procedures used by the special education teacher or counselor, particularly how to reinforce a newly learned skill. For example, Walker and his colleagues (1975) developed a program for training regular classroom teachers in many of the strategies used in special classrooms. You also can develop a program to encourage staff, relatives, and friends to use similar strategies and to reinforce newly acquired behaviors.

Another method that shows considerable promise for facilitating generalization and maintenance of social skills is to teach the students to evaluate their own social performance or academic work and classroom conduct. For example, Rhode, Morgan, and Young (1983) taught students to rate their own conduct on a six-point scale ranging from excellent to totally unacceptable. They first were taught to rate their behavior every 15 minutes in the special education (resource) classroom. When a student's rating matched the teacher's, the student was given an extra bonus point that could be exchanged later for various reinforcing activities. The time intervals for self-ratings gradually were extended, and the frequency with which the teacher checked each student's ratings against his or her own gradually thinned out, too. Once an average of at least 80-percent appropriate behavior was achieved in the resource room, the students also rated their behaviors in the regular classroom. Ratings were done every 30 minutes at first, but they gradually lengthened until they were completely phased out. As a result of extending the self-evaluation procedures in the regular classrooms, the students transferred *and* maintained high levels of appropriate classroom behavior.

Generalization also is more likely to occur when a skill is taught in several situations. Self-evaluation was taught and reinforced not only in the resource room in the Rhode et al. (1983) illustration, but also in the regular classroom. Similarly, as mentioned earlier, Goldstein et al. (1980) assigned homework to students. After the students role played a set of social skills, they were to try them out in real-life situations, such as the classroom or school yard. Some schools in the Los Angeles unified school district have set up "halfway" classes that share characteristics of both environments, to make the transition from special to regular classrooms more gradual. Rather than producing an abrupt environmental change, other districts known to us gradually introduce students into regular classroom settings a few class periods at a time, usually starting where the student is most competent and likely to succeed. Such a transition permits the reinforcement schedule to be diminished slowly, while the special education teacher temporarily supplements the comparatively leaner reinforcement schedule and stricter requirements of the regular classroom.

Notice that as in other programs of behavior change, generalization over time or *maintenance* of recently acquired skills should be planned systematically by gradually and progressively fading antecedent cues; reducing the frequency of reinforcement; adjusting the quality of the reinforcer so it eventually resembles the reinforcer inherent to the situation in which the behaviors are to be practiced; and introducing delay of reinforcement and diminishing the amount. For Tyrone, who probably would need powerful motivation to alter his social behaviors, Mr. Lee might start by using a token system and instructing, demonstrating, and guiding Tyrone's acquisition and practice of his social skills. The tokens could be traded for special rewards and privileges. Once a skill was firmly acquired, Tyrone

might receive fewer tokens and/or receive them less frequently, yet get a good deal of praise when he practiced the skill. When all necessary skills were learned, Mr. Lee could begin to remove the token system, substituting praise, smiles, and other gestures of approval for the previous rewards and privileges. Maintenance also might be supported by teaching Tyrone to rate his own performance, for example, by providing him with a checklist that he and his teacher could score at the end of each class period. As usual, reinforcement for accurate self-assessment is critical, so Tyrone's teacher or Mr. Lee would have to reinforce accurate self-evaluation until it became firmly established.

If your concern is teaching social skills to be practiced outside of school or in less structured social settings within school, you should try to follow similar procedures to promote maintenance and generalization. The likelihood of successful transfer to the real world may be expected to diminish, though, as your control of contingency arrangements lessens. If you were Marissa's counselor, you should recognize that your best efforts to help her handle her relationships with young men could fail, as it would be very difficult to alter her social environment outside of school. If a few friends were willing to lend support, though—like her friend Jeana—you might have more cause for optimism. One such instance of success was reported by Edward Sulzer (1965). In that case, a young man was experiencing extreme problems due to excessive consumption of alcohol. An analysis of his social environment revealed that his job entailed visiting bars, where he often would join friends for social conversation while consuming liquor. Several procedures were applied, one of which involved enlisting the help of his friends. They agreed not to converse with him if he were drinking hard liquor, but they would interact if he drank nonalcoholic beverages or nothing at all. The intervention was apparently successful, as the young man was able to return to his regular daily activities, free of drunkenness.

By following the foregoing advice, you may find that the newly acquired skills are much more likely to persist in the natural setting. Further, once patterns of reciprocal reinforcement are established between students and their peers, parents, or teachers, with each supporting change in the other, then training can be reduced or withdrawn altogether. In fact, often such programs have resulted in major changes in the way that a teacher and a pupil interact. Instead of reacting negatively to one another, the teacher and pupil reinforce each other's positive behavior. Reports on change from both parties have been enthusiastic. The teacher sees the pupil as virtually a changed person, while the pupil says that the teacher is much nicer than previously (Graubard et al., 1971; Polirstok & Greer, 1977). Everyone seems to benefit by such an approach.

Notice, however, that success is not guaranteed in social skills training any more than it is in other realms of application. Do not assume all the blame if your efforts fail to produce the generalization you were anticipating. Others sometimes experience a failure of training to generalize. For instance, Berler, Gross, and Drabman (1982) taught their subjects various social skills in the presence of some of the students' teachers and peers, yet generalization did not occur. Do not be discouraged, either, if you try a method you read about in a journal and it doesn't work for you. There may have been subtle differences between the procedures you used and those used by the authors; also, your clients surely have different learning histories, physical attributes, and home and school environments from theirs. Other researchers may have tried certain techniques already without success; perhaps their reports were not submitted for publication or maybe they were submitted and rejected. There well may be a bias in favor of publishing successful treatment outcomes in preference to unsuccessful ones.

EVALUATING THE EFFECTIVENESS OF YOUR SOCIAL SKILLS PROGRAM

To permit you to assess whether or not your program is working, as we consistently recommend in this book, you should repeatedly collect measures of performance. These could be frequency counts of subskills expressed without prompting or some other measure. Changes too subtle to be noted moment by moment or day by day will be revealed by the graphs you plot. Naturally, you will need to collect baseline measurement over a period of time sufficient to enable you to obtain a reasonably valid picture of ongoing behavior prior to treatment. Then you can institute training for a while for one behavior, reserving training for others, assuming that the others will not covary with the first. Then, should the data on the treated behavior demonstrate an improvement, you could try with the next, and so on, in multiple-baseline fashion as described and illustrated in Chapter 3. Alternatively, you could test your procedure across different students, delaying treatment for a while for each while continuing to record their baseline performance. Then, in either situation, if change occurs *when and only when* the treatment is put into effect, you can become increasingly more certain that it was the treatment that was related to the change; that is, that the change was a *function* of your treatment.[1]

Showing that the training program is responsible for the change is of critical importance, but there are other factors to consider in evaluating a social skills package: how general and enduring the changes are and how satisfied your consumers are with the results. The generality and durability of change can be assessed by collecting observational data in other settings and continuing to collect the data, at least intermittently, following termination of the formal program. When Stevenson and Fantuzzo (1984) collected these data for an underachieving student, they found generalization of newly learned self-control skills across behaviors, settings, and time, as well as positively affecting the behavior of another student who sat adjacent to him. Sometimes you may find you must provide periodic review sessions to support adequate maintenance (Luiselli, Colozzi, Donellon, Helfen, & Pemberton, 1978). To assess consumer satisfaction, you might interview partici-

---

[1]We do not suggest that you use a withdrawal (reversal) or a multiple-baseline-across-settings design for evaluating social skills training. In the first case, because you are dealing with skill acquisition rather than rate, you would not expect the behavior to diminish substantially when treatment is removed. In the latter case, you might well observe cross-setting generalization to occur without specific planning. This happy surprise will nullify the power of the multiple baseline design.

pants, teachers, parents, and other staff. Or you could ask them to complete a questionnaire. A nice supplementary measure of consumer satisfaction is to see if the students choose to engage in other activities with you in the future or if their friends or acquaintances show enthusiasm in response to your invitations to involve them in a similar program.

Social skills training often is used as a preventive service, as in easing students' transfer from special to regular classes. If you have records of the number of referrals for assistance with academic and management problems prior to training, these can be compared with the number per similar time period after the training program. The analysis could provide some important cost/benefit data as to the value of the program.

Summary

A variety of social skills are critical to achieving success in school. Students who have not learned appropriate social skills tend to have more difficulty with peer relations, misbehave more often, and do worse academically. In this chapter, we described a step-by-step approach for teaching social skills, including identifying specific social skill deficits; examining the environment to determine how well it will support change; designating objectives; obtaining consent; teaching the social skills; promoting generalization and maintenance; and evaluating the effectiveness of the program. Suggestions for facilitating generalization and maintenance included:

1. **Trying to keep the training conditions as similar as possible to the natural setting or gradually increasing the similarity between the two. When possible, teach the social skills in the environment where it is to be practiced such as the classroom itself.**

2. **Teaching the students to evaluate their own classroom behavior accurately.**
3. **Providing practice of the skill in a variety of settings.**
4. **Teaching the students to prompt for reinforcement and to reinforce appropriate behaviors of their teachers, parents, or peers.**
5. **Teaching the students to reinforce their own behaviors.**
6. **Encouraging those in the natural environment to reinforce newly learned behaviors.**
7. **Gradually withdrawing your instructions and reinforcement.**

Because of the critical nature of these social skills, we no longer can ignore them or assume that our students have learned them. Social skills need to be recognized as an integral part of the curriculum, and their acquisition no longer should be left to chance. The knowledge and skills now are available to teach them.

Study Questions

1. Describe in detail two approaches to pinpointing and eradicating problem behaviors.
2. List several social skills that are important prerequisites for successful academic performance.
3. Mr. Anderson plans to use a behavioral program to teach Peter several important social skills. The school psychologist suggests he begin by assessing Peter's performance and the environment in which he is and will be functioning. Explain the importance of performing these tasks.

4. (Refer to the previous question.) Mr. Anderson has assessed Peter's performance and his environment. What steps should he follow next?

5. State three social skills that should be obvious to the teacher.

6. Dale's social deficits are extremely difficult to pinpoint. Describe in detail a good way to initiate the process of identifying the skills he should be taught.

7. List the nine behaviors that Mesibov and La Greca (1981) identify as important areas for social skills training.

8. Provide 13 skills that may predict social acceptability.

9. Mr. Laker would like to pinpoint the important social deficits for the students he is counseling, but does not want to use an inventory to accomplish this task. Describe in detail two alternative methods he could use.

10. Define *sociometric instrument*.

11. (a) Provide an original narrative illustrating that not all social skills should be targeted for change.
    (b) Justify your selection.

12. The school psychologist wants to use a behavioral program to enable several students to develop a set of classroom social skills. Discuss the considerations critical to the success of the program.

13. (Refer to the previous question.) She also wants to ensure that the teachers are likely to cooperate.
    (a) Describe several ways to increase cooperation by teachers.
    (b) Identify the advantages of targeting behaviors such as friendliness and expressions of appreciation for assistance.

14. Rhoda will be mainstreamed into a regular class soon. State at least one type of social skill that is particularly important to target for her.

15. You will be mainstreaming a child into a regular classroom.
    (a) State in detail what you anticipate may happen.
    (b) Support your answer.

16. Peggy is learning to solicit teacher attention and feedback in socially productive ways. Tell her the many benefits she could receive from being able to perform this skill.

17. (a) Provide an original example and (b) label the critical features of a behavioral objective in the area of social skills.

18. Provide a guideline for setting the standard for evaluating success of a treatment program.

19. Examine your behavioral objective in question 17. Be sure that it has a frequency dimension. If it does not, rewrite it.

20. Provide the three criteria to use when selecting a measurement scale.

21. State (a) the advantages and (b) the disadvantages of using a rating scale.

22. Identify the steps that should be completed before collecting baseline data.

23. Provide at least one reason for identifying the antecedents and consequences of a behavior.

24. List the four basic steps in the most common approach to teaching social skills.

25. Describe in detail the information that should be discussed with a client before beginning social skills training.

26. Kim is participating in social skills training to learn to share. Develop a skill card for her.

27. (Refer to the previous question.) (a) Describe a fictitious student who would be a good model for Kim. (b) Justify your selection.

28. Provide guidelines for the effective use of role playing.

29. Sam has attempted to imitate the behavior of a model. Give a thorough list of the remaining steps that should be included to ensure that the program will be a success.

30. List at least three survival skills.

31. State the three aspects of survival skills training.

32. (a) Illustrate an instance of effective generalization in social skills training.
    (b) State the circumstances under which it is most likely to occur.

33. List the steps that can be taken to facilitate the generalization and maintenance of newly acquired social skills.

34. Describe an additional method for facilitating maintenance and generalization.

35. Mrs. Draper was told that she should systematically plan for maintenance of newly taught social skills. Explain.
36. A withdrawal design was planned to assess the function of Mrs. Draper's intervention. What do you think?

37. Monica has demonstrated that the change is a function of her training program.
(a) State the two other factors that she needs to consider in evaluating her social skills package and (b) describe how she can accomplish that end.

References

Berler, E. S., Gross, A. M., & Drabman, R. S. (1982). Social skills training with children: Proceed with caution. *Journal of Applied Behavior Analysis, 15*, 41–53.

Blom, D. E., & Zimmerman, B. J. (1981). Enhancing the social skills of an unpopular girl: A social learning intervention. *Journal of School Psychology, 19*, 295–303.

Bornstein, M. R., Bellack, A. S., & Hersen, M. (1977). Social-skills training for unassertive children: A multiple baseline analysis. *Journal of Applied Behavior Analysis, 10*, 183–195.

Brophy, J. E., & Good, T. L. (1970). Teachers' communication of differential expectations for children's classroom performance: Some behavioral data. *Journal of Educational Psychology, 61*, 365–374.

Bryan, T. S. (1974). An observational analysis of classroom behaviors of children with learning disabilities. *Journal of Learning Disabilities, 7*, 35–43.

Bryan, T. S., & Wheeler, R. (1972). Perception of children with learning disabilities: The eye of the observer. *Journal of Learning Disabilities, 5*, 484–488.

Cartledge, G., & Milburn, J. F. (1978). The case for teaching social skills in the classroom: A review. *Review of Educational Research, 1*, 133–156.

de Groat, J. R., & Thompson, G. A. (1949). Study of the distribution of teacher approval and disapproval among sixth grade pupils. *Journal of Experimental Education, 18*, 57–75.

Deinzer, R., Feudo, V. J., & Shook, G. L. (1982, May). *The effects of multi-piece and single-piece toys on the sharing behavior of mentally retarded preschoolers.* Paper presented at the Eighth Annual Convention for Behavior Analysis, Milwaukee, WI.

Drabman, R. S., Hammer, D., & Rosenbaum, M. S. (1979). Assessing generalization in behavior modification with children: The generalization map. *Behavioral Assessment, 1*, 203–219.

Eisler, R. M., Miller, P. M., & Hersen, M. (1973). Components of assertive behavior. *Journal of Clinical Psychology, 29*, 295–299.

Fink, W. T. (1977). *An investigation of teacher consequation in unstructured social interactions with mildly handicapped, moderately handicapped, and "typical" children.* Unpublished doctoral dissertation, University of Oregon.

Goldstein, A. P., Sprafkin, R. P., Gershaw, N. J., & Klein, P. (1980). *Skillstreaming the adolescent.* Champaign, IL: Research Press.

Gottman, J., Gonso, J., & Rasmussen, B. (1975). Social interaction, social competence, and friendship in children. *Child Development, 46*, 709–718.

Graubard, P. S., Rosenberg, H., & Miller, M. B. (1971). Student applications of behavior modification to teachers and environments or ecological approaches to social deviancy. In E. A. Ramp and B. L. Hopkins (Eds.), *A new direction for education: Behavior analysis.* Lawrence, KS: Support and Development Center for Follow Through, pp. 80–101.

Gresham, F. M., & Nagle, R. J. (1980). Social skills training with children: Responsiveness to modeling and coaching as a function of peer orientation. *Journal of Consulting and Clinical Psychology, 48*, 718–729.

Hoehn, A. (1954). A study of social class differentiation in the classroom behavior of nineteen third-graders. *Journal of Social Psychology, 39*, 269–292.

Lancioni, G. E. (1982). Normal children as tutors to teach social responses to withdrawn mentally retarded schoolmates: Training, maintenance and generalization. *Journal of Applied Behavior Analysis, 15*, 17–40.

Liberman, R. P., King, L. W., DeRisi, W. J., & McCann, M. (1975). *Personal effectiveness: Guiding people to assert themselves and improve their social skills.* Champaign, IL: Research Press.

Liberman, R. P., Lillie, J., Falloon, I. R. H., Harpin, R. E., Hutchinson, W., & Stoute, B. (1984). Social skills training with relapsing schizophrenics. *Behavior Modification, 8*, 155–179.

Luiselli, J. K., Colozzi, G., Donellon, S., Helfen, C. S., & Pemberton, B. W. (1978). Training and generalization of a greeting exchange with a mentally retarded, language-deficient child. *Education and Treatment of Children, 1,* 23–28.

Mesibov, G. B., & LaGreca, A. M. (1981). A social skill instructional model. *The Directive Teacher, 3,* 6–7.

Nesbit, M. J. (1977). Effects of social skill training and group counseling on adolescent self and peer perceptions. Doctoral dissertation, University of Texas at Austin, 1976. *Dissertation Abstracts International, 37,* 7645–7646.

Oden, S., & Asher, S. R. (1977). Coaching children in social skills for friendship making. *Child Development, 48,* 495–506.

Polirstok, S. R., & Greer, R. D. (1977). Remediation of mutually aversive interactions between a problem student and four teachers by training the student in reinforcement techniques. *Journal of Applied Behavior Analysis, 10,* 707–716.

Rhode, G., Morgan, D. P., & Young, K. R. (1983). Generalization and maintenance of treatment gains of behaviorally handicapped students from resource rooms to regular classrooms using self-evaluation procedures. *Journal of Applied Behavior Analysis, 16,* 171–188.

Risley, T. R., & Hart, B. M. (1968). Developing correspondence between the nonverbal and verbal behavior of preschool children. *Journal of Applied Behavior Analysis, 1,* 267–281.

Rogers-Warren, A., & Baer, D. M. (1976). Correspondence between saying and doing: Teaching children to share and praise. *Journal of Applied Behavior Analysis, 9,* 335–354.

Senatore, V., Matson, J. L., & Kazdin, A. E. (1982). A comparison of behavioral methods to train social skills to mentally retarded adults. *Behavior Therapy, 13,* 313–324.

Seymour, F. W., & Stokes, T. F. (1976). Self-recording in training girls to increase work and evoke staff praise in an institution for offenders. *Journal of Applied Behavior Analysis, 9,* 41–54.

Stevenson, H. C., & Fantuzzo, J. W. (1984). Application of the "Generalization map" to a self-control intervention with school-aged children. *Journal of Applied Behavior Analysis, 17,* 203–212.

Stokes, T. F., & Baer, D. M. (1977). An implicit technology of generalization. *Journal of Applied Behavior Analysis, 10,* 349–367.

Stokes, T. F., Fowler, S. A., & Baer, D. M. (1978). Training preschool children to recruit natural communities of reinforcement. *Journal of Applied Behavior Analysis, 11,* 285–303.

Strain, P. S. (1977). An experimental analysis of peer social initiations on the behavior of withdrawn preschool children: Some training and generalization effects. *Journal of Abnormal Child Psychology, 5,* 445–455.

Strain, P. S., Shores, R. E., & Timm, M. A. (1977). Effects of peer social initiations on the behavior of withdrawn preschool children. *Journal of Applied Behavior Analysis, 10,* 289–298.

Sulzer, E. S. (1965). Behavior modification in adult psychiatric patients. In L. P. Ullmann & L. Krasner (Eds.) *Case studies in behavior modification.* New York: Holt, Rinehart and Winston.

Sulzer-Azaroff, B., & Pollack, M. J. (1983). The modification of child behavior problems in the home. In A. Bellack, M. Hersen, & A. Kazdin (Eds.), *International Handbook of Behavior Modification and Therapy* (pp. 917-958). New York: Plenum.

Thompson, R. H., White, K. R., & Morgan, D. P. (1982). Teacher-student interaction patterns in classrooms with mainstreamed mildly handicapped students. *American Educational Research Journal, 19,* 220–236.

Walker, H. M., & Buckley, N. K. (1972). Programming generalization and maintenance of treatment effects across time and across settings. *Journal of Applied Behavior Analysis, 5,* 209–224.

Walker, H. M., Hops, H., & Johnson, S. M. (1975). Generalization and maintenance of classroom treatment effects. *Behavior Therapy, 6,* 188–200.

Wolf, M. M. (1978). Social validity: The case for subjective measurement or how applied behavior analysis is finding its heart. *Journal of Applied Behavior Analysis, 11,* 203–214.

Young, C. C., & Kerr, M. M. (1979). The effects of a retarded child's social initiations on the behavior of severely retarded school-aged peers. *Education and Training of the Mentally Retarded, 14,* 185–190.

19 Improving attendance among students and staff

Goals

After completing this chapter*, you should be able to:

1. Define each of the following terms:
   a. School phobia
   b. Behavioral contract
   c. Daily report cards
   d. Systematic desensitization
2. Describe a reasonable absenteeism average and contrast that to the rate reported in many schools.
3. List the problems caused by excessive absenteeism of:
   a. Students
   b. Teachers
4. Identify and discuss the punitive factors contributing to attendance problems.
5. List and illustrate four factors that contribute to school phobia.
6. Identify factors that may contribute to excessive teacher absenteeism.
7. Describe the importance of examining the records and determining the scope of the problem prior to implementing a program.
8. Describe why it is important to analyze the system prior to implementing a program.
9. Tell what to consider when setting priorities for attendance goals and objectives.
10. Identify the behaviors to measure in an attendance program, and explain how to collect the information.
11. Describe the importance of identifying antecedents and consequences that influence attendance in a specific setting.
12. Discuss why the authors emphasize positive approaches to dealing with attendance problems rather than punitive approaches.
13. Illustrate each of the following techniques for reducing student attendance problems:
    a. Commendations
    b. Phone calls or letters
    c. Attendance contests
    d. Rewarding activities
    e. Drawings
    f. Use of natural consequences
    g. Self-recorded and publicly posted data
    h. Reentry programs
    i. Behavioral contracts
    j. Daily report cards
14. Identify and discuss the guidelines of successful behavioral contracts for improving attendance and punctuality.
15. Describe a number of ways to deal with school phobia.
16. Illustrate and discuss the following techniques for reducing staff attendance problems:
    a. Pay incentives or bonuses
    b. Involvement in program development
    c. Lottery prizes
    d. Informational feedback

*The authors would like to express their gratitude to Mrs. Mary Nafpaktitis for providing us with a partial review of attendance literature

17. Describe a method of evaluating an attendance program.

18. Describe methods for maintaining good attendance and punctuality.

"Isn't it a glorious day, Mr. Truax!" exclaimed Mrs. Olsen. "Here you are, early again. You really seem to be enjoying school lately."

"You know, this year seems to be better than any of the others," he answered. "Look at Billy, for instance. Here I'd just about given up hope, and now he's caught up almost a full grade level in reading and there are still a few months left to go."

They watched as the students bounded out of the bus.

"Hi, Mrs. Olsen, Mr. Truax," shouted Billy. "Look what I got." He pulled a book with a crisp new cover out of his backpack. "Look. It's got stories of all my favorite baseball stars. Here's Reggie Jackson. I can't wait to read about him."

"Wow. That does look impressive. I'm delighted that your parents have been pleased enough to buy you such an exciting gift. I've been looking over the attendance chart posted in your classroom and noticed that you haven't missed a day in the past month. No wonder you've been doing so well."

"Gee, thanks," he said as he rushed into the building, book in hand, as Mrs. Olsen turned to several other children to greet them and say how pleased she was to see them.

It wasn't just by accident that Mrs. Olsen had been standing at the door that spring morning. For the past several months, she had made it a daily practice to do so. She had come across an article describing how school attendance was improved simply by the principal's systematically congratulating students for good attendance (Copeland, Brown, & Hall, 1974). Because she had charted attendance for several years, she matched dates against the previous years. It became clear that this spring's attendance was substantially better, although improvement had been gradual. The staff, too, was coming to school more regularly, and even she, herself, had resisted the temptation to call in sick a few times. Things definitely were improving.

Mrs. Olsen's practice of greeting students and staff each day provided only part of the picture. Other things were going on, as well. Probably most critical was the fact that children were learning more successfully and enjoying school more. In a few cases, where truancy and tardiness had proved long-standing difficulties, she negotiated individual contracts with students and applied other strategies too.

Success in reversing the trend toward increased absenteeism and tardiness should not be dismissed lightly. Truancy, class cuts, and tardiness are a costly national educational problem. In California, for instance, absenteeism in the secondary schools runs about 18 percent. Levante (1979) has reported that although it is reasonable to expect an absenteeism average of 5 percent for legitimate reasons, in some high schools the figure rises to as much as 25 percent.

Official reports of student absenteeism may actually constitute underestimates. Recognizing that school districts generally receive substantial funding on the basis of average daily student attendance, we presume it unlikely that reports of absenteeism would suffer erroneous inflation. Also, skipped classes may well go unreported. Regardless, absenteeism can cost schools considerable revenue. One large high school in Los Angeles County, for example, reported a loss of state reimbursement of about $200,000 during a single calendar year.

Financial loss is one issue, but what about the loss in instructional time and consequential unfulfilled opportunities to learn, both for the absent student and for classmates as well? Not only do students who are absent miss instruction but, on their return to school, the teacher must digress to make up for the loss. Either that, or the student falls out of step with classmates.

What youngsters are doing while they are not in school is also a critical social concern. Unstructured time can lead to trouble. How many acts of juvenile crime are traceable to a search for relief from boredom — classic instances of negative reinforcement!

Students aren't the only ones whose absence is problematic. Nonattendance by staff is also a matter of concern. For example, absenteeism among teachers has been increasing nationally (Manlove & Elliott, 1979), producing all sorts of educational hardships: lost instruction; diversion of the principal's time toward seeking substitute teachers; increased expenses for substitutes' pay; postponement of staff meetings; distress to students and colleagues who often must cover for the absent teacher until a substitute arrives; and a general erosion of morale and the credibility of the teaching profession (Lewis, 1981; Manlove & Elliott, 1979). Clearly, reductions in rates of teacher absenteeism would be advantageous financially, socially, and educationally.

Coping with the problem of absenteeism among students and staff can be accomplished in various ways: by identifying and eradicating factors that contribute to attendance problems, and/or by implementing programs to make regular attendance more reinforcing than absenteeism. In the sections that follow, we present a discussion of some factors that contribute to attendance problems and offer suggestions that you might use to design your own program for coping with this knotty issue.

FACTORS CONTRIBUTING TO ATTENDANCE PROBLEMS

By now you are well acquainted with students like Lucinda, Juan, Tyrone, Billy, Richard, and others who have experienced histories of failure in school. Reminisce about your own school days, and you'll probably identify one experience they all share: an abundance of punishment. Students like these are the ones who are scolded, treated to sarcasm and derision, and penalized in various ways. This treatment is natural, for their teachers and peers are re-

acting to students whose performances are aversive or nonreinforcing to them. You can see how this generates a vicious cycle; the student performs poorly or misbehaves. Teachers or peers respond with punishment. This, in turn, is followed on the student's part by — you guessed it — either counter-aggression or escape. For the teacher, delivering punishment can be its own source of reinforcement. Either the irksome behavior is terminated (negative reinforcement), or as Dubanoski[1] has contended, the student's expression of pain cues reinforces the dispenser of punishment. Punishment increases, and the punitive classroom climate accelerates. What better conditions can you think of to encourage nonattendance?

Documentation that the school climate often tends to be punitive is provided by the American Association of School Administrators (Brodinsky, 1980). The association contends that schools invest more time and energy implementing punitive measures than preventive ones in dealing with misbehaving students. Direct observation in classrooms has demonstrated that many teachers tend to use verbal disapproval many times more often than approval (Heller & White, 1975; Thomas, Presland, Grant, & Glynn, 1978; White, 1975), although the reverse may also be the case (Nafpaktitis, Mayer, & Butterworth, in press). While these statistics surely vary, the fact remains that the atmosphere in many classrooms is punitive, which may well be conducive to student absenteeism.

Another factor is likely to contribute to producing a school climate so punitive that individual students may be provoked to stay away: a mismatch between students' levels of academic skills and their assignments. Work too difficult can cause distress; too easy, boredom. According to Brodinsky (1980, p. 6), "Many administrators attest to a direct relationship between the kinds of subject matter and instructional material used, on the one hand, and the number of classroom disruptions, acts of defiance against teachers, apathy and absenteeism, on the other."

---

[1]Richard A. Dubanoski, personal communication.

Under some circumstances, students may avoid school because they have failed to learn to interact positively with their peers and teachers or to participate constructively in the school program. Schools may alleviate that situation by providing social skills training for such youngsters. Our impression, however, is that schools that regularly take this approach toward diminishing absenteeism are the exception rather than the rule.

Sometimes individual youngsters display severe reactions to being required to attend school, to the extent that their bodily functioning is affected. They may complain of headaches, stomach aches, nausea, or dizziness. When their reactions are so serious that they are regularly permitted to remain at home, they may be diagnosed as **school phobic.** Several factors contributing to school phobia have been postulated (Kennedy, 1965; Lazarus, Davison, & Polefka, 1965; Tahmisian & McReynolds, 1971). Among them, school phobia may be an escape reaction to an aversive or punitive stimulus, such as a scolding teacher or threatening peer. The reaction also may have generalized to the extent that all stimuli associated with school become aversive. Remaining at home may be reinforcing, not only because the youngster successfully avoids the punitive experience, but also because the parents often provide attention and sympathy as a consequence of witnessing their child's distress. Further, under some circumstances, the child's presence in the home is reinforcing to the parent, which could lead parents to further inadvertently reinforce the absenteeism.

Teachers, too, can be adversely affected by a negative school climate. Besides the unpleasantness doled out by their unsuccessful or misbehaving students, they may be punished by nonsupportive supervisors, poor peer relationships, or other nonreinforcing circumstances. In fact, it has been concluded that teacher absenteeism tends to be high when there is low community support and high discord among staff regarding school policies—regardless of material incentives or pleasantness of the physical environment (Manlove & Elliott, 1979; Spuck, 1974).

FACTORS TO CONSIDER IN DESIGNING THE PROGRAM

We have seen many cases in which changes in the school environment have led to changes in how students and staff behave. If an analysis of your school setting indicates that truancy, class cuts, tardiness, and teacher absenteeism are problems, you undoubtedly will want to initiate action to remedy the situation. From what we have observed, changes in the curriculum and in the consequences of student performance often may accomplish the purpose among students. Enabling teachers to work toward *mutually* established goals, while they regularly receive positive feedback from community members, supervisors, and one another, should encourage teachers to attend consistently. In the following sections, we offer some guidelines that you might follow in designing a program to promote improved attendance by students and staff.

Assessment: examine the records and determine the scope of the problem

Start by determining the frequency and pattern of unexcused and total absences. Do most teacher absences occur on Monday or Friday, as Manlove and Elliott (1979) have reported? Are those students who are most frequently absent academically delayed or advanced? Do students with social skills deficits represent a major portion of the absentees? (See Chapters 2 and 18 for ways to assess social skills.) Are any so distressed about attending school that they could be labeled "school phobic?" Answers to such questions will help you determine the nature and scope of the problem. They also will provide data against which you can measure change as a function of the program you subsequently implement.

Analyze the system

As always, before implementing any program, you need to consider the organizational system within which change is to take place. Contingencies to impede or support change can be found within the entire network of interacting elements: the students, their families, the community and its powerful spokespersons, the school administration, teachers, professional and paraprofessional staff, and many others. Ask yourself if the system will support a program to reduce absenteeism. For example, Mr. Forsyth, Bennie's teacher, may be just delighted that Bennie doesn't attend school regularly. The classroom routine runs so much more smoothly when Bennie is absent. So inadvertently (or possibly not), Mr. Forsyth might sabotage a program designed to ensure Bennie's presence in class. For a program to work successfully in this case, you would need to enlist the teacher's cooperation and also plan a method for making Bennie's presence more reinforcing for his teacher.

Besides assessing the interaction between teacher and students, you should inquire about the policies and practices of the school district, the school administration, and other groups of people whose activities influence school attendance. Often, it is possible to supplement ongoing programs with a seemingly minor yet critical strategy. For instance, your district superintendent may make it a practice to send attendance officers to the homes of students suspected of truancy. It might be possible, while in the neighborhood, for the officer to contact families of students whose attendance has improved and to convey congratulations. Rather than instituting a totally new program, this revision might be preferable, especially if the practice is one considered by all concerned to be readily manageable. Practices that bear resemblance to familiar ones are more apt to be continued, whether or not you remain in the picture.

It is always important to find out how much help you can anticipate from attendance personnel and from district and school administrative staff. Work collaboratively with attendance officers. This is their territory. Seek their advice and enlist their participation. Be certain to obtain the endorsement of the district administrators, along with any assistance they are willing to supply, such as providing data, personnel, procedural modifications, and so on.

Principals can furnish valuable support, morally or materially, or they can impede efforts to remedy school attendance problems. If, for example, the only time Mr. Rodriguez ever inquired about his teachers' health and well-being was following a day when they hadn't been at school, some unplanned reinforcement might be going on. Those contingencies should be rearranged. Principals and their secretarial staffs generally manage data on attendance, which will be crucial to assessing the effectiveness of any program. These people also are the ones who interact most frequently with parents and the public. Thus, their actions in relation to attendance are critically important. They can enlist the cooperation of parents, teachers, students, and members of the community, or they can alienate them. Prudence would tell us that it is best to work closely with the administrative staff in a school, so that its members cooperate and provide the kind of aid necessary for a program to succeed.

Other groups can be enlisted to combat problems related to attendance: special and auxiliary personnel, parents, and community organizations. These people may collaborate in implementing programs to improve attendance by providing material assistance or their own time. Examine the potential wealth of resources in your school and community. You may be pleasantly surprised at the gold mine available. Consider a situation in which local shop owners have been plagued by youngsters who, rather than attend school as they should, loiter about the shops. Losses due to shoplifting are at a peak at those times. The shopowners' association may be delighted to cooperate by supplying material goods to be used as rewards for students whose records of school attendance show improvement.

Assuming that you will want to capitalize on as many potential resources as possible in designing and implementing a program to improve school attendance, you might remind yourself about the factors to consider by referring back to Table 3.1. Included are such people as the superintendent, principals, clerical, professional, and other staff; also space, community resources, and others. As you analyze the role and characteristics of each, examine how each is functioning currently and how each might support or impede your attendance program in the future (see p. 43).

Specify and select goals and objectives

Among the possible goals you might select for a program designed to remedy attendance problems are decreasing rates of student truancy, class cuts, tardiness, unpermitted early departure, and teachers' absenteeism. You also might include some goals related to factors you hypothesize may influence absenteeism rates: decreasing punitive management practices and increasing positive ones, and promoting closer correspondence between students' capabilities and interests and their academic assignments.

You may not be able to realize all of those goals from a practical perspective, so you will need to set some priorities. To guide you in this process, always recognize how important your success will be. Reassess current and potential resources and support networks, and only proceed to work on those goals that you are convinced can reasonably be met.

Let us suppose that you have decided to assign highest priorities to reducing truancy and tardiness among a specific group of students and absenteeism among several teachers. It is time to specify the objectives for those particular individuals.

1. The students involved in the program will reduce their rates of absenteeism by at least 25 percent for the remainder of the school year.
2. These students will reduce the number of times they arrive late to class by at least 30 percent within a month, then maintain that level throughout the school year.
3. The teachers involved will reduce their absenteeism rates to half of the previous year's for the rest of the school year.

Measure the behavior

Whether or not an individual is present or absent is readily discernible. It also is easy to identify which people arrive late. Truancy is another matter, as determining deception is often difficult. We therefore recommend that you focus on attendance or tardiness per se, and not truancy, as the key measures. Where truancy is suspected, handle it within the treatment program by involving the concerned individuals. For example, Brooks (1974) worked out a system with a high school student who was frequently absent without official permission, using attendance as the key measure. The guidance counselor initialed a card each day the student attended. Each initial counted toward various rewards to be delivered by the student's parents. To verify the accuracy of the recording, a form was distributed to each teacher daily. Figure 19.1 displays a facsimile of such a form.

As discussed earlier, personnel in some classes or schools are more careful than others in reporting attendance data. Because you will want valid measures, you may need to find a way to verify reports. We caution you, though, to be certain to do this only with the concurrence of those involved: the administrative and attendance staff and cooperating teachers. In working toward the objectives identified above for students, you might ask their teachers to provide you with their own recordings of those students' attendance. These data then could be assessed for agreement against administrative records. It probably would be best to start out with only a few teachers to test the waters. If things progressed smoothly, other teachers gradually could be involved. In terms of teacher absenteeism, check in advance to be certain that the school keeps accurate records of these data. Otherwise, negotiate an alternative record-keeping system and delay any treatment until an adequate baseline is established. Although this may take several additional months or years, it is the only way you will be able to demonstrate change validly.

IDENTIFY ANTECEDENTS AND CONSEQUENCES THAT CURRENTLY INFLUENCE ATTENDANCE

Earlier in this chapter, we presented a set of factors that often are related to problematic attendance

DAILY ATTENDANCE VERIFICATION

| Last Name | | First Name | Date |

PERIOD	SUBJECT	POSITIVE COMMENTS	TEACHER'S SIGNATURE
1			
2			
3			
4			
5			
6			

This form must be completed and signed by all teachers and returned to the Counselor's Office immediately after 6th period.

Counselor's Signature _____

Student's Signature _____

Figure 19.1
Sample attendance card.

rates. In your setting, conduct an inventory to see if you can identify the same or different factors that influence your students' and staff's attendance. If a punitive climate and a mismatch between students' abilities and academic assignments can be ruled out, try to find out if other factors are at work. Maybe you are located in a farming community and the students are involved in the harvest. Climatic or transportation problems may play a role. Perhaps students are poorly nourished and suffer frequent illness. Are there attractive nuisances in the neighborhood, such as movie theaters or video game arcades that admit youngsters during school hours? Depending on what you identify, the approach to treatment would be quite different. In a farming community, the problem might be ameliorated by altering the school calendar; in another, by teaching students good nutritional habits; in another, it might be necessary to enlist the cooperation of local business people, and so on. No one set of antecedents or consequences will affect attendance universally. You need to look into your own situation closely.

PROGRAMS OF INTERVENTION: ALTERING ANTECEDENTS AND CONSEQUENCES OF ATTENDANCE

By using reliable data on attendance that span a sufficient number of months or years, you will have sufficient information for a reasonable baseline without needing to wait any longer. Then, having obtained the necessary cooperation and support, you are ready to plan and implement a program of change. The most obvious thing to do is to try to alter the antecedents and consequences that you suspect have been promoting absenteeism by modifying them in some way or substituting others of more promise.

Identifying and selecting antecedents and consequences

Table 19.1 lists a sampling of antecedents and consequences that have been altered to improve attendance among students, teachers, and employees

from other occupational settings. We have included the latter because few experimental studies have been conducted to manage absenteeism and tardiness among teachers. You may find it feasible to modify some of those events to meet your own particular requirements. For example, the daily schedule in your district may be unalterable, so you might dismiss "flexitime" as irrelevant to your situation. Yet some aspects of the school program may well be flexible: in-service training schedules, committee meetings, preparation times, and so on. Perhaps bonuses aren't permitted by district regulations. Yet lotteries for extra instructional equipment or supplies may be. Whether or not you find these particular strategies useful, others are available. Carefully reexamine the antecedents and consequences that seem to be controlling attendance and punctuality among students and teachers, and you may discover a set of events that can be managed successfully.

In the following sections, we describe a number of programs that have been used effectively by school districts within specific schools and with individual students and staff. In these descriptions, notice how many basic principles of behavior analysis have been incorporated.

Illustrative programs

In attempting to remedy problematic behavior, you have two basic choices: to punish it directly or to reinforce its desired alternative. Punishing absenteeism makes little sense, for as you already know, punitiveness produces avoidance and escape. It is like attempting to decrease a child's crying by spanking him. The method evokes exactly the behavior you are attempting to halt. Why would a habitually truant youngster want to return to school if returning meant trouble for her? So in this situation, it is almost mandatory to turn to reinforcing attendance and punctuality instead. (Not that mild punishment wouldn't work for the occasional transgressor. It can, but for all the other reasons we have outlined throughout this text, we prefer to emphasize the positive.) Let us, then, describe several illustrative applications of positive approaches to improving attendance and punctuality.

Table 19.1
Improving attendance and punctuality

Population	Strategy	Source
Students	Special reading laboratory plus token economy.	Adwere-Boameh, 1975
	Changes in curriculum.	Neel & DeBruler, 1979; Wilson, 1977
	Tutoring and social skills training.	Fiordaliso, Lordeman, Filipczak, & Friedman, 1977
	Revising disciplinary policies: clearly communicated, fair, individualized; increasing praise, reducing punishment, correctly implementing behavioral procedures by teachers; improving relations between instructional and administrative staff.	Butterworth, Mayer, Nafpaktitis, & Hollingsworth, 1982
Students	Money for lunch from resident staff contingent on either individuals or group attending all classes.	Alexander, Corbett, & Smigel, 1976
	A party and a specific number of "fun rooms" contingent on perfect or near-perfect attendance.	Barber & Kagey, 1977
	Privileges and cash from parents for meeting terms of attendance contracts.	Brooks, 1974
	Tokens (to be used in a lottery) for attending classes and for positive comments from teachers.	Brooks, 1975
	Tokens for being on time and for good attendance, exchangeable for cash.	Brown, Copeland, & Hall, 1972
	Positive phone calls to parents for improved attendance.	Fiordaliso et al., 1977
	Loss of course credits for absenteeism or tardiness.	Garcia, 1979
	Daily report cards, contracts, points toward grade contingent on punctuality.	Potthoff, 1979
	Course credit, discussion of topics to be on quiz contingent on attendance.	Lloyd, Garlington, Lowry, Burgess, Euler, & Knowlton, 1972
	Access to family car, pool hall, privileges, movies, time with peers, contingent on school attendance.	MacDonald, Gallimore, & MacDonald, 1970

Table 19.1
Improving attendance and punctuality (*continued*)

Population	Strategy	Source
Teachers	Monetary incentives for month of perfect attendance.	Nord, 1970
	Suggested: reward good attendance with bonus from money saved; praise in person or in writing; include data on attendance in evaluation reports and letters; requiring documentation for absences; involving teachers in monitoring; evaluating teacher absences.	Manlove & Elliott, 1979
	Suggested: "Dinners, cash awards, paid tuition for courses, attendance at special workshops— whatever works for you."	Lewis, 1981 (p. 40)
Employees in nonschool settings	Cards from poker deck for punctual attendance; highest poker hand at end of week wins $20.	Pedalino & Gamboa, 1974
	Commendation letter for reaching preset attendance criterion; supervisory counseling and a lottery system.	Shoemaker & Reid, 1980
	Token economy and feedback.	Kent, Malott, & Greening, 1977
	Weekly and yearly bonuses contingent on attendance.	Orpen, 1978
	Pay scale adjusted as a function of attendance.	Kopelman & Schneller, 1981
	Cash prize drawings for no absenteeism during specific time periods.	Stephens & Burroughs, 1978
	Workers involved in development of incentive program.	Lawler & Hackman, 1969
	Permitting employees flexible work schedules.	Reid, Shuh-Wear, & Brannon, 1978; Pierce, Hoffman, & Pelletier, 1974; Kim & Campagna, 1981

Commendation. The simplest system, and one often used, is to give public recognition to students whose attendance is exemplary by awarding them certificates, pins, or other tokens. Figure 19.2 displays a perfect attendance award issued to students who attended Meller Junior High School in Los Angeles County for a particular number of consecutive days. Attendance awards often are distributed at the end of the school year, a rather lengthy delay, particularly for students attempting to remedy a poor

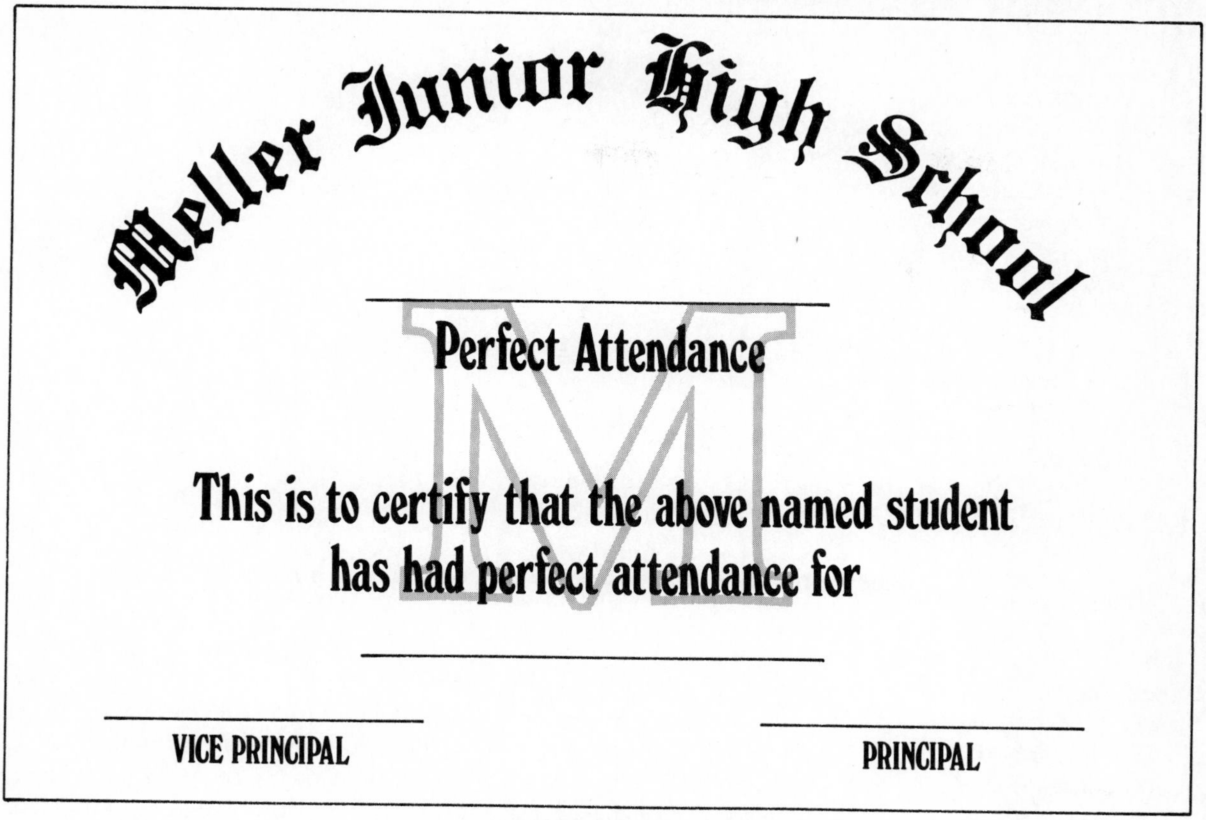

Meller Junior High School

Perfect Attendance

This is to certify that the above named student has had perfect attendance for

---

VICE PRINCIPAL   PRINCIPAL

Figure 19.2
Attendance certificate.

attendance record. Also, the first absence signals the loss of the award. It is important, then, to modify the time schedule so *approximations* to perfect attendance can be rewarded.

Fiordaliso et al. (1977) handled this challenge by adjusting positive consequences to the individual student's current pattern of attendance. Besides following the standard practice of informing the student's parents of their child's absence, and expressing concern, the school contacted the parents by phone or letter to offer congratulations when the child's attendance improved. (A sample letter is shown in Figure 19.3.) Contacts were gradually and progressively extended in time, an ideal arrangement for supporting maintenance. For example, while the absence rate was high, (i.e., six or more days per month) the student was recognized with a

positive phone call or letter for every three consecutive days of attendance. This procedure was continued until the student achieved two consecutive weeks with no absences. Once that criterion was achieved, recognition was given after four consecutive days of school attendance. After another two consecutive weeks of zero absences, five consecutive days were required for the positive recognition. The schedule continued to be extended until absenteeism stabilized at one or less over two months. The authors of the study also reported a special advantage — this program can be carried out by a single aide, under supervision, in about an hour a day.

High school students often enjoy a competitive situation. In one such school, South High in Torrance, California, attendance was compared within and across class periods and departments. A winner

---

Dear Parents:
I am happy to inform you that your son/daughter, _____, has
been on time to _____ period for _____ days in a row. This is a marked
improvement. I anticipate that he/she will experience greater success in
class as a result.
  Thank you for working together with your child and the school to achieve
and maintain improved attendance.

Sincerely,

Counselor or Teacher

Figure 19.3
Sample letter to parents—improved attendance.

was declared for each period—first, second, third, and so on—over a two-week interval. The winners within each period then competed across periods over the next two weeks. Winners representing departments then competed for the title of all-school champion. (In the meantime, classes eliminated from the tournament were not ignored. They were permitted to enter an attendance improvement contest. Thus, classes with 100 percent attendance *and* those showing an improvement over the previous two weeks also were eligible to win.) At South High, winning classes received a framed certificate initially. To this, stars were affixed for each subsequent victory. Other rewards for winners included publication of the students' names in the school newspaper, tickets for a drawing to be held at the end of the competition, special pencils, and movies. The vice-principal reported that attendance increased significantly.

Tardiness was a serious problem at a junior high school (Butterworth, 1980). Between 6 and 10 percent of the students were tardy to their first and fifth class periods. To counteract this, the fifth-period homeroom class showing the best record of punctuality was promised a trip to the local arboretum. Also, any student who was punctual nine times out

of ten won a free ticket to the school dance. Every student but four won the tickets, and punctuality was perfect in the winning homeroom class. When the program was extended later to the first period, results were similar, showing an increase from 83 to 95 percent of the students arriving to their classes on time.

Here is how a junior high school in Southern California handled its difficulties with attendance and punctuality: rewarding activities were set up in special rooms during each class period one day every two weeks. These included film showings, a talent show, a fashion showing of sewing projects by the home economics classes, and various free or low-cost rewarding activities provided by the school and local community. All students who punctually attended the corresponding period each day for two weeks were excused from that regular class period to attend one of the activities. The others were required to complete their class assignments instead. Students with perfect records in all classes were able to attend several special reward sessions on that day.

At another junior high school, a drawing was held biweekly. Each class was assigned an identifying numeral. Five numbers then were chosen at random, signifying the classes eligible for the next phase. Students in each eligible class were assigned new numbers, and those numbers were pooled for the drawing. When a number was drawn, the student was identified and his or her attendance record over the past two weeks checked. If it was perfect, the student was awarded a prize. If not, another number was drawn for that class until a winner was found. Absenteeism among seventh graders diminished from an average of approximately 45 to 10 or less.

In another junior high school, the pool of names was generated by computer and a potential winner selected from each grade level. Again, to win, the students had to have perfect records in the interim. Prizes included items from the school store and an attendance award. The names of winners also were published in the weekly bulletin, and parents were called and congratulated. In both of these cases, the schools achieved a major impact with a minimum of effort and time. An average decrease of 7 percent in unexcused absences occurred over the previous year's level (Mayer et al., 1983).

Consequences natural to the school program also can be arranged to promote punctuality and attendance. Some teachers we know write the answers to an upcoming quiz or homework assignment on the board before the beginning of the period, erasing information when the bell rings to signal the start of class. Others administer short quizzes first thing. In one school, students who received five tardy marks were suspended. To convert this situation into a more reinforcing one, the teacher and class successfully negotiated a practice of removing a tardy mark from a student's record in exchange for each sequence of five consecutive days on which the student arrived promptly (a nice example of negative reinforcement). By pairing this procedure with a great deal of praise for punctuality, the teacher was able to diminish tardiness to nearly zero for the remainder of the school year. Some teachers send letters to parents informing them when their children are tardy regularly, but they *also* follow with other letters commending demonstrated improvement.

Punctual attendance at extracurricular and other special activities is often a problem, especially because no powerful consequences control the behavior; neither grades nor promotion are at risk. Again,

self-recorded and publicly posted data can come to the rescue. McKenzie and Rushall (1974) found themselves in such a predicament with a competitive community swim team, consisting of youngsters from 9 to 16 years of age. The problem was virtually eliminated when students recorded their attendance on a large display board, first for simply attending, next for attending punctually, and ultimately for remaining throughout the full session. [In a second phase, the same procedure was used to promote the development of specific skills, which resulted in the team's moving from "relative obscurity to provincial prominence" (McKenzie & Rushall, 1974, p. 205).] You might try to use this sort of procedure to promote regular and timely attendance at remedial, social skills, and other special classes, clubs, and other volunteer activities. Figure 19.4 displays an illustrative attendance poster.

Reentry programs. Students who are *chronically truant* present a particularly challenging problem for themselves and their teachers and classmates. Besides taking up the teacher's time and attention in an effort to catch up, the students probably recognize that they have fallen out of step with their peers, a situation most easily avoided by not returning in the first place. One way of handling this is a *reentry* program—a special class set up to provide these students with intensive instruction in the subject areas in need of remediation. If, as is often the case, the chronic truants in your school also experience difficulties in relating interpersonally with their peers and teachers, they also might be included in a program designed to assist them to develop the social skills they are lacking (see Chapter 18). As they begin to show substantial progress academically and socially, it should be possible *gradually* to mainstream them back into their regular classrooms.

Behavioral contracts. Individual students with histories of problematic attendance and punctuality often can receive the boost they need by means of a **behavioral contract.** As we've seen earlier, the contract stipulates goals and procedures with sufficient clarity and detail that all in-

ATTENDANCE

DATE—NOVEMBER

CONSECUTIVE DAYS OF ATTENDANCE

NAME	2	3	4	5	6	9	10	11	12	13	16	17	18	19	20	23	24	25	26	27	CURRENT	BEST
Gerald	✓	✓	✓	✓	✓																5	5
Margarita			✓	✓	✓																3	5
Elizabeth				✓																	1	4
Tom	✓	✓	✓	✓	✓																5	5
Ray	✓	✓	✓	✓	✓																5	5
Mary	✓	✓	✓	✓	✓																5	5
Pam	✓	✓	✓	✓	✓																5	5

PERFECT ATTENDANCE!

Figure 19.4
Public recognition of attendance.
(Developed by Mary Nafpaktitis)

volved are aware of their mutual responsibilities and benefits. Beware, though. Contracts function best only under certain circumstances; simply negotiating and writing a contract is but the beginning. Here are some important guidelines for you to review if you hope for success in using contracting to improve attendance and punctuality.

1. *Stress the positive.* Emphasize what *will* be done, not what should not be done: "Billy will attend school daily, punctually at 8:15 A.M." (Not— "Bennie will not play truant or be tardy.")

2. *Request and reinforce small improvements.* You need to follow the basic rule of shaping here: reinforce successive approximations. It is important to succeed regularly, both for the student's sake as well as your own. Starting where the student is and moving forward in small steps is the way to proceed. Billy only attended school 50 percent of the time. The first contract stipulated that he should attend at least three days a week. (Later contracts required four out of five days; nine out of ten, and so on.)

3. *Clarify the terms of the contract.* All concerned must know exactly what is required of them within what time period, what consequences each will provide and when, how, and how much they will assist: "Each day Billy arrives at

school on time he is to go immediately to Mrs. Olsen to have his card signed. Then he will show the signed card to his teacher, Mr. Truax, who will compliment his punctual attendance. At the end of the two-week period, if Billy has signatures, Mr. Truax will send a note home to his parents. After receiving five such notes, his parents will buy him a book of his choice."

4. *Reinforce the target behavior immediately.* You already know the importance of immediate reinforcement. Under a contractual arrangement, though, immediate reinforcement also helps the student to discriminate that meeting the terms of the contract is paired with reinforcement. (Note just above how immediately reinforcing events are used to bridge the time gap between Billy's attendance and the tangible reward of a book.)

5. *Include an option to withdraw or modify the terms of the contract.* When you negotiate the terms of a contract, you are, after all, collectively making your best guesses about what circumstances are likely to produce success. If your predictions have been imperfect, so be it. The terms of the contract need to be modified. Perhaps, in Billy's case, one of the schedules was overly ambitious. The contract could be renegotiated to enhance chances for success. Permitting participants to withdraw from contractual arrangements also would be reasonable under certain circumstances, but those circumstances need to be spelled out. Billy might reach the point when he felt he no longer needed such a contrivance. A clause such as the following would allow for that: "At such a point that Billy has attended school punctually for four weeks in a row, except in cases of documented emergencies, he may opt to discontinue the contractual arrangement for a trial period of one month. Assuming his good record continues, no further contracts need be negotiated."

6. *Weigh costs and benefits for all participants.* When costs are too great or benefits too small for any participants in a contractual arrangement, the program has little chance of long-range success. People will drop out or neglect to meet their obligations. To avoid this problem, pause to take inventory of both. Itemize the immediate and long-range academic, social, and personal advantages to the student, as well as the benefits to school officials, staff, teachers, parents, and the public. Also list costs in terms of time, money, effort, and even such subtle factors as loss of power or control. If the latter clearly outweigh the former, modify the program to make it more practical. When an initial conference was held among Billy, Mrs. Olsen, Mr. Truax, and Billy's parents, the adults asked Billy what sort of reward he would like for attending school regularly. Billy asked to be taken to the World Series, a request his parents obviously would be unable to fulfill as it was well beyond their financial means. Instead, Mr. Truax helped them negotiate the arrangement described above—the prize of a book.

Contracts can vary in format. No ideal standard exists. You may wish, though, to see a sample contract. The illustration in Figure 19.5 depicts a contract developed by Brooks (1975) and successfully used by a group of truants. Figure 19.6 is a contract form used by a school district where one of the authors consults. Regardless of the formality involved—from an oral agreement to an officially notarized document—the attendance contract is a device that has demonstrated its potential as a tool to help control attendance and punctuality problems.

Daily report cards. The **daily report card** system is particularly well suited to the improvement of attendance and punctuality. The daily report card is a device for informing parents about particular aspects of their children's performance on a particular day. Unlike the traditional report card, it focuses on the positive and usually incorporates an agreement between home and school as to the consequences the parents will deliver as a function of what is recorded on the card that day.

The card that Billy brought home to his parents was a form of a daily report card, despite the fact that he didn't bring it home every day. It isn't essential that the card be sent home every single day. The

Name _____

Date _____

Problem: During the first 8 weeks of school I have had ____ days of truancy. I agree that this is excessive and will follow the procedures below so that I might reduce the number of days truant.

Provisions: I, _____, agree to the following:

1. I will attend school every day. If I miss school it will be for an excused illness or doctor's appointment and I agree to bring a note from home.
2. At the end of each school day I will record my attendance on a chart in the counselor's office.
3. Each morning I will pick up a green attendance card in the counselor's office, complete the card, have it initialed by each teacher for each class I attend, and exchange the card with my counselor according to the provisions of the reward schedule posted in the counselor's office.
4. I agree to attend all scheduled group meetings. I understand that this is a binding contract and I agree to abide by all the provisions herein.

_____
(Student's signature)

Counselor's Statement and Agreement:
I understand that this is a binding contract between _____ and my-self, and I agree to the provisions herein.

_____
(Counselor's signature)

Reward Schedule

Provisions:
In order to help you develop habits of attendance you will be rewarded for the classes you attend. Gradually, the rewards that you earn will be withdrawn in the hope that other rewards (success in class, less nagging by parents, freedom from that feeling of "getting caught" for skipping) will take over. During this 8-week project you will be rewarded in the following manner for attending classes.

Weeks 1, 2, and 3
1. For each signature you receive on the green card you will be given a ticket for the drawing at the end of the 3 weeks.
2. For each positive (good) comment written by a teacher on the green card you will be given a bonus ticket.
3. For every 5 full days of class you attend without missing any classes you will receive five bonus tickets the first 5-days, ten bonus tickets for the second 5 (10 in a row), and fifteen for the third 5 (15 in a row). If you attend 15 days without missing a class you will have earned thirty bonus tickets.
4. A drawing will be held at the end of the first 3 weeks. If you attended all your classes for 3 weeks you would have been given at least 120 chances. So you can see the more you attend the better chance of winning the prizes listed below:
   First prize $10.00
   Second prize   5.00

Figure 19.5

Attendance contract. [From Brooks, B. D. (1975). Contingency management as a means of reducing school truancy, *Education, 95,* 206–211]

Third prize	3.00
Fourth through tenth prizes	1.00 each

Weeks 4, 5, 6, and 7
  The same procedure as weeks 1, 2, and 3 will be followed. The prizes are listed below:

First prize	4 tickets to drive-in movie
Second prize	2 tickets to Cinema Theatre
Third prize	2 albums (33⅓)
Fourth prize	1 album (33⅓)
Fifth through tenth prizes	$2.00 gift certificates

Week 8
  During the last week no prizes will be awarded. We will have two group meetings during which we will discuss attendance and related topics. You must continue, however, to turn in your green card daily.

Figure 19.5
Attendance Contract (*continued*)

system may function just as effectively and even be preferred by parents and teachers when cards are delivered intermittently, as Saudargas, Madsen, and Scott (1977) found. We recommend that you carefully examine the student's current level of functioning when planning a schedule for sending home the report card. If it is important to harness substantial support from parents early in a program, you might start out sending the card each day, later on diminishing the schedule to a less frequent one.

Several cases in which daily report cards have been used to manage attendance have been reported in the literature. Brooks (1974) found the device helpful in his work with junior high school truants. Similarly, Schumaker, Hovell, and Sherman (1977a,b) reported its successful use by counselors who assisted junior high school students to attend school more regularly and improve their conduct and academic performance.

Programs for school phobics. The approach for dealing with school phobia depends in part on the student's reaction and the variables controlling it. If the behavior appears strictly to be one of avoiding an unpleasant situation, you would attempt to alter the punitive stimuli that have become associated with the school. If the parent's actions reinforce the child for remaining home, then you would have to work cooperatively with the parents so those consequences can be altered. Approaches

like these have been applied by Ayllon, Smith, and Rogers (1970), Doleys and Williams (1977), and others. For example, parents have been instructed to commend their child for attending school or for commenting positively on the experience, and to withhold reinforcement for not attending school or for commenting negatively about it. When school personnel and parents act in similar ways, the desired results are more likely to be achieved.

You may be faced with a different sort of challenge when the school phobic suffers intense and pervasive anxiety in response to stimuli associated with school. Teachers and guidance counselors or psychologists can work together to help these children. They might supplement the strategies suggested above with a treatment designed to deal directly with the anxiety per se. **Systematic desensitization** is one such method (Wolpe, 1958). With systematic desensitization, the client learns to relax[2] in the presence of the formerly feared stimuli: first, stimuli associated with the feared event are arranged in a hierarchy from the least to the most feared (e.g., seeing pictures of a school, hearing a bell resembling the one at school, seeing the school bus, getting on it, arriving at school, seeing the building, getting off the bus, entering the building, entering the classroom, and so on). Each individual's hierarchy of feared stimuli

[2]See J. R. Cautela and J. Groden (1975).

This contract is between＿＿＿＿＿＿＿＿＿＿＿＿＿＿＿＿＿＿ (student)
and＿＿＿＿＿＿＿＿＿＿＿＿＿＿＿＿＿＿＿＿＿＿ (teacher, friend, other)
Date: from＿＿＿＿＿＿＿＿＿＿＿＿to＿＿＿＿＿＿＿＿＿＿
                (this date)   (contract expiration)
Following are the terms of the contract:
＿＿＿＿＿＿＿＿＿＿＿＿＿＿ (student) will＿＿＿＿＿＿＿＿＿＿
＿＿＿＿＿＿＿＿＿＿＿＿＿＿＿＿＿＿＿＿＿＿＿＿＿＿＿＿＿＿＿
＿＿＿＿＿＿＿＿＿＿＿＿＿＿＿＿＿＿＿＿＿＿＿＿＿＿＿＿＿＿＿
＿＿＿＿＿＿＿＿＿＿＿ (teacher, friend, other) will＿＿＿＿＿＿
＿＿＿＿＿＿＿＿＿＿＿＿＿＿＿＿＿＿＿＿＿＿＿＿＿＿＿＿＿＿＿
＿＿＿＿＿＿＿＿＿＿＿＿＿＿＿＿＿＿＿＿＿＿＿＿＿＿＿＿＿＿＿
When this contract is completed, the contractee will be able to＿＿＿＿＿
＿＿＿＿＿＿＿＿＿＿＿＿＿＿＿＿＿＿＿＿＿＿＿＿＿＿＿＿＿＿＿
＿＿＿＿＿＿＿＿＿＿＿＿＿＿＿＿＿＿＿＿＿＿＿＿＿＿＿＿＿＿＿
＿＿＿＿＿＿＿＿＿＿＿＿＿＿＿＿＿＿＿＿＿＿＿＿＿＿＿＿＿＿＿
＿＿＿＿＿＿＿＿＿＿＿＿＿＿＿＿＿＿＿＿＿＿＿＿＿＿＿＿＿＿＿

＿＿＿＿＿＿＿＿＿＿＿＿＿＿   ＿＿＿＿＿＿＿＿＿＿＿＿＿
Contractee   Contractor

＿＿＿＿＿＿＿＿＿＿＿＿＿＿
Witness

This contract may
be terminated by
agreement of parties
signing this contract.
New contract(s) may be
negotiated by the same
parties.

Figure 19.6
Sample contract form.

may be different from another's. Treatment starts by teaching the client to relax in the presence of either the actual or imagined stimulus. If you plan to attempt this method, try to use the actual stimulus to facilitate generalization. Once the student is able to relax in the presence of the least feared stimulus, proceed on to the next, and so on, until he or she is able to relax in the presence of the most feared stimulus. Naturally, it makes great sense to reinforce each progressive step as it is accomplished. In this way, systematic relaxation is combined with shaping to enhance the total effectiveness of treatment.

Prout and Harvey (1978) have outlined several steps to follow in treating school phobics. We have summarized them below:

1. Train the student in relaxation procedures.
2. Attempt to remove all sources of reinforcement for staying home.
3. Implement desensitization. (We also would recommend using a shaping procedure.)
4. Reinforce progress.
5. Implement program daily.

Programs for staff

As mentioned previously, little experimental evidence can be found documenting effective programs to manage absenteeism among school personnel, although some evidence exists among employees of other organizations. Here we describe a few approaches for you to consider adapting to your own school setting.

Pay incentives or bonuses have been found to be successful in several instances (Lawler & Hackman, 1969; Orpen, 1978; Pedalino & Gamboa, 1974). In one of those programs (Lawler & Hackman, 1969), the authors also investigated the importance of involving the affected workers in the development of the program. For three groups, workers devised the incentive plan; for another two, this same plan was imposed on them without their involvement in its development; four other groups received no treatment at all. The plan had an immediate and significant impact on the three groups who participated in devising the plan, but none on the others. This finding once more underscores how important it is to encourage those involved to participate in developing procedures of staff management that will affect them.

Before dismissing the notion of including an incentive plan in your organization, consider what the parents and school board members of Agua Fria High School in Phoenix, Arizona did in an attempt to reduce staff turnover. They formed a nonprofit foundation through which to solicit funds to be used to recognize outstanding teachers. Recently, five teachers were awarded $1,200 each, a gesture that would surely help them feel appreciated (Mayer et al., 1983).

Absenteeism among staff at residential institutions for clients with special needs is often a major problem. Shoemaker and Reid (1980) successfully implemented an inexpensive program designed to discourage unnecessary absences and use of sick leave at such a setting. A group of chronically absent staff members was counseled at four-week intervals. During the sessions, the counselor reviewed the staff member's attendance record for the intervening period and delivered positive or corrective feedback, as appropriate. Those with a perfect record for the previous four weeks were given letters of commendation and were eligible to participate in a lottery. Prizes included being treated to lunch by the supervisor; relief from lunchroom duty for a day; being allowed to rearrange their schedule; or receiving coverage for a client-training session by the supervisor. It would take little imagination to translate those practices into the school program. For example, the principal could take over lunch duty or substitute for a period in class as a reward for good attendance.

At a residential treatment center for the retarded, staff members were asked to identify a nonmonetary reward they might receive for reduced rates of unscheduled leave ("defined as the number of hours any staff member was not at work on the unit as previously scheduled," Durand, 1983, p. 108). The staff selected an additional eight hours of scheduled leave, provided the staff member did not use unscheduled leave during the entire month. When this contingency was put in place, the mean of unscheduled leave diminished by 3.3 percent, while the mean percentage of scheduled leave increased by only about half that amount—for an excellent net savings. Even more impressive was the finding that when the intervention was in effect, 16 of the 27 residents of the target unit displayed major decreases in disruption (greater than 15 percent), while the deportment of most of the others remained the same. Even if staff members were sick, the loss for that month would not be so crucial that they would feel compelled to come to work if they were seriously ill. Next month, another opportunity to earn extra leave would present itself.

Should a school district balk at the idea of permitting extra scheduled leave (although the idea seems reasonable to us, as the net gain could be significant), other rewards might be considered: released lunchroom, bus, study hall, or playground duty; preferred class or committee assignments; or many of the other reinforcers mentioned elsewhere in this chapter and in Chapter 22. It would be interesting to see if school staff would respond as the instititional staff did. Perhaps improved student deportment and productivity would also accompany improvements in teacher attendance. That would be a pleasant discovery!

Informational feedback often produces amazing results. Silva, Duncan, and Doudna (1981) simply charted attendance and posted it in a conspicuous place in the working area. As a result, absenteeism diminished by 50 percent.

EVALUATING PROGRAMS FOR IMPROVING ATTENDANCE AND PUNCTUALITY

Obviously, much research remains to be done in the area of absenteeism and punctuality, especially among school personnel. A reasonable starting place would be to try implementing those procedures that have shown promise elsewhere, in other educational or organizational settings. If you decide to test one of those with your students or staff, we hope you will be certain to establish a solid baseline first and then test the procedure sequentially across different groups (i.e., multiple baseline design), withdraw it temporarily to show a drop-off, and then replace it (i.e., withdrawal design) or use a control group to demonstrate the validity of the outcomes. Then, assuming the results are promising, they should be communicated to the profession and the public.

MAINTAINING CHANGE

Change will not maintain by magic. As in dealing with other areas of problematic performance, attendance and punctuality will sustain over time only with environmental support, which is most apt to happen in a school atmosphere in which students are achieving successfully and management and motivation practices are positive. Contrived reinforcers, especially tangible rewards, may produce eventual satiation, although this isn't always the case. You might try shifting to enjoyable activities and events more intrinsic to the school program after the problem has been alleviated reasonably. Also, adjust the schedule of reinforcement to make it gradually more intermittent and build in delay of reinforcement gradually, continuing to support the change with natural, unobtrusive reinforcers in the interim, like pleasant greetings, praise, and others so familiar to you by now. In this way, both students and staff will find the quality of their life in school much enhanced.

Summary

Coping with absenteeism and tardiness among students and staff constitutes a particularly serious concern for school officials. Attempts to deal with truancy and tardiness have ranged from no systematic plans to carefully arranged contingencies. Unfortunately, such arranged contingencies frequently tend to be punitive. We recognize this practice to be self-defeating, as punishment may further contribute toward escape and avoidance in the form of absenteeism and tardiness, the very problems one is attempting to prevent. To reverse this trend, two major strategies need to be addressed:

1. Sources of punishment within the school program that may be provoking attendance problems need to be identified and eliminated.
2. Reinforcement for accomplishments on the job, in academic and social performance, and especially for improvements in attendance and punctuality needs to replace a reliance on punishment.

Exchanging a punitive for a reinforcing school environment is no small feat. As we've seen elsewhere, support must be obtained from many sources: the community, parents, administrators, pupil personnel specialists, teachers, and the students themselves. Though a formidable task, it is not impossible. In this chapter, we have shown how this end can be accomplished in a variety of ways, and in many sorts of educational and other organizations. We hope that some of the suggestions will be applicable to your situation. Give them a reasonable try. You may find, to your delight, that your school environment has become a more pleasant place of work for staff, students, and for yourself.

Study Questions

1. List several educational hardships produced by teacher absenteeism.
2. Identify two ways of coping with the problem of absenteeism among students and staff.
3. Describe the vicious cycle that is generated by students whose scholastic performance is punishing or nonreinforcing.
4. Explain in detail how delivering punishment can become its own source of reinforcement.
5. Discuss in detail the fact that the social environments of many classrooms are conducive to student absenteeism, as well as the relation between absenteeism and the level of academic assignments.
6. Charlie does not interact positively with his peers and frequently is absent from school. Offer a suggestion to help solve this problem.
7. Define *school phobia*.
8. State several factors thought to contribute to school phobia.
9. Several of the teachers at the Wilson Street School are adversely affected by the negative school climate. Describe in detail factors that may be related to this problem.
10. You believe that absenteeism is a problem at your school, and you would like to use a behavioral program to improve the situation. State several questions that you should attempt to answer before beginning a program.
11. List the forms of assessment you should complete before implementing a program.
12. Mr. Foss believes that he should try to improve an ongoing program before instituting a new one. Present an argument in support of his opinion.
13. Identify the people whose help you should solicit and the resources you should check when designing a program to reduce absenteeism. (You may find it helpful to refer back to Table 3.1.)
14. State several reasons for including principals and their secretarial staffs in your plans.
15. Staff members feel that they need additional help and resources to combat the attendance problem at their school. Suggest several people or places outside of the school to which they can turn for assistance.
16. Review Figure 16.1 and list those individuals

or groups whom you would not want to overlook if you were designing a program to reduce attendance problems.

17. (a) State one goal for a program to remedy attendance problems and (b) provide the criteria you used to make that decision. (c) Specify the objectives for the students involved in your program.

18. Discuss the importance of measuring the target behavior.

19. Provide an original narrative illustrating that both an antecedent and a consequential event can be related to an attendance problem.

20. Compare the effectiveness of punishment and reinforcement in reducing absenteeism.

21. Design a simple original program using reinforcement to reduce (a) absenteeism and (b) tardiness in your school. (Be sure to include approximations to the desired response.)

22. (a) Define behavioral contract. (b) State the guidelines for successful behavioral contracting.

23. Discuss the purpose of using a daily report card.

24. Andrea says she has school phobia but does not suffer from intense and pervasive anxiety in response to stimuli associated with school. Describe a plan to solve her problem. (Be sure to involve the teacher and parents.)

25. Wendy is severely affected by her school phobia. She gets sick and has migraine headaches each morning before school. Her parents have heard that systematic desensitization might help, but do not know anything about it. Briefly describe the procedure as you would explain it to them.

26. Outline several steps to follow in treating school phobia.

27. Provide an original plan to increase teacher attendance.

28. List three ways to demonstrate the validity of the outcomes of your program.

29. Discuss in detail ways to ensure that the change will be maintained.

30. Describe in detail a *reentry program*.

31. List several consequences that are natural to the school environment and may be used to reduce tardiness and absenteeism.

References

Adwere-Boameh, J. (1975). *Project MACK*. Final evaluation report 1974–75. Oakland Unified School District, CA.

Alexander, R. N., Corbett, T. F., & Smigel, J. (1976). The effects of individual and group consequences on school attendance and curfew violations with pre-delinquent adolescents. *Journal of Applied Behavior Analysis, 9,* 221–226.

Ayllon, T., Smith, D., & Rogers, M. (1970). Behavioral management of school phobia. *Journal of Behavior Therapy and Experimental Psychiatry, 1,* 125–138.

Barber, R. M., & Kagey, J. R. (1977). Modification of school attendance for an elementary population. *Journal of Applied Behavior Analysis, 10,* 41–48.

Brodinsky, B. (1980). *AASA critical issues report. Student discipline, problems and solutions.* AASA, 1801 N. Moore St., Arlington, VA 22209 (#021-00334).

Brooks, B. D. (1974). Contingency contracts with truants. *Personnel and Guidance Journal, 52,* 316–320.

Brooks, B. D. (1975). Contingency management as a means of reducing school truancy, *Education, 95,* 206–211.

Brown, R. E., Copeland, R. E., & Hall, R. V. (1972). The school principal as a behavior modifier. *The Journal of Educational Research, 66,* 175–180.

Butterworth, T. (1980). *Strategies for reducing violence and vandalism. Prevention through remediation of contributing factors.* Office of the Los Angeles County Superintendent of Schools. 9300 E. Imperial Highway, Los Angeles, CA, 90242.

Butterworth, T., Mayer, G. R., Nafpaktitis. M., & Hollingsworth, P. (1982). *Constructive discipline: Improving attendance and reducing disruption and vandalism costs.* Office of the Los Angeles County Superintendent of Schools. An ESEA, Title IV-C end-of-year evaluation report.

Cautela, J. R., & Groden, J. (1975). *Relaxation: A Comprehensive manual for adults, children, and children with special needs.* Champaign, IL: Research Press.

Copeland, R. E., Brown, R. E., & Hall, R. V. (1974). The effects of principal-implemented techniques on the behavior of pupils. *Journal of Applied Behavior Analysis,* 7, 77–86.

Doleys, D. M., & Williams, S. C. (1977). The use of natural consequences and a make-up period to eliminate school phobic behavior: A case study. *Journal of School Psychology,* 15, 44–50.

Durand, V. M. (1983). Behavioral ecology of a staff incentive program. *Behavior Modification,* 7, 165–181.

Fiordaliso, R., Lordeman, A., Filipczak, J., & Friedman, R. M. (1977). Effects of feedback on absenteeism in the junior high school. *Journal of Educational Research,* 70, 188–192.

Garcia, E. J. (1979). Instant quarter-credit concept—an answer to class cutting? *NASSP Bulletin,* 63, 39–43.

Heller, M. C., & White, M. A. (1975). Rates of teacher verbal approval and disapproval to higher and lower ability classes. *Journal of Educational Psychology,* 67, 796–800.

Kennedy, W. A. (1965). School phobia: Rapid treatment of 50 cases. *Journal of Abnormal Psychology,* 70, 285–289.

Kent, H. M., Malott, R. W., & Greening, M. (1977). Improving attendance at work in a volunteer food cooperative with a token economy. *Journal of Organizational Behavior Management,* 1, 89–98.

Kim, J. S., & Campagna, A. F. (1981). Effects of flexitime on employee attendance and performance. *Academy of Management Journal,* 24, 729–741.

Kopelman, R. E., & Schneller, G. O. (1981). A mixed-consequence system for reducing overtime and unscheduled absences. *Journal of Organizational Behavior Management,* 3, 17–28.

Lawler, E. E., III, & Hackman, J. R. (1969). Impact of employee participation in the development of pay incentive plans: A field experiment. *Journal of Applied Psychology,* 53, 467–471.

Lazarus, A. A., Davison, G. C., & Polefka, D. (1965). Classical and operant factors in the treatment of a school phobia. *Journal of Abnormal Psychology,* 70, 225–229.

Levante, J. (1979, October). High school absenteeism. *National Secondary School Principals' Bulletin,* pp. 100–103.

Lewis, J., Jr. (1981). Do you encourage teacher absenteeism? *The American School Board Journal,* 168, 29–30.

Lloyd, K. E., Garlington, W. K., Lowry, D., Burgess, H., Euler, H. A., & Knowlton, W. R. (1972). A note on some reinforcing properties of university lectures. *Journal of Applied Behavior Analysis,* 5, 151–155.

MacDonald, W. S., Gallimore, R., & MacDonald, G. (1970). Contingency counseling by school personnel: An economical model of intervention. *Journal of Applied Behavior Analysis,* 3, 175–182.

Manlove, D. C., & Elliott, P. (1979). Absent teachers . . . Another handicap for students? *The Practitioner,* 5, 2–13.

Mayer, G. R., Butterworth, T. W., Spaulding, H. L., Hollingsworth, P., Amorim, M., Caldwell-McElroy, C., Nafpaktitis, M., & Perez-Osrio, X. (1983). *Constructive discipline—building a climate for learning. A resource manual of programs and strategies.* Los Angeles: Office of the Los Angeles County Superintendent of Schools, Downey, CA.

McKenzie, T. L., & Rushall, B. S. (1974). Effects of self-recording on attendance and performance in a competitive swimming training environment. *Journal of Applied Behavior Analysis,* 7, 199–206.

Nafpaktitis, M., Mayer, G. R., & Butterworth, T. (In press.) Natural rates of teacher approval and disapproval and their relations to student behavior in intermediate school classroom. *Journal of Educational Psychology.*

Neel, R. S., & DeBruler, L. (1979). The effects of self-management of school attendance by problem adolescents. *Adolescence,* 14, 175–184.

Nord, W. (1970). Improving attendance through rewards. *Personnel Administration,* 33, 37–41.

Orpen, C. (1978). Effects of bonuses for attendance on absenteeism of industrial workers. *Journal of Organizational Behavior Management,* 1, 118–124.

Pedalino, E., & Gamboa, V. U. (1974). Behavior modification and absenteeism: Intervention in one industrial setting. *Journal of Applied Psychology,* 59, 694–698.

Pierce, P. S., Hoffman, J. L., & Pelletier, L. P. (1974). The 4-day work week versus the 5-day work week: Comparative use of such time and over-time by direct-care personnel in an institutional facility for the severely and profoundly retarded. *Mental Retardation,* 12, 22–24.

Potthoff, J. O. (1979). Three techniques to reduce tardiness in secondary learning handicapped students. *Teaching Exceptional Children,* 11, 146–148.

Prout, H. T., & Harvey, J. R. (1978). Applications of desensitization procedures for school-related problems: A review. *Psychology in the Schools,* 15, 533–541.

Reid, D. H., Shuh-Wear, C. L., & Brannon, M. E. (1978). The use of a group contingency to decrease absenteeism at a state institution. *Behavior Modification,* 2, 251–266.

Saudargas, R. W., Madsen, C. H., Jr., & Scott, J. W. (1977). Differential effects of fixed- and variable-time feedback on production rates of elementary school children. *Journal of Applied Behavior Analysis, 10,* 673–678.

Schumaker, J. B., Hovell, M. F., & Sherman, J. A. (1977a). An analysis of daily report cards and parent-managed privileges in the improvement of adolescents' classroom performance. *Journal of Applied Behavior Analysis, 10,* 449–464.

Schumaker, J. B., Hovell, M. F., & Sherman, J. A. (1977b). *Managing behavior: Part 9. A home-based school achievement system.* Lawrence, KS: H & H Enterprises.

Shoemaker, J., & Reid, D. H. (1980). Decreasing chronic absenteeism among institutional staff: Effects of a low-cost attendance program. *Journal of Organizational Behavior Management, 2,* 317–328.

Silva, D. B., Duncan, P. K., & Doudna, D. (1981). The effects of attendance-contingent feedback and praise on attendance and work efficiency. *Journal of Organizational Behavior Management, 3,* 59–69.

Spuck, D. W. (1974). Reward structure in the public school. *Educational Administration Quarterly, 1,* 18–34.

Stephens, T. A., & Burroughs, W. A. (1978). An application of operant conditioning to absenteeism in a hospital setting. *Journal of Applied Psychology, 63,* 518–521.

Tahmisian, J. A., & McReynolds, W. (1971). Use of parents as behavioral engineers in the treatment of a school phobic girl. *Journal of Counseling Psychology, 18,* 225–228.

Thomas, J. D., Presland, I. E., Grant, M. D., & Glynn, T. (1978). Natural rates of teacher approval in grade-7 classrooms. *Journal of Applied Behavior Analysis, 11,* 91–94.

White, M. A. (1975). Natural rates of teacher approval and disapproval in the classroom. *Journal of Applied Behavior Analysis, 8,* 367–372.

Wilson, A. (1977). Development and implementation of a structured program for the systematic reduction of factors contributing to students dropping out of school. ERIC Document Reproduction Service (ED 154 268).

Wolpe, J., (1958). *Psychotherapy by reciprocal inhibition.* Stanford, CA: Stanford University Press.

20 Reducing school violence and vandalism

Goals

After completing this chapter, you should be able to:

1. List and explain three major factors that serve as setting events for school violence and vandalism.
2. Describe how to determine a need for programs to reduce vandalism and/or violence.
3. Describe the importance of analyzing a system prior to planning and implementing programs for it.
4. Differentiate between process and outcome goals, and give an illustration of each.
5. Discuss why it is important to set priorities for goals.
6. State an objective for preventing vandalism.
7. Describe how you can measure vandalism, violence, and related events.
8. List deterrents to vandalism and violence, and describe how each should be used if selected.
9. Discuss why coercive deterrents should be used as temporary expedients.
10. Describe several methods for preventing (a) vandalism and (b) violence.
11. Describe the method suggested, and its rationales, for changing the total school environment.
12. Describe the method suggested for accurately evaluating the effectiveness of a program designed to reduce violence and/or vandalism.

The whining roar of the fire engines faded into the distance and the crowds began to disperse, but the acrid, smoky aroma still hung in the air around Rolando Elementary School.

George turned to his buddy Sam, "Do you think they'll have school tomorrow?"

"Yeah. All they managed to get was the area around the janitor's closet and a few brooms and mops."

"Remember when we used to go here, how in fourth grade some kid or another was always talking about wanting to burn the place down?" George asked. "I wonder if one of them did it."

"I bet—and in a way, I don't blame them. That old crab Mrs. Greene was always yelling and complaining." Sam then mimicked her in a high-pitched voice, "'Won't you ever learn to pay attention and stop wiggling?' 'Give me that paper, George. You are insolent and forever wasting time with your doodling.' 'I swear, you students are a bunch of ignoramuses. None of you will ever amount to anything.'"

"And that time you got caught for chalking her picture and all those dirty words on the front wall? If you weren't so good at drawing they would never've found out."

The two boys roared with laughter, punching one another good humoredly.

Yet, as the sour odor of the fire's aftermath again drifted by, the two boys quickly sobered.

"No matter how mad I got, I'd never do anything like this. Whoever did it must be nuts. Somebody could've gotten hurt," said Sam.

"I know," George agreed. "Besides, I don't feel like that about school anymore. You may think I'm crazy, but I like it now."

"Me too. But don't tell anybody or I'll kill you," Sam whispered.

In the not too distant past, Washington Street School had suffered similarly. Intentionally broken windows, furniture, and fixtures had been commonplace. But since the faculty had modified its methods of instruction and classroom management, such damage gradually diminished. Assaults also had decreased. Simultaneously, the teachers seemed to grow more patient and students worked harder to earn access to special activities. As they were rewarded with events like interesting films, parties, music, festivals, trips, sports competitions, and assemblies, their grades improved and they felt better about themselves.

In contrast with those in the inner city, schools like Franklin High, out in the plusher suburbs, and Willow Grove, nestled away in its rural locale, experienced less severe vandalism and violence. Nevertheless it existed in those places as well. Broken windows, damaged lockers and lavatory fixtures, and angry messages scratched into furniture and walls were commonplace there and elsewhere.

In fact, school vandalism is a continually escalating problem affecting all areas of the United States, regardless of socioeconomic factors. More than $500 million was spent annually during the 1970s to repair damage by vandalism (National Institute of Education, 1978). Current costs are estimated to be much higher. For instance, property losses resulting from school vandalism in California alone approached $100 million annually during 1980 (Deukmejian, 1981). Insurance premiums and deterrents such as security guards and alarm systems require further expenditures, often exceeding the costs of repairing the results of vandalism. For instance, repair and replacement of property lost through vandalism, arson, theft, and burglary in school districts throughout Los Angeles County cost more than $8 million during the 1980 to 1981 school year. Those same districts spent more than $20 million on security during the same year (Office of the Los Angeles County Superintendent of Schools, 1982). Violence

also is committed by students against their peers and school personnel at similarly alarming rates.

FACTORS CONTRIBUTING TO VIOLENCE AND VANDALISM

School violence and vandalism are complex, multifaceted problems for which numerous explanations have been offered. Some blame the juvenile justice system; others indict parents, excessive violence on television, racial tension, and drugs. While each of these factors probably does contribute in some degree, many of them are beyond our control as educators. Our attempts to address them often have resulted in frustration or apathy and led us to conclude that our efforts will not make a difference.

Are there factors within the school that might influence direct or displaced violence, as we hinted in the episode opening this chapter? Because they have been temporally remote from the acts of vandalism, such factors have been difficult to identify. However, based on some of our own current research (Butterworth, Mayer, Nafpaktitis, & Hollingsworth, 1982; Mayer & Butterworth, 1979; Mayer, Butterworth, Nafpaktitis, & Sulzer-Azaroff, 1983; Mayer, Nafpaktitis, & Butterworth, 1985) and extrapolating from our knowledge of behavioral principles, some of the factors that serve as **setting events** for vandalism are beginning to be identified. The extent of punitiveness that characterizes the school environment is one such factor. Included here are an overuse of punitive methods of control, mismatches between students' reading levels and the reading difficulty of assigned materials, and an unclear disciplinary policy with poor administrative support.

An overuse of punitive methods of control

A punitive school climate is one factor that may well be responsible for provoking school vandalism (Mayer & Butterworth, 1979; Mayer et al., 1983). In Chapter 9 we pointed out that aggressive behavior is a predictable reaction to punishment and can occur in the form of violence directed against peers, teachers, and/or property. Nevertheless, probably because constructive alternatives are unknown to them, or for reasons outlined earlier, teachers depend heavily on punishment to control student behavior. Additionally, a survey by the American Association of School Administrators (Brodinsky, 1980) indicated that school districts have invested more time and energy in implementing punitive measures than they have in implementing preventive measures to deal with student misbehavior.

Many classroom teachers, like Mrs. Greene, rely heavily on punitive measures to gain control over their classes. Several studies have reported that many teachers use verbal disapproval in some cases as often as three times more frequently than approval (Heller & White, 1975; Thomas, Presland, Grant, & Glynn, 1978; White, 1975). By contrast, Mayer, Butterworth, and colleagues (1979; 1981; 1983) found that vandalism costs decreased in several elementary, junior high, and high schools once teachers increased their ratios of approval to disapproval and implemented other changes in the school environment.

Mismatch of reading material

Punishment can take more subtle forms than disapproval or reprimands by teachers. It also can derive from a poor match between individual students' levels of preparedness and the level of the materials they are assigned to study. Think how Howard Parker might react if he were required repeatedly to study primary level arithmetic texts or if Billy, who couldn't read beyond the second-grade level, were assigned to work from a history text written at the seventh-grade level. Yet such circumstances are not unusual. Whether because of insufficient time for tailoring assignments to individual students' abilities, school policy, inadequate instructional resources, an unawareness of the difficulty, or a combination of these factors, teachers often do assign material that is too difficult or too easy for their students to handle. The result can be failure (i.e., punishment) or boredom (i.e., extinction). Many students respond to such situations by acting

aggressively against their classmates, their teachers, or their physical surroundings. Others, as we discussed in Chapter 19, attempt to escape by being truant or dropping out of school.

Support for this contention derives from several sources. Greenberg (1974) has indicated a strong relation between delinquency and reading ability. Similarly, Mayer, Nafpaktitis, and Butterworth (1985) found that relatively higher rates of vandalism occurred in schools in which reading levels and assigned materials showed a high discrepancy when compared with schools in which the match was closer.

Other factors

A number of other factors probably contribute toward the level of punitiveness of a given school environment. One is an *unclear discipline policy* or one that is *inadequately supported* by the administration (Mayer et al., 1985). When disciplinary policies are unclear or receive inconsistent support, both positive and negative consequences tend to be dispensed arbitrarily. Discriminative control is difficult to achieve, because it becomes impossible to guess what will result from different occurrences. Anticipated reinforcement may fail to be delivered while punishment may be dispensed when least expected. This combination of extinction and punishment, as we know, bodes poorly, with aggression as a predictable by-product.

Another likely culprit is a paucity of reinforcement within the school setting. Even though punishment per se might be minimal, the stimuli associated with nonreinforcement (i.e., extinction) alone can acquire aversive properties and, as we have just noted, might well provoke vandalism and violence. Also, *it is especially important that the level of reinforcement be kept reasonably high if reductive procedures, such as response cost and timeout, are to be used effectively.* A good case in point here was a study of timeout by Solnick, Rincover, and Peterson (1977). The procedure was designed to reduce tantrums, spitting, and self-injury by two developmentally delayed children. The authors found that the strategy the staff had labeled "timeout" was not timeout at all, but negative reinforcement instead. The instructional environment lacked sufficient reinforcing properties, while the mislabeled "time-out" circumstances provided a respite from the aversiveness of the instructional setting. Removing the students from that setting, then, actually *increased* the maladaptive behaviors until the environment was enriched by adding instructional and recreational materials and more frequent praise.

It is difficult to verify our suppositions directly, as most acts of vandalism and many of violence tend to be committed in our absence. No simple A-B-C contingency or sequence analysis will serve. We cannot count the acts reliably, but instead must focus on their presumed products — damage, destruction, or injury — determining how those outcomes change as a function of changes within the school program. (Accidental damage cannot be sorted from damage caused intentionally. We can assume only that as the absolute amount decreases, some unknown proportion attributable to vandalism is included.) Yet we are quite certain that improvements in the school climate will lead to concomitant decreases in violence and vandalism. Follow along with us to see one model that administrators, attendance and other specialized personnel, and teachers might collaboratively apply toward this end.

ASSESSING THE NEED

Before involving others in setting up a program to reduce vandalism and/or violence, you as the administrator or pupil personnel specialist who is to conduct the program should be able to demonstrate to all involved that there is a need for the program. Vandalism costs and the number of episodes should be estimated. Figures on which those estimates are based usually are recorded periodically by the school principal or district office. Figure 20.1 illustrates a form used by Mayer et al. (1983) to collect monthly vandalism data. Violence can be measured by recording fights, assaults against staff and students, and injuries or referrals for medical treatment.

It also is helpful to determine the location of the episodes, as illustrated in Figure 20.1. When evidence of vandalism is found in one section of the campus in particular, structural changes may be sufficient to help reduce the problem. For example, a washroom was being vandalized regularly in a junior high school in which one of us consulted. The entrance was obscured, as it was located around the corner from the main hallway that contained the classrooms. Relocating the washroom's entrance to the main hallway reduced the vandalism. Data of these sorts, then, can help you to determine the scope of the problem — not only to decide if there is need for a program, but also to use the data to constitute a baseline as a basis for comparison should you subsequently implement a program.

ANALYZING THE SYSTEM

As emphasized in Chapter 3, it is critical to consider the total system in planning and implementing programs designed to remedy violence and vandalism, if you hope to obtain the kind of ongoing support you are sure to need. Otherwise, your efforts may come to naught. Additionally, examining the system can help you to identify organizational factors that may influence the effectiveness of your program. Remember to conduct this analysis at several levels.

First, contact the people in charge — the superintendent and whoever is in charge of security — to obtain their approval. Clarify their roles, how much material and administrative support they will supply, and what data they will make available (e.g., repair costs, injury records). Be sure you know about the school system's currently operating programs and policies with regard to violence and vandalism. If possible, try to work within those structures; otherwise, see to it that a mechanism for modifying them is negotiated collaboratively.

Because you are dealing with potential criminal acts, you will want to learn something about the laws governing those acts and how they tend to be

	CLASSROOM BUILDING		CAFETERIA		WASHROOM		OTHER (please specify, e.g., library, playground, administrative building, bus)	
	Date of Occurrence(s)	Cost*	Date of Occurrence(s)	Cost*	Date of Occurrence(s)	Cost*	Date of Occurrence(s)	Cost*
BROKEN GLASS								
EQUIPMENT THEFT								
FIRE DAMAGE								
PROPERTY DAMAGE (Graffiti, smashed furniture, fixtures torn off wall, carved desks, miscellaneous ruination)								

*Be sure to include labor cost. If precise dollar figures are not immediately available, estimate cost in pencil. When accurate figures are available, indicate in ink.

Figure 20.1
Recording sheet for occurrence and cost of vandalism.

administered among juveniles in your locale. You might find it advantageous to contact juvenile authorities to find out how legal contingencies operate. Similarly, it is important to discover how community leaders and parents respond to those problems; and what roles and influence are manifested by business, civic, and parent organizations. Often, these people are willing to help. We know of instances in which businesses have supplied prizes, gift certificates, admission passes, and other material rewards. In Burlington, Vermont (Barrera, 1984), the operator of a video game arcade currently is permitting children to earn tokens to operate his machines by accomplishing academic tasks. Parents and civic groups often are willing to donate time or funds to support reinforcing activities, such as trips to circuses and other forms of entertainment, prizes, and so on. They realize that in the long run all in the community benefit when violence and vandalism diminish.

Within the school itself, you naturally will need the support and assistance of many: the administration and its support staff, nurses and/or doctors, and students. These people control many important contingencies and may possess important data that could be made available to you. Their cooperation is crucial. If your district is unionized, the impetus for doing something to handle this problem may well have derived from the union membership, as these problematic areas tend to be of especially serious concern to teaching personnel. It is they who must cope with such difficulties, and often they who are the victims of student violence. Regardless of the source of the decision to counter violence and vandalism, though, the union leadership will have to be involved, or at least informed, as the program is planned. The cooperation of student leaders can be similarly important.

If used appropriately, such an analysis of the system should provide information that will improve your chances of success, while an absence of such information and support can result in failure. If you would like to prepare an environmental analysis form, you can simply modify the one we presented in Chapter 3 (Figure 3.1, page 43).

SPECIFYING AND SELECTING GOALS AND OBJECTIVES

Once you have determined that there is a need and that environmental support exists for a program, you should formulate specific objectives. A first step is to specify possible goals. Decreasing the number of episodes, injuries, and various costs of violence and vandalism is probably your basic **outcome goal.** Other goals may be related to the process or treatment itself. For example, we identified several possible setting events to vandalism. If you determine that one or more of those setting events need to be addressed, then you might develop several **process** or **treatment goals,** such as:

- Teachers will increase the proportion of approving to disapproving statements.
- The discrepancy between students' reading levels and assigned academic materials will be narrowed to less than ±2 on the average.
- Relations will improve among staff and administrators (e.g., instructional materials will be provided when requested; prompt action will be taken on disciplinary referrals; administrators will communicate verbally or in writing their appreciation of good teaching and classroom discipline practices).
- A written discipline policy will be developed that is stated clearly and allows for individual differences.

Once you have listed tentative goals, you need to assign priorities based on the time and resources available to accomplish your goals and on the cooperation and support you can obtain from others within the system. *Do not* try to accomplish too much at once. Select one or two high-priority goals with which to begin. Once those are accomplished, you can always add others. Don't forget that you must have the necessary time, resources, and support or you will be not only wasting your time but that of others as well.

Let us assume that you have determined which goals have the highest priority and support. Your next step is to specify your *objectives.* Here are some samples:

- Compared with the previous academic year, this year the costs of property damage, theft, and fire will be reduced by at least 25 percent (adjusted for inflation).
- The number of assaults on instructional staff for the year will be half of the previous three-year average.
- Before shifting to a maintenance program, selected teachers will increase by at least 25 percent their rates of approval and decrease by at least 25 percent their rates of disapproval, for five consecutive days.
- The students' in selected classrooms will decrease their absolute reading discrepancy scores by at least 25 percent within three months. That level will be maintained over the next three months.
- Ratings by selected teachers of disciplinary policies and relations among staff and administrators will improve by at least 25 percent, then stabilize at that level according to trimonthly evaluations for the remainder of the academic year.

MEASURING SCHOOL VANDALISM, VIOLENCE, AND RELATED EVENTS

Vandalism

As we said earlier, it is usually impossible to observe acts of vandalism directly. Thus, we must use indirect measures, such as the products of vandalism. For example, to obtain an estimate of the number of occurrences, we can measure the cost required to repair damage, or count each day during which new damage is done.

We have used the monthly costs of repairing and replacing vandalized property (e.g., Mayer & Butterworth, 1979) as illustrated in Figure 20.1. Vandalism was defined as broken glass, equipment theft, fire damage, and property damage. Further, we transformed this information to costs per 100 students to help make the data more comparable among the various schools in which we were working. In most school districts, data must be obtained from an administrator, which can be problematic. First, we have found that many administrators tend to minimize the costs they report, to make their school look better. Second, custodians in many schools paint over graffiti and repair other damage as part of their normal duties. A proportion of the cost, then, can be hidden in the salaries of support staff or in other budget areas, making accurate measurement difficult.

Violence

Certain acts of interpersonal violence are observed and can be counted: fights in class or elsewhere on the school grounds; assaults against students or staff, with or without weapons. Often such episodes are recorded and occasionally reported to police. These records can serve as a data source. Otherwise you will want to arrange to collect such data, noting the circumstances surrounding the fights or assaults, the victims and any consequential injuries to them, and the immediate and delayed consequences to the assailants. (Sometimes parents commit violence in schools. In the unfortunate event that this happens in your area, keep those records, too.) To avoid focusing exclusively on such distressing data, we also suggest that you record and graph time periods in which violence did not occur, which will remind you to appreciate moments of respite.

Related events

As we noted earlier, we strongly suspect that certain factors are related to vandalism. One, *teacher rates of approval and disapproval* have been measured frequently (Heller & White, 1975; Nafpaktitis, Mayer, & Butterworth, in press; Thomas et al., 1978; White, 1975). Most of the investigators included only verbal behavior in their measurement. However, Nafpaktitis et al. (in press) included both verbal and nonverbal behavioral measures. Approval was defined as verbal praise, rephrasing what a student had said, approving gestures, gentle physical contact, positive recognition, and delivery of token or tangible rewards. These forms of approval were recorded only when the approval was given as a consequence of students' paying attention or being involved in their assigned activities. Disapproval was defined as "verbal criticism, disapproving gestures, and implementation of punitive contingencies, such as isolation, penalties and fines." The teacher was observed for ten-second intervals, and each behavior was recorded as it occurred within that interval. Several behaviors could be recorded within a single interval.

Reading discrepancy scores can be determined by subtracting each student's reading test score [such as that obtained from the California Test of Basic Skills (CTBS)] from the readability grade of the student's textbook. The latter can be obtained by using a readability formula such as the SMOG for factoring in the number of polysyllabic words (McLaughlin, 1969; Vaughan, 1976). A positive reading discrepancy test score of two or more grades indicates that the textbook is too difficult; a similar negative score indicates that it is too easy.

Disciplinary policies and relations among staff have been measured through the use of the school environment survey (Mayer et al., 1985) included in Chapter 3 (Table 3.2, page 44). The test-retest coefficient obtained for the survey was .87, supporting its reliability as an instrument, and it correlated −.43 and −.39 with school vandalism frequency and cost, respectively, showing that the more positive the school environment, the lower the rate of vandalism.[1]

Other means of measuring this area could involve a description of changes that occurred, tabulations of positive notes sent to teachers by administrators, or direct observations of many of the items listed in the school environment survey. Collecting direct observational data would provide a more objective measure and allow you to gather input data on only those factors that appear most relevant to your situation. However, as such an activity does involve personnel time, consider the extent to which this information will contribute to the potential effectiveness of the program.

Once you have selected your measurement system(s) and have allowed for adaptation where necessary, you are ready to start collecting your baseline data. In addition, personnel permitting, you should obtain frequent interobserver agreement checks on any direct observational system you are using to reduce the possibility that observer bias might distort the validity of the data, guard against *observer drift*, and increase the believability of the data.

DESIGNING AND CONDUCTING THE TREATMENT PROGRAM

You have determined the scope of the problem and the degree of support and cooperation you are likely to obtain. Mutually acceptable objectives have been specified, and baseline measures have been obtained. Now you are ready to design and implement the treatment strategy.

---

[1]Note that a correlation of this type means that two sets of scores tend to vary together. It does *not* indicate that change in one *causes* a change in the other. Only an *experimental analysis* of the kind frequently advocated throughout this text is capable of revealing that change in one set of dependent variables (e.g., vandalism rates) is a *function* of the changes in the independent variables (e.g., a more positive school climate). See the discussion on evaluating the effectiveness of the program below, where the multiple baseline is recommended as the design for conducting such an experimental analysis.

No single treatment program has been totally effective in eradicating violence or vandalism. In this section, then, we will discuss a variety of approaches to preventing and reducing vandalism—some that we have helped to develop, and others that have appeared in the literature. We also will review a few suggestions for preventing or reducing violence. However, we would like to remind you again that what we describe probably will have to be modified to meet the specific needs of your particular setting. Also, because of space limitations, we have kept program descriptions brief. However, if you have followed the steps as we have outlined them, you should be in a good position to develop your own program, based on the information we have provided throughout this book.

Deterrents and punishment

The first options to which many school administrators turn when faced with excessive violence and vandalism are short-range strategies involving coercive *deterrents* or methods of detection and punishment (Brodinsky, 1980). Many deterrents are antecedents designed to *inhibit* violent and/or vandalistic acts. They include hiring security personnel, installing alarm systems, involving community members in various school watch programs, and posting various punitive consequences (Butterworth, 1980).

If security personnel are hired, their role should be viewed primarily as preventors of crime, not just as enforcers of the law. Scrimger and Elder (1981) point out that the more successful security personnel programs provide a balance of educational and security functions. How well security personnel are trained, then, influences their effectiveness. Training should include not only technical preparation for the job but also knowledge of the local gangs and behavior management problems, and skill in the use of reinforcement.

There are a wide variety of alarm systems, ranging from a single bell activated by intruders to a system that notifies a protection or security agency. Because of the diversity of needs among schools, it is best to obtain the help of an independent security consultant in designing the best system for your school, rather than going to a commercial alarm distributor.

School watch programs are designed to alert community members to the problems of vandalism and to solicit their support and assistance in reducing occurrences of graffiti, broken windows, theft, fires, and other damage to school property. Local residents are requested to report to the police anything suspicious, such as vehicles on or near the school grounds during nonschool hours, people on roofs of buildings, unusual lights or noises, smoke coming from the school, or individuals observed stealing or destroying school property. A sample handout given to community members is included in Figure 20.2.

The presence of such deterrent programs serves as a warning to potential perpetrators that they are likely to be reported, caught, and punished if they vandalize or commit assaults. These deterrents suppress vandalism rather than remedy it.

Students and their parents also need to know that committing assaults on school personnel and other students cannot be condoned, and policies for treating such episodes must clearly be communicated and consistently implemented. Because you will not want to model violence yourself, you probably will avoid using corporal punishment and instead select alternative punitive strategies, such as loss of privileges and other forms of response cost, timeout, contingent effort, or overcorrection.

Deterrents of this kind rely, of course, on the administration of *aversive consequences*. Typically, several penalties are posted and used when a student has been caught assaulting someone or vandalizing property. They might include requiring the student and his or her parents to pay for the damage (i.e., restitution), suspension, expulsion, or referral to the criminal justice system.

Sometimes the use of such deterrents and punishment are necessary to protect people and property and to make conditions safe for students and staff. However, if you depend exclusively on these methods, you can anticipate several problems. First, as we pointed out in earlier chapters (e.g., see Chapter 9), punitive procedures tend to be overused because they produce rapid results. The paradox here is that the more that punitive measures are used, the less effective they become, often requiring increasingly harsher punishments to achieve similar results. Second, such deterrents and punitive consequences do not address the factors that may be provoking violence and vandalism in the first place. In fact, coercive deterrents or punishments usually have the opposite effect in the long run—they add to the punitive nature of the school environment. Perhaps this is why Greenberg (1974) and Scrimger and Elder (1981) reported that campus security forces often appeared to aggravate rather than to deter violence and vandalism. Thus, if a crisis requires that you select a deterrent program, view it as a temporary expedient to augment your implementation of long-term preventive strategies.

Preventing vandalism and violence

A variety of antecedents have been employed by Mayer and his colleagues (Mayer & Butterworth, 1979; Mayer et al., 1983) to help *prevent* violence and vandalism at the elementary, junior high, and high school levels. These have included:

- Increasing rates of teacher-delivered praise and other forms of positive recognition for constructive classroom behavior.
- Reducing teachers' use of punitive classroom control procedures.
- Reducing the mismatch between students' reading levels and the reading difficulty level of assigned materials.
- Reducing the misuse of behavior management procedures (e.g., helping teachers to avoid using timeout with a student who is misbehaving for the purpose of not having to do an aversive assignment).
- Improving relations among staff members and administrators.

FOR EMERGENCY
POLICE SERVICE
CALL

911

Be sure to give the exact
location of the incident
you are reporting.
CALLERS NEED NOT GIVE NAME.

The above phone number connects you with the Communications Center of the Oakland Police Department. On receipt of your message, a School Security patrol car or an Oakland Police Department patrol car will be dispatched by radio to investigate the incident. We appreciate your cooperation and help.

George Hart
Chief of Police

Figure 20.2
Sample school watch announcement.

- Revising disciplinary policies so that they are clearly communicated, fair, and flexible enough to adjust to individual differences.

Typical *reinforcing consequences* that have been incorporated in programs to reduce vandalism include:

- Student committees deciding how to spend a percentage of the money saved through reduced vandalism costs (Butterworth, 1980).
- Praise and tickets given to students for picking up trash and keeping the campus looking attractive. (The tickets were used in a lottery. Winners received various privileges and tangible items — see

Chapter 21 [page 351] for a detailed description.)

If you watch students who frequently commit assaults, you may notice that they exhibit patterns as they work their way up to their outbursts. Lucinda was one of these. First she would clench her fists, and her whole body would stiffen. She would begin to breathe rapidly and audibly, and her face would flush. Sometimes the teacher would try to calm or distract her before the eruption came, and occasionally that worked, but other times there was no holding her back. Once Lucinda lost control, her teacher could not restrain her. Is there something that might have worked to interrupt the chain of responses that ended in violence?

One very promising method has been demon-

OAKLAND PUBLIC SCHOOLS
Security Section
1025 Second Avenue, Oakland
836-8450

Dear Neighbor:

The Oakland Public Schools earnestly seeks your cooperation in controlling vandalism at our schools. Should you observe any unusual activities that cause you to suspect vandalism, or a break-in, please call the Emergency Police Number listed on the other side of this card. Such activity might include:

    People on roofs of buildings
    Rowdyism of any kind
    Unsupervised play after dark
    Throwing rocks or shooting of any kind of weapon
    Playing with fire (in case of actual building fire, call the Oakland Fire Department, 444-1616)
    Operating or parking motor vehicles in the schoolyard
    Alarm bell ringing

Please do not hesitate to call, as it may save many dollars of taxpayers' money. Help us to protect your schools. Callers need not give name.

Robert W. Blackburn
Interim Superintendent of Schools

---

strated to us at the Behavioral Development Center in Providence, Rhode Island. Children with very serious behavioral difficulties attend this training program. Many have long histories of expressing violence toward themselves or to people and objects in their surroundings. Such children have learned to induce themselves to relax at those times instead of continuing inexorably toward expressing their rage. We even have seen this practice used by children whose development has been very severely impaired. They learn this skill systematically, just as they learn social, motor, or other skills. The staff uses a training manual developed by June Groden (one of the directors of the center) and Joseph Cautela (1978). Relaxation is broken down into its component parts and each part is shaped as described in Chapters 6, 7, and 8. The children learn to practice the skill on cue from an adult and sometimes by cueing themselves.

Observing closely also can assist you in other ways to prevent violence. Try to notice if particular events predictably lead to outbursts. For some children, slanders about their race, nationality, or family are predictable precursors. Others overreact to being touched, even accidentally. (Recall how, in an earlier chapter, Lucinda shoved sweet, gentle Amy into the coat closet for accidentally bumping into her?) Many children—and adults, too—covertly produce stimuli for themselves that ultimately lead to violence, such as repeatedly rehearsing distressing images and statements to themselves. These can be based on reality or distortion. Such obsessions or delusions indeed can set the occasion for overt aggression.

Each of those types of precursors potentially can be managed, usually with the assistance of a psychologist or other pupil personnel specialist. The child can be taught to ignore taunts or real or imagined insults by substituting alternative responses, such as walking away, laughing, or relaxing. Similarly, people, including young ones, can learn to terminate their obsessive thoughts and delusional images, and to substitute other more adaptive ones, such as rehearsing pleasant experiences or accomplishments. [See the extensive list of references in Cautela and Groden (1978), for example.]

Developing effective school-wide treatment strategies, however, requires that you not restrict your focus to one or two individual students, but rather that you consider the total school environment. Thus, we recommend that a team be formed consisting of an administrator, pupil personnel worker, three or four teachers, and two or three students to provide leadership in the selection and implementation of programs to reduce violence or vandalism. We also recommend that you first test any method you select by working with a few carefully chosen teachers, rather than with the entire staff. The task will be more manageable, as (1) you will be able to provide closer supervision and more frequent feedback; (2) you will have a chance to make improvements in the program while it is being piloted in a few classrooms; and (3) once the selected teachers have implemented the programs successfully, they can serve as models and resource persons for those staff members who are interested in implementing similar programs.

We also would suggest that you select those teachers to work on the team who have:

- Demonstrated a willingness to share new ideas.
- Gained the respect of their fellow staff members (enhancing their effectiveness as models to other teachers).
- Expressed a willingness to commit the time to work with administrators and others involved with the project.

Our research (Mayer & Butterworth, 1979; Mayer et al., 1983) has indicated that the total school climate can be affected by working initially with the *strong, influential* members of a school staff.

Much can be done in our schools to reduce violence and vandalism. For example, as we saw at Washington Street School, the level of reinforcement was enhanced (see Chapters 4 to 6) and other behavior management procedures such as Alt-R (see Chapter 9), modeling, DRL, and DRO (see Chapter 10) began to be used to correct minor infractions that occurred both in the classroom and on the school grounds. Consequently, the staff reduced the punitiveness of the school ambience and made it a more pleasant place by approving and otherwise increasing reinforcement. The arbitrary use and misuse of punitive procedures (see Chapters 11 and 12) diminished.

At places like Franklin High School, academic materials need to continue to be adjusted to students' levels of functioning while still capturing their interest (see Chapters 7, 8, and 13 to 17). Use of the materials also should be paired with considerable positive reinforcement, such as recognition for progress, if aggression is to be reduced. In addition, programs can be implemented to improve relations and morale among educators and students (see Chapters 5, 19, and 22) and to upgrade the school discipline program. For example, a behavior code could be developed at Franklin High that stresses *how* students should behave and the rewards for such behavior rather than emphasizing what not to do and the consequences for violations. Similarly, it must be recognized that at times consequences must be tailored to specific individuals. The same consequence does not work for all.

In summary, it appears that violence and vandalism can be reduced by applying most of the principles described in this book, although this is no easy task. But then, neither is teaching. A program can be designed initially to accomplish one or two high-priority treatment or process objectives. Once the initial objectives are met, other treatment programs can be added to accomplish additional objectives. Although it may sound like a monumental task, when such approaches have been undertaken, dramatic success has been achieved (Mayer & Butterworth, 1979; Mayer et al., 1983).

MAINTAINING PREVENTIVE PROGRAMS

The factors that influence violence and vandalism often relate to the behavior of educators. For that reason, as we discuss maintenance of the program, our focus is on maintaining the behavior of administrators and teachers — because how they respond has so much influence on the school environment.

In Chapter 5, we discussed the need to reinforce staff frequently *over a period of time,* and then *gradually to thin out the reinforcement* rather than moving on before the change has firmly taken hold. This approach is particularly necessary when attempting to implement preventive programs, as such programs tend not to provide immediate reinforcing consequences to those who use them in the same way that deterrents and punishment do. Consequently, staff may require supplementary positive reinforcement — from one another, consultants, administrators, and community members — if preventive programs are to persist and become part of the school's natural environment. In Chapter 22, we discuss a variety of ways to reinforce the performance of staff members. We also suggest that you review the section in Chapter 5 on the frequent delivery of reinforcement with staff.

EVALUATING THE PROGRAM'S EFFECTIVENESS

As stated earlier, school vandalism is not an easy variable to evaluate because it usually is impossible to observe the occurrence of such incidents. Thus, as we discussed previously, we have to rely on indirect measures, such as the cost and frequency of that damage, which can interfere with an unbiased evaluation. For example, one method frequently used to evaluate the effectiveness of a vandalism program is to compare the cost and frequency of various types of vandalism (i.e., property damage, fire, theft) each month during and following program implementation against cost and frequency figures from the previous year. Yet, once a program is implemented, the accuracy of the vandalism data tends to be scrutinized more closely, as people involved in the program begin to double-check the figures given to them by administrators: "Did you include the cost of the broken window in Building A? Remember, somebody threw a rock through it." Such vigilance can promote more accurate reporting during treatment than during baseline or pretreatment conditions, obscuring actual improvement to an unknown extent.

To counter these difficulties, a withdrawal design (see Chapter 3) could be implemented. If it could be shown that vandalism decreased during treatment, increased during withdrawal, and then decreased again during reimplementation of treatment, you would have reasonable evidence that the treatment program, and not something else, was effective in remedying the problem. However, such a design might be difficult to justify ethically as well as monetarily. Who would want to take the chance of bringing about a temporary increase in vandalism? An alternative possibility would be to use a multiple-baseline design across schools (see Chapter 3), which would involve collecting baseline data in several schools and then implementing the selected treatment first in one, then in another, and perhaps later in yet another. If it can be shown that vandalism changes maximally in each school only after treatment is applied, then the evidence favors the treatment rather than some other influence.

We prefer this multiple-baseline design for evaluating programs directed toward either reducing vandalism and/or violence. It seems to be a natural approach because if the problem decreases in one school after your program has been implemented, then the next logical step would be to try the program in another school to see if similarly positive results could be achieved. If you do this, take care to obtain data that is as accurate as possible. Try to enhance the accuracy by using *two independent* reporters during *both* baseline and treatment phases (Mayer et al., 1983). Not only could disagreements be discussed and resolved following observational recording sessions, resulting in more believable data, but interreporter agreement indexes could be calculated.

Other related objectives could be evaluated in a similar fashion by using the multiple-baseline design. For increasing the use of positive reinforcement by teachers at places like Washington Street School, and lowering student reading discrepancy scores at schools like Franklin High, we would suggest that a small number of teachers be involved initially, and others added later. Thus, a multiple-baseline design, across teachers and classrooms, could serve nicely to evaluate the programs' effectiveness, assuming that the teachers in the delayed condition are not exposed to the program until the proper time.

Changes in disciplinary policies and staff relations can be presented descriptively and in detail, permitting us to see if the onset of the treatment coincided with a reduction in the problems. Detailed descriptions also permit later replication of the treatment program. Other evidence of change also might help. For example, you might want to record and graph the number of positive notes sent to teachers by school administrators, and then compare baseline with treatment rates.

Summary

We have stressed the need to implement preventive programs for dealing with school violence and vandalism. Most schools have relied on deterrents and punitive measures, several of which we have described briefly. However, the paradox is that some of those measures inadvertently can cause the situation to worsen; their addition makes the environment more punitive, thereby generating events that set the occasion for the very problems the measures are intended to improve. Thus, aversive deterrents and punitive measures should not be used unless combined with positive practices to prevent, reduce, or eliminate the factors that evoke acts of vandalism or violence.

Several possible setting events were identified that appear to contribute to vandalism and violence. Because of their remoteness in time to such aggressive acts, these setting events can be hard to identify. The time lag also makes it difficult to treat the problem. The average innocent onlooker sees a logical rationale for punishing a student for vandalizing a school, thereby supporting a punitive program. However, it may be difficult for that person to see the link between vandalism and the teacher's use of reinforcement and disapproval. The two elements are not immediately associated in time; one does not immediately precede or follow the other. Thus, the connection is more difficult to identify and explain. Many, therefore, find themselves unable to support a given program of prevention because it doesn't make sense to them. Take care, therefore, to educate your school staff as to the relevance of setting events. Because setting events can function powerfully, they all must be identified and dealt with effectively if we are ever durably to prevent, rather than just temporarily suppress, violence and vandalism in our schools.

Study Questions

1. List at least three possible factors that serve as setting events for school vandalism.

2. Discuss in detail the relationship between a punitive school climate and school vandalism.

3. Present an argument for matching assigned materials to the individual students' levels of preparedness. (Be sure to use data to support your argument.)

4. (a) Identify two problems associated with school discipline policies and (b) discuss how they contribute to the level of punitiveness of a given school.

5. Mrs. Jones frequently uses extinction and response cost in her classroom. Describe a possible relationship between her classroom management procedures and vandalism.

6. Mr. Sanders would like to determine how damage and destruction change as a function of the changes he has made in the school program. Pinpoint several problems that might arise as he attempts to do this.

7. You would like to demonstrate a need for a program to reduce vandalism in your school. List the information you should record before making your presentation.

8. Provide another reason for recording the information you listed in the previous answer.

9. Discuss the importance of considering the total system in planning and implementing programs designed to remedy violence and vandalism.

10. Identify the people who should be contacted when a program to reduce vandalism is being designed and describe the information you will need to obtain from each of them.

11. Provide at least one example of (a) an outcome and (b) a process or treatment goal.

12. You have tentatively listed goals. Describe in detail your next step.

13. Provide an original example of a behavioral objective related to reducing violence or vandalism.

14. Discuss the problems associated with obtaining the costs of vandalism from the school administrator.

15. List the data on violence that could be recorded.

16. Identify three frequently recorded major events related to school vandalism.

17. Discuss the difficulties of collecting direct observational data on vandalism.

18. Present an argument for obtaining frequent interobserver agreement checks on the direct observational system you are using.

19. Describe in detail the first options to which many school administrators turn when faced with excessive violence and vandalism.

20. Discuss (a) the role of security personnel and (b) the type of training they should receive.

21. Your school administrators would like to install an alarm system. How should they proceed?

22. Describe the purpose of a school watch program.

23. List several ways to communicate that you do not condone assaults on students and school personnel.

24. Discuss the problems associated with using aversive consequences to reduce vandalism.

25. List the six antecedents employed by Mayer et al. (1983) to help prevent violence and vandalism.

26. The teachers at the North Street School would like to incorporate reinforcing consequences into their program to reduce vandalism. Offer two ways that this end could be accomplished.

27. Paul's violent outbursts are always preceded by the same chain of responses. Describe one possible way to prevent his violence.

28. List several possible causes of violent acts that may be discovered by close observation.

29. Maureen frequently reacts violently when she doesn't obtain what she requests. Provide a list of alternative behaviors she could learn.

30. Identify the individuals who should be included on a team selected to implement programs to reduce violence and vandalism.

31. Discuss the advantages of only selecting a few teachers when you first test your program to reduce violence.

32. Mr. Guarro will be selecting the teachers to work on his team. Provide him with a list of guidelines to ensure that he makes a wise selection.
33. Design an original behavioral program to improve relations and morale among educators and students.
34. You want to ensure that your staff continues to implement the school's programs for preventing violence and vandalism. Provide a list of guidelines to increase the likelihood of the program's continuation.
35. Describe a hypothetical episode in which you used a multiple baseline design to evaluate a program designed to curb violence or vandalism in your school.

References

Barrera, R. D. (1984, August). *Programmed supplemental grammar instruction in the video arcade.* Paper presented at the Annual Meeting of the American Psychological Association. Toronto, Canada.

Brodinsky, B. (1980). *AASA critical issues report: Student discipline, problems and solutions.* AASA, 1801 N. Moore St., Arlington, VA, 22209 (#021-00334).

Butterworth, T. (1980). *Strategies for reducing violence and vandalism: Prevention through remediation of contributing factors.* Office of the Los Angeles County Superintendent of Schools, 9300 E. Imperial Highway, Los Angeles, CA, 90242.

Butterworth, T., Mayer, G. R., Nafpaktitis, M., & Hollingsworth, P. (1982). *Constructive discipline: Improving attendance and reducing disruption and vandalism costs.* Office of the Los Angeles County Superintendent of Schools. An ESEA, Title IV-C end-of-year evaluation report.

Cautela, J. R., & Groden, J. (1978). *Relaxation: A comprehensive manual for adults, children, and children with special needs.* Champaign, IL: Research Press.

Deukmejian, G. (1981, July). *School security handbook: Get a handle on a vandal.* School Safety Center. Office of the Attorney General, 555 Capitol Mall, Suite 655, Sacramento, CA, 95814.

Greenberg, B. (1974). School vandalism: Its effects and paradoxical solutions. *Crime Prevention Review, 1,* 105.

Heller, M. C., & White, M. A. (1975). Rates of teacher verbal approval and disapproval to higher and lower ability classes. *Journal of Educational Psychology, 67,* 796–800.

Mayer, G. R., & Butterworth, T. (1979). A preventive approach to school violence and vandalism: An experimental study. *The Personnel and Guidance Journal, 57,* 436–441.

Mayer, G. R., & Butterworth, T. W. (1981). Evaluating a preventive approach to reducing school vandalism. *Phi Delta Kappan, 62,* 498–499.

Mayer, G. R., Butterworth, T., Nafpaktitis, M., & Sulzer-Azaroff, B. (1983). Preventing school vandalism and improving discipline: A three year study. *Journal of Applied Behavior Analysis, 16,* 335–369.

Mayer, G. R., Nafpaktitis, M., & Butterworth, T. (1985). A search for the elusive contingencies of school vandalism: A correlational study. Manuscript submitted for publication.

McLaughlin, G. H. (1969). SMOG grading—a new readability formula. *Journal of Reading, 12,* 639–646.

Nafpaktitis, M., Mayer, G. R., & Butterworth, T. (In press). Natural rates of teacher approval and disapproval and their relations to student behavior in intermediate school classroom. *Journal of Educational Psychology.*

National Institute of Education. (1978). *The safe school study.* Washington, D.C.: U.S. Department of Health, Education and Welfare, Office of Education.

Office of the Los Angeles County Superintendent of Schools. (1982). Attendance, pupil and administrative services. *1981–82 annual bulletin.* General bulletin #55 APAS 5-81-82. Downey, CA.

Scrimger, G. C., & Elder, R. (1981). *Alternatives to vandalism: Cooperation or wreckreation.* Sacramento, CA: School Safety Center, California Department of Justice.

Solnick, J. V., Rincover, A., & Peterson, C. R. (1977). Some determinates of the reinforcing and punishing effects of timeout. *Journal of Applied Behavior Analysis, 10,* 415–424.

Thomas, J. D., Presland, I. E., Grant, M. D., & Glynn, T. (1978). Natural rates of teacher approval in grade-7 classrooms. *Journal of Applied Behavior Analysis, 11,* 91–94.

Vaughan, J. L., Jr., (1976). Interpreting readability assessments. *Journal of Reading, 19,* 635–639.

White, M. A. (1975). Natural rates of teacher approval and disapproval in the classroom. *Journal of Applied Behavior Analysis, 8,* 367–372.

21 Improving conduct outside the classroom

Goals

After completing this chapter, you should be able to:

1. Identify, describe, and illustrate each step in the Mayer, Nafpaktitis, and Butterworth model for dealing with behavior problems and litter in the lunch area.
2. List criteria for selecting those goals that should be given the greatest priority.
3. List each step in setting up a program to change behavior outside the classroom.
4. Illustrate each step as you describe a program for maintaining peace and cleanliness in the lavatory.
5. Describe a method of increasing bus ridership.
6. Describe a method for decreasing disruptive behavior on the bus for normal and for handicapped youngsters.
7. Describe how time might be used more efficiently on the bus.
8. Illustrate what can be done for each step in goal 3 to improve the playground environment.

Watch out! You'd better protect yourself from flying objects when you enter this school cafeteria. Bunched-up paper napkins, crusts of bread, sweaters, and an occasional tennis shoe are flying through the air. Amy lowers her head, clutching her tray tightly to protect her bowl of peaches. Sidestepping the remains of a well-trodden peanut butter sandwich, she edges toward the area patrolled by Mrs. Burnes. The girl watches despairingly as her favorite teacher scrambles from table to table pleading with the youngsters to settle down and behave. Kate Burnes holds grimly to the certainty, based on long years of experience, that as soon as the bell rings to signal the end of lunch period, the students will fall into ragged formation and the chaos will lessen. As lunch period ends, Amy hangs back and offers to help Mrs. Burnes clear her tray, sharing with her a few brief moments of peace.

In another school, you'd have no need to protect yourself. All the students are seated quietly eating, or their hands are folded on the table before them. Two teachers patrol, their expressions stern, their demeanor commanding. One boy covers his mouth with his hand and whispers something to the boy next to him, who giggles. One of the patrolling teachers strides up to the second boy, takes him by the collar and leads him to face the corner of the room.

The apparent stark contrast between these two schools is deceptive, because they have something very important in common: in both situations, fear prevails. In the former case, the danger is clear and imminent. In both, instead of functioning as a welcomed, relaxing break in the daily routine, lunch time becomes an experience to be tolerated grimly by both students and teachers. Problems of this sort tend to arise during other unstructured times: while students are in the lavatory, playground, and in the school bus. In this chapter we illustrate a number of behavioral strategies that have improved conduct effectively during unstructured times.

IMPROVING CONDUCT IN THE LUNCHROOM

A colleague, Mac Horton,[1] was consulted to assist in helping to restore order in the cafeteria of an elementary school. The children had been throwing food, running about the room, shouting, and poking one another. Targets for change included remaining seated except to obtain food or water, go to the lavatory, or clear one's tray from the table; speaking softly; not throwing objects or hitting. Dr. Horton formulated and explained the definitions of each of those target behaviors in detail, describing exactly what constituted noisy talk, hitting, and so forth, so that everyone clearly understood what was expected.

It was decided to try a dual approach, permitting members of a group of classes to earn special privileges when they adhered to the rules and generating competition between groups at the same time. A chart was posted near the exit; groups were indicated as row headings, the individual rules of conduct as column headings. First the consultant, and later the cafeteria supervisor, walked around the lunchroom recording the behavior of students in each group, then checked the chart as each group prepared to exit. In this case, students earned free time and an occasional treat when their groups had accumulated a sufficient number of positive checks. A student announced over the loudspeaker the identity of the group with the most checks and awarded it a banner to be displayed in its own area of the building for a week. The improvement was instantaneous, and peace reigned thenceforth.

Some of the teachers had worried that children would pressure or coerce one another, but fortunately that never happened. Banners had been used previously to reward other group accomplishments; so in this case, the procedure dovetailed nicely with

[1]Personal communication, Arthur MacNeil Horton.

an established tradition. Most encouraging was the fact that it was possible for a single individual, the cafeteria supervisor, to administer the entire program on her own.

Let's take a moment to analyze this clever solution. First, the need for the program derived from several sources: the principal, various teachers, and the cafeteria supervisor. It seemed that the students also welcomed a promise of improvement in the situation. Because everyone agreed on the necessity for change, any jointly designed program that proved feasible would tend to receive continuing support, even after the consultant left the scene.

The enducements of terminating misconduct and regaining peace apparently were not sufficiently enticing to induce change. Consequently, the points, backup rewards, and awarding of the banner were added to supplement those potential, naturally reinforcing consequences. The posted rules helped guide the students' performance while the points were *consistently* and *immediately* delivered and could be exchanged for reinforcers that were *functionally effective* with those students. (Those conditions, you'll recall from reading about the effective use of reinforcement in Chapter 5, promote change optimally.) The public announcement of the winner prompted congratulations from students and teachers, and the banner reminded everyone that the group had accomplished something laudable. Restricting the duration of the display of the banner probably kept it from losing its appeal, as it would be hung for only one week. As for operating the system, that could be accomplished with minimal cost in terms of funds, effort, and personnel. The recording method was clear and simple, and only the services of a single staff member, who required little training and supervision, was needed. Programs like these—elegant in their simplicity—have the greatest likelihood of persisting.

Planning a behavioral management program for your lunch area

Do your students bring lunch from home, or are they served hot or cold lunches at school? Are their meals subsidized, or do they pay the full price? Are they able to choose food items, or is the menu fixed? Where do students eat — in a large common room such as a cafeteria, auditorium, or gym, or in classrooms or out of doors? How are the acoustics? Is noise the major problem, or are you more concerned with general disorder, food wastage, litter, or poor nutritional habits? Do teachers eat in the same location as students? Who supervises? Obviously, problems in the lunch area vary from location to location, so no specific set of procedures is appropriate to all.

Recognizing this fact, Mayer, Nafpaktitis, and Butterworth (1981) developed a general model for dealing with behavioral problems in the lunch area. Here we summarize that model and offer some illustrations using frequently cited problems: noise, throwing and wasting food, pushing, and littering. Perhaps some of these are concerns of yours. (In the event that none of these examples is typical of your particular situation, you still should be able to utilize the model by applying the principles of behavioral change that we have provided in Part I of the text.)

The steps in the model consist of:

- Clarifying the problem.
- Establishing a planning team.
- Setting goals.
- Measuring the severity of the problem.
- Formulating behavioral objectives.
- Planning strategies for achieving objectives: logistical and organizational arrangements, behavioral management strategies.
- Training lunch area supervisors.
- Implementing and maintaining the program.
- Phasing out the program.

We shall describe and illustrate each step below.

Clarifying the problem

All that Mrs. Burnes knew was that lunch time was awful, that something had to be done. She discussed the general problem with the other teachers, all of whom agreed that things were out of hand. They requested a meeting with the counselor, Mr. Lee, and the principal, Mr. Rodriguez.

Everyone seemed to be speaking at once.

"It's the noise I can't stand!"

"I'm afraid someone might get hurt — one of the students, or even me!"

"What bugs me the most is that here we have all these youngsters who probably haven't had a balanced meal in a year, and what happens when we try to provide them with nutritious food? Most of it ends up in the wastebasket."

"It's the filth that gets to me."

"Wait a minute," said Mr. Rodriguez. "Let's take things one at a time and go about this systematically. Mr. Lee, can you suggest how we might proceed?"

Mr. Lee suggested that they conduct a *needs assessment* to help pinpoint the problems. A few teachers volunteered to observe systematically, noting:

1. The time and place at which incidents occurred.
2. The methods used to resolve those problems.
3. The outcome.

They would not only concentrate on problem incidents but also try to hunt for examples of successful episodes. Figures 21.1 and 21.2 illustrate the type of information they collected. A lunch area fact sheet also was filled out, along with a map of the normal traffic pattern, as illustrated in Figures 21.3 and 21.4, permitting the physical arrangement of the environment to be examined to see if changes might be indicated in that realm.

Establishing a planning team

While the *needs assessment* was underway, Mrs. Burnes and several other teachers joined Mr. Lee in organizing a planning team. They also invited the cafeteria supervisor and a student representative to take part. (If you organize such a team in your school, try to involve a few people who are enthusiastically committed to constructive improvement in the lunch room — for instance, those who most conscientiously attend meetings on the topic or have already participated in other ways.)

Observer M.N. Date 10/3/ Time 11:15–12:15

Problems Observed	Place	Time	Method Used to Resolve Problem	Outcome	Comments
Long line waiting to get lunch.	Cafeteria window	11:30	Teacher tells students to keep hands to selves.	Pushing when teacher looks elsewhere	
Student throwing orange peels at another.	Bench	11:38	Supervisor shrugs shoulders and ignores.	Peels hit student—fall to and remain on floor.	Occurs daily. Ignoring is not working.
Student walks to another table, almost bumping into student entering from cafeteria line.	Central area	11:40	Supervisor calls loudly for first student to sit down.	Student goes to his friend first, then back to his own table.	
Litter.	Whole area under and around tables	12:15	Custodian sweeps up after lunch.	Cleanliness lasts only a few minutes. New deposits of litter occur at second lunch period.	
Students shouting, loud laughing, banging trays and utensils.	Every-where	Entire period	Supervisor "shushes" repeatedly. Teachers shout "quiet" every few minutes. Mr. M. blows whistle when noise level is unbearable.	No change. Momentary reduction in noise. Quiet for about a half minute, then gradual recovery in noise level.	

Figure 21.1

Lunch area needs assessment—problems. (Mary Nafpaktitis developed Figures 21.1 through 21.4. We appreciate her willingness to allow us to include them in this chapter.)

Setting goals

When the Washington Street School planning team met, members examined the data that had been collected over the previous week. Based on that information, they generated a list of potential goals:

- To eliminate pushing, throwing food, and litter on the floor.
- To reduce congestion.
- To reduce noise.
- To reduce food waste.
- To increase the time students remain seated quietly or talking in reasonable, conversational tones.
- To teach students to try unfamiliar foods.
- To increase consumption of nutritious food.

As the list grew, it became apparent that they would have to set priorities. In deciding how to proceed, Mr. Lee suggested that the participants identify some criteria that would direct their choosing. The resulting questions were noted, including:

Observer M.N.   Date 10/3/   Time 11:15–12:15

Assets Observed	Place	Time	Response to Student Behavior	Outcome	Comments
Group of six students eating together, talking in normal voices.	Bench	11:22	None	Continues.	Perhaps noon supervisor could compliment students.
Two students walk to trash can to deposit papers.	Trash can area	11:34	None	Trash not on floor.	Thanks by noon supervisor would be appropriate.
Student raises hand to be excused from lunch area.	Bench	11:40	Supervisor smiles and promptly signals the student to leave.	Supervisors consistently excuse students with raised hands.	Seems to work well.

Figure 21.2
Lunch area needs assessment—assets.

"Will the goal be difficult to achieve? Do we have the time, energy, skills, and resources to tackle it?"

"Can it be accomplished by some simple means, such as changes in schedule or a rearrangement of traffic patterns?"

"Have others successfully solved the problem, and can we use their methods?"

Size of room:

Number of tables:

Number of trash cans:

Total number of students:

Number of students bringing lunches:

Number of students purchasing lunches:

Number of lunch periods:

Period   Period   Period
   A   B   C
Time:

Number of students:

Notes on floor plans and traffic patterns:

Figure 21.3
Lunch area fact sheet.

"How likely are the instructional and cafeteria staff to cooperate?"

A few members of the team offered to check out the literature to see how others with similar problems might have selected their goals.

One reported what happened in one case in a Cleveland, Ohio, elementary school. Aides recruited from the neighborhood supervised the students over the lunch hour (MacPherson, Candee, & Hohman, 1974). These aides were responsible for overseeing the children for 60 minutes, consisting of a 10-minute lavatory break, a 20-minute eating period, and a 30-minute recreation period. Apparently, disruption was a serious concern. A six-point rating scale of ten misbehaviors was distributed to the aides to clarify the specific nature of the problem. *Talking while the aide speaks*, *being out of seat*, and *quarreling* received the highest ratings. Each of those items then was defined more precisely. For example, "*Quarreling* was defined as a child verbally annoying another child, disrupting an activity by throwing or snatching a player's equipment, name calling or shouting verbal disagreements while eating or engaging in one of the reinforcement activities" (MacPherson, et al. 1974, p. 288). Because it cost so much in time and money, littering in the school lunch area was identified as a major concern in a junior high school with

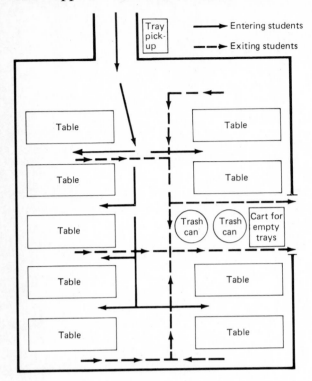

Main entrance and main exit bottlenecks are well separated.
Some conflict exists in traffic patterns in central area.

Figure 21.4
Diagram of lunchroom floor plan and traffic patterns.

a student body of 844 and in an intermediate school of 680 (Mayer et al., 1981). In each case, inordinate efforts were expended in attempting to prevent or cope with the problem.

Management of *noise* in the lunchroom was identified as the goal of several studies. For instance, LaRowe, Tucker, and McGuire (1980), Mayer et al., (1981), and Michelson, Dilorenzo, Calpin, and Williamson (1981) tackled noise directly in the lunchrooms, respectively, of an elementary school, an intermediate school, and in an inpatient program for emotionally disturbed/learning-disabled children.

When these examples were reported back to the planning team, its members felt they were ready to go ahead. They would work toward eliminating pushing, throwing food and litter on the floor, and

reducing the noise level, assuming that the next step, measuring the severity of the problem, indicated those goals to be warranted.

Measuring the severity of the problem

"Why do you think it is important to measure how severe the problems are that we've isolated?" inquired Mr. Lee.

"Because they may not actually be as bad as we think. Maybe we're barking up the wrong tree. Maybe this is our problem, not theirs," Mrs. Burnes replied.

"Yes. It's apparent you understand the rationale for collecting baseline data before attempting to cure the situation. Now, let's discuss how we might measure these behaviors. How did they do it in the studies you just reported?"

Team members then told how the problems had been measured. (You learned about those measurement systems in Chapter 2, pp. 23 to 32.)

Formulating behavioral objectives

By the end of a couple of weeks, the data convinced everyone that all the problems they had selected, indeed, could stand to improve, so a set of behavioral objectives was formulated. For a month, the frequencies of pushing and food throwing were to be reduced to no more than once per five-minute intervals. Litter was to be eliminated entirely in at least 30 of the 36 zones. Noise was to be kept below the threshold during 90 percent of the lunch period. It was then time to plan a way to accomplish those objectives.

Planning strategies for achieving objectives

Logistical changes. Two of the problems, pushing and noisiness, might be alleviated to some extent by a few logistical and organizational changes, the planning team reasoned. One obvious modification would be to shorten the lunch lines by staggering the times classes would arrive. Another was to examine the traffic pattern to see if the flow could be altered to prevent crowding. It was found, for instance, that paths from the counter to the tables crossed those from the tables to the trash receptacles, and also that tables were so close to one another that only one person could navigate comfortably past them at a time.

The planning team also considered distributing litter bags, an activity shown to be successful in a sports stadium by Baltes and Hayward (1976), and adding several trash receptacles closer to the tables, an effective method, as shown by Luyben and Bailey (1979).

Behavioral management strategies.
The modification in schedule did alleviate some of the congestion, as did a rearrangement of tables and trash receptacles. Pushing and noise levels diminished, the reduction leveling off after a few weeks. At that point, the team decided to try to change the students' behavior directly. Again, the literature was consulted for ideas.

Different intervention techniques have been used to curtail noise in the lunchroom. LaRowe et al. (1980) rigged up their monitoring system to a simulated traffic signal that permitted each color — green, yellow, and red — to activate at correspondingly increasing levels of noise. Large enough to be seen by all, the traffic light informed everyone when noise was at an acceptable level by flashing green; when it was increasing toward an unacceptable range it flashed yellow; and when the noise level was intolerably loud, it sounded a bell, audible above the din, and flashed red. This information was sufficient to reduce noise considerably. Even further reductions were accomplished when a group contingency was combined with the feedback. For the group contingency, a card was handed to each class indicating whether or not the criterion for acceptable noise levels during their period had been met. If so, the teacher permitted the class to participate in some especially enjoyable classroom activities.

The noise detection system that Michelson et al. (1981) used emitted an audible click when the noise level exceeded the preset level. The children were informed that if the machine did not click too often,

they would receive ice cream during their mid-afternoon snack. Apparently ice cream was a pretty powerful reinforcer for those institutionalized children, as the contingency was accompanied by a major reduction in noise.

Various strategies have been attempted to reduce *littering* in neighborhoods and parks and also within institutions and schools (Bacon-Prue, Blount, Pickering, & Drabman, 1980; Chapman & Risley, 1974; Hamad, Bettinger, Cooper, & Semb, 1980/1981; LaHart & Bailey, 1975). In an intermediate and a junior high school cafeteria, a lottery system seemed to provide a reasonable solution over a period of several weeks (Mayer et al., 1981). Tickets were distributed to children as they placed litter in trash receptacles. The children were asked to write their names on the tickets and deposit them into a decorated coffee can for their respective grades. At the end of the week, a drawing was held and children with winning tickets received special prizes that had been provided from funds allocated by the student council. Additionally, the grade level receiving the most tickets was treated to a special assembly featuring special events such as magic shows or performances by rock bands. Not only did the appearance of both cafeterias improve dramatically, but also social interactions between students and aides appeared to improve as well.

Having reviewed the literature and referred back to their knowledge of principles of behavior, the Washington Street School planning team designed a system for controlling noise, food throwing, pushing, and littering. A noise-guard meter was installed. On days when the meter showed a reading below the preset threshold, students would be permitted privileges, such as extra recess, special assemblies, access to ordinarily restricted sports equipment, and others. Children who had lunched in zones in which no fighting or food throwing had been observed, and which contained no more than one piece of litter, would be dismissed early from the lunchroom and permitted to go outside or to play in the gym. Any children who were directly observed fighting or throwing food would be given one warning to stop. Following the second such episode, they would be assigned to copy a mediational essay like one of those used by MacPherson et al. (1974). The essay consisted of four questions requiring answers that specified the consequences of the particular misbehavior and of the alternative behavior. The questions were: "What did I do wrong? What things happen that I don't like when I do wrong? What should I do? What pleasant things happen when I do what I should?" (p. 290).

As in every behavioral intervention, the team knew to specify a clear set of rules of acceptable performance in the lunchroom, involving student representatives in the process. They also selected the consequences they had observed to be effective, and now they needed to assure that these were delivered appropriately. One way to achieve that result would be to train the supervisory staff of the lunchroom, the next step in the model developed by Mayer et al. (1981).

Training lunch area supervisors

The success of any program depends on the precision and consistency with which change strategies are implemented. Informing teachers or other staff who supervise the lunch period about the planned procedures is just the beginning. They also need to demonstrate that they can implement the program as planned, meaning that they consistently present the selected consequences and, of course, that positive consequences are accompanied by specific praise. Praising improvement does not always come naturally, particularly when one's nerves are frayed by the commotion caused by remaining miscreants. So a system of planned practice and supervision usually needs to be conducted. Once supervisors are performing their new roles consistently, the trainer gradually can withdraw guidance until he or she just occasionally mentions the importance of and reinforces continued adherence to the procedure, with praise and/or evidence of its effectiveness. Staff members can forget just how awful things used to be. Data do not! (See Chapter 22 for a discussion of staff training.)

Among the skills that the Washington Street

School planning team pinpointed for training was the delivery of specific praise. A series of workshops were set up for lunchroom staff and other interested personnel, and participants were supplied with the rules for using specific praise:

- Make direct eye contact and smile.
- Use a pleasant, sincere, and enthusiastic voice.
- Include a specific statement describing the positive aspects of the student's performance. For instance, "Great! You've cleaned up every scrap from the floor. See how nice you've made it look."

Role-playing episodes were arranged. Some played the role of students; some of supervisors. The others watched and offered feedback of their own.

Trainers gave specific praise as well, following suggestions by Schumaker, Hovell, and Sherman (1977, p. 35):

If they do something inappropriately (e.g., use a sarcastic voice tone, or forget to use descriptive words) ask them to try it again making a slight adjustment in the specific problem area. Always compliment first and mention deficiencies second. For example, for the supervisor who forgets to smile, you might say, "You remembered to look at me, you used a very sincere voice tone, and you beautifully described three areas of improvement. I didn't see much of a smile, though. It's important to show a child that you are happy with the improvement and you'll do that with a smile as well as your tone of voice and the words you use. Let's try it again and this time see if you can smile as you tell me about the card. O.K.?"

Then the group went out into the lunchroom. With actual students, the trainer showed how to deliver specific praise that described which rules the students were following. Others also tried out their skills and followed up by commenting on their own performance and on the performance of the others.

When the group judged that it had mastered that aspect, it practiced filling out forms and other administrative aspects of the program. Once it was apparent that everyone had acquired all the necessary skills, they were ready to go; and the team selected a starting date. It was time to move on to the next step: implementing and maintaining the program.

Implementing and maintaining the program

During this most crucial stage of the program, it is essential that roles and responsibilities be precisely designated and that all participants indicate their clear comprehension of who is to do what, when, and with whom. The trainer or consultant is present to see how things are progressing, to ensure that observational data are continuing to be collected as planned, and that procedures are being implemented properly. Following each of the first few sessions, a brief postmortem is held. That is the time for staff problems to be aired, questions addressed, feedback delivered. After things are operating smoothly, those meetings can be scheduled less frequently and more informally. The data will tell you about the success of the program. If progress has been measured, you can conclude reasonably that the program is being implemented successfully. Lack of progress might mean that the intervention was not appropriate for the situation or that the program was not being implemented as planned. Only careful observation and supervision will enable you to decide which of the two may be responsible. Surely, the latter should be addressed first. If a program is implemented as planned, yet is not producing results in the desired direction, give it a fair trial of a few weeks. If progress still is not forthcoming, then consider altering your strategies.

Don't forget to double-check with any other people who might be involved. The Washington Street School plan called for involvement of classroom teachers, so their follow-through with delivery of privileges would need to be checked and reinforced. Appropriate assignment of the mediating essays could be verified by arranging to have the essays filed. As always, it is primarily cooperation with the program that is emphasized and praised. Lapses are handled gently, as problems to be solved, not as if they were major calamities. When dealt with in a reasonable fashion, participants usually are pleased to collect materials and report things as they actually did occur.

Phasing out the program

Sooner or later, if feasible, contrived management strategies may be phased out and replaced by more natural methods. It is best to wait for the desired change to occur and stabilize — say over several consecutive weeks. Then more intrusive artificial reinforcing consequences such as prizes can begin to be delivered less often, while the more natural ones continue as usual. You also will want to plan some gradual delay in delivering rewards, such as switching extra recess time to later in the day instead of right after lunch, and so on. It is the responsibility of the person in charge of the program to see that data continue to be recorded and that any major disruption in performance is handled by a temporary return to a previously more effective set of conditions or some substitute for that set.

Here you have seen how one general model for dealing with behavioral problems in the lunchroom can operate. By no means is this the only way to manage conduct during school mealtimes. Different models might include these steps in different order, or with their components altered. Yet a model such as this does have generality beyond coping with mealtime disruption. Take a few moments to consider how you might apply it to:

- Taking a class trip.
- Running an open classroom.
- Organizing and conducting a student governance program.
- Other behavioral problems of concern to you.

As you read the following sections on conduct in the lavatory, on the school bus, and in the playground, consider how you could fit the suggested procedures into a similar programmatic format.

IMPROVING CONDUCT IN THE LAVATORY

"I swear, I'm going to go home for lunch just so I can use the bathroom. That place is a pit!" wailed Monica.

"I know what you mean," responded Angela. "Paper towels plugging up the toilets — wet paper wads stuck to the ceiling. The things kids write and draw all over the walls are disgusting. It's gross!"

"Yeah, and you can hardly find your way through the smoke, and it's not just cigarettes," Monica said.

Wanda had similar complaints about the school bus.

"Gosh I hate going home on the school bus," she sighed. "I can't wait to get my driver's license next year."

"What's the problem?" asked her mother, Mrs. Lanz.

"Oh, I don't know. It's just such a drag. The driver seems so unfriendly and the ride takes so long."

"If that's all you have to complain about, it can't be that bad," responded Mrs. Lanz. "I was talking to Mrs. Hughes, Karl's mom, the other day. I hear that things are much worse over on the east side of town. The kids are misbehaving something awful. They run around, pester each other, and make such a commotion that the bus drivers can't concentrate. One driver has been pulling over to the side until things quiet down. But as soon as he starts up again, so do the kids. It sounds pretty dangerous to me. If I were the driver, I'd be afraid of getting so distracted that I might not be able to drive safely!"

At the Willow Grove School, a distressing thing has been happening lately. Many of the older youngsters have taken sides with one of two groups — those who live in town or those who travel in from the surrounding farms. No one knows exactly when the controversy began, but it seemed to have started with some good-natured teasing that got out of hand. Soon the teachers found themselves breaking up fistfights and imposing themselves between members of the warring factions who were baiting one another. Students would be mysteriously tripped, their books and papers strewn about, their family members insulted. Consequently, they would retaliate.

Maybe you are not beset with difficulties as severe as these. Perhaps the only problems of this sort that you face in your school are noise or an occasional altercation on the bus or playground.

Regardless of how serious conditions are for you, these difficulties are amenable to effective treatment by means of behavioral methods. As usual, whether the behavior takes place in the lavatory or bus or on the school grounds, you first must pinpoint what problems exist. Next, find out (1) how to measure them, (2) generate appropriate rules of conduct, (3) arrange for consistent consequences for following or disobeying the rules and for engaging in alternative productive behaviors, (4) implement the program, (5) measure change, (6) revise it as necessary and (7) verify the influence of the system you've selected. Finally, be sure to switch back gradually to natural contingencies whenever feasible.

Maintaining peace and cleanliness in the lavatory

At a school in California the lavatories were a complete disaster. Toilets and washbasins were plugged up. Graffiti and paper wads festooned the walls and ceilings. Water was left running. In an effort to remedy the situation, the school counselor met with members of the teaching and custodial staff and representatives from the student council. Together they formulated a set of rules:

1. Always flush the toilet after use.
2. Don't throw paper. Place all paper towels in the trash cans.
3. Don't kick doors.
4. Don't stand on toilets or washbowls.
5. Keep the walls and ceilings clean.
6. Always turn off the water after using it.

While custodial staff members agreed to continue their regular duties of cleaning the lavatories daily and keeping them supplied, several members of the student council were selected to help manage the conduct of those using the restrooms. The student patrol members were given identification belts and were assigned to stand outside a lavatory during recess and lunch. They were instructed to enter the lavatory approximately every five minutes to score the condition of the room according to a set of criteria, and they also recorded the names of any students who were observed violating the rules and reported them to their teachers. (An alternative would be to report the names of those teams for whom no violations were observed—a DRO procedure.) Teachers agreed to make sure that marking implements remained in the classroom and to instruct students to follow—and to encourage each other to follow—the rules. They also would ask their students to report any infractions to the patrol members or teachers.

The counselor trained the patrol members to evaluate the lavatories. First he demonstrated how to evaluate, then he watched patrol members rating, finally he compared the patrol member's scores with his own until they totally agreed. Later on he supervised by checking for accuracy daily, eventually cutting back to every once in a while. The patrol students earned stickers exchangeable for treats such as cupcakes or ice cream; and, of course, they received liberal praise for carrying out their duties appropriately. At the end of each month of participation, they also were awarded certificates for continuing to fulfill their responsibilities.

During the first phase of the intervention, patrol members were to score a plus if the walls were free of marks or graffiti; otherwise they assigned a minus. In the second phase, a requirement that walls and ceilings be free of paper wads was added. During the third phase, in addition, floors and washbasins had to be clean of refuse.

Patrol members recorded scores daily on a chart posted in the lunchroom. When their scores matched those of the counselor's, the team they represented was awarded bonus pluses. When the scores did not match, a penalty was imposed, and pluses were subtracted. Those strategies were designed to prevent coercion by the other students or excessive rigidity by the scorer.

At the end of each week, the team with the most pluses earned an extra recess period. If both teams had perfect scores, both earned the extra recess. In the case of a tie between two teams with less than perfect scores, both teams won, but one minute was deducted from the total time of the extra recess for each minus assigned.

Within a week, change was apparent; within several weeks, minuses rarely were awarded. As time progressed, the reinforcement program was phased out slowly, as proper behavior in the lavatory became established.

Depending on your situation, a low-cost method like this can be modified to meet your own requirements. In the early stages, you might choose to add a component that provides reinforcers for the students who use the lavatory appropriately. For instance, a monitor could be stationed in the room with a checklist, the contents of which also are publicly posted. Students who perform according to the posted rules would be awarded checks, points, or tokens exchangeable for some special privilege. This reward system would enhance the reinforcing value of the monitors' jobs, as the patrol members would be mediating positive in addition to punitive consequences.

IMPROVING CONDUCT ON THE SCHOOL BUS

Discomfort and disruption on school buses are prevalent. Improving conduct and social interactions among students and also between the students and the driver would make the ride safer and more enjoyable, and they would help the school day to start on a positive note. In your circumstances, is behavior on the school bus problematic? If so, you might appreciate finding out how others have treated this concern successfully.

Programs for improving conditions on the school bus

Sometimes a simple courtesy, such as exchanging hellos and farewells, can make the bus ride a more positive experience. For example, two bus drivers who transported high school students to and from school reported that their passengers never greeted them (Edwards & Johnston, 1977). Data recorded by the drivers during twelve baseline sessions corroborated that fact. What they did to change things was very simple. Each time the bus stopped to pick up a group of riders, the driver greeted the first student. If any of the other students in the group picked up the cue and greeted the driver, he responded with a return greeting. That's all there was to it. Can you imagine what happened? You're right. The students gradually increased the number of times they greeted the driver. The same thing happened, though to a lesser extent, when the driver primed and reinforced farewells. Interestingly, a survey found that students who rode these experimental buses rated their drivers as more friendly and the ride as more favorable than did students who rode control buses on which greetings and farewells never occurred.

If your campus is anything like many familiar to us, private autos often are used in preference to freely available group transportation, causing excessive consumption of fuel as well as parking problems. Perhaps if Wanda rode on a bus driven by a friendly driver, she might be willing to continue riding it even after she were able to drive to school. Another method for increasing bus ridership is to provide supplementary reinforcement to passengers. In one case (Ritchl, Mongrella, & Presbie, 1972), taped rock and roll music was played during the ride; in another, tokens were distributed to bus riders (Everett, Hayward, & Meyers, 1974). The tokens could be exchanged for items dispensed by local businesses. Adding those features increased ridership considerably.

In case your response is, "Who wants to increase the number of students riding our buses? Fewer students mean less trouble," then you probably are more concerned about disruption on the bus. Ritchl et al. (1972) managed disruption very simply by playing the music only when all students were seated. If your buses are intolerably noisy, the program designed by Greene, Bailey, and Barber (1981) might suggest some potential solutions. About 44 sixth through eighth graders rode the bus. From time to time, some caused serious disruptions. Because the driver was too occupied to operate the entire musical reward system, it was designed to operate mechanically. A *noise guard*, a meter similar to that used to monitor noise in the lunchroom, and four speakers were installed. Students could suggest music to be played. When noise exceeded the specific threshold level, a light was activated and the music stopped. Observers counted the number of times the threshold was exceeded and if they recorded no increase over previous days, the students were eligible to participate in a raffle. Four winners earned coupons exchangeable for burgers. Following five consecutively successful days, a raffle for ten movie passes was held. To avoid group repercussions from any single student's deliberate activation of the system, students were told that the perpetrator would be reported to the principal. Under those conditions, outbursts of noise were almost eliminated. Additionally, although not treated directly, the time spent out of seat and roughhousing by students, and the number of coercive comments by the bus driver, also diminished substantially. A second experiment showed that just the lights and contingent music were sufficient to reduce noise dramatically and even to diminish substantially the untreated out of seat activity and roughhousing, and the driver's coercive comments.

Programs for students with special needs

Are children with special needs riding your buses and giving you cause for concern? Here is how such idiosyncratic problems have been handled by others.

An eight-year-old profoundly retarded girl kicked, cried, banged her head on the seat, and fell to the floor of the bus when it slowed down or accelerated (Barmann, Croyle-Barmann, & McLain, 1980). Her caretakers tried to soothe and calm her at those times. For the first formal intervention, they withheld those forms of attention, but nothing changed. Next, they tried a different form of soothing—playing music over headphones. Again nothing changed. Next, a therapist sat beside the child and the music was continued, but each time the child engaged in any of the disruptive behaviors, the therapist removed the headphones, returning them only after the child was quiet for five seconds. That produced a major decrease in disruption. Ultimately, each of the components of the reward system were removed gradually. First the headphones were removed, but the music continued to be audible directly from the recorder. Next the volume and duration of the music gradually were diminished. Finally the therapist sat further and further away, eventually no longer riding the bus with the client at all. The driver was requested to play music from time to time when the client was seated quietly. Eight weeks of follow-up data showed that disruptive behavior remained close to zero.

A fading procedure was used to teach an autistic child to board a school bus without reacting with severe emotional outbursts (Luiselli, 1978). Remaining calm because both the mother and therapist were along, the child boarded the bus when it was parked outside the school. After a number of such trials, all three boarded the bus together a short distance away from school with the same success. Gradually they traveled longer distances and the mother and therapist spent less and less time with the child, until eventually the child successfully rode alone.

Two days of training and several days of supervision on the bus were sufficient to instruct a bus driver to employ a token system effectively with a ten-year-old retarded boy (Chiang, Iwata, & Dorsey, 1979). The bus driver was provided with a counter that she could press each time the bus reached a prespecified point on the route, such as a particular traffic light. On reaching each point, if the boy had behaved properly within the previous segment of the route, the driver praised him and advanced the counter. If the child had been aggressive, destroyed equipment, left his seat, stimulated himself, or vocalized inappropriately, the driver explained why the counter would not be pressed. At the end of the trip, the numeral on the counter was converted to points that were recorded on a card, and each card was given to the boy to hand to his teacher or parent. The points could be combined with others earned at school and home to purchase special rewards.

Within a short time, the child hardly disrupted at all on the bus.

With very young or severely handicapped children, improper conduct on the bus may not be a management issue at all—it simply might result from a skill deficit. Perhaps they simply don't know how to board, sit on, or exit from a bus. If you suspect that this might be the case, or if you are preparing children to ride buses for the first time, you can teach those skills right in the classroom, as Neef, Iwata, and Page (1978) have done. Training consisted of asking the subject to perform the correct response component by manipulating a doll on a posterboard model and saying what the doll was doing. Teachers gave corrective or positively reinforcing feedback. Subjects also were shown a set of slides representing correct and incorrect stimuli or behaviors, and were asked about the appropriateness or inappropriateness of particular situations or responses. A role-playing sequence also was included, in which subjects pretended to board a bus consisting of rows of chairs. Progression from one training phase to another depended on several criteria selected to assure mastery of the response components. When compared with an alternative training procedure that took place on an actual bus, the simulated training fared just as well and cost much less in terms of time, funds, and effort.

Using time on the bus efficiently

Have you noticed that practically all the strategies we have reported here have dealt with reducing disruption? Yet the school bus easily could provide an opportunity for recreation or learning. The old standbys used by camp counselors and parents—group singing, games such as I Spy or Twenty Questions, or other absorbing activities—well might prevent disruption in the first place. When one of the authors took her family on long trips, the children could earn points for each half hour during which they adhered to jointly specified rules; the points were exchangeable for money with which the youngsters could buy souvenirs. Participating in word games and instructional experiences, such as those just mentioned, made it much easier for the points to be earned and for time to pass quickly. Perhaps a systematic analysis of those sorts of techniques will be reported in the literature before long.

Just as Hart and Risley (1975) used incidental teaching for children with learning deficits by responding selectively to the children's use of increasingly more elaborate vocabulary, the bus ride could provide an excellent opportunity for incidental teaching. Peer tutors could be assigned to help other children to label objects and events that they pass along their route, increasing the complexity of responses over time.

IMPROVING CONDUCT ON THE PLAYGROUND

The use of peer involvement has resulted in effective improvements in other areas of behavior as well. Peer monitors have cooperated toward improving social interactions on the playground.

Trouble on the playground during recess and loosely structured activity periods is not unusual. When released from the confines of the classroom, youngsters naturally seize recess as an opportunity to let off steam. That's fine when their activities permit them to exercise and play to the mutual pleasure of themselves and their friends. But sometimes the play gets out of hand, as we saw with the students at Willow Grove. Then those of us who are responsible for their welfare must take over responsibility so that no one is harmed. As the trouble escalated at Willow Grove School, the staff realized that threats and scolding achieved little, so they decided it was time to intervene more systematically.

Recently Mrs. Olsen had attended a regional meeting on behavior analysis and classroom management. She returned with some really good ideas about reward systems and discussed them with the other teachers. Together they decided to design some "good citizen" tokens. Using a rubber stamp of a smiling face, they stamped several sheets of posterboard and cut them out. The tokens would be distributed to children in the corridors and lunchroom, and on the playground, when they were observed

sharing, playing together cooperatively, or performing some visible form of kindness. To identify the token as theirs, the children initialed them in ink. The tokens could be exchanged later for special privileges: films, local trips, extra desserts, free time, and so on. When they tried it out, the system worked.

Procedures such as these closely resemble those you would use on the school bus or in the lavatory, lunchroom, or other settings in which activities do not tend to be rigidly planned. What we shall address, instead, are a couple of pragmatic issues: the problem of staffing the programs of intervention and the logistics of assessment in an open field environment. Then we'll briefly mention opportunities for learning not only social interaction skills but also physical motor skills during periods scheduled for the playground.

Staffing

In many schools, the recess period serves as a break, not only for the students, but also for the teachers. In our experience, the children may be left almost entirely on their own or be supervised by one or two staff members and/or monitors. To recommend intervention procedures that would require the attention of many instructional staff people probably would be resented, thus proving impractical. Teachers do need a few minutes of reprieve from the continual vigilance required of them. Methods that minimize the necessity for many teachers to be present, then, would seem ideal.

You've probably anticipated what we're about to suggest, as you have heard it before: involve the students! "What! My students aren't equipped to handle difficult youngsters like Juan, Tyrone, or the town bully," you might contest. Please hold your judgment for a few moments and consider what Mullins, Fowler, and Paine (1982) did.

During recess, two mildly retarded children started fights and grabbed things belonging to other children. Following social skills training, which consisted of reading prepared scripts, modeling, and role playing, a point system was established. The boys could earn points for appropriate conduct and lose them for rule violations. They also received praise for positive cooperative social interactions. Individuals and groups could earn rewards concurrently for good behavior. First, the school consultant administered the program; then the classroom teacher took over, and next classroom peers handled it. Eventually, the first child himself was trained to serve as a monitor of the second; later, the second monitored a third, and so on. With each succeeding change in the agent who administered the program, improvement continued or was sustained, with particularly dramatic results when the target children performed as managers of the program for their peers. What's more, their social standing, as measured by sociometric instruments, also improved! Here was a case in which an intensive short-term effort by the staff paid off by enabling them eventually to fade themselves out of the picture.

Are you wondering how on earth you can measure change in performance when you're dealing with large numbers of nameless people who move in and out of the setting? The playground is a case in point. At Willow Grove School, lunchtime is scheduled for 11:45, 12:00, and 12:15, respectively, for each of the three classes. Around noon the corridors are filled with students entering and exiting the lunch area. By 12:30, everyone in the school is out on the playground whooping it up.

"How are we to know if Mrs. Olsen's system works or not? It's just about impossible to keep track of any single individual. They flit in and out so," one teacher complained. The faculty considered assigning students to specific tables and areas of the playground and requiring that they remain in a particular order in line in the corridors. That idea was rapidly rejected. "They're cooped up for hours on the bus and in the classroom. I don't think they need any more regimentation than they already have," remarked Mr. Truax. The others agreed. So, recalling how the behavior of people within a particular area at a given time could be counted, they decided to measure the performance of the group by using a zone system.[2] (Refer back to Chapter 2, page 29, to remind yourself how this system can be implemented.)

Opportunities for learning on the playground

The playground is an ideal place for students to learn physical skills, and, as we have asserted repeatedly, students involved in productive learning are less apt to misbehave. With a semblance of order restored on the Willow Grove playground, conducting practice in physical skills would be a constructive way to prevent further difficulties while enabling the students to enhance their abilities. (Refer to Chapter 17 for some suggestions here.)

---

[2]This episode is based in part on a program designed by the members of the Clifford D. Murray School in Azusa, California. The observation system was designed by Elizabeth V. Smith, Judy Jones, and G. Roy Mayer. A similar observational system has been used to record safe and unsafe performance by large numbers of factory workers (Sulzer-Azaroff & Fellner, 1984).

Summary

This chapter completes our presentation on applications of behavior analysis to conduct by discussing the topics of behavior in the lunchroom, lavatory, bus, and on the school grounds. Illustrative behavior management programs were provided for each topic. When developing a program for your school, though, be sure to remember to design it around the uniqueness of your setting, staff, and students.

A step-by-step approach to reducing disruptions and mayhem in the lunch area included: (1) clarifying the problem; (2) establishing a planning team; (3) setting goals; (4) measuring the problem; (5) formulating objectives; (6) planning the treatment program; (7) training lunch area supervisors; (8) implementing and maintaining the program; and (9) phasing out the program. The discussion on improving conduct on the school bus included bus etiquette, increasing bus ridership, programs for students with special needs, and methods for using the time spent on the bus efficiently. For the school-grounds we talked about staffing, assessment, and some opportunities for learning social and physical-motor skills.

Frequently, many of the topics covered in this chapter are overlooked. However, they can influence the quality of the students' environment, and impact on how both students and staff respond to the school climate. Effective programs for these areas can help make the school a more desirable place in which to learn and work.

Study Questions

1. (a) Identify the people who should be consulted when determining if there is a need for a program to improve conditions in the lunch area, and (b) discuss the advantage of consulting these individuals.
2. Several teachers have agreed to conduct a needs assessment. List three things they should note during their systematic observations.
3. Provide a guideline for selecting people to serve on a planning team.
4. Review the list of potential goals and record any that you might overlook when designing a program for the lunch area.
5. You have created a list of goals for your school's lunch area, but realize that you will need to set priorities. Identify the questions you could ask yourself to make your task simpler.
6. Mr. Nickerson would like to learn how other people have solved problems similar to those at his school. Tell where he could find this information.
7. Discuss the rationale for collecting baseline data before attempting to solve a major school-wide behavioral problem.
8. Provide an original example of a behavioral objective for a program in the lunch area.
9. (a) Identify and (b) provide an original example of each of the two planning strategies for achieving objectives.
10. Narrate a novel noise reduction program using token reinforcement.
11. T/F Behavioral procedures are generally ineffective for reducing litter in neighborhoods. Support your answer.
12. Design your own intervention using positive reinforcement for a program to reduce the number of papers on the floor. (Be sure to involve the students.)
13. Your students are requested to write an essay when they misbehave in the lunch area. List the four questions that they should answer in the essay.
14. Identify the techniques that have been tried successfully to train personnel precisely and consistently to implement specific skills.
15. Describe the appropriate way to give praise.
16. Discuss the important considerations and steps that should be taken during the implementation of a lunch program.
17. (a) What are *postmortem* discussions? (b) Tell how frequently they should be held.
18. Steve found that progress was not being made in his program. Discuss (a) the possible explanations and (b) the steps he should take in the future.
19. T/F Lapses in cooperation by staff should be thought of as major problems and handled accordingly. Support your answer.
20. Describe the correct way to phase out management strategies.
21. Mr. Kane began to set up a behavioral program to improve conditions in the rest rooms. He pinpointed the problems and devised a measurement system. List the six steps that he would follow subsequently.
22. Student patrol members have been recording infractions. Data show that many of the recordings are inaccurate. Offer a solution to the problem.
23. The bus driver wants to participate in a pro-

gram to make bus rides enjoyable. Design a procedure to involve her.

24. Develop an original program to increase bus ridership.
25. Identify a method for reducing noise levels.
26. Amy, a retarded five-year-old, will not remain seated and fails to get off at the appropriate bus stop. Data reveal that these behaviors are not in her repertoire. Describe in specific detail how you will teach her these skills.
27. Students pretended to board the bus in a role-playing sequence to teach them acceptable bus boarding. This (select the best answer):
    (a) requires that the students reach a criterion level before progressing
    (b) is very time consuming
    (c) can be more expensive
    (d) requires more effort of the staff than if a real bus were used.
28. T/F   The bus can provide an opportunity for recreation and learning. Support your answer.
29. Discuss how bus riding can provide an opportunity for *incidental learning*.
30. Design a procedure that involves peer monitors to reduce trouble on the playground.
31. T/F   Retarded children are incapable of being peer monitors. Support your answer.
32. Provide two advantages of using peer monitors.
33. (a) Narrate a description of the procedure you would use in measuring behavior within zones. (b) Explain your reasons for choosing the zone system.
34. List five desirable behaviors children can learn on the playground.
35. List at least one advantage of teaching physical skills on the playground.

References

Bacon-Prue, A., Blount, R., Pickering, D., & Drabman, R. (1980). An evaluation of three litter control procedures: Trash receptacles, paid workers, and the marked item techniques. *Journal of Applied Behavior Analysis, 13,* 165–171.

Baltes, M. M., & Hayward, S. C. (1976). Application and evaluation of strategies to reduce pollution: Behavioral control of littering in a football stadium. *Journal of Applied Psychology, 61,* 501–506.

Barmann, B. C., Croyle-Barmann, C., & McLain, B. (1980). The use of contingent-interrupted music in the treatment of disruptive bus-riding behavior. *Journal of Applied Behavior Analysis, 13,* 693–698.

Chapman, C., & Risley, T. R. (1974). Anti-litter procedures in an urban high-density area. *Journal of Applied Behavior Analysis, 7,* 377–383.

Chiang, S. J., Iwata, B. A., & Dorsey, M. F. (1979). Elimination of disruptive bus riding behavior via token reinforcement and a "distance-based" schedule. *Education and Treatment of Children, 2,* 101–109.

Edwards, K. A., & Johnston, R. (1977). Increasing greeting and farewell responses in high school students by a bus driver. *Education and Treatment of Children, 1,* 9–18.

Everett, P. B., Hayward, S. C., & Meyers, A. W. (1974). The effects of a token reinforcement procedure on bus ridership. *Journal of Applied Behavior Analysis, 7,* 1–9.

Greene, B. F., Bailey, J. S., & Barber, F. (1981). An analysis and reduction of disruptive behavior on school buses. *Journal of Applied Behavior Analysis, 14,* 177–192.

Hamad, C. D., Bettinger, R., Cooper, D., & Semb, G. (1980/1981). Using behavioral procedures to establish an elementary school paper recycling program. *Journal of Environmental Systems, 10,* 149–156.

Hart, B., & Risley, T. R. (1975). Incidental teaching of language in the preschool. *Journal of Applied Behavior Analysis, 8,* 411–420.

LaHart, D., & Bailey, J. S. (1975). Reducing children's littering on a nature trail. *Journal of Environmental Education, 7,* 37–45.

LaRowe, L. N., Tucker, R. D., & McGuire, J. M. (1980). Lunchroom noise control using feedback and group contingent reinforcement. *Journal of School Psychology, 18,* 51–57.

Luiselli, J. K. (1978). Treatment of an autistic child's fear of riding a school bus through exposure and reinforcement. *Journal of Behavior Therapy and Experimental Psychiatry, 9,* 169–172.

Luyben, P. D., & Bailey, J. S. (1979). Newspaper recycling: The effects of rewards and proximity of containers. *Environment and Behavior, 11*, 539–557.

MacPherson, E. M., Candee, B. L., & Hohman, R. J. (1974). A comparison of three methods for eliminating disruptive lunchroom behavior. *Journal of Applied Behavior Analysis, 7*, 287–297.

Mayer, G. R., Nafpaktitis, M., & Butterworth, T. W. (1981). *Dealing with disruption and mayhem in the school lunch area.* Office of the Los Angeles County Superintendent of Schools, Downey, CA.

Michelson, L., Dilorenzo, T. M., Calpin, J. P., & Williamson, D. A. (1981). Modifying excessive lunchroom noise: Omission training with audio feedback and group contingent reinforcement. *Behavior Modification, 5*, 553–564.

Mullins, B. S., Fowler, S., & Paine, S. (1982, May). *Recess revisited: The use of peer monitors to reduce negative interactions on the playground.* Paper presented at the meeting of the Association for Behavior Analysis, Milwaukee, WI.

Neef, N. A., Iwata, B. A., & Page, T. J. (1978). Public transportation training: *In vivo versus* classroom instruction. *Journal of Applied Behavior Analysis, 11*, 331–344.

Ritchl, C., Mongrella, J., & Presbie, K. J. (1972). Group time-out from rock and roll music and out-of-seat behavior of handicapped children while riding a school bus. *Psychological Reports, 31*, 967–973.

Schumaker, J. B., Hovell, M. R., & Sherman, J. A. (1977). *Managing behavior. A home-based school achievement system.* Lawrence, KS: Excel Enterprises, Inc.

Sulzer-Azaroff, B., & Fellner, D. J. (1984). Searching for performance targets in the behavior analysis of occupational safety: An assessment strategy. *Journal of Organizational Behavior Management, 6*, 53–65.

V Organizational management: promoting and sustaining effective educational change

"Hey, K. C.," called the principal. "Your in-service program was a smashing success. I haven't seen such a surge of optimism among the staff for many years."

"I'm so pleased they enjoyed the meetings. There is good reason for optimism too, provided, of course, that the behavioral strategies are practiced consistently."

"Why? Don't you think everyone's going to try?"

"It's not their intentions that should concern us. It's how effectively they carry out the rules for good teaching. Don't forget that even for educationally sophisticated people like ourselves, rule-governed behavior is effective only to a certain point. We are no different from other creatures, in the sense that the contingencies of reinforcement we have experienced govern our behavior even more forcefully. If our schools are to enable students to learn successfully and with enjoyment, then we must arrange our own environments to help keep us applying the strategies."

This last chapter describes some methods for helping you to organize your environment for yourself and/or your staff. As always, please use the suggestions primarily as illustrative examples. Then, as you progress, try to employ the behavioral principles you have learned as a basis for devising strategies appropriate to your own particular setting.

22 Staff development strategies

Goals

After completing this chapter, you should be able to:

1. State briefly the way to go about maximizing your staff's accomplishments.
2. Specify and discuss the first step in creating a staff development program.
3. Define and provide examples (other than those illustrated) of four basic communication techniques.
4. Offer answers to each frequently posed question concerning the behavioral approach.
5. Describe and illustrate methods for developing measurable objectives for staff.
6. Discuss why staff development, planning, and training teams should have broad representation.
7. List the individuals who should be members of the staff development team, and describe how and why each should be selected.
8. Explain why the senior administrator is an especially essential member of the staff development team.
9. Describe how the authors use the term *staff development*.
10. Describe the importance of arranging for reinforced practice as part of the staff development program.
11. Illustrate how shaping can be used during consultations with staff members.
12. Describe why student progress has been reported to be insufficiently reinforcing for changes in teacher behavior.
13. Describe and illustrate how prompts and cues can be used to teach or foster the transfer to the classroom of behavior learned during training.
14. Describe and illustrate how artificial support for staff members' performance is faded.
15. Discuss why it is important to provide a variety of reinforcers to support and maintain staff behavior.
16. List and describe several ways of providing reinforcement within the natural environment to staff members to promote transfer and maintain their performance.
17. Describe why it is important to provide a variety of reinforcers to support and maintain staff behavior.
18. Respond to six frequently asked questions about the behavioral approach.

Fingers snapping, hips twisting to the beat of a Latin melody, Ms. Thomas's class has formed a circle to watch Juan and Carmen perform a series of intricate movements.

"Man, I just wish I could dance like that," sighs Sam, as he struggles to duplicate Juan's steps. "Hey, Ms. Thomas, this sure beats doing our regular work."

"I'm glad you people are having fun. You earned your party all right—and this is the first time that every single member of the class worked well enough to attend one of our special events. We should all be proud."

"Yeah!" echoed a chorus of the students who stood within hearing range. A few glanced briefly at the chart verifying that all of them had completed at least 90 percent of their class and homework assignments acceptably.

Inadvertently caught up in the musical beat, Ms. Thomas found her own head nodding and fingers snapping as she reminisced with wonder. How had it all come about?

Much as we wish we could attribute the minor miracle totally to the in-service lectures provided by Mr. Lee, we must confess that much more was involved: With his guidance, the members of the staff repeatedly practiced the skills under simulated and real circumstances, receiving from him considerable reinforcement initially and a diminishing amount as their proficiency increased.

You too will want to find out about tactics of staff development beyond reading and lectures. For although your knowledge of behavioral strategies undoubtedly has grown as a result of studying our material, you too will need to receive and provide opportunities for reinforced practice if your performance or that of your staff is to change durably.

PROGRAMMING STAFF CONSULTATION AND TRAINING

You have seen how the staff members of our three model schools have sought to learn methods for improving their skills in managing, motivating, and instructing their pupils through coursework, formal and informal consultation, books and journals, and in-service training. The regular use of these traditional tactics has persisted for a reason: they can be useful. For example, in upper New York State, one teacher of difficult-to-manage 12- and 13-year-olds had requested consultation and training in how to decrease misbehavior and lead discussions (Burka & Jones, 1979). After several months passed and the teacher still hadn't received the desperately needed help, the principal gave her a text on token econo-

mies. This book plus a set of instructions apparently aided her, because the teacher was able to implement a very successful token system. (We hope our text will be similarly useful for you.)

There is a sequel to the story of that teacher, though. About a month later, she finally received formal training via didactic instruction and role playing in a mock classroom. As a result, just as with her colleagues who had received similar training earlier, her class improved much more dramatically than it had the previous time, with disruptions during class discussions eliminated almost completely. Therefore, if you wish to maximize your own or your staff's accomplishments, it may not be sufficient to supply them with reading material or lectures only. You probably should supplement them with other instructional methods.

How can this be accomplished? By using the very same principles with staff that we have found helpful with our students, and by arranging the environment so that positive change is most likely to happen and keep happening. That means approaching the topic systematically, knowing where you want to go and how to get there, and receiving adequate support along the way.

Assess the system

Earlier we have seen many instances of staff members seeking out consultation and training opportunities in an effort to remedy emergency situations. That is understandable. We all try to *avoid* and *escape* from aversive circumstances. Yet if trying to extinguish brush fires were our only basis for learning educational skills, our progress would be neither effective nor efficient. There would be little opportunity to design a system to *prevent* problems in the first place and to *enhance learning*. In contrast, we should plan our programs of staff development with the same amount of forethought as we would any other program of behavior change, which means starting out by assessing the system.

As you will recall from Chapter 3, you should begin by conducting a *needs assessment*. If you are in charge of consultation services or staff development and are deciding how to proceed, make contact with your superiors, staff, parents, students, and members of the community. Find out what they want of their schools and in what order of priority. (Refer back to the instruments displayed in Figures 3.4 and 3.5 for some ideas.) Among the differences of opinion, you probably will find some major points in common — for example, those concerning academic performance, social deportment, and vocational preparation. Focus on the points in common with the highest priorities, as they should be supported most heavily, particularly by those most directly involved. Touch bases with those same key people so you can determine if the methods you are considering are acceptable; otherwise, negotiate others that *are* mutually acceptable. If Mrs. Olsen had decided to train the other teachers at Willow Grove to institute peer tutoring and the teachers and parents were unalterably opposed to both the concept and methods, the plan would have little likelihood of success. Yet, it was precisely because the requests for in-service training and consultation came from the Washington teaching staff that Mr. Lee found everyone so cooperative.

In case you are functioning in a consulting role, the demands on your services can become inordinate, so you may have to set some priorities for yourself if you are to survive. Yet you want to do the most good possible for your system. With which staff and students will you choose to intervene? How do you decide? Melahn and O'Donnell (1978) offer an objective data-based strategy you might find useful. What they did was to conduct behavioral observations in a large number of Head Start classrooms on the island of Oahu, Hawaii. There they developed a behavioral code and norms for 32 behaviors, comparing age, sex, exceptional status, and other factors. They found out a great deal about their population, including that cooperative activities, talk, and silence changed as a function of age; that boys were more active than girls; and that the exceptional children engaged in more antagonistic interchanges with peers. Heavily represented in referrals were boys who were quieter and girls who were noisier than their peers. The authors assert that normative observations of this type can be useful for three main reasons: first, to determine if the referral is appropriate, that is, whether data support the presence of identified problematic behaviors; second, to ensure that the consultant observes a wide range of the students' behaviors, not just those identified by the referring teacher; and third, to compare the performance of referred pupils to that of their peers in their own particular cultural setting. They also suggest that if you are aware that particular forms of conduct are likely to improve simply as a function of time, then treating those would best be postponed.

Establish rapport

If you are to be successful in providing training and consultation, you need to establish good relations with your trainees and clients. You need their respect so your instruction holds discriminative control (e.g., functions as discriminative stimuli), and your attention and approval must be reinforcing. It might prove helpful for you to teach yourself and practice some of the communication techniques that have derived from the counseling field (Goodwin & Coates, 1976; Ivey, 1974; Ivey, Miller, & Gabbert, 1968): reflecting, clarifying with "I" statements, summarizing, and communicating nonverbally in a positive manner. Table 22.1 defines and illustrates each of those techniques.

Although the logic and evidence of the effectiveness of behavioral strategies tend to convince even the most serious skeptic over time, you may find that your initial contacts are impeded temporarily by concerns about the morality, generality, and technology of the approach. In Table 22.2 we present some frequently voiced concerns and our responses to them. Perhaps you too will find them useful while you are establishing rapport with your trainees and clients.

Specify objectives and measures

Assuming you now are communicating effectively with the other staff members, you and your trainees should be ready to set objectives and measures. The objectives will derive directly from the goals you identified by means of the needs assessment, observations, and interviews. As you assemble the goals,

Table 22.1
Communication techniques

Techniques	Definitions	Illustrations	Comments
1. Reflecting	a. Repeating verbatim what was said.	a. Teacher: "I'm thinking about quitting teaching." Consultant: *"You're thinking about quitting teaching?"*	The use of this reflecting technique should be restricted to situations of disbelief or confusion.
	b. Repeating the last couple of words.	b. Teacher: "I just feel as though I have taken on too much." Consultant: "Too much?"	This second reflecting technique can serve as a reinforcer by informing the teacher that you have heard what was said, and as an S^D to cue the teacher to continue discussing the situation.
	c. Paraphrasing: Communicating in your own words what you have heard the teacher say.	c. Teacher: "I just feel as though I have taken on too much." Consultant: "Right now you're really feeling overwhelmed and down."	This is the most helpful of the three in communicating understanding.
2. Clarifying	a. Seeking additional information by expressing your confusion or need for clarification.	a. Teacher: "Yes, Tyrone was really hyper today." Consultant: "Hyper? I'm not sure I understand what he was doing."	This communication technique is used to help you, the consultant, to understand more clearly the actual situation, the behavior(s) of concern, and the goals sought by the teacher. It promotes greater specification or operationalization of the behaviors. This technique also helps to avoid an overreliance on questions to obtain such information. An overuse of questions can, at times, seem intimidating and evaluative.
	b. Confirming your tentative understanding.	b. Consultant: "Hyper? Do you mean he was throwing things, yelling, and jumping out of his seat a lot again?"	
3. Summarizing	Stating the major points that have been discussed in a sequence analysis (A-B-C) format.	Consultant: "Let me see if I understand things so far. During the beginning of class (A), Tyrone tends to yell and jump more than at other times (B). Your response has been to ignore such behavior or to tell him to settle down (C). Is that right?"	Summarizing frequently serves to refocus the consulting session by communicating where you are so far in working on the problem. It also clarifies the A-B-C relationship.
4. Nonverbal	a. Demonstrate attention.	Make eye contact. Nod following verbalizations that you agree with and/or understand.	

Table 22.1
Communication techniques *(continued)*

Techniques	Definitions	Illustrations	Comments
	b. Take notes in an A-B-C format.	List the behavior(s) of concern under B, the antecedents under A, and the consequences under C. Do the same for the goal behavior(s).	Note-taking helps to focus the session on analyzing and solving the problem, and provides you with a record of what transpired.
	c. Sit at a 90-degree angle to the teacher.		Sitting this way permits the teacher to see what you are writing.*

*We also have found it helpful to verbalize what we are writing to inhibit the teacher from talking while notes are being taken. It avoids, then, the problem of trying to write notes of something previously said while the teacher is discussing an important new point. It also focuses the attention on the A-B-C analysis.

set priorities based on long-term as well as short-term considerations plus whatever objective data you may have or can obtain. If you are like most others we know, you will be tempted to be overly ambitious at first, wanting to accomplish everything at once. Instead, resist the temptation and try to identify outcomes that should be achievable within a reasonable time period, so you and the participants will receive fairly rapid reinforcement for your efforts. Select measures and criteria levels with the same factors in mind:

- "Within a month following training, Mr. Truax will have involved at least three students in peer tutoring for at least one subject three times a week."
- "Each teacher will have developed a set of class rules and corresponding consequences by the end of the last week of the first month of the semester."
- "All pupil personnel specialists will have visited at least three classrooms for a minimum of ten minutes for two weeks in a row."
- "The frequency of individual educational plans prepared by each special service team [according to Maher's (1981a) seven criteria for an evaluable plan] will increase to five per month."

Each of those objectives probably can be measured and achieved fairly readily. To graph progress, you would define the behavior operationally, specify measures, and record and plot the data as a function of such conditions as baseline, training, and maintenance over time (see Figures 22.1, 22.2, and 22.3).

Select staff

You need a staff for several purposes: to plan, implement, evaluate, and provide follow-up management. Either different individuals or the same ones may be included, depending on the specified activities.

The planning team. This team should be composed of individuals representing all of the constituencies involved. These may include students, teachers, pupil personnel specialists, administrators, and parents. Sometimes other specialized personnel are involved: attendance officers, lunchroom or playground supervisors, bus drivers, street crossing guards, or others depending on the nature of the program. Several educators (Mayer & Butterworth, 1979; Mayer, Butterworth, Nafpaktitis, & Sulzer-Azaroff, 1983; Nafpaktitis, Mayer, Hollingsworth, & Butterworth, 1982) included on their planning teams three carefully selected teachers, along with the school's administrator, psychologist and/or counselor, one to three students, one or more parents, plus other specialized personnel members as needed. The team's responsibilities were to design, carry out, and monitor school-wide conduct-manage-

Table 22.2
Frequently posed questions about the behavioral approach and our responses

1. "Isn't what we're doing a form of bribery?"

It might be, if we were using our methods, as the dictionary says, to pervert the judgment of or to corrupt the people whose behavior we were attempting to manage, and if our ends were to our own advantage but to their detriment. On the contrary, however, we see behavioral strategies as being applied for those people's benefit. Also, we systematically reinforce their doing schoolwork with the kinds of events that we ourselves experience in our own everyday lives: praise, recognition, and material rewards. How long would we continue working at our jobs if we received no recognition or remuneration? Why should our students and clients be expected to be any different than we are?

2. "Are you saying I should reinforce students to get them to do something they should be doing anyway?"

Our perspective says that we concern ourselves more with what *is* rather than what should be, within, of course, ethical and humanitarian constraints. If, for example, our students are performing satisfactorily, and their progress seems to be supported adequately by the natural consequences of success, then it is not necessary to arrange formal reinforcing events. Instead, we would continue to praise and recognize their accomplishments intermittently as merited.

If, on the other hand, our students and clients are not performing satisfactorily, we feel that the responsibility for attempting to remedy the situation is ours. Collaboratively, where possible, we need to try to rearrange the environment and turn things around so we promote success. This objective could be accomplished by providing them with support services, transferring them into a different environment, or modifying their current environment. In many cases, we will need to adopt the very same reinforcing consequences that we already are dispensing unsystematically (e.g., attention, assistance, privileges) and scheduling their delivery more precisely. In other circumstances, we may need to augment the natural reinforcing events with others more powerful for the individual, to encourage movement in the desired direction. When progress is well established, though, we begin gradually to dispense with those artificial supports, using the individual's patterns of behavior to guide our actions. In essence, behavioral strategies are among the most important teaching tools we can use.

3. "How do I find the time to do all this?"

How much time and effort are you currently expending in attempting to cope with problem situations, to motivate your students, and to remediate their learning deficiencies? Often you only need to redistribute your energies in these more constructive directions. Any extra investment during start-up phases should be compensated for rapidly as your students begin to progress and the social climate of your classroom starts to improve.

4. "I would feel phony and awkward using behavioral strategies. What should I do?"

Such reactions are to be expected. Did you feel natural or confident when you first started driving, speaking a foreign language, or playing tennis? If we only did the things with which we felt comfortable, we would learn very few new skills. Learning new skills often takes time, effort, and the patience to overcome initial periods of awkwardness. As progress is reinforced, the skill begins to feel more natural. Also, as with many skills, once we become proficient in applying them, either because of their intrinsic properties and/or because of the reaction from the environment, they begin to become reinforcing in their own right. Watch, for example, the expression of pleasure from a student who has been recognized for a well-deserved accomplishment and you will see how giving recognition can be reinforced naturally.

5. "Do behavioral principles apply to everyone?"

Yes. However, the specific details of their application must vary with the individual. Each person is a composite of genetic endowment and other physical characteristics, learning history, and current circumstances. For this reason, strategies must be arranged to suit the individual's requirements under particular sets of conditions. Fortunately, with informed and creative planning, it is often possible to identify procedures that are suitable for groups of individuals.

Table 22.2
Frequently posed questions about the behavioral approach and our responses (*continued*)

6. "Isn't it unfair to treat students differently?"

First, we need to realize that we already do that by paying attention to troublesome behavior. Also, for the reasons just stated, if we treated everyone alike, the effect on their behavior would not be uniformly beneficial. Next, consider a number of other factors:

a. By being singled out for special attention for accomplishing something, the student's social status often improves, which provides a reasonable antidote to the impaired status the student may have suffered as a result of being scolded or corrected for past wrongs.

b. Special attention should be phased out over time, slowly, as performance improves. Then it will be possible to turn that attention to others in need of it.

c. If you plan carefully, the others also can be given a share in the reinforcing events that are dispensed to the individual student: group celebrations or entertainment, special class activities, and so on. Just shifting from aversive to reinforcing consequences can help to make the classroom atmosphere more pleasant and rewarding for everyone.

d. Reinforcement is dispensed for *improvement* in performance, and everyone can stand to improve in some manner. If you worry that one student is getting special privileges but the others aren't, you can consider doing something similar for them. Ask the others to identify some areas in which they themselves feel they would like to improve, and plan currently or in the near future to initiate special procedures for them.

e. It doesn't hurt to explain to your students that each of you is unique and that each has special interests, skills, and areas of weakness (yourself included). Often they will understand that it makes sense to focus on different behaviors to change and to use different methods.

f. Finally, often it is a great relief to the individual students' classmates when help is finally on the way. The classmates may have been suffering from their peers' difficulties and may recognize that they stand to benefit from the intervention. Sometimes it helps to point this benefit out to them and reinforce their supportive efforts.

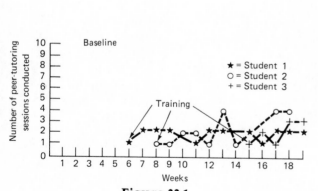

Figure 22.1

The number of peer-tutoring sessions conducted each week in Mr. Truax's class. Each symbol refers to a different student.

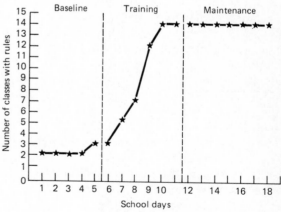

Figure 22.2

The number of classes posting rules of conduct plus consequences. Notice that the number increased dramatically during training and continued during management.

371

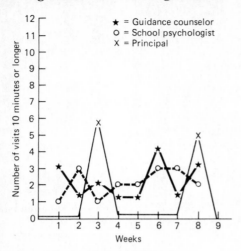

Figure 22.3
The number of classroom visits by the principal, school psychologist, and guidance counselor over an eight-week period.

ment programs and to implement in-service meetings for the entire staff of the school.

Why involve such broad representation? By sharing their varied perspectives, these individuals can help to set priorities and define objectives and measures. They also can react to proposed methods, voicing approval or suggesting modifications. Additionally, as we have seen repeatedly, *involvement promotes change.* Just as including workers in the development of pay incentive plans improved their attendance (Scheflen, Lawler, & Hackman, 1971), and allowing students to collaborate in generating rules or participate in selecting consequences seemed to enhance programmatic effectiveness (Mayer & Butterworth, 1979; Mayer et al., 1983; Nafpaktitis, et al., 1982; Sulzer, Hunt, Ashby, Koniarski, & Krams, 1971), we would expect that involving representatives in planning staff training programs would promote their groups' cooperation and support. There is good reason for this assumption because the groups they represent are going to be affected. During planning, it becomes clear how this involvement will occur, so the ultimate arrangement should be seen as mutually beneficial.

The *senior administrator* of the organization—in

schools, the principal; in districts, the superintendent—is an especially essential member of staff development programs. He or she can participate directly, as in one case in which the principal helped to mediate a timeout procedure among disruptive junior high school students (Nau, Van Houten, & O'Neil, 1981). Although, due to other time demands, the administrator may not always be able to join in quite so actively, he or she must be included in planning if this person is to be expected to encourage and support programs of change.

Administrators at all levels are often prestigious models, and they control many of the contingencies necessary for success. If they do not actively endorse your activities, your attempts probably will be thwarted. This assertion is supported in at least one case in which we have been involved (Mayer, Butterworth, Komoto, & Benoit, 1983). When we examined vandalism rates in various schools, we found that decreases were experienced in those schools in which consultants reported that the administrative staff was highly involved and supportive; on the other hand, those in which administrators were less involved suffered an increase. We make it a practice to limit our own participation only to programs in which administrators or managers have expressed their complete endorsement of our activities and preferably participate as needed, because their active involvement tends to produce much better results.

In addition to the senior and other administrators, what particular individuals should be selected to represent the various constituencies? In many instances, there is just one possible individual: a school psychologist, counselor, resource specialist, reading specialist, or truant officer, perhaps. In other cases, the constituency is large: pupils, parents, and teachers, for example. In the latter situation you should apply what you have learned about selecting effective models. Try to identify highly prestigious individuals who share common characteristics with their peers and thus are more likely to be imitated by them. This method of selection will encourage the cooperation of the groups represented and also will prove useful later on, for when training is carried out some of those very same people can serve a key role.

The training team. While we recognize that it can be useful to recite strings of words to guide ourselves in carrying out particular actions, the reinforced practice is what counts the most. We must rehearse the skills we want to acquire, preferably with help and guidance. Now the matter could become more complicated. From where will such assistance derive? Even were Mr. Rodriguez and Mr. Lee willing to invest a substantial portion of their time in this endeavor, the amount they have available is finite. How could they possibly provide adequate supervision to more than a dozen teachers? They need to examine available resources, and so do you.

We suggest that the training team be composed of the same people as the planning team. In the event that this is not possible, you may need to search elsewhere for participants. Look about and see who—in addition to your professional consultant and supervisor—might be available to perform some of the necessary training, program implementation, and evaluation functions you require.

Starting at the beginning, there is *you*. You certainly could participate in the selection of training objectives and instructional resources for yourself. You also can collect your own data, assuming that the skills you are teaching yourself are not too complicated. As an example, in a study by Nelson, Hay, Hay, and Carstens (1977), several fourth-, fifth-, and sixth-grade teachers learned to record their own use of positive statements accurately by operating a clicker worn about their necks. (Their self-recording of negative statements was not quite so accurate, and in addition they found that recording them appeared to heighten the frequency of negative statements, so you probably wouldn't want to do that anyway.)

Then there are your *students*. Students, as we have seen, often have been trained and supervised to perform various important instructional functions, such as tutoring peers and serving as aides to classroom teachers (Loos, Williams, & Bailey, 1977). Examples also have been reported in which students have served as observers (Whyte, Van Houten, & Hunter, 1983) and have modified not only their own performance but that of their teachers as well (Graubard, Rosenberg, & Miller, 1971). In the latter case,

those students were successful in increasing their teacher's positive contacts with them by contingently smiling and making positive comments. We request that our students compliment us, the authors, when they hear us as being polite but firmly refuse to undertake too many outside responsibilities—and that really helps!

Parents and *paraprofessionals*, such as undergraduates, volunteers, teacher's aides, and others, also may prove helpful as data collectors and contingency managers. As community representatives, parents who participate also can increase support from that realm. They can correct misunderstandings that might arise among their neighbors and sometimes contribute materially as well, for instance by providing tangible and social reinforcers for students and staff. Parents often are included in home-based reinforcement systems, like the **daily report card** method, by providing reinforcing events according to plan (Bailey, Wolf, & Phillips, 1970). Also, many of the papers published on training and supervision of school personnel report involving the members of the research team, many of whom are graduate and undergraduate students, in helping to conduct the program. (That is one reason it often pays to welcome behavioral researchers into school settings.)

Just as we have suggested that you train peers, paraprofessionals also should receive training and supervision, if they are to perform their roles well. Several investigators (Offner, Faught, Dark, Crow, & van den Pol, 1983) have developed a system for utilizing paraprofessionals in a preschool setting. Included in the program are methods for assessing competent performance, procedures for refining trained skills, tactics for ensuring transfer of skills to the teaching environment, strategies for assessing and enhancing skill maintenance, and systems for providing evaluative feedback.

One of the most useful and constructive sources of personnel support is your *peer group*. Just as student peers can help one another, professional colleagues can assist by providing instruction, modeling, and feedback. Here is a fine example of this concept: in all, 12 teachers from two elementary inner-city schools in Rochester, New York, were involved in training (Jones, Fremouw, & Carples, 1977). First, three of the teachers were instructed via a package including modeling, role playing, and other elements in a set of classroom management skills. Then they, in turn, each trained three of their fellow faculty. While improvement was quite substantial, those first-tier teachers who had benefitted least from their initial training showed major gains once they had performed as coaches for their peers. A similar model was used to train 45 institutional direct-care staff by first training three of their supervisors (Page, Iwata, & Reid, 1982), while another application of the method was used with peers who taught their fellow employees safety-related skills at a developmental disabilities center (van den Pol, Reid, & Fuqua, 1983).

When educational personnel serve as trainers and managers among their colleagues, they are functioning in the manner of *master teachers*. Because they may share their own experiences, they are also *resource* people and, of course, they act as *models* who have much in common with those they are training. These peer-trainers also benefit as well. They are likely to learn the skills even better than before, and they also gain prestige and possibly other rewards as a consequence of serving in that role. When you identify staff members to serve as peer-trainers, therefore, you probably will find it advantageous to rotate the job among highly skilled, resourceful, and respected individuals. If those qualifications are carefully and objectively defined, candidates can be selected fairly. Other staff will know what skills they need to perform to qualify and can aim toward achieving them. Although the prestige of being a peer-trainer may be sufficient reinforcement to encourage participation, nevertheless we suggest that you consider offering some incentive pay for these extra duties, not only to augment the reinforcement for participation but also to make the position especially attractive to others.

Veteran teachers who supervise student teachers play a particularly crucial role in training future teachers. As Baer and Bushell (1981, p. 267) point out

> Most behavior analysts will appreciate that the real power to determine a future teacher's teaching

is the first period of apprenticeship, practicing teaching in an actual classroom with real students, under supervision of a real (and usually veteran teacher). . . . If behavior analysis is to appear in the teaching behaviors of teachers, it will have to survive the moment of apprenticeship. That means that the veteran teacher must model, explain, and reinforce the same logic that was taught in concept.

If you are a veteran teacher, you systematically will reinforce good teaching practices, without delay, regularly and often. (Of course, if you are a trainer of teachers you will see to it that your students not only learn the concepts of behavior analysis, but that you reinforce their application of those concepts during their student teaching.)

Naturally the *pupil personnel specialists* are going to be especially active in this area. It is probably apparent to you by now that we feel that training, consultation, and management should constitute a major portion of the guidance counselor's, social worker's, and psychologist's activities. Limiting themselves to serving students directly places severe restrictions on the number that can be served. By assuming a position of leadership in staff development and supervision, pupil personnel specialists can multiply their coverage many times over.

Direct line supervisors sometimes can play an especially helpful role in implementing programs in the school environment. We already have seen how a principal participated in a timeout program (Nau et al., 1981). In another case, Souweine, Sulzer-Azaroff, and Frederickson (1977) studied how a principal's positive comments might influence teacher's rates of praising. The teachers first were trained in a workshop to apply specific praise in their classrooms. Initially their rates of praise were high following training, but they began to drop off gradually during a phase in which the principal dropped by regularly to comment on other matters. When the principal began to comment positively on the teacher's use of praise, however, the rates increased back to the high posttraining level.

At a state center for multihandicapped retarded people, an in-service program was implemented to teach staff appropriate methods of interacting with and stimulating residents (Montegar, Reid, Madsen,

& Ewell, 1977). Training alone was insufficient to sustain the practice of the skills; when the supervisor commended and attended to staff members for interacting with residents, however, performance increased substantially. At a similar type of facility, Fox and Sulzer-Azaroff (1983) also found that after supervisors began to deliver performance feedback to them, staff members increased the number of fire evacuation training trials they conducted with residents. Once more we see the importance of active involvement of supervisors or administrators in staff development activities.

IMPLEMENTING STAFF DEVELOPMENT ACTIVITIES

You may have noticed that our use of the term staff development is rather broad. Its activities may take place within group sessions for staff, as with the in-service lecture-discussions of Mr. Lee, or during consultation sessions in a specialist's office, as you saw with Dr. Levy, the Parker family, and teachers at Franklin High. Or it might and often does take place directly in the setting in which the skills are to be practiced: the classroom or other locations for school-related activities.

Let's consider Ms. Thomas's experience, the one result of which we saw at the opening of this chapter. During the later in-service training sessions, she and Mr. Lee worked together directly in the classroom to develop a management system. After discussing their alternatives, Mr. Lee showed her how to plan with the class. Together all of them developed a point system for increasing academic output. Mr. Lee continued to help for a while—visiting, checking on the recording system, and providing Ms. Thomas with a good deal of reinforcing feedback. As performance improved, Mr. Lee was able to diminish the amount of help he gave, while Ms. Thomas and the class carried on, as you saw, quite successfully.

Lest you be skeptical that this sort of event is too fanciful, you should know that a number of its key aspects are based on an actual case experience. In that case, however, the school psychologist initiated the program and it actually was carried out by a first-year graduate and a senior undergraduate student working under the direction of one of the authors (Alavosius, Brown, & Sulzer-Azaroff, 1983).

Arrange for reinforced practice during training

Our anecdote was designed to describe how lecture formats generally serve as jumping-off points rather than as complete training packages. For as we have mentioned repeatedly, saying is not the same as doing. For this reason, verbal instruction constitutes the first in a series of elements of a behavioral consultation or training program. With the addition of the other elements—those that provide for active involvement plus consequences—performance improves much more.

One example was a study (Flanagan, Adams, & Forehand, 1979) comparing the effectiveness of four strategies to teach parents how to use timeout in the home. The strategies were written instructions, lectures, videotaped modeling, and role playing. While all helped to increase parents' *knowledge* of the procedures, only the two latter methods were found to produce major transfer of the appropriate use of timeout in the home.

Maher (1981b) also found that active participation and feedback were especially effective in a study with educational personnel. Several public school managers were trained in a program that included discussion, behavioral rehearsal, social reinforcement, and feedback. The results compared favorably with a format that emphasized only lectures and discussions. In another study that same year (Maher, 1981a) the members of special service teams were taught successfully to increase their frequencies of developing "evaluable educational plans" (i.e., educational plans capable of being objectively evaluated) by means of exercises, behavioral rehearsals, and discussions of the seven essential ingredients of such plans. In a similar manner, Krumhus and Malott (1980) demonstrated that modeling and feedback enhanced the use of descriptive social reinforcers by tutors, over and above their rates under instructions alone; and Adams, Tallon, and Rimell (1980) showed that role playing was better than lectures as a device for training staff to continue implementing behavioral procedures. You saw earlier how this was also the case with the teacher who began her own token economy while awaiting training (Burka & Jones, 1979). In our own preservice training of educators and psychologists, we use an extensive array of training materials that call for active responding and provide for feedback under simulated and real-life circumstances. [See Sulzer-Azaroff and Reese (1982) for a training manual designed for this purpose.]

Reinforce successive approximations and response sequences

As with students, a staff member's performance of choice may be absent from his or her repertoire, so reinforcement alone will not help. In that case, you can teach the skill by using *shaping* and *chaining* strategies. Here is an actual case illustration reported by Mayer and McGookin (1977): a teacher requested help in coping with her rowdy class. After observing several times it became clear to the consultant that the teacher scolded and corrected the students very frequently, but never complimented or praised them. When faced with the prospect of substituting praise of good behavior for the negative feedback, she expressed strong reservations, protesting that she would not have the time for such unnecessary frills. So the consultant instead suggested a bonus response cost system, which the teacher agreed to implement. Each student started out with a set number of points, one of which was crossed off each time the teacher observed the student misbehaving. Points could be exchanged for time in an activity center that the consultant helped the teacher to set up in the rear of the room. After a few days, the deportment of the class began to improve and the teacher did not need to scold and correct as often. Then the consultant advised that following a period of 10 to 15 minutes during which all the students were on task, the teacher might dispense a bonus point to each member of the class. Next the teacher was convinced to spend a bit of the free time made available complimenting those students who were performing well.

Specific examples were described, and the teacher grudgingly agreed to try. At the end of each session, the consultant pointed out the improvements that had accrued as a result of the teacher's efforts, and little by little the class continued to progress. Eventually, the teacher was complimenting her students fairly regularly. Class deportment was much improved, and the students reported to a formerly skeptical principal that they enjoyed school much more because their teacher wasn't always yelling at them.

Arrange for continued reinforcement, transfer, and maintenance

Here we come to the most challenging aspect of staff training: promoting transfer of skills into the natural setting and keeping them going. Unfortunately, we cannot assume that this transfer will happen automatically, or even after once being applied successfully that student progress will be sufficient to sustain the practice of those skills. In a study by Craigie and Garcia (1978), when students' behavior improved as a function of therapy, the teacher's daily ratings of the children also improved; but behavioral improvement by students did not appear to change the way the teacher interacted with the students. Much the same findings were reported by Coles and Blunden (1981), for although there had been an increase in the engaged behavior of residents of a hospital for the mentally handicapped in Wales, the improvement did not lead to maintenance of the program by the staff. It actually may be the case that certain forms of student progress are sufficiently reinforcing for teachers—for instance, progress that is clearly discernible and obviously tied to the teacher's practice of newly acquired skills. If the skill that the teacher is acquiring, though, is one that requires considerable effort and concentration, then imperceptible, mild, or delayed changes in student performance may be insufficient. In such instances, it would be necessary to supplement, perhaps temporarily, with auxiliary S^Ds and reinforcers. Among the most promising of these are prompts and cues on the antecedent stimulus side and feedback (via self-recording or the assistance of others), private and public acknowledgment, praise, special privileges, and rewards on the consequent side. A few illustrations follow.

Prompts and cues. The primary form of training in the classroom study by Alavosius et al. (1983) consisted of modeling procedures for the teacher in the classroom. After watching once or twice, she was able to implement them herself. You too might try a similar approach. If, instead, the staff member really seems to have learned the skill well and just needs to be reminded to implement it, then you could use some form of cueing system. Such techniques were employed by Hall, Lund, and Jackson, (1968) using a colored piece of paper; and by Zeilberger, Sampen, and Sloan (1968), who used head nods to remind teachers to apply reinforcement. Often just your presence functions as an S^D for your trainee, because while you were present during the original training you presumably dished out considerable reinforcement in the process. In case the trainee is too preoccupied to glance in your direction, you might consider resorting temporarily to a bug in the ear, a radio transmitter with a receiver that plugs into the ear like those we use for listening to television without disturbing others. We know of cases in which such devices have helped busy classroom teachers to catch particular students being good and student teachers to coach motor skills in large gymnasiums.

Readily visible checklists can guide your trainees to remember to perform each subtask of the skills they are practicing. In the Mastery Learning Center at the University of Massachusetts, as daily reminders, staff members post a list of their duties and responsibilities on the wall directly next to their desks. Their supervisor does the same thing, listing tasks to accomplish that particular day. At Western Michigan University, a checklist system also is used to improve task performance among staff of an instructional program (Bacon, Fulton, & Malott, 1982). These authors, as well as Burg, Reid, and Lattimore (1979), provided their participants with prepared checklists, which presumably not only eased their task of self-recording but also served as effective S^Ds or prompts.

If you are trying to increase the frequency of a particular teaching practice, you can indicate directly on the list the number of times the skill should be practiced during a given time period. Providing a separate box for each check also should help to prompt the response. Figure 22.4 displays an example of a file card that Mr. Genovese kept in his pocket. The darkened boxes were to be ignored, while the blank boxes were to be checked. During this particular week, assuming that they merited it, he planned to compliment the students at least once when they entered, also when they got down to work, and during wrap-up. He also would compliment them at least four times when he observed them doing their work during class. The following week he would darken one box less for the work period, to remind himself to increase the rate to five times that week.

Sometimes prompts and cues are an integral aspect of your program. For instance, if you are conducting a token economy, then as you are delivering tokens you probably will be reminded to praise, a side effect a number of investigators have noted (Mandelker, Brigham, & Bushell, 1970). Something similar should happen if you present daily report cards or notes to parents, give out certificates, or use a wall chart to chart or graph student accomplishments. The delivery of praise tends to be cued when reinforcing events and items are delivered.

The use of very precise guidelines also can help. For instance, a high school teacher agreed with Far-

Date ________ Class period ________

SKILL	NUMBER OF TIMES DONE								TOTAL
Complimenting orderly entry									
Complimenting getting to work									
Complimenting work during period									
Complimenting orderly wrap up									

Figure 22.4
Checklist for teacher as a personal reminder to catch students being good.

ber and Mayer (1972) that he would praise at least one student who was behaving appropriately during the first minute of the period. He also would select two time blocks of approximately five minutes each during which he would circulate about the room, dispensing praise where appropriate. In another case, the parents of a teenage boy, with whose family one of us was consulting, found it difficult to find anything to praise in their son's deportment. During a meeting, we practiced identifying some of the boy's positive actions. The parents then were given the assignment of identifying and writing down each evening three things that the boy had done well during the day. The parents reported that they found themselves praising the child much more frequently, which probably resulted from their close monitoring of his behavior and finally noticing that there was much to praise.

Sometimes just specifying *target dates* is sufficient to set the occasion for increases in staff performance (Cronin, 1982). Ten home supervisors in a developmental center had been given a set of blank forms and instructed to complete behavioral data reports weekly. The tendency was to hand in the reports very late, nearly 20 days late on the average. When the management system was modified only slightly, by supplying blank forms one day in advance of the date by which the form was to be turned in, performance turned around. The average number of days late dropped to two and then to one.

Fading prompts and cues. If a prompt is integral to a program, there will be no reason to arrange to fade it. Otherwise, eventually you will want to dispense with the artificial support. The staff member's performance should be controlled by circumstances natural to the setting, so you will apply your fading techniques here just as you did in establishing stimulus control: gradually, and moving from the most to the less obtrusive prompts. If you use a card or a bug in the ear, pause temporarily and see if the skill is performed in its absence; be sure, of course, to reinforce. Then extend the pauses, recording to assure yourself that the level of performance is sustained. Once those devices are eliminated entirely, continue to be on hand for a number

of sessions and then begin to fade your own presence, turning over data recording to someone else, possibly the trainee. Similarly, checklists and task analyses probably will not be necessary forever and slowly can be faded by suggesting that they be checked intermittently rather than continuously.

Reinforcing trainee behavior. This lesson has been emphasized so thoroughly that by now it could be superfluous. But, please bear with us one more time. More often than we like to admit, we overlook the obvious, particularly when it comes to applying reinforcement with those people with whom we interact most closely in our daily lives: our families, friends, colleagues, and ourselves. Somehow we seem to assume that such people are different and don't require the same reinforcement as those on the outside. Is this the message of the saying, "Familiarity breeds contempt?" Here, with the most important individuals involved, we may be overlooking this terribly important aspect.

Like most other behavioral phenomena, this oversight probably has a behavioral explanation: we have had so many trials of interacting with these folks in a certain way that the patterns are particularly resistant to change. So if you want to turn that problem around, you may need to program reinforcement very carefully, particularly when a staff member is learning a new skill. (Remember that effective reinforcement implies frequent application of a *variety* of reinforcers during the early acquisition period. Only after the behavior is well established should you *gradually* begin to thin those out.) Here, then, we describe a few strategies for reinforcing trainee behavior that staff developers have found helpful.

With little extra effort, you can deliver feedback that is based on performance just observed or recently recorded on video or audio tape. *Performance feedback* like that often can be provided naturally. Charts and checklists not only cue, but they also supply feedback. As the number of checks on your list grows, these become more and more reinforcing, signaling that the job is approaching completion. Your trainees, too, can be taught to provide themselves with covert verbal feedback and praise, complimenting themselves for skills well practiced. You also can teach them to solicit positive feedback from those about them in a gentle and socially acceptable manner. They can do this by describing something that they accomplished without unduly emphasizing their own role or by sharing products, such as students' papers, projects, or graphs showing clear improvement.

Formal systems of feedback have been found to be especially useful for promoting all types of employee performances. [See Prue and Fairbank (1981) for an extensive review of the topic.] As an educator, you may be particularly interested in some of the feedback systems that have special relevance for school personnel.

Two teachers of multihandicapped deaf children first were taught to set objectives and measure pupil performance (Hundert, 1982). Next, they were given a training manual to teach them a general problem-solving approach to developing behavior change programs for their students. Teachers then scored their own methods of dealing with the target behaviors by referring to the definitions for each of seven teaching variables. They also corrected any incorrect aspects of their performance and could request comments from the trainer. The trainer's comments were limited to indications of errors and to praise for correct application of training. Measures of pupil performance showed that the teachers were able to design and implement successful programs of behavior change.

The role of the school psychologist has expanded to include not only assessment but also consultation and participation in the development of behavioral management programs. In one study, by asking two school psychologists to record their activities and independently verify those records via the teachers they purportedly served, each of the two was found to be conducting less than four of either type of service — consultation or management program developments — weekly (Maher, 1981a). As an intervention, the director of psychological services provided written feedback by means of a summary sheet (Maher, 1981a, p. 32) "that described the frequency and range of the service activities engaged in by the school psychologist during the previous week rela-

tive to particular performance goals set by the psychologist for that week." As a result, each psychologist showed major increases in her rates of providing each service. You should notice that *feedback in this study was tied to preset performance goals*, a tactic that many successful businesses and industries also are using as effective management strategies. We can understand why it works so well — because the S^Ds and consequences are tied to the performance of concern.

Teachers in two elementary schools were responsible for generating the daily instructional program of one handicapped pupil and for planning and evaluating that pupil's mainstreaming instructional program each week (Maher, 1981/1982). They did this sporadically until a performance feedback sheet was introduced by the principal and checked each week if the duties had been performed. The feedback from the principal markedly increased the percentage — to nearly 100 percent — of instructional programs and evaluation recordings that were conducted.

The 19 teachers of a junior high school in Nova Scotia carried out their before- and after-school supervisory duties inconsistently (Whyte, Van Houten, & Hunter, 1983). So a 13-year-old student was enlisted, and she, along with the experimenter, separately checked a roster of the teachers present for supervision. During the baseline period, only about 60 percent were there for morning duties and only about 30 percent for afternoon duties. As an attempted remedy, a large bristol board poster covered with plastic laminate displayed the percentage of staff attending during morning sessions and the best record to date. Attendance rose to nearly perfect as a result. When the same method was employed for the afternoon duties, attendance doubled. The teachers, unfortunately, were not pleased with the system until the purpose of the study was explained to them. (Because of the nature of the study, staff members were not informed beforehand as to its objectives.) For this reason, the authors cautioned that prior to implementing a public posting feedback system of this type, it is important to invite the participation of those involved during planning and intervention, a point with which we heartily concur.

Notice that in several of these programs, feedback was paired with praise, and for good reason too. It tends to improve the results further. In one case (Cossairt, Hall, & Hopkins, 1973), the investigators reported that when they delivered feedback to teachers, some of the teachers may have found it aversive — results were inconclusive; but when praise was added, performance improved substantially. In another study (Shook, Johnson, & Uhlman, 1978), care givers in a human service setting were encouraged to keep their graphs of client progress current. Group and individual feedback brought graphing up to date; but adding praise (e.g., "It's great that you graphed your data today") increased the rates even further. In a similar study in industry (Chandler 1977), a supervisor was informed that the productivity of his shift and his negative comments were being recorded. Although feedback and praise were delivered as a consequence of production increases and not for reductions in negative comments, production rose *and* negative comments dropped out almost entirely.

Consultation is an activity that also can serve a reinforcing function. After two certified special education teachers were provided with a list of ten program-relevant behaviors to be implemented during small group instructional sessions (Maher, 1981a), it was found that their frequencies of applying those elements remained low. However, when they added an intervention consisting of weekly consultation meetings with the school psychologist to discuss implementation methods and review problems, almost all of the elements were applied consistently.

The cases just cited generally have involved feedback, either directly face to face, or indirectly in writing by people employed within the setting. What happens, as with the three Willow Grove teachers, when trainers and consultants are separated geographically from those they serve? When you are employed in a sparsely populated area and have responsibility over a broad geographical region, you often face this problem. We have, in rural areas of southern Illinois and Massachusetts, as have others of our acquaintance elsewhere around the world. Here are some techniques that have been used to promote *behavior modification by long distance*.

A third-grade teacher, Ms. J., who lived 500 miles away from Philip Bornstein of the University of Montana, contacted Bornstein for assistance in managing the inappropriate out-of-seat behavior of one of her students (Bornstein, Hamilton, & Quevillon, 1977). Communicating only by means of the mail and telephone, and with the assistance of a classroom aide who functioned as a reliability observer, they were able to institute collaboratively an effective positive practice program.

Beverly Holden coordinated an intensive program for children with learning difficulties at Southern Illinois University (Holden & Sulzer-Azaroff, 1972). The students would attend her program for several months, during which time they were assessed and provided with remedial instruction. Once their progress was judged reasonable, the children were returned to their own local systems, carrying with them a set of prescriptive instructional materials plus a set of daily checklists, on which teachers were to note the number of prescriptive assignments they had administered each day. Recognizing that the teachers probably would require some support to continue to apply the prescriptive materials, yet unable to visit those locations herself, Ms. Holden phoned from her office. She called the teachers, either weekly or daily, to inquire as to how things had been progressing in general and how many assignments were completed in the interim. She also commented positively on their accomplishments. More assignments were completed with the daily calls, but levels were also reasonably acceptable with the weekly ones. Probably over time, teachers might become satiated with daily calls but not with weekly ones, so you might consider using a weekly schedule yourself, at least during the latter stages of your maintenance program.

In another case, Sharon Hunt (Hunt & Sulzer-Azaroff, 1974) was teaching a class of multihandicapped children assembled from a wide geographical region. Each mother of these youngsters agreed to help her child with a prewriting activity at home and to send the completed work back to school in the child's lunch box the next day. Only a few of the mothers complied, until following each completed assignment Ms. Hunt enclosed a note of thanks for the youngster to return to the parent. Before long, all were following through quite consistently.

The foster mothers of several developmentally disabled clients resided in rural areas of western Massachusetts. Each had selected some self-help skills and volunteered to teach them to her child (Fox & Sulzer-Azaroff, 1981). After the program supervisor prepared a task analysis and taught the mothers how to conduct the instruction, maintenance was accomplished by means of regularly scheduled telephone and mail contact.

The Big Sky Early Education Center (van den Pol, 1982) is a program designed to serve preschool children in remote areas of Montana. The goals of the program are to prepare handicapped youngsters to go to school and function in groups, provide them with formal instruction and therapeutic services, and train and support staff. Volunteers and parents are involved heavily and receive training and support as well. Role playing, checklists, and data sheets on teacher performance and child progress are among the materials used to train and support instructional personnel as they function in isolated regions of the state. [See van den Pol, Crow, and Offner (1982) for a description of the staff development and support system.]

Performance feedback and either direct or indirect consultation, as we have seen, can function as effective reinforcers in a variety of circumstances. We suspect that they operate most effectively when the time or effort required of the trainee is not too formidable. When the change you seek is substantial or when the less intrusive events just described fail to accomplish the purpose, you may solve the problem by selecting *extrinsic reinforcers*. Such reinforcers historically have been found to promote effective behavioral change among staff.

Salaries and bonuses, tied to performance objectives, offer potential for improving the performance of school personnel, just as they have been shown to in industry (Gaetani, Hoxeng, & Austin, 1983; Orpen, 1978). We suggest if you plan to try such a method that, to be equitable, performance objectives be based on prior performance of the staff and students involved and be designated and assessed mu-

tually by management and staff. You also might try to establish the forms of group contingencies that are based on cooperation and support. [See Hake and Vukelich (1972) and Litow and Pumroy (1975) for an analysis of the social effects of group contingencies.] For example, teams could set objectives and then distribute incentive pay evenly among team members when those objectives were met.

Many *other potential reinforcers* exist in addition to those presented above. Some, such as a group's preferred work schedule (Reid, Shuh-Wear, & Brannon, 1978), flexitime (Ronen & Primps, 1980), commendations, supervisory counseling, a lottery system (Shoemaker & Reid, 1980), token economies (Kent, Malott, & Greening, 1977), extra leave time (Durand, 1983), and other reinforcing contingencies have been found effective in controlling staff absenteeism.

A number of other possibilities that have been suggested by school personnel include public recognition of faculty and student accomplishments, such as during staff meetings, over the public address system, and in newsletters and the press; notes of praise and letters of appreciation, commendation, and recommendation; release from extra duties; time to attend in-service training, meetings, and conferences; rapid responses to suggestions and requests for assistance or materials; opportunities to teach peers; and various other special privileges and tangible rewards.

In selecting reinforcers for school personnel, remember that these personnel/"subjects" are always right, as are all other student-client/"subjects." If an event fails to increase an individual's rate of responding, it is not sufficiently reinforcing. Turn, then, to other possibilities until they show their effects. If you need to use some intrusive system of reinforcement, try always to tie it to the more intrinsic forms of reinforcement, such as feedback, and an emphasis on improved performance by the trainees and their students.

Again, we must remind you that while many potential sources of support and reinforcement are available to you as an educator, there will be times when no matter what you do, it will not help. Events are and have occurred beyond your purview and over which you have little or no control. Staff members at Washington Street School may or may not have the resources or control of the contingencies that can supersede Lucinda's history as an abused child, or those at Franklin the wherewithal to counter Marissa's current social and sexual reinforcers. They should set a reasonable estimate of time and costs during which they will do their best. If the anticipated improvements do not come to pass, they should turn elsewhere, at least temporarily.

EVALUATING PROGRAMS OF STAFF DEVELOPMENT

Accountability, the hallmark of behavior analysis, applies to programs of staff development as well as to those affecting students directly. You want to know whether your efforts are producing the intended results so you can continue on, revise your activities, or shelve them in favor of alternative methods. You also want to be able to communicate your accomplishments to the consumers of your services and to your supervisors. (Be careful, though, when you tell people who are unfamiliar with behavior analytic terms and concepts what you have accomplished. Make sure you avoid excessive use of technical terms and jargon. We know we are in trouble when we say "in-seat behavior" instead of "sitting down.")

To assess progress, you can record and chart skills practiced by staff, as we showed in the hypothetical data in Figures 22.1 to 22.3, and the progress being made by their students, as illustrated elsewhere in this book. You also may want to record other *process variables*, such as specific training skills performed, attendance and punctuality during training sessions, subjective reactions of trainees, the regularity with which training was held, and other such elements. But the key measures always will be the ultimate *outcome variables*—the performance of students, particularly as they begin to succeed academically, personally, and socially. That is education's bottom line!

Summary

If students are to succeed educationally, the school staff that serves them must competently practice effective strategies of management, motivation, and instruction, which requires that it possess and consistently apply good teaching skills. Such skills, although sometimes practiced intuitively, normally need to be acquired, expressed, and regularly supported by the school environment. To teach and reinforce these skills, we advise that you conduct an ongoing program of staff development.

Effective staff development takes careful planning and execution. Before you begin, conduct a needs assessment to determine current problems and practices and to discover the degree of existing support you might anticipate for proposed programs. Then, **because involvement promotes support, form teams that include representatives of all constituencies involved. Such teams will be responsible for planning, implementing, and evaluating the staff development programs.**

Next you need to provide appropriate experiences to enable the staff to acquire and regularly apply effective skills. To achieve that end, you can use the same strategies among staff as with students: teaching, consulting, supervising, and managing by applying principles of effective behavior change. Yes, you inform; but you also prompt, shape, and reinforce skills when they are appropriately rehearsed in the training setting and when they are performed in the classroom or elsewhere in the school.

In this book, we have seen how our fictitious characters were aided by means of behavioral strategies: how Juan learned to interact effectively with his peers, and how promising plans were developed to enable Richard to overcome his academic difficulties. We have witnessed Tyrone's initial entry into the mainstream and Billy's improvement in reading. We have seen how the staff members in our three schools have found more effective ways of managing, motivating, and instructing their students, thereby finding their jobs so much more rewarding; and we have observed numerous actual episodes based on the authors' experiences and cases reported in the literature to show that just about all of us and our students can change for the better. So let us set challenging but reachable goals for ourselves and apply the most suitable and promising strategies toward attaining them within our settings. And then let us congratulate ourselves, not only as we effectively prevent and treat problems, but particularly as we and our students jointly progress toward achieving educational excellence.

Study Questions

1. You have been asked to design a program of staff development. Identify the first step you will take.
2. (Refer to the previous question.) List the people you should contact.
3. Although the people with whom you consult will have different opinions, you will find some major points in common.
   (a) State three points in common you are likely to discover, and
   (b) provide a guideline to aid in selecting the one upon which to focus.
4. Discuss the advantages of doing normative observations.
5. (a) List and (b) briefly define each of the four communication techniques that have derived from the counseling field.
6. (a) List each of the six concerns listed in Table 22.2, and (b) in your own words provide a brief answer to each question.
7. Provide a list of guidelines for setting objectives, measures, and criteria.
8. Discuss the purpose of selecting staff for development activities.
9. (a) Discuss and (b) identify the responsibilities of the planning team.
10. Present an argument for having a broad representation on a planning team.
11. Discuss the advantages of including a senior administrator in a program of staff development.
12. (a) Identify the people ideally suited for the training team, and (b) list those individuals you could involve in the event that you are unable to obtain the help of your first choice.
13. List several settings in which staff development activities may take place.
14. State two procedures for teaching skills not in a staff member's repertoire.
15. Identify the most challenging aspect of staff training.
16. List a set of prompts and cues you might include in a program of staff training.
17. Identify the circumstances under which you (a) should and (b) should not fade prompts and cues.
18. Provide a possible reason why people tend to forget to reinforce the performance of those closest to them.
19. Discuss in detail ways to encourage your trainers to provide feedback and praise.
20. Design an original program that combines feedback with praise.
21. T/F Consultation can serve a reinforcing function. Support your answer.
22. Describe an original staff supervision pro-

gram that could be implemented from 200 miles away.

23. Provide a list of guidelines for tying salaries and bonuses to performance objectives.

24. Identify several potential reinforcers for school personnel.

25. The _____ are always right. Elaborate on the statement above.

26. T/F There will be times when no matter what you do, it will not help. Explain your answer.

27. List several (a) process variables and (b) outcome variables. (c) State which variables are more important.

References

Adams, G. L., Tallon, R. J., & Rimell, P. (1980). A comparison of lecture versus role-playing in the use of positive reinforcement. *Journal of Organizational Behavior Management*, 2, 205–212.

Alavosius, M., Brown, C. S., & Sulzer-Azaroff, B. (1983, October). *Increasing academic productivity in a sixth grade class*. Paper presented at the annual conference of the Berkshire Association for Behavior Analysis and Therapy, Amherst, MA.

Bacon, D. L., Fulton, B. J., & Malott, R. W. (1982). Improving staff performance through the use of task checklists. *Journal of Organizational Behavior Management*, 4, 17–25.

Baer, D. M., & Bushell, D. Jr. (1981). The future of behavior analysis in the schools? Consider its recent past, and then ask a different question. *School Psychology Review*, 10, 259–270.

Bailey, J. S., Wolf, M. M., & Phillips, E. L. (1970). Home-based reinforcement and the modification of predelinquents' classroom behavior. *Journal of Applied Behavior Analysis*, 3, 223–233.

Bornstein, P. H., Hamilton, S. B., & Quevillon, R. P. (1977). Behavior modification by long-distance: Demonstration of functional control over disruptive behavior in a rural classroom setting. *Behavior Modification*, 1, 369–380.

Burg, M. M., Reid, D. H., & Lattimore, J. (1979). Use of a self-recording and supervision program to change institutional staff behavior. *Journal of Applied Behavior Analysis*, 12, 363–375.

Burka, A. A., & Jones, F. H. (1979). Procedure for increasing appropriate verbal participation in special elementary classrooms. *Behavior Modification*, 3, 27–48.

Chandler, A. B. (1977). Decreasing negative comments and increasing performance of a shift supervisor. *Journal of Organizational Behavior Management*, 1, 99–103.

Coles, E., & Blunden, R. (1981). Maintaining new procedures using feedback to staff, a hierarchical reporting system, and a multidisciplinary management group. *Journal of Organizational Behavior Management*, 3, 19–33.

Cossairt, A., Hall, R. V., & Hopkins, B. L. (1973). The effects of experimenter's instructions, feedback, and praise on teacher praise and student attending behavior. *Journal of Applied Behavior Analysis*, 6, 89–100.

Craigie, F. C. Jr., & Garcia, E. E. (1978). Effects of child behavior change on teacher verbal behavior and rating of student behavior. *Journal of Applied Behavior Analysis*, 11, 308.

Cronin, J. (1982). A comparison of two types of antecedent control over supervisory behavior. *Journal of Organizational Behavior Management*, 4, 37–47.

Durand, V. M. (1983). Behavioral ecology of a staff incentive program: Effects on absenteeism and resident disruptive behavior. *Behavior Modification*, 7, 165–181.

Farber, H., & Mayer, G. R. (1972). Behavior consultation in a barrio high school. *The Personnel and Guidance Journal*, 51, 273–279.

Flanagan, S., Adams, H. E., & Forehand, R. (1979). A comparison of four instructional techniques for teaching parents to use time-out. *Behavior Therapy*, 10, 94–102.

Fox, C. J., & Sulzer-Azaroff, B. (1981, May). *A program to train and maintain geographically distant foster-parents' teaching*. Paper presented at the Association for Behavior Analysis, Seventh Annual Convention, Milwaukee, WI.

Fox, C. J., & Sulzer-Azaroff, B. (1983). *Effectiveness of performance feedback from a supervisor vs. a non-supervisor in promoting paraprofessionals' implementation of basic fire-evacuation training*. Paper presented at the Association for Behavior Analysis, Ninth Annual Convention, Milwaukee, WI.

Gaetani, J. J., Hoxeng, D. D., & Austin, J. T. (In press). A productivity analysis of commission compensation replacing salary compensation at a small business. *Journal of Organizational Behavior Management,* 7.

Goodwin, D. L., & Coates, T. J. (1976). *Helping students help themselves.* Englewood Cliffs, NJ: Prentice-Hall.

Graubard, P. S., Rosenberg, H., & Miller, M. B. (1971). Student applications of behavior modification to teachers and environments or ecological approaches to social deviancy. In E. A. Ramp & B. L. Hopkins (Eds.), *A new direction for education: Behavior analysis, 1971* (pp. 80–101). Lawrence, KS: University of Kansas.

Hake, D. F., & Vukelich, R. (1972). A classification and review of cooperation procedures. *Journal of Experimental Analysis of Behavior, 18,* 333–343.

Hall, R. V., Lund, D., & Jackson, D. (1968). Effects of teacher attention on study behavior. *Journal of Applied Behavior Analysis, 1,* 1–12.

Holden, B., & Sulzer-Azaroff, B. (1972). Schedules of follow-up and their effect upon the maintenance of a prescriptive teaching program. In G. Semb, D. R. Green, R. P. Hawkins, J. Michael, E. L. Phillips, J. A. Sherman, H. Sloane, & D. R. Thomas (Eds.). *Behavior analysis and education—1972* (pp. 262–277). Lawrence, KS: University of Kansas.

Hundert, J. (1982). Training teachers in generalized writing of behavior modification programs for multihandicapped deaf children. *Journal of Applied Behavior Analysis, 15,* 111–122.

Hunt, S., & Sulzer-Azaroff, B. (1974, September). *Motivating parent participation in home training sessions with pre-trainable retardates.* Paper presented at the American Psychological Association, New Orleans, LA.

Ivey, A., Miller, C., & Gabbert, K. (1968). Counselor assignment and client attitude: A systematic replication. *Journal of Counseling Psychology, 15,* 194–195.

Ivey, A. E. (1974). The clinician as teacher of interpersonal skills: Let's give away what we've got. *The Clinical Psychologist, 27,* 6–9.

Jones, F. H., Fremouw, W., & Carples, S. (1977). Pyramid training of elementary school teachers to use a classroom management "skill package." *Journal of Applied Behavior Analysis, 10,* 239–253.

Kent, H. M., Malott, R. W., & Greening, M. (1977). Improving attendance at work in a volunteer food co-operative with a token economy. *Journal of Organizational Behavior Management, 1,* 89–98.

Krumhus, K. M., & Malott, R. W. (1980). The effects of

modeling and immediate and delayed feedback in staff training. *Journal of Organizational Behavior Management, 2,* 279–293.

Litow, L., & Pumroy, D. K. (1975). A brief review of classroom group-oriented contingencies. *Journal of Applied Behavior Analysis, 8,* 341–347.

Loos, F. M., Williams, K. P., & Bailey, J. S. (1977). A multielement analysis of the effect of teacher aides in an "open"-style classroom. *Journal of Applied Behavior Analysis, 10,* 437–448.

Maher, C. A. (1981a). Improving the delivery of special education and related services in public schools. *Journal of Organizational Behavior Management, 3,* 29–44.

Maher, C. A. (1981b). Training of managers in program planning and evaluation: Comparison of two approaches. *Journal of Organizational Behavior Management, 3,* 45–56.

Maher, C. A. (1981/1982). Performance feedback to improve the planning and evaluation of instructional programs. *Journal of Organizational Behavior Management, 3,* 33–40.

Mandelker, A. V., Brigham, T. A., & Bushell, D., Jr. (1970). The effects of token procedures on a teacher's social contacts with her students. *Journal of Applied Behavior Analysis, 3,* 169–174.

Mayer, G. R., & Butterworth, T. (1979). A preventive approach to school violence and vandalism: An experimental study. *The Personnel and Guidance Journal, 57,* 436–441.

Mayer, G. R., Butterworth, T., Komoto, T., & Benoit, R. (1983). The influence of the school principal on the consultant's effectiveness. *Elementary School Guidance & Counseling, 17,* 274–279.

Mayer, G. R., Butterworth, T. W., Nafpaktitis, M., & Sulzer-Azaroff, B. (1983). Preventing school vandalism and improving discipline: A three year study. *Journal of Applied Behavior Analysis, 16,* 355–369.

Mayer, G. R., & McGookin, R. B. (1977). *Behavioral consulting.* Downey, CA: Office of the Los Angeles County Superintendent of Schools.

Melahn, C. L., & O'Donnell, C. R. (1978). Norm-based behavioral consulting. *Behavior Modification, 2,* 309–338.

Montegar, C. A., Reid, D. H., Madsen, C. H., & Ewell, M. D. (1977). Increasing institutional staff to resident interactions through inservice training and supervisor approval. *Behavior Therapy, 8,* 533–540.

Nafpaktitis, M., Mayer, G. R., Hollingsworth, P., & Butterworth, T. (1982). *Constructive discipline: Improving attendance and reducing disruption and vandalism* costs. (End of year evaluation report, ESEA Title IVC #5867) Downey, CA: Los Angeles County, Superintendent of Schools Office.

Nau, P. A., Van Houten, R., & O'Neil, A. (1981). The effects of feedback and a principal-mediated timeout procedure on the disruptive behavior of junior high school students. *Education and Treatment of Children*, 4, 101–113.

Nelson, R. O., Hay, L. R., Hay, W. M., & Carstens, C. B. (1977). The reactivity and accuracy of teachers' self-monitoring of positive and negative classroom verbalizations. *Behavior Therapy*, 8, 972–985.

Offner, R., Faught, K. K., Dark, S., Crow, R., & van den Pol, R. (1983, May). *Staff management: A system for utilizing paraprofessional and volunteers in a handicapped preschool setting*. Paper presented at the Association for Behavior Analysis, Ninth Annual Convention, Milwaukee, WI.

Orpen, C. (1978). Effects of bonuses for attendance on absenteeism of industrial workers. *Journal of Organizational Behavior Management*, 1, 118–124.

Page, T. J., Iwata, B. A., & Reid, D. H. (1982). Pyramidal training: A large-scale application with instructional staff. *Journal of Applied Behavior Analysis*, 15, 335–351.

Prue, D. M., & Fairbank, J. A. (1981). Performance feedback in organizational behavior management: A review. *Journal of Organizational Behavior Management*, 3, 1–16.

Reid, D. H., Shuh-Wear, C. L., & Brannon, M. E. (1978). Use of a group contingency to decrease staff absenteeism in a state institution. *Behavior Modification*, 2, 251–266.

Ronen, S., & Primps, S. B. (1980). The impact of flexitime on performance and attitudes in 25 public agencies. *Public Personnel Management*, 9, 201–207.

Scheflen, K. C., Lawler, E. E., III, & Hackman, J. R. (1971). Long-term impact of employee participation in the development of pay incentive plans: A field experiment revisited. *Journal of Applied Psychology*, 55, 182–186.

Shoemaker, J., & Reid, D. H. (1980). Decreasing chronic absenteeism among institutional staff: Effects of low-cost attendance program. *Journal of Organizational Behavior Management*, 2, 317–328.

Shook, G. L., Johnson, C. M., & Uhlman, W. F. (1978). The effect of response effort reduction, instructions, group and individual feedback, and reinforcement of staff performance. *Journal of Organizational Behavior Management*, 1, 206–215.

Souweine, J. D. W., Sulzer-Azaroff, B., & Fredrickson, R. H. (1977). *Maintaining increased teacher praise through principal attention*. Paper presented at the Association for Advancement of Behavior Therapy, Atlanta, GA.

Sulzer, B., Hunt, S., Ashby, E., Koniarski, C., & Krams, M. (1971). Increasing rate and percentage correct in reading and spelling in a fifth grade public school class of slow readers by means of a token system. In E. A. Ramp and B. L. Hopkins (Eds.), *A new direction for education: Behavior analysis* (pp. 5–28). Lawrence, KS: University of Kansas, Follow Through, Department of Human Development.

Sulzer-Azaroff, B., & Reese, E. P. (1982). *Applying behavior analysis: A program for developing professional competence*. New York: Holt, Rinehart and Winston.

van den Pol, R. (1982). *The Big Sky Early Education Center*. Final report. (Grant # G008000191). Missoula, MT: Montana University Affiliated Program.

van den Pol, R. A., Crow, R. E., Dark, S. L. & Offner, R. B. (1982). *The staff utilization and support system*. Unpublished manuscript, University of Montana.

van den Pol, R. A., Reid, D. H., & Fuqua, R. W. (1983). Peer training of safety-related skills to institutional staff: Benefits for trainers and trainees. *Journal of Applied Behavior Analysis*, 16, 139–156.

Whyte, R. A., Van Houten, R., & Hunter, W. (1983). The effects of public posting on teachers' performance of supervision duties. *Education and Treatment of Children*, 6, 21–28.

Zeilberger, J., Sampen, S. E., & Sloane, H. N., Jr. (1968). Modification of a child's problem behaviors in the home with the mother as therapist. *Journal of Applied Behavior Analysis*, 1, 47–53.

Glossary

A-B-C model   Viewing behavior (B) as a function of its consequences (C) and its antecedents (A).

Abscissa   The horizontal or x-axis on a graph. In applied behavior analysis, the abscissa usually depicts successive trials or the passage of time, such as days.

Accountability   Objective demonstration and communication of the effectiveness of a given program: behavioral outcomes, cost benefit, consumer satisfaction, and so on.

Across-behavior multiple-baseline design   A within-subject or intensive experimental design that involves: (1) obtaining pretreatment measures (baseline) of several *different behaviors;* (2) applying the intervention or experimental procedure to *one* of the behaviors until it is changed substantially, while continuing to record the baseline measures of the other behaviors; (3) applying the intervention to a second behavior as in (2) above, and so on. This procedure is continued until the investigator determines whether or not each class of behavior changes systematically as a function of the intervention.

Across-individuals multiple-baseline design   A within-subject or intensive experimental design that involves: (1) collecting baselines on the same behavior of several *different individuals;* (2) applying the intervention first with one individual while the baseline conditions are continued with the other individuals; (3) applying the intervention to the second individual's behavior as in (2) above. This procedure is continued until the investigator determines whether or not each individual's behavior changes systematically as a function of the intervention.

Across-situations multiple-baseline design   A within-subject or intensive experimental design that involves: (1) collecting baselines on a behavior of one or more individuals across *different situations;* (2) testing the effects of the intervention *(independent variable)* first in one situation while the baseline conditions are continued through the other situations; (3) applying the intervention to the second situation as in (2) above. This procedure is continued until the investigator determines whether or not each individual's behavior changes systematically only in the situation in which the intervention is applied.

Activity table   A table on which a variety of reinforcing activities is displayed. Students earn access to time at the table for accomplishments, such as completing their work or following various classroom rules.

Adaptation Following the initial reaction to altered circumstances, the gradual change in behavior that often occurs after an individual is placed in a new environment or when novel stimuli are introduced into a familiar environment. When the behavior has stabilized, adaptation is assumed to have been accomplished.

Adaptation period The phase in a behavior analysis program during which *adaptation* takes place.

Advocate A person or group that serves to protect a student's interests rather than serves as an agent of other individuals, an organization, or institution. Advocates, who may be community representatives such as clergymen, law students, a panel of interested citizens, and so on, consider a program's goals and procedures in terms of what is best for the *individual* student and argue on the student's behalf.

Alt-R See Reinforcement of alternative behaviors; Reinforcement of incompatible behaviors.

Antecedent stimulus A stimulus that precedes a behavior and may or may not exert discriminative control over that behavior.

Applied behavior analysis A system derived from the principles of behavior analysis, designed to investigate the ways in which a particular set of conditions (e.g., strategies, interventions) function to change behavior in a precisely measurable and accountable manner; restricted to those interventions that include an experimental design to assess their functions. See also Behavior modification.

Applied behavior analysis program A program that includes the full behavior analysis model (see Figure 1.1). It entails establishment of behavioral objectives; selection and application of valid and reliable measures; regular recording; consistent application of selected procedures based on principles of behavior; plus an experimental evaluation of results. An applied behavior analysis program sometimes is referred to as a *behavior analysis program, behavioral program,* or a *behavior modification* or *therapy program.*

Applied behavior analyst An individual who has demonstrated the professional competencies of designing, implementing, evaluating, and communicating the results of an applied behavior analysis program.

Applied research Research that is directed toward an analysis of the variables that can be effective in improving the behavior under study.[1] In applied behavior analysis, it is confined to the examination of behaviors that are socially important. Applied research often is conducted in a natural setting rather than in the laboratory.

Artificial discriminative stimulus A prompt or discriminative stimulus that is not usually present in the environment. Because an artificial stimulus is contrived or intrusive, usually it should be faded or gradually eliminated before the goal is judged to have been achieved (e.g., verbal instructions serve as artificial stimuli as a student learns a new motor skill like a tennis serve and are faded as the behavior is accomplished and integrated).

Artificial reinforcer A contrived reinforcer that is not usually present in the natural setting or is not a natural consequence of the behavior. For example, trinket rewards serve as artificial reinforcers in many school programs.

Aversive stimulus A stimulus, also called a *punisher,* that has the effect of decreasing the strength (e.g., rate) of a behavior when it is presented as a consequence of (is contingent upon) that behavior; a stimulus that the individual will actively work to avoid. The contingent removal of an aversive stimulus results in an *increase* in the rate of the behavior. Nontechnically: an unpleasant object or event. See also Negative reinforcer; Punisher. (Note: There is no *d* in the word aversive.)

---

[1]Baer, D. M., Wolf, M. M., & Risley, T. R. (1968). Some current dimensions of applied behavior analysis. *Journal of Applied Behavior Analysis, 1,* 91–97.

Avoidance behavior A behavior that increases in rate when it postpones or avoids completely an aversive stimulus. Nontechnically: staying away from or doing something to keep from getting punished.

Back-up reinforcer An object or event that already has demonstrated its reinforcing effect on an individual. It is received in exchange for a specific number of tokens, points, or other exchangeable reinforcers. For example, points might be exchanged for the back-up reinforcer of free time.

Backward chaining procedure Promoting the development of a behavioral chain of responses by reinforcing the last response, element, or link in the chain first; the last two next; and so on, until the entire chain is emitted as a single complex behavior.

Baseline The strength or level (e.g., frequency, intensity, rate, duration, or latency) of behavior before an experimental variable or procedure is introduced. Baseline measurements are continued prior to implementing the treatment procedure until performance has stabilized and can be used as a basis of comparison to assess the effects of the experimental variable or treatment.

Behavior Any observable and measurable external or internal act of an organism. A response. See also Response.

Behavior analysis procedures or strategies Interventions that are used to bring about behavioral change through the application of behavioral principles. Behavioral procedures or strategies are used to prompt, teach, maintain, increase, extend, restrict, inhibit, or reduce behaviors. They serve as the core of most applied behavior analysis programs.

Behavior modification Interventions that are designed to change behavior in a precisely measurable manner; derived from the principles of behavior analysis. Often used interchangeably with the terms *applied behavior analysis* and *behavior therapy*. However, applied behavior analysis is restricted to those interventions that also include an experimental design to assess treatment effects. Behavior modification and behavior therapy often are comprised of only three phases: (1) baseline; (2) treatment; and (3) follow-up. When respondent procedures are emphasized, one tends to use the term *behavior therapy*.

Behavioral contract The negotiated goals and procedures of a behavior analysis program, mutually agreed on by the student and other involved persons and modifiable by joint agreement. Also called a *contingency contract*.

Behavioral goal See Goal.

Behavioral measurement See Precise behavioral measurement.

Behavioral objective Precise specification of a goal, including three essential elements: (1) behavior; (2) the situations or conditions under which the behavior is to occur; and (3) the standard of acceptability or *criterion* level of performance. When the objective is related to formal instruction, it is called an *instructional objective*.

Behavioral rehearsal Practicing a complex skill under simulated conditions; usually reinforcement is integral to the procedure. Role playing is one form of behavioral rehearsal.

Brainstorming Generating a large list of items, such as solutions to problems, examples, and so on. To accomplish this, participants come up with suggestions as rapidly as possible, unfettered by requirements for practicality or other restrictions.

Chain A behavioral sequence consisting of two or more behaviors that occur in a definite order.

Chaining procedure A procedure in which simple behaviors already in an individual's repertoire are reinforced in sequence to form more complex behaviors that occur as a single cohesive unit.

Coded interval recording sheet An observation form, with letter codes for each behavior of concern designated on it, allowing for the simultaneous recording of several behaviors. The presence or absence of each behavior is scored by making a slash mark through the letter symbolizing that behavior. This form can be used with one or more subjects.

Coefficient of agreement See Reliability.

Coercion The use of threats, oppressive contingencies, or disproportionately powerful incentives. Coercion emerges as incentives and threats gain strength, and the client becomes progressively less involved with goal selection.

Collateral behaviors Behaviors that are not treated intentionally in a particular situation, yet their frequency of occurrence or rates may change as the targeted behavior is treated. Also, behaviors, other than those directly treated, that might be influenced by the treatment.

Complete stimulus control See Stimulus control, complete.

Complex behavior Behavior consisting of two or more subsets of responses. (Almost all the behaviors with which educators are concerned are complex behaviors.)

Concept The shared characteristics of otherwise different ideas or things.[2] Roundness is a concept as it is a property shared by a ball, the earth, a sphere, a globe, and so on.

Conditioned aversive stimulus (S^p) A stimulus that initially has no aversive properties but acquires them as a result of repeatedly accompanying or being presented just prior to (1) the withdrawal or absence of reinforcers, or (2) the delivery of unconditioned or other conditioned aversive stimuli.

Conditioned reinforcer (S^r) A stimulus that initially has no reinforcing properties but, through frequent pairings with unconditioned or strongly conditioned reinforcers, acquires reinforcing properties. Also called *secondary reinforcer*.

Contingencies The specified dependencies between behaviors and their antecedents and consequences. Contingencies can occur naturally or can be arranged as stimuli are presented, withdrawn, or withheld by people to affect either their own behavior or the behavior of others.

[2]Lahey, B. B., & Johnson, M. S. (1978). *Psychology and instruction*. Glenview, IL: Scott, Foresman.

Contingency analysis See Sequence analysis.

Contingency control The ability to manipulate the environmental antecedents and consequences of a given behavior to achieve a specific behavioral goal.

Contingency managers Individuals—for example, parents, nurses, teachers, counselors, therapists, and/or the clients themselves—who conduct the day-to-day operation of a behavioral program by systematically applying behavioral strategies or procedures to influence the client's behavior.

Contingency package See Treatment.

Contingency-shaped behavior Behavior that has been learned by experiencing the consequences directly.

Contingent effort A requirement that the individual physically exert effort as a consequence of a misbehavior. This technique is found in procedures such as overcorrection and contingent exercise.

Contingent exercise A contingent effort procedure in which the individual is required to perform an exercise routine such as standing up and sitting down rapidly ten times following each occurrence of the infraction.

Contingent observation A reductive procedure that contains elements of timeout. The individual is placed a few feet away from the reinforcing activity so that observation of it is possible but participation in it is not. Used as a mild form of timeout; see also Timeout.

Contingent reinforcement A reinforcing event that occurs only as a consequence of the specified behavior.

Contingent relation The relation between a behavior and the antecedents that precede it or the relation between a behavior and the consequences that follow it.

Continuous behavior A response that does not have a clearly discernible beginning or end. Pouting, smiling, eye contact, and other behaviors often are treated as continuous responses because it is difficult to determine when the behavior begins and terminates.

Continuous reinforcement (CRF) A schedule of reinforcement in which each occurrence of a response is reinforced.

Control The condition that exists when there is a *functional relation* between a performance and a particular event or independent variable. For example, if a child usually or consistently asks for ice cream while driving past the local ice cream stand, the response, requesting ice cream, is controlled by the antecedent event, passing the ice cream stand.

Countercontrol The action taken by an individual in response to powerful or perhaps troublesome control by another. When both individuals are able to arrange contingencies that strongly affect each other's behavior, reciprocity may develop. However, when contingency control is primarily available to only one member of the pair, countercontrol will be weak and coercion or exploitation may occur. In such instances, social regulations may be necessary to protect the rights of the individual being exploited.

Criterion level The standard used to indicate when a behavioral goal has been reached; or the specification of an acceptable level of performance that a student is to achieve. Criteria are used to evaluate the success of a given behavior analysis program.

Critical features The distinctive properties of stimuli, such as size, shape, position, color, and so on, that enable one stimulus class to be discriminated from another. When a set of stimuli share a number of critical features, those features can be grouped to characterize a particular concept. For example, stimuli sharing the features of being alive; having fur, a backbone, and spinal cord; and suckling young characterize the concept *mammal*. Yet some critical features, such as particular shapes, habits, genetic qualities, and so on help to distinguish one species of mammal from another. See also Concept.

Daily report card A contingency arrangement among the educational personnel, student, and his or her family. It is designed to coordinate the contingencies provided in the student's different settings. In one setting (usually the school), a card is marked contingent on the occurrence of the target behavior. The report is sent each day to the other setting (usually the home), where a delayed consequence is presented.

Delayed prompting When the natural stimulus fails to evoke a given response, an artificial S^D (prompt), usually the correct answer, is inserted to occasion the behavior so it can then be reinforced. Teaching progresses by gradually delaying the time when the prompt is presented, until the student responds reliably in advance of the prompt. For example, the problem "4×4" might be presented on a flash card (the natural stimulus) followed by "16" (the artificial S^D) spoken orally by the teacher to occasion the student's correct response "16." Each time the problem "4×4" is presented, the instructor waits a few additional seconds before giving the prompt "16." Each time the student says "16," the response is reinforced. Eventually, the 4×4 should occasion the student's saying "16" before the teacher says it. We can then say that stimulus control has been transferred from the prompt "16" to the problem "4×4." See also Transfer of stimulus control and Progressive delay.

Delphi method A strategy for identifying the best examples of any particular class of items. For instance, each member of a panel of experts independently suggests a list of prototypical items. These are pooled, and each member then independently rank-orders them. This process continues until a select set of items rises clearly to the top. The Delphi method can be used to identify high-priority goals and objectives, lists of recommended readings, key examination items, and so on.

Dependent variable A variable that is measured while another variable (the *independent variable*) is changed in a systematic way. When changes in the independent variable are accompanied by changes in the dependent variable, we say that the two are *functionally related* — that the level or value of the dependent variable is in fact dependent on the level or value of the independent variable. In behavior analysis, the dependent variable is usually behavior, and the independent variable is some condition or treatment procedure that may affect the level of that behavior.

Deprivation The withholding of a reinforcer for a period of time or the reduction of its availability, designed to increase the effectiveness of the reinforcer.

Desensitization See Systematic desensitization.

Differential reinforcement (1) The reinforcement of one class (or form or topography) of behavior and not another; (2) the reinforcement of a behavior under one stimulus condition but not under another stimulus condition. Also, the reinforcement of one behavior under one stimulus condition while other behaviors are reinforced under different stimulus conditions.

Differential reinforcement of diminishing rates (DRD) Selectively reinforcing a sequence of repeated responses occurring below some preset rate. As long as the number of responses in a specified period of time is less than a set limit (e.g., no more than three talk-outs during the period), reinforcement is delivered; otherwise it is withheld.

Differential reinforcement of high rates (DRH) A schedule that involves selective contingent reinforcement of a grouping of responses that occur in rapid succession. High rates are differentially reinforced, while low rates are not.

Differential reinforcement of low rates (DRL) A behavior is reinforced only if it is expressed following a pause for a specific period of time. For example, a student waits three minutes before participating again to allow others to have their turns. If the student fails to wait at least three minutes, reinforcement is withheld.

Differential reinforcement of the non- or zero-occurrence of a behavior (DRO) A procedure in which the individual receives scheduled reinforcement *except* when he or she engages in a specified behavior *during* a specified period of time. This procedure, which

also is called *omission training*, usually results in a decrease of the specified behavior.

Dimensions of behavior Measurable descriptive characteristics of a behavior, such as number of occurrences, intensity, duration, topography, and accuracy.

Direct Instruction A system of teaching and a published set of curriculum materials (often referred to as DISTAR) that involves: (1) following a very carefully organized and detailed sequence of instruction; (2) teaching skillfully in small groups when appropriate; (3) being able to evoke unison responses; (4) using signals to encourage all students to participate; (5) pacing presentations quickly; (6) applying specific techniques for correcting and preventing errors; and, (7) using praise.

Direct observational recording A method, sometimes called *observational recording*, in which a human observer records behavioral data as they occur. Event and time sampling are both direct observational recording systems.

Discrete behavior A behavior that has a clearly discernible beginning and end. Lever presses, sneezes, and written answers to addition problems are examples of discrete responses.

Discrimination The restriction of responding to certain stimulus situations and not others. Discrimination may be established by *differentially reinforcing* a response in one stimulus situation and extinguishing or punishing that response in other situations, or by the reinforcement of other behavior in the other situations.

Discriminative control A particular antecedent has discriminative control when it reliably evokes (i.e., sets the occasion for) a given response. For example, every time a student sees the letter b, he responds, "b." However, when he sees the letter d or any other letter, he does not respond, "b." The letter b is said to have discriminative control.

Discriminative stimuli Stimuli are said to be discriminative when, after several pairings with consequential stimuli, their presentation or removal is accompanied by reliable changes in the rate of response. Thus, their presence influences the behavior they precede. There are three types of discriminative stimuli:

S^D—A stimulus in the presence of which a given response is likely to be reinforced. An S^D operates to prompt a particular response in that it signals the likelihood of reinforcement.

S^Δ (S-delta)—A stimulus in the presence of which a given response is not reinforced. An S^Δ signals nonreinforcement and functions to inhibit or suppress the response.

S^{D-}—A stimulus in the presence of which a given response is likely to result in a consequence of punishment, timeout, or response cost. An S^{D-} signals the likelihood that an aversive consequence will follow the response and functions to reduce the subsequent rate of the response.

DISTAR Curriculum material used in Direct Instruction.

Distributed practice "Spreading study time out into short periods with breaks in between" (Lahey & Johnson, 1978, p. 361). For example, practicing a few unknown spelling words at a time, rather than a whole long list at once (massed practice).

DRD See Differential reinforcement of diminishing rates.

DRH See Differential reinforcement of high rates.

DRI See Reinforcement of incompatible behaviors.

DRL See Differential reinforcement of low rates.

DRO See Differential reinforcement of the non- or zero-occurrence of a behavior.

Duration recording Recording the elapsed time during which an event occurs. For example, an observer could record the amount of time a youth spends on a task or talks on the phone.

Elicit In respondent or classical conditioning of reflexes, a verb that denotes the effect of a conditioned or unconditioned stimulus on a conditioned or unconditioned response. In describing the salivary reflex of a dog, we would say that meat *elicits* salivation. Following conditioning, another stimulus, such as a tone, also might elicit salivation. See also Respondent behavior.

Emit In operant conditioning, a verb that describes the occurrence of behavior in the absence of any known (classical) eliciting stimulus. In this text we tend to use the more familiar verbs express, perform, respond, and behave instead.

Error correction procedure A procedure in which students are told that the response is wrong and are presented with the correct response. The student then is requested to repeat the task (e.g., to reread the sentence over again) correctly.[3]

Errorless learning Acquiring a particular discrimination by means of instruction in which a sequence of artificial discriminative stimuli are carefully arranged and slowly and systematically faded so that only correct responses are occasioned or evoked.

Escape conditioning See Negative reinforcement.

Ethical responsibility Operating according to ethical precepts: providing for voluntariness and informed consent; arranging the least intrusive or restrictive and most benign and effective procedures; obtaining, maintaining, and continuing development of competence; and so on.

Event recording A procedure in which an observer records the number of occurrences of a specified discrete behavior, such as times tardy, answers correct, or bites received by a peer, over a specified period of time. The interval may be, for instance, a classroom period, a day, or the duration of a meal or of a TV program.

Experimental analysis of behavior A scientific analysis designed to discover the func-

---

[3]Delquadri, J., Whorton, D., Elliott, M., & Greenwood, C. R. (1982, May). *Peer & parent tutoring programs: A comparative analysis of the effects of packages on opportunity to respond, reading performance, and achievement scores of learning disabled disadvantaged children.* Paper presented at the Eighth Annual Convention of the Association for Behavior Analysis, Milwaukee, WI.

tional relation between behavior and the variables that control it.

Experimental design An aspect of an experiment that is directed toward experimental control or demonstration of a functional relation. Several single-subject (within-subject) designs may be employed to demonstrate the existence of a functional relation between the *dependent variable* (the dependent or treated behavior) and the *independent variable* (usually the *intervention strategy* or *procedure*).

Extinction A procedure in which the reinforcement of a previously reinforced behavior is discontinued. In nontechnical language, extinction often is referred to as the appropriate withholding of rewards or attention, or as the nonrecognition of behaviors that interfere with learning or development.

Extinction-induced aggression Aggressive behavior that often accompanies the early phases of an extinction program, in the absence of any other identifiable precipitating events.

Fading The gradual removal of discriminative stimuli (usually artificial or contrived), such as directions, imitative prompts, physical guidance, and other cues. Fading is used to foster independence from auxiliary stimulus control that may be necessary during the early stages of learning. It facilitates the assumption of responsibility, as constant reminders and suggestions are no longer required.

Feedback Information transmitted back to the responder following a particular performance. Feedback can include seeing or hearing the results, being told how well the job was done, and receiving statements of specific praise. Feedback may be reinforcing or punishing and/or it may serve a discriminative function by guiding subsequent performance.

Flexitime A flexible arrangement of a schedule of work time, usually negotiated between employers and employees. (Sometimes called flextime.)

Forward chaining Developing a behavioral chain of responses by training the first response or

link in the chain first, the second next, joining them together, and so on until the entire chain is emitted as a unitary complex behavior.

Frequency The number of times a behavior occurs. Usually expressed in relation to a given period of time.

Freeze technique Instructing students to maintain the topography of their behavior while ceasing movement. It is used to teach students to discriminate positive and negative examples of good motor form.

Functional relation A lawful (predictable) relation between values of two variables. In behavior analysis, a *dependent variable* (treated behavior) and a given *independent variable* (intervention or treatment procedure) are *functionally related* if the behavior changes systematically with changes in the value of the independent variable or treatment. For example, the greater the intensity of an aversive stimulus, the greater the response suppression.

Functional skill A skill that is age appropriate, socially significant, and is likely to be reinforced or supported by the natural environment in both the short *and* long run.

Generalization, response (Induction) The spread of effects to other classes of behavior when one class of behavior is modified by reinforcement, extinction, and so on. For instance, the way a particular letter is shaped or formed may vary in ways that are similar but not identical to the formation of the letter as it was originally reinforced.

Generalization, stimulus The spread of effects to other stimulus situations when behavior is modified, reinforced, punished, and so on, in the presence of one stimulus situation. Generalization occurs when stimulus control is absent or incomplete. (The child who calls all quadrupeds "doggie" is generalizing.)

Generalization training A procedure designed to prompt in another stimulus situation a behavior emitted in one stimulus situation; programming for stimulus generalization. For instance, students who learned skills in one setting (e.g., the resource room) would be taught to apply those skills in other settings (e.g., the classroom).

Generalized reinforcer   A conditioned reinforcer that is effective for a wide range of behaviors as a result of having been paired with a variety of previously established reinforcers. Due to this history, its effectiveness does not depend on any one state of deprivation. Money is a generalized reinforcer. It has been paired with (and can purchase) a variety of other reinforcers.

Goal   The end toward which effort is directed to change the target behavior. Usually presented as a statement of how the target behavior is to be changed: increased, decreased, maintained, developed, expanded, or restricted. A goal should be translated into a set of behavioral objectives prior to designing a program.

Goal, outcome   A specification of the end product or behavior sought as a result of the treatment program. Examples include decreases in vandalism cost or reductions in the number of absences.

Goal, process (or treatment)   A goal whose accomplishment serves to enable the achievement of an outcome goal. For example, increasing a teacher's rate of giving approval might be a *process goal* to enable the *outcome goal* of improving his or her students' scholastic achievement.

Goal setting   Identifying in advance the values or levels to be reached, often by a particular time. A goal might be set at a certain number of accomplishments, level of quality, percentage of correct answers, and so forth. A term used in organizational management.

Good Behavior Game   A group treatment package. The group is divided into two or more teams, and rules are specified. In its original form, a team received a check against it if a member violated one of the rules. Reinforcers were provided for each team with fewer than the criterion number of marks or for the team with the fewest marks at the end of a preset period. Now its use frequently involves reinforcing consequences as well as punishment, such as providing points exchangeable for reinforcers for a team when its members act according to the rules.

Graduated guidance   The combined use of physical guidance and fading, resulting in a systematic gradual reduction of physical guidance.

Grandma's rule   A rule that declares if first you engage in less pleasant behavior, then you may do the more preferred: "first you work and then you may play"; "after you eat your spinach you may have your dessert."

Group contingencies   Arrangements in which consequences are delivered to some or all members of a group as a function of the performance of one, several, or all of its members.

Guiding   See Physical guidance.

Imitation   Matching the behavior of a model, or engaging in a behavior similar to that observed.

Imitative prompt   A discriminative stimulus in which behavior by a model is designed to prompt an imitative response.

Incidental teaching   A teaching procedure applied in natural situations in which a student indicates an interest in an item or topic (e.g., teaching is initiated when a child requests, "I want the truck."). The teacher prompts an elaboration that when supplied is contingently reinforced. In this instance, the teacher asks, "What color truck?" When the child says, "I want the *red* truck," the teacher gives the child the truck.

Incompatible behavior   A specific alternative response (Alt-R) or behavior that cannot be emitted simultaneously with another behavior; behavior that interferes with the emission of specified other behavior.

Incomplete stimulus control   See Stimulus control, incomplete.

Independent variable   The variable that is manipulated. In behavior analysis, the independent variable is often a behavioral procedure, package, or other intervention or treatment strategy.

Instructional objective   See Behavioral objective.

Intensive designs   See Within-subject experimental design.

Intermittent reinforcement A schedule of reinforcement in which some, but not all, of the occurrences of a response are reinforced.

Interobserver agreement (IOA) assessment A method for estimating the reliability of a behavioral observation system. Two or more independent observers compare the number of times they agreed in proportion to the number of observations they scored.

Interval spoilage See Partial interval time sampling.

Intervention See Treatment.

Intrinsic motivation A hypothetical state inferred by observing an individual expressing a particular behavior at high rates in the absence of observable or extrinsic reinforcing consequences; presumably emitting the behavior is itself reinforcing.

Irrelevant features Those properties of stimuli that do not permit one stimulus class to be distinguished from other stimulus classes. The size of a letter is a feature irrelevant to its identification, while its shape is a critical feature.

Latency The time that elapses between the presentation of an antecedent stimulus and the response.

Learning Any enduring change in behavior produced as a function of the interaction between the behavior and the environment. Often used to describe motor or cognitive skills, but also may refer to social, affective, personal, and other behavioral categories.

Learning history The sum of an individual's behaviors that have been conditioned or modified as a function of their interaction with environmental events.

Link The response or performance that is combined with others in the development of a behavioral chain.

Maintenance procedures Strategies to promote the persistence of behaviors under natural environmental conditions, such as applying schedules of reinforcement, altering reinforcers, fading artificial prompts, teaching self-management, and so on.

Massed practice Repetition of a block of activities without a break (e.g., cramming). Often this form of practice results in lessened effectiveness of learning the activity.

Matching to sample A task in which a student selects a stimulus that matches or corresponds to a standard or sample, from two or more alternatives.

Model A person whose behavior is imitated.

Modeling procedure A stimulus control procedure that uses demonstrations or modeling to prompt an imitative response; colloquially, a *show procedure*.

Momentary DRO A variation of the DRO procedure in which reinforcement is delivered at a particular preset moment, provided that a particular behavior is *not* being expressed—best reserved for *maintaining* rather than for initially evoking a low rate of responding.

Momentary time sampling A time sampling procedure in which a response is recorded only if it is occurring at the moment the interval terminates. For example, a timer goes off at the end of a ten-minute interval, and the observer checks to see if the youngster has his thumb in his mouth *at that moment*.

Multielement design A within-subject or intensive experimental design that involves alternate presentations of independent variables, independent of changes in the dependent variable. Different procedures, each correlated with a different specific stimulus, are applied successively to the behavior. The effects of the treatment procedure(s) then are observed by comparing differential performances. For example, one might wish to analyze the function of three contingencies on completion of a task: treatment A = no extra recess; treatment B = extra recess time with planned activities; treatment C = extra recess time with free play. The treatments could be alternated from day to day. Assuming that the students had information available about the condition to be in effect (A, B, or C) on any given day, the influence of each on task completion could be compared and evaluated after several weeks of implementing the experimental comparison.

Multiple-baseline designs A within-subject or intensive design in which the experimenter repeats an intervention, attempting to replicate the effects of a procedure (treatment or intervention) across (1) different subjects, (2) different settings, or (3) different classes of behavior. The intervention is introduced independently to each subject (or setting or class of behavior) in succession. See also Across-behavior multiple-baseline design; Across-individuals multiple-baseline design; Across-situations multiple-baseline design; Within-subject experimental design.

Narrative recording A written running account of behavior in progress. The events then can be ordered into a *sequence analysis* that specifies a behavior and its antecedents and consequences.

Natural discriminative stimulus A nonintrusive discriminative stimulus that is present in the natural environment, not one artificially introduced. The printed word is a natural S^D for reading the word. The beginning of the period is a natural S^D for taking one's seat and starting to work.

Natural reinforcer A nonintrusive reinforcer that is not artificially introduced and is present in the natural environment. A smile or a good mark is usually a natural reinforcer in a school setting.

Needs assessment A systematic method for identifying goals to target for programmatic change. Needs assessments may include observations, tests, interviews, questionnaires, and other sources of input.

Negative reinforcement A procedure that involves the removal of an aversive stimulus as a consequence of a response; it results in the maintenance or an *increase* in rate of the behavior. A behavior has been negatively reinforced if it *increases* or is *maintained* due to the contingent *re-*moval or *reduction* of a stimulus. This procedure sometimes is referred to as *escape conditioning*. For example, when a child does as asked, the teacher stops nagging. The child's behavior, doing as requested, has been negatively reinforced by the removal of the nagging.

Negative reinforcer A stimulus that, when removed or reduced as a consequence of a response, results in an *increase* in or *maintenance* of that response. See also Aversive stimulus, which is used in this text in place of the term *negative reinforcer*.

Neutral stimulus An object or event that is neutral with respect to some property that it later may acquire. A neutral stimulus does not affect behavior reliably in a particular context until it has been paired sufficiently often with some event that does have controlling properties (i.e., it has not yet developed into an S^D, reinforcer, etc.).

Objective measurement Recording behavioral data unbiased by the observer's feelings, interpretations, or other extraneous factors.

Observational recording See Direct observational recording.

Occasion To increase the likelihood of the emission of a response by arranging prior stimulus conditions. It also is used as an action verb in reference to operant behavior, where the response bears a probabilistic relationship (not a one-to-one relationship, as with *elicit*) to the occurrence of the S^D. In this text we sometimes use the terms evoke, promote, and other synonyms instead.

Omission training See Differential reinforcement of the non- or zero-occurrence of a behavior (DRO).

Operant behavior Behavior whose rate or probability of occurrence is controlled (at least in part) by its consequences.

Operant level The strength (e.g., rate or duration) of behavior prior to any known conditioning. (Baseline, which subsumes operant level, refers to the strength of behavior before the introduction of an experimental variable, but does not preclude earlier conditioning.)

Operational statement The product of breaking down a broad concept, such as aggressiveness, into its *observable* and *measurable* component behaviors (frequency of hitting or biting others, duration of scream, and so on). Sometimes referred to as a *pinpointed* or *targeted behavior.*

Ordinate The vertical or *y*-axis on a graph. In behavior analysis, the response measure (e.g., frequency) usually is plotted on the ordinate.

Outcome goal See Goal, outcome.

Outcome variables Those measurable factors that characterize the outcome goal, such as improved academic and social performance.

Overcorrection A reductive procedure that is a subcategory of contingent effort. Overcorrection consists of two basic components: (1) *restitutional overcorrection* (or restitutional procedure) requires the individual to restore the environment to a state improved in a major way from that which existed prior to the act; and (2) *positive-practice overcorrection* (or positive-practice procedure) requires that the individual repeatedly practice a positive behavior. When no environmental disruption occurs, only the positive-practice procedure is used.

Package See Treatment.

Paraprofessionals Staff members who perform teaching, training, and/or management functions but who do not have formal professional training and/or job status.

Part method of chaining Teaching a few links in a chain at one time, gradually adding other links; preferable to the *whole method of chaining.*

Partial-interval time sampling A time-sampling procedure (often labeled *interval recording* alone) that records the presence of a response when the response occurs even momentarily during the interval. The response need not occur throughout the entire interval, as in *whole-interval* time sampling. Partial-interval time sampling sometimes is called *interval spoilage*, because any instance of the behavior spoils the interval.

Performance feedback See Feedback.

Permanent product recording A behavioral recording method in which products of a behavior, such as the number of windows broken or homework problems handed in, percentage of test questions correct, and so on are assessed. This observational method cannot be used on *transitory behaviors.*

Personalized System of Instruction (PSI) A method of teaching that usually is characterized by:

"(1) The go-at-your-own-pace feature, which permits individual students to move through the course at a speed commensurate with their ability and other demands upon their time.

"(2) The unit-perfection requirement for advancement, which lets the student go ahead to new material only after demonstrating mastery of that which preceded.

"(3) The use of lectures and demonstrations as vehicles of motivation, rather than sources of critical information.

"(4) The related stress upon the written word in teacher-student communication; and, finally:

"(5) The use of proctors, which permits repeated testing, immediate scoring, almost unavoidable tutoring, and a marked enhancement of the personal-social aspect of the educational process."[4]

Also known as the Keller Plan, after its originator.

Physical guidance A form of response priming in which the appropriate body part or parts are physically guided through the proper motion by another person. For example, a swimming coach who guides the movement of a youth's arm to demonstrate the proper stroke is using the physical guidance procedure. Such guidance should be faded gradually, as the student gradually assumes greater responsibility for executing the correct movement (see Graduated guidance).

PLA-Check (Planned Activity Check) An observational recording system developed by Risley and Cataldo (1973).[5] Every

---

[4]Keller, F. S. (1968). Good-bye teacher. *Journal of Applied Behavior Analysis, 1,* 79–89.

[5]Risley, T. R., & Cataldo, M. F. (1973). *Planned activity check: Materials for training observers.* Lawrence, KS: Center for Applied Behavior Analysis.

given number of minutes the observer counts the number of students engaged in the assignment activity at that moment. See Momentary time sampling.

Planned ignoring Deliberate withholding of attention as a consequence of an infraction. Assuming that the attention is reinforcing, this would be a type of extinction procedure.

Planning team Individuals representing various involved constituencies—administrators, counselors, teachers, parents, students, etc.—who meet together to design, carry out, and monitor school programs.

Positive practice (overcorrection) See Overcorrection.

Positive reinforcement A procedure that maintains or increases the rate of a response by contingently presenting a stimulus (a positive reinforcer) following the response.

Positive reinforcer A *stimulus*, such as an object or event, that follows or is presented as a consequence of a response and results in the rate of that response increasing or maintaining. Praise, attention, recognition of achievement and effort, special events, and activities serve as positive reinforcers for many people. Nontechnical terms for positive reinforcers include incentives, rewards, or strokes.

Praise See Positive reinforcer; Qualitative praise.

Precise behavioral measurement The selection and implementation of accurate, clearly defined operations for recording and quantifying behavior. Precise measurement allows change to be measured and evaluated unambiguously.

Precision Teaching A formal, individualized instructional method that emphasizes rate building and charting of performance, plus the need to design and implement teaching and to reinforce each specific behavior under all the conditions in which it is expected to occur.

Premack principle A principle that states that contingent access to high-frequency behaviors (preferred activities) serves as a reinforcer for the performance of low-frequency behaviors.

Primary reinforcer See Unconditioned reinforcer.

Probe A phase in a behavior analysis experiment designed to test the effect of a given intervention. A *withdrawal* phase is a probe because the intervention is removed for a period of time to test behavior in the absence of the intervention.

Process goal See Goal, process.

Process variables Those measurable factors that enable an outcome goal to be achieved (e.g., attending school is requisite for optimal learning).

Programmed instruction The selection and arrangement of educational content based on principles of human learning.[6]

Progressive delay procedure A procedure, sometimes called *stimulus delay* or *delayed prompting*, designed to teach a behavior by manipulating the time between the presentation of the natural and an artificial discriminative stimulus. Initially, the natural discriminative stimulus is presented concurrently with a currently effective artificial S^D or prompt to evoke and reinforce a response. Then, systematically, the time is gradually increased between presentation of the natural S^D and the artificial prompt over successive trials, until eventually the responder anticipates—that is, expresses the response before the prompt is given. For example, you might hold up a ball and say, "What is this? ... Ball," and deliver reinforcement when the student then says "ball." After doing this several times, you would hold up the ball and say, "What is this?" then wait a few moments before saying, "ball." You would progressively delay delivery of the cue "ball" until the student responds "ball" to the question, "What is this?" before you supply the name. (See also Delayed prompting.)

Prompt An auxiliary discriminative stimulus presented to occasion a given response. Prompts usually are faded before the terminal goal is judged to have been achieved. (For example, the "ff" sound serves as a prompt in "2 + 2 are ff ——." The "ff" sound must be faded completely for the teacher to conclude that the student has achieved the goal of knowing how to add 2 + 2.)

[6]Taber, J. K., Glaser, R., and Schaefer, H. (1965). *Learning and programmed instruction*. Reading MA: Addison-Wesley.

Punisher A stimulus that, when presented immediately following a response, results in a *reduction* in the rate of the response. In this text, the term *aversive stimulus* is used interchangeably with *punisher* or *punishing stimulus.*

Punishment A procedure in which a punisher or aversive stimulus is presented immediately following a response, resulting in a reduction in the rate of the response.

Qualitative praise The delivery of praise paired with the rationale or reason for its delivery. For example, rather than just saying, "I like that," one would say, "I like that because . . . (e.g., you looked at what you were doing)." This technique both reinforces a given behavior *and* assists the learner to discriminate the conditions under which the response is to be emitted. Often called *labeled* or *behavior-specific praise.*

Rate The average frequency of behavior emitted during a standard unit of time. Formula: number of responses divided by the number of time units. For example, if 20 responses occur in 5 minutes, the rate is 4 responses per minute.

Reactivity The effect, often temporary, produced by experimental activities other than the independent (treatment) variable. For example, just the presence of an observer in the classroom may influence the dependent variable(s) or distort the validity of the data, as when a teacher uses more verbal praise than usual in the observer's presence.

Reductive procedure A procedure, such as Alt-R, DRL, punishment, response cost, and time-out, used to reduce the occurrence of behavior.

Reentry program A method for dealing with chronic truants that provides them with intensive instruction in the subject areas in need of remediation and possibly in social skill deficits.

Reinforcement density Frequency, magnitude, intensity, and/or rate with which responses are reinforced. The lower the ratio the greater the magnitude or intensity or shorter the interval required by a given reinforcement schedule, the denser the reinforcement.

Reinforcement history See Learning history.

Reinforcement of alternative behavior or response (Alt-R) A reinforcement procedure usually designed to reduce a given behavior by increasing specific behaviors that are (acceptable) alternatives to the behavior to be reduced.

Reinforcement of incompatible behaviors (DRI or differential reinforcement of incompatible behaviors) A specific Alt-R procedure designed to increase the rate of a behavior or behaviors that cannot coexist with a behavior that has been targeted for reduction. For example, reinforcing work toward the completion of a task reduces those forms of disruption that are incompatible with working.

Reinforcement procedure Arranging for presentation of a reinforcing event or removal of an aversive event to follow as a consequence of a behavior, resulting in an increase in or maintenance of the behavior. Reinforcement is defined solely by its effect upon increasing or maintaining behavior. This book discusses two basic reinforcement procedures: *positive reinforcement* and *negative reinforcement.* Both increase or maintain behavior.

Reinforcement reserve The unconsumed quantity of reinforcers in the possession of an individual or group. This term frequently refers to a number of tokens or other exchangeable reinforcers.

Reinforcer A consequential stimulus occurring contingent on a behavior that increases or maintains the strength (rate, duration, etc.) of the behavior. A reinforcer is defined solely by the fact that it increases or maintains the behavior on which it is contingent. See also Conditioned reinforcer and Unconditioned reinforcer.

Reinforcer sampling A procedure that enables a person to come in contact with a potential reinforcer to experience the positive characteristics of the stimulus. The procedure is useful in developing new reinforcing consequences for a given individual.

Reliable measurement Consistency of measurement that occurs when the measuring device remains standard regardless of who uses it and what conditions prevail during its use. See also Reliability.

Reliability coefficient (interobserver or coefficient of agreement) A mathematical estimate of the consistency of measurement. In applied behavior analysis, reliability often is estimated by assessing the agreement between two or more independently scored data records of the same episodes, preferably by different observers. The coefficient of agreement often is calculated as a percentage by dividing the number of agreements by the number of agreements plus disagreements, and then multiplying the fraction by 100. When feasible, agreement measures should be reported for each phase of a within-subject design. When estimating reliability of interval recording systems, only *scored* intervals should be included in the calculation.

Repertoire, behavioral "The behavior that a particular organism, at a particular time, is capable of emitting, in the sense that the behavior exists at a nonzero operant level, has been shaped, or, if it has been extinguished, may be rapidly reconditioned."[7]

Replicate To repeat an experimental procedure for the purpose of reproducing a particular finding.

Respondent behavior A response that is elicited by antecedent stimuli. Also, reflexive behavior; an autonomic response that requires no previous learning, though such responses may be conditioned, as in Pavlov's famous experiments with the conditioning of dogs' salivation responses. See also Elicit.

Response A directly measurable behavior. Used interchangeably in this book with *behavior* and *performance*.

Response cost A reductive procedure in which a specified amount of available reinforcers are contingently withdrawn following the response. Usually these reinforcers are withdrawn from the student's reserve, as with loss of points or yardage or the imposition of fines. However, in a modification of this procedure, *bonus response cost*, the reinforcers are taken away from a pool of potential bonus reinforcers that the student will receive if all are not withdrawn.

Response delay A procedure in which reinforcement is contingent on a preset time intervening between the S^D and the response. Response delay helps to manage impulsiveness (e.g., the student is shown a math problem but is not permitted to begin solving it until a given time interval elapses).

Restitutional overcorrection See Overcorrection.

Reversal design An experimental design in which the effects of the *independent variable* are tested by introducing a phase (e.g., an Alt-R or DRO treatment phase) in which the direction of the change reverses (e.g., reinforcement of being out-of-seat instead of being seated).

Role playing Performing a sequence of responses to simulate the action of another individual or the same individual under other circumstances. A method of *behavioral rehearsal*.

Rule-governed behavior Behavior under the control of (i.e., behavior that reliably follows) such S^Ds as rules and instructions, rather than that shaped by reinforcing or aversive contingencies.

Satiation The reduction in performance or reinforcer effectiveness that occurs after a large amount of that type of reinforcer has been delivered (usually within a short time period) following the behavior.

Schedule of reinforcement The response requirements that determine when reinforcement will be delivered; that is, how frequently, what particular responses it should follow, and so on.

School phobia A severe anxiety reaction to school, often characterized by nausea and complaints of headaches, stomach aches, and dizziness.

S^D See Discriminative stimuli.

S-delta (S^Δ) See Discriminative stimuli.

[7]Catania, A. C. (1968). *Contemporary research in operant behavior*. Glenview, IL: Scott, Foresman.

Secondary reinforcer See Conditioned reinforcer.

Self-control Managing the contingencies that influence one's own behavior. For instance, postponing immediate reinforcement in favor of delayed positive reinforcement (e.g., completing a work assignment instead of watching TV, allowing time to visit friends on the weekend, or avoiding the pressure of a last-minute rush). Sometimes referred to as *self-management*.

Self-instruction Guiding one's own learning, usually by reciting a sequence of verbal prompts or using other prompting, fading, and reinforcement strategies.

Self-management A procedure in which individuals change some aspect of their own behavior. It generally involves four major components: (1) self-selection of goals; (2) monitoring one's own behavior; (3) selection of procedures; and (4) implementation of procedures.

Self-modeling A form of modeling in which individuals are shown videotaped samples of their own best behavior; external prompts and poor performances are edited out. Self-modeling is designed to prompt imitation of one's own exemplary performance.

Sequence analysis A description of an individual's behaviors and the events that appear to precede and follow those behaviors. Used to provide clues about the possible functional properties of various environmental stimuli. Sometimes called *contingency analysis*.

Setting events External or internal stimulus events that exert general control over other stimulus-response interactions. Setting events may precede and/or overlap with other discrete stimulus-response (S^D-R) relationships. (For example, noisy surroundings could adversely influence the interaction between a work assignment and a student's performance. Similarly, food deprivation could set the occasion for general irritability, impeding a variety of social interactions.)

Shaping A procedure through which new behaviors are developed by systematic reinforcement of *successive approximations* toward the behavioral objective. Sometimes PSI or individualized instruction are referred to as shaping methods.

Show procedure See Modeling procedure.

Single-subject designs See Within-subject experimental designs.

Skill card A card used in training that contains the steps or components of the skill to be learned (e.g., the steps to follow in learning a new social skill).

Slot machine game A game of chance in which participants receive reinforcers as prizes. Several cups are placed upside down, concealing paper slips on which the names of reinforcing items or events are written. Each participating student or staff member who has earned the opportunity selects one cup, receiving access to the indicated reinforcer.

Social reinforcer A reinforcing stimulus mediated by another individual within a social context. Praise (e.g., "That's a good job") usually functions as a social reinforcer.

Social skills training Systematic instruction in constructive social interactional responses.

Specific praise See Qualitative praise.

Spontaneous recovery The reappearance, following an extinction procedure, of a response that had not been emitted for an extended time interval. Robert Epstein (personal communication) prefers the term *resurgence* because the phenomenon is not random but controlled by the state of the organism's conditioning history and current circumstances, as are all forms of operant responding.

Sr See Conditioned reinforcer; Positive reinforcer; Reinforcement.

S^R See Unconditioned reinforcer.

Staff development Educational activities for staff that may occur within group sessions or during individual consultation away from or within the setting in which the skills are to be practiced.

Step size The number of new responses in a subset, or the extensiveness of the change in topography (shape or form) that constitutes a *successive approximation* in a specific shaping procedure. For example, the step size for teaching one youngster to use a swing on a playground might consist of approaching, touching, sitting down, and following verbal instructions to pump; for another child, pumping might have to be broken down into smaller steps including physical guidance, modeling, and so on.

Stimulus A physical object or event that does or *may* have an effect on the behavior of an individual. Stimuli may be internal or external to the person. Stimuli that frequently are arranged in behavior analysis programs include *reinforcing stimuli*, *aversive stimuli*, and *discriminative stimuli*.

Stimulus control Systematic effects of an antecedent stimulus (or set of stimuli) on the probability of occurrence of a response. Thus, the response form or frequency is different under one controlling stimulus or set of stimuli than another. These controlling stimuli are referred to as *discriminative stimuli*. See also Discriminative stimuli.

Stimulus control, complete A phenomenon, inferred by observing, that the behavior has a high (almost perfect) probability of occurring in the presence of a particular antecedent stimulus (or stimuli) and a very low probability of occurring in its absence. For most drivers, stopping is under complete control of a red light stimulus.

Stimulus control, incomplete A phenomenon, inferred by observing, that the antecedent stimulus does not consistently regulate the behavior (i.e., the behavior regularly does not occur or fail to occur, respectively, in response to the presence or absence of the stimulus). When the teacher says "Finish your work," Mary complies inconsistently. The teacher's instruction exerts incomplete stimulus control.

Stimulus delay procedure See Delayed prompting and Progressive delay.

Stimulus fading See Fading.

Stimulus generalization See Generalization, stimulus.

Stimulus presentation procedure Presenting a discriminative stimulus to influence the probability of occurrence of the response.

Stimulus property An attribute of the stimulus such as topography, texture, volume, size, color, position, intensity, and so on.

Subset of behavior The group of simpler response components that form a more complex behavior.

Successive approximations Behavioral elements or subsets, each of which more and more closely resembles the specified terminal behavior.

Supplementary reinforcers Reinforcers used in addition to the major contingent reinforcer.

Systematic desensitization A procedure in which stimuli associated with a feared stimulus are arranged in a hierarchy from the least to the most feared by the client. The client then is taught to relax in the presence of the least feared stimulus, then the next, and so on until he or she learns to relax in the presence of the most feared stimulus.

Target behavior The behavior to be changed.

Task analysis The act of breaking down a complex skill or behavioral chain into its component behaviors, subskills, or subtasks. Each component is stated in its order of occurrence and sets the occasion for the occurrence of the next behavior. Task analyses are particularly useful in planning specific stimulus control and chaining procedures.

Tell procedure A stimulus control procedure that involves using verbal or written instructions or rules to prompt a response under appropriate conditions so that reinforcement may be delivered.

Terminal behavior The behavior that is to be achieved at the end of a behavior-analysis program. The terminal behavior is described according to all its relevant behavioral dimensions and usually is assigned a criterion by which an acceptable level of performance is to be judged. Often used interchangeably with *behavioral* or *instructional objective*, *goal*, and *target behavior*; occasionally denoted by the noun *pinpoint*.

Timeout (TO) A procedure in which access to the sources of various forms of reinforcement is removed for a particular time period contingent on the emission of a response. The opportunity to receive reinforcement is contingently removed for a specified time. Either the behaving individual is contingently removed from the reinforcing environment, or the reinforcing environment is contingently removed for some stipulated duration.

Timeout room; timeout booth; timeout area; quiet place   A physical space that is arranged to minimize the reinforcement that an individual is apt to receive during a fixed time period. Procedures for using such facilities must conform to ethical and legal requirements.

Time sampling   A direct observational procedure in which the presence or absence of specific behaviors is recorded, within short uniform time intervals. For example, an observer may observe for ten seconds and record during the following five seconds the occurrence or nonoccurrence of a behavior. This procedure may continue for a specific 30-minute period each day. There are several time sampling variations: (1) *whole-interval time sampling*, (2) *partial-interval time sampling*, and (3) *momentary time sampling*.

Token economy   A contingency package. Tokens (exchangeable reinforcers) are given as soon as possible following the emission of a target response. The tokens later are exchanged for a reinforcing object or event.

Token reinforcer   A symbol or object (e.g., check marks or poker chips) that can be exchanged at a later time for a back-up reinforcer in the form of an item or activity; an *exchangeable reinforcer*. For example, money is a token. The extent to which tokens are reinforcing depends on the individual's experience and on the back-up items available.

Topography of response   The configuration or form of a response. The correct topography of a behavior can be determined by photographing an expert performing the behavior.

Training team   Individuals within an organization, such as a school, representing the various constituencies who are responsible for evaluating, presenting, and providing in-service workshops,

consultation, and other educational experiences for the staff.

Transfer of stimulus control   A process in which, instead of a previous antecedent stimulus, a new antecedent stimulus begins to evoke a response. In applied behavior analysis this is often deliberately arranged by using *fading* or *delayed prompting*.

Transitory behavior   A behavior that does not leave an enduring product (e.g., smiling, paying attention, or teasing). Such a behavior needs to be observed and recorded as it occurs or else preserved via film or videotape.

Treatment   The behavioral procedures, intervention, program, or independent variable(s) being applied. May be referred to as a *treatment* or *contingency package* when specific behavioral procedures are combined into a unitary treatment.

Treatment goal   See Goal, process.

Treatment phase   The period of time during which the intervention is in effect.

Unconditioned aversive stimulus (S^P)   A stimulus, object, or event, such as a painful electric shock, a bee sting, or a sudden loud noise, that functions aversively in the absence of any prior learning history (i.e., its contingent occurrence is punishing).

Unconditioned reinforcer (S^R)   A stimulus, such as food, water, or sexual activity, that usually is reinforcing in the absence of any prior learning history; often used interchangeably with *primary reinforcer*.

Valid measures   Measures that actually do measure what they are presumed to measure, without distortion.

Variable   Any condition, including stimuli, in the individual's internal or external environment or a behavior that may assume any one of a set of values. See also Dependent variable; Independent variable.

Voluntariness   The degree to which an individual agrees to pursue a behavioral goal or program in the absence of coercion. Voluntariness is presumed to be present when the individual chooses and/or initiates action toward a goal in the absence of strong threats or unusually powerful incentives.

Weak stimulus control   See Stimulus control, incomplete.

Whole-interval time sampling   A time sampling procedure, often referred to simply as interval recording, that requires the response to be emitted throughout the entire interval for its presence to be scored. See also Time sampling.

Whole method of chaining   Teaching all links in sequence at one time; as opposed to the more effective *part method of chaining*.

Withdrawal design   An experimental design that involves the removal of the intervention to test its effect. For example, one frequently utilized withdrawal design involves: (1) obtaining a base rate of the target behavior; (2) applying the intervention or procedure; (3) withdrawing the intervention, so conditions are the same as those that were in effect during the baseline period; and (4) reapplying the intervention. This design is used to determine whether or not the effect of the intervention can be reproduced. Often abbreviated as ABAB design.

Within-subject experimental designs   Research designs, sometimes referred to as *intensive designs*, developed to evaluate unambiguously the effects of the independent variable on the behavior of a single organism. See also Experimental design; Multielement design; Multiple baseline design; Withdrawal design.

X-axis   See Abscissa.

Y-axis   See Ordinate.

Zone system   An observational system similar to partial-interval time sampling in which space, such as the school yard, is divided into specific predesignated areas. Each area or zone is relatively small and provides equivalent opportunities for the target behavior to occur in. The observer watches *all* performance within a particular area. If evidence of one or more instances of the targeted behavior is recorded within that zone during the observational interval (e.g., ten seconds) that interval is scored to designate its occurrence. The observer scores behavior within one zone several times before moving on to the next.

Name index

Subject index

*Italicized page numbers refer to glossary

Peer (student) involvement, in programs to improve playground conduct, 358–9

Peer reinforcement, benefits of, 88; elements of, 88–90; examples of, 87–91 passim

Performance feedback (*see* Feedback)

Permanent product recording, 24, 34, 39, *398*; advantages of, 24; examples of, 23–4; other recording methods compared to, 33; use of, in DRO procedure, 159

Personalized System of Instruction (PSI), 5, 270, *398*; effectiveness of, at different grade levels, 85; features of, 85; peer tutoring important to, 91; preparation of study materials for, 270–3 passim; use of, 272–3

Personnel (*see* Staff)

Physical guidance, 93, 107, *398*; examples of, 93, 123; use of, in contingent effort procedures, 181; *See also* Graduated guidance

PL 94.142 (*see* Education for All Handicapped Children Act)

PLA-Check (*see* Planned Activity Check)

Planned Activity Check (PLA-Check), 32, *398–9*; examples of, 38, 48; *See also* Momentary time sampling

Planned ignoring, 104, *399*; examples of, 168–9 passim; *See also* Extinction

Planning team, *399*; example of, 20–1, 56; selection of (for lunch area program, 347, 349–50, 359; for staff development program, 369, 372–5)

Playground, programs to improve conduct on, 358–9

Positive practice (*see* Overcorrection)

Positive reinforcement, *399*; applications of (to compositional writing skills, 209–10; to handwriting, 192, 194–6 passim; to reading, 221–2; to social skills training, 291; to spelling, 198–202; to staff development program, 378–82); as part of differential reinforcement, 105–6; aversive procedures combined with, 184; critical features of, 104, 116; delayed, 84, 86–7; delivery of, 92–3; effectiveness of, 83–94, 255; ethics of, 11–2, 93, 370; evaluation of, 94; examples of, 63–4, 66, 71–6 passim, 82–94 passim; frequency of, 87–92; games to promote, 72–5; group, 69–70; immediate 84–7; intermittent, 91–2; lack of, as setting event for school vandalism, 331–2; peer, 70–5, 87–91; principles of successful, 78–9; role of, in enforcing rules, 113–5 passim; self-, 76–7; staff, 73–4, 91–2; timing of, 84–7; use of, in chaining procedure, 133; use of, in shaping procedure, 135–8

Positive reinforcer, 65–6, 69–70, *399*; selection of, 67–8; *See also* Premack principle

Praise (*see* Qualitative praise)

Precise behavioral measurement, 15, *399*; applications of (to instructional output, 276–7; to lunch area, 350; to staff development program, 369, 371–2; to social skills training, 292–3, 300–1); methods of, 23–32; techniques applied to, 8–9; *See also* Assessment, behavioral; Assessment of environment; Record-keeping

Precision Teaching, 255–6, *399*; concepts of, 273; use of, 273

Premack Principle, 67–8, *399*; examples of, 68; *See also* Reinforcer

Preparation through Responsive Educational Programs (PREP) approach, 275

Primary reinforcer (*see* Unconditioned reinforcer)

Probe, *399*; *See also* Withdrawal design

Process goal (*see* Goal, process)

Process variables, 382, *399*; vs. product, 257

Proctoring (*see* Tutoring)

Programmed instruction, *399*; development of materials for, 5, 270–3; effect of personal computers on, 85, 273; features of, 85

Progressive delay procedure, 122, *399*; example of, *399*; use of, in stimulus control, 122–3; *See also* Delayed prompting

Prompt, 93, *399*; applications of (to handwriting, 193–6 passim; to reading, 225–8; to staff development program, 377–8); examples of, 93, *399*; sample of, in programmed instruction, 272; *See also* Prompting strategies

Prompting strategies, applications of (to arithmetic skills, 249–50; to compositional writing skills, 211; to handwriting, 192; to reading, 225–8; to social skills training, 296); self-, 121–2; types of, 117–22; use of, in chaining procedure, 133–4; *See also* Fading; Response delay; Verbal antecedents

PSI (*see* Personalized System of Instruction)

Punctuality (*see* Attendance programs)

Punisher, 64, *400*

Punishment, 65, 104, 144, 181, *400*; as classroom management strategy, 144–5, 146; as factor in attendance problems, 307, 312; as setting event for school vandalism, 330–1; corporal, 166, 182; disadvantages of, 112, 145–6, 150; effective and ethical use of, 144–5, 150, 181–4, 255; examples of, 144–6 passim, 181–2; reinforcement of alternative behaviors vs., 143–7, 150–1, 162–3; rule enforcement by, 113–5 passim; vandalism and/or violence prevented or reduced by, 336–7; *See also* Avoidance behavior; Reductive procedure